The Academy of St. Martin in the Fields

The War Artists
(published in association with the Tate Gallery
and the Imperial War Museum)

Opera Today

Sheathing the Sword:
The Demilitarization of Japan 1945–52

A Pilgrim Soul:
The Life and Work of Elisabeth Lutyens

SOLDIERS OF THE SUN

SOLDIERS OF THE SUN

THE RISE AND FALL OF THE
IMPERIAL JAPANESE ARMY

Meirion and Susie Harries

Random House

New York

This work was originally published in slightly different form by
William Heinemann Ltd., London, in 1991.

Library of Congress Cataloging-in-Publication Data
Harries, Meirion
    Soldiers of the sun: the rise and fall of the Imperial Japanese
Army/Meirion Harries and Susie Harries.—1st ed.
        p.   cm.
    Includes bibliographical references and index.
    ISBN 0-394-56935-0
    1. Japan—History, Military—1868–1945. 2. Japan. Rikugun—
History. I. Harries, Susie. II. Title.
DS838.7.H37 1992
952.03—dc20   91-52684

Manufactured in the United States of America

2 4 6 8 9 7 5 3

First U.S. Edition

This book was set in 11/13 Bodoni Book.

Designed by Richard Oriolo

PREFACE AND
ACKNOWLEDGMENTS

T he Imperial Japanese Army had been in existence for only seven
decades when on November 30, 1945, General Douglas MacArthur, Supreme Commander of the Allied Forces in Japan, signed the
order for its dissolution. Yet in that short span it had redefined the
meanings of both heroism and barbarity.

No one can doubt the courage of the Japanese soldier. The defenders of Saipan and Iwo Jima gave their lives on a scale unimaginable to
the soldiers of the West. Where Allied troops surrendered at the rate of
one prisoner for every three dead, on the Japanese side 120 died for each
soldier who surrendered.

How was it possible for an organization displaying the highest of
soldierly qualities to possess such a capacity for barbarism? How is the
heroism of the defenders of Saipan to be reconciled with the starvation
and torture of prisoners, with experiments in biological warfare carried
out on thousands of human beings, and with the creation of a narcotics
empire that reached into America and Europe to pay for the weapons of
war?

This paradox, still unresolved, lies at the heart of Western suspicions of Japan. The exhaustive and cathartic examination of the Holocaust by Germans in recent years has no Japanese equivalent. There has been no easy explanation of Japanese atrocities, no Nazi party to act as the scapegoat for collective war guilt. Because the Japanese have not come to terms with their own past, neither have others. Many Asians remain deeply suspicious; many Westerners either avert their gaze from the military past and fix it firmly on the commercial present and future, or explain the Japanese war record as well as they know how—often in crudely racist terms. Barbaric behavior, it is tacitly implied, is in some way "natural" to the Japanese; an essential inhumanity is perhaps the cornerstone of their economic success.

In telling the story of Japan and the Imperial Army, we have tried to shed some light on these issues, and throughout the research and writing of this book we have received a great deal of help from former Imperial Army personnel, present-day scholars, and the custodians of national archives and libraries.

We should like to thank Professor Louis Allen, General Seizo Arisue, Holloway Brown, Paul Cornish, Grant Eustace, Ichiro Fujisaki, Yoriko Fujisaki, Mikiko Fujiwara, Professor Ikuhiko Hata, Mrs. Reiko Hayashikawa, Professor Kiyoshi Ikeda, Dr. Akifumi Ikeda, Professor Masamichi Inoki, Jane Irisa, Professor Hisao Iwashima, Fumiyo Kitamura, Toshiaki Kitamura, Professor Shigekatsu Kondo, Dr. Dominic Lieven, Lady Marriner, General Makoto Matsutani, Jinnosuke Miyai, Professor Toshio Morimatsu, Seiichi Nakata, Dr. R. John Pritchard, Sir Julian Ridsdale, Phil Reed, Professor Kahei Rokumoto, Heyden Rostow, Shuichi Sakai, Professor Yoshiyuki Sekiguchi, General Hiroshi Shimizu, Frank J. Shulman, General Ichiji Sugita, Professor Hisashi Takahashi, Professor Eiji Takemae, Takahiko Tanaka, General Yoshio Tanaka, John Taylor, General Ichiro Tsuchiya, and Shuichi Wada.

We should also like to thank the staffs of the National Diet Library, Tokyo; Kokusai Bunka Kaikan, Tokyo; the National Institute for Defense Studies, Tokyo; the Archives of the Service Historique de l'Armée, Vincennes; the Archives of the Foreign Ministry, Paris; the National Archives, Washington, D.C.; the London Library; the British Library; the Public Record Office, Kew; the Centre for Japanese Studies, Sheffield University; the Imperial War Museum; the Institute for the Study of Drug Dependency; the International Institute for Strategic Studies; the London School of Economics; the Ministry of Defence; and the School of Oriental and African Studies.

PREFACE AND ACKNOWLEDGMENTS

We owe a particular debt of gratitude to Hugh Hanning, chairman of the Fontmell Group for International Disaster Relief; Brigadier Kenneth Hunt, OBE, MC, Vice-President of the International Institute for Strategic Studies; and General Katsuichi Tsukamoto, Executive Director and General Secretary of the Research Institute for Peace and Security, in Tokyo.

We should like to offer special thanks to Professor Ryoichi Tobe of the National Defense Academy, Japan; Professor Kanji Akagi of Keio University, Tokyo; and Professor Ian Nish, CBE, of the London School of Economics, each of whom gave us help, encouragement, and precious time, and read a late draft of this manuscript in whole or part. They gave us much information we would not otherwise have found, corrected errors of fact, and provided invaluable suggestions. But, given the sensitivity of some of the material, we would like to stress that none is in any sense responsible for the interpretations and opinions we have expressed about the Imperial Japanese Army.

Last, we would like to thank Robert Loomis for his unfailing courtesy, his patience, his continuing help in supplying documents and information that we would otherwise have missed, and his meticulous and constructive editing, without which this book would be far poorer.

MEIRION AND SUSIE HARRIES
June 24, 1991

CONTENTS

CONTENTS

PART IV: DIVIDED ARMY, 1932–1937

PART V: THE CHINA WAR, 1937–1941

PART VI: THE STRIKE SOUTH, 1939–1941

PART VII: THE PACIFIC WAR: THE ATTACK

CONTENTS

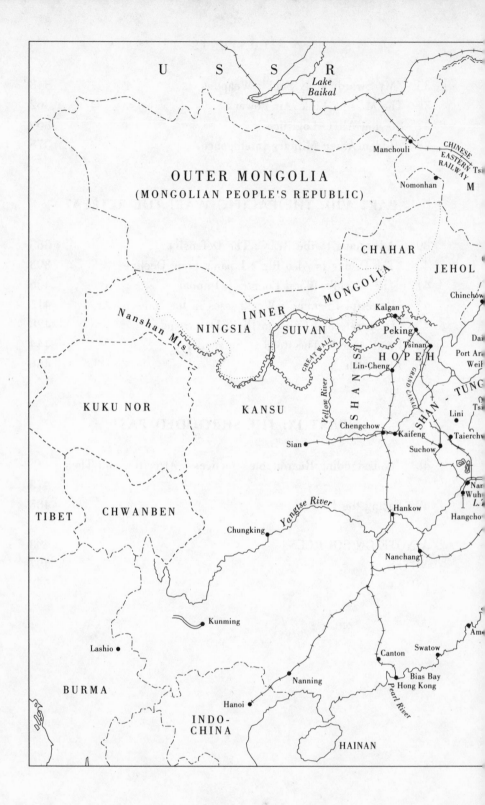

U S S R

Lake Baikal

Manchouli

CHINESE
EASTERN
RAILWAY

Tsi

M

OUTER MONGOLIA
(MONGOLIAN PEOPLE'S REPUBLIC)

Nomonhan

CHAHAR

JEHOL

Chinchow

Nanshan Mts.

INNER

MONGOLIA

NINGSIA

SUIVAN

Kalgan

Peking

Dai

Port Ar

Weil

GREAT WALL

Tsinan

Yellow River

S
H
A
N
S
I

HOPEH

Lin-Cheng

KUKU NOR

KANSU

Chengchow

Sian

Kaifeng

Suchow

GRAND CANAL

S
H
A
N
-
T
U
N
G

Lini

Tsi

Taierchw

TIBET

CHWANBEN

Yangtse River

Chungking

Hankow

Nar

Wuh

L.

Hangcho

Nanchang

Kunming

Lashio

Canton

Swatow

Ame

Nanning

Bias Bay

Hong Kong

Pearl River

BURMA

Hanoi

INDO-
CHINA

HAINAN

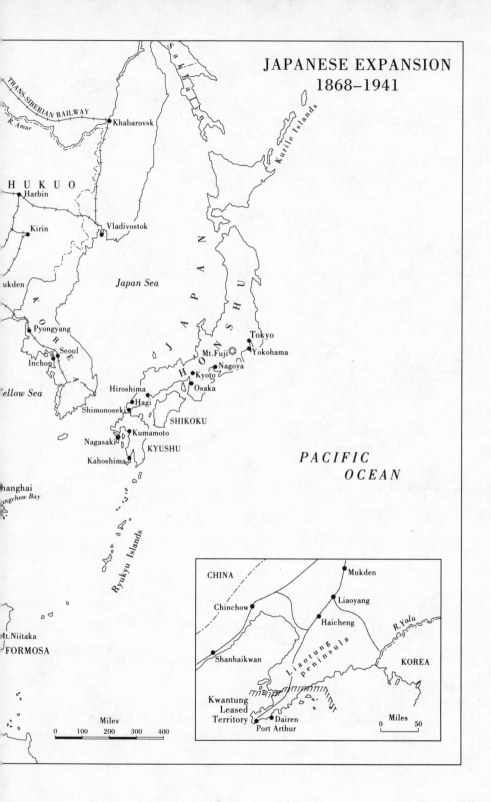

JAPANESE EXPANSION
1868–1941

TRANS-SIBERIAN RAILWAY

R. Amur

Khabarovsk

Sakhalin

Kurile Islands

H U K U O

Harbin

Kirin

Vladivostok

ukden

K O R E A

Japan Sea

J A P A N

H O N S H U

Pyongyang

Seoul

Inchon

ellow Sea

Hiroshima

Hagi

Shimonoseki

Nagasaki

Kumamoto

Kahoshima

SHIKOKU

KYUSHU

Mt.Fuji

Nagoya

Kyoto

Osaka

Tokyo

Yokohama

PACIFIC
OCEAN

hanghai

ngchow Bay

Ryukyu Islands

Mt.Niitaka

FORMOSA

Miles

0   100   200   300   400

CHINA

Chinchow

Mukden

Liaoyang

Haicheng

R. Yalu

Shanhaikwan

Liaotung peninsula

KOREA

Kwantung
Leased
Territory

Dairen

Port Arthur

Miles

0   50

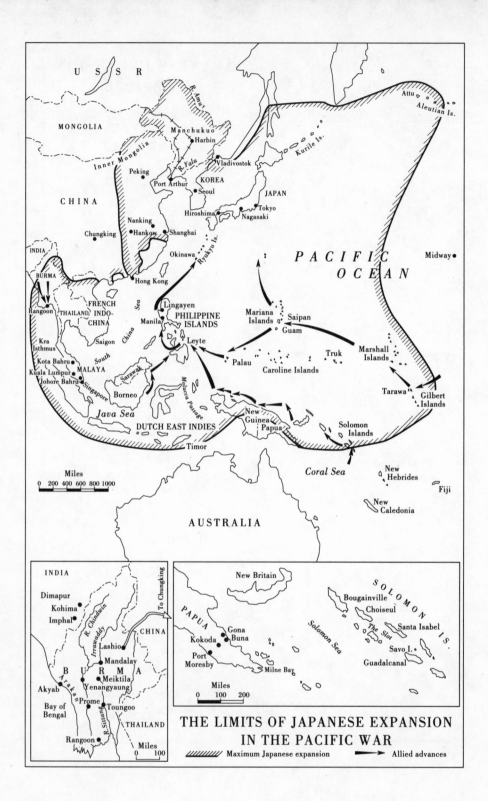

U S S R

MONGOLIA

Inner Mongolia

R. Amur

Manchukuo
• Harbin

R. Yalu

Vladivostok

Kurile Is.

Attu
Aleutian Is.

CHINA

• Peking

Port Arthur
• Seoul

KOREA

JAPAN

PACIFIC
OCEAN

• Midway

Chungking •
Nanking •
Hankow •
Shanghai

Hiroshima •
Nagasaki •
Tokyo

INDIA

BURMA

Okinawa

Ryukyu Is.

Rangoon •

FRENCH
INDO-
CHINA

THAILAND,

Hong Kong

Lingayen

Manila

PHILIPPINE
ISLANDS

Mariana
Islands

Saipan
Guam

Kra
Isthmus

Saigon

China
Sea

Leyte

Kota Bahru •
Kuala Lumpur •

MALAYA

South

Palau

Caroline Islands

Truk

Marshall
Islands

Johore Bahru •
Singapore •

Sarawak

Borneo

Molucca Passage

Tarawa

Gilbert
Islands

Java Sea

DUTCH EAST INDIES

New
Guinea
Papua

Solomon
Islands

Timor

Coral Sea

New
Hebrides

Fiji

Miles

0 200 400 600 800 1000

New
Caledonia

AUSTRALIA

INDIA

Dimapur •

Kohima •

Imphal •

R. Chindwin

R. Irrawaddy

To Chungking

CHINA

Lashio •

Mandalay •

B U R M A

Meiktila •

Akyab •

Yenangyaung •

Arakan

Prome •

Bay of
Bengal

Toungoo •

R. Sittang

THAILAND

Rangoon •

Miles

0   100

New Britain

PAPUA

Gona
Kokoda • Buna

Port
Moresby

Milne Bay

Solomon Sea

S O L O M O N

Bougainville •
Choiseul

The Slot

Santa Isabel

Savo I. •

Guadalcanal

I S.

Miles

0   100   200

THE LIMITS OF JAPANESE EXPANSION
IN THE PACIFIC WAR

///////// Maximum Japanese expansion   ——▶ Allied advances

PART I

CREATING THE IMPERIAL ARMY
1868-1890

1

SAMURAI AND SQUINT-EYED BARBARIANS

The Imperial Japanese Army was created quickly and with single-minded determination during the 1870s and 1880s. It was a modern military organization. Command structure, weaponry, support services, conscription methods, and educational infrastructure were all based on the best of Western models. It seemed as though in only twenty years Japan had cast off her samurai heritage without a backward glance. But had the thirteenth-century samurai who defended Japan's shores with bow and sword against the Mongol hordes of Kublai Khan been able to see their successors awaiting the Americans on Attu, Iwo Jima, or Saipan, they would have found nothing novel or alien in the grim resolve to achieve victory or endure annihilation. In appearance up-to-date, the Imperial Army was suffused with a spirit of feudal origins. In many ways the soldiers of the sun were in the twentieth century, but not of it.

The potency of Japan's military tradition in the mid–twentieth century was due to the extraordinary emphasis given to martial virtues during the evolution of Japan, to the quirk of history which ensured that

3

the tradition remained in full flower until little more than a hundred years ago, and to the use to which the creators of the Imperial Army put it. Until the middle of the nineteenth century, Japan remained a feudal society untouched by the industrial revolution. In consequence, the technological basis of warfare in Japan—the sword, bow, and spear—remained virtually unchanged for two millennia, and so, too, did the philosophy of war.

"To attempt an estimate of the Japanese Army," wrote an American infantry officer in 1942, "is something like attempting to describe the other side of the moon." It was true. In the West, feudal attitudes toward honor, death, and the very purpose of a soldier's life had vanished centuries before. But the men who created the Imperial Army had themselves been raised in the feudal tradition. They knew that the repeating rifle had made the sword obsolete, and so they built an army based on the rifle unit—but they did not abandon their own heritage, the ethos that had made the samurai so formidable. America's enemy in the Pacific was an uneasy blend of ancient thought and modern methods, a matrix of unresolved tensions fueling the extremes of heroism and barbarity.

The origins of this spirit lay in Japan's distant past. The tribes that ultimately coalesced to become the Japanese people were warriors, invaders thrusting into the archipelago from the Asian continent. They colonized the main island of Honshu, probably in the first century A.D., at the expense of the indigenous Ainu people, who were pushed west and north, out of the rich agricultural plains. Unrelenting warfare on the frontiers bred toughness; Korean writings of the fourth century attest to the fearsome reputation of the Japanese fighting man.

The *Tenno*, or Emperor, chief of the dominant Yamato clan from whom the present Emperor of Japan claims notional descent, was both temporal and spiritual leader of the Japanese people. Chinese texts mention a coalition of tribes ruled over by the Empress Pimiko, who was both priestess and witch. By the eighth century, the Emperor was firmly established as Japan's religious leader. Proof of his status was provided by the great chronicles, the *Kojiki* and the *Nihongi,* which recorded the Imperial line's descent from the most powerful of the Japanese deities, the Sun Goddess, Amaterasu. By writing down what were in essence the creation myths of Japan, the Imperial family ensured exclusivity for their version of Japan's origins and guaranteed that the Throne would remain a unique and irreplaceable part of Japanese life down to modern times.

The seventh and eighth centuries were the apogee of the Emperor's temporal rule, with power consolidated by a shift away from the original alliance of clans toward a centralized conscript army under the Emperor's command. But from the process of pushing back the frontiers of the Empire there slowly emerged a group of powerful lords, each with his private army of retainers. Gradually, these retainers transferred their personal allegiance from the Emperor to the individual lords who gave them the land on which their existence depended. This evolving feudal structure had by the ninth century created beneath the lords a warrior class of men known as samurai, "those who serve," who became the true arbiters of power in Japan.

For eight hundred years, from the twelfth century through the middle of the nineteenth, Japan was dominated by a succession of these powerful military dynasties. The head of the ruling family took the title "Shogun" and exercised power through a bakufu or "tent government"—a term deriving from the original, literal military encampment—on behalf of the Emperor. The fact that each notionally acknowledged the Emperor's authority was to be extremely significant in the story of the Imperial Army. The explanation for this acknowledgment seems to be that no Shogun could usurp the place of the Imperial line in Japan's religious life without denying that the Emperor was descended from the Sun Goddess—which would entail a denial of the fundamental precepts of Japanese religious life; and by "ruling on the Emperor's behalf," the Shogun's own regime gained in legitimacy.

Brought to power by the sword, each Shogun held sway over a country where warfare was virtually epidemic. In the crucible of war, the samurai began to evolve an extraordinary code of unquestioning loyalty, and through their exploits on the battlefield established the tradition of transcendent courage by which the modern Japanese soldier would live and die.

In these centuries the arts of war and of weapons evolved naturally. The samurai took what advantage they could from the world's military technology; by the sixteenth century, they were using rudimentary firearms—a development that in turn affected castle design and battlefield tactics. Given the samurai willingness to adapt, the military tradition in Japan might well have followed the path of the West, edged weapons giving way to the rifle and artillery as sail had before steam.

But then, in the late fifteenth and early sixteenth centuries—crucially, just before the dawn of modern weapons development—Japan was brought under the control of a new military dynasty, the Tokugawa, which sealed the country away from outside influences, including imports of weapons. For 250 years—the centuries of the industrial revolution and the restructuring of the battlefield in the West—Japan kept to the ways of the sword and bow.

Under the Tokugawa, as in preceding centuries, Japan was divided into 260 or so regional domains, each ruled by a dynastic family supported by its samurai, with the lords—daimyo—in their turn swearing allegiance to the Tokugawa Shogun. With the regional divisions the samurai kept their sense of clan identity. And among those clans that had originally resisted the Tokugawa's rise to power, the spirit of opposition remained alive.

Preeminent among the dissidents were the clans of Choshu and Satsuma, and from their samurai would come the men who founded the Imperial Army and shaped the course of modern Japan. Satsuma, the second-largest of the domains, with its capital at Kagoshima, lay on the remote edge of Kyushu. It was a rugged, mountainous region, which bred some of Japan's toughest warriors. Despite the poor agricultural land, the domain was rich, because traditionally the king of the Ryukyu Islands, which include Okinawa, paid tribute to the Satsuma lord; also, considerable trade had evolved between the Ryukyus, China, and Satsuma. Flanked by mountains, Satsuma maintained a strong sense of independence, the inhabitants' regional identity reinforced by the particularly archaic dialect they spoke (a dialect used by members of the Japanese Foreign Ministry in international telephone calls during the run-up to Pearl Harbor, because the speakers believed that U.S. intelligence would not be able to translate it).

Choshu, on the western edge of Honshu with its capital at Hagi, was the ninth-largest of the domains. It was little more than half the size of Satsuma, but better farmland gave it an equivalent productive capacity, which in turn supported one of the largest samurai populations. But Choshu had once been considerably larger, and it was a source of undying resentment toward the Tokugawa that they had taken away Choshu land. In Choshu, children were put to sleep at night with their feet pointing insultingly in the direction of the Tokugawa capital, Tokyo. And in both Satsuma and Choshu, the knowledge that they were opposed to the Tokugawa was passed down the generations. For 250 years, on the first day of the year, a deputation of clan elders would visit the Choshu lord and ritually inquire: "Has the time come to begin the subjugation of the Tokugawa?"

The Tokugawa succeeded in holding Choshu and Satsuma in check by a carefully devised balance of power; but though this ensured 250 years of peace, it also generated enough tension to keep the samurai in a state of perpetual martial preparedness. The traditional samurai spirit did not wither. Rather, it deepened into the all-encompassing ethic now known as Bushido, the Way of the Warrior.

Under the twin influences of Confucianism and Zen Buddhism, the Way of the Warrior developed into an ethic of absolute loyalty and unhesitating sacrifice. The *Hagakure,* one of the great Bushido texts of this period, emphasizes the transcendence the samurai achieved over his own mortality. "I have found that the way of the warrior is death," wrote Jocho Yamamoto.

This full flowering of the samurai ethic was the ghost in the modern machinery of the Imperial Japanese Army. But on occasion the ghost proved stronger than the machine. Though armed with rifle and served by complex weapons systems that distanced the soldier from his enemy, the Imperial Army acted on precepts designed to maximize the effectiveness of a man fighting hand-to-hand with a sword. This led naturally to an affection for the cold steel of the bayonet, and justified the suicidal banzai charge—an insane dissonance between the nature of the weaponry and its use that was to make the Japanese soldier a surreal-seeming figure.

A second and equally important development in these centuries was the growth of direct loyalty toward the Emperor. The Tokugawa Shoguns, like their forebears, paid lip service to the notion that they ruled on behalf of the Emperor, whom in fact they kept semi-captive in Kyoto. But by adopting Confucianism as their philosophy of state they were unwittingly creating the conditions in which a fundamental reconsideration of the Emperor's position was inevitable. Their intention was very different: to exploit the Confucian precepts of obedience and the loyalty of servant to master as a form of social control. "Morality," one of the Tokugawa's chief advisers cynically wrote, "is nothing but the necessary means for controlling the subjects of the empire [and] may be regarded as a device for governing the people."

By the nineteenth century the Japanese people as a whole were thoroughly imbued with this Confucian ethic. But so, too, were the scholars, and those who examined Japan's history from a Confucian perspective could not help but conclude that the Emperor, not the Shogun, was the person to whom ultimate loyalty was owed.

This conclusion was tailor-made to appeal to clans that were seeking to justify their opposition to the Tokugawa. By the nineteenth century the old animosities of domains like Choshu and Satsuma had become wedded, in the minds of radical samurai, to the idea of restoring to the Imperial line the sovereignty that had been denied it for a thousand years. Of course, truly threatening opposition, even with the Emperor as its center, was still a chimera while the Tokugawa held the balance of power in Japan. But in the nineteenth century, the foundations of Tokugawa predominance were being undermined by the incursion of Western nations into Asia.

Both the Tokugawa and the daimyo kept a weather eye on developments in the West. Through the handful of Dutch and Chinese permitted to trade at Nagasaki during the seclusion, through watching China's suffering at the hands of imperialist powers, and on a theoretical level through translation work at the Shogun's Institute for the Investigation of Barbarian Books, the more progressive of the samurai had come to comprehend how much more powerful was the West. Japan had no science or technology; its soldiers, drawn exclusively from the samurai class, were armed with the sword, bow, and lance. And unlike Western nations, Japan had no national military organization, merely an inefficient net of feudal obligations which bound each daimyo to field a certain number of samurai when the Shogun called.

Many samurai feared that Japan might fall prey to Western predators. In 1844, King Willem II of Holland wrote to the Shogun, warning him of the burgeoning strength of Western military organizations and urging that Japan end her seclusion. The Tokugawa needed to keep Japan isolated for their regime to survive; nevertheless, they turned to Western arms for self-defense.

In the 1840s, after the Opium War in China, the Shogunate embarked on a program of reforms under the slogan "Be frugal and love arms." Guns were bought in increasing quantities from the Dutch, and students of "foreign learning" now concentrated on military technology rather than medicine, astronomy, or languages. Individuals were permitted to buy and sell weapons, and the first primitive forms of machine production were introduced in order to accelerate arms manufacture.

The threat from the West and the obvious potential of modern weapons combined to galvanize the more radical of the Tokugawa's opponents. For two centuries the authority of the Tokugawa had ultimately depended on their ability to field numerically superior forces. But, as the students of Western military science became aware, rifles deployed in disciplined units were force multipliers. It was not inconceivable that a single clan army, armed and trained on Western lines, might successfully challenge the massed power of the Tokugawa. As the nineteenth century wore on, the potential to overthrow the Shogunate and restore the Emperor using Western-style forces became increasingly obvious.

Fatefully, there now appeared in Choshu a charismatic teacher and prophet who combined deep reverence for the Throne with a full appreciation of the power of modern weapons. To Shoin Yoshida's school under the pines came the men who in the years to follow would fulfill his vision and create a new Japan defended by a powerful imperial army.

According to Robert Louis Stevenson, Yoshida was dirty, disfigured by smallpox, and slovenly, with food-stained clothes and matted, filthy hair. His appearance concealed a legendary intellect, and so fanatically devoted to his studies was he that in the drowsy heat of summer he would put mosquitoes up his sleeve to help him concentrate, and on winter nights run barefoot through the snow to keep himself awake and thinking. Yoshida saw Japan as a nation, not—as it was in his time—an aggregation of semi-autonomous domains. He inspired his pupils with *yamato damashii*, the national spirit of Japan, which for him was focused on the Emperor. He taught, too, that Japan must master the science of the Western powers and use it as a tool against them, and he put his pupils through a rudimentary basic training in weaponry and infantry tactics.

The need for defense against the West was becoming increasingly urgent. Until the mid–nineteenth century, the Tokugawa policy of seclusion remained viable largely because Japan lay well north of the trade routes followed by sailing ships. However, as sail gave way to steam, the country's coasts became easily accessible to the ships of the West; and, though not conspicuously rich, Japan was not without its temptations—coaling stations, refuge for shipwrecked whalers, a new market for the manufactures of the industrialized world, and, in Britain's case, a vantage point from which to keep an eye on Russia in the aftermath of the Crimean War.

America, with her growing Pacific coast trade, had a particular interest in the shrouded nation across the ocean. In 1846, a U.S. Navy vessel under Commodore James Biddle tried and failed to open contacts with the Tokugawa—but America was not deterred. President Millard Fillmore, in his message to Congress on December 6, 1852, sounded the death knell of the Tokugawa seclusion policy. "The general prosperity of our states on the Pacific," he said, "requires that an attempt be made to open the opposite regions of Asia to a mutually beneficial intercourse. It is obvious that this attempt could be made by no power to so great an advantage as by the United States, whose constitutional system ex-

cludes every idea of distant colonial dependencies. I have accordingly
been led to order an appropriate naval force to Japan under the command
of a discreet and intelligent officer. . . . He is instructed to obtain from
the government of that country some relaxation of the inhospitable and
anti-social system which it has pursued for about two centuries.''

The ''discreet and intelligent officer'' was Commander Matthew
Perry, and he succeeded where the others had failed. The Tokugawa
signed treaties with him and opened the floodgates to other Western
countries—Britain, Russia, Germany, and France—a process that led to
full-blown commercial treaties heavily and humiliatingly biased in favor
of the foreigners.

With the benefit of hindsight, it now seems inevitable that Japan's
seclusion should have ended as modern communications began to shrink
the world, but wisdom after the event should not detract from Matthew
Perry's achievement. In preparing for the expedition, he read all the
available literature on Japan and deliberately adopted a strategy based
on power play. He gained an initial advantage from the shock to the
Japanese psyche of ships belching black smoke as his flotilla steamed
into the heat and haze of Tokyo Bay in July 1853: Japan's first sight of
steam power.

He then proceeded to perform as a man of outstanding eminence
and authority, playing on what he understood of the ingrained Japanese
sense of hierarchy. He refused instructions to divert to Nagasaki; he
insisted on dealing only with high officials; he warned off the Shogun's
guard boats, which surrounded the U.S. squadron (and which, incidentally, gave Shoin Yoshida the opportunity to stow away on Perry's
flagship). Perry sent the *Mississippi* up Tokyo Bay to menace the Shogun's capital, and when meeting the Shogun's representatives to present
the President's letter, he ensured that his men looked as aggressive as
possible. ''Sixty or seventy of them suddenly entered the building,''
recorded one Japanese eyewitness. ''They were all wearing a sword and
a loaded . . . pistol. They stared at [us] and were ready to attack. Those
[of us] in charge of the reception entrance were almost trampled over.''

Keen eyes watched every move made by the newly arrived Americans. The samurai were particularly intrigued by the fact that all of
Perry's men were military effectives; all carried arms, even the sailors
manning the launches. When a samurai force assembled, less than two
in ten were fighting men; each samurai warrior would have a retinue of
armor bearers, bow carriers, lance carriers, grooms, sandal carriers, box
and parcel carriers. American weaponry was also of considerable inter-

est; and when Perry presented the Shogun with the latest U.S. cavalry rifle, it was promptly borrowed by the lord of the Satsuma clan, who had comprehensive drawings made before returning it.

The success of the Perry mission dealt a fatal blow to the Tokugawa. Their response was to appease and adapt, study and emulate, and, within careful limits, open to the foreign invader the country that had been closed for so long. There was no realistic alternative, but the Tokugawa's opponents were disgusted by what they saw as irresolute kowtowing. "What a disgrace to our country," wrote one of the Satsuma clan leaders, "that we are not able to say to the newly arrived foreigners as we did to [the seventeenth-century Dutch traders] at Deshima, 'Fear, tremble, and obey!' " The Shogun's traditional epithet, they pointed out, was "barbarian-subjugating," and if he had no intention of subjugating barbarians, then he no longer deserved to lead.

The Emperor-centered opposition gathered force. The Tokugawa themselves unwittingly aided the process by decreeing that the plain around Kyoto was forbidden to foreigners and calling samurai from all over Japan to defend the area from Western intrusion—overtly making the court the symbol of national resistance. "Revere the Emperor and Expel the Barbarian!" became the nationalists' rallying cry. But resistance to the foreigner was soon shown to be futile. In June 1863, Choshu zealots fired on American, French, and Dutch vessels at the port of Shimonoseki with some newly acquired artillery pieces. With little ado, the U.S.S. *Wyoming* sank several Choshu ships, and French expeditionary forces bombarded and stormed coastal forts—a lesson that was repeated the following year, when Choshu once again tried to close the straits to Western shipping. Satsuma also had its capital, Kagoshima, bombarded and half destroyed by a British squadron in retribution for the murder of a British subject by Satsuma samurai.

The patent impossibility of expelling the barbarian changed the character of Japan's internal politics. From now on, the movement to restore the Emperor became an end in itself—and the foreigner supplied the means.

In response to the foreign threat, from the 1840s to the mid-1860s both the Tokugawa and the rebel domains had been modernizing their forces. "The commonest sound in [Tokyo] is the musket and artillery practice of the soldiers," reported an eyewitness in 1860. By 1862 the Tokugawa, whose survival was predicated on an unchanging feudal society, found themselves obliged to begin planning for a Western-style army, divided into the three branches of infantry, cavalry, and artillery.

11

Of the foot soldiers, the greater proportion were to be heavy infantry armed with old-fashioned guns and swords, but approximately a quarter were to be light infantry equipped with modern European rifles, with an elite group of marksmen, trained in Western techniques, surrounding the Shogun.

As for the opposition, the Satsuma domain, which had been among the first to show interest in Western learning, had built a cannon factory as early as 1854, and in succeeding years traded busily through Shanghai to earn the money to buy arms. Choshu already possessed one of the strongest of the clan armies, and produced some of the most gifted military innovators, such as Uemon Yamada and Shinsaku Takasugi. Yamada was fascinated by the Western rifle unit, at once compact and flexible, and he urged commanders in Choshu's clan army to achieve the same degree of mobility, maneuvering their men "as one moves hands and feet." He also advocated a far greater uniformity of equipment. The hodgepodge of bow, pike, sword, and rifle currently in use made any formation unwieldy—"like a gathering of crows," Yamada said.

Takasugi, a young Choshu zealot with a remarkable knowledge of Western artillery, was more interested in creating rifle units outside the regular clan army, which was wholly samurai-based. These new units, he proposed, should be a mixture of samurai and peasants; in other words, the privilege of bearing arms and fighting for one's lord should no longer be restricted to the traditional warrior class. This was not a novel idea. Peasant militias had been assembled by various clans in the past to meet specific threats, and it was increasingly widely felt that duty to the nation should transcend narrow class loyalties. Even the Tokugawa were, by this time, prepared to consider drawing upon the strength of their commoners. But Takasugi was the first to turn theory into regular practice.

By the start of 1864 the first of Takasugi's mixed rifle units, or *shotai,* had been formed under the title of *Kiheitai,* "shock troop." At its core was a group of radical samurai; around them clustered commoners eager to secure the symbols of the samurai class—distinguishing titles, status, and the right to carry swords. Subsequent *shotai* included men of every class and profession—hunters, fishermen, sumo wrestlers, and Buddhist monks, as well as agricultural workers. But it would be misleading to regard them as "revolutionary" troops; they were led by samurai, and they represented the samurai creed of fighting for the honor of the clan.

Among the *shotai* officers was Aritomo Yamagata, the man who more than any other was to shape the Imperial Army. In these years, he was a reserved, cautious youth with a thin voice, stiff manner, and a predisposition to chronic indigestion. He had neither the temperament nor the magnetism to be a popular hero or a well-loved leader, but he had an extraordinary intellect, the highest political skills, and a passionate commitment to reshaping Japan. He took his place willingly among the Choshu *shishi*, the "men of spirit" gathered at the feet of Shoin Yoshida, and risked his life for his beliefs.

Yamagata was a member of the *Kiheitai* from its inception, and eventually became a commander—a position that was to be the foundation of his rise to political power. Like the other radical samurai with whom he enlisted, he first saw the *Kiheitai* as a weapon to be turned against the foreigner. Yamagata had witnessed foreign arrogance while still a boy, when the crew of a British vessel had come ashore and seized water and supplies from a small Choshu village. Yamagata wrote angrily, "The ugly English barbarians behaved with extreme disorder and uncontrollable uncouthness. . . . When we unsheath our swords and kill them, they . . . will be thrown into the deep sea like bits of seaweed." But at Shimonoseki, Yamagata was forced to see that these were empty words. During both of the Western attacks on the port Yamagata was in command of one of the captured forts. He bore a scar on his forearm for the rest of his life, and he was never again to make the mistake of underrating Western armed strength.

By the mid-1860s Yamagata, like the rest of his *shotai* comrades, had begun to focus on the Tokugawa as the immediate threat. Relations between Choshu and the Tokugawa began to deteriorate steeply, and by the end of 1864 the Shogun was threatening to send an expeditionary force against Choshu. The Choshu conservatives then in power surrendered meekly, demolishing fortifications, forbidding the wearing of a particular type of shoe characteristic of battle dress, and even ordering officials to use feminine grammatical forms in their correspondence as a symbol of submissiveness.

This capitulation was the spur to action for the radicals, such as Yamagata and Takasugi, and they used the *shotai* to take control of Choshu, defeating the regular clan army in the process. In a maneuver that must have given him considerable satisfaction, Yamagata used against the regular Choshu army the tactics of bombardment and flank attack employed against him only months before by the French at Shimonoseki.

Once in power within Choshu, the radicals swore a blood oath to take direct action against the Shogun. As the Tokugawa themselves began to recognize the seriousness of the threat, an arms race exploded, which in the years 1864–1868 brought well over 100,000 new rifles into Japan, a profitable trade for Western arms dealers. Weapons were the currency of influence, and the British Foreign Office pointed disapprovingly to American agents selling arms, but was less forthcoming about Jardine, Matheson and Company's gunrunning activities in Nagasaki and a certain shopping trip to London by members of the Satsuma clan.

The Tokugawa now invited direct participation in their military buildup. Their tentative inquiries met with little response from Britain, whose sympathies, such as they were, inclined toward the rebel clans to whom they felt the future belonged (particularly now that anti-foreign feeling had taken second place to anti-Tokugawa action). So, taking advantage of traditional European rivalries, the Tokugawa turned to the French, from whom they secured a large loan with which to develop foundries and dockyards at Yokosuka, and the promise of a military training mission in the near future.

Meanwhile, the new Choshu regime had appointed a new adviser to rationalize the *shotai* and bring them under central control. Masujiro Omura was a leading scholar of European military science and had recently translated a work on strategy written from the standpoint of German military theory. He placed heavy emphasis on discipline and morale, and rapidly set about standardizing training and weapons. In this he was helped by a consignment of 7,300 rifles (4,300 of them Miniés left over from the American Civil War) bought from an English merchant at Nagasaki. Satsuma leaders were very helpful in arranging this purchase; common antipathy to the Tokugawa was fostering increasingly close relations between the two domains, and in March 1866, through the intercession of the Tosa and Hizen clans, Satsuma and Choshu negotiated a formal alliance that aimed to restore the Emperor.

The alliance could not have come at a more critical time. The Shogun had been expecting Satsuma support for another proposed expedition against Choshu, and their refusal to help proved a crippling blow. In the summer of 1866, the new, streamlined *shotai*, led by Yamagata, Takasugi, and Omura, proved that modern weapons had indeed altered the balance of power in Japan. Despite numerical inferiority, the *shotai* fought the Tokugawa army to a humiliating standstill, casting real doubt on the Shogun's continuing ability to rule.

This weakening of Tokugawa authority was at the same time fatally damaging to the samurai military tradition. Defeat had demonstrated to the Shogunate the urgent necessity of accelerating its military reforms.

The existing system still relied heavily on levies of vassal samurai, slow to mobilize and difficult to coordinate. In 1867, the Tokugawa embarked on a new program of reform, which envisaged a cadre of foreign-trained officers and men supplemented by an embryo conscript force. Instead of providing armed men, vassal clans would be required to pay a tax, which could be used to buy the modern weapons the regime so badly needed.

But it was too late. Even the French military mission that arrived later that year could not speed the modernization program sufficiently. Though there was some talk of introducing conscription, the authorities continued to rely on voluntary recruitment, which was discouragingly slow. Nor, when the troops were eventually assembled, was their training straightforward. In the uniforms supplied by the French mission, the new soldiers were a curious sight. "They still wore their two swords," reported the mission commander, Charles Chanoine, "in a sort of hybrid fashion between Japanese Yakunin and a Parisian Gendarme. The trousers did not fit, the boots were large and heavy which the old habit of dragging the sandal made difficult for them to wear; the coats were made of black cloth profusely covered with silver lace, and a slit up the back to allow the long sword to stick out behind." Farmers faced with the prospect of this motley crew drilling on their land rallied to the sound of the conch horn and drove the soldiers off with bamboo spears.

By now Choshu and Satsuma had extended the scope of their alliance to include joint military action. Yamagata had had a meeting with some of Satsuma's own "men of spirit"—among them Takamori Saigo and Toshimichi Okubo, both destined to play crucial roles in the new Japan—and with the clan daimyo, who gave him a six-shooter and suggested that they all now take more direct steps to plan for the benefit of the nation.

In an attempt at moderation, the Tosa clan proposed that the Shogun be persuaded to resign peacefully. In November 1867 he finally abdicated, though still retaining sufficient power to ensure Tokugawa dominance of the proposed council of clan leaders that was to replace the Shogunate. For Choshu and Satsuma, half measures were not enough. They occupied Kyoto, declared the Restoration of the Emperor Meiji, and in January 1868 advanced from Kyoto to fight the assembled Tokugawa army.

The two forces met at the villages of Toba and Fushimi, on the road to Osaka. The most potent force overall was the Choshu contingent, which, though not the largest, commanded the highest proportions of modern weaponry and of troops trained in Western fighting techniques.

The Satsuma forces, highly motivated and skillfully deployed, were fighting with a more motley collection of arms, making it harder to integrate their attacks. As for the Tokugawa, their most devoted supporters were at once a glory and a critical weakness. The samurai swordsmen of the Aizu clan fought on long after all hope of victory had evaporated. Yet it was the Aizu men, committed to hand-to-hand combat to the death, whose strength failed first and broke the line.

After their victory at Toba-Fushimi, the rebel army moved west to Tokyo (proclaimed the new capital at the end of 1868) and from there into the territories of the northeastern clans led by the diehard Aizu. Yamagata was Chief of Staff of the Imperial expedition to the north. Resistance was dogged—the Shogun's supporters, after all, had everything to lose—and Yamagata has been accused of great brutality in the methods he used to suppress it. Brutality would not have been entirely out of character; the northern rebels were all that stood in the way of an objective he had been pursuing unremittingly for over ten years. But if the claims are true, this was one of very few occasions in his disciplined life when he could ever be accused of excess.

Other clans had not proved as loyal as the Aizu. Chanoine reported in March 1869 that many indisciplined bands of samurai had defected from the Tokugawa forces, but not, he was pleased to add, any French-trained troops. Indeed, in October 1868 an artillery captain named Jules Brunet, who was a member of the French mission itself, had joined ranks with Takeaki Enomoto, one of the Shogun's admirals, in proclaiming a rebel republic in the northern island of Hokkaido.

Brunet had been a popular instructor, was attached to his pupils and to the Tokugawa cause, and believed he had a mission to perpetuate French influence in Japan. (He consistently referred to Hokkaido as "his" island; "I am all-powerful," he wrote.) He was, nevertheless, violating the official French policy of neutrality, and succeeded only in prolonging an ultimately futile campaign that cost many lives. When defeat seemed imminent, he instantly deserted his Japanese allies and hurried home. The arrogance of Western attitudes to Japan at this point is well illustrated in the French decision to "punish" Brunet for fomenting civil war in another sovereign state by suspending him from active duty for a year. He finished his career as a general in the French army.

In the sixteen years since Perry's unopposed landing in Japan, both the Shogun and his opponents had made remarkable progress in reshaping their armed forces. But the Tokugawa, hamstrung by a failing economy, could not accumulate enough of the weapons they knew they needed. And they faced more widespread resistance to change from samurai retainers who clung to their traditional status, refusing to drill alongside peasants, refusing to exchange their swords for the plebeian rifle, failing to recognize the threat of extinction as a class until it was too late. It was the Choshu and Satsuma clans that acted first and adapted best; and it was these two clans that were to take the lead in constructing Japan's modern military machine.

2

EMPEROR AND ARMY

For Japan, 1868 was a historic year. From one perspective, the Meiji Restoration—the triumph of the forces that had fought the Tokugawa Shogunate in the name of the Emperor Meiji—was a transfer of power by traditional means. Victory had been achieved by force of arms, not through popular uprising; the defeat of the Shogun was at most a palace revolution. But here continuity with the past ended. The men now installed in Tokyo Castle had more in view than simply establishing dynastic supremacy. Their objective fell little short of encouraging the rebirth of Japan as a modern nation on Western lines. Only through rapid and wholesale modernization could Japan become strong enough to end the humiliation of the unequal treaties imposed in the 1850s and to preserve herself from further depredations by the West. "Rich Country, Strong Army" became the public slogan and private objective.

To be modern, to be rich, to be strong, Japan had first to become truly unified. In 1868, however, she consisted of the patchwork of domains and the caste-divided society inherited from the Tokugawa. If

these impediments could be swept away, powerful forces would be un-
leashed to help in the nation-building process.

Geography was on the nation builders' side. As a cluster of islands,
the homeland had an immediate and coherent physical identity. Her
people shared a common language and ethnic mix; and after two thousand years of development uninterrupted by invasion or large-scale immigration, they possessed a remarkably homogeneous culture. Hostility
to Western intruders was a further coagulant.

But the main instrument of national self-recognition was the Imperial Throne. The present incumbent was a sixteen-year-old boy—but he
embodied the charisma of an institution dating back to the creation. The
new government worked hard to buttress the Throne as the epicenter of
the new Japan, the capstone of a new unified hierarchy that replaced
regional with national loyalty. In 1868, the Emperor transferred his
court from Kyoto to Tokyo, a gesture symbolic of the reunion of temporal
and spiritual leadership after a millennium apart. In his "Restoration
Rescript," he proclaimed "a return . . . to the government used at the
time of Jimmu Tenno, the founder of Japan and the first Emperor of the
Japanese people."

In propagating the Emperor's spiritual preeminence, the authorities
were quite ruthless. Competing religions were attacked; Buddhism,
which in the Tokugawa era had been the state religion, was disestab-
lished and priests were defrocked, temple lands forfeited to the state,
Buddhas and ritual objects taken for scrap. Christianity, which had been
proscribed by the Tokugawa, had nevertheless survived in secret among
communities in an isolated area near Nagasaki. Overestimating the open-
ness of the Restoration period, Christians at Urakami declared themselves. Thirteen of them were promptly beheaded, and the government
ordered Christians to apostatize or face exile or execution.

Shinto, the collection of beliefs on which the Emperor's divinity
depended, was made the official faith of the new state, but it was not a
perfect propaganda tool. It was not a well-organized religion, nor did it
have coherent isms or ologies; so the government was obliged to manufacture some. Between 1870 and 1884, ten thousand evangelists were
employed in a massive campaign to promulgate the "Three Great Principles" which naturally included "love of country, reverence for the Emperor and obedience to the will of the Court." During this Great
Promulgation Campaign, shrines and traditional festivals were placed
under government supervision, and attendance was made compulsory. In
Tokyo, a new national Shinto shrine—the Yasukuni Shrine—was

erected to the spirits of all those who died in the service of the Emperor.

To mobilize this sense of national identity, rooted in racial integrity and Emperor worship, and make it work towards the creation of a modern Western-style state, Japan's new rulers needed a national administrative framework. Over the two decades following Toba-Fushimi, they dismantled the Tokugawa system of government, centralized the administration under powerful national bureaucracies, instituted a modern tax system, stimulated industrial development, railway building, telegraph systems, shipbuilding, and banking and financial services, and introduced a nationwide education system.

Much of what the rulers did in the early years was based on trial and error. They studied the knowledge and skills of the industrialized world, experimented with them, and took the version that best suited their purposes. Though at the time the Meiji leaders may have seemed confused, bedeviled by factional rivalries and lacking a coherent program for change, in retrospect their achievement seems extraordinary. By the 1890s, this new nation, so recently escaped from the time warp of feudalism, had American congressmen railing against the "barefoot coolies" whose low wages meant unfair competition for American businesses.

The bedrock of power in the new state, however, was the same as it had always been—military strength, albeit in a new guise. In 1868, the government consisted simply of the representatives of a handful of clans that between them possessed sufficient strength to defeat potential opponents. "Men of spirit" like Yamagata now urged the importance of working toward a single national force.

Efforts at centralization began immediately, directed by Masujiro Omura. He had been one of the architects of the victorious Choshu army, but had no hesitation in enlisting the military talent that had been available to the Shogun. Perhaps the most valuable adviser was Amane Nishi, a prominent member of the Shogun's Institute for the Investigation of Barbarian Books and Japan's leading interpreter of Western ideas. For the Shogun he had expounded "barbarian" military science; for Omura and Yamagata, he advised on international diplomatic practice and military capabilities, and he was appointed a lecturer to the Emperor on Western thought in general.

Omura also used the Shogun's French-trained officers to set up a military school in Kyoto through which to propagate his ideas. He favored the method (French-influenced) of having samurai officers, trained in Western techniques, lead troops drawn from the population at large. Omura's ideas were not revolutionary; the monopoly of the samurai had already been invaded during the struggle to overthrow the Shogunate, when soldiers from other social classes had fought on both sides. But they were still risky, and in 1869 Omura was assassinated by an outraged Choshu samurai.

His philosophy was reinforced the following year, however, when several influential figures who had made expeditions abroad returned infused with similarly progressive notions. Even before the fall of the Shogun, a few individuals had traveled to the West to get the measure of the enemy. Choshu's Hirobumi Ito was in London when he read in *The Times* of his clan's first attack on foreign ships at Shimonoseki in 1864, and hurried home, too late, to warn them of the retribution they might expect. Now that the years of seclusion were over, the new regime encouraged an increasing stream of study missions.

Yamagata, who had been one of Omura's assistants, was in Europe at the outbreak of the Franco-Prussian War in 1870. So too was one of his own Choshu protégés, Taro Katsura, a young military officer and veteran of the campaigns of the 1860s, who had decided to go to France on his own initiative and at his own expense to improve his knowledge of modern military methods. On his way to Paris, Katsura heard that the city had fallen to the Prussians and, deriving the obvious moral, he instead headed for Berlin, where he was to spend the best part of the next three years.

Yamagata returned to Japan in 1870, deeply impressed with what he had learned of Prussian military organization and skills, and of the relations between the military and the state. In October, under the momentum of Omura's last efforts before he was assassinated, the government lurched briefly in the opposite direction and ordered all clans to adopt the French military system, only days before the news broke of France's crushing defeat by the Prussians at Sedan. But this was at least a move towards standardization.

Progress towards a national force was under way; but it was too slow for those in the government, who were acutely aware of their own insecurity. As a short-term buttress, the Imperial Guard was created in 1871—still exclusively a samurai force, and still drawn only from the three leading clans. At Yamagata's insistence the Imperial Guard was put under the command of Satsuma's Takamori Saigo, one of the principal fighting heroes of the war against the Shogun. Saigo was a towering, bulky, rash, individual extremist in a country where the slight, cautious conformist is more common; paradoxically, he was much loved for his rejection of the orthodox, and Yamagata, himself the complete antithesis, had a profound respect for Saigo.

At the same time, the government's combined forces were organized into four garrisons (increased to six in 1873) at strongpoints throughout the country; the troops were centrally controlled, and to weaken regional loyalties, men were invariably posted away from their own areas.

There were now two forces working directly to central authority: the Imperial Guard and the garrisons. But these represented only a tiny fraction of the potential military strength of Japan. Alongside them there still existed the old clan armies, a lingering threat to the stability of the government. The daimyo of Tosa, for example, had some 9,000 troops, seven times the maximum prescribed for the clan by the government.

There could be no genuinely unified army, no really potent national force, without a genuinely unified state. Now was the moment to push for the abolition of the feudal domains, a step that had always been in the minds of the new regime. "Rather than face collapse as we do today," wrote Toshimichi Okubo, "we can only make a bold and decisive commitment to change." In 1871, with the Imperial Guard at their backs as an enforcement agency, and the Great Promulgation Campaign in full swing, the government took the plunge. The old domains were replaced with a network of prefectures under government administrators, which cut across old loyalties and substituted new chains of allegiance all leading directly to the Emperor.

The individual lords' claims on their retainers' services perished with the clan system, releasing every man in Japan to answer the call of the state and removing any alternative focus of loyalty. Now the door was open for the introduction of universal conscription—a crucial development in the eyes of soldier-statesmen like Yamagata, for only on the foundation of a national army could a strong, modern, Western-style nation be built.

Already at the end of 1870, following Yamagata's return from Europe, new "Conscription Regulations" had proclaimed that men of all classes who were over five feet and between the ages of twenty and thirty were eligible for military service. In February 1872, Yamagata drafted his "Opinion Favoring a Conscript Army," which shortly afterward was translated into the first Conscription Law. Now all men between seventeen and forty were liable for three years' active service, two further years in the first reserves (subject to periodic training) and two more in the second reserves (on standby, subject to call-up in an emergency). All those men eligible for service but exempted for one reason or another might eventually, it was thought, form a "national army" of part-time militiamen.

The exemptions themselves were based to a large extent on those that had been employed by the French. All officials of central and local government were exempt, all students of education, engineering, and medicine, all scholars studying abroad, all heads of families, and all only sons, oldest sons, or oldest adopted sons. In addition, exemption could be bought for the reasonably substantial sum of 270 yen—a provision forbidden in Prussia and in fact largely abolished in France by this time. Where upper-class youths were concerned, exemption was often achieved simply through "the discretion of the examiners in the conscript examination"; as was perfectly obvious even at the time, the system ensured that military service appeared to be the duty primarily of the lower classes.

But the burden was initially light. While all those eligible may have taken the necessary physical examination, only a small proportion even of those who passed and entered the ballot were actually called up— between 11 percent and 18 percent in 1880–1881, for example. For some years it seemed more important to establish the principle underlying conscription than to use the system to anything like its full extent. Conscription was quite skillfully presented as a democratic gesture rather than an autocratic imposition. The authors of the conscription laws were at pains to insist that conscription was not a novel or revolutionary measure but was rooted in Japanese historical tradition. In ancient times, they pointed out, the sturdy yeoman had tilled his fields in time of peace and in war leapt to the support of the central government; such a reaction was so instinctive as to be virtually a law of nature. "Every country should be equipped with an army," claimed the Imperial Rescript proclaiming conscription, "and if an army is there, the people should naturally serve in it. In this respect a militia system is nothing else but a natural principle, and not an accidental or artificial one."

Soon, however, it was clear that the people failed to regard the opportunity to bear arms as an honor. Military service was a burden that took the fittest young men from the land and threatened them with unknown rigors. Particularly unfortunate was the Imperial Rescript's metaphorical reference to a "blood tax"—which, taken literally, started rumors that the blood of recruits was to be used for various arcane purposes, including the dyeing of the new uniform hatbands. (The telegraph wires that had recently begun to go up throughout Japan were alleged to be its conduits.) The call-up was regularly evaded, some conscripts even resorting to deliberate self-mutilation, and widespread discontent sometimes flared into open protest.

The new army needed a new ethos. For this it needed at its heart a cohesive and permanent officer corps, with the ability constantly to regenerate itself by passing on its skills through specialized educational institutions. The second French military mission to Japan, which arrived in 1872, was invited primarily to train an officer cadre and to set up a full-fledged system of military schools. In 1873 the Toyama School was established, replacing Omura's organization, to produce noncommissioned officers qualified to train the rank and file. Then in 1875, the Military Academy was founded, on the model of the French academy at St. Cyr, giving officer cadets a modern science-based education virtually unobtainable elsewhere in Japan. The officer corps that emerged was remarkably unitary. Among the senior commanders and officers—a permanent professional cadre of volunteers—the prevalence of men from Choshu and Satsuma provided more than enough cohesion; indeed, it was not long before others were bitterly inveighing against the "tyranny of the clans."

At the lower level, too, an infusion of spirit was necessary. Reluctant conscripts lowered the army's military efficiency. The government needed to provide them with a sense of common purpose and drew upon their own samurai tradition—Bushido, the "Way of the Warrior"—but they did so selectively. Bushido was originally a subtle, refined complex of beliefs centered on the concepts of loyalty, obedience, honor, bravery, and simplicity. In the Tokuho, the Soldiers' Code, promulgated in 1872, the seven duties of the soldier were spelled out as loyalty, unquestioning obedience, courage, the controlled use of physical force, frugality, honor, and respect for superiors. But while similar in many respects to Bushido, the Tokuho nevertheless lacked its spiritual underpinning and its elements of compassion and sensitivity. "A military man without poetry is a savage, not a samurai," wrote the Christian teacher Kanzo Uchimura.

Ten years later, a fuller expression of the army's ethos, different again, would be given in the Imperial Rescript to Soldiers and Sailors. At the heart of this Rescript, too, were the traditional samurai virtues—obedience, fidelity to one's word, frugality, and bravery of a rational and willed kind. "To be incited by mere impetuosity to violent action cannot be called true valor," the Rescript warned. "If you affect valor and act with violence, the world will in the end detest you and look upon you as wild beasts. Of this you should take heed." These were to be prophetic words.

The soldier's paramount duty was loyalty unto death: "Duty is weightier than a mountain, while death is lighter than a feather." The credo of the nobility of death in action was to dominate the Imperial Army ethos through to the end of the Pacific War. "If someone should enquire of you concerning the spirit of the Japanese, point to the wild cherry blossom shining in the sun." The soldier who, while still in his full vigor, gave his life for his Emperor and nation achieved the glory of the short-lived cherry blossom, which fell while its flower was still perfect.

The virtues cited in the Imperial Rescript of 1882, however, had a different quality from those in Bushido and Tokuho. They had been elevated to the status of sacred obligations—and here the final version of the Rescript diverged from its original draft by Amane Nishi. His emphasis had been upon the loyalty and obedience owed by the soldier to his superior officers. But a new hand—probably that of Confucian scholar and bureaucrat Kowashi Inoue—inserted the concept of absolute loyalty to the Emperor and made it all-important.

The religious aura surrounding the duties of the soldier was to prove particularly compelling among recruits from the rural areas, who made up the bulk of the Imperial Army. They had a strong instinctive faith in the *kami,* or spirits, of the land, with the rice *kami* naturally one of the most important spiritual forces. One element of the Emperor's national ceremonial functions was particularly effective in commanding the rural recruits' devotion. Once a year, at the time of the harvest, the Emperor ritually ate a meal of the first rice crop; in the process, he imbibed the rice *kami* and made its power his own—a far more direct source of divinity than his descent from the Sun Goddess, Amaterasu.

For such recruits, the Emperor's promise to worship at Yasukuni the "nation-protecting" *kami* of soldiers who died in his service held immense potency and energized the Imperial Army until its end. "We'll meet at Yasukuni!" the young Japanese conscripts shouted to each other as they watched American landing craft approaching the beaches in the Pacific War.

3

THE END OF THE
SAMURAI

There were many casualties in Japan along the road to modernization, not least the samurai's existence as a coherent caste. The men
who provided Japan's leadership were all samurai themselves, and they
certainly had not intended to destroy their own heritage, but the goals
they set themselves were inconsistent with the survival of a class dependent on feudalism. The abolition of the domains in 1871 made the
samurai rootless, and the replacing of clan armies with universal conscription broke their stranglehold on the right to bear arms. They were
denied many of the traditional privileges of rank. Entry into the new
bureaucracy and the Military Academy was through competitive examination—though here at least their educational standards did help ex-
samurai to succeed, and the expansion of the education system absorbed
numbers of the more literate among them as teachers in the new establishments.

Japan's new leaders had considerable sympathy with the samurai's
plight. "I think there are some methods which are almost cruel and not

suitable for dealing with the samurai. I ponder deeply over what method will be best for Japan's future," wrote Takayoshi Kido, who had ordered the Urakami Christians to be executed. But awareness and compassion did nothing to defuse samurai resentment. Omura's murder was not their only hostile gesture. Less dramatic but equally threatening was the suggestion put forward in the very early years of the new government that the country should indeed have an army equipped and organized on national lines—but that the soldiers should be exclusively samurai.

Progressives like Yamagata knew that such a system would perpetuate feudalism and work against the creation of a modern state. Unfortunately, the proposal came from Takamori Saigo, the huge, charismatic samurai from Satsuma who, at Yamagata's own request, had been appointed the first commander of the Imperial Guard. Saigo saw the opportunity to create his kind of army in 1873, at a moment when most of the nation's top leaders, led by Tomomi Iwakura, were on a tour of the world's capitals (including Washington, D.C.) seeing at first hand what the modern world was like and attempting to renegotiate the unequal treaties.

It fell to Saigo, among others, to decide how to respond to the first international crisis faced by the Meiji regime. The occasion was, this time, not some rupture in the delicate relationship with the West, at present in the hands of the Iwakura mission, but Korea's aggressive and insulting refusal to recognize the Restoration regime. Saigo saw an opportunity to preserve a role for the samurai in the defense of Japanese honor by proposing an armed expedition to put Korea in its place. Others saw this as a means of channeling unruly samurai energies away from the government, and threw their support behind him. With more temperate leaders away, the pro-invasion lobby was able to establish a majority.

Volunteers pressed forward. The samurai of Kanagawa presented a petition begging to be allowed to redeem their relative inaction at the time of the Restoration: "We have not yet been able to return the infinite debts that we owe to the state and perform our duty of cooperating with the people. . . . The state has become increasingly stable, and men like us, having no assignments to perform, simply wind up useless."

Pressure for an expedition was reaching a peak when the senior members of the government returned—and they vetoed the project. Toshimichi Okubo, in particular, had the vision of overwhelming Western superiority fresh in his mind. The Japanese government, he argued, had far better devote its limited funds and energies to reform and consolidation at home. An adventure on the Asian mainland would give the Western powers scope and excuse to interfere. Britain, as the major creditor of the penurious Meiji regime, might object to the spending of her money on a military expedition, and—in the not unlikely event that Japan defaulted on the loans—intervene to make her "another India." And a weakening struggle with Korea might simply expose both nations to attack from their neighbors: "If we open fire on Korea, Russia will fish out both the clam and the bird and get a fisherman's profit."

Saigo and several other leaders resigned in disgust. But although they had been outvoted at government level, they commanded a great deal of support throughout the country, which over the next three years would manifest itself in sporadic uprisings. That the regime took these protests seriously, though they were quite easily suppressed, is suggested by the Formosan expedition of 1874, which had all the signs of being a substitute for action in Korea, but without any of the risks.

The pretext for the expedition was the murder by Formosan aborigines of fifty-four natives of the Ryukyu Islands, claimed as nationals by Japan. In fact, the intervention was largely instigated by the American minister in Tokyo, anxious to promote discord between Japan and China (Formosa's suzerain) and thus prevent an Oriental alliance against the West. When this minister was replaced by one more judicious or less paranoid, American support was withdrawn, but nevertheless, the expedition went ahead—badly organized, inconclusive, and costly, for without medical support the expeditionary force was decimated by disease.

Not surprisingly, this debacle had little effect in tempering samurai discontent, which was multiplied exponentially in 1876, when within the space of six months samurai had the remaining shreds of both status and security torn away. In March the wearing of swords was finally prohibited. In August the government, under acute financial pressure, compulsorily commuted the samurai's annual stipends into one-off capital payments in the form of government bonds of questionable value.

From the government's perspective, the assumption, on the dissolution of the domains, of the former lords' obligation to pay their samurai had become an unjustifiable burden. The new government had inherited an empty exchequer from the Tokugawa and was having to finance Japan's transformation largely from current income: taxes, and these imposed on a barely self-sufficient peasant population. In the Tokugawa period, each lord had paid his samurai according to their status in the clan hierarchy, which in turn reflected the level of military service each was obliged to provide, a high-ranking samurai being expected to provide several warriors for his lord's army. However, in the new Japan, military service was performed by the individual conscript, and consequently the samurai was offering nothing in return for his stipend.

But from the samurai perspective, the stipends were private property handed on from generation to generation and it was not open to the government to deprive them of their birthright. Relations between samurai and government reached flashpoint, and the explosion came in Satsuma. After his resignation in 1873, Saigo became a lodestar for samurai who bitterly disapproved of what they saw as the willful destruction of traditional values. Returning to Satsuma, he founded a military school for the preservation of samurai virtues. Kindred spirits flocked to join him, similar schools multiplied, and within three years Saigo commanded thousands of supporters. He gathered an able cadre of officers around him, many of them ex-members of the elite Imperial Guard. Some of the schools employed foreign military instructors and possessed their own looms, foundries, and powder mills. In his diary, the Choshu leader Takayoshi Kido apprehensively described Satsuma as "a sort of independent country," whose officials paid more attention to Saigo's schools than to the government in Tokyo.

Even after the formal dissolution of the clans, the men of Satsuma had vigorously asserted their individuality. The government in far away Tokyo—which included a significant proportion of Satsuma leaders—had generally found it easier to humor them, allowing them a degree of independence in their administration, high positions in the army, police force, and executive, and even suggesting that Satsuma stipends might be dealt with differently from those of other samurai. As the British representative, Sir Harry Parkes, observed early in 1877, "Although observing outwardly to some extent the recent decree of the government prohibiting the wearing of swords, the samurai of Satsuma have never been disarmed, and under the name of establishing schools for this particular class, they have formed and maintained among themselves a formidable military organisation."

Fear of what this formidable organization might have in mind made the government attempt a preemptive raid to empty the arsenal at Kagoshima, the Satsuma capital. The plan was clumsily executed: The small government naval force sailed into Kagoshima harbor and docked close to the arsenal, whereupon it was attacked by a group of Satsuma activists, who seized the arms themselves and for good measure occupied government installations in the town. If the central authorities had been looking to provoke a showdown, they had succeeded.

At this point the rebels were not led by Saigo, and for some time the government even had hopes that he would remain loyal; Yamagata in particular found it hard to believe that he could do anything else. But in Kagoshima the rebels seized some fifty government "spies," one of whom confessed to having been ordered by Toshimichi Okubo to murder Saigo. After this there was no holding back, and Saigo himself took command.

He turned the incident into a plan to march on Tokyo to "put questions" to the government. In answer to Saigo's call, the warriors of Satsuma, some of them boys of fourteen and fifteen, poured into Kagoshima from the military schools in the country districts. All were required to equip themselves with arms and with money for the journey to Tokyo, though some funds came from the schools and wealthy individual supporters.

On February 17, 1877, with snow falling, Saigo and his army of samurai left Kagoshima and marched north toward the government stronghold of Kumamoto. By now, it seems, he was planning not merely to question but to attack the government in Tokyo, and Kumamoto Castle was the first obstacle in his path. It was also his downfall, for the garrison, manned by Imperial Army conscripts, held out: For fifty days and nights they fought off the unrelenting suicidal attacks of the Satsuma men, giving the government time to mobilize in great strength and corral Saigo on Kyushu.

Saigo's samurai had expected the conscript troops within Kumamoto Castle to be afraid "to encounter in arms their social superiors of the old fighting class." Even the government in Tokyo was not confident of automatic support from its troops. "Political thought was not yet developed," wrote one Imperial Army officer later. "Those who felt thankful towards the government hardly existed at all." But the new military system met its first real challenge with credit. The conscripts demonstrated that they could be relied upon in a crisis and that military skills were not the sole preserve of the hereditary samurai class.

The credit due to the conscripts was the greater for their having faced samurai whose skills were still in their finest flower. Indeed, during the Satsuma Rebellion, hand-to-hand combat between individual samurai made its last authentic appearance in Japanese history. The government commanders' response to Saigo's march had been admirably rapid, allowing them to seize an initiative that they never subsequently lost. They committed their serving troops and their first reserves to battle immediately—but as these died in the bloody fighting, the government was left without trained reinforcements. One obvious solution was to recruit ex-samurai from other clans. Yamagata was greatly opposed to diluting the conscription system, or in way displaying a lack of confidence in it; but to make up numbers he devised a plan for taking the ex-samurai into the country's police forces, rather than directly into the army.

These samurai paramilitaries were regularly sent to bear the brunt of the battle. Much of the fighting was taking place in mountainous and inaccessible terrain, where the serried ranks of the new infantry found it impossible to advance. "The bravest and strongest among the Tokio policemen are sent for to take the van," Parkes noted. "Armed with swords they attack the rebel works and rush in among the rebels while the troops are firing at the latter from a distance."

Parkes claimed the need to employ samurai had arisen because the new recruits were not yet practiced enough with rifle and bayonet. The foreign minister told him, he maintained, that the government was "in need of men who knew the use of their weapons, implying thereby that the new troops of the regular army who have been trained to the rifle and bayonet are not familiar with their arms. It is indeed reported that they are unequally matched with the Satsuma samurai when the latter rush upon them with their swords."

This may on occasion have been true. But in general the rebels, however adept and ferocious, were simply outgunned. Pinned between the garrison at Kumamoto and the government relieving force, Saigo's troops were without reinforcements and soon without supplies, having reduced the surrounding area to famine. In April 1877 Parkes reported that the government had already fielded 43,000 men to Saigo's 18,000. The regular army had better arms—Krupp field guns, rifles, Gatling guns, mortars—more ammunition, and better communications, having revolutionized their field communications with Japan's first military use of the telegraph.

Casualties were rising steeply on both sides; appeals were made to "women of rank" to emulate European gentlewomen in the Crimean and Franco-Prussian wars by providing comforts and bandages for the wounded. At last a detachment of defenders broke out of Kumamoto Castle and joined the relieving force in putting the rebels to flight. Saigo handled his southward retreat superbly, even contriving to put the government forces on the defensive at Kagoshima, where Parkes recorded the use of prototype trench warfare—"rifle pits, each pit being able to hold fifty men, and being protected with earthen or sandbag ramparts." But the final outcome was rarely in doubt, and in September 1877, cornered and wounded, Saigo commanded a comrade to behead him.

Throughout the campaign, Yamagata had forbidden his men to

speak ill of the enemy leader. Now he was reported as having had Saigo's head, decently washed for burial, brought to him and, while holding it in his hands, to have said, "Alas, your face looks serene. For your sake I have not been at ease for half a year. Now, I am at peace, but you were one of the greatest heroes of our land." Saigo was the paradigm of the "noble failure" for whom the Japanese have always had a particular regard. Immediately after his death a star in the night sky began to sparkle more brightly; this, many believed, was his resting place. Within a few years of the crushing of the Satsuma Rebellion the "traitor" was a national hero, loved as neither Yamagata nor any of the other "successful" Meiji rulers would ever be.

Yamagata's conclusions in the aftermath of the war were mixed. The conscription principle itself had been vindicated, but glaring weaknesses had been revealed elsewhere in the new military organization. In difficult terrain the transport system had been poor, resulting in enormous bills for the use of peasants and pack animals. The artillery had been generally ineffectual, the old muzzle-loading mountain guns and field guns failing frequently and disastrously. The reserve system had broken down, with the untrained second reserves proving almost useless at short notice.

The Satsuma Rebellion had also set a precedent for military overspending that was to hold for another seven decades. At the outbreak of hostilities Yamagata had called for a special advance of 200,000 yen, only to be told that it was simply unavailable. The Meiji government did not yet have independent revenues, and had paid for the War of Restoration with irregular levies from reluctant clans and with loans from wealthy merchants like the Mitsui family. The government also resorted to the lavish overissue of paper money, which inevitably led to an outflow of metal currency and to serious trade imbalances. Twice already in the 1870s, with domestic loans beyond redeeming, large additional loans had been raised in London. By 1878 Japan's international debt had soared to 47.5 percent of her total national expenditure. The government was forced to economize, and by 1880 even the army's budget was affected—though the head of the French military mission reported that most of the "cuts" were derisory, like the decision to replace the clerical staff's tea with hot water.

Most serious of all, the campaign had exposed deficiencies in operational planning. The French advisers had so far only taught command at company level. They had concentrated on tactics while postponing strategy and command studies—and even these instructions may have been imperfectly digested. While the fighting was building to a climax in March 1877, Parkes had observed that the government appeared to be avoiding a general engagement, at least partly because of "the want of familiarity on the part of the commanders . . . with the foreign military tactics which they now try to practice."

The French themselves acknowledged that their pupils' training was far from complete, and would remain so for several years to come. The Japanese army was only "le commencement du commencement," bearing no comparison with even the British sepoy force, let alone the Sikhs or Gurkhas. The Japanese soldier, claimed the mission leader, was far harder to discipline than either the Indian or the Chinese, balking at rigorous treatment and resenting correction. Men and officers alike tended to be flighty, capricious, overconfident, and careless. What they desperately needed was practical training—route marches and simple maneuvers employing the weapons whose use they had mastered in theory. But what they much preferred was the cultivation of physical strength for its own sake, in gymnastics and kendo; and they had a weakness for expensive and pointless mock battles. "La fantasia est trop dans le goût des Orientaux," snapped the French representative, Bougouin, in 1881, "et l'Empereur prend trop d'intérêt aux simulacres de combat pour que l'on renonce a ces manœuvres bruyantes."*

Bougouin's role was by this time that of an observer. To the disgust of the French (which may partly explain their disparaging comments) the Japanese had decided they had no further need of the mission's services, and it returned to France in 1880. One of the prime movers behind its dismissal may well have been Taro Katsura, who had returned in 1878 from three years as military attaché in Berlin to become one of Yamagata's principal advisers as an advocate of Prussian methods.

Yamagata first appointed Katsura to investigate the performance of the Japanese army during the Satsuma Rebellion. Katsura believed that the weakness of its operational planning was due to the fact that the Imperial Army, thanks to French influence in its earliest years, lacked a central nucleus for planning and operational command—a General Staff, such as that developed by the Prussians.

In the 1870s, thanks to Prussia's crushing defeats of the Austrians in 1866 and the French in 1870, her army's General Staff had achieved

---

*"Grotesque display is too much the style of these Orientals, and the Emperor takes too much interest in exhibition battles to give up these noisy exercises."

an almost mystical prestige. Foreign military experts—from Italy, Greece, Russia, Turkey, even from defeated France—streamed into Berlin to study the general-staff system, with a view to returning home and creating a similar organization.

Yamagata himself had been exposed to the charisma of the Prussian General Staff during his European tour in 1870, and had begun to work toward a specialized agency of this sort. He redoubled his efforts in 1874 when the government, faced with a serious outbreak of samurai discontent, to his fury appointed a civilian to lead the official forces against the rebels. In disgust, Yamagata resigned from his position as army minister—but took to himself the leadership of both the Imperial Guard and the existing planning and operations bureau within the ministry. Then, with effective control of all the military forces in Tokyo, he urged upon his colleagues a "Staff Bureau" that would defend the prerogatives of the military specialist against civilian meddling.

The Staff Bureau was in existence when the Satsuma Rebellion put the army to the test, and a separate field headquarters, answering directly to the Bureau, was set up in Kyushu. But the general administrators within the ministry still had overall control, and the result was militarily inefficient command. So Katsura recommended a clean break between the administration and command spheres of the army. The recommendation was put into effect, and in 1878 the army was given an independent General Staff with its own headquarters separate from the Army Ministry—and with Yamagata as the first Chief of Staff.

Other measures were also taken on Katsura's advice to strengthen the military machine. In 1879 the length of service in the first and second reserves was extended from four to seven years, with a view to prolonging training and increasing the army's strength in depth. As far as armaments were concerned, 1,400,000 yen was immediately committed to improving artillery. A reverberatory furnace was built at Osaka in 1882, and Japan produced its first domestic breech-loading field gun. Japanese arsenals had already begun mass-producing the new rifle designed in 1880 by Major Tsuneyoshi Murata—the first modern small arms actually made in Japan.

4

THE NATION IN ARMS

B y the end of Imperial Japan's first ten years, at the close of the 1870s, the army had survived the direct challenge of the samurai but was now to face a different and more unexpected threat from the ordinary people of Japan. The drive for modernization had permitted a crop of Western ideas and ideologies to be sown across Japan, and some of the seeds had taken root. Party politics had begun germinating in 1875 with the formation of the Freedom and People's Rights Movement by several of the antigovernment figures who had resigned with Saigo in 1873 to take up not the sword, but the cause of democracy. In Yamagata's view, the pursuit of Western "enlightenment" had led to frivolity and superficiality as craze followed craze—whist, velocipedes, Mesmerism, waltzing, planchette. Far more seriously, it had implanted notions about Western-style government where power lay with the people—and by 1881, popular feeling had grown so strong that the government was obliged to announce that a constitution would be drawn up and implemented over the next decade.

To Yamagata, the political jockeying that now began in earnest was potentially the most corrupting, degrading, and subversive influence within the new Japan, a deadly threat to the spirit of corporate unity that he felt must characterize the nation, and the military in particular. He was determined to counter it, and his position was strong. At the time of the Meiji Restoration he had been in the second rank of leaders, but now age and the toll of assassinations had pushed him well to the fore. At this critical phase in the development of parliamentary government Yamagata was the man in charge of Japan's home affairs. And he became prime minister in the first elected assembly under the new constitution.

Determined on principle to contain civilianism in Japan, Yamagata was particularly anxious to insulate the army from its corrupting influence. Lip service was paid to the notion—novel in a country that had had a military government for some eight hundred years—that the military should not exploit its power by interfering in civilian affairs. Far more genuine was the conviction that the military should not be contaminated by contact with politics.

This credo had respectable intellectual roots in Amane Nishi's theory of two societies, civilian and military, distinct though peacefully coexisting. The military, Nishi felt, must be isolated from the ideological currents buffeting civilian society—egalitarianism, libertarianism, parliamentarianism—in order to keep it strong enough to protect that society. He added the crucial rider that the military should be subject to civilian control; but like many of his doctrines, his notion of a separate military subculture was to be taken over by men less liberal than himself and turned into something more sinister.

Yamagata knew that political involvement had considerable appeal for many soldiers. Conscription was itself a form of involvement in the political process, and many rank-and-file soldiers took an interest in the rights they assumed must be theirs in return for the duty they had undertaken. Nor were officers immune. In August 1878, there had been a serious mutiny among the elite Imperial Guard, from which many officers were drawn. The reason the rebels gave for their action was the government's failure to reward them adequately for their efforts in the Satsuma Rebellion. But the authorities found more worrying an undercurrent of sympathy with the Freedom and People's Rights Movement and resentment of continuing domination by officers from the Choshu and Satsuma domains. Yamagata was determined to discourage these sentiments and to keep military affairs and politics strictly separate.

The following month, he issued an "Admonition to Soldiers and

Sailors." In it he criticized spiritual weakness and urged the threefold military virtues of bravery, loyalty, and obedience—with the stress heavily on the last two. It was not for the soldier to question the policy of the government, any more than he would question an order given him by a superior officer; there was to be no "deploring the times" or "imitating the scandalous behavior of students." No reference should ever be made to the Emperor's name, and officers should not mix socially with the rank and file. In 1880 the Admonition was reinforced with regulations formally proscribing political activity among soldiers; and 1881 saw the formation of a military police force to ferret out dissidents—the *kempeitai*, later one of the most dreaded instruments of repression in the Japanese military state.

Most important of all, Yamagata kept civilians at bay by making the command function of the General Staff independent of political controls. In 1878 the command function had been separated out from the multitude of administrative duties with the creation of a separate General Staff. Now the Supreme Command was placed—in theory—directly in the hands of the Emperor. In practice the military was self-governing from the very beginning.

By 1885, as part of the preparation of the constitution, it had been agreed that the Emperor possessed two separate military powers: *gunrei*, the power of command, which covered strategy, discipline, training, and the disposition of troops (and was to be laid down in Article 12 of the constitution); and *gunsei*, the power of military administration, which included the right to determine the size of the army and to regulate armament supplies and conscription (*gunsei* was to be laid down in Article 13).

It was also agreed, tacitly at least, that where administration was concerned, the Emperor was to be advised by the army minister. More significantly, in planning and strategy (which could be taken to mean most aspects of military foreign relations as well as the conduct of wars) the Emperor was to take advice directly from, and exercise his power directly through, the Chief of Staff, without reference, necessarily, to prime minister or Cabinet. This arrangement was not actually specified in the constitution itself, which mentioned only the powers, not the channels through which they were to be exercised. The role of the Chief of Staff was enshrined only in *military* regulations, but it contrived to be generally respected nevertheless.

The result was that "a senior officer who was subject to no government control, as any cabinet minister might be, enjoyed direct access to the Emperor and was charged with carrying out the Emperor's commands after suggesting to him what these orders should be." At this point even the Prussian Chief of Staff was not entrusted with such power, having direct access to the Kaiser only in wartime; perhaps the position of the Japanese Chief of Staff was the result of a deliberate extension by Yamagata and Katsura with a view to avoiding the fierce rivalry that had grown up between Bismarck, leader of the Prussian state, and Moltke, Chief of its General Staff.

In the 1880s Yamagata was sufficiently well placed to do more than merely shield his beloved army; he also had the power to confine the Freedom and People's Rights Movement. For the entire decade he was to straddle the whole political spectrum in Japan, with a foot in both the military and the civilian camps, allowing the influence of the army to percolate into national policy.

In 1883 he was appointed home minister, and gradually made the ministry the heart of the country's administration, the spider at the center of an authoritarian web. Local government, in Yamagata's opinion—an opinion shaped yet again by a Prussian adviser, Albert Mosse—was akin to conscription, a form of national service, not a vehicle for political expression. Real authority was centralized; all senior officials were appointed by the government, not elected by the people, and local representative assemblies had purely advisory powers.

The police, too, were reorganized to give the central government tighter control. The traveler Isabella Bird, touring Japan in the early days of Meiji, had judged the police to be "very gentle to the people . . . a few quiet words or a wave of the hand are sufficient. . . . The entire police force of Japan numbers 23,300 educated men in the prime of life, and if 30 percent of them do wear spectacles, it does not detract from their usefulness." Now a training school was set up on the German model to raise standards and increase efficiency; previously existing quasi-garrisons were broken up and policemen dispersed to a network of local stations and village-level police boxes.

The ruling elite had no scruples about employing censorship. During the Satsuma Rebellion, the press avoided mentioning heavy government casualties, and throughout the Meiji era political activities were closely regulated. Students, teachers, and some local government officials were banned altogether from party politics; and those citizens who did indulge were carefully monitored. Private individuals were forbidden "persistently to advocate foreign ideas" or even to discuss Japan's new laws as they entered the statute books.

As for the Freedom and People's Rights Movement, it operated from the start within predefined limits, and even these seemed to some to be too liberal. At the end of 1887, alarmed by the increasing violence of its more extreme opponents, the government introduced a "Peace Preservation Ordinance," which outlawed all secret societies and assemblies, authorized the police to halt any meeting, and gave the Home Ministry the power to expel political suspects from Tokyo. That Yamagata was alive to the measure's extraordinary harshness is shown by the precautions he took. The night before the ordinance went into effect, he stationed troops round the Akasaka Palace and for six hours walked around the darkened city from one potential trouble spot to another, on the alert for signs of popular revolt. It never came, and within a week he had banished 570 dissidents from the capital.

But Yamagata had a wider purpose in mind than simply entrenching authoritarian government rule. The Freedom and People's Rights Movement, and Western liberal thought in general, were the most serious threats to his plans to buttress Japan's strength through the creation of a nation-in-arms. In the nineteenth century, military power was understood to rest not solely on a head count of soldiers, nor even on the technical attributes of their weaponry, but on a "remarkable trinity" of government, army, and people, each with an equal contribution to make. This was the "nation-in-arms," a society molded to sacrifice everything willingly for the sake of the nation when the call came.

"Every great nation," wrote the Prussian military philosopher Clausewitz, "must prepare in time of peace for total effort in time of war." His ideal, one shared by Yamagata, was the strong centralized state that guaranteed the soldierly education of its people and harnessed their full strength to the needs of war. The French had shown during the Revolution what the *levée en masse* could achieve—but the Prussians had demonstrated that a nation could also be inspired to willing sacrifice within an authoritarian framework.

During the debate in Japan over the Formosan Expedition of 1874, Taneomi Soejima had indicated the hierarchy's familiarity with the Prussian nation-in-arms when he spoke of "a free people militarily organised on the North German plan." When Yamagata, Katsura, and others were in Berlin, they were exposed to the ideas of Clausewitz as implemented by Moltke. Certainly Yamagata witnessed the fervor and commitment of the Prussian people on the eve of war with France. "In the olden days of the throne," declared Emperor Meiji in November 1875, "there was no distinction between soldiers and citizens: every man was a soldier.

This honor must be revived. . . . For the future I wish the army to consist of the whole nation."

At the heart of the nation-building program was the Imperial institution and the government's campaign to make it the focus of the nation. This they had originally hoped to achieve by making Shinto the official state religion. But despite the ruthlessness with which they set about the task, and the funds they poured into the Great Promulgation Campaign, they met with little success. Somehow, the myriad evangelists expounding the virtues of paying taxes, complying with conscription, compulsory education, and the solar calendar failed to arouse popular enthusiasm.

State Shinto and the preeminence of the Emperor remained the objectives, but in its efforts to provide a coherent value system for the people as a whole, the government turned away from the shrines and put its trust in the educational system. From the beginning, it had given education a high priority, aiming at providing a network of 54,000 elementary schools offering places to all Japanese children. By the 1880s, the basic tenets of a nation-in-arms philosophy were surfacing in education. The duty of teachers to the state was now considered more important than their own educational ideas. In 1886 elementary-teacher training was organized on quasi-military lines, with the student-teachers billeted in barracks and subjected to strict discipline and indoctrination. The individual fulfillment of the child was irrelevant; schools were not run for the benefit of the pupils, declared the minister of education, but for the good of the country. New elementary-school regulations spelled out the objectives of education: moral training, the cultivation of the national essence, and the pursuit of knowledge—in that order.

Then, in 1890, the year of Japan's first parliament, came the document that was effectively the charter of the nascent nation-in-arms—the civilian equivalent of the codes governing the ethos of the army. The Imperial Rescript on Education was aimed not just at teachers and pupils but at every man and woman in Japan. The "education" to which it referred was not confined to schools, but was the lifelong process by which the loyal Japanese citizen was formed.

The Rescript was a set of ethical principles intended to govern every aspect of the relations between citizen and state, and to foster the automatic respect for authority on which Imperial rule depended. "Know ye, Our Subjects: Our Imperial Ancestors have founded Our Empire on a basis broad and everlasting and have firmly implanted virtue; Our Subjects ever united in loyalty and filial piety, have from generation to generation illustrated the beauty thereof. . . . Herein . . . lies the source of Our education. . . . Advance public good and promote common interests. . . . Should emergency arise, offer yourselves courageously to the State and thus guard and maintain the prosperity of Our Imperial Throne coeval with heaven and earth."

From now on, moral education based on the Imperial Rescript was to be an integral part of the elementary-school curriculum. A copy of the Rescript itself was kept in every school, locked away reverentially with the portrait of the Emperor and taken from its shrine every morning to be read aloud; more than one teacher, having the misfortune to stumble over the words, was reputed to have committed suicide to atone for the insult to the sacred document. Collections of *shushin*, moral tales or maxims expanding and illustrating the Rescript, were compiled for study in special lessons; more insidiously, "approved" ideas were woven into the teaching of other subjects and into every aspect of school life. History teaching was tailored to illustrate the growth of the Japanese Empire, geography to place Japan at the center of the world, and Shinto mythology to portray the Japanese people as one large family tree, with the Imperial line as the trunk and the people the branches.

The army reinforced the "family" idea in its dealings with new recruits, with the unit receiving the conscript presented to him as an extension of his family. Before he even arrived in barracks his commanding officer would have written to his parents asking for personal details and soliciting their help in perfecting the young man's education, "with the company and your home forming a complete circle." The cherry tree in the barracks square was there as a daily visual reminder of home. The service regulations of 1909 set out the responsibilities of the company commander as father to his family of conscripts. "He cultivates their qualities, develops their knowledge and their aptitudes, sees to it that regulations are strictly observed . . . and inculcates in every man the virtue of perseverance unto death." Under him, each junior officer was a mother to the recruit, ensuring that his material needs were met; every other man in the company was his brother. French observers commented in some astonishment that the Japanese soldier did not appear to mind being confined to his barracks, which were to him as a family hearth.

Between 1868 and 1890, Yamagata and the other Meiji leaders had splintered a tradition of military-civilian relations spanning two millennia, and put in its place a new relationship defined by the constitution but regulated in practice by a constricting external apparatus of repression and control. In the future, Yamagata hoped that the Japanese state would coalesce as a Prussian-style nation-in-arms, and he had instituted the means of persuasion, the machinery for indoctrination that the military leaders of the 1930s would inherit and exploit. However, there was a striking contrast between present reality and future prospects as Japan's new parliament, the Diet, held its first session.

Yamagata had failed to completely insulate the army from the political process because it was paid for from the public purse. Under the constitution, the Diet had the power to debate budget appropriations, and the right to reject the army's estimates—though not to deny funds entirely; if the estimates were rejected, the previous year's budget figure would operate. In its first session, military power and expenditure was one of the principal issues on which the Diet chose to flex its muscles. Pointing out that Japan was already allocating to the armed forces a larger proportion of its national expenditure than were the leading imperialist powers of Europe, the first Diet made a spirited attempt to challenge the military budget, as it assumed was its right.

The government responded by declaring this move contrary to the constitution. According to Article 67—a vaguely worded provision recently "clarified" by Yamagata—expenditure already fixed could not be altered without government agreement. Thanks again to Yamagata, military expenditure had been specifically "fixed," before the Diet had come into existence, at a level high enough to underwrite a seven-year expansion plan. Disgusted by the fait accompli, the Diet rejected the budget outright—and was dissolved.

Popular government was in direct conflict with the nation-in-arms ideology. Far from working in harmony, the army and the people's representatives snapped and snarled at each other. Yamagata's gloomiest forebodings about the disruptive potential of political parties had been realized, and he had no hesitation in trying to rig the elections that followed the Diet's dissolution, to ensure a more amenable assembly. He organized large-scale disruption of the polls, in which 25 people died and 388 were wounded, even according to government figures.

As it turned out, the sabotage, a major stain on Yamagata's reputation, was futile. The new Diet was no more amenable and when in 1892 the navy presented sharply increased estimates, the Diet turned them down flat. At this point, with representative government in dire trouble before it had really got going, the Emperor intervened. He offered 300,000 yen from the Imperial purse every year for six years toward the navy's expansion program; and he ordered all government officials to make a "donation" of 10 percent of their salaries for the same purpose. Diet and government were temporarily shamed into compromise; but the battle had only just begun.

5

A MODERN ARMY
EMERGES

The determined opposition of civilian elements in the Diet at the start of the 1890s was a major obstacle across the path the army had been charting since the Satsuma Rebellion in 1877. Up till that point, the army was little more than an unusually heavily armed police force, regionally deployed in static garrison units whose primary function was to maintain domestic calm. Now, in the 1880s, with armed samurai opposition at an end, it became a more versatile instrument, organized on a divisional basis and capable of large-scale operations abroad.

The creation of a General Staff in 1878 had been the first step on the road to flexible deployment. Then in 1881 Yamagata prepared a radical memorandum on Japan's national security in which he defined the concept of "security" to include the possible need for territorial expansion. "I am of course not a lover of upheavals," he wrote. "I merely want to make sure people do not forget there are upheavals"—and to guard against international turbulence Japan should make herself a "floating fortress," prepared to "exercise power in all directions." By the following year, his memorandum had been translated into an Imperial edict on the need for Japan to expand her military strength. For a decade, Yamagata had argued that the army would sooner or later turn its attention to the outside world; and in the 1881 memorandum, he directed its gaze to Japan's immediate neighbors: China and Russia.

Japanese attitudes toward China had for a millennium been respectful, admiring, imitative. Between the eighth and sixteenth centuries, Japan had absorbed political institutions, religious ideas, educational practice, legal theory, and the basis of her language from China. But now, in the late nineteenth century, she was acutely aware of the pressure being successfully applied to a crumbling empire. In 1850 the ruling Ch'ing dynasty had been shaken by a series of internal rebellions that exposed China's military weakness. By 1858 the French had taken Saigon and pushed into Cochin China (now part of Vietnam) and Cambodia. In 1858 the Tsar annexed the north bank of the Amur, and in 1860 claimed extensive lands east of the Ussuri River, depriving China of a large stretch of Pacific coastline and creating a common border for Russia with Korea. At the other side of the empire Britain had designs on upper Burma and on Tibet.

Japan's leaders were determined that she should not miss the opportunity, amid the process of Chinese disintegration, to establish her own foothold on the continent. In 1871 they concluded a commercial treaty on more or less equal terms with China; and soon afterwards were disputing her claims to the Ryukyu Islands, off the southwest tip of Japan. The main point of contention, however, was China's tributary Korea.

Korea's importance to Japan was predominantly strategic, as the peninsula was the only point from which an invasion of Japan might realistically be launched. It was very much in Japanese interests that Korea remain neutral if not actively friendly, and strong enough to resist seizure by an enemy. The Japanese saw little chance of this state of affairs persisting under China's suzerainty. For Korea to be able to defend herself, modernization was essential—and here as elsewhere, China was committed to the preservation of the status quo, even though in Korea that meant nurturing a reactionary monarchy that was both corrupt and inefficient.

After abandoning the Korean expedition in 1873, the dominant faction in the Meiji leadership set about securing concessions from the Korean regime by means short of war. In 1875 an opportunity presented itself—perhaps not without a little stage management—when Korean coastal batteries opened fire on "peaceful" Japanese survey vessels. Japan promptly sent an armed expedition to demand an apology—and, more to the point, the opening of Korean ports to Japanese trade. Under the Treaty of Kanghwa, signed in February 1876, three ports were opened and Korea was officially declared "independent"—that is to say, free of Chinese claims.

Japan was now in a better position to cultivate her influence in the former "Hermit Kingdom." There was, however, no single policy emerging from Japan, but a multiplicity of influences. Korean dissidents found vigorous support at the two extremes of the Japanese political spectrum. Liberals like Yukichi Fukuzawa and Taisuke Itagaki had genuine aspirations for political reform in Korea, which they hoped would somehow infect Japanese society with a desire for similar change. On the other hand, ultranationalist groups like the Genyosha, or "Dark Ocean Society," saw the overthrow of the Chinese-backed Korean government as Japan's first stepping-stone to power in Asia.* But between the two poles, there was almost certainly also covert assistance from the army ministry to anti-Chinese groups.

Meanwhile, China was hardly a passive spectator. In 1882 the Chinese-backed former regent of Korea, the Taewon-gun, was induced to lead an anti-Japanese, antireform revolt in which Japanese nationals were murdered and their minister was put to flight; the following year China reasserted Korea's tributary status. It was thus Japan's turn to underwrite or at least condone the next coup, in 1884—but China held her position and once again the Japanese minister retreated.

Under the Treaty of Tientsin in 1885, China and Japan agreed mutually to withdraw their troops and give advance notice of any intention to send troops back to Korea in future. Generous protestations of belief in Korea's "independence" were exchanged—but in fact China, with her regent, Yüan Shih-k'ai, in place, had the upper hand. On the basis of surveys carried out by the General Staff, the Japanese government decided that the Imperial Army was not yet strong enough to act.

For some years, therefore, Japan's policy in Korea was necessarily to be one of conciliation. But beneath the relatively tranquil surface, pressure for a more "forward" policy was building up. Katsura, for one, found the inactivity galling. Rising fast within the military bureaucracy,

*The ultimate goal was the seizure of Manchuria; hence the reference in the group's name to the "dark" or muddy waters of the Amur River, Manchuria's northern border.

he was now the commissioner of the General Staff; and he had the vigorous support of Soroku Kawakami, a high flyer on the staff side whose conception of Japan's role in Asia, and her policy toward Korea in particular, was frankly expansionist.

Meanwhile, it had escaped no one's attention that China was no longer the only enemy to be faced in Korea. In 1884 the Korean government had concluded a commercial treaty with the Russians, who feared, as Prince Alexei Lobanov-Rostovsky would later explain, that any Japanese presence on the Asian continent would spread like "a drop of oil on a sheet of blotting paper."

For their part, the Japanese had perceived Russia as a threat since her ships had first started appearing off the Japanese coast in 1779. By the middle of the nineteenth century, Russia's territorial gains in China—first the lands north of the Amur, then the crucial acquisition of the Maritime Province and the founding of Vladivostok, the "Ruler of the East"—had brought the menace very near. In 1861, the British representative in Japan concluded apprehensively: "To annex a territory with nearly three hundred leagues of sea coast, and this without war or expense, beyond the pay of a few agents preparing the way by their 'scientific' explorations, must be considered [a] triumph. . . . The Russians themselves seem to regard the recent stride down the Chinese coast as the great turning point of their destiny." During the early years of foreign intervention in Japan, the Russians had been suspected of harboring designs on both Hokkaido and the island of Tsushima, strategically placed in the strait between Korea and Japan.

Russia desperately needed a warm-water port to give her constant access to the Pacific, and few doubted where she hoped to find one. "Allow me to assure you," wrote the British representative in November 1862, "that whenever the Captain of a Russian man-of-war leaves with sealed orders from the Admiral, his destination is invariably Korea."

With good reason, Japan's strategic planners in the 1880s focused their gaze outward. What is less clear is whether the new posture was defensive or aggressive. From one perspective, the whole thrust of Japan's modernization looks defensive, undertaken in response to the threat from the West. Until the very end of the nineteenth century, Japan's overriding aim in foreign policy was to secure the revision of the prejudicial treaties she had been obliged to sign by the Western powers—in other words, to secure equality, not advantage.

But the powers Japan was trying to rival were themselves aggressive, nationalist, and colonialist. As Katsura and Kawakami pointed out, only the second-class Western nations were content merely to defend their frontiers. The goal of every truly great nation was "to radiate military power and in times of trouble call upon the soldierly strength of all citizens, thus taking insult from no quarter." There was certainly great popular support for the notion of a Japan "radiating military power." Overtly expansionist groups had powerful allies both inside and outside government, within the business community, industry, the Foreign Ministry—and, undeniably, the military, for whom any swing toward a more aggressive national policy meant a larger share in the shaping of that policy and, by implication, in government as a whole.

By the mid-1880s, Meiji Japan was on the alert, if not the attack, in Korea; and beyond, was becoming increasingly aware of her interests in Manchuria, the vast northern territory now encircled by a horseshoe of Russian menace. Actually part of northeast China, Manchuria was controlled by a dynasty (the Manchus) that did its best to disown Chinese claims on the area, making it easier for other nations with their own ambitions there to do the same. Russia had long been encroaching piecemeal on Manchuria, an advance that Japan viewed with intense suspicion—at the same time noticing herself the area's attractions as a rich source of soybeans, coal, and iron ore. More importantly, the Liaotung Peninsula, the southernmost point of Manchuria, was coming to be viewed as the key to the security of neighboring Korea.

The need to defend Japan, against Russia in particular, was undoubtedly genuine. The desire to extend Japan was equally undeniable, at least in some quarters. With both objectives in view, Japan was always likely to go into action on the Asian mainland as soon as she was militarily strong enough to do so. But whether the new Imperial Army was a defensive or an aggressive force, it was unquestionably becoming an ever more skilled and sophisticated one.

The 1880s were the years when the army evolved and entrenched a professional establishment, capable of gathering intelligence, formulating policy, planning and directing operations, and recruiting, training, equipping, transporting, and administering a modern armed force. But by opting for a conscript rather than a samurai army, a totally new system rather than a reworking of the old, Yamagata and his colleagues had placed a great deal of onus on the cadre responsible for training the new forces.

Early in the 1880s it was clear that the men available were too few and too inexperienced for the job. There was an urgent need for skilled officers who could raise the caliber of lower ranks, and in particular there was a need for a staff corps as the *fons et origo* of military expertise. In 1883, at the instigation of the General Staff, a Staff College was set up at General Staff Headquarters. It was a timid venture at first, teaching tactics but neither organization nor logistics. But it nevertheless offered the advocates of reform an opportunity to bring in foreign instructors again—and this time they turned to the victors, not the losers, of the Franco-Prussian War.

Across the whole spectrum of its modernization, Japan would be eclectic in her choice of models—America for the beginnings of her educational system, Britain for her railway network and her navy, France for her centralized banking methods. But in the crucial spheres of politics and military matters, she turned regularly if not exclusively toward Germany.

Given the pro-Prussian sympathies of Yamagata and others as early as 1870, the French mission's survival for almost ten years was remarkable. Even after it departed in 1880, its influence persisted in some areas with the help of powerful supporters like Iwao Oyama, a Satsuma member of the inner circle of government and a senior member of the army General Staff. But in 1884 Oyama left for Europe at the head of a mission whose objective was specifically to compare the military organizations of the Western powers. In its absence a powerful lobby came into the open to push for the use of Prussian teachers at the Staff College.

Among those accompanying Oyama were Katsura and Kawakami, who no doubt seized every opportunity to draw to his attention the advantages of the Prussian military system. By the time the mission returned, Oyama had been either convinced or outweighed. On the strength of connections formed during his term as military attaché in Berlin (possibly even on the advice of Moltke himself), Katsura was able to recommend a specific candidate for the Staff College. Major Jacob Meckel was to the casual observer the stereotype of a Prussian officer—tall, stiff-backed, a holder of the Iron Cross from the Franco-Prussian War, interested in drinking and German opera. He was also an exceptionally effective teacher, with years of experience at the Prussian Staff College.

Meckel arrived in Japan in 1885, at the age of forty-three, to assume a dual role as Staff College lecturer and adviser to the Japanese army General Staff. With his arrival, Katsura and Kawakami (now respectively vice-minister of the army and vice-chief of the General Staff) established a committee to investigate army organization and strategy, chaired by Gentaro Kodama, another of Yamagata's protégés. In close collaboration with Meckel, the three pushed ahead a program of reform that reached into every cranny of the old system and reshaped the Imperial Army as an offensive force.

"It is rather difficult to get accurate information about the Japanese army," complained Rudyard Kipling, writing for the *Civil and Military Gazette* in the late 1880s. "It seems to be in perpetual throes of reorganisation." Meckel's suggestions embraced every aspect of the military system, including the abolition of virtually all exemptions to conscription.

In 1888, the army took the crucial step of moving the basis of its organization from that of the garrison to the division. Static accumulations of troops, French-style, were replaced by mobile, self-sufficient operational units combining infantry, cavalry, artillery, engineers, and supply troops. This, Yamagata felt, was a major step toward preparedness for operations on the Asian continent; and it is perhaps no coincidence that at the same time arrangements were made for closer cooperation with the Imperial Navy.

Meckel had firm opinions about the direction these continental operations might take. Korea, he declared, was a dagger pointed at the heart of Japan, and his teaching was based from the start on the premise that this army was to be used for campaigning abroad. The French had concentrated mainly on small-unit training and the inculcation of fighting spirit. Meckel's concern was large-scale operational planning, such as would be needed in a major conflict with a powerful enemy—the deployment of a field army, entailing the command of entire divisions.

Meckel did not, so far as is known, include training in intelligence gathering in his courses at the Staff College. But spying and intelligence had been quite sophisticated under the Tokugawa shoguns, and the Japanese built on these foundations during Meckel's era. Military staff were attached to their legations overseas as "language officers"; besides learning European languages, their job was to profit from Europe's experience in spying and intelligence and, as needed, gather intelligence about the host countries themselves. In the 1880s the most usual destination for army officers, not surprisingly, was Germany.

Meckel did not overlook the possibility that trouble in Korea might even mean the threat of an invasion of the home islands, and he emphasized the urgency of building a foolproof mobilization system with the logistic capacity to concentrate troops fast at any point in Japan. The Japanese had originally believed that the lack of a railway system was actually a good defense, denying an invader the means of rapid advance. Needless to say, Meckel did not subscribe to this theory—the Prussian General Staff having learned the value of railways from studying the

American Civil War—and throughout the decade and beyond, railways were extended and improved.

By 1891 all the main military strongpoints were joined, if just by a single-line, narrow-gauge track, and maneuvers held to test the network were entirely satisfactory. At the same time, the supply system was revolutionized. An Army Service Corps was created in 1888, and sweeping changes to administrative methods within the Army Ministry meant improvements in purchasing, storage, accounting, rationing, and distribution of food and equipment. Overseeing the organization as a whole was an inspectorate-general with wide powers, on a par with the Army Ministry and the General Staff.

In the realm of battlefield tactics, Meckel's teachings were more questionable, as he favored theories that were already being discarded in Europe. There, mainstream thought favored the use of columns that fanned out as they reached the firing line. This extended the fighting area, and Meckel felt that it diluted the assault. Worse, having seen in the Franco-Prussian War whole companies taking cover in the undergrowth, he believed it undermined the fighting spirit. Closed ranks advancing into fire, regardless of cost, to deliver the maximum "shock" to the enemy appealed far more to his temperament, with its near-compulsive stress on discipline and obedience. The more enlightened ideas of the great Clausewitz, with their stress on flexibility and common sense rather than absolute rules based on historical precedent, were not, it seemed, being passed down the line stretching from Clausewitz to Moltke to Meckel. In later years, when war with Russia eventually came, the choice of Meckel as a mentor was to prove appallingly costly to the Japanese infantry as they tried to advance en bloc through barbed-wire entanglements in the teeth of artillery and machine-gun fire.

Nevertheless, in 1890, Yamagata felt he had a military machine worth displaying to the world. That spring, in the Grand Maneuvers at Nagoya, the Imperial Army went through its paces for the benefit of foreign diplomats and an admiring Japanese public, parading the largest body of troops ever assembled for such an occasion. Entirely new was the effective use of rail as well as sea transport, and a high degree of cooperation with the navy. The French observer considered the amphibious efforts especially remarkable. The German diplomats thought overall strategy rather weak and coordination imperfect, though the Japanese commanders made good tactical use of terrain and their deployment and control of firepower were excellent. There was praise and criticism from the foreigners, but none could deny the remarkable truth that here, on the edge of Asia, a modern army had been born.

PART II

THE ARMY AT WAR
1890-1918

LINE OF ADVANTAGE:
THE FIRST SINO-JAPANESE
WAR

I n 1890, the year of the Nagoya maneuvers, Yamagata made one of
his most influential statements on Japan's strategic position. He did
not directly incite military expansion or advocate war, and yet he made
both more likely by clarifying the issues, pinpointing the enemies, and
highlighting the options. He distinguished between Japan's "line of
sovereignty" and her "line of advantage." The former was the border
of territories she actually possessed. The latter demarcated nearby territories whose fate could have the most crucial influence on her strength
and safety.

As Yamagata spoke, Japan's "line of advantage" lay in Korea.
Friendly, the Korean peninsula was a buffer against invasion from the
continent; hostile, it was, as Meckel had said, a dagger to Japan's heart—
and in the early 1890s both Chinese and Russian hands threatened to
seize the dagger's hilt. Since the Treaty of Tientsin in 1885, ostensibly
a "stand-off" agreement, China had generally got the better of the
discreet tussle with Japan for influence and economic opportunity in

Korea. And in 1891 with the start of work on the Trans-Siberian Railway, Russia took its first menacing step toward Japan's danger zones. Yamagata sounded the alarm. "In order to defend oneself by remaining stationary," he declared, "one must have enough strength to launch an attack." In the event, the target of this "offensive defense" was China.

The spur to war was the Korean government's response to a revolt by the native Tonghak religious sect. The Tonghaks had the support of Japanese ultranationalists—support that was somewhat double-edged, since the Tonghaks, as defenders of traditional values, sought the expulsion of foreigners from Korea, while the Japanese reactionaries hoped that the insurrection would pave the way for Japanese expansion on the peninsula.

The Korean government lost little time in appealing to China for help, and China promised to send troops. Japan at once invoked her right under the Treaty of Tientsin to send a corresponding force. By the time the Chinese and Japanese contingents arrived, the Tonghak Rebellion had in fact been contained, and the two "protectors" of Korea could have withdrawn their troops without in any way compromising the peace; but neither did so.

For her part, Japan decided to push for the reform of the Korean regime—either jointly with China, or unilaterally if cooperation were not forthcoming. She proposed a sweeping program of "reforms"—to Korea's police, her army, judicial system, educational framework, currency, and tax structure—which were all to be undertaken under Japan's aegis and which would have guaranteed a considerable measure of Japanese control. And when China, predictably enough, rejected the proposals, the Japanese resorted to force. On July 23, 1894, Japanese troops attacked the royal palace in Seoul, and the Taewon-gun was once more induced to take over the government. On July 25 the Japanese navy sank the *Kowshing*, a British vessel chartered to carry Chinese reinforcements to Korea, drowning more than a thousand men. On August 1, tardily, war was declared.

This apparently logical sequence of events was in fact a blend of the deliberate and the accidental, the product of a tangle of conflicting motives and ambitions. No single figure or faction on the Japanese side could be labeled the prime mover, because war suited many people's purposes, not least those of the ultranationalists whose machinations had paved the way to the conflict. For a decade army leaders had had provisional plans for a confrontation with China in Korea, though in 1894 Yamagata was not optimistic about Japan's chances in a head-on clash with China. Kawakami, by now preeminent within the General Staff, poured contempt on Yamagata's opinion. "How could this old fellow understand soldiers?" he asked. Deeply involved in intelligence gathering on the mainland—both the "official" operations of the army and the "unofficial" activities of ultranationalist societies—Kawakami was convinced the time had come when Japan could present her giant neighbor with a realistic challenge.

Outside military circles, a key ally in forcing the issue to the point of war was Foreign Minister Munemitsu Mutsu. He saw war as a safety valve for the disruptive energies generated by the new Diet and as a means of rallying public support behind the government; and he also hoped that if military action was initiated early enough, overall strategy might remain within the control of the civilian authorities rather than the General Staff.

Mutsu was among the first to advocate sending troops; he almost certainly contrived to conceal from Prime Minister Hirobumi Ito the fact that even before the troops landed, they were no longer needed to suppress disorder; he may even have conspired to trick Ito into increasing the size of the Japanese force. Once the troops were in Korea, he believed that they could not be withdrawn without the government looking foolish. Preferring war to political humiliation, by mid-July he was writing to Japan's minister in Korea, "You will commence active movement on some pretext, taking care to do what is least liable to criticism in the eyes of the world." But Mutsu had to some extent been maneuvered into adopting this hard line by the military men he had hoped to preempt.

On the basis of firsthand reports from his agents in Korea, and even before the Cabinet had met to discuss the question, General Kawakami urged Mutsu to recommend sending troops. And it was he who is said to have presented Mutsu with the means of tricking Ito into sending a genuinely effective strike force. Kawakami's plan was to inflict enough damage on the Chinese to provoke them into sending more troops, thus justifying the dispatch of a Japanese force large enough to fight a full-scale campaign for Korea. For this he felt he needed an initial body of 7,000 men. Mutsu objected that Ito, anxious to avoid alienating foreign opinion, was unlikely to authorize so large a force. According to one story, Kawakami came up with a ploy. "Let us present it as a brigade," he suggested. "Since the premier knows that a brigade is composed of 2000 troops, he will probably not disapprove. But if we send a *mixed* brigade, it will have 7–8000 troops." Whether or not this was the means by which Ito was persuaded, the larger force was duly sent, and the fuse of war was lit.

Kawakami was a figure of great charisma—a soldier's soldier, in contrast to military bureaucrats and politicians like Yamagata and Katsura. But his effectiveness in this situation, overcoming the misgivings of the ruling elite, was more than simply a personal triumph; it was a symptom of the generally growing influence of the army. And this was perhaps the point at which the military first began to play a crucial part in determining Japan's foreign policy.

In the years immediately following the Meiji Restoration, the army had been hardly distinguishable as a separate force in government, so great was the overlap of military and civilian leadership. The civilian government included many figures with military rank, past and present, from the ex-leaders of Choshu *shotai* to generals in the new army.

Then had come the creation of the separate General Staff in a conscious effort to establish the independence of the army. In theory these newly "liberated" military officials had no role in government; in practice they exerted a constant influence, thanks largely to their continuing personal ties with the inner circle of Meiji leaders.

By 1890 this inner circle was composed of seven genro, "elder statesmen"—special advisers to the Emperor, his guides through the political minefield at a time when the new structure of cabinet and constitution was complete but insecure. The genro were the principal survivors of the original Meiji ruling elite. Their position was extraconstitutional and informal, but their prestige was immense, and their power was reinforced by the intricate network of contacts that bound them tightly together: bonds of clan (all were either Choshu or Satsuma); bonds of marriage and adoption; shared links with business and the bureaucracy.

The genro's ties with the military were obvious. Three of the seven held senior ranks in the military hierarchy. Almost to a man, military leaders shared the genro's suspicion of political parties. And the "Satcho" (Satsuma-Choshu) monopoly of power was as pronounced in the armed forces as it was among the genro—Kawakami, Oyama, and others from Satsuma; Yamagata, Katsura, Kodama from Choshu. As the power of the genro reached its peak at the turn of the century, it helped to entrench the influence of the military, paving the way to power for men like Kawakami.

The other conspicuous display of the military's new muscle came with the setting up of the first Imperial General Headquarters at the beginning of June 1894. Normally a headquarters of this sort would be organized only during actual hostilities, for the direction of operations. This one was established fully two months before war was formally declared, with the barely concealed ulterior motive of wresting the initiative in policy-making from the civilian government and preventing civilian interference in military matters. Significantly, however, the central military authorities were not in absolute control of their own officers in the field; though under instructions to stay aboard their transport vessels at Inchon until an advance was ordered, a proportion of the mixed brigade landed regardless, on its own initiative, and moved on Seoul.

The war that was to follow was, in the phrase of one contemporary observer, "an encounter between such tactics as were employed by Agamemnon at Troy and those that might have been conceived by Moltke." The Japanese forces, nearing a peak of potency in 1894, were confronting an enemy in stagnant decay.

After the Meckel era, the Japanese army was a compact and well-organized unity. Its brain, the General Staff, served by efficient intelligence, could count on having its instructions swiftly implemented through a comprehensive system of mobilization, transport, supplies, and communications. Its officer cadre was increasingly well trained and its men were adequately if not magnificently equipped. Japan was moving toward self-sufficiency in arms production. Quick-firing field guns, smokeless powder, and Murata repeating rifles were being manufactured in large quantities (though only two field divisions were actually equipped with the rifles at the outbreak of the First Sino-Japanese War, and none had ever been used in combat). A precision instrument factory had been set up in Tokyo under the aegis of an Italian artillery major, turning out binoculars, range finders, and other modern military aids. And the arsenals were even making a small number of weapons for export; in 1892 Japan sold a consignment of sabers and small arms to the officials of the City of Melbourne.

In contrast, the Chinese forces could scarcely be described as a single army at all. Nominally divided neatly into two—the Yungchun and the Lienchun Forces—the so-called army was in practice a cluster of separate regional contingents in varying degrees of disrepair; some were little more than volunteer constabulary. The local militias—embryo warlord armies—which had been effective in mid-century had rapidly declined in the 1870s. Organization, equipment, and morale were all lamentable. The uniform of the typical Chinese enlisted man consisted of "baggy trousers and a brightly coloured, but ill-fitting jacket, topped by a turban or conical bamboo hat. This unmilitary appearance was often accentuated by the addition of a fan and umbrella." Chinese military efficiency was undermined by neglect of the troops—underfed, housed in dirty, inadequate huts, debilitated by enforced idleness, and likely to be addicted to gambling and opium. There was no central budget, no General Staff, no national feeling. When war came in 1894, there was still no coordinated central command, no mobilization or transport system. The vast resources of manpower at China's disposal remained largely untapped.

The Chinese entered the war with a hodgepodge of antiquated and incompatible weapons, and military leadership that ranged from the mediocre to the abysmal. The Belgian representative, Baron Jules Joseph d'Anethan, detailed their arms: serviceable modern weapons which too often lacked matching ammunition; Krupp mountain guns alongside bows and arrows; cannonballs made of painted mortar, designed originally to fool the commissariat at stock-taking time; "enormous, formidable-looking sabres whose blades were made of tin—veritable harlequins' bats"; ammunition filled with coal dust or sawdust instead of explosives. As for their officers, many had achieved their rank through nepotism, and most were poorly trained. Some were arrant cowards. The Chinese soldiers' invariable custom, reported one military attaché, was "to fire off all their remaining ammunition at full speed and to follow their officers to the rear (also at full speed) as soon as the attacking force came within a certain distance of their entrenchments. I have heard Japanese Officers say to each other, 'Now they are off' as soon as the fusillade . . . commenced."

Japan had made herself strong in response to an acutely painful recognition of her vulnerability to the West. In contrast, China's safety was fatally compromised by "a sense of self-assurance that at times bordered on the megalomaniac." The Chinese paid attention to few other nations and showed no signs of taking seriously the threat from the neighboring "dwarf pirates." Knowing nothing of her present strength, they viewed Japan as a tributary rather than one of the Great Powers. The thoroughness of Japanese preparations and the discipline and hardihood of the Japanese soldier came as an unpleasant surprise. "We operate on our own territory," lamented one Manchurian official, "and yet do not know the topography, but they all carry maps individually and move over obscure paths and waterways as if they were old familiar roads"—a tribute to the intelligence network of Kawakami and others.

Even after hostilities had begun, many Chinese took little or no notice, showing more interest in the plans for the Empress Dowager's sixtieth-birthday celebrations. Meanwhile, in Japan popular sentiment was solidly behind the war. "So many old samurai dusted off their fathers' swords and asked to be sent to the front that an Imperial Rescript was issued telling them to get back to work at their jobs." Yamagata himself was overjoyed to be in command of the First Army, and wrote several poems describing his happiness at finding himself once more on active service.

On September 16, six weeks after the declaration of war, the Japanese won a decisive victory at Pyongyang. Yamagata stage-managed a swift and well-disguised advance culminating in an attack on three sides, which put the Chinese to flight within hours. Official Japanese figures listed their own casualties at 700 as compared with China's 6,000. The following day, in the Battle of the Yellow Sea, the Japanese navy virtually annihilated China's northern fleet. In less than forty-eight hours, Japan had effectively taken control of Korea and of the seas around it—a double blow from which the Chinese leaders never recovered.

The approaches to North China by land and sea were now clear, enabling the Japanese army to go ahead with a two-pronged advance on Manchuria. The ultimate objective—of the military if not the civilian authorities—was the invasion of Hopei province and an attack on Peking. By October 9 the last Chinese troops had been driven from Korea; on October 24 the Japanese First Army crossed the Yalu River and entered Manchuria in hot pursuit. At the end of the month the Second Army made an amphibious landing on the Liaotung Peninsula, and headed for the key ports of Dairen and Port Arthur at its tip. Disastrously, the Chinese commanders failed to defend the narrow neck of the peninsula, where the Japanese advance might most easily have been checked. On November 6 Dairen fell, and Port Arthur was taken two weeks later.

The Liaotung offensive made the reputation of one of Japan's most revered but controversial military leaders: General Maresuke Nogi. Nogi's early career had taken a catastrophic turn during the Satsuma Rebellion, when his regiment lost its battle standard—a disgrace which he took so personally that he decided to kill himself and was only restrained by direct orders from a superior officer. Years of drink and debauchery followed as he brooded on the debacle. But he reached the rank of general notwithstanding; and in 1887 a tour of duty in Germany revived his sense of dedication to the military ideal and the samurai tradition.

He would appear also to have absorbed Prussian doctrines of strategy and tactics, for the taking of Port Arthur from the Chinese was a textbook operation that would have gladdened Meckel's heart. The Japanese infantry advanced in perfect order regardless of casualties—the officers suffering particularly severely in leading from the front, as Meckel had decreed—and took the stronghold in a single day.

The triumph was marred only by reports in the foreign press of atrocities committed as the Japanese swept through the town. Between two thousand and three thousand people, soldiers and civilians, men, women, and children were said to have been shot and hacked to death. "More of these piteous deaths we saw," wrote the London *Times* correspondent, "unable to stay the hands of the murderers, until sick and saddened beyond the power of words to tell we slowly made our way in the gathering gloom to headquarters. There at the Chinese general's pavilion, facing the spacious parade-ground, Field-Marshal Oyama and all his officers assembled amid strains of strange music from military bands, now weird, now lively, and ending with the impressive national anthem, 'Kimi ga yo,' and a huge roar from 20,000 throats of Banzai Nippon. The contrast was horrible, insufferable."

With an eye to the good opinion of the outside world, Japan had been anxious to go to war "in Christian style," ensuring that the troops were accompanied by Red Cross representatives and lawyers versed in international conventions. The allegations were absolutely denied. The reports may well have been exaggerated in the more sensational newspapers; Baron d'Anethan considered that they were. Other commentators justified the barbarities as retaliation; troops entering the town found the heads and mutilated corpses of Japanese prisoners hanging near the gates. But military attachés and Red Cross officials confirmed the more sober charges. Whatever the truth may have been, for the first time a sinister question mark had been raised over the character of the modern Japanese fighting man.

In the meantime Yamagata and the First Army were looking towards Haicheng on the southwestern border of Manchuria, apparently with a view to continuing the advance toward Peking. But Ito, the prime minister of the day, now struck a blow for civilian moderation. Using Yamagata's ill health as an excuse—the general was suffering from his recurrent stomach trouble—Ito had him recalled.

At the same time, Ito proposed as an alternative to Peking an advance on the Shantung Peninsula, an area of both economic and strategic interest to Japan. In January and February, despite pleas for peace from China, troops landed in Shantung and occupied the treaty port of Weihaiwei. Meanwhile, the First and Second Armies had combined to push the Chinese up the Liaotung Peninsula and out of Manchuria across the Liao River. Now Japan called a halt; the question being asked was not whether the Japanese would win the war, but how they should best handle the peace.

Japan's victory revolutionized her standing in the region, if not in the world. It altered the way the Great Powers regarded her. "The spectacle of this Eastern nation," mused the *Illustrated London News* condescendingly, "fighting and manoeuvring and organizing with a *verve* and intelligence worthy of a first-class European war has sent a thrill of admiring wonder through the military world." Perhaps more important, it altered the way Japan regarded herself.

The Sino-Japanese War of 1894–1895 marks the start of Japan's career as an imperial power. For the first time she was not afraid to express and pursue territorial ambitions—ambitions that developed hugely as the war progressed and success followed success. Japan's "line of advantage" no longer seemed to lie in Korea, but had been pushed outward to include the Liaotung Peninsula and Formosa; and many looked farther, to Fukien province in the south, central Manchuria in the north, and even to Peking.

In 1866, after the Battle of Königgrätz, which opened the way to the unification of Germany, Bismarck had written to his wife: "If we are not excessive in our demands and do not believe that we have conquered the world, we will attain a peace that is worth our effort . . . I have the thankless task of pouring water into the bubbling wine." In 1895 some elements in Japan—the fierier military leaders in the field, with enthusiastic if ill-informed popular support—appeared to believe that they had conquered the world. In fact resources were running low and casualties high; though the official figures only admitted to 1,000 Japanese killed and some 5,000 wounded, almost 17,000 had died of disease. More important, while the Japanese had conclusively defeated China herself, they could not hope to sustain a confrontation with the Great Powers, which had well-established interests in China. It was the task of Ito, Yamagata, Mutsu, and others to moderate their nation's demands in accordance with these realities, and to achieve a settlement that would bring Japan genuine advantages without provoking suspicion and retaliation. In the end they failed to resolve the equation correctly—a misjudgment that would crucially affect Japanese history in the twentieth century.

As early as January 27, 1895, Ito had predicted that any but the most modest peace terms would lead to outside intervention. On February 16 the Russian minister to Japan confirmed Ito's forebodings by advising against seeking the concession of any territory in mainland China. On March 8 the German minister echoed the Russian warning. On March 20 the peace conference opened at Shimonoseki, with Japanese troops still poised to march on Peking. After four days of negotiations the Chinese plenipotentiary, Li Hung-chang, was shot and seriously wounded by a Japanese assailant. In some embarrassment, the Japanese offered a cease-fire as a gesture of good faith—but not before Japanese troops had occupied the Pescadore Islands.

The cession of both Formosa and the Pescadores came near the top of the list of demands presented to the Chinese at Shimonoseki; the Japanese were extremely anxious to stop these key strategic islands from falling into the hands of Western powers. Then came the inevitable demand for Chinese recognition of Korean "independence"—the original casus belli—and for a large indemnity to cover Japan's war expenses. So far there was little to which the Great Powers took exception, and China herself was in no position to resist. But despite the warnings, the Japanese had decided to push their luck, and they went on to demand the best part of the Liaotung Peninsula, including Port Arthur, which had particular significance both as an ice-free port and as the base for China's Northern Fleet. From the army's point of view, Liaotung was of unique strategic importance. Not only was it the key to control of Korea, it was also the gateway to Manchuria and ultimately to Peking. Japan had fought hard for this immensely valuable territory and had won; but given the realities of the existing balance of power in the region, to attempt to keep it was hubris.

On April 17, China, having little bargaining power of her own, signed the treaty of Shimonoseki, accepting all Japan's demands. But throughout the negotiations the Chinese had made sure that all interested parties were aware of the extent of Japan's ambitions. On April 23 the Japanese observed that all Russian warships in their ports had been placed on the alert to set sail at twenty-four hours' notice. That day the ministers for Russia, France, and Germany appeared at the Japanese Foreign Ministry and offered their "friendly advice." The Japanese claim to the Liaotung Peninsula would be a constant threat to Peking and to peace in East Asia, and they should immediately renounce it.

This "Triple Intervention" was impossible to resist. By combining their naval forces, the three nations could cut off the Japanese armies, which were still in Manchuria. On May 5, in return for an additional indemnity on top of the original substantial sum, Japan agreed to relinquish the territory that had been its modern army's first and most valuable prize. It was a bitter blow.

7

THE RUSSIAN MENACE

The Triple Intervention was crucially important in shaping the way the Japanese looked at the outside world in the twentieth century. Thirty-five years later, Inazo Nitobe would write: "We are under an illusion that in diplomacy we are always beaten or cheated. The illusion is so ingrained in us that no diplomatic move has been made by us without arousing resentment in one quarter or another."

Japan's sense of competition was whetted by humiliation. Tadasu Hayashi, then vice-minister of foreign affairs, was the official obliged to receive the three foreign ministers and their "friendly advice," and accordingly privileged to witness three different brands of European arrogance in action. Hayashi had no doubts about the remedy Japan should seek. "At present Japan must keep calm and sit tight so as to lull suspicions nurtured against her," he wrote. "During this time the foundations of national power must be consolidated, and we must watch and wait for the opportunity in the Orient that will surely come one day. When this day arrives Japan will decide her own fate, and she will be able not only to put into their place the powers who seek to meddle in her affairs, she will even be able, should this be necessary, to meddle in their affairs."

The years following the intervention saw Hayashi's program implemented with a vengeance. In 1896 a new Ten-Year Plan for building up the army was proposed. Five more divisions were authorized, as well as a composite brigade for the occupation of Japan's new colonial possession, Formosa. This trebled the army's potential strength to 600,000, and meant that its actual strength had doubled since Meckel's day. The period of conscription was extended once more, to twelve years and four months of combined active and reserve service.

To pay for these huge increases, Yamagata pressed for a steeply raised budget; with the Diet's resentment deflected away from the government and toward the insolent foreigner, he got it. Between 1896 and 1903 military expenditure virtually doubled, from 20 million yen to over 38 million; during these years it averaged 40 percent of Japan's total budget, reaching a peak of 51 percent in 1898—a staggering contrast with the meager 5.3 percent spent by the Shogun in the last year of his rule.

At the same time, the industrial revolution was taking hold in Japan, providing the army with a sound material base. At the outset, military growth had acted as the motor for industrial development. The military imperative was far stronger than ordinary economic imperatives, and the government willingly poured money into mines, shipyards, foundries, railways, textiles, and telephones. Factories making military-related products were government-owned or carefully protected with large contracts at generous fixed prices. By the mid-1890s the principal heavy industries were solidly founded—and Japan's armed forces were moving ever nearer to self-sufficiency in weapons and equipment.

Most important in the political strengthening of the military was the regulation, introduced in 1900, decreeing that the army minister must be a serving general or lieutenant general. This was designed to ensure that he would be subject to military discipline, even control; he would be in touch with current army thinking, his primary loyalties and priorities would be military rather than political, and he would have no party political connections or incentives. Most significant of all, the army was now in a position to nominate its own minister—or to refuse to nominate one, making it impossible for the prime minister to form a cabinet. One simple and logical-sounding administrative regulation had given the army the power to bring down governments.

Since the majority of serving officers still came from Choshu or Satsuma, the new provision also had the effect of strengthening the *hanbatsu,* or dominance of the old clans. In particular, it enhanced the position of the Choshu elite; for after the First Sino-Japanese War several key Satsuma figures, including Kawakami, died "as if by sudden epidemic," leaving Choshu, with Yamagata at its head, preeminent.

The last years of the century were the years of Yamagata's greatest power, and years that saw the apparently irresistible rise of the military clique around him. This rise took much of its impetus from developments in the international situation that seemed to cry out for a more forceful approach to foreign policy. Between 1895 and 1898 Japan saw the progress she had made on the mainland whittled away to vanishing point, while thieving foreign powers prospered.

Shortly after the beginning of the war with China, Japan had signed a treaty of alliance with the Taewon-gun's government in Korea, with the sworn objective of expelling China and maintaining Korean independence; Japan would do the fighting, Korea provide the facilities. Under genro Kaoru Inoue, her new representative in Korea, Japan initiated the program of reforms that China had so contemptuously rejected in the summer of 1894. Some of the measures were worthwhile, like the principle of employing able people in government regardless of their family background. Others were needlessly provocative—in particular the compulsory cutting of the topknot, a hairstyle that had been worn for centuries in Korea as the sign of a mature man and had become a symbol of national identity. In the event, the entire reform program was soon abandoned, largely because Japan was not prepared to pay the administrative costs.

The Triple Intervention, a disastrous blow to Japanese prestige, encouraged her Korean enemies, led by the Taewon-gun's daughter-in-law Queen Min, to look for help elsewhere. Min turned to the Russians, who now replaced the Chinese as the principal challengers for power in Korea.

When the reform program for Korea failed, Inoue had been replaced by General Goro Miura, who appeared in Korean eyes as a "bully-like samurai," going to extraordinary and disreputable lengths to resist the court's anti-Japanese maneuvering. At the end of 1895, almost certainly with Miura's complicity (though probably without the approval of the Japanese government), Queen Min was murdered by members of the pro-Japanese faction with the aid of Japanese soldiers stationed in Seoul. *Soshi,* or Japanese "strong men," burst into the palace and ran-

66

sacked it. They found the queen hiding in a side room and slashed her to death with their swords. The body was then wrapped up in a silk quilt and taken to a grove of trees not far distant; the assassins piled over it, poured on kerosene, and set the pyre alight.

Queen Min was far from well-loved by her people; but Japanese involvement in her murder transformed the incident from an unattractive sideshow in a domestic power struggle into an international incident, one of the mainsprings of Korean nationalism, and started a precipitous decline in Japanese influence. In February 1896 the Korean king took refuge at the Russian legation in Seoul. Russia's stock rose sharply, and the brief supremacy in Korea which the Japanese had earned by military victory was over. They were forced to settle in 1896 for effective partition of the peninsula with Russia, and mutual recognition of separate spheres of influence. In 1898 the Russians conceded to Japan commercial and industrial rights in the south. But by 1900 they had negotiated a secret treaty with the Korean government to lease a site near the key port of Masampo on the tip of the peninsula nearest Japan—in Japanese eyes, very much the thin end of a wedge that might irrevocably separate Korea from Japan.

At the same time, Russia was closing in on Manchuria, being well entrenched both on the Amur and in the Maritime Provinces. The Chinese found themselves unable to pay Japan the indemnity negotiated at Shimonoseki; they borrowed from Russia. In return, the Russians demanded and were given the right to build the Chinese Eastern Railway across Manchuria direct to Vladivostok. The following year they extracted the right to build the South Manchurian Railway down the length of the Liaotung Peninsula to Port Arthur. By 1898 they had expropriated the town and demanded a lease on the peninsula. This time there was no one to intervene to "safeguard" the security of East Asia, and Japan had to stand by while the motives behind Russia's "friendly advice" to evacuate the Liaotung Peninsula became glaringly apparent. Germany had already acquired Kiaochow and rights in the Shantung Peninsula in 1897; in the scramble for a stake in China, Japan was visibly being pushed to the back.

Meanwhile, in Formosa, the one overseas possession she had managed to retain, Japan's troops were faring little better than they had twenty years before in the expedition under Takamori Saigo. The mountainous and forest-covered island provided perfect terrain for partisans and bandits alike, and the epidemic diseases that had decimated Saigo's expeditionary force continued to kill Imperial troops by the hundred.

Faced by a sullen and uncooperative population, the Japanese resorted to brutal tactics of "pacification" and coercion. "The Japanese, sent to Formosa," remarked the Belgian d'Anethan disapprovingly, "show themselves arbitrary, arrogant and cruel." And the British in Amoy, on the mainland across the straits, alleged the slaughter of "several thousand" Chinese civilians, as well as the murder of several of their own subjects.

On every side Japan's position seemed to be deteriorating. It was urgent that she decide where her primary interests lay. Were they to the north, in northeast Asia and especially in Korea? Alternatively, should Japan be looking to the south, at South China, and specifically at Fukien province, as a base for trade in China and the South Seas? The question was to be posed directly in 1900 when, for the first time standing shoulder to shoulder with the other imperialist powers, Japan once more flexed her military muscles on the mainland.

In the clearest possible demonstration of the eagerness of foreign powers to stake their claims on the decaying Chinese empire, a joint expeditionary force of British, Americans, Russians, Germans, French, and Japanese was organized to suppress a violently anti-Christian religious sect that surfaced in North China at the end of the 1890s: the Boxers. Their hatred of foreigners and their suspicion of the ruling Ch'ing dynasty made them popular among the peasantry and sparked a chain of hideous attacks on missionaries and increasingly serious riots. Fearing for its own safety, the imperial court under the Empress Dowager chose to deflect the Boxers' aggression toward the foreigners, and by June 1900 trouble had spread to Peking.

By June 4, Boxer troops were roaming the countryside around Peking, and had cut rail and telegraph lines. On June 11 the chancellor of the Japanese legation set off toward a railway station on the outskirts of the city in the hope of welcoming reinforcements. He was intercepted, killed, and decapitated by Chinese government troops. On June 13 the Boxers entered the capital and the siege of the foreign legations in Peking began. Allied forces already in the region now seized two forts on the Yellow Sea coast southeast of Peking. In response to what it called an "invasion," the Chinese court resolved to make war and authorized a full-scale onslaught on the capital's legation area. On June 20 the German minister to China was killed by the Boxers and the foreign representatives abandoned all hope of extricating themselves peacefully.

The allied powers now had to act fast, and hasty preparations were made for a full-scale international expeditionary force. Japan was patently eager to enter the "club" of Great Powers; her participation in the Boxer expedition was to be partly paid for out of resources that appear in her accounts of government spending as an "Educational Fund." The military also welcomed a possible opportunity to pursue their interests in South China.

"The foreigners are like fish in the stew pan," remarked the Chinese Empress Dowager. Swollen by hundreds of missionaries and Chinese converts from the surrounding areas, the foreign community was packed into the Legation Quarter of Peking. As the siege progressed, the area they could defend became ever smaller, and the hope of relief began to fade. For weeks the outside world had little reliable news of what was happening; on July 16 the London *Daily Mail* published a report headed "The Peking Massacre," claiming that the siege had come to a grisly end with all inside the legations "put to the sword in a most atrocious manner." A memorial service in St. Paul's Cathedral was arranged for July 23, and canceled only hours before it was due to start, when the U.S. Department of State received a telegram from the American minister in Peking begging for immediate help.

By this time the besieged were reduced to eating their horses, even dogs and crows, and had little hope of being able to hold out for more than a fortnight. Still the allied expeditionary force failed to move. Then, on August 4, it left Tientsin; the following day the Japanese contingent played a key role in the decisive battle of Peitang, and took an early lead in the march on Peking. On August 14 some 22,000 men, including 8,000 Japanese (as compared with 4,000 Russians, 3,000 British, and 2,000 Americans), entered Peking and relieved the legations, not without a good deal of undignified international jockeying for the kudos of arriving first—an honor eventually claimed, to universal irritation, by the British. (The Russians had initiated the first attack, jealously followed by the Japanese. The Americans were next, but according to Russian accounts, they could find nowhere to hoist the Stars and Stripes, as all of the most obvious vantage points on the wall were already occupied by Russian flags; the Russians last saw them trudging off in search of a fitting flagpole. Meanwhile the British entered, almost unopposed, through a sewer, their only fatality a victim of heatstroke.)

The Boxer expedition was to some extent a competitive exhibition of military power. From the initial stages of the competition at Peking, the Japanese emerged strongly. They had shown themselves to be not merely disciplined but brave and determined fighters, well to the forefront in the attack and absolutely undaunted in defense. They had many of the virtues on which Western soldiers most prided themselves, the officers calmly smoking cigarettes as the shells burst around them and the gunners cracking jokes when enemy fire got too hot.

Colonel Shiba, the military attaché leading the Japanese effort from inside the walls, emerged as one of the individual heroes of the siege. His men spearheaded the struggle to hold the palace of Prince Su (known as the Fu) which faced and effectively gave access to the British Legation. "Luckily for us it is the Japanese who are defending the Fu," remarked one diplomat. "If it had been the Italians or Austrians it would have been taken long ago, and all would have been UP." "The Japs are perfectly splendid," enthused another, "like little terriers, as keen and plucky as can be. . . . Their whole arrangements are so wonderful. If a Jap is hit, there's always a doctor on the spot, mounted well, with panniers with the very latest surgical jinns [magic cures]."

In the aftermath of battle, too, the Japanese attracted praise from all sides. They were the only troops not to join in the bloody scenes of retribution that followed the lifting of the siege; and though they were not immune to the temptation of looting the treasures to be found in the foreign settlements, even here they were commended for their good taste. "The Japanese," wrote correspondent Henry Savage Landor, "were the only soldiers in the field who showed any natural and thorough appreciation of art and of things artistic. They—like everybody else, of course—looted, but they did it in a quiet, silent and graceful way, with no throwing about of things, no smashing, no confusion, no undue vandalism. They helped themselves to what they fancied, but it was done so nicely that it did not seem like looting at all.

"I went into a house," Landor continued, "which had been entered by a number of Japanese privates. They had found a cabinet of old china, and each soldier was revolving in his supple fingers a cup or a vase or dish, and carefully examining the design. 'Lovely, isn't it!' exclaimed one soldier, looking into the work with the eye of a connoisseur. 'Yes, indeed. First rate!' announced his neighbor, drawing in his breath in sign of admiration, while he tried to decipher the mark on the bottom of each cup. . . . One could not help being struck, especially when small, delicate articles were handled, by the dainty, artistic touch of the Japanese soldiers as compared with the clumsy, sausage-like fingers of the American, Russian, French or British soldier . . . The Yankee, or the French or the British or Russian, not to mention the German, could touch nothing that was not solid bronze or stone without breakage or twisting or soil or injury of some sort."

Unfortunately, the admiration was not mutual. The Japanese soldier in fact developed a low opinion of some of his Western counterparts at Peking. Many observers commented on the open friction between the Japanese and the Russians during the siege; but the Japanese contingent also seemed to despise Britain's native troops as inefficient and cowardly. The Japanese press aired these views with little tact, and Western observers began to regret their first kind words about the Japanese performance.

"The real reason for the Japanese opinion," reported the British military attaché indignantly, "may be traced to their fixed idea that a 'good fight' is to suffer casualties, and their eagerness, amounting to rashness, to get in with the bayonet. The Indian troops, when under fire, assumed the extended formations they are taught to take up from the day of their enlistment, and this in conjunction with the tactical dispositions of a General experienced in savage warfare, resulted in our casualties being out of all proportion to those sustained by the Japanese, who presented their usual close targets to the enemy's fire. The Japanese apparently failed to understand this disparity in losses, and attributed it to the over-cautiousness of our General and to a want of dash in our troops."

Each of the allied powers was anxious to impress the others with its strength, because each had its own ambitions in China. It was too much to hope that once the immediate objective of relieving the legations was achieved they would withdraw their troops at once. Instead, as Yamagata angrily pointed out on August 20, a week after the lifting of the siege, "Russia has quickly built up its forces and naval strength in Manchuria, Britain in the Yangtze and Germany and France likewise. All give abundant evidence of lurking evil intentions."

Yamagata's righteous wrath was not entirely justified, as even before the lifting of the siege, Japan was planning its own expansionist enterprise. On August 10, Katsura had ordered Gentaro Kodama, governor-general of Formosa, to prepare an expedition to the port of Amoy in Fukien province on the southeast coast of China, immediately opposite Formosa, as part of a southward-looking policy for Japan. Transports were loaded on Formosa and warships were already on their way when Kodama received a telegram from Tokyo ordering him to delay the invasion. As days passed, the opportunity for "a quiet, inconspicuous act of aggression" was lost.

Once again military authorities on the spot would seem to have gone farther and faster than the civilian government wanted. Yamagata had not envisaged so large an intervention, and was distracted by the simultaneous threat to Japanese power in the north. It seemed highly likely that Russia, instead of withdrawing her troops, would mass them in Manchuria, where they would constitute a menace to Korea. That the invasion of Amoy should so nearly have taken place despite hesitation and even opposition in Tokyo was due primarily to the enthusiasm and initiative of Kodama in Formosa. In later years the central government's control over its officers in the field would become ever more tenuous.

Many may have felt that Japan would do better to capitalize on the goodwill she had earned by her actions at Peking. The time had come for Japan, as a power with something tangible to offer, to seek allies and attempt to play a full part in the power game in East Asia. Advocates of Westernization within Japan wanted her to break away from the decadent East and take her place in the "club" as a quasi-Western nation. Woodblock prints by Japanese artists of battle scenes from the Sino-Japanese War had subtly exaggerated the contrast between the combatants; the Chinese soldier had steeply slanting eyes, a wide nose, a tight pigtail and garish clothes, while his Japanese counterpart was markedly taller, pinker, more aquiline, more European.

Politically as well as culturally, many Japanese felt it would be wise to put some distance between themselves and the Chinese, to counter European fears of a "Yellow Peril"—an ungodly alliance of China's unlimited manpower and natural resources with Japan's military skills and industrial strength. Kaiser Wilhelm II expressed these fears crudely but convincingly in the notorious picture—which he himself painted—of a Buddha, mounted on a dragon, bursting through the smoke billowing from a burning European city, while in the foreground the Archangel Michael exhorts Europe to unite. German merchant ships carried reproductions of this masterpiece to the corners of the earth.

The most obvious means of exorcising the specter of the Yellow Peril was an alliance with a major Western power. Some, like Ito, argued that there was still time to defuse Russia as an enemy, at least temporarily, by wooing her as a friend. Others, led by Yamagata and including virtually all military men, believed that the only realistic strategic option in the long term was to recruit the strongest available ally against her. Britain, though she no longer led the world industrially, was still the preeminent naval power, and by combining their forces the Royal and Imperial navies would outweigh the Russian and French fleets by some 70,000 tons.

The advantages were equally obvious to Britain, weakened and almost friendless in Europe after the Boer War. Japanese ships would enable British naval forces protecting the China trade to be redeployed in European waters, where the German navy was expanding at an alarming rate. Japan had shown herself to be an ally worth having. "As long as Japan indulged in the gentle arts of peace, she had been regarded as barbarous," one Japanese observer remarked sharply, "but victory in war had induced the foreigners to call Japan civilized."

The Anglo-Japanese Alliance of 1902 was largely negotiated by Tadasu Hayashi, now Japan's minister in London. Since his outburst over the Triple Intervention, he had already seen his short-term advice carried out, with the strengthening of the army. Now it seemed he was helping to implement the long-term policy of putting Japan in a position to meddle in other countries' affairs.

The alliance was not in itself offensive, but it did help to make Japan's approach to the world more aggressive. By committing Britain to go to war if Japan was opposed by two or more powers, it made a repetition of the Triple Intervention impossible, and Japan was the bolder in her foreign affairs as a result. By supporting Japan's rights to defend her interests in Korea, in return for the recognition of British concerns in South China, Her Majesty's Government helped pave the way for renewed expansion into the peninsula—the most encouraging of welcomes to the imperialist club.

8

WAR WITH RUSSIA

I n the first years of the twentieth century, the main question hanging over Japan and Russia was not whether they would go to war but when. Boosted by the ten-year program launched in 1896, the Imperial Japanese Army was reasonably well equipped, though inevitably it still trailed behind the leaders in weapons development. It had reached a peak of training and organization; it had acquired vital experience of campaigns on the mainland; and it was buoyed up by popular support of a kind it would never enjoy again.

For the moment, too, Japan's hostility toward Russia was partly shared by the Western powers, because the peaceful "slicing of the Chinese melon" in the wake of the suppression of the Boxers was being sabotaged by Russian intransigence. At the end of 1900, with thousands of Russian troops still in Manchuria, the Tsar's government issued China with a set of extortionate demands, including Russia's rights to veto territorial concessions to any other powers and to approve the Chinese police and armed forces. Someone in Japan would seem to have taken

careful note of the kind of demands that might be made of China, as
many of the salient features of the Russian proposal were echoed fifteen
years later in Japan's notorious Twenty-one Demands. Nevertheless,
resistance was fierce and immediate, and the Russians were forced to
back down.

But they did not remove their troops. In 1902 a three-stage withdrawal was agreed with China, but only the first stage was ever carried
out. Russia's stake in Manchuria was increasing all the time. Tsar Nicho-
las II, acutely aware of the internal stresses at the heart of his empire,
was eager for success in Asia. He was also anxious to protect the Manchurian stretches of the Trans-Siberian Railway, which had been a huge
capital investment and was not yet paying its way.

April 8, 1903, the date fixed for the second troop withdrawal, came
and went, and Russia's only action had been to appoint a viceroy for the
East, based at Port Arthur; this made her intention of staying all too
clear. The Japanese could not ignore the threat to their interests—not
so much in Manchuria, though they still had aspirations there, but in
neighboring Korea, where their influence had declined alarmingly.

"It is inevitable that we should keep Korea under our thumb by
force whatever happens," declared a Cabinet resolution. "Our Korean
policy . . . depends either directly or indirectly on conducting military
operations." Military leaders saw no reason why these operations should
be confined to Korea. If Russia refused to withdraw peacefully from
Manchuria, then she must be forced out, in the cause of national security—and if in the process Japan recovered her self-respect and some
vital commercial advantages, then so much the better.

Japan did not plunge headlong into war with Russia in 1904, any
more than she had rushed toward war with China ten years earlier. Those
who wanted to strike immediately, before Russia could move more troops
to Manchuria and take delivery of more warships from Britain, were
curbed for some time by the genro, who persisted throughout 1903 in
working for a peaceful settlement long after army officers in the field had
assured them that it was impossible. The advocates of action were
younger men, a second generation of political leaders coming up behind
the genro, and more junior members of the General Staff.

These younger officers joined forces with like-minded men in the
Navy General Staff and the Foreign Ministry to form a pro-war pressure
group, the Kogetsukai—on the surface a dining club taking its name
from the restaurant where it met, but in reality a cabal existing solely
to lobby the genro and government for war.

The Kogetsukai had one particularly useful ally: Army Minister Gentaro Kodama, whose career had woven in and out of the story of the Imperial Japanese Army almost from its beginnings. In his early twenties he had been badly wounded fighting to suppress the 1874 Saga Rebellion (an early samurai rebellion, led by Shimpei Eto); three years later he survived the siege of Kumamoto Castle as a youthful major. At thirty-five he was head of the Staff College and in 1886 he was one of the triumvirate principally responsible for putting Meckel's ideas on army reform into practice. During the First Sino-Japanese War he was the army vice-minister. Then in 1898 he was sent as governor-general to Formosa, where he gradually curbed the brutality of his forces and laid the foundations of orderly if illiberal colonial rule. It was Kodama who had initiated moves against Amoy in 1900.

Kodama was "gifted with a lively intelligence," according to the French military observer, "a good organizer, commanding ready obedience, very popular in the army," affable, charming, and frivolous. He was the only one of Yamagata's most favored protégés who would fail to become prime minister, thwarted by an early death at the age of fifty-four, which the French attributed to "notorious intemperance."

In October 1903, two months after Japan opened negotiations with Russia, the vice-chief of the General Staff died suddenly and Kodama took his place. On paper the move involved demotion from quasi-ministerial level, but back in the bosom of the General Staff, he could play a far more important part in formulating army policy against Russia. His plan entailed an early invasion of Korea, and he worked hard to rally support. He used his Choshu contacts to apply pressure on other staff officers; he cultivated prominent members of the business community; and when he failed to get immediate agreement for the invasion, he tried to mobilize public sentiment by deliberately leaking information damaging to the Russians.

Public opinion was by now a force with great potential for both good and evil. Chauvinist ambitions and suspicions, already simmering at the time of the First Sino-Japanese War, had been brought to the boil by the Triple Intervention. Russia's seizure of the Liaotung Peninsula gave the government an opportunity to channel nationalist zeal. The slogan "We must defeat Russia" was taught in the schools and became the theme of popular songs and writings. The widespread success of the propaganda showed when the government began raising war loans: nearly 50 million yen of the 452 million total came in payments of 200 yen or less.

By the end of 1903 war could not be postponed for much longer. Every week of negotiations gave Russia the chance to move still more troops along the Trans-Siberian Railway to the sensitive areas of the Liaotung Peninsula and the Korean border. The Japanese proposals were presented once again on December 21, but this time more as a ploy than with any real hope that they would be accepted. Japan wanted a further delay—but with a view to completing her preparations for war.

On December 28 a Supreme War Council was established. On January 13, 1904, Japan delivered her final proposals to Russia with an ultimatum. The popular press was baying for blood, and commercial interests, who might have seemed to have much to lose by a violent disruption of the peace, seemed impatient for a showdown. The Belgian attaché, d'Anethan, commented, "It is unusual for bankers and capitalists to express warlike sentiments. Yet in Japan there is this surprising phenomenon."

He went on to describe a remarkable banquet given at the end of January by some of these "capitalists" for the benefit of American and British military attachés and press correspondents. "A female dancer, dressed like an ancient samurai, is sitting leaning on her sword; another female dancer arrives carrying the head of the Britannic Lion; she is followed by a third female dancer, dressed like . . . John [Bull]. The Britannic Lion gives the samurai a warship and John a bag of flour. . . . They begin to sing this war song . . . : 'The bear who wants to choke us can dance and howl. . . . His grimaces do not deceive us. Let us march, let us march, now is the time to crush him.' "

On February 1, Chief of Staff Oyama informed the Emperor of the army's intention to launch a preemptive strike. One of the most famous of the great samurai swordsmen of the past, Tsukahara Bokuden, had defeated many opponents with a single devastating sword-stroke delivered straight from the scabbard—the *i-ai* stroke, designed to cripple the enemy before battle had even begun. It was a tactic the Japanese would repeatedly favor over the years.

Still the Russians stalled, apparently unable to believe that Japan would really presume to go to war. On February 9 a Russian gunboat was involved in a mêlée with a Japanese vessel outside the Korean port of Chemulpo, and fired two shots. The following day, without warning, the Japanese navy under Admiral Heihachiro Togo attacked Port Arthur.

In sharp contrast with popular opinion, the mood among Japan's leaders was hardly one of unbridled aggression and rampant self-confidence. Against so huge an enemy, the army felt it had at best an even chance of winning; the navy expected to lose half its forces, but hoped to win with the other half. Before the war even began, the government, acutely conscious of its precarious finances, had started to investigate the possibility of an early peace. The day the Imperial conference formally decided on war, an envoy left for America to promote good relations with the power most likely to offer to act as mediator in peace negotiations.

But there was actually more cause for optimism than anyone thought. Geography often vitiates apparent strength, as the American naval genius Admiral Alfred Thayer Mahan pointed out; and Russia's great size, which gave her inexhaustible supplies of soldiers, also made it impossible to mobilize them effectively. One army corps coming from European Russia needed no less than 267 trains to move, and these had to cover vast distances on a railway system that was incomplete and inadequately supplied with coal. Long stretches were single-track, there was no loop around Lake Baikal, and with nobles and generals claiming precedence for their trains, fighting troops were accustomed to spending long hours in their trucks in sidings.

These European Russian soldiers were badly needed in Manchuria. Outside opinion was sharply divided as to the quality of the Russian fighting man, but all were agreed on the superiority of the more highly trained European soldiers to the Siberian frontier guardsmen who made up the majority of troops in Manchuria. Unfortunately for the field commanders, the Tsar, faced with the threat of Polish revolt and a rising tide of industrial and revolutionary unrest, retained in the west all the crack regiments and the whole of the regular standing army.

The typical Russian soldier whom the Japanese faced in Manchuria was brave, stalwart, and hard to shift, but unskilled and rumored not to be very intelligent. (Even the famous Cossack cavalry were unreliable; they had to provide their own uniforms, equipment, and horses, and were careful not to risk them unnecessarily.) "Lions led by asses" was the opinion of Western military observers. Too many of the staff officers were lazy and incompetent, promoted through string-pulling. Too often, seniority counted more than talent, and some of the most influential officers in the Russian army were too old for their jobs—hesitant, sluggish, first indecisive and then inflexible. Many were baffled by recent developments in warfare, and were unable to use the new technology, preferring runners to heliography or wireless telegraphy.

Russia at this time was also industrially backward, and levels of equipment in the army were uneven. Crucially, in 1903 the artillery was in the middle of reequipping. The navy, too, would have been stronger if war could have been delayed; the Russians had five battleships completing in 1904, which would have given them a convincing numerical advantage. But the fleet varied in quality; because Russia had global interests, her ships had to be able to travel long distances, and many had large coal bunkers at the expense of armament. Like the Japanese, the Russians were building submarines, but not yet using them. The limits of their understanding were revealed in the instructions issued to a Russian officer for dealing with the new technology: "Seize the submarine by its periscope, then smash it by blows with a mallet so as to blind its crew. Better still, wrap a flag or a piece of canvas around it; or lastly—and this is probably the best way of all—tow the said submarine by its periscope into the inner harbour."

But the most serious defect in Russia's war readiness was her total underestimation of Japanese strength. She was perhaps the most notable victim of Western preconceptions about the Japanese. The Russian army commander, General A. N. Kuropatkin, would later claim that the only accurate intelligence reports on Japanese military strength in 1903 were pigeonholed because senior generals refused to believe them. The information on which they preferred to rely paid no attention to reserves, with the result that Russian estimates put the Japanese army at about a third of its actual strength. From casualty figures released after the war, it became obvious that the Japanese had lost more men than the Russians had originally thought they could field.

Russian knowledge of the Japanese forces was based less on secret intelligence than on observation of the public annual maneuvers, from which headquarters staff drew some heartening conclusions. Japanese officers, they reported, had trouble identifying definite objectives in the assault. They tended to use direct frontal attacks without turning movements. They had no faith in the power of cold steel. In general, their senior officers were incapable of command. These were assessments that Kuropatkin would later have serious cause to resent.

Fortunately, others within the Russian War Office disagreed: "In discipline, élan, patriotism and absolute callousness to death, the Japanese are well up to European standards." Kuropatkin commented enviously that the average Japanese noncommissioned officer was superior to his Russian counterpart, thanks to the widespread education of the poorer classes. The cavalry, however, attracted universal scorn. In Europe, cavalry officers were usually drawn from the upper classes, those who could afford to provide their own mounts; but in Japan the cavalry failed to attract the best recruits. "The saddest thing of all," wrote Kipling of a Japanese cavalry training exercise, "was the painful con-scientiousness displayed by all the performers in the circus. They had to turn these rats into cavalry. They knew nothing about riding, and what they did know was wrong." Natural terrain of mountains and paddy fields, commented the French, made it hard to train the horse as a weapon of war, and Japanese horses were often clumsy, tired, dirty, and ill equipped.

Generally, Japanese equipment was adequate, though it had its weaknesses. By 1902 Japan was virtually self-sufficient in arms produc-tion, and the Anglo-Japanese Alliance enabled her to fill most gaps. Both the rifle and the field gun had been redeveloped in 1897–1898, though most troops had had little opportunity to use them in action. Nitroglyc-erin and dynamite had recently been tested; both railway and telegraph battalions had gained valuable experience during the Boxer Expedition. (Modern communications remained something of a novelty; an American observer attached to the Japanese First Army commented in awe on the activities of a mounted telegraph squad, "one of the men carrying a staff with two prongs like a pitchfork, terminating in polished balls, and communicating through the body of the staff to a sounder, from which messages were taken from the wires when desired.")

It was in information about their enemy and the terrain on which they would be fighting that the Japanese had their greatest advantage. Intelligence had been a well-organized activity since Meckel's day. "Con-tingency funds" begin to show up in government accounts from 1886 onwards, rising steeply in 1893 just before the First Sino-Japanese War. They appear in the budgets of the Foreign Ministry as well as the Army and Navy General Staffs, and there is evidence to suggest that they were applied at least in part to intelligence-related activities.

The army's spy network was undoubtedly the most effective. "The Foreign Office generally sends out men with less brains and less money than the General Staff," commented one British observer. Certainly the army had some remarkable brains at its disposal. Yasumasa Fukushima, in 1903 a leading member of the Kogetsukai, had once crossed Siberia alone on horseback on an "intelligence ride" to gather information about Russia's plans for the Trans-Siberian Railway—information that had much to do with the military escalation of the mid-1890s.

Another key operative was Giichi Tanaka, a man who was to play an extremely significant part in the army's affairs over the next twenty-five years. Tanaka was a Choshu protégé of Yamagata, a talented officer with a taste and flair for politics and a firm belief in the unified military state. In the strained years after the Triple Intervention, he was sent to St. Petersburg on "study leave," first as a language officer and then as military attaché, and conducted a thorough investigation of the condition of the Russian army and its relations with the people. He created an invaluable network of contacts with Russian dissidents; and when his period of "study" had expired, he chose to journey back to Japan the long and informative way, through Siberia and Manchuria. On the Trans-Siberian and Chinese Eastern railways, on boats up and down the Sungari and Amur rivers, across to Vladivostok and down to Port Arthur, he busily accumulated the makings of a coordinated strategy for war.

Motojiro Akashi, his successor as military attaché in St. Petersburg, was well fitted to build on the foundations Tanaka had laid. At the outbreak of war, his mission was to distract the attention of the Russian government and discourage it from sending its crack troops to the war in the east, by supporting its opponents at home, ethnic minority groups and nascent revolutionary parties alike. His contacts with the Bolsheviks were too tenuous for Akashi to be credited with influencing the Russian Revolution of 1917; but Japanese money and machinations undeniably contributed to the lesser revolution of 1905, which in its turn had an effect on the outcome of the Russo-Japanese War.

Under the direction of men like these, the army infiltrated dozens of agents into Russian strongholds in China, as barbers, tailors, merchants, coolies, taking advantage of the European inability to distinguish Japanese from Chinese. "At great self-sacrifice," Kuropatkin remembered ruefully, "many officers were performing the most menial duties in our employ in the Far East in order to study our ways at a time when our military representatives in Japan were looking upon their nation with immense condescension!" It was not simply Russian mores that interested the Japanese moles, but the progress of the Trans-Siberian Railway, the mobilization and deployment of troops, the strength and siting of armaments. The Russians discovered after the war that for years, officers billeted at the key Manchurian port of Newchwang had been shaved and coiffed by a captain in Japanese intelligence.

It was not particularly surprising that the Japanese should duplicate in 1904 the strategy that had proved so successful against the Chinese ten years earlier. The plan was first to neutralize the enemy fleet and secure communications with the mainland. Then one army would invade Korea and advance overland to Manchuria across the Yalu; meanwhile a second army would land on the Liaotung Peninsula and attack Port Arthur. The two armies, in company with a third, which would have landed in between them, would converge and advance up the line of the Chinese Eastern Railway to Mukden in the Manchurian plain.

What was remarkable was that the Russians should in their turn have duplicated many of the Chinese mistakes. The general strategy employed by Kuropatkin was one of passive defense. The more time he could gain by checking the Japanese advance, the greater the strength he could muster. He had drawn his line of forward defense well over to the west of Manchuria, at the town of Liao-yang.

The Japanese general principle, on the other hand, which they had learned from Clausewitz via Meckel, was that of bringing superiority to bear at a given point. They seized the initiative by attacking Port Arthur, and they would never really lose it. The Russians were obliged constantly to respond, rather than shaping the campaign for themselves, and found themselves defending several fronts at once. They took few risks—and scored even fewer successes.

Given the Russians' unpreparedness, more might have been expected of Admiral Togo's naval assault on Port Arthur. On the day of the attack, diplomatic relations had already been broken off, and a Japanese ship removed the last of the Japanese residents from the town—yet few of the Russian ships even had their torpedo nets out.

But Togo failed not only to obliterate the Russian Pacific fleet but even to pen it immovably within the harbor. The long-term threat to Japanese transport and supply lines remained; and if the Russians could somehow bring their Baltic fleet to reinforce the beleaguered squadron, they would have a potentially overwhelming force. If the navy could not block the harbor effectively or defeat the surviving Russian ships at sea, then the army's role in taking Port Arthur from the land would become critical.

But for the time being, the Russian fleet was unable to interrupt the Japanese landings on the mainland. The First Army, under General Tamemoto Kuroki, landed at Chemulpo in Korea on March 14 and progressed smoothly up the peninsula. For this they had to thank not only inert Russian commanders, but also Meckel and the other General Staff officers who had transformed the army's logistical support services. The troops found quarters ready for them and supply lines well established, with a huge and well-paid coolie army standing by—a system that inspired the respect and envy of their counterparts in neutral countries. American observers in particular seem to have used the virtues of the

Japanese army as a stick with which to beat their own administrators. In glowing terms, army surgeon Louis Seaman compared the Japanese field medical system with the arrangements made, or not made, by the U.S. Army during the Spanish-American War.

The Japanese, he pointed out, promoted advanced ideas like "scientific massage and surgical gymnastics" [sic]. They had bacteriological laboratories in the field, which did much to forestall epidemics. "Malaria is malaria and typhoid is typhoid in the Japanese Army, and not 'Fever' caused by inappropriate and irritating rations." He had in mind the fat pork, beans, and fermenting tomatoes beloved of U.S. Army cooks, all of which aggravated diarrhea and enteritis. The Japanese diet of dried fish, tinned vegetables, and rice, though deficient in nitrogen, was generally better balanced, and far better suited to battlefield conditions.

The Japanese soldier was also well prepared for the rigors of campaigning in the hostile conditions of Manchuria, alternately hot and humid and freezing cold. Army surgeon Seaman detailed some of the health instructions issued to the troops: Have every wound examined immediately; keep your nails clean; oil your shoes to prevent blisters; don't eat or drink anything left by the enemy; don't talk too much when marching into the wind; carry a leaf in the mouth to check the feeling of thirst on the march; use snow as an entrenchment to keep off the wind, but don't sleep in it; don't drink sake in the cold, as it cools the inside of the body and induces sleep.

On April 1, the First Army reached the Yalu River, the border with Manchuria and the line for Kuropatkin's covering force. Kuroki's original plans for getting his troops across the river were based on those used in the First Sino-Japanese War, but he was dismayed to find that changes in the streams and mudbanks had made them virtually useless. He now had quickly to organize an alternative crossing that would take the Russians by surprise.

This was made easier for him by the Russians' fatal overconfidence. Dug in behind a broad and swiftly flowing river, they barely bothered to camouflage guns and trenches, and Kuroki's spies, some of them plying the river as fishermen, had little trouble in identifying their order of battle. In contrast, Kuroki erected screens of trees and dried kaoliang (a tall, densely growing cereal crop) to conceal his troop movements. He then set up a skillful feint attack well west of the point at which he actually intended to cross, and kept the Russian gunners busy bombarding a decoy bridge made of native boats anchored with Korean plows.

Meanwhile his troops established the real bridgehead and crossed on the night of April 30. In the battle that followed, the Russians were outnumbered and their badly hidden batteries eliminated. The Japanese had won a convincing victory; but the price of launching a mass attack with closed ranks in the teeth of modern weaponry was seen to be rising. Kuroki had lost 1,000 men killed or wounded, most of them during the advance across a tributary of the Yalu once the main river had been forded; with their dark-blue uniforms standing out starkly against the sandy background, the Japanese infantry made clear targets as they waded shoulder to shoulder through chest-deep water. Nevertheless, after the battle Kodama sent a telegram of thanks to Meckel on behalf of the Japanese General Staff.

The repercussions of the Battle of the Yalu were disproportionate. At the back of Japanese minds, commented General Sir Ian Hamilton, there had existed "a certain vague apprehension lest in some undefined inexplicable way the European might after all prove the better man when they met him on the battle field. That feeling is now gone, and gone never to return."

The Russians had certainly considered themselves the better men, and this defeat was disastrous for morale both in the field and at home, where there had never been any real popular support for the war. After the war Kuropatkin would point to "the cooperation of the (Japanese) nation with the army and the Government" as one of the principal factors bringing Japan victory. Meanwhile, America and Britain were persuaded to supply Japan with badly needed loans.

The war zone in 1904, as in 1894, was confined to the extreme south of Manchuria, to the Liaotung Peninsula jutting into the Yellow Sea between Korea and the Chinese mainland, and an arc of territory immediately above it, cut by the South Manchurian Railway running from Port Arthur at the tip of the peninsula northward to Harbin.

From the moment of their defeat at the Yalu River, the Russians retreated westward across this arc, toward Kuropatkin's line of forward defense at the town of Liao-yang one-third of the way up the railway and close to Manchuria's border with Jehol. This strategy both isolated the Russian garrison at Port Arthur and allowed General Yasukata Oku to land the Second Army on the Liaotung Peninsula anywhere he chose. The Japanese were themselves taking a chance in opening a second front, pushing down toward Port Arthur as well as across to Liao-yang. But besides the need to curb the Russian Pacific Fleet, there was the symbolic significance of retaking Port Arthur to wipe out the memory of the Triple Intervention.

The Imperial Army should never have been able to reach Port Arthur. The Kwantung Peninsula, on which the town is built, is separated from the bulk of the Liaotung Peninsula by an isthmus little more than two miles wide at high tide. Bestriding the isthmus are the Nanshan Heights, which the Russians had fortified with heavy artillery, barbed-wire entanglements, mantraps, and electrically detonated mines, and which they should have had no trouble defending.

But the Russians now encountered the Japanese determination to win at absolutely any cost. The early advances on Nanshan were easily repulsed. "They melt away from the glacis [slope]," wrote the London *Times* of one sortie, "like solder before the flame of a blow pipe." But the assault was constantly renewed. Nine times the Japanese charged that day, and finally the Fourth Division, advancing down the coast on the right flank, took to the sea and, wading waist-deep in water and thick mud, broke through. "When the Russians finally retreated," reported Reuters, "the water was literally crimson."

In taking the Nanshan Heights, the Second Army lost 4,300 men, among them the elder son of General Nogi. "There is to be no funeral ceremony," the general announced, "no mourning until the end of this war, when my surviving son and myself will be among the mourners or the mourned." The Japanese had also used more ammunition in this single battle than in the whole of the First Sino-Japanese War. But the way to Port Arthur lay open; by the beginning of May the port would be besieged from the land as well as the sea.

General Maresuke Nogi, leading the Third Army, was both an obvious and a disastrous choice to command the siege of Port Arthur. By 1904, when he was recalled for duty, he had already been retired for three years; he was reclusive and depressive, even suicidal. The last time he had attacked the citadel, in 1894 when it was in Chinese hands, he had taken it in a day with the loss of sixteen men. His mental picture of its defenses was based on the impressions he had formed then—and poor reconnaissance and intelligence work ensured continued overconfidence. Equally disastrously for his men, he seriously underrated the Russians, whom he despised, and his notions of strategy had not altered since 1894.

In consequence, for many weeks he would hurl wave after wave of infantry at the forts and walls around Port Arthur, with little perceptible result. In fairness, he was greatly handicapped by the loss of eighteen large siege guns, sunk in June 1904 when the Russian squadron at Vladivostok broke out and raided the Japanese coast. He was also under crushing pressure from home to seize the coveted emblem of Japanese pride. But the price he was forced to pay in other men's lives would haunt him until his death.

"The story of the Siege of Port Arthur," wrote Ellis Ashmead Bartlett of the London *Times*, "is the story of a succession of Charges of the Light Brigade, made on foot by the same men over and over again, with the scientific destructiveness of modern weapons thrown into the scale. . . . The Japanese soldiers were called upon to face death in so many different ways that each soldier could make choice of what he considered to be the most honourable method, and succumb accordingly. There were bullets—hardly noticed, and treated with contempt—there were common shells, shrapnel, and pom-poms. There were mines, hand-grenades, and torpedoes; pits filled with fire, and with stakes pointed at the end; masses of rock and poisonous gases." There were also dysentery, typhoid and beriberi, afflicting the besiegers as badly as the besieged.

At home the Japanese public had the flags and lanterns of victory ready and waiting. But in the natural amphitheater of Port Arthur, with the world's press and military observers looking on in fascination, the Japanese soldier was caught up in siege warfare that looked back to his country's middle ages and forward to the trenches of World War I. In the heat and pouring rain he advanced against both boiling oil and electrified wire, against planks with nails hammered through them to spear his feet in the dark and the new weapons of the searchlight and the magnesium flare. The searchlight, wrote Ashmead Bartlett, "blots out everything in front, causing the men to wander aimlessly about seeking shelter from this terrible enemy. The rays follow their every movement, and the machine gun follows the rays."

Nogi's attack on Port Arthur's outer defenses—the fortified hills to the northwest and northeast of the town—made progress, though at a cost. But at the middle line of defense—the old Chinese wall, strengthened by new and formidable forts of whose existence Nogi had been ignorant—the advance bogged down. Bodies piled up in gullies, cushioning the path of big guns frantically seeking fire positions; in some attacks uphill, corpses were used to build parapets behind which to shelter. The "yellow races," Ashmead Bartlett noted with interest, turn green in death. Humidity accelerated the decomposition of the first to fall, making conditions intolerable for those coming behind them; sentries had to be issued rags soaked in ammonia to enable them to stay at their points for even half an hour.

The stalemate at Port Arthur greatly increased the pressure on the Japanese armies advancing toward Liao-yang in the north. If the campaign was not to lose momentum and popular support, striking victories were needed in Manchuria. Fortunately for the Japanese, their opponents had a far more serious morale problem, which reached right up to the top ranks of the leadership.

Kuropatkin's instinct was to withdraw gradually to Liao-yang or even beyond and wait for heavy and unanswerable reinforcements. But while he saw delay as a key element in his strategy, his political masters were anxious for quick victories to divert the attention of an increasingly disaffected public, and he was compelled to stand and fight battles that were neither in places nor at times of his own choosing. Against him came Oyama, now the Japanese Commander in Chief—a worldly man with a large, round, pitted face like a bath sponge and a taste for poetry and old porcelain. As Kuropatkin havered, Oyama decided to attack across the whole front.

Slowly the three armies—First, Second, and Fourth (the latter organized from troops that had landed in May)—converged on Liao-yang, pushing the Russians from a series of apparently impregnable defensive positions. Time after time the Russians pulled back without committing their reserves to the full, caught in a spiral of demoralization, timidity, defeat or retreat, and more demoralization.

The Battle of Liao-yang, which lasted from August 25 until September 3 (taking in the anniversary of Sedan, fought on September 1, 1870), has been described as the first of the twentieth century's great battles. In many respects it anticipated the shape of warfare to come. Huge armies met along an extended front, and day after day battered each other with weapons of unprecedented power. In its timing and geographical position, Liao-yang may be seen as the hinge on which the Russo-Japanese War turned.

The Russian aim was to hold the Japanese for as long as possible, falling back in careful stages on the main stronghold of Liao-yang itself while a counteroffensive was prepared. The Japanese intended simply to drive the Russians out of Liao-yang. In the event, it was the Japanese who achieved their objective. As so often during the campaign, the Russians found it impossible to move from a defensive to an offensive stance; the counteroffensive never materialized, and the Russians retreated toward Mukden. But, in a pattern that repeated itself throughout the campaign, Japanese losses were appalling, and significantly higher than the Russians'. After one day's fighting, three major generals—

among them the father of Hideki Tojo—were demoted for their inflexible, doctrinaire tactics. It sometimes seemed that the Imperial Japanese
Army won its battles mainly by accepting a price in human life that other
nations were not prepared to pay.

Without this particular victory, the entire campaign might have
been lost. With Port Arthur in deadlock, all four Japanese armies would
have fought themselves to a standstill, bleeding heavily. As it was, the
First, Second, and Fourth Armies now turned to pursue Kuropatkin's
forces to Mukden. For a conclusive victory, they needed every available
soldier, and Oyama looked for reinforcements to Port Arthur, where
General Nogi was still battering bloodily at the walls with his Third
Army.

The pressure on Nogi for a quick victory was already intolerable.
Against all the odds, the Russian Baltic Fleet was planning to set sail
for Manchuria. Port Arthur must be taken, to destroy the Pacific Fleet
if for no other reason. In the autumn of 1904 Nogi's arm was strengthened by the arrival first of desperately needed siege guns and then of
Kodama, sent to take charge of strategy.

Nogi had at first seemed unable to conceive of any alternative to the
massed frontal attack—a strategy that in mid-August had lost him
20,000 men in less than a week. Then he took the advance underground
with a system of sapping and mining. Kodama, however, advocated
concentrating on a renewed attack overground on 203 Metre Hill, a hill
with two peaks to the west of the town, from which the harbor and the
Russian fleet were fully visible.

The French considered Kodama overrated, and deprecated the label
"the Japanese Moltke" that some attached to him. Nevertheless, the
capture of 203 Metre Hill proved to be a turning point. It would take
more than two months. During the final onslaught, at the start of December 1904, the Japanese kept up an artillery barrage so intense that the
hill resembled an erupting volcano. The Russians had never had more
than 1,500 men on the hill at once, but they lost 3,000, as they kept
pouring in reserves. When the Japanese finally took possession, on one
peak there were only three Russians left alive. As for the Japanese
themselves, in eight days they had suffered 8,000 casualties.

The press were tolerated by the Japanese commanders at Port
Arthur, on the strict condition that they would send back not one word
about the fighting until the siege was over, lest they frightened Japan's
creditors into cutting off support. Allowed onto 203 Metre Hill after the
battle, reporters could not believe what they saw: "Here the corpses do
not so much appear to be escaping from the ground as to be the ground

itself. Everywhere there are bodies, or portions of bodies, flattened out and stamped into the surface of the earth as if they formed part of it, and several times in the ascent I was on the point of putting my foot on what seemed to be dust when I recognized by the indistinct outline that it was a human form stretched and twisted and rent to gigantic size by the force of some frightful explosion."

At once, Japanese observers on the summit of 203 Metre Hill began directing the fire of the heavy siege guns toward the remnants of the Pacific Fleet penned in the harbor by Admiral Togo's ships offshore. Within days the Russian ships had been sunk, and the strategic need to capture Port Arthur was gone. But the emotional commitment was stronger than ever, with thousands of Japanese dead piled around the walls.

Inside the garrison, medical supplies were running out, scurvy was widespread, and horseflesh the only meat available. Conditions were disgusting—but they were not desperate. The Russians still had ammunition and almost 25,000 men fit to fight; they also had a commander who had already shown himself to be vain, self-seeking, and unintelligent. General Anatoly Stössel now displayed an eagerness to surrender which infuriated his colleagues (whom he did not consult) and astonished the grateful Nogi. (It was widely rumored in the Far East that Stössel had been bribed by the Japanese.) On January 2, 1905, the white flag was sent out of Port Arthur. During the 240 days of the siege, the Russians had suffered over 31,000 casualties, representing 70 percent of the officers and 64 percent of the men. The Japanese had suffered almost twice as many losses. Nogi's other son was among the dead.

The Third Army was now free to join the struggle in the north. Immediately after the Battle of Liao-yang in September, Kuropatkin had once again been forced against his will to launch a southward offensive, rather than a northward retreat, in an effort to relieve pressure on Port Arthur. This had resulted in a defeat so crushing that for once Russian losses were markedly heavier than Japanese. Over the winter of 1904, the conflict in Manchuria was stalled in prototype trench warfare.

Russian morale was ebbing fast. The ordinary soldier, taught to despise the Japanese as "leather-skinned dwarves," had been obliged, repeatedly and often mysteriously, to retreat before them. Drunkenness, looting, venereal disease, and virulent criticism of the leadership were not confined to the rank and file. News from home was all of the swelling discontent that would break out and be brutally repressed in the Winter Palace massacres of "Bloody Sunday," January 22, 1905.

But at least reinforcements for the Russians were continuing to arrive. The Japanese had no such resources to draw on. They had already been forced to amend their Conscription Law to spread the net wider. Reserves were running low, and those who were coming now were older, less fit, less thoroughly trained. Many were urban reservists, far more resistant than rural recruits to patriotic indoctrination. Enormous quantities of ammunition had disappeared into the bottomless pit of Port Arthur. With the Russian Baltic Fleet approaching, and fears mounting that foreign aid would soon be suspended, Oyama needed a swift, conclusive victory.

The final confrontation, which took place at Mukden in March 1905, was the biggest battle in history before World War I. The front initially stretched for a hundred miles; along it 300,000 Japanese faced 350,000 Russians. Tactics, too, were modern, in the sense that at last the Japanese seemed doubtful of the wisdom of the massed infantry attack, and in the approach to enemy lines made intelligent use of looser formations.

Oyama, like most of the General Staff, had immersed himself in the teachings of Clausewitz and the campaigns of Moltke. His dream was to rival Moltke's achievement at the battle of Sedan—to outflank the enemy and envelop him entirely. He almost achieved his goal. Skillful disinformation had helped to convince Kuropatkin that the main attack on Mukden would come from the Third Army in the mountains to the east, and an apparent outflanking movement drew his reserves in that direction. Meanwhile, Nogi and his army had actually arrived undetected in the west, to turn the Russians' right flank and encircle Mukden. Once more a Russian counteroffensive was canceled, and Kuropatkin's forces performed the maneuver at which they were most adept: the retreat.

But again Oyama had been denied his crushing victory. The Russians had lost 89,000 men (as opposed to the 16,000 Japanese killed and 54,000 wounded); but the remainder had escaped to fight another day, and it was becoming increasingly hazardous for the Japanese to pursue them. Shortages of men, money, and ammunition were far more acute than the public at home suspected or was prepared to believe. The much-vaunted support services were degenerating, too—standards of hygiene were collapsing and lines of transport breaking down.

War loans had distorted the Japanese economy, triggering hectic fluctuations in prices and interest rates, undermining industry and ruining the trade balance. The war was accounting for 53 percent of the nation's annual budget. Industrialization could barely keep pace with military consumption; steel production in particular was inadequate to meet the army's needs.

Japanese victories continued, it was true, on both land and sea. In April and May 1905 the Russian Baltic Fleet under Admiral Zinovi Rozhdestvenski had completed the 3,500-mile voyage from its home ports in the Baltic. The voyage was both heroic and astonishingly badly organized, not helped by the activities of revolutionary saboteurs among the crews; but by the time it arrived in Asian waters, Port Arthur had fallen, depriving Rozhdestvenski of a base from which to engage the Imperial Navy under Admiral Togo.

The two fleets were evenly balanced in the single respect that both were spearheaded by four sophisticated battleships. But Togo had commanded the Japanese navy for eight years; five of his vice-admirals and seven of the rear admirals were his pupils; and he worked his force as a confident, practiced, and well-integrated unit. Togo gambled on Rozhdestvenski taking his fleet through the Tsushima Strait between Japan and Korea, and he guessed correctly. On May 27, 1905, as the encounter began, Togo, aboard his British-built flagship, the *Mikasa,* passed the message to his fleet, ON THIS ONE BATTLE RESTS THE FATE OF OUR NATION. LET EVERY MAN DO HIS UTMOST, paying homage to his British mentors with this paraphrase of Lord Nelson.

The Russians were able to read this signal as Togo maneuvered his fleet into their path, briskly crossing Rozhdestvenski's T. He turned his ships once more, bringing them onto a course opposite and parallel to the Russians'—and then wheeled them hard to port, one after another. The aim was to bring his fleet up alongside Rozhdestvenski's, enabling him to concentrate his fire. The risk was that as each ship turned on the same point, within Russian gunshot, it masked the fire of the one following. So bold was the maneuver, and in the event so successful, that it became known as the Togo turn.

At a cost of three torpedo boats and 110 Japanese lives, Togo sank or captured all eight Russian battleships and most of the rest of the Baltic Fleet. Of the Russian sailors, 4,830 were killed and another 8,862 taken prisoner or interned. The Battle of Tsushima was the first major sea battle in almost eighty years, the first major battle between steamships, and the last encounter in the last naval war to be fought on the surface only, with neither air nor submarine assistance.

This remarkable victory was greeted with jubilation at home and a reassessment of Japanese naval prowess abroad, but it had only limited significance for the outcome of the war, which was essentially won by this point. The defeat was, however, devastating for the Russian leadership, which had pinned exaggerated hopes on Rozhdestvenski's mission. Public morale, already desperately low, plunged still farther after the *Potem-*

kin mutiny at Odessa in June. And in July the Japanese seized the island of Sakhalin—the first Russian territory (as opposed to Chinese or Korean) to fall into their hands.

But precisely because of the revolutionary ardor encouraged by the defeats at Mukden and Tsushima, and fostered by men like Akashi, the Russian regime could not permit the humiliation of unconditional surrender—and the Russians could afford to delay a settlement. Japan's position could only get worse; Russia's, in Kuropatkin's opinion, would have improved all the time as the mobilization system at last established itself.

What success at Port Arthur, Mukden, and Tsushima bought Japan was not the overwhelming victory for which the populace was screaming, but merely the opportunity of an early peace. The majority of the military leaders who had been most anxious for war to start—Kodama, Yamagata, Oyama—were now most eager for the fighting to stop. At the beginning of June 1905 the Japanese played the joker that they had stored up their sleeve the day the Imperial conference had decided for war. They invoked the aid of Theodore Roosevelt in getting the two belligerents to the negotiating table.

By the Treaty of Portsmouth (New Hampshire) signed on September 5, 1905, Japan achieved many of the objects for which the war had been started. Russia acknowledged Japan's unlimited freedom of action in Korea and agreed to withdraw her troops from Manchuria, ceding to Japan Port Arthur and the Liaotung Peninsula. Japan also gained control of the newly completed Pusan–Seoul railway in Korea, and a significant stretch of the South Manchurian Railway leading north from Port Arthur, both of which would serve as a bridgehead for the later penetration of Manchuria and Inner Mongolia.

But to the man in the street, these gains were less impressive than the concessions the negotiators had been forced to make. There was to be no indemnity, though many had seen such restitution as the only hope of ending the privations brought by the war; Japan was to receive only the southern half of Sakhalin; Vladivostok was not to be demilitarized; and, perhaps most galling of all, the Japanese armies were to withdraw from Manchuria proper, tamely relinquishing territories won at dreadful cost. Once again, the ultranationalists and political agitators argued, Japan had fought the armies of the West and won—only to be cheated by her diplomats.

As the treaty was signed in Portsmouth, thousands of antipeace protesters rallied in Tokyo's Hibiya Park and marched toward the Imperial Palace to declare their patriotic discontent to the Emperor. Nervously, the police moved in, and riots erupted; police stations, newspaper offices, churches, and buses were burned, hundreds of policemen were hurt, and order was only restored by the imposition of martial law. A week later Togo's flagship, the *Mikasa,* blew up in dock. The explosion could have been caused by unstable ammunition or by a drunken crew trying to dispose of industrial alcohol spilled in the bilges. But many preferred to see it as a gesture of disgust against the men who had won the war but lost the peace.

9

THE ARMY UNDER
ATTACK

"What o'clock is it in Japan?" asked Inazo Nitobe rhetorically in November 1905, two months after the signing of the Treaty of Portsmouth. The time in Spain, he declared, where the high noon of civilization had been reached in 1600, was now five in the afternoon. In France, where the sun had been at its highest under Louis XIV, the Sun King, it was three in the afternoon. In England, "the sun is right overhead, and while we are watching, we notice it slowly passing the meridian." In Germany, it was not yet eleven in the morning, and the people were warming to their work. In America it was ten in the morning. In China it was still dark: "The 400 million pigtailed heads are resting on their pillows, dreaming of gold and a past millennium." But in Japan the sun was just rising.

Ironically, in some respects the zenith of the Imperial Japanese Army had already been reached. In terms of popularity, overall technological efficiency, and harmonious cooperation with the civilian government, it would never again be as fit for war. But that was far from obvious in 1905. In the eyes of the world Japan had achieved enough in the Russo-Japanese War to join the ranks of the Great Powers in the East, and abroad her army was now regarded with a mixture of admiration and fear.

In "I Was There" memoirs, press articles, monographs on strategy, and a flood of books on "the new Japan," analysts pored over the details of the war in the effort to understand and perhaps emulate the Japanese success. Failing to explain the victory over Russia in material terms, the commentators began attributing it to "spirit"—unique qualities of character, morals, and temperament. The Japanese soldier became a symbol of all that Westerners feared their armies might be losing, and all that Easterners hoped their armies might become—an icon of dutiful courage and endurance. In Asia the victory had a profound impact on the psychological development of emerging nationalist leaders like Nehru and Sukarno.

Westerners seemed sometimes to be admiring the Japanese in spite of a thinly veiled physical condescension, even revulsion. The lanky General Hamilton was both a perceptive and a pro-Japanese observer, but he still showed a tendency to pigeonhole the Japanese soldier with other small, yellowish warriors. From experience of "the gallant little Gurkhas," he wrote, "imaginatively I carry a key which gives me the entree right into the heart of the (Japanese) machine." Kipling also found the comparison with Gurkhas a useful one. No giant himself, he persisted in referring to the Japanese military as "little anatomies," "handy little men . . . with the easy lope of the rickshaw coolie"; but his attitude was fundamentally less affectionate. "If you meet Japanese infantry, led by a Continental officer," he wrote, "commence firing early and often and at the largest range compatible with getting at them. They are bad little men who know too much."

In his appearance, the Japanese fighting man was consistently found wanting in Western eyes; he was scruffy and inelegant. The discomfort of foreign uniforms was much to blame in the early days; peasant recruits, quite unused to Western clothing, would put on their trousers back to front and suffer agonies from army boots, heavy and unyielding after clogs or sandals. Western drill techniques, too, often sat uneasily on the Japanese frame. French observers derided the mediocre results of the close-order drill, copied slavishly from the Prussians. "I have still not been able to grasp," wrote one, "what the Japanese officers could possibly like about the parade-ground pace they teach their infantry. Their soldier, too supple and well-trained in all the gymnastic skills to be able to make himself stiff, throws his leg forward without bending it, puts his foot down generally askew in such a way that all his shoes are worn down on the outer edge, balances his torso from the hips in the most comical manner, at the same time swinging his left arm far too widely to be natural."

Later, the disregard for appearance would become something of a matter of principle, a contempt for superficialities. Officers considered it effeminate to shave more than once or twice a week; and their men were stubbled, with patched uniforms and unpolished boots and buttons. Marching was slovenly, with little effort to keep strictly in step. Nevertheless, all observers noted that whatever the terrain or weather, the march was unusually effective.

In other words, beneath the unprepossessing exterior lay extraordinary mental and moral qualities. It was here that the myth of the Japanese "superman" began. What most immediately impressed all Western observers about the Japanese soldier was the fanatical bravery and utter disregard for personal safety, which seemed at once admirable and sinister to the Occidental. But in this war the Japanese soldier was also seen as magnanimous—generous in his respect for brave enemies and chivalrous in his treatment of their casualties. Some Russian prisoners were sent home on parole, some wounded given medical treatment; and "pinned on the breast of one of their dead," recorded Hamilton, "was a slip of paper, on which was written, in English, 'Brave Japanese, bury our dead.' I may add that the Japanese not only complied with this touching request, but put flowers upon these Russian graves."

Nitobe's *Bushido, the Soul of Japan,* setting the modern Japanese warrior in the context of traditional samurai virtues, became a best-seller in the West. New military heroes and legends were created, not just for home consumption but also by and for foreigners. One of the most popular of the new totems was Genjiro Shirakami, the valiant bugler boy who died sounding the charge and was found on the field of battle with his bugle, still at his lips, pointing heavenward. The German "F. Schroeder" hymned Gen in a moving verse epic:

> *Another rush, as again rings the signal.*
> *Advance, ad—! What is that, out of breath, little Gen?*
> *We look back, he totters, yet his lips to his bugle:*
> *Ad-vance!—why, your bugle is red, little Gen!*

And so on.

Americans were just as ready to recognize Japanese strengths, but their reactions were considerably less maudlin. True, Theodore Roosevelt was said to have bought no less than sixty copies of *Bushido, the Soul of Japan* to give to his friends, and adopted jujitsu as part of his program of the strenuous life. Nevertheless, he could still write, in December 1904: "I wish I were certain that the Japanese down at bottom did not lump Russians, English, Americans, Germans, all of us, simply as white devils inferior to themselves not only in what they regard as the essentials of civilization, but in courage and forethought, and to be treated politely only so long as would enable the Japanese to take advantage of our various national jealousies, and beat us in turn."

The American Reuters correspondent Willard Straight was more forthright in his mistrust of "the real yellow man. Not the pleasant fellow you meet at Harvard, not the very likeable men I knew in Tokyo, in the Foreign Office, but the real Jap, the kind there are pretty nearly thirty million of. . . . The Japanese will have to change a good deal before they cease to cause one to look for the tail."

America had itself recently passed through a phase of full-blown nationalism for the first time, with the annexation of both Hawaii and the Philippines in the 1890s. One of the symptoms of this new national sensitivity was a growing anxiousness to "Americanize" the huge numbers of immigrants to U.S. shores—and among the groups most resistant to this process was the rapidly increasing Japanese community on the California seaboard. Britain conducted its relations with Japan across half the world, and could afford to indulge in an idealized and sentimental vision of the Japanese fighting man. Many Americans, rightly or wrongly, perceived a direct and immediate threat from Japan to their livelihoods and even their lives—and the greater Japan's success, the greater this threat seemed to become.

Japanese laborers were seen as a threat to American jobs. Worse, they might even be disguised soldiers—an advance guard to be mobilized when Japan's imperialist designs came to fruition. In contrast with the patient and submissive Chinese, they were aggressive and virile, and they were employed everywhere—on the railways, in the public services, as navigators along the coast. A remarkable number of American citizens wrote to Roosevelt warning him of the potential security risks; Japanese had been spotted sketching Fort Knox, poring furtively over maps of Kansas City, paying close attention to lessons on the use of explosives. Several letters suggested collusion between the Japanese and "the Negroes."

At the start of the Russo-Japanese War, American sympathy for

Japan had still been perceptible, bolstered by distaste for the brutality and anti-Semitism of the Tsarist regime. The picture of the Japanese soldier presented by American cartoonists was that of the samurai locked in combat with the Russian bear—an image light-years removed from the buck-toothed ape of the Pacific War. But as Japan's victory became ever more likely, and the consequences of that victory more obvious, sympathy was replaced by open suspicion. In 1905 the California state legislature denounced Japanese immigrants in "Would you want your daughter . . ." terms, and in San Francisco a Japanese and Korean Exclusion League was founded. The following year, Japan was the most generous single donor of aid to the victims of the San Francisco earthquake—but two Japanese seismologists visiting the city were attacked and beaten up.

Exaggerated though the fears may have been, and unpleasant as their manifestations became, they were not entirely without foundation. Among the incentives for Japanese traveling to America—money, space, freedom, classlessness—was the desire and even the duty of racial expansion. The Japanese had absolute faith in their ethnic superiority; some already believed it was their destiny to spread Japanese culture to the four corners of the earth.

Certainly, through the efforts of the Imperial Army, Japan as a whole now seemed to be entering a period of unprecedented international prestige, strength, and growth. Through armed conflict, she had become an imperial power. To Formosa, her prize from the First Sino-Japanese War, she had added the Liaotung Peninsula, important railway concessions, and a recognized sphere of interest in Korea. Up to this point, her advance onto the mainland had been powered mainly by her concern for her own security; now businessmen began taking a serious interest in foreign investment and even migration, and the strategic incentive for expansion was reinforced by an overt economic incentive.

Underpinning both was the constant pressure of public opinion in favor of aggression in Korea and Manchuria. Japan's embryonic empire had already cost her 100,000 men and 2 billion yen. The whole nation had made sacrifices in war, and to question the cause in which they had suffered was considered to be treachery. The ultranationalist societies gained in strength; from them and from others emerged an ideological justification for empire.

Asia, the imperialist rhetoric ran, was fundamentally one huge community, bound together by culture, trade, religion, and way of life, all of which were under threat from the West. Japan was best qualified, by her unique national essence and her military and economic prowess, to lead Asians in the battle against Western imperialism. The countries of Asia should be politically united, and their resources and energies carefully channeled; and if Japan had to conquer some of them in order to fit them for the fight, then this was in their own best interests.

Pan-Asianism was not as completely hypocritical a creed as it now sounds. In the early years of the century, many Japanese thinkers genuinely felt a responsibility for the enlightenment and modernization of countries whose progress had not been as startling as their own. Korea, for instance—"a poor, effeminate people with no political instinct, with no economic 'gumption,' with no intellectual ambition"—had become, in Nitobe's opinion, "the Brown Japanese . . . Man's Burden."

The choice of Hirobumi Ito as the Japanese resident-general in Korea, when a protectorate was first set up after the war, bears out the claim that some Japanese were genuinely committed to reform. The Army General Staff may have decided as early as 1902 that Korea must be annexed—hence the fighting talk of keeping Korea "under the Japanese thumb" by force. During the war the army had subsidized the Ilchinhoe, a Korean group in favor of a "merger" with Japan. For five years Ito staved them off and struggled to encourage the Koreans to reform themselves. But his position became impossible in 1907, when the Korean king's emissary made a dramatic appearance at the second international Hague Peace Conference and appealed for help against the Japanese imperialists. The Japanese were already directing Korean foreign policy; the king's behavior gave them the excuse to assume control of domestic affairs as well.

In the process, they attempted to disband the Korean army. This was seen as a lethal strike against Korean independence, and violent resistance broke out, led by groups known as the Righteous Armies. The Japanese response was heavy-handed, for which much of the blame has been laid on Akashi, now the director of police affairs in Korea. Over three years, almost 18,000 Koreans would be killed. By 1909 Ito's moderate approach was under strong attack from all sides. "For the next step in our policy," wrote Katsura to Yamagata, Ito would have to be replaced. Almost certainly, the "next step" was to be annexation.

In June 1909 Ito resigned; by September a policy of annexation had been officially approved. Weeks later Ito was assassinated by a Korean nationalist, and popular support for annexation flared higher. In July 1910, the new military governor-general, Masatake Terauchi, arrived in Seoul. "It was as though a chill had passed over the city," wrote one Korean. With Akashi as his principal aide, Terauchi presided over a period of repressive authoritarian rule, the first real warning to the outside world of the potential menace of Japanese military government.

All public officials, including elementary-school teachers, were obliged to wear uniforms and sabers; all political organizations were dissolved, the press was censored, and Christian leaders were persecuted. "The world can enjoy peace only when all countries reach the same level of civilization," declared the Tokyo *Mainichi* newspaper in August 1910. "It cannot permit such a thing as low civilization countries."

Meanwhile, with the Korean frontier secure, Japan pushed feelers ever farther into Manchuria. After the Boxer Rebellion the Japanese had righteously protested against Russian encroachment on Chinese territory; this did not prevent them from joining hands with Russia in 1905 to exploit Manchuria jointly.

In accordance with the Treaty of Portsmouth, both pulled their troops out of Manchuria proper. Japan withdrew to the Liaotung Peninsula, now known as the Kwantung Leased Territory, and in 1905 set up the Kwantung government administration. In 1906 the Kwantung Army was created from the troops which had been occupying South Manchuria. The army acted as a department of the Kwantung government, to guard the Leased Territories and the South Manchurian Railway zone from Port Arthur to Changchun.

But in practice, the government delegated a great deal of responsibility to the South Manchurian Railway administration, which was from its inception in 1906 very much more than a mere railway company, involving itself in the running of ports, harbors, tax collection, utility companies, and mines. Modeled on the East India Company, the S.M.R. turned the railway zone into something resembling an independent state, another Japanese colony on the mainland.

Too often in these years the Japanese in Manchuria, both military and civilian, were greedy and corrupt. The London *Times* correspondent, J.O.P. Bland, reported mounting hostility to "our gallant little allies" the Japanese. "The aggressive little people, the 'deliverers of Manchuria,' are rapidly alienating the sympathy of natives and foreigners alike and creating for themselves an atmosphere of dislike and distrust—all same as in Corea [*sic*]." The American consul-general in Mukden, reported Bland, "moves off whenever one [i.e., a Japanese] comes near him because he's afraid he might hit him." Nevertheless, through the combination of the Kwantung government and army and the S.M.R., Japan was establishing a sphere of influence, which by 1907 was formally recognized by other powers—a major step forward on the imperial path.

In this climate, it was not difficult for the army to consolidate its strength at home. In 1907 Yamagata and Giichi Tanaka between them produced a new Imperial National Defense Policy, calling for another rapid buildup like the one that had followed the First Sino-Japanese War, to protect Japan's new interests in Korea and Manchuria.

The defense policy carefully distinguished the aims and duties of army and navy, simultaneously stressing the urgent need for effective cooperation between the two forces. For the navy, the most likely enemy was America. To maintain superiority over the U.S. fleet, sixteen capital ships were ideally needed—two fleets, each with eight warships at its head—which would mean an increase of fourteen new ships. For the army, the principal enemy was Russia, the likely battleground northern Manchuria, and the strength desired to counter her there, twenty-five divisions—an increase of four divisions, of which two were authorized immediately. To meet these new needs, the military budget leaped from 37 million yen in 1906 to well over 65 million yen in 1908.

Some of this money was devoted to the upgrading of arms and equipment. Koseki's Army Branch Information (an English-language paraphrase of Japanese newspaper reports) for 1909–1910 chronicles various experiments and innovations—snowshoes for the cavalry, a new field kitchen that could filter water and cook bean sauce, bulletproof cloth made of cotton wadding coated with lacquer. At the same time, the authorities were concerned at the lack of Japanese inventiveness. Captured weapons were distributed to shrines and schools to promote study—and, presumably, imitation—of them.

The Japanese were well aware of the significance of the new weapons that had proved themselves during the Russo-Japanese War. Each infantry regiment now had its machine-gun detachments; artillery regiments were changing over to rapid-fire weapons as quickly as they could afford to; there had been experiments with military automobiles; in 1909 the Nambu light automatic rifle, which would become standard issue, was submitted for the Emperor's inspection.

But a far more powerful weapon was being forged for the Imperial Japanese Army in this period. In 1909 a new set of service regulations was issued, which laid extraordinary stress on the importance of "military spirit," and explicitly held up Bushido as a model. This appeal to the military past of the Japanese was part of what a French observer described as "their respect—which has recently become a real obsession—for national traditions. . . . It is not at all unusual to read in their newspapers . . . this affirmation of an almost childish conceit—that Japan is the last corner in a corrupt world where moral purity is preserved."

The Japanese had come, like their foreign admirers, to believe that they owed their success to their national temperament. "The cold-steel principle is one of the mental features of the Japanese nation, and is the reason why the bravery of Japanese troops has no equals in the world." From now on the military spirit would be ferociously cultivated in order to compensate for material weaknesses, and relied upon to an unrealistic degree.

The new regulations were permeated with the concept of obedience—an obedience that through training had to become instinct, not merely habit. The strengths and weaknesses of this orientation became apparent almost at once. Between 1908 and 1911 statistics of crime within the army fell by almost 50 percent. At the same time, the number of casualties in training increased. On a twenty-four-hour forced march carried out by an Osaka regiment in the blazing heat of July 1909, the men never stopped to rest or eat their rations, nor were they allowed to take off helmets or unbutton coats. Water bottles were kept sealed; villagers on their route, appalled by their condition, offered them tea, but they were not allowed to accept. Two men died of heart failure during the march, and eighty collapsed, with nine left in critical condition.

By the time Korea was annexed in 1910 the Imperial Japanese Army had developed in both potential and ambition. But as it strengthened, the forces ranged against it strengthened too.

Opposition to the rapid growth of military power had always existed within the Meiji state. On purely ideological grounds, Christians, socialists, and Marxists found Japan's aggressive foreign posture repugnant; pacifism had fine but tenacious roots in Japan. For more practical reasons, the political parties were broadly opposed to the military establishment as an undemocratic—even antidemocratic—power in the state, and a serious drain on its finances.

This opposition had never posed a serious threat as long as the ideas and objectives of the military had coalesced with those of the genro, who kept the parties firmly in check. But now, gradually, the solidarity of the old ruling class was crumbling—as is clear from the changing position of Yamagata himself, the standard-bearer of Japanese military power for so long.

Yamagata would live for seventeen years after the Russo-Japanese War, and he was by no means a spent force. General Hamilton met him in 1904, and was much impressed: "A handsome old warrior, with clean, clearcut features; a great deal of gold in his teeth, which flashes out

whenever he smiles, and a determined aquiline type of countenance
. . . perfectly charming to meet, and he spoke to me with all the keenness
of a gunner-major about the vexed question of mobility and weight of
metal for field guns."

Both soldier and statesman, Yamagata had been crucial in binding
together and balancing the military and civilian elements in the nation-
at-arms; during the Russo-Japanese War, he had kept genro, Cabinet,
and General Staff together. But now, like the rest of the genro, he was
retiring from direct participation in government, and would never again
hold Cabinet office.

To the fore came a second generation of leaders, eager for a share
of power—men like Taro Katsura, "a rotund, contented, but intensely
clever-looking little man," who inherited from Yamagata the leadership
of the "military" clique, while Ito's successor as head of the "civilian"
group within the ruling elite was Kimmochi Saionji. But the preeminence
of the military clique was by no means as well established under Katsura
as it had been under Yamagata.

Katsura was personally unpopular and had no real base of support.
Throughout the first decade of the twentieth century, he was forced to
alternate in power with Saionji, to whom Ito had passed the torch of
parliamentary democracy. The political parties—among them the Seiyukai, which Ito himself had founded in 1900—were growing stronger; and
much of their newfound influence was directed against the military.

Sometimes the military establishment was attacked as the nucleus
of Choshu-Satsuma power, increasingly resented and challenged. The
army, the parties said, was becoming a "haunted house" infested with
favoritism and corruption. The army was charged with undue influence
in civilian affairs. In February 1910, the *Mainichi Dempo* complained
that the army consistently lobbied for rail routes that avoided the coasts
and ran inland through mountains—more secure from naval bombardment, but far less useful for trade. Later that year came interference with
the development of tramways, which, according to the army, must have
sufficient space on either side to allow a gun carriage to pass.

But the root of civilian hostility was quite simply money. Japan's
financial situation by the 1900s was precarious, and the people's representatives were justified in concluding that military expenditure was
largely to blame.

"Japan is much in the position of a private individual who having
raised his social position finds himself obliged to spend more money,"
commented the British in 1902; Great Power status had its price. By the

end of the Russo-Japanese War, interest on foreign debts amounted to almost 25 percent of total national expenditure. Meanwhile, the enormous loans raised at home were virtually unmanageable. Some were never redeemed at all; the Finance Department's accounts included an item for "building of fireplace for destroying withdrawn securities belonging to National Debt Consolidation Bureau." "Special" taxes levied during the war—on sake, soy, salt, sugar, land, mining, inheritances—had to be maintained in peacetime; and the government made savage economies. Under the heading of "extraordinary income" in 1906 came the proceeds from the sale of government properties: buildings, provisions, cattle, and night soil.

The hardship of the postwar years furthered the cause of the political parties. The task of pushing military budgets through the Diet became ever more difficult—and the army could not look to its sister service, the Imperial Navy, for help. From the beginning their paths had diverged. Clan rivalry played its part—Satsuma predominating in the navy and Choshu, generally speaking, in the army—but it was one factor among many. The army was the senior service—older, better financed, more popular, with far deeper roots in Japanese history. Army leaders openly disparaged the navy, sometimes seeming to regard it as little more than a ferry service for the troops, with a minor role in coastal defense. Until 1872, when the Navy Ministry was created, the navy was not even a distinct department. In 1878 a General Staff was established for the army, but the navy had to wait another fifteen years.

Naval men naturally disputed this lopsided view of the relative importance of the two services; and their attitudes differed in other ways from those of the army. Unable to hark back constantly to an ancient tradition, they prided themselves on being more liberal, even progressive; they certainly felt more acutely the need to keep pace with Western technology, since a greater proportion of their strength rested in their armaments and less in their manpower. They also involved themselves less avidly in politics—partly, perhaps, because they were British-trained rather than German-trained; partly because, as a volunteer and not a conscript force, they had less interest in a mass power base; and partly because they were engineers and technicians, first and foremost.

What set army and navy most bitterly apart, however, was competition for funds and the two services' sharply divergent views of strategic priorities. In the 1890s naval development accelerated all over the world; in Japan, though the army, being a much bigger force, still accounted for a larger share of the budget, the relative increase in the navy's spending was more precipitous, and the navy absorbed a considerable proportion of the Chinese indemnity. This rankled with the army—the more so because the navy proposed to use its new strength to pursue independent and even antipathetic objectives.

The navy had little interest in territorial possessions on the Asian mainland; influenced by the American strategist Mahan, who saw trade and commerce as the key to defense, Japanese naval leaders favored cooperation rather than conflict on the continent. Rather than the strike north over land, toward Manchuria and beyond, the navy advocated a move into Southeast Asia and the Pacific, "choice territory that Heaven had placed temporarily in the custody of other countries." Their strategy entailed not only a different division of labor—for in a Pacific war the navy would naturally assume the key role—but also a different enemy.

To the army, the United States had always seemed more of an irritant than a serious threat. In China the Americans wanted no more than an "Open Door"—equal economic opportunities for all, without compromising China's territorial integrity—and Japan had found herself quite able to subscribe to this ideal on paper without sacrificing any of her real ambitions on the continent.

But by 1890 the United States had become the world's leading industrial power and very near the forefront in naval technology. Her ships had forced Japan's coasts once before, and the Imperial Navy sensed a new menace in American power in the Pacific; a purely commercial rivalry took on strategic dimensions. When the Americans annexed Hawaii and took control of the Philippines, Guam, and Wake Island, the navy's suspicion deepened.

By 1906, the year the San Francisco school board voted to segregate "Asiatic" children, suspicion of America was becoming more general in Japan. In a fascinating change of tune, Yamagata warned of the threat from America and proposed an entente with Russia, the traditional enemy. At about this time, the first draft of the Imperial National Defense Policy, drawn up by Giichi Tanaka, included plans for hostilities against the United States in the Philippines.

In 1907 Roosevelt staged a show of strength. "I had been doing my best," he wrote later, "to be polite to the Japanese and had finally become conscious of a very, very slight undertone of veiled truculence in their communications in connection with things that happened on the Pacific slope; and I finally made up my mind that they thought I was afraid of them. . . . I definitely came to the conclusion . . . it was time for a showdown." He sent his "great white fleet" on a world tour, which anchored for some time in Yokohama. Japan and Russia now formed an entente that amounted to a conspiracy against other powers in Manchuria, where America had significant commercial interests. Meanwhile Roosevelt was formulating secret proposals for an Anglo-American coalition against Japan.

But even though many in the army now conceded that America was an opponent to be feared, there was to be no rapprochement with the navy—with the result that when it faced the most serious political crisis of its life so far, the army stood alone.

In 1911 the second Cabinet to be headed by Saionji voted to reduce the military budget. The army was incensed at the threat to its expansion program and in particular to the two new divisions that were to protect Korea. These divisions had been authorized under the 1907 Defense Plan, and the army had, at Saionji's request, made economies to help pay for them. But the way in which its representatives handled their legitimate complaints showed a catastrophic lack of tact, shining a bright light on the fault line that ran between the civil and military elements within government.

The death of the Emperor Meiji in 1912 seemed to give the army a heaven-sent opportunity to get its way by exerting influence over his young successor, Yoshihito (whose reign name was Taisho). Army Minister Yusaku Uehara made a crude and unsuccessful attempt to push the budget through, and was forced to resign—whereupon the army played the card it had had up its sleeve since 1895, and refused to nominate another minister. The Saionji Cabinet was obliged to leave office, and at Yamagata's insistence the genro selected Katsura as prime minister once more.

The army would have preferred General Masatake Terauchi to represent its interests and fight for its two divisions. Katsura's situation, caught between the army and the political parties, was extremely difficult. He was already suspected of having used his position at the Imperial Court—he had been chosen as the young Emperor Taisho's grand chamberlain—to regain the prime minister's office; Taisho was mentally feeble and easily convinced. For centuries the true rulers of Japan had used the charisma of the Throne to bolster their own power; but they had been careful to observe certain niceties. None had shown the flagrant contempt for both people and Throne that Katsura now betrayed as he fought for his political life.

The navy, jealous as ever of its share of the military budget and outraged by the army's cavalier use of its "Cabinet" card, decided to play its own, and refused to nominate a navy minister to the new government. Katsura's response—a fatal mistake—was to obtain a rescript from the Emperor forcing the navy to nominate.

The genro had often been criticized for an arbitrary use of power that was essentially extraconstitutional, but never had one of them flaunted it as crassly as this. The Diet was in an uproar when the Rescript was announced, and very soon the people's representatives had passed a vote of no confidence in the government.

Katsura was already a sick man. Losing his head completely, he went begging to the Emperor again for a rescript overruling the censure motion. The remains of his support melted quietly away; a man like Yamagata, whatever his bonds with Katsura might once have been, could not tolerate either his disrespect for the Throne or his political stupidity. By February 1913, Katsura had been forced ignominiously to resign and before the year was out he was dead.

Nineteen thirteen was not a good year for the political fortunes of the military. Katsura had been accused of promoting the interests of Choshu, the genro, and the army at the expense of the nation. He was succeeded as prime minister by Admiral Gonnohyoe Yamamoto of Satsuma, heading a navy cabinet that found time to disallow the army's two divisions and promise future naval expansion, before itself falling precipitously from grace on corruption charges.

At the end of October 1913, a confidential typist employed by the German engineering firm of Siemens and Shukert was sacked. In revenge, he took with him a clutch of confidential papers, which he sold to Reuters, presumably for publication. But the Reuters agent, having read the stolen documents, decided on a little private enterprise of his own.

The papers detailed "commissions" paid by Siemens and other European firms with a view to securing orders. The recipients were a variety of Japanese naval officials including the vice-minister for the navy, the controller of the navy, the director of naval ordnance, the chief naval constructor and the engineer in chief. The Reuters agent's attempt to squeeze Siemens was entirely inept, with the result that the papers fell back into the hands of the Japanese Admiralty—but not soon enough for the scandal to be suppressed. Yamamoto was not personally implicated, but he chose to resign, and the navy's moral superiority was badly dented.

Nineteen fourteen opened with a Cabinet in which the balance seemed to tilt away from the military and back toward the political parties, represented by Prime Minister Shigenobu Okuma, who had been associated with the popular-rights movement for thirty years. His Cabinet took the opportunity to revoke the rule that the army and navy ministers must be serving officers, breaking the hold of the General Staff over these posts.

But Okuma was not consistently opposed to military expansion; the army was rapidly recovering its political influence, and within months the sagging fortunes of the armed forces would be bolstered still further, by the arrival of the greatest conflict the world had ever witnessed.

10

FALLING BACK:
THE GREAT WAR

A t the outbreak of the First World War in the summer of 1914,
some Imperial Army officers expressed strong sympathy with their
German mentors. There was, however, no real threat to the Anglo-
Japanese Alliance. Indeed, the army was believed to be behind an approach made to a Canadian insurance company in September 1914 to
discover the premium on sending 100,000 to 500,000 troops by sea from
Japan to the Western Front. In the opening months of the war, however,
England and her dominions had little immediate need of Japanese help,
and were on balance more afraid of self-serving Japanese interference.
They hoped to confine Japanese action to naval patrols against German
raiders in the western Pacific, and when a request for assistance was
made, it was presented in these restricted terms.

But having resolved to support the Allied cause, Japan found the
lure of German possessions in China irresistible. "Japan must take the
chance of a millennium (to) establish its rights and interests in Asia,"
the government declared. In terms strongly reminiscent of the Triple

Intervention, Japan demanded that Germany hand over the territory of Kiaochow on the Shantung Peninsula, a German colony since 1898, when China had been forced to offer the lease as compensation for the murder of two German missionaries.

Kiaochow held numerous benefits for Japan, strategic and economic. Tsingtao, the major port of the Kiaochow Leased Territory, was one of the strongest fortified ports in the East, and with Port Arthur would give Japan control over the sea approaches to northern China. A foothold on the Shantung Peninsula, commercially valuable in itself, would also act as a lever in bargaining for concessions in Manchuria, Mongolia, and the Yangtze Basin.

On August 11, 1914, the German representative in Tsingtao sent a less than inscrutable telegram to his minister for foreign affairs: "Engagement with Miss Butterfly very probable." By the end of August, a joint naval blockade of Tsingtao had been established by Japan and Britain. Then, on September 2, in the midst of an appalling two-week storm that made nonsense of the plans of both attackers and defenders, Japanese troops landed on the Shantung Peninsula, preempting by three weeks the much smaller British contingent then being hastily assembled.

At once Japan's intentions became clear. For while one body marched on Tsingtao and laid siege to it from the landward side, another set off up the railway toward Tsinan in the heart of Shantung province. The Japanese minister in China had warned strongly against infringing Chinese neutrality in this way, and even the Army Ministry doubted the wisdom of such open provocation. But the General Staff was not to be dissuaded; it offered only the feeble claim that the railway, German-built, was German territory and therefore a fair target.

In Tsingtao itself, the garrison of 4,000 Germans—incorporating a motley crew of reservists from all over China—was without prospect of reinforcement, and after little more than six weeks' resistance they surrendered. Though the campaign was fought in the worst possible weather conditions, the Japanese army behaved in a well-disciplined fashion. At the end there was some looting, particularly when caches of alcohol were found, but generally behavior toward the Germans was restrained, even friendly. During the operations, many officers had sent messages into the garrison "wishing their German friends and former tutors luck and safety during the siege."

The first German prisoners to be sent back to Japan were given an extraordinary reception. The Emperor sent an army representative to receive them, and invited the officers to keep their swords; eager crowds shouted "Banzai!" and waved German and Japanese flags. Unaccustomed to the Japanese way of life, German soldiers found conditions in the prison camps cheerless; ceilings were too low, walls too thin, heat from the charcoal braziers inadequate, crowding acute, and diet scanty. But only in the worst cases, when discomfort bred disobedience, did the Japanese guards respond roughly.

The Japanese showed far less regard for their British allies. During the fighting the Japanese had lost 415 dead and 1,451 wounded, as against German losses of 199 dead and 294 wounded—and, more significantly, as compared with 13 British dead and 61 wounded. As at Peking, the Japanese fighting beside the British complained that they were slow to advance. Furious, the British commander accused the Japanese of pro-German sympathies and of oversensitivity to the suggestion that Japan was a second-rate power. The British for their part tended to regard their Japanese counterparts as coolies in uniform, and disliked serving under Oriental officers.

From a rather low-key, one-sided encounter, the Japanese army derived most benefit from the opportunity to test in action their fledgling air forces. For some years the Japanese had been observing with fascination the development of flying machines in Europe. In 1909 Japanese aviators were training in France and Germany, and at home there had been a spate of hopeful inventions. The Yamada triangular airship was vaunted as being safer than the Zeppelin in a sidewind, and the Narahara airship was designed to convert into an automobile on landing. Soon afterwards an Institute of Military Aero-Investigation was set up to examine the whole question of dirigibles.

In the meantime, as elsewhere in the world, amateur enthusiasts in Japan were promoting their own designs for aircraft. "It will serve as a darting missile," reported the *Hochi* newspaper of the work of one inventor, "taking the advantage of the extraordinarily high speed of it and destroy hostile aeroplanes freely; it has numerous sharp-edged tools on the outside for the same purpose. What suggested ideas to Mr. Uchida for his grand invention were birds, arrows, kites and butterflies. According to his explanation, birds are natural aeroplanes, having motors in their abdomens." The Uchida plane had no steering gear, and was sprung like a paper lantern, which increased elasticity. Perhaps fortunately, it had not progressed beyond the idea stage, as Uchida could not afford to build one and had to wait for foreign inventors to take up his design.

By 1913, the army possessed only five planes, and four of them were imported—a Blériot, a Wright, a Grade, and a Farman. No nation had yet used airplanes in battle, with the exception of the Italians, who had employed a single machine from which to throw grenades during the invasion of Libya in 1911–1912. But at Tsingtao, the Japanese navy used seaplanes to bomb ships and wireless installations, flying off an "airplane ship," a converted merchant vessel, while the army had three planes operating from an improvised airfield. These were largely for reconnaissance, but were also engaged in what must be counted the first aerial combat in history, when the Japanese fliers and the Germans' lone pilot circled cautiously, firing pistols at each other from their cockpits.

The British attitude toward Japanese participation in the war changed as 1914 wore on. In the Pacific, where there was a perpetual perceived threat of Japanese expansion, Japanese intervention must be limited as far as possible; in Europe, beyond the Japanese sphere of influence, the Allies needed all the help they could get. By December, both Churchill and Lloyd George were supporting a request for Japanese troops to be sent to the Western Front in order to release British troops for the Dardanelles. Later, war correspondent Colonel Charles à Court Repington would present proposals for the Japanese to help in Russia. In February 1915 a private patriotic association in Tokyo planned to send a corps of Japanese "Byrons and Lafayettes" to the war in the cause of personal liberty.

But bureaucrats on both sides were quick to point out the difficulties. The Japanese soldier, argued the Japanese Foreign Ministry, was conscripted to defend his homeland, not to fight thousands of miles away against a power that was no longer a threat in Asia. Public opinion, too, was against it. If the army could spare thousands of men to fight in Europe, how could it claim to need the famous extra two divisions? Then, so many ships would be required to transport the troops and their supplies that overseas trade would be at a standstill.

In time the Japanese navy would send warships as far as Malta to help curb German submarines in the Mediterranean—and, incidentally, to study European naval techniques and technology. But from 1915 to 1918 the Japanese army was primarily concerned with building on the foothold it had gained in China.

Since humiliation in the First Sino-Japanese War and the indignities endured at the time of the Boxer Rebellion, the old Imperial order in China had been sliding ever quicker toward collapse. Revolutionary groups and provincial warlords shared a profound distaste for the ruling Manchu dynasty; and when in 1911 serious disturbances exposed the total impotence of central government under the boy-emperor Pu-yi, both sets of dissidents established alternative regimes. Revolutionary leader Sun Yat-sen was elected president in Nanking; warlord general Yüan Shih-k'ai was appointed prime minister in Peking. In 1912 Pu-yi was induced to abdicate, and in order to unite the country, Sun conceded authority to Yüan as president of the Chinese Republic.

Japan's approach to the Chinese situation was ambiguous and almost entirely self-serving; the military at least was prepared to support any faction that promised to advance Japanese interests. Well before the revolution of 1911, the army (in the teeth of Foreign Ministry opposition) had been interfering in China. Continental adventurers were plotting uprisings to establish independent regimes in Manchuria and parts of Inner Mongolia. These the army supported clandestinely in the hope that Japanese forces might somehow be sucked into military clashes in these territories; the restraint of the civilian government and its refusal to intervene thwarted and infuriated the military, which did not yet feel confident enough of its power to take unilateral action.

Then, after the revolution, Yamagata, anxious to take advantage of China's weakness, proposed sending two divisions to southern Manchuria. But the Saionji Cabinet refused, on the grounds of expense and the offense it would give to foreign powers. "We have missed a god-given opportunity," complained Yamagata, "and I am truly and mightily indignant for the sake of our country."

Official policy at the beginning was generally to favor Yüan Shih-k'ai as the lesser of two threats. Sun's republicanism, it was felt, could lead either to a stronger, united China or to Western intervention, both of which were highly undesirable from Japan's point of view. In 1913 Yüan defeated the "Second Revolution" of Sun and his Kuomintang party, abolished the parliamentary system, and laid the foundations of a new monarchy. But the stronger Yüan became, the more inclined were many Japanese to throw their weight on the other side of the scales, and the army helped some of Sun's defeated rebels to escape.

The capture of the Kiaochow Leased Territory and occupation of the railway through the Shantung Peninsula both augmented Japan's holdings in China at a time when the Great Powers (except for the United States) were preoccupied in Europe. For the Tokyo elites, military and civilian, the time had come to reach a consensus on policy toward China and to act while the opportunity remained. Through the latter part of 1914, the debate turned into a spiral of opportunism and greed as each faction added its desires to the growing list of demands to be made on the Chinese government.

As early as August 1914 Motojiro Akashi, now vice-chief of the

General Staff, had recommended sorting out all "pending questions" in China. In November, the Cabinet formally adopted a list of twenty-one demands. Most straightforward were the transfer of Germany's lease of Shantung, and the extension to ninety-nine years of the Manchurian leases that Japan had taken over from Russia in 1905 and that were now nearing expiry. Then came joint Sino-Japanese control of the giant Hanyehping mining and smelting complex; an agreement that China would accept Japanese advisers throughout the whole spectrum of her financial, political, and military affairs; unrestricted missionary activity; the right to build railways; and joint control of the police "where necessary." Earlier in the year, the General Staff had presented the army minister with an outline treaty it would like to see imposed on the government in China. When the official list of demands was presented to the Chinese in January 1915, the army made sure that the most significant of its desires were included—notably the appointment of military advisers, but also the approval of certain kinds of strategic building using foreign capital, and China's agreement to buy half of its munitions from Japanese arsenals.

Altogether, the Twenty-one Demands, as they became known, were an anachronistic exercise in old-style imperialism, successful because the timing was right. For almost three months, Yüan conducted a rearguard action of negotiation and appeals to international sympathy. He succeeded in mobilizing grass-roots opinion in the United States, and President Woodrow Wilson himself intervened to force the Japanese to abandon the last seven demands—which were principally those formulated by the Imperial Army. (Anticipating trouble, the Japanese government had expressed these as "desires" rather than outright demands.) But the Japanese hard-liners were not to be denied completely; and with the war in progress in Europe, there was no power to stop them. In May 1915, Japan issued China an ultimatum, to accept the Demands on pain of war, and on May 25 a "treaty" was signed.

For the fledgling Chinese republic, May 25 was thereafter known as the "Day of National Humiliation" and marked each year by anti-Japanese demonstrations. The rising tide of Chinese nationalism washed now on Japanese shores, and boycotts, riots, murders, and demonstrations were permanently to sour relations between the two Asian countries. The Twenty-one Demands, coupled with Japan's reluctance to help with the war in Europe, would also have profound effects on her future relations with the world powers, as events at the Versailles Conference were to show. From now on, Americans would show a marked preference for China, and the defense of Chinese interests by President Wilson and Secretary of State William Jennings Bryan was at the core of a resistance to Japanese expansion that paved the way to the Pacific War.

With time, in the pacifist climate of the years following the First World War, Japan could conceivably have drawn a moral from the episode of the Twenty-one Demands—that old-style imperialism was dead. She might have pulled back and found an honorable place in the community of nations. But it was not to be. The lesson the Imperial Army chose to learn from the Great War was not that imperialism did not pay; on the contrary, they concluded that it had become a vital ingredient in the survival of a country as resource-poor as Japan. The age of total war had arrived, and the army set its face toward equipping the nation to compete.

PART III

IN THE AGE OF TOTAL WAR
1918-1932

RETHINKING WAR

On the eve of the First World War, Japan had an army in the first rank among world powers. Four years later, having been little more than a spectator of events, the Imperial Army was marooned, an obsolescent relic in a new world of war. The very terms "army" and "nation-in-arms" had taken on new meanings in the crucible of the Western Front. No longer was war simply a duel between professional armies enlarged by an influx of willing conscripts; now it pitted whole nation against whole nation in a protracted war of attrition. Every resource that could be mobilized—science, technology, blood, and treasure—was applied in quest of the unconditional surrender of the enemy. The "nation-in-arms" had become the "nation at war." Civilian populations and civilian industry were required to be as regimented and centrally controlled as the armed forces, and in Japan, where there were no constitutional checks upon the military sphere, the Imperial Army would come to perceive its role within the state as virtually without limit.

In strictly military terms, the visible results of the change to total war were vast armies engaged in conflict on a scale that dwarfed the Battle of Mukden, vast consumption of matériel, and an extraordinary advance in all the technologies of warfare, from medicine and poison gas to tanks and aircraft. While the victorious powers of the Western Front ended the war equipped for the twentieth century, Japan languished in the nineteenth. Relatively, the Imperial Army was as clearly inferior to those of the West as it had been in the early 1880s, when Meckel had judged that one Prussian division could have cleared Japan in a single sweep.

Without the mortal imperatives of the Western Front to compel change, "doctrinal stodginess" had survived in the upper echelons of the Imperial Army. Yusaku Uehara, chief of the General Staff from 1915 to 1926, and other senior planners clung to the weapons and tactics of the past on emotional and moral rather than practical grounds. To men brought up to honor physical courage and self-sacrifice, hand-to-hand combat and leading from the front, such devices as tanks and periscopes seemed distinctly unheroic. Foreign observers at the Grand Maneuvers of 1918 criticized obsolete tactical formations, indifferent and unintelligent use of artillery, apparent incomprehension of the principles of camouflage or the use of gas, and a dearth of machine guns, tanks, aircraft, and motor vehicles. "The fact is," wrote one Western intelligence officer, "that the mechanical mind has not yet been evolutionized in Japan, and in case of a modern war of any duration it would probably be through this failing that they would lose. Their one strong point is telephones."

Imperial Army strategists were well aware of their nation's fundamental unpreparedness. Japanese officers observed the gargantuan national mobilization programs of Britain, France, Germany, and America, and witnessed the bloodbaths engendered by this material strength. Horrified by the scale of the conflict, in their dispatches home they spelled out the bitter truth that their own nation had, virtually overnight, become impotent in this new game of war.

The message got through to the highest levels. The prime minister, General Masatake Terauchi, declared on July 2, 1918: "For the achievement of ultimate victory the cooperation of the whole nation is necessary as is proved by the present European War." This was corroborated by General Giichi Tanaka, in a speech to the Imperial Military Reservist Association: "The outcome of wars of the future will not be determined by the strongest army, but by the strongest populace."

Japan was once again at a crossroads. Would she seek new strength along the new path defined by the West? Or would she accept that the tide of Western progress had washed her into the ranks of the second-class military powers in Asia and elsewhere? In the Imperial Army, the samurai tradition lived on. As early as 1917, plans were being laid for Japan's recrudescence as a twentieth-century military power of the first rank.

But the challenge that pride was prompting the army to take up was one of grotesque proportions. A nation needed five essential attributes to wage total war successfully: a compliant and motivated population; secure supplies of raw materials; an industrial base to process those materials into weapons of war; a research-and-development infrastructure for qualitative improvement, including a scientific capability rapidly to evolve new weapons technologies during the war itself; and, arching over the whole, a detailed mobilization plan to maximize the nation's strength within the shortest period. Measured against her potential enemies, Japan was weak in all categories except the first.

All could be remedied in time, though access to secure supplies was the hardest problem to solve. Japan's difficulty was that all her supplies had to be imported, as the home islands were virtually devoid of resources. From the home islands, Japan could in peacetime spare some sulphur for export and possibly be self-supporting for copper, zinc, and mica, but could not provide any important fraction of wartime requirements. Yamagata himself, now in his seventies, seems to have been aware of the resource crisis as early as 1915. To please him, Motojiro Akashi, now a general, sent a survey team to look for oil in northern Yunnan in the far interior of China.

The Asian mainland was the obvious place for Japan to find self-sufficiency. In 1917 Giichi Tanaka toured China and Manchuria for two months, producing a report ominously entitled "The Exploitation of China's Resources." His protégé Kazushige Ugaki urged the policy makers to impress upon the Japanese people that the Yangtze valley was "a limitless treasure trove." In the words of Japan's first postwar long-range defense plan, dated February 1923: "China's abundant natural resources are an indispensable element in both our economic development and our defense." In fact, in the circumstances of modern war, economic development *was* Japan's defense.

Seizure of Germany's Kiaochow Leased Territory in 1915 had opened a gateway to China through the Shantung Peninsula. Tsingtao offered a good harbor, excellent road and rail communications with the interior, access to sources of vital raw materials, a base for propaganda, and an opportunity to interfere in Chinese politics. Three days after the German surrender at Tsingtao, Japan set up a military administration with jurisdiction over taxation, customs, policing, postal services, and the Tsingtao–Tsinan Railway. For some seven years, this administration, supplemented in 1917 by a civilian authority, would control the best part of the Shantung Peninsula.

During this time, economic penetration of the area—the setting up of joint-stock companies and manufacturing concerns, the capturing of a generous share of markets—was rapid and thorough. Elsewhere in China, including the "limitless treasure trove" of the Yangtze valley, Japan had secured or confirmed valuable rights through the Twenty-one Demands. Then loans made to Tuan Ch'i-jui, the warlord who had risen to temporary power within the Chinese government after Yüan Shih-k'ai's death in 1916, had bought notional control of vital railway lines linking Korea and Manchuria, speeding Japan's passage to the heart of North China.

Besides China, Japan appeared to have another avenue to explore in the quest for resources. In the chaos of the Bolshevik revolution, the Russian Far East seemed easy prey, and the eyes of the total-war advocates turned to the north. "It is by the grace of heaven that we are given this opportunity," declared Tanaka.

In February 1918 a Siberia Planning Committee was formed jointly by the General Staff and the Army Ministry. The ultimate aim was to turn the Russian Far East into a Japanese-controlled buffer state. It was a huge undertaking; the strategy proposed by the army committee involved advancing on two fronts from Vladivostok to Khabarovsk and into the Amur valley, and along the Chinese Eastern Railway due west to the six-hundred-mile-long Lake Baikal, the natural boundary of the Russian Far East.

The civilian government, now headed by Kei Hara, the first commoner prime minister, had more moderate ideas. Hara favored intervention only in cooperation with other powers and for less selfish ends, if at all. But acrimony was avoided, or at least postponed, by an invitation from Washington to participate in a joint expedition to Siberia to rescue a corps of Czechoslovak troops, cut off by the collapse of the eastern front, now slowly battling their way out. Then the genie was out of the bottle. Japan went into Siberia within a framework of international cooperation, but insisted on a large degree of independence—she would not, for instance, permit her troops to be put under American command—and kept her own interests clearly in view.

Army policy on the Siberian venture continued to diverge sharply from that of the civilian government, and for several years it was the army in the field that had its way. Indeed, well before any official decision to intervene, the army in Manchuria seems to have been lining up an anti-Bolshevik force on its own initiative, in close contact with White Russian leaders in the area. In January 1918 General Masatake Nakajima was sent to Vladivostok to build a similar network.

Then, once the expedition had been authorized, the General Staff ensured that Japanese participation was on a far larger scale than any of her allies could have anticipated. Originally expected to provide about half the Allied contingent of 24,000, the Japanese eventually deployed some 70,000 troops, justifying each new extension as a "response to local conditions."

The Americans had envisaged action only in the area of Vladivostok; but before long Japanese troops were ranging far and wide in the Amur and west into Buryatia, as far as the shores of Baikal. Within months, the army had in its grip a region abounding with mineral wealth. By the middle of 1920, many of the *zaibatsu*, including Mitsui, Mitsubishi, and Suzuki, had opened branches in Vladivostok, Khabarovsk, Harbin, Chita, and Nikolaevsk, bringing with them some 50,000 Japanese settlers.

Having extracted the Czechs, the United States and Britain withdrew their troops, but the Japanese—and a few Americans manning a top-secret wireless listening post on an island in Peter the Great Bay—stayed on. The Japanese claimed to be protecting their nationals; in fact, they were losing no opportunity, however dubious, to consolidate their economic gains, extend their hold on mines, forests, fisheries, and railways, and "integrate the economy of the region with that of Japan." Observers noted sourly that the Japanese had an enormous number of fresh interests at stake—"The Japanese have been buying up real estate among other things"—and could see no withdrawal in the near future.

Political opposition at home ensured that the army could not simply annex the Russian Far East. Instead, they had to use the White Russian regimes in the region: that of Admiral Aleksandr Kolchak until his capture and execution by the Bolsheviks in 1920, and thereafter, of Ataman Semenov, a Tatar Cossack, half-Russian and half-Mongol. These regimes were hastily formed and inherently unstable, and by 1922 were on the verge of collapse. Only the Imperial Army's intervention prevented the Bolsheviks from advancing to Vladivostok. In March and April 1922 the Japanese repulsed the Bolshevik advance, but with all hope gone of establishing a buffer state the army was obliged to choose between withdrawal and the prospect of prolonged, expensive warfare. International opinion had turned sour, and at home—where for two years the army had absorbed half the domestic budget—there was an irresistible outcry for an end. "Nearly four years have passed since the occupation," thundered the *Asahi Shimbun*, "with the only result that Russian enmity towards Japan has been greatly increased."

Grim proof was provided in May 1920. In Nikolaevsk, the entire Japanese population of seven hundred men, women, and children was subjected to torture and rape by Bolshevik troops before finally being murdered. In retribution, the Imperial Army occupied parts of northern Sakhalin, with its enormous coal, oil, and timber reserves.

On June 24, 1922, Japan finally announced that it would withdraw from everywhere except Sakhalin by the end of October. By way of a goodwill gesture, the Japanese government neutered Semenov's militancy against the Bolsheviks by the simple expedient of denying him access to his hoard of gold and platinum in Japanese banks. (He had deposited his wealth not in his own name but under the titles of "Commander of the Front" and "The Pohodny Ataman of All the Cossacks," to neither of which he could now lay claim.)

The Imperial Army was at last, it seemed, acting in conformity with the international community's expectations. But to the puzzlement of Western observers, though Japan's withdrawal was unilateral, the Bolsheviks nevertheless agreed to negotiate a basis for it. Then, on June 27, a British agent, code-named "Black Jumbo," passed over a secret Japanese document that asserted that the Bolsheviks wanted to reopen negotiations and had agreed to most of Japan's conditions for withdrawal. And the reason? If the Bolsheviks at Chita were to sign the Japanese proposals they would, by August 15, have delivered to them "the arms and ammunition now impounded by our forces at Vladivostok."

The "arms and ammunition at Vladivostok" made up the largest stockpile of war munitions ever made. The allies, for the purposes of the Siberian expedition, had accumulated 84,000 rifles, 200,000 grenades, 30 million pounds of powder, 9,300,000 artillery shells, 364 artillery pieces, and other ordnance, which now sat in Vladivostok under Japanese guard.

With Bolshevik revolution to the north and west and political chaos to the south, this stockpile gave the Japanese extraordinary leverage over both the Chinese warlords competing for power among themselves, and the ill-equipped Bolsheviks. The eventual fate of the stockpile is not clear. It was deteriorating—the Vladivostok nights were punctuated by random explosions—but it was certainly not destroyed, despite pleas from both the American and British governments—so presumably, when the Bolsheviks finally entered Vladivostok, a large proportion of the stockpile fell into their hands.

Long before that, however, significant quantities had been deployed by the Imperial Army in the attempt to secure their position in northeast China. The beneficiary of their largesse was Chang Tso-lin, perhaps the most remarkable of all the modern-day Chinese warlords. He was a tiny man, illiterate, an opium addict, but ruthless and shrewd. By 1922, Chang—the "Old Marshal," as he was known—had gained control of the three northeastern provinces that form the bulk of Manchuria. He knew the Japanese were in Manchuria to stay, and that his survival depended on a working relationship with them, in particular with the Imperial Army. Here, it seemed, was some profit for the army from the Siberian expedition. A separate Manchuria ruled by a man dependent upon Japan at least promised to guarantee Japan's primacy in the region of China where her interests were strongest.

12

THE GREAT DIVIDE

R unning hand in hand with the search for secure supplies of resources on the continent was the process of domestic reorganization. Six months before the end of the Great War, Japan had an
Industrial Mobilization Law, which empowered the government to utilize
or expropriate factories and workshops, regulate the use and importation
of raw materials and fuel, and requisition labor. This single shift of
policy was of great significance for the evolution of the Imperial Army.
From being an element external to the development of Japan as a whole,
the mailed fist quite separate from the body politic, the army now sought
integration, in effect a "Japan Incorporated."

Foreign military attachés were startled. "Nothing of any importance
has hitherto been achieved by private factories in Japan in the manufacture of war-like stores. . . . The military authorities have always professed
to believe that nothing but inferior workmanship was to be expected from
private enterprise. The lessons of the war have evidently come home to
them."

126

But while the blueprint for a nation at war was slowly emerging, enthusiasm among industrialists for working more closely with the army was minimal. Army planners found themselves looking enviously at the high degree of "voluntariness" shown by American industrialists during the Great War. Marumiya Shoten, a soap-making company in Osaka, was urgently requested to make additional glycerine for the manufacture of dynamite, as imports became scarcer. The glycerine failed to materialize in the required quantities because, Marumiya explained, the order "interfered with their profits."

Significantly, despite the powers granted to them by the Industrial Mobilization Law, the army did not attempt to coerce Marumiya. In the years immediately following the Great War, its influence politically and among the people at large was in decline. The days of easily fired sentimental enthusiasm among the Japanese people were long over. The Great War, primarily a European battle, aroused little popular interest in the form of songs, books, or heroic tales. The fighting at Tsingtao had been brief and comparatively unspectacular, nothing to compare with the siege of Port Arthur, and the action in Siberia had been far from glorious. The official conduct of the Siberian expedition would later be bitterly attacked in the Diet, with Tanaka accused of grossly misrepresenting the size of the force sent and even of misappropriation of secret funds.

Public feeling turned against the army, given impetus by the spread of ugly rumors of atrocities committed by Japanese troops. The army had also associated itself with some very dubious anti-Bolshevik forces— among them, the "Mad Baron" Roman von Ungern-Sternberg, a Russian major general who believed himself to be the reincarnation of Genghis Khan. In pursuit of his dream, he waged a campaign of conspicuous sadism, roasting would-be deserters alive and lynching Jews and the deformed. Before he was finished, he declared, he would plant an avenue of gallows from Mongolia to Moscow.

In Korea, too, the rebellion of 1919 had been repressed with great brutality; and again in 1920, when bandits attacked the town of Hunchun near the border between Korea and Manchuria, killing fourteen Japanese, the army sent six battalions, who burned churches and schools and murdered almost four hundred Koreans.

The loss of public support in Japan was reflected in draft-dodging on a previously unimaginable scale. Only in rural areas did the army retain popular support. Since the 1870s, there had been a constant cycle of rural conscription and supply (particularly of horses and forage) and intimate family connections, father to son, with the local regiment. But

127

in the cities, military service was no longer considered especially honorable or even respectable; many officers preferred not to wear their uniforms off duty. This new hostility was partly due to the use of the army against the public from which it was drawn. By 1918 the cost of living had risen 130 percent in four years; when large-scale rice hoarding was discovered, with a strong whiff of establishment profiteering, there was serious and widespread rioting, and the troops were called out to suppress it.

But more generally, suspicion of the military was just one symptom of rapid fluctuation in the political climate of Japan. In the early 1920s there was more scope for dissent and challenging of authority than at any other time from the Meiji Restoration to the Pacific War.

This apparent liberty flowered within carefully defined boundaries. The centralized and authoritarian Meiji state remained as strong as ever; and though in 1925 the Diet would grant universal male suffrage, it was accompanied by a new Peace Preservation Law granting the government even more extensive powers to curtail free speech and suppress "undesirable" political activity with its omnipresent thought police.

Nevertheless, "acceptable"—as opposed to extremist—politics prospered. Japan was moving into the era of full-fledged conservative party government, and the military's right to intervene in policy-making was fiercely challenged. Kei Hara, prime minister from 1918, was neither a genro nor the protégé of one, neither Choshu nor Satsuma; he was the first head of government to hold a seat in the lower house and to lead a Cabinet formed from the majority party. Hara was no leftist, and was not opposed in principle to the military as the spearhead of overseas expansion. But on the subject of its political influence, he was adamant. Policy-making was the sole preserve of the civilian government of Cabinet and ministries—and that applied not only to domestic affairs but also to foreign and even military policy.

Ever since the acquisition of the Liaotung Peninsula and the recognition of Japanese predominance in Korea in 1905, the army had tended to feel that mainland affairs were its exclusive preserve. Men like Saionji had challenged this belief, and public suspicion of uncontrolled military adventurism on the continent was widespread. The rift between the foreign policies of the military and the Foreign Ministry was no secret; but Hara was determined that "dual diplomacy" should be stopped.

The Emperor, he declared, should be "unburdened" of some of his responsibilities by the Cabinet—including some as head of the army. In sharp contrast with the procedure at the start of the Russo-Japanese War, no separate Imperial Headquarters was established for the Siberian expedition. Though the General Staff of course directed operations, the Army Ministry controlled objectives, giving the Cabinet some scope to set the overall limits of action. During Hara's premiership, with Giichi Tanaka as army minister under him, there would be repeated clashes between the ministry and the General Staff; it was even possible for Finance Minister Korekiyo Takahashi to suggest in 1920 the total abolition of the General Staff.

Hara had good grounds for his determinedly antimilitary stance. Japan could not afford to exacerbate international opinion, which had already branded her selfish and untrustworthy—not least because of her behavior during the war. "Japan's prosperity may be justly taken as a measure of the extent to which she has been assisting the Allies, and a compliment to her rather than a condemnation," argued one Japanese representative optimistically. The Allies were not convinced. "So far as Japan and the war are concerned," the *London and China Telegraph* had written in October 1916, "the old proverb that it is an ill wind that blows nobody any good has never perhaps been better exemplified. While the other belligerents are pouring out blood and treasure to a degree never before paralleled in history, our Far Eastern Ally is making enormous profits as the result of Armageddon."

Reveling in the absence of competition, Japan had traded busily with all sides, moving in on markets—cotton, textiles, shoes, shipping, chemicals—previously dominated by powers whose attention was distracted by war. Her entire industrial capacity was devoted to fulfilling war orders from powers more deeply involved in the fighting; there was a certain satisfaction in being able to redeem the debts left by the Russo-Japanese War with money made from selling arms to Russia. By 1918 gold reserves had been doubled, the entire foreign debt cleared, and the trade balance righted, and there was money to invest in industrial growth and to plow into Kwantung and the South Manchurian Railway. "Financially the war has placed Japan in a position beyond her dreams of avarice," concluded the *Telegraph*.

But the principal grievances of the international community focused on the behavior of the army in Siberia and also on Japan's conduct in China, where there was intense resentment of the Twenty-one Demands, manifested in damaging trade boycotts and an outcry for the return of Shantung. America too was infuriated with Japan on China's behalf, as well as on her own account. For years war between America and Japan had been a possibility which neither could ignore; in 1914, for example,

Japan had detailed plans for an invasion of the Philippines in the event of hostilities with the United States. Gradually, the uneasy entente, based on well-worn and hollow formulae—fidelity to the principle of the Open Door on one side, recognition of Japan's special standing in Korea on the other—was submerged in a rising tide of naval competition and racial ill-feeling. Consequently, by 1920 Japan had attached to herself the rooted dislike and distrust of what was now the richest and most highly industrialized nation in the world, whose presence in East Asia was beginning to predominate.

The British, too, had radically revised their opinion of the nation which was still their ally. Their sensibilities had been outraged by Japanese criticisms of their performance at Tsingtao and thereafter. Of the defeat of General Sir Charles Townshend by the Turks at Kut-el-Amara in April 1916, the *Hochi* had written condescendingly, "The Japanese cannot understand why a great army of 10,000 men should have surrendered. It may perhaps be explained by the difference between the temperaments of east and west, and for this reason we are unwilling to judge England too hardly." The *Yamato Shimbun* had no such reticence; the Turks, it wrote, no longer regarded the British as a nation to be feared, and other Eastern peoples might similarly be expected to see the light.

But even more serious than Japan's arrogance—displayed at its worst in the Twenty-one Demands, of which Britain received no warning—was her lack of sympathy with her ally's needs and objectives. She had rejected urgent appeals for help at a time when Britain and France were in desperate straits on the Western Front. "Apart from the selling of guns and ammunition to the Russians and ourselves," commented Admiral John Jellicoe furiously, "Japan is not taking a full share in the war." Not content with this, she had damaged the Allied cause further by actively threatening British interests in India.

This was not merely a question of commercial competition. Political agitators campaigning for Home Rule were finding both moral and material support in Japan. Pan-Asian ultranationalists provided shelter, seditious literature, and even arms; one group was strongly suspected of collusion with Germany in gunrunning to India. But subversion was not confined to the extremist fringes; former prime minister Okuma was also a vocal supporter of Indian Home Rule, and had been singularly unhelpful when asked to expel Indian dissidents taking refuge in Japan. The British suspected Japan of operating an elaborate system of espionage and intrigue throughout Asia—supplying arms to the Dalai Lama in

Tibet, infiltrating into Nepal, spying in northern Australia and in Persia, fomenting local unrest in the Dutch East Indies in the hope of creating a situation where she might officially intervene.

The scales, it seemed, had fallen from British eyes. "Prior to the war," commented the British ambassador to China, "there was a tendency to look upon Japan as a model of all the international virtues. Abroad, the Japanese were loosely spoken of as a virile enterprising little race, who, shaking off the dust of two thousand years, were advancing by leaps and bounds to the status of a First Class Power. In England they were extolled as the best and most devoted of Allies. . . . That was at the time when the Powers viewed each other through a glass darkly, but now they see each other face to face. Today we have come to know that Japan—the real Japan—is a frankly opportunist, not to say selfish, country, of very moderate importance compared with the Giants of the Great War, but with a very exaggerated opinion of her own role.

"Japan is at heart Asiatic," he added, voicing the suspicions of all the Great Powers, "and need not be expected, apart from motives of self-interest, to favour one European nation over another, or to bind herself to any Western Power a moment longer than it suits her to do so." He went on: "As long as Great Britain was able to maintain her prestige in the Far East, Japan was enthusiastic for the Anglo-Japanese Alliance; but when the hour of our distress arrived, and we began to pay the penalty for our national unpreparedness, she wavered. It will perhaps be kindest to leave it at that." Better now, he thought, that Britain should rebuild her own power in the East. Once the war was over, she should seek to build up the navy in the Pacific, expand trade and supplant German shipping lines. "Above all things let us keep the control of important raw materials in our own hands. So long as we do this Japan is at our mercy."

The Japanese had come face to face with the accumulated acrimony of the Allies in 1919 when they arrived in Versailles to negotiate their share of the spoils; they seem to have been surprised by the bitterness. Most obviously hostile were the Americans, who were not only reluctant to concede Japanese possession of Shantung and the mandated Pacific islands but were also instrumental in the defeat of Japan's proposal for a racial equality clause to be inserted into the charter of the League of Nations. (The most virulent opponent of the clause was the prime minister of Australia; but by insisting that voting on the issue must be unanimous, Woodrow Wilson played straight into his hands.) Not without reason, Japan construed this as meaning that the Americans rejected the notion that the Japanese were their equals, and instead planned to restrict their immigration in the United States.

The pressures and tensions in the triangular relationship among the United States, Japan, and Britain were coming to a head. In particular, the Anglo-Japanese Alliance was no longer tenable. It had originally evolved to meet a set of circumstances that no longer existed. To many Japanese the raison d'être of the alliance had vanished when Russia was defeated in 1905. The nation against which Japan now seemed most likely to need help was America—and she was specifically excluded from the terms of the alliance, as Britain had no desire to find herself at war with the United States on Japan's account. Some Japanese even saw the association with Britain as an obstacle to their expansion in Central China, where British interests were strongest, and a threat to the cause of Pan-Asianism.

In addition, brakes had to be applied to a naval arms race that was rocketing rapidly out of control. America had also profited substantially from the war, and plowed much of the proceeds into a formidable navy. Japan lacked the capital, natural resources, and productive capacity easily to compete, but she could not afford to let the American expansion go unchallenged; in 1918 the naval budget took off, and kept climbing.

The 1921–1922 Washington Conference, called by America to discuss East Asian affairs and naval arms limitation, revealed once again the determination of the world's leading powers to keep Japan in her place. Existing American and British naval strength was approximately equal, Japanese strength roughly three-fifths as great. The aim of the Western powers was to limit the size and firepower of capital ships and peg their tonnage at these levels. Japan's objective was to achieve a ratio of seven Japanese to ten British to ten American vessels overall, which would give her practical superiority in Asian waters.

Unfortunately for the Japanese, American cryptologists had broken a Japanese cipher which revealed that they would concede a ratio of 6:10:10 if absolutely necessary. The required pressure was applied, and the navy minister accepted the status quo. At the same time the Japanese government reached a compromise with China on the return of the former German territory at Kiaochow and withdrawal from the rest of the Shantung Peninsula, and announced Japan's readiness to withdraw from Eastern Siberia.

Though the acceptance of a 6:10:10 ratio had been against the wishes of the navy's General Staff, there were some compensations. America undertook to stop constructing fortifications on Guam, Britain likewise in Hong Kong. With no Western presence west of Hawaii or north of Singapore, Japan—which also continued to hold the German Pacific colonies of the Caroline, Marshall, and Mariana islands—now had security in her home waters.

The system for regulating international relations in Asia that emerged from the Washington Conference emphasized agreement to respect existing rights in the Pacific, and in particular to maintain China's territorial independence. The ruling principle was free trade within a framework of conciliation and cooperation, a restatement of America's Open Door policy.

From the army's perspective, the naval détente and disarmament produced by the Washington Conference put a welcome curb on the navy's share of the military budget. But the army's own scope for expansion in China was also curbed. In seeking political and economic cooperation with America and Britain, Baron Kijuro Shidehara, the new foreign minister and one of the dominant civilian figures of the 1920s, closely reflected the thinking of Japanese industrialists. In their view, far greater immediate rewards were to be gained from peaceful trade than from the kind of military pressure that had resulted in the Twenty-one Demands and the Siberian expedition—and in the cause of Japan's economic well-being, Shidehara was prepared to renounce all intervention in China's domestic affairs.

"The age of Machiavellian aggressive state policy is over," Shidehara argued vehemently. "Foreign policy must be conducted in accordance with the great principles of peace and justice." Japan's participation in the League of Nations and the Washington Conference was a resounding victory for civilian, internationalist values, but a direct challenge to those in the pursuit of total-war preparedness. Shidehara was denying the army all opportunity of acquiring secure sources of raw materials on the Asian continent, while condoning an increasingly pluralistic political system at home.

The army was under attack. Under the terms of the Washington Conference, all the gains it had made during the war and its aftermath—Tsingtao, Shantung, Vladivostok, North Sakhalin—were relinquished. The Anglo-Japanese Alliance was terminated, leaving Japan without a formal ally; and at home, disenchantment with the army and a sharp economic depression made economies in military spending imperative.

Between 1921 and 1923 military appropriations dropped from 49 percent to 30 percent of total national expenditures. For the time being, the navy bore the brunt; the sharpest cuts for the army were still to come.

In 1921 the army possessed twenty-one divisions. During his term in office, Army Minister Hanzo Yamanashi achieved quite substantial troop reductions under cover of the withdrawals from Siberia and Shantung. He did it without reducing the number of divisions, on the principle that, in better times, it would be easier to expand existing divisions, however skeletal, than create new ones.

But the Yamanashi cuts were not enough. In 1923, when a violent earthquake (and subsequent fire and tidal wave) killed almost 150,000 people and devastated much of the Tokyo-Yokohama area, martial law was declared and the army was set to work clearing the wreckage, providing relief, and restoring law and order. Though their efforts did something to increase their popularity, the financial drain made further economies inevitable. In 1924 the new army minister, Kazushige Ugaki, bit the bullet and cut four divisions in their entirety—the first reduction in the size of the army since its foundation.

13

COUNTERATTACK

With the conclusion of the Washington Conference and Shidehara's strictures against "Machiavellian aggressive state policy," the army's hopes of preparing Japan for total war fell into abeyance. Even the Munitions Bureau and Council—the prototype administrative system created in 1918—had both been abolished, and responsibility for "stocktaking of national industries" had passed to individual civilian ministries. The High Command was forced to recognize that there were limits and alternatives to the exercise of military power. In 1923 Iwane Matsui (later hanged by the Allies for ordering the Rape of Nanking) circulated a top-secret memorandum: "We must substitute economic conquest for military invasion, financial influence for military control, and achieve our goals under the slogan of co-prosperity and co-existence, friendship and co-operation."

But the flame had not died: on February 16, 1925, General Baron Oi, former Commander in Chief in Siberia, reopened the offensive in the House of Peers by inquiring whether there was any intention of establishing a Council of National Defense. He was told that the civilian ministries had not yet succeeded in carrying out investigations to clarify the actual condition and strength of the country and "its relation with the natural resources of foreign countries"—both necessary preliminaries to general-mobilization planning.

What was needed was an organization to carry out these basic researches. In October 1926, with some of the money saved by the Ugaki cuts, a new "Equipment Bureau" was created at the Army Ministry. Despite its unimpressive title, the Equipment Bureau had important responsibilities, including requisition and control of munitions and "the conversion of the industrial resources of the nation to a war footing." The man Ugaki chose as bureau chief, Tetzusan Nagata, was to become the high priest of total-war preparedness, dominating army thinking for almost a decade.

Tetzusan Nagata, aged forty-two at the time of his appointment, was a slightly built, myopic, austere-looking intellectual, a theorist rather than a fighting soldier. His family roots were in Nagano Prefecture, where his father was a successful doctor. Nagata first came to the attention of the upper echelons when he proved himself the brightest of the crop of young officers in the last years of Meiji. The turning point in his carreer came during the Great War, when he was posted to neutral Scandinavia to gather information on Germany's conduct of hostilities. He stayed on in Europe afterward, learning at close quarters the price of Germany's failure to win in total war.

Nagata saw that not only had the nature of war changed, so, too, had the nature of defeat. The pattern of events in the Sino-Japanese War or even the Russo-Japanese War—peace paid for by treaty, indemnity, and economic concessions—had no application to the Germany of the early 1920s. Defeat in the age of total war meant total catastrophe for the entire nation. In January 1919 the mark had been worth 8.9 U.S. dollars; by November 1923 the dollar was worth 4,200,000,000,000 marks. Germans starved, begged, turned to prostitution, and yet still died by the thousands of malnutrition. And feeding on the misery was the specter of communism—250,000 card-carrying Germans by 1923, with the near prospect of successful revolution.

The nation that had been military godfather to Japan was here driven to the verge of moral, physical, and financial extinction by the combined power of enemies possessing a superior productive capacity and superior resources. Nagata was to dedicate his life to preserving Japan from a similar fate. In 1927, *Kaikosha-kiji*, the journal of the officer corps, carried two significant and highly influential memoranda in which Nagata and his chief, Naosuke Matsuki, argued the case for total war, pointing out that a nation can maximize its strength only by utilizing every last resource. The irony of the Great War was that while to civilians it was "the war to end war," to soldiers it meant the creation of nothing less than a garrison state. It was a radical message, and one Nagata repeated at greater length and to a wider audience in his book *Total National Mobilization,* published the following year.

In May 1927, after retired general Giichi Tanaka became prime minister, the quest for total-war capability passed another milestone with the creation of an integrated body for general mobilization, under the direct control of the prime minister—a body the British saw as the equivalent of their own Committee for Imperial Defence, the highest planning and coordinating body in the British Empire.

This organization, the Resources Bureau, brought total-war planning to the highest levels; its members included the prime minister, the army minister, the minister for commerce and industry, the vice-chiefs of the army and navy General Staffs, the chief secretary of the Legislative Bureau, and the vice-ministers of finance, foreign affairs, and communications. Its secretariat, which kept in communication with Nagata's Army Ministry Equipment Bureau, was housed in offices just outside the Palace gates, where it carried out the detailed work of "control and direction of the entire personnel and material resources of the Empire, including drawing up schemes for the general mobilisation of the nation for war."

Industrial mobilization required a comprehensive national plan, which in turn required both information and experience. On December 1, 1929, the means of gathering information was created: "Regulations for the Investigation of Resources" made each minister of state responsible for detailing resources within his own sphere.

Unlike previous legislation, these regulations prevented bureaucratic obfuscation by spelling out to a remarkable level of detail exactly what information was required. On the home minister's list was the number of chauffeurs in the country; the foreign minister was expected to supply the number of Japanese resident abroad, the nature of their businesses, and the condition of foreign businesses under Japanese management; and the finance minister was to monitor government warehousing of rice.

But critically, the regulations did not give the planners unrestricted access to the leading edge of the nation's technology, such as it was. The influence of the *zaibatsu* ensured that "inventions and special processes officially recognised as such" could be protected. Here, in the 1920s, began internecine conflict that ensured that Japan, unlike the United States, would never create the technological capacity and momentum sufficient to upgrade or revolutionize her weapons systems during the Pacific War itself.

Efficient planning required some hands-on experience, which Japan's brief involvement in the Great War had not provided. Accordingly, the Commerce and Industry, Home, and Army Ministries arranged a series of practical exercises. The first, in the summer of 1929, started from the hypothesis that the "country" next to the Osaka region had declared war on its neighbor at one P.M. on June 23; at eight A.M. on the following day the chief of the Resources Bureau ordered industrial mobilization.

Boy Scouts requisitioned motor cars, reservists supervised the enforcement of a blackout, Youth Association members directed traffic. Bombers flew over Osaka, and anti-aircraft guns blazed away at them with blanks from the roofs of offices and department stores. The radio airwaves were full of propaganda, and in Osaka, Kyoto, and Kobe, hundreds of factories were mobilized to manufacture, or act as if they were manufacturing, a huge range of materials necessary in time of war: shells, boots, X-ray machines, canned beef, aspirin and other chemicals, various oils and acids, automobiles, and aircraft.

It was a huge operation, which awoke the Osaka conurbation to the new face of war. But old men sitting in the teahouses of Kyoto and Osaka, watching the frenzy of activity around them, would have recalled a time six decades before, when the area had been used to pilot another military scheme—something called conscription.

The Osaka mobilization experiment was symbolic of a crucial shift in the balance of power in Japan. In just five years, the power of the civilian internationalist consensus had seriously weakened. The foundation of the internationalist order—an open world economy—was crumbling. In October 1924, the finance minister had called for national retrenchment to deal with the "grave crisis" confronting Japan's finances. In 1927, there was a serious bank crisis, from which the economy had barely recovered before the Great Depression struck Japan. A return to the gold standard in 1929 ensured that goods for export remained costly, while markets abroad shrank. Between 1929 and 1931, exports fell by 40 percent, leaving a trail of bankruptcies and growing queues of unemployed. Rural areas, the army's heartland, were devastated: Most farmers depended on producing raw silk for the American market, and when the appetites of the Roaring Twenties vanished overnight, agricultural communities faced starvation. So desperate was the situation that the old practice of selling daughters into prostitution made a reappearance.

Conciliation and cooperation had failed to feed the people. Nor could it guarantee Japan's security against the upsurge of Chinese nationalism or the reemergence of Russia as a major military power. As the 1920s drew to a close, the Soviet Union was becoming "a land of metal," in Stalin's phrase, and only a decade after the Bolshevik revolution its leaders were boasting that they could challenge the economic supremacy of the United States. The Soviet Union had natural autarky; through central planning, Stalin quickly and with a ruthlessness that defies description built the infrastructure of a powerful defense state.

In December 1927, the Fifteenth Communist Party Congress resolved that the first Five-Year Plan (to begin in 1929) would concentrate on developing those sectors of industry that would contribute most to defense and economic security in the event of war. This was the kind of political will toward national defense that Nagata and the other advocates of total war sometimes despaired of finding in Japan, but the fact that the Soviet Union, the real threat to Japan, was progressing toward total-war preparedness only confirmed the accuracy of Japanese army planners' perceptions of national security. While in 1916 the concept of total war could have been criticized as inapplicable in the Asian context (since there was so little industry to mobilize), by the end of the 1920s it had become the sine qua non of national salvation and the mainspring of the army's elite.

Even as the Five-Year Plan took shape, the Soviets were already harvesting the fruits of their efforts in the 1920s to build military-industrial strength. Since 1922, the German army had been secretly giving the Russians aircraft, tank, and poison-gas technologies for bases on Soviet soil, where Germany might build up its strength away from the eyes of the Western Allies. For Japan, the resulting advances in Russian aircraft development had particular significance: In 1929, a modified Soviet heavy bomber (the TB-1, stripped of its armor) flew from Moscow to New York, over Siberia and through Japanese airspace. The potential for bombing Tokyo was all too obvious.

While building military strength at home, Stalin exported the virus of Communist ideology to sap his enemies abroad. Where Lenin had seen Russia as an instrument of world revolution, Stalin saw world revolution as a tool of the Soviet state. In March 1919 in Moscow, Lenin and Trotsky had called into being a new international revolutionary organization: the Communist International, or "Comintern." This now fell into Stalin's hands as the principal instrument for furthering covertly the aims and policies of the Politburo.

The Comintern was active throughout the Japanese Empire. As an ideology, communism was remarkably persuasive in these years; anathema to the Emperor system, it was a political alternative tailor-made to suit Japanese society. The way in which it operated—as a pyramid of small cells of activists bound together by ties of personal loyalty and obedience to higher authority—cloned existing Japanese social organization. To Japanese youth in particular, communism offered release from the morbid obsessions of Emperor-based propaganda. Far from Tokyo, the hotbed of 1920s radicalism, and deep in army territory at Kumamoto, the police regularly staged surprise raids on the dormitories of the local high school in search of "dangerous" literature. Some 25 percent of the students there studied communism seriously, and on average ten students a year were expelled and twenty-five suspended.

To set against communism, Japan had only an artificial mythology centered on the Emperor, which attracted none but the Japanese, and, in the era of Taisho democracy, few enough of them. Consequently, Communists made inroads into many areas of Japanese life—among the young, the intellectuals, the workers of the industrial cities, the upper echelons of the South Manchurian Railway Company, even Cabinet circles.

Particularly alarming to the High Command was the sight of the Comintern undermining Japan's security position by aiding the national-regeneration movement that had grown up in China following the 1911 overthrow of the Ch'ing dynasty. Because Stalin did not believe China to be capable of Marxist-Leninist revolution, he directed the energies of Comintern agents (like the young Ho Chi Minh, posted to Canton as secretary to the principal Comintern agent) to help not the fledgling Chinese Communist Party of Mao Tse-tung, but the Nationalist movement spearheaded by Chiang Kai-shek. To Stalin, a Nationalist China could do as much damage to Japan as a Communist China, and, given the charisma of Chiang Kai-shek, the Nationalists were a far better bet.

Chiang's destiny was to die embittered and confined on the island of Taiwan; but in the 1920s he was a folk hero, the living symbol of China's blossoming aspirations toward democracy and regeneration. "A genius . . . a slim, unassuming young officer . . . willed by a will as stern as the Great Wall, as irresistible as the flood of China's rivers," was how Han Su-yin saw him during her childhood in Peking and later, when she was the wife of one of his officers.

Chiang had himself studied in Moscow. In the 1920s Soviet agents trained his officers and Moscow armed his troops. And when he advanced north from Canton to unify China by military force, ahead of him went Comintern propagandists—spreading the message not of communism, but of the Nationalist party. On the crest of this wave, Chiang's triumphant "northern expedition" had reached Nanking by 1927 and by 1928 was knocking on the gates of Peking itself.

In the mere five years since Japan's withdrawal from Siberia, her security position had been completely transformed as new military powers materialized to menace her vested interests on the Asian mainland. And military threat was compounded in China by the Nationalist-inspired popular movement to recover the rights China had been forced to concede to outside powers, Japan included. Of all the imperialist nations in China, Japan had most to lose from this Nationalist ambition. "The peculiar element in the situation of Japan," noted the British Foreign Office, "is the extent to which her economic fortunes are bound up with the development of China. Nearly all her eggs are in the China basket. To America, trade relations with China mean very little, to Britain they are of the greatest importance, to Japan they are vital."

The particular focus of Japan's concern was Manchuria, where two-thirds of all her investment in China was to be found. Though supported by the army since the Siberian expedition, the "Old Marshal," Chang Tso-lin, had not proven quite the ally he had once seemed. In May 1927, he notified the Japanese government that "in the light of the Washington Conference principles, he could not recognise Japan's interest in Manchuria." He did not hesitate to oppose Japanese interests where they impinged on his own. He sponsored, for instance, a Chinese railway and harbor system that bit deeply into the profits of the South Manchurian Railway. Nor would he countenance the thought of Manchuria being used to provide *Lebensraum* for the overflow of the Japanese Empire.

Worse, from the Imperial Army's perspective, was Chang's ambition of founding a new dynasty to rule China. Against instructions (which the Japanese called advice), he advanced his army south of the Great Wall and took Peking. There, in the Forbidden Palace, the tiny opportunist wove his opium-induced fantasies of emperorship. This was a dangerous move for Japan as well as for Chang himself. Manchuria, shielded by mountain ranges, is naturally defensible. But once he had entered the open North China plain, the Old Marshal was vulnerable to Chiang Kai-shek—and his defeat would lay the whole of Manchuria open to the Nationalists.

At this crucial moment, on April 20, 1927, Giichi Tanaka, now retired from the army, became prime minister of Japan. He had been chosen to head a political party, the Seiyukai, in order to take a hard line against the Nationalists—the first sign of public dissatisfaction with the "weak-kneed" policies of Shidehara. Tanaka sent troops into Shantung province to protect Japanese interests, and at Tsinan in 1928 some 3,500 of Chiang Kai-shek's forces were killed for refusing to evacuate the city.

For all the Old Marshal's faults, he remained the cornerstone of Tanaka's China policy. In his heart, Chang knew his army was no match for the Nationalists, and as Chiang Kai-shek advanced, Tanaka was able to persuade the Old Marshal to give up Peking and return with his army to Manchuria, where his security (and from Tanaka's perspective, his obedience) could be guaranteed.

Unfortunately for Tanaka, this solution did not meet with the approval of Imperial troops in Manchuria and North China, in whose sides the Old Marshal had been a thorn for too long. The commander of the Japanese garrison at Tientsin suggested that the time had come to be rid of him; the Kwantung Army's senior staff officer, Daisaku Komoto, obliged. At 5:23 A.M. on June 4, 1928, as Chang's train approached Mukden, it was blown up. The Old Marshal died, and along with him went Tanaka's China policy.

In Tokyo, his Cabinet gave way to that of Osachi Hamaguchi, who brought Shidehara once again to the Foreign Ministry. From the army's perspective, there could have been no more provocative a combination. Shidehara was passive and conciliatory abroad; Hamaguchi, known as "the Lion," was strong at home and hard to handle. He had once been finance minister, and his Cabinet now determinedly pursued policies of fiscal retrenchment.

Once again military budgets were a prime target, and in particular the navy's shipbuilding program. Against the advice of the navy General Staff, Hamaguchi forced through acceptance of a new naval arms control treaty signed in London in 1930. The London Naval Treaty extended beyond capital ships the Japanese-American-British ratio fixed in Washington in 1923. Alleging that Hamaguchi had interfered with the navy's right of command, the chief of the navy General Staff resigned. Hamaguchi escaped the political shafts, but in November 1930, as he boarded a train at Tokyo station, a bullet from an ultranationalist's pistol found its mark.

Undaunted by this violent evidence of hostility to Cabinet policy, Shidehara continued to insist on respect for China's sovereignty. Nothing could have alarmed the army more—particularly as they watched the new Manchurian warlord chart an errant course.

Chang Tso-lin had been succeeded by his son, Chang Hsüeh-liang. The "Young Marshal" was another confirmed opium addict, as ruthless as his father. His right of succession as warlord had been challenged by the Old Marshal's Chief of Staff—a problem the young Chang resolved by calling the officer to his residence for a meeting, pulling out his revolver, and shooting him through the forehead.

Chang Hsüeh-liang continued the attacks on foreign interests in Manchuria with reckless abandon. He selected what he thought was the weakest of the powers, the Soviet Union, as his first target. Despite their anti-imperialist rhetoric, the Bolsheviks had clung fast to the Chinese Eastern Railway running east–west across Manchuria—like the South Manchurian Railway, an indispensable economic tool, and of strategic value in providing the means of transporting troops and munitions rapidly to Vladivostok should the need arise. Alleging Comintern activity in the Russian legation at Harbin, the Young Marshal deployed his troops along the Chinese Eastern Railway, arrested Russian citizens, and suspended operation of Soviet trade organs in Manchuria.

Chang's estimate of relative strengths in Manchuria in 1929 had not been unreasonable—except that in relegating the Soviets to last place he had discounted Bolshevik willpower. General Vasily Blücher (only lately military adviser to Chiang Kai-shek on the "northern expedition") was appointed commander of a new Special Far East Army of 113,000 men equipped with the products of the "land of metal": artillery, tanks, and aircraft.

On October 12, Blücher struck, smashing through Chinese opposition. Finally, on November 17, Soviet forces encircled and crushed the Young Marshal's forces at Manchouli. Fortunately for Chang, Stalin contented himself with enforcing the return of the Chinese Eastern Railway and did not exploit his victory to the full.

The Imperial Army, surprised by the power of the Soviet Union, paid careful attention. Their own military estimates had been much in line with that of Chang Hsüeh-liang, and they had hastily to revise their opinion of the Bolsheviks. Perhaps more significantly, they also revised their opinion of Chang. No longer could a Chinese warlord be expected to protect Japanese interests in Manchuria. From now on, Manchuria had to be the exclusive domain of the Imperial Army, and issues like building the strategically valuable railway lines north to the Soviet border assumed an even greater significance.

The Manchouli defeat might have been enough by itself to end Chang's potential usefulness to the Imperial Army, but he compounded his problems by turning on Japan. He not only continued the economic warfare pioneered by his father but added to it the political dimension that Japan most feared: He joined the Nationalists.

On December 29, 1928, the "blue sky–white sun" flag of the Nationalists flew over Manchuria. From being an independent warlord, the Young Marshal had become the Nanking-appointed commander of the Northeastern Frontier Defense Army. China was unified, on paper at least—and the rights recovery movement sponsored by Nanking moved into a higher gear.

These were times that sharpened the fears of men like Nagata. Even as the shadow of the Soviet Union fell over the northeast, Japan's access to the resources of the region, without which she could not withstand war with the Soviet Union, was being denied. And above all, Manchuria, it seemed, was slipping from Japan's grasp.

14

THE HARD CHIEF AND
THE VISIONARY

When Daisaku Komoto planned Chang Tso-lin's assassination, he had hoped to provoke the Old Marshal's troops into attacking Japanese soldiers, giving the troops in the Kwantung Leased Territory, the Kwantung Army, an excuse to intervene in Manchuria on a grand scale. The timing of the decision to murder Chang gave him too little time to prepare, and the Kwantung Army did not go into action at all. For Komoto, it was a debacle—he was transferred to other duties—but the lessons of his failure were valuable to his replacement, Seishiro Itagaki. In alliance with Kanji Ishiwara, another total-war enthusiast recently seconded to the Kwantung Army, Itagaki began making new plans for army domination of Manchuria.

Komoto had in fact been fortunate that his failure had been complete. With Manchurian troops outnumbering local Imperial forces by twenty-five to one, a ragged attack by Imperial troops would have resulted in their annihilation. To deal with the Chinese numerical superiority, Itagaki and Ishiwara adopted tactics based firmly on traditional

Japanese infantry virtues: the surprise attack, at night, at the heart of the opponent's strength. This was blitzkrieg—the bold stroke to dislocate the enemy's defensive system, preventing his mobilization for resistance or counterattack. The key to the Young Marshal's strength lay in Mukden, where his best troops were housed in Peitaying Barracks; and there, when the time came, hostilities would begin.

Itagaki and Ishiwara made a formidable team, ideally matched. Itagaki, then aged forty-six, is remembered as "a hard chief, determined and probably ruthless"; self-reliant, hard-drinking, skilled at kendo and always ready for action, he was "one of the tough type of Japanese officer." (In 1948 he would be hanged by the Allies for withholding food and medicines from prisoners of war.) Ishiwara stood always in Itagaki's shadow and turned to him frequently for protection. But though Itagaki could provide solid administrative skills, and could be relied upon to plan and execute staff work efficiently, he lacked the charisma to convince others of the need for independent army action—and here Ishiwara came into his own, flamboyant, visionary, even messianic, a brilliant, persuasive orator.

While the Kwantung Army staff focused closely on events in Manchuria, a wider consensus for action began to take shape at home. As the Great Depression hit Japan, and both the domestic and international situation seemed to deteriorate daily, key elements in the officer corps began conspiring to end the policy of cooperation with the civilian government and instead take direct action to solve the problems facing Japan.

Both at an official level within the High Command and behind the scenes, in the restaurants and teahouses, wherever field-grade officers gathered they argued about how best to achieve total-war preparedness. By this time, the last vestiges of restraint on military involvement in politics had gone—a fact underlined in 1931 by General Kazushige Ugaki. Although soldiers should neither be led astray by current opinions nor meddle in politics, he reminded divisional commanders, referring to the Imperial Rescript of 1885, equally they must not lose sight of their responsibility for national defense. Sometimes the need to defend the nation would override the requirement to stay out of politics.

There was in fact a strong lobby within the High Command for fulfilling this "responsibility for national defense" by coup d'état. During a posting to Turkey, Colonel Kingoro Hashimoto had seen a dedicated officer corps spearhead miracles of modernizing reform in the state. On his return he urged his brother officers to renovate Japan in the same way, and founded an association of field-grade officers from both General Staff and Army Ministry to work toward this goal. Known as the Sakura-kai ("Cherry Blossom Society") the group would have a strong and damaging influence on relations between the army and the state.

Their opportunity came when Prime Minister Hamaguchi failed to recover from the wounds received during the assassination attempt in 1930. As Hamaguchi lay fatally ill, Prince Kimmochi Saionji, the last genro, and Count Nobuaki Makino, the Lord Keeper of the Privy Seal, toyed with the idea of recommending General Ugaki as prime minister but ultimately decided a civilian nominee would better suit Japan's present circumstances. However, several army generals—Ugaki's vice-minister, his military affairs bureau chief, the vice-chief of the General Staff and the intelligence division chief—refused to let the idea of his nomination drop; in January 1931, they ordered Colonel Hashimoto to plan a coup that would bring Ugaki to power.

Hashimoto did more than go through the motions. He stockpiled munitions and consulted extremist organizations about orchestrating an "incident" at the Diet that would require troops to be called out. But to his chagrin, as his plot reached the point of no return his seniors decided the time was not yet ripe. On the orders of Ugaki himself, the coup was abandoned.

Ugaki had several reasons for caution—not least the hope that soon he might become the new head of the ruling Minseito party and might therefore become prime minister by constitutional means. However, the opinion of the advocates of total war seems also to have weighed heavily in the balance. Just before aborting the plot, Ugaki had a long conversation with Nagata's immediate subordinate, Teiichi Suzuki. What was said remains obscure, but the thrust of Suzuki's argument is likely to have been that the military dictatorship proposed by the Sakurakai was a recipe not for strength, but for national weakness. National defense required partnership, not dictatorship, and power in Japan rested with a handful of elites—industrialists, bureaucrats, court officials—from whom the army could expect only resistance if it seized power. And the army by itself simply could not supply the vast range of administrative, managerial, financial, and technical skills required to sustain a modern industrialized state.

Ugaki was well aware of this. In July 1929 he had advocated "tightening the links between military forces and the industrial world." The benefits would not all be on one side. The army wanted the coopera-tion of industry, and were prepared to surrender autonomy in large areas of military production. News emanating from the Army Ministry in January and February 1931 indicated the transfer of production to private hands of a range of military products, including nonclassified artillery materials, clothing, army medicines, and food.

Collaboration with Japan's bureaucrats, who possessed formidable power, was already close enough to be called partnership. The Osaka experiment in industrial mobilization had been a joint operation between the Ministry of Commerce and Industry, the Home Office, and the army. As the Depression bit ever more deeply and the failure of Shidehara-style internationalism and the sterility of civilian economic ideas became more apparent, the mandarins of the Ministry of Commerce and Industry came to believe that the country was in need of stronger direction, that free enterprise could not solve the problems afflicting the economy. Out of this conviction grew a consistent economic policy—a discreet bureaucratic sculpting of the industrial landscape—which in its turn became infected by the militarist desire for the "renovation" of the nation. In an age where foreign nations were erecting tariff barriers, the army's proposals for securing resources and markets for Japan's exclusive use became increasingly attractive to a wide audience of industrialists and bureaucrats who were looking to promote corporate and national prosperity at a time when exports to the the United States, Japan's largest market, had virtually ceased.

Inside Japan, the High Command had more to gain from working within the system than from using military strength to grab the reins of power. Only weeks away from the statute books was the Important Industries Control Law, under which defense-related industries could be nurtured and brought on quickly through a combination of special finance, protection, and rationalization. Abroad, however, it was a different matter. Itagaki's and Ishiwara's plans for action in Manchuria were well known at the higher levels, and had strong support within the Army Ministry and General Staff which the arguments for restraint at home did nothing to dilute. There was one particularly powerful lobby for military action to solve the "Manchuria-Mongolia" question. The Issekikai was an informal association of forty of the most brilliant of the field-grade officers. Its membership reads like an elite *Who's Who* of the High Command in the 1930s and 1940s: Hideki Tojo, prime minister at the time of Pearl Harbor; Tomoyuki Yamashita, the "Tiger of Malaya"; Daisaku Komoto, Chang's assassin; Ishiwara and Itagaki, architects of the Manchurian Incident; and of course, Tetzusan Nagata, the high priest of total war.

The power of these officers and of their sympathizers among the generals had been demonstrated most clearly in 1929, when they had been influential in preventing Giichi Tanaka from punishing Komoto for Chang's murder. It was a revealing episode in many ways; in particular, it betrayed precisely how the army elite (as distinct from run-of-the-mill officers) perceived the new Emperor, Hirohito, and just how lightly opinions expressed by him—his personal wishes or those of his advisers—ultimately weighed in the balance of army decision-making.

The army could never work with Hirohito. Apart from disliking many of the leaders intensely as individuals, he personally believed, contrary to army dogma, that Japan was a constitutional monarchy and himself merely an organ of state. He rarely acted independently, making his decisions only on the advice of government and court officials; and the army elite saw him as a man manipulated by one of their principal opponents—Prince Kimmochi Saionji, who had undoubtedly molded the Emperor's political views as Hirohito grew to manhood.

The relationship between Prince and Emperor resembled that of master and pupil. Saionji had immense prestige. He and the Emperor Meiji, Hirohito's grandfather, had played together as children growing up in the secluded palaces of Kyoto, and Saionji now survived as the living emblem of the Meiji Restoration. He also possessed supreme political skills, far beyond the youthful inexperience of the twenty-eight-year-old Hirohito. And where finesse was not enough, he could, and did, simply prevent pertinent information from ever reaching the Emperor's ears.

But though Saionji insisted that the Emperor act "constitutionally"—that is to say, on the advice of his counselors—at all times, he could not resist using the Throne for his own purposes when it suited. Saionji saw the Old Marshal's murder as an opportunity to call the army to heel; and so, fatally, he had Hirohito order army leaders to "strictly enforce army discipline."

Prime Minister Tanaka promised Hirohito that he would carry out the Imperial wishes. But he had two problems: His Cabinet, for both domestic and international reasons, did not want the assassination pinned firmly to Japan; and the assassin, Komoto, was one of the leading proponents of total war. The Issekikai, and the senior officers supporting them, closed ranks, and Tanaka found little cooperation at army headquarters and none at all from the Kwantung Army. The best they were prepared to offer was to punish Komoto for not guarding the railway adequately.

149

The Cabinet approved the proposal with some relief, and Tanaka took it to the palace. "This is different from what you told me first, is it not?" were the Emperor's only words as he humiliated Tanaka by striding from the audience chamber in disgust.

But the downfall of Tanaka clouded the real significance of the Komoto incident. Even by using Imperial prestige, Saionji could no longer curb the army; he had played his trump card and seen it fail. Worse, he had allowed, even encouraged the army to become fully aware of its own growing autonomy at a critical time for Japan.

Through the summer of 1931, pressure grew for a more "positive" policy on the mainland. The Kwantung Army repetitively demanded immediate action, and was able to point to a progressive worsening of the Japanese position. In May, the Nanking government announced that extraterritorial rights in China would be unilaterally abrogated on January 1, 1932. In Manchuria, Chang Hsüeh-liang's troops murdered an Imperial Army staff officer. Korean farmers—Japan's colonial subjects—clashed with Chinese over water rights. And Japanese colonists called for Manchurian autonomy.

As summer gave way to autumn, and still no move was made, time seemed to be running out for Ishiwara and Itagaki, who knew that in the normal course of events they could soon expect to be transferred. More pressure was put on Tokyo. Itagaki even provided finance for a propaganda campaign in the home islands: "Wake Up for National Defense," urged leaflets scattered from army planes.

At last the High Command was persuaded to agree, in principle, with the Kwantung Army. A policy document drawn up in June 1931 by Major-General Yoshitsugu Tatekawa (a key figure in the abortive Ugaki coup) was endorsed by senior figures in the General Staff and Army Ministry. This set spring 1932 as the date for action, leaving a few more months in which to persuade Chang Hsüeh-liang to cooperate and at the same time to seek international and domestic approval for forceful action should he fail to do so.

But events were moving quickly, and by early August powerful figures in the High Command were beginning to lend their voices to the Kwantung Army's chorus of "Action Now." They included all the original instigators of the March coup and, not without reservations, some of the total-war campaigners, including Tojo and Nagata.

Domestic worries sharpened the cries for action. By mid-1931, Japan's economic ailments had made military budgets a target for cuts once more—and it seemed that there might be worse to come. On the horizon was the World Disarmament Conference, whose objective was, in President Hoover's words, to find a way of reducing "the overwhelming burden of armament which now lies upon the toilers of the world." Hoover's stated intention was that "all tanks, chemical warfare and all large mobile guns . . . all bombing planes should be abolished" and naval tonnage should be reduced by half.

To the Imperial Army, facing the twin challenges of Russia and China, such sentiments were anathema. The new army minister, Jiro Minami, publicly and provocatively questioned civilian authority to reduce the army's appropriation, reviving echoes of the London Naval Treaty furor of the preceding year. The prospect of trouble in Manchuria was a valuable weapon with which to defend not just army budgets, but the very concept of Japan as a militarily self-reliant nation.

"When is war to begin in Manchuria?" the press asked eagerly. It was a question close to Saionji's own heart. Such was his concern that he again decided to use the Throne to restrain the army. On September 11, Hirohito summoned Minami to the palace. The grand chamberlain, Kantaro Suzuki, reported later that Minami was well prepared. Before the Emperor could ask a question, Minami volunteered the information that "recently some of the young officers have been criticizing the weakness of foreign policy," and reassured the Emperor that he need have no fears. Army leaders recognized that "foreign policy is national policy" and disapproved of the statements and actions of the hotheads.

On September 14, Minami visited Saionji and was left under no illusion as to his opposition to the army's obvious plotting. "It is extremely bad to be sending villains and roughnecks and members of right-wing terrorist groups to Manchuria," Saionji warned. "As head of the army and with responsibilities as a Minister of State, you must be discreet and control this kind of thing."

The Saionji counteroffensive seemed to produce a concrete result. A high-ranking General Staff officer was dispatched to Manchuria under orders to caution the Kwantung Army against rash action. But unfortunately for Saionji, the officer who left Tokyo on September 15 was none other than Major General Tatekawa. Before he left Tokyo, his office telegraphed details of his ostensible purpose to Itagaki at Mukden. By his interference, Saionji had presented Itagaki and Ishiwara with a simple choice: now or never. Once Tatekawa had delivered his Imperially sanctioned order, the Kwantung Army would not easily be able to strike; and the decision was made—for action.

Tatekawa traveled by train, and was met with ceremony by Itagaki on the evening of September 18. He could have flown, but by taking the train he gave the Kwantung Army activists three precious days. Tatekawa accepted Itagaki's offer of hospitality, postponing business until the next day; together the two went to a restaurant, the Kikubumi in Mukden, where they dined cheerfully—until about ten P.M., when Itagaki made his excuses and left the general to enjoy the rest of the evening.

That night there was no moon over the central Manchurian plain. By torchlight, just as Itagaki was leaving the Kikubumi, Lieutenant Suemori Kawamoto and his seven-man detail worked quickly to strap the guncotton—forty-two packs—required to blast apart a joint on the railway line to Mukden station.

Between 10:15 and 10:20 P.M., the fuse was lit and the detachment took cover. The explosion was very loud—"like a signal," one of the residents of Mukden was later to recall. So, too, was the sound of the approaching express Kawamoto was intending to derail. Anxiously, Kawamoto's men braced themselves for the grinding crash and flames of the express leaping from the rails to its doom. Suddenly, it was upon the saboteurs, and in a moment gone—passing untroubled on its way into Mukden.

By a miracle, the train had taken the 1.5-meter break in the line in its stride. There was no derailment, no outrage against Japanese lives and property, and no "serious incident" for the Kwantung Army to exploit. The site of the blast had been carefully chosen: well concealed but, more importantly, no more than 1,200 yards from the huge Peitaying Barracks near Mukden, home to Chang Hsüeh-liang's best troops. The derailment had been intended as a magnet to draw Chang's men out from Peitaying to the site of the outrage—where they would find themselves facing the righteous anger of the Kwantung Army.

Chang had always feared that friction between his men and the Kwantung Army would lead to something more serious, and for that very reason had forbidden night patrols. Something very dramatic was needed to lure his men out. To atone for his failure on the railway, Kawamoto led his men up to the barracks and fired at the guards on the western gate, who, being armed only with bamboo spears, retreated rapidly behind the ten-foot mud wall enclosing the barracks.

For the next half-hour, the northeastern and southwestern corners of this rectangular enclosure were subjected to feint attacks by the Japanese detachment, now reinforced. These were designed to create "consternation and disorder," and were entirely successful. Then, at eleven P.M. two howitzers concealed in sheds within the Kwantung Army's own barracks compound in Mukden began intermittently to shell Chang's beleagured troops.

The Chinese inside were badly shaken by the attacks and the barrage. They were incapable of mounting a defense, partly because their weapons had been locked away after the evening parade, and partly because they were bound by Chang's standing orders not to resist—passivity being Chang's main strategy for avoiding conflict with the Kwantung Army. At the time of the assault, he was away in Peking, dining with the British minister; when informed of the attack, he merely repeated the order not to resist.

His studied nonchalance was to cost him his domain. As their overlord continued to enjoy British soup and fish, Chang's levies cracked and ran. About a third of them broke open the armories and stole weapons—not to resist, but to equip themselves for the life of banditry that they knew they would now be forced to follow if they were not to starve to death.

At 1:30 A.M., three Japanese companies attacked the west wall in earnest. They broke into barrack rooms and stores and killed many of those they found inside. According to badly wounded survivors of one barrack block, the Japanese went "back and forwards among the wounded, shooting them again until they had assured themselves that no-one remained alive." By four A.M. the barracks were in Japanese hands.

The city of Mukden also held Chang's arsenals and headquarters. By this point these too had fallen, along with the airfield, and there only remained the walled city itself. From positions along the south wall, Japanese machine-gunners raked the streets with bullets. The city police put up some resistance, but they could not prevail against trained and highly motivated infantry. A few died in the attempt and the rest were disarmed. Chang's military headquarters were ransacked and the banks and offices of his provincial government occupied. By ten A.M., Mukden was under control and notices reading OCCUPIED BY JAPANESE were pasted in conspicuous places on every public building.

Over the next few days, the Kwantung Army demolished the remnants of Chang Hsüeh-liang's power in central Manchuria. In the early hours of September 19, the infantry and artillery of the Chinese Kirin Army were swept from their barracks at Changchun, an important rail depot up the line from Mukden. On the twenty-first, the Kwantung Army occupied the city of Kirin itself. On the twenty-second, they seized the eastern terminus of the Kirin–Tun-hua railway and with it control of Chientao, a region riddled with Communist agitators. Finally, the Japanese deprived Chang of his principal source of revenue by occupying key points of the regional Chinese railway system.

At a stroke, one of the most powerful men in China had been pushed to the verge of insignificance. Only in the northwest, at Tsitsihar, capital of Heilungkiang province, and in the far south, at Chinchow, just north of the Great Wall itself, did Chang still possess troops capable of organized resistance. The rest of Manchuria belonged to Japan.

Despite the dismal failure of the derailment attempt, the Kwantung Army continued to assert the legitimacy of their response. "Proof" was provided to the world's journalists. After a delay of twelve hours, during which the site of the explosion was sealed off, they were taken to see the carefully arranged bodies of several Chinese soldiers, shot in the back and lying facedown, heads pointing in the direction of Peitaying Barracks—toward which, the tableau suggested, they were fleeing when a hail of bullets from alert Japanese infantry cut them down.

15

TURNING SOUR IN
SHANGHAI

The strategy devised by Itagaki and Ishiwara proved to have been well judged. Minimum force achieved major returns: The single blow to crush the Young Marshal's Mukden base was followed by low-key piecemeal operations against strategic points in southern Manchuria. Japanese armored trains prowled the rail network. At Newchwang, on the day following the Mukden coup, a Japanese force of 500 arrived to disarm the Chinese garrison and police, and to occupy the railway station, banks, and government offices. Four days later this force withdrew, leaving a compliant administration in its place. It was a pattern repeated all over central Manchuria.

Both the army and the civilian authorities in Tokyo—who remained ignorant of the true cause of the fighting—stuck publicly to the proposition that the incident had been provoked by Chinese nationalists and that Japan was only acting to protect herself and her interests. Privately, none of the Western powers believed the story, because of the clockwork precision of the army's response—and because the line was blown up north of Mukden. "To have any point at all, it would have [had] to be south of the city," had Chinese saboteurs intended to disrupt Japanese business.

Nevertheless, in the immediate aftermath of the capture of Mukden, the Japanese action found widespread sympathy abroad. In October, President Hoover, while castigating Japan's "immoral" and "outrageous" behavior, acknowledged that Japan had a good case in her efforts to protect her interests and maintain order. Britain, the major investor in China, did not regard Japan's action to be at all "inimical" to British interests: "On the contrary, it may be regarded as likely to induce the Chinese in future to pursue a more reasonable line." The Soviets, debating how Japan might be ejected from Manchuria, were of the opinion that "if Japan were forced to withdraw by the action of the Great Powers, the first and most important result would be that China would become impossible to deal with. The Chinese would become convinced that if the Japanese could not force them to respect agreements, no other power could do so and Chinese arrogance would increase accordingly."

But the Soviet argument was purely hypothetical; for a Japanese withdrawal was nowhere in sight. The Kwantung Army's strategy had been predicated on the well-founded belief that in the autumn of 1931 there would be no resistance from foreign powers. On September 23, British military intelligence put in a report agreeing with the Japanese analysis: "The Soviet Union is probably neither willing nor prepared to undertake external military adventures at the present time. The preoccupation of the rest of the world with their own internal affairs makes it unlikely at present that any power would take serious measures to interfere with the development of Japanese policy in South Manchuria. America could, if she desired, exert strong economic pressure but it may be doubted whether this would be sufficient." The forecast proved to be substantially correct.

As for China herself, the powers, led by Britain, used every means at their disposal to prevent her declaring war on Japan—not that this was ever really a serious risk. At this point, China's internal affairs were chaotic. Two competing "national" governments were squaring up for civil war; the Chinese Red Army was successfully holding out against Nanking's anticommunist campaign in Kiangsi; and there had been catastrophic flooding in the Yangtze Basin. True, the disparate elements in China found common cause in opposition to Japanese action in Manchuria, and a fragile government of national unity came into being; but it never had the strength to take on Japan. In early December, an envoy from Chiang Kai-shek told the Young Marshal bluntly that "the financial condition of the country could not bear the strain of military preparations and that war against Japan was out of the question."

Instead, China's strategy was twofold: at home, boycotts on Japanese goods, which hurt in the already depressed conditions of 1931; and abroad, an appeal to international opinion through the League of Nations, in the hope of forcing the Kwantung Army to pull back to the railway zone. The League was quite willing to direct the Japanese government to withdraw its troops as a necessary condition for negotiations to start, and attempted to set a deadline of November 16. But Japan promptly rejected the resolution for a deadline. There was no means of enforcing the directive, and Washington regarded the strategy as a mistake, the State Department informing diplomats in Washington that it did not think that Japan "can possibly meet this demand."

The State Department was right, and November 16 passed unregarded. By early December, Chiang Kai-shek was advising the Young Marshal that "Nanking had made up its mind that direct negotiations with Japan would sooner or later have to take place and that (the Young Marshal) should explore all possible avenues of approach to the Japanese."

The Kwantung Army had placed the Young Marshal in an unenviable position. He still had a toehold in Manchuria, having relocated his administration in the southern town of Chinchow. But though he achieved some irritant effect by organizing guerrilla bands posing as bandits to attack Japanese and Korean settlements, his forces could realistically hope neither to hold Chinchow nor to advance against the Imperial Army—and now he knew he could expect no support from Nationalist forces.

Time was running out for both sides. Banditry and boycotts were together forcing Japan's hand; the Young Marshal had to be evicted from Chinchow and order restored before Manchuria collapsed in chaos. On December 5, British intelligence intercepted a telegram from the Japanese minister in Peking, in which he informed Tokyo that, following his instructions, he had met Chang Hsüeh-liang and pointed out that the Young Marshal was in "a very precarious position and that if (he) did not come to some amicable agreement with Japan, he was in danger of losing everything."

Diplomatic pressure produced the required results. British military intelligence in Tientsin reported an "unusually reliable source" as confirming that an understanding had been reached and Chang would be permitted to keep his army intact and retain control of the province of Hopei. The price was paid in January 1932. Under the watchful eye of reconnaissance aircraft from an Imperial Navy carrier cruising off Chinwangtao, Chang's divisions moved, unmolested by Imperial troops, to Shanhwaikuan and south through the Great Wall. By mid-January, the southern half of Manchuria was firmly in Japanese hands.

Northern Manchuria presented different problems. Cutting across the terrain, roughly from Manchouli to Tsitsihar and on to Harbin and Vladivostok, ran the Russian-controlled Chinese Eastern Railway. Only two years before, the Soviets had shown themselves willing to defend their interests with alarmingly effective military power, and the Japanese High Command were nervous of provoking another confrontation. The problem was to interpret precisely how the Soviets defined their interests.

It appears from intelligence intercepts at Tientsin that the Soviets had had full warning of what was to happen at Mukden. On September 7, Vice-Commissar of Foreign Affairs L. M. Karakhan had warned the Soviet consulate in Tientsin "to watch Japanese activities in China very carefully, since Moscow had information that Japan was trying to provoke an incident in Manchuria which would give her an opportunity of armed intervention on a large scale." On September 17, Tientsin received another telegram stating that the Japanese would move the following day, and that "Moscow had notified Tokyo that provided the Japanese occupation stopped at Tsitsihar the Soviets would take no action against it, but that if Japanese troops occupied Tsitsihar Russian troops would enter Manchuria."

How serious was the Soviets' threat? In the debate over strategy for acquiring the north of Manchuria, the Kwantung Army wanted to call their bluff with a display of strength. Tokyo disagreed and opted instead for the counterbluff. In Moscow, while the Japanese ambassador, Koki Hirota, was being presented with Soviet proposals for a Soviet-Japanese Nonaggression Pact, his military attaché was sending a telegram urging the General Staff to recognize that it was Japan's "unavoidable destiny to clash with the USSR. . . . Considering the capacity of the USSR for national defense and the situation of the other powers, the sooner the Soviet-Japanese war comes, the better for us."

The Kwantung Army was continually edging toward the "unavoidable destiny," the central government continually pulling it back. The army employed a local warlord to fight Ma Chan-shan, the Young Marshal's final military ally in the North, who, it was believed, was being supported with Soviet arms. Then, when the puppet failed to defeat Ma, Japanese troops did indeed advance to Tsitsihar. Within a day, however, they had been evacuated on orders from Tokyo.

The British were entirely cynical about this game of brinkmanship. They had intercepted a private letter from the German councilor in Moscow, assuring General Hans von Seeckt (a former head of the Reichswehr) in Berlin that "there will be no question of strained relations between Japan and the Soviets, since the Russians will use their neutrality as a lever for getting economic advantages from the Japanese." Certainly in the end the north came under Japanese control by political and not overtly military means. One and a half million dollars from Tokyo oiled the regional administrators' slide from allegiance to Nanking in the direction of Manchurian "autonomy." A "free" Manchuria, the republic of Manchukuo, came into being on March 1, 1932, firmly under Imperial Army control. As Staff Officer Tadashi Katakura noted in his diary: "Today the state is dragged on by the army, and the army by us—the Kwantung Army."

For a few brief weeks, a certain smugness was justified. The Manchurian problem seemed to have been given a permanent solution. There had been no resistance from the "Great Powers" and little from China; the Soviet bear had merely growled. Even the League of Nations had temporarily shelved the issue by appointing a commission of inquiry under Lord Lytton—to which Japan was confident of presenting a reasonable case, given the extent of treaty violations by the Chinese.

But then, disastrously, events farther south in Shanghai turned the Manchurian adventure into a nightmare. Where the army had been bold and shrewd, the Imperial Navy, responsible for policing Japan's interests in Shanghai—aggregating 25 percent of all Japanese investment on the mainland—now blundered and butchered and destroyed any chance that the international community might eventually accept Japanese control of Manchuria.

Throughout China, the "Manchurian Incident" had raised anti-Japanese sentiment to a new peak. Japanese goods were boycotted—in 1932, Japan's exports to China dropped by an average 90 percent—and Japanese nationals were intimidated, beaten up, even murdered. Shanghai was no exception. Portraits of Hirohito with paper swords stuck through his heart were paraded in the streets, and Japanese residents lived in fear of the mob. On January 19, 1932, five Japanese Buddhist priests were attacked. When one of the victims died, four hundred members of the Japanese Youth League sought revenge. In the fracas, one was shot dead by a Chinese policeman, who in turn was stabbed to death.

The next day, the Japanese consul-general demanded from the Chinese mayor of Shanghai an apology, compensation, and an end to anti-Japanese agitation. The Imperial Navy's commander in the area, Admiral Shiozawa, confident in the knowledge that an aircraft carrier would arrive on January 24, backed the demand with a threat to "take appropriate steps" to protect the rights and interests of the Japanese Empire. The British believed that the Japanese were deliberately seeking a pretext to take Shanghai, the major commercial center of China, and thereby deny Chiang Kai-shek his principal source of financial backing. Perhaps with this same suspicion in mind, the mayor was overanxious to avoid trouble, and gave way well before the Japanese deadline expired. But he was too late to prevent the foreign powers in Shanghai from mobilizing troops to defend their settlements.

Japan had an extensive settlement in Shanghai, and duly mobilized both civilian volunteers and a detachment of marines. And then, according to eyewitnesses, Admiral Shiozawa deployed his forces in a highly provocative manner, starting at midnight on January 28 with airplanes dropping flares to frighten the opposition. "The Chinese did not understand what was happening, they thought the Japanese were advancing to capture the city and put up stout resistance causing many Japanese casualties. The Japanese then resorted to bombing to destroy the armoured train from which they were being sniped at. . . . As a result the North Station was destroyed and a number of houses burnt down."

The Japanese military had reached the brink and were teetering on it. The marines were opposed by the crack Chinese Nineteenth Route Army, and though the British managed to arrange a temporary cease-fire, mutual hostility swelled in the days that followed. Japanese arrogance was felt to be intolerable. "They have quite unnecessarily established a (military) post in the British sector and have installed many machine-gun posts in the American sector . . . without deference to local commanders." The Chinese for their part began rewriting the events of January 28 for external consumption. Now the Japanese had "incessantly and indiscriminately" bombed the densely populated workers' area known as Chapei, killing "countless civilians."

On February 1 an artillery duel started. The fighting soon escalated beyond the capacity of a handful of marines, and the Imperial Army felt obliged to send in ground troops—which by the end of February numbered 50,000 men under General Shirakawa. The battleground was a nightmarish maze of narrow winding streets and inlets from the river Whangpoo. The Nineteenth Route Army fought unflinchingly, and only by encircling them was Shirakawa able to win a military victory and force a truce. But there was no glory in this victory. The political cost to Japan proved to be more than Manchuria was worth—ruinous both to Japan's position in China and to her image in the eyes of the world.

As far as opinion within China was concerned, though Chiang Kai-shek would not engage in war with Japan at this time, a limited conflict in Shanghai—even one he had lost—served his purposes well. The risks of serious escalation were, after all, minimal: Shanghai was the center of Western investment and Chiang was confident that the powers would act firmly to protect their interests. And by demonstrating a will and capacity to resist, he had consolidated his own position as the supreme Chinese leader.

Internationally the fighting awoke passionate Western prejudice against the Japanese, which would carry through to the Pacific War. There were thousands of foreign eyewitnesses to describe the events in Shanghai, and the Western media relayed the horrors of vicious urban warfare in words, pictures, and newsreels. *The New York Times* painted an appalling picture of the bombing of civilians, and told of Japanese soldiers firing indiscriminately at the shell-shocked survivors. Outraged Americans organized themselves to confront the problem of Japan, pressuring Secretary of State Henry Stimson to institute sanctions. President Hoover vetoed the proposal, but Stimson's own feelings were clear and unambiguous. Only nine years later, long before he had had time to forget, Stimson would again be in a position of influence in Washington at a critical point in the formulation of policy toward Japan.

The reaction of Thomas W. Lamont, a partner in J. P. Morgan, fiscal agent for the Japanese government, was typical of the shift of Western opinion. In the weeks following the bombing at Mukden, he defended Japan in public and private, asserting that "China has conducted the most lawless and aggravating course possible." After Shanghai, he could only view Japan as the aggressor. As for the American financial community, Lamont wrote that it would now be "quite impossible to arrange any credit, either through investment or banking circles."

Most seriously for Japan, the open wound in U.S.-Japanese relations inflicted at Shanghai would never be permitted to close. Anti-Japanese sentiment in the United States provided a platform on which both Chinese and Russian propagandists could build. As early as 1918, Lenin had sought to cultivate U.S.-Japanese rivalry, and it was equally in

Stalin's interests to promote it. There is even a suggestion that the Shanghai incident itself was aggravated by Communist cadres firing from both sides of the line in order to inflame anti-Japanese feeling.

Whether or not that is true, the Shanghai incident undeniably marked the beginning of a ten-year propaganda war between Moscow and Nanking on the one hand and Tokyo on the other for the hearts and minds of the American people. The Japanese lost this war; to some extent, the "infamy" of Pearl Harbor was no more than a confirmation of America's darkest suspicions. It would have taken much less to bring the people of America, as distinct from their leaders, to the pitch of hatred requisite for war.

The keystone of the propaganda edifice was one of the most successful "dirty tricks" of the twentieth century—a bogus document so brilliantly conceived that thirty years later Westerners were still taken in by it. In 1960, Soviet premier Nikita Khrushchev warned the people of Indonesia of continuing Japanese ambitions in Asia. The foundation for his claims was, he said, the Tanaka Memorial.

The Memorial purported to be a plan for world domination submitted to the Emperor in 1927, having been mapped out at a high-level conference held that year in Tokyo under Prime Minister General Giichi Tanaka. "In the future, if we want to control China," it read, "we must first crush the United States just as in the past we had to fight in the Russo-Japanese War. But in order to conquer China we must first conquer Manchuria and Mongolia. In order to conquer the world, we must first conquer China. If we succeed in conquering China the rest of the Asiatic countries and South Sea countries will fear us and surrender to us. Then the world will realise that Eastern Asia is ours and will not dare to violate our rights. This is the plan left to us by Emperor Meiji, the success of which is essential to our national existence."

The Memorial first appeared in Peking in September 1929, and though not then taken up, was given new life by the Imperial Army's actions in Manchuria. The full text, in English, appeared in a Shanghai newspaper six days after the Mukden bombing, and was subsequently published and widely distributed in the United States as a free pamphlet. It would even scale the heights of Hollywood, providing the inspiration for a wartime masterpiece entitled *Blood on the Sun,* in which James Cagney infiltrates Japan to steal the enemy's master plan (the Memorial) and thereby save the world. But though the document originated in China, its antecedents may have been Russian. In 1926, the British ambassador to Peking was shown a map by his Russian counterpart,

Karakhan, purporting to be Japanese plans for the annexation of Manchuria.

The butchery at Shanghai and the international propaganda offensive both contributed to the isolation of Japan, which increased from 1932 onwards. The Lytton Commission, when finally it made its report, was less heavily inclined against Japan than had been been expected, acknowledging that China had provoked Japan to a certain extent and that China's sovereignty over Manchuria was less than absolute. But when the League of Nations adopted the report, Japan chose to regard it as an unacceptable vote of censure, and, in 1933, withdrew from the League.

PART IV

DIVIDED ARMY
1932-1937

16

THE OFFICER CORPS
DIVIDES

International ostracism notwithstanding, the total-war planners could look back on the decade following the Washington Conference with some satisfaction. At home, the army had asserted its independence from the civilian powers, had even succeeded in controlling them. To the nation, suffering acutely in the throes of the Depression, only the army appeared to offer a plausible way out, and the people united behind the policy of aggression in Manchuria—"so much so that any Minister who weakened now would probably be assassinated." The dragon's teeth of the nation-in-arms, sown in the Meiji era, were beginning to produce their deadly crop.

Prince Saionji, who had made such vigorous efforts to restrain the army before the seizure of Manchuria, now decided not to risk the prestige of the Throne again by trying to force the army to disgorge its gains. Hirohito wanted to call the prime minister and army minister together in an attempt to work out a compromise acceptable to the League of Nations. Saionji suggested he first speak to Foreign Minister

Shidehara; and he told Shidehara to "talk to the Emperor at length and in such a way as to avoid worrying him"—in other words, to calm him down and choke him off.

By the early 1930s, radicals on both the right and the left agreed that capitalism, internationalism, and democracy were now sterile and moribund, and Japan must seek a new path, more carefully directed and regulated. Even among those nearer the center of Japanese political life, especially within the bureaucracy, there was a growing sense of a need for "renovation" in the country—a sentiment harnessed by Nagata in his drive for total-war preparedness. The fear shared by the more moderate renovationists and those on the extreme right was that the collapse of the present system would lead inevitably to communism. The reins of state must be taken firmly in hand before all control was lost.

The *zaibatsu* themselves, flag-bearers of capitalism and free enterprise, underwent a kind of *tenko,* or spiritual conversion, during this period. The times were such that it was possible for a senior figure in the Ministry of Commerce and Industry (forerunner of the Ministry of International Trade and Industry) to write in 1935: "Modern industries attained their present development primarily through free competition. However, various evils are gradually becoming apparent. Holding on to absolute freedom will not rescue the industrial world from its present disturbances. Industry needs a plan of comprehensive development and a measure of control."

For the total-war officers whose work over the preceding decade underlay the Manchurian Incident, fulfillment came on April 11, 1932: "regardless of the consequences," the Cabinet agreed to organize the new state of Manchukuo in such a way as to achieve "a self-sufficient economic unit" in combination with Japan. Here at last was the long-desired expression of political will to compete in the world of total war, through the creation of industrial power.

But appearances were deceptive; Japan was not really ready to march to the tune of the total-war planners. Even as Nagata was rising to prominence, the army was changing in ways that would prejudice integrated policy-making. The officer corps was no longer the cohesive social unit it had once been. In 1877, all but three of the 158 officers graduating from the first class of the Military Academy were of samurai descent. By 1907, following the Russo-Japanese War, less than half the officers were samurai—and by 1931, descendants of samurai made up only about 15 percent. Nor were they all of rural origin. By the mid-1930s, half were from urban areas, and from widely differing socioeconomic backgrounds.

Nor was authority within the officer corps unitary. Choshu no longer provided the backbone of the army hierarchy. In theory, this should have been beneficial—indeed, one of Nagata's ambitions as a young man had been to break the feudal grip of Choshu on right of passage into the upper echelons. With regional favoritism removed, the way should have been open for the emergence of a professional, egalitarian officer corps.

In practice, however, monolithic Choshu dominance was replaced by a kaleidoscope of personal cliques and pressure groups, like the Issekikai, all maneuvering for advancement and power. It was an unhealthy development with serious implications not only for policy-making, but also for discipline. Loyalty to individuals or ideologies became more important than obedience to legitimate orders—and from time to time, the High Command lost control of whole sections of the army.

Perhaps the most significant change during the 1920s and 1930s, however, was the gulf that had opened between the total-war strategists and the majority of their own officer corps—a severing of the brains from the body of the Imperial Army. In the midst of planning for warfare in the twentieth century, the High Command had to acknowledge that the Imperial Army still belonged to the nineteenth, and perpetuate some recognizably outdated features whilst introducing such changes as they could.

Full modernization might still have been out of reach in this intermediate stage, but given the power of twentieth-century weapons, some immediate change in tactics was unavoidable. The nineteenth-century doctrine of the attack was upgraded to produce highly mobile, highly committed infantry tactics designed to strike the enemy before he had time to collect his superior mechanized forces. Mobility was all the more crucial because the projected theater of war was northern Manchuria and Siberia, and trench warfare was virtually ruled out by the intense cold of winter. The attackers increased their chances of catching the enemy unawares by advancing at the double, over great distances, saving time by giving, receiving, and executing orders without breaking the momentum.

There was a premium on fitness. In full marching dress, less rifle, second-year conscripts were expected to run 100 meters in 16 seconds and 1,500 meters in under 6 minutes; long-jump 3 meters 90 centimeters; and throw a grenade over 35 meters. During maneuvers, a regiment would be expected to march 25 miles a day for 15 days with only 4 rest days. The usual pattern on the move was to march for 55 minutes and rest for 15, averaging 2½ miles per hour, but with an easy acceleration to 4 miles per hour. One statuesque British officer was unimpressed by their pace on the flat, but pointed out enviously that short legs gave a man "lower gearing" and a tremendous advantage on hills.

For such tactics to be effective, the officers in the front line had to possess the highest level of élan and ready sacrifice, coupled with blind obedience to the rule book—just as had their nineteenth-century counterparts in the frontal assaults on the defenses of Port Arthur. And in terms of ethos, officer education was much the same in the 1920s and 1930s as it had been forty years earlier.

The molding of a cadet began at school, in the aura of the Imperial Rescript on Education, and accelerated at about the age of fourteen when the cadet passed into one of the six regional military preparatory schools, which had been set up on the German model after the return of the Oyama mission in 1884. At seventeen the cadet progressed to the central preparatory school in Tokyo for training, which would include some service in the ranks. (By entrance examination, the school also accepted graduates of ordinary middle schools who had not been to a military preparatory school.)

There were four "grand principles" of education in the military preparatory schools: to form "a strong constitution" through physical exercise; "to fill the heart with loyalty and patriotism"; "to inculcate knowledge beneficial to Civilization"; and "to produce the strength of will necessary for military men."

Physical strength came first, for "action depends on health." Drill, gymnastics, fencing, riding, swimming, and musketry were all compulsory, and occupied the recreation periods as well; the playing of games and competitive sports was not permitted. But the object of physical culture was mental strength—"the harmonious growth of muscle and mind." Many of the characteristic Japanese physical skills had a mental and moral dimension lacking in Western sports.

Then came intellectual improvement—for "the character and civilization of a country are the reflection of the knowledge possessed by the nation." Sitting rigidly to attention and taking notes only when instructed to do so, the cadets covered a wide curriculum. The Japanese and Chinese classics took pride of place, the materials carefully selected to exclude "anything containing conceited, frivolous, unsound, or superstitious ideas." Then came foreign languages (French, German, or Russian, for English was widely taught in middle schools and the army needed a variety of languages at its disposal), mathematics, science, logic, drawing, and penmanship. Geography and history were used to reinforce moral instruction:

Comparisons will be drawn from foreign histories, as far as possible, with reference to the sanctity of our Imperial family, the excellence of our national organization, the grand work of our ancestors, our faithfulness and devotion, etc. In giving lessons in foreign history, an instructor must always try and draw parallels from facts or epochs of Japanese history, and must pay attention to those periods in which Oriental and Occidental histories are brought into contact.

Most important of all was the development of "a will which knows no defeat." This was expected to permeate everything the cadets did; and it continued as a central motif as they progressed through the system. "The rules and codes of training," ran the "Admonition to Soldiers and Sailors" of 1878, "are the physical body of bones and flesh while the spirit is the brain and nerves that activate the physical body. Thus the spirit of the military is the foundation of the entire army."

Individual ambition was strictly discouraged. There were no permanent leaders; each cadet in turn acted for twenty-four hours as subordinate company commander, a system which did less to promote initiative and other leadership qualities than to generate an atmosphere of cohesion and cooperation. The Japanese, foreign observers noted sagely, were excessively discouraged by failure; examination results were not generally made public in any detail, to avoid the risk of suicide among less successful candidates.

To become an officer, the cadet had to pass through the Military Academy at Ichigaya. In the 1920s the Academy was still using the original two-story French-style barrack blocks built in the 1870s; these had survived the great earthquake of 1923, and continued to offer little comfort to the cadet. Cut off from his family, he lived in spartan, overcrowded barrack rooms with no semblance of privacy. In winter he shivered over his desk in an unheated study room, and did physical training bare-chested. The quality of food remained poor. In the 1920s the average cadet, passing from adolescence to manhood during his training, gained on average only three pounds (to weigh around 128 pounds) and grew only half an inch (to be five feet four inches tall).

Even on an adequate diet the daily schedule would have been punishing:

05:30	Reveille
06:30	Breakfast

07:00–08:50	Private study
09:00–11:50	Lectures
12:00	Lunch
13:00–16:00	Gymnastics, fencing, jujitsu, equitation, drill, and lectures on the training manual
16:00–17:00	Free exercise
17:00–17:50	Private study
18:00	Supper
19:00–21:20	Private study
21:30	Roll call
22:00	Lights out

The ten-minute intervals between lectures were "fully taken up by the collection of books, falling in and being marched over to the new lecture hall. The lecture halls are often a considerable distance from each other (so) all this frequently has to be done at the double." And any other spare moments in a day incorporating ten hours of study were filled by cleaning boots, kit, clothes, weapons, accoutrements, and the Academy's buildings. Even had there been time, little recreation was allowed. Reading matter was strictly censored; and when on Sundays, after meticulous inspection, the cadets were allowed out of the Academy's precincts, they were forbidden to smoke, drink, or go into cafés or cinemas.

The intensity of Japanese officer training was most obvious by comparison with the standards imposed in Western military academies after the Great War. In England, an officer would have been given approximately 1,372 hours of classwork and 245 hours of private study. In Japan an officer was commissioned after 3,382 hours of classwork and 2,765 hours of private study. In addition he would have spent 301 days in camp or training outside the barracks, against which the British officer had nothing to set.

Bowed under the exhausting pace of work, the trainee was ground down further by constant anxiety, amounting often to neurosis, about success. His whole future career—in the first instance, the arm of the service to which he was attached—would be determined by his progress and his position in class at graduation. A poor result was not just a personal disappointment, but a betrayal of his parents, to whom he owed a duty to work hard. The depth of this responsibility was encapsulated in a poem in common currency at the Academy in the 1920s:

The young man, having made a firm resolve,
   leaves his native home,
If he fails to acquire learning,
   then even though he die, he must never return.

Though not as blatant as Soviet "reeducation," training for life in the Imperial Army constituted classic psychological preparation for deep indoctrination, and the message imprinted on these defenseless minds was devotion to the Emperor. The Inspector-General's Rules and Regulations for the Military Academy stated: "As officers are the backbone of troops, the source of martial spirit and discipline, the axis on which the will and energy of the country moves, during the education of cadets at the Academy, particular attention must be paid to . . . fostering a spirit of loyalty and patriotism."

All the courses at the Academy other than strictly military instruction were structured to serve this end and permeated with an overpoweringly moralistic flavor. The inspector-general of military education designed a program of instruction to impart the fundamental moral principles and demonstrate how the Imperial Rescript on Education and the Tokuho, "Soldiers' Code," both developed naturally out of them. At the center was a basic ethics course on the principal themes of the all-embracing Rescript—a monolith kept in place by quasi-academic buttresses.

Science, for example—a British military observer noted disapprovingly that it was "distorted and its disfigured shape used to substantiate the moral training. . . . That this is a race morally superior to all others is driven in, followed by an extra knock to the effect that the soldiers of this race are again a thing apart."

History as taught at the Academy, the same observer noted, was "an instrument to hand, which after very considerable doctoring is used to cultivate only pride of country and national confidence. . . . Japan does not stand first, it always stands alone in the splendour of its glory. Of her sons, and especially of her officers, she demands service in keeping with her history. Clio, the Muse of History, must indeed weep here in Japan, to such ends is she prostituted." While no nation presents its history unvarnished, the version of Japanese history taught at the Academy was indeed exceptionally distorted.

After graduating from the Military Academy, cadets selected for the different branches or specializations—air, artillery and engineering, cavalry, medicine, communications, intelligence, *kempeitai*—went on for further training at specialist schools. But in the infantry, not all officers proceeded to further education. By far the largest branch of the army, the infantry required more officers than the Infantry School at Chiba could possibly accommodate. So at Chiba cadres of officers were trained in skills that they could then disseminate through the regiments. The school was also a place for experimentation in tactics and weapons, and its research function appears to have created a more liberal regime. But the Infantry School was a small enough chink in the armor of regimentation.

Even at Staff College, the pinnacle of the army educational edifice, open only to the select few, notions of initiative, creativity, originality, and individual force of character were stifled. At what was effectively the university for the Imperial Army's intellectual elite, the generals of the future, there was no real preparation for leadership. There was no general discussion, no attempt to make the students talk freely, just more learning by rote—and this for men of thirty to thirty-five, few of them below the rank of captain. When asked a question in class, the Staff College student "immediately sat at attention and shouted 'Sir!', firmly grasping each side of the chair on which he sat—and fixing his eyes on the small of the back of the person immediately in front of him, he proceeded to bawl out at the top of his voice what appeared to be a carefully prepared answer."

Battles of the Russo-Japanese War were still being appraised in 1937. Even though it was conceded that "the study of a battle which occurred as long ago as 1904, before the advent of air power and modern equipment, was of little tactical value," it was felt nevertheless that "great spiritual value was derived from the knowledge of the action of subordinate commanders." According to one observer, "methods of instruction approximate to the methods in use at the British Staff Colleges before the Great War."

For the bulk of infantry-officer cadets, the path from Military Academy led directly to their assigned units, where, after a short probationary period, they were admitted into the hallowed ranks. The objective was reached, as one Western observer pointed out in awe, "after 3 years in the Military Preparatory School, 2 years in the Military Academy Junior Division, 6 months attached to their unit, 1 year and 10 months in the Senior Division, and finally 2 months in their unit again. . . . After seven and a half years of the most strenuous, the most exacting and the most spartan of all military training, they at last reach the rank of 2nd Lieutenant. During these impressionable years they have been walled off from all outside pleasures, interests or influences. The atmosphere of the narrow groove along which they have moved has been saturated with a special national and a special military propaganda. Already from a race psychologically far removed from us, they have been removed still further."

17

THE SPUR TO ACTION

While physical prowess and deep indoctrination were necessary to compensate for material deficiencies, they did not sit comfortably on a peacetime army. The young officers were prepared for death, preferably in heroic circumstances, not for stagnating on a base in Sendai or Aomori or Niigata. But because Japan's involvement in the First World War was so truncated, the bulk of the Imperial Army saw no action of any consequence for three decades. For high-flyers like Nagata and other army planners, absorbed in total-war planning, the early decades of the century were a crucial and challenging period. But for rank-and-file officers, the years passed drearily and slowly. In terms of their own ethos, they were failing to justify their existence; and to make matters worse, in the 1920s critics outside military circles also began to question their raison d'être.

The Yamanashi and Ugaki cuts merely underlined the fact that the world was poised on the threshold of an era of demilitarization. In the cities, the Japanese people had thrown off feudal restraints and were tasting individual liberty, experimenting with Western fashion, dance, and theater—and, more important, Western politics: democracy, socialism, communism. Most seriously for the army, Japanese civilians showed a strong tendency toward pacifism. Increasingly, these thought currents sweeping the country divided soldier and civilian. Civilians regarded military values as fifty years out of date, while the officer corps regarded modern political activism of any sort as a straightforward denial of loyalty to the Emperor. Civilians asserted that the democracies had won the Great War—but they did not understand the degree to which democracy had been suspended in the process.

On the whole, the Emperor-based indoctrination at Ichigaya insulated the officer corps against contrary ideologies drawn from Western sources, but it did not provide all-around protection. Ironically, it made the young officers particularly vulnerable to a menacing, indigenous ideology built from the elements of the indoctrination itself. *A Plan for the Reorganisation of Japan,* a book by Ikki Kita, son of a rich brewery owner, called for a revolution akin to the restoration of the Emperor Meiji.

Kita saw Japan as a land of "state socialism" ruled over by Imperial prerogative, where private property would have to be returned to state ownership by the usurpers—industrialists, landowners, and even some members of the Imperial Family itself. He poured scorn on the "effeminate pacifism of doctrinaire socialism," preaching instead the "gospel of the sword." Once Japan's polity had been restored, she might go on to offer to "our seven hundred million brothers in China and India" a path to independence, and herself "lift the virtuous banner of an Asian league and the leadership in a world federation which must come."

This vision of a loyal and militarily strong Japan, preeminent in Asia, struck a deep and lasting chord with the officer corps, and Kita's book (though in fact banned by the authorities) was widely read and debated. Within an organization obsessed with authority and obedience, Kita's ideas took hold because he identified the way to state socialism as lying through military dictatorship headed by the Emperor. More specifically, he recommended that this dictatorship should be achieved by a coup d'état executed by junior officers of the Imperial Army.

One of the brightest students of the Military Academy class of 1923 was Mitsugi Nishida, the son of a sculptor from Tottori prefecture. While others of similar caliber, like Nagata, focused on war's material requirements, Nishida seems to have been in thrall to the nation-at-arms ideology even before entering the Academy. Then, while still a cadet, he met

Kita and became his disciple; the "gospel of the sword" gripped him.

Nishida was himself highly charismatic; after two frustrating years on the fringes in base camp at Hiroshima, he resigned his commission and developed his own circle of followers among army officers. These young men were alienated from civilian society, and passed harsh judgment on what "modern" Japan was becoming. With the onset of the Depression, Nishida's group found common cause with the rapidly multiplying reactionary groups in Japan who directed their energies toward "the realisation of a system of Fascist dictatorship," in the view of the British Embassy, "based upon aggressive militarism, chauvinism and the destruction of all liberal principles of government."

The ultranationalist movement was particularly threatening, the report continued, because of the very large number of "dangerous patriots"—extremists who found a haven within or affiliated to the larger and more respectable reactionary societies. Fringe groups like the Saitama Young Men's Patriotic Storm Troops and the East Asia Supremacy Association turned the years after the shooting of Prime Minister Hamaguchi into a period of "government by assassination" during which "dangerous patriots" of all hues plotted and murdered in the name of loyalty to Japan.

Early in 1932, for instance, the Blood Pledge Corps of Nissho Inoue, a long-standing intimate of the Young Officers, attempted a string of politically motivated murders, succeeding with former finance minister Junnosuke Inoue and Baron Takuma Dan, director of the Mitsui company. (At his trial in September 1934, Nissho turned the dock into "a pulpit for reactionary oratory and semi-religious exhortation." The vernacular press was unanimously sympathetic and the court received 300,000 pleas for clemency. Neither Nissho nor any of his followers was sentenced to death.)

The army officer corps had natural sympathy with the mood of violent protest. Though officers were drawn equally from rural and urban areas, 80 percent of their men came from fishing and farming communities, and the officers knew at first hand the miseries that ordinary people were suffering during the Depression. This was the period when farmers in areas faced by starvation resorted to the old practice of selling daughters into prostitution, and common soldiers took the unheard-of step of deserting their units to be with their starving families.

As for Nishida's group, the Young Officers, they made their own first attempt at action late in 1931, after some ten years of talking and planning. Within weeks of the start of the Manchurian adventure, they joined forces with Kingoro Hashimoto and the Sakurakai (planners of the aborted Ugaki coup in March) in plotting a new coup d'état to take place in October 1931.

This time there were no senior officers involved, and the plot was on a far more violent and grandiose scale than the March debacle. Its aim was to assassinate the entire Cabinet, seize key points in Tokyo, and arrest a selection of the "traitors around the Throne." The political vacuum thus created would be filled by the conspirators, who would force Prince Saionji to recommend General Sadao Araki as prime minister.

The rebels' faith in Araki was based on his reputation as a man of action. In the uncertain days following the murder of Chang Tso-lin in 1929, Araki had urged the High Command to send the army to overrun Manchuria. Since the mid-1920s he had headed the 40,000-strong Kodogikai, an organization based on the philosophy of *Kodo,* the "Imperial Way." *Kodo* harnessed the type of Emperorism implanted during military training to fuel a program of reform at home and expansion abroad. "There is a shining sun ahead for Japan," prophesied Araki.

With his chiseled features and handlebar moustache, Araki looked the part of the Prussian militarist. But appearances were deceptive. He was a highly intelligent and sophisticated man, with an "unusually attractive" personality and a taste for philosophical discussion—no mindless fanatic, but one of the army's intellectual elite, much admired by Nagata. His advocacy of *Kodo* was functional—a spur to military sacrifice and a shield against Communist infiltration. Just as Nagata was shaped by his experiences in Europe, so Araki was never to forget his service in Russia during the Bolshevik revolution; he perfectly understood the fatal attraction of communism for the poor and starving.

The October coup was suppressed and Hashimoto transferred from Tokyo. But the attempt had established Araki's popularity among the radical officers, and when a new government came to power on December 13, 1931, he was appointed army minister.

Araki's rise to power proved disastrous for Nagata and for total-war planning. Araki firmly believed that the growing strength of the Soviet Union would lead to war with Japan no later than 1936, and he advocated immediate short-term rearmament. Others in the High Command, including Nagata, shared his concern over the Soviet threat, but believed it was best met by building a strong industrial base first, as the Soviets were themselves doing. Nagata represented mainstream opinion in the army; but once Araki had been promoted, Nagata found himself no longer a ministry theorist but a bewildered regimental commander in charge of live soldiers, well away from the planning power base.

Meanwhile Araki, playing the High Command's brand of personal

politics, exploited his newfound strength to build an individual following. His clique (which included a new inspector-general of military education, General Jinzaburo Mazaki) called itself the Kodo-ha, "Imperial
Way Faction." With a single focus, the Kodo-ha was strong, while its
opponents, like Nagata, were united only in their broad disagreement
with the Kodo-ha strategic view. The opposition was called the Tosei-ha,
or "Control Faction," by the Kodo officers, but this was not a name the
Tosei officers themselves used. Nor did they recognize themselves as
being a clique.

Without ado, the Kodo-ha began its preparations for war. Hot from
the Army Ministry's presses came an unending stream of highly charged
militarist propaganda on the theme of the "crisis of 1936" in Japan's
relations with Russia. Araki vigorously stirred loyalist sentiment within
the officer corps. He personally revived the ancient craft of sword-
making, which had virtually died in the nineteenth century when
Yamagata decided on mass-produced swords for the new army.

Communists became a particular target for nationalist fervor. Three
thousand were arrested in 1933 and fifteen hundred in 1934, to be held
in prison until they repented. The situation looked rather like "a Shinto
inquisition stamping out a communist heresy."

More concretely, Araki put short-term military preparations in
hand. The government formally recognized Manchukuo and strengthened its southwestern and southern flanks by taking Jehol province and
the key Shanhaikuan Pass, forcing China to concede the creation of a
demilitarized zone in northeastern Hopei.

At home, the Army Ministry began a program of large-scale imports
of war resources. British intelligence reported Mitsubishi as having been
active, secretly, on behalf of the Japanese government in the purchase
of "certain metals." On the London metals markets Japan bought zinc,
lead, nickel, and aluminum, and there was also an "intimation" that
America was buying up large quantities of tin in the hope of resale to
Japan. From the French colony of New Caledonia the Japanese bought
three shiploads of chrome—a significant purchase, in the British view,
because "the last time a large shipment was taken from there was just
before the [1914–1918] war when Germany ordered a similar consignment."

From Germany and Belgium came imports of spikes for barbed
wire, from England tank engines, and from Sweden ball bearings at a
rate sufficient to equip six hundred aircraft engines and fifty tanks per
month. In September 1932, the Japanese warned Ford and General

Motors that their factories in Japan might be requisitioned and taken over "at any moment." Nippon Jidosha, a Japanese motor-vehicle company, was working flat out manufacturing "three-wheeled carriers for a military order." Even as the Japanese were withdrawing from the League of Nations, the activated-charcoal industries of British Malaya and the Dutch East Indies were enjoying unprecedented prosperity supplying Japan with filters for gas masks.

These preparations were not, however, sufficiently dramatic for the Young Officers, who rapidly grew disenchanted with Araki. For his part, he complained of ill health caused by the constant interruption of his privacy, day and night, by junior officers demanding progress toward the Showa Restoration. In January 1934 he accepted elevation into the ranks of the Supreme War Councilors and out of day-to-day practical politics. The new army minister, General Senjuro Hayashi, immediately restored the fortunes of a grateful Nagata, who resumed his preparations for total war—the first step being to purge Araki's appointees.

From the Young Officers' perspective, this was definitely a retrograde step, and their disillusionment with the High Command was complete. It was compounded in July 1935, when Mazaki (popular with the Young Officers since the 1920s, when he had been principal of the Military Academy) was relieved of his post as inspector-general of education and "promoted," like Araki, to the Supreme War Council.

Two of the Young Officers circulated a memorandum identifying Nagata as being responsible for Mazaki's downfall and blaming him generally for the army's failure to achieve the Showa Restoration. This so incensed one member of the Kodo-ha, Lieutenant Colonel Saburo Aizawa, that he sought out Nagata at the Army Ministry building and personally protested Mazaki's removal. Nagata had him listed for transfer to Taiwan; but on the day scheduled for his departure, August 15, 1935, Aizawa returned. Entering Nagata's office with drawn sword, he slashed at and wounded him. Nagata, who had been deep in conversation with the chief of the Tokyo Military Police about discipline in the army, jumped up and ran for the door. The gendarme tried to hold Aizawa, but he broke loose and slashed and stabbed wildly at Nagata, pinning him briefly to the door before the dead weight of the corpse jerked the sword to the floor.

Araki and Mazaki, in their undesired eminence as Supreme War Councilors, were powerful enough to insist on a public trial for Aizawa, where his dissatisfaction and that of others like him might be aired. Even more damaging, the venue for this explosive trial was to be the depot of the First Division, the epicenter of Young Officers agitation. Expecting trouble, Army Minister Hayashi hastily arranged for the First Division to be transferred to Manchukuo, but this could not be effected before Aizawa had had his day in court. "Our object is everlasting evolution," he said.

With passions running at fever pitch and several of their leaders threatened with imminent removal from Tokyo, the Young Officers found themselves facing the choice that had confronted Ishiwara and Itagaki only four years before: now or never. True to all they had been taught as officers of the Imperial Army, they had little doubt as to what their decision must be.

18

THE FEBRUARY 26 REVOLT

The Young Officers were optimistic as they foregathered in the house of Lieutenant Yasuhide Kurihara on the evening of February 22, 1936, to finalize arrangements for their coup d'état. They were still at liberty despite an interview published in the mid-February edition of *Nihon Hyoron,* in which they had confirmed that they intended drastic action. Even the mock attack five nights before, on Tokyo Metropolitan Police Headquarters, had not drawn down the wrath of their military superiors. On the pretext that this was a rehearsal for action in Manchuria, troops of the Third Regiment had charged howling, with bayonets fixed, up the front steps.

Nor had the authorities acted against the uncontrolled outburst by one of their number, Captain Ichitaro Yamaguchi, the previous month. Before a captive audience of 600 new recruits to the First Infantry Regiment, their parents, and their brothers, he had declared that the Cabinet of Prime Minister Keisuke Okada had "no sincerity toward clarification of the national polity," and that for one of Okada's colleagues, the veteran finance minister Korekiyo Takahashi, his "hatred was without bounds." The tirade made the national press; interviewed later, Yamaguchi explained ominously that "clarification of national polity is the foundation of loyalty to the Emperor, and loyalty is the first duty of the soldier."

It was precisely to fulfill the "first duty of the soldier" that the conspiracy had been put in hand. The conspirators' "Manifesto" proclaimed that this special polity had been fully expressed in the Meiji Restoration, but now, because of the encroachments of "evil and selfish people" on the Emperor's authority, it required to be "strengthened and expanded." Therefore, the rebels concluded, "we have risen to smash the traitors and save Japan."

On the evening of the twenty-second, the conspirators had a final run-through of their list of targets. From the Cabinet, Prime Minister Keisuke Okada and Finance Minister Korekiyo Takahashi were to die; from the tight circle of advisers to the Emperor, they had earmarked the Lord Keeper of the Privy Seal, Makoto Saito; Grand Chamberlain Baron Kantaro Suzuki; Count Nobuaki Makino; and the last genro, Saionji himself. This was a remarkable roll call of the men at the hub of civilian power in Japan; the only military name on the list was that of the new inspector-general of military education, Jotaro Watanabe, who had replaced the conspirators' beloved General Jinzaburo Mazaki.

Following these executions, the conspirators intended to seize control of the Palace grounds, isolating the Emperor, and to halt the national administration by occupying the key governmental district in the heart of Tokyo. Then, with their forces stretched to the limit, they would appeal for support to the Tokyo Garrison.

To this point, the plot was carefully planned and prepared. If they succeeded they would create chaos—but the exploitation of this chaos would be left to others. As they sat and talked on the night of the twenty-second, they were well aware that they had no definite promises of support from anyone in the upper echelons of the establishment. They considered that the Kodo-ha generals Araki and Mazaki might both be well disposed, but there was nothing definite. Prince Chichibu, the oldest of Hirohito's brothers, who had been in the same class at Ichigaya as Mitsugi Nishida, is alleged to have once said, "When you rise up, come for me with a company of men"—but in February 1936, he was neither aware of the rebellion nor even near enough to Tokyo to be of immediate help.

Nevertheless, firmly convinced of the righteousness of their cause, the conspirators had founded on the shifting sands of a vague sympathy the belief that their masters would "awaken" and make a reality of their dreams of social and political revolution. It was the strategy of young men and idealists. Of the nineteen conspirators ultimately to be executed, seventeen had passed through Military Academy and thirteen were still serving Imperial Army officers, none above the rank of captain; their planning reflected both their indoctrination at Ichigaya and their position in the military hierarchy—tactically sound, strategically blind.

For the murders and the occupation of the palace and city center they needed the services of some fifty men from the Third Infantry Regiment of the Guards Division, 1,350 men from the First and Third Regiments of the First Division, and about a dozen men from the Seventh Field Artillery Regiment. None of the soldiers appears to have questioned his orders. "I went poking around a bit during the fuss," reported the British military attaché in Tokyo. "I spoke to a good many of the sentries of the 3rd Infantry Regiment. They were polite and I don't think they knew what they had been involved in."

Indeed, what made the revolt possible was the willingness of the rebels' men to obey the most far-reaching orders without seeking superior authorization. This was a legacy of the nineteenth century. The ethos of the army based obedience on irrational awe, making it a deadly weapon in the hands of those who could mobilize it. The Japanese soldier more than any other was discouraged from thinking about what he was doing. Individual conscience was not, in any case, a Japanese concept, but in the military sphere it was specifically proscribed. "A subordinate should never fail to respect and obey his superior," ran the "Admonition to Soldiers and Sailors," "even when the latter's orders may seem unreasonable."

The action began in the early hours of February 26, 1936. Snow was falling, shrouding the city in an ominous silence. The killers of Count Makino had farthest to go. Makino, second son of the assassinated Meiji leader Toshimichi Okubo, was then aged seventy-four and living as an invalid in a wing of the Itoya Inn at Yugawara, some sixty miles away. His assassination squad of seven men, commanded by Captain Hisashi Kono, set off at 12:40 A.M. in two cars, carrying two light machine guns, pistols, and swords. They arrived at the inn at about five A.M. and burst into Makino's wing. A policeman on guard duty was shot dead, and Makino's nurse, Suzue Mori, was wounded in the hand. They could not find Makino, and assuming the old man was still hiding inside, they went out into the snow and set the hotel ablaze, shooting at anyone who tried to put out the fire.

A blood frenzy then gripped them. They machine-gunned the burning building. They thought they saw the count in every group of people trying to escape the mayhem (he was, in fact, in one group), and shouting "Penalty of Heaven!" the would-be assassins fired indiscriminately at men, women, and children. More police arrived; in the fighting, Captain Kono was severely wounded. His men took him to the army hospital at Atami and then surrendered themselves. Makino, meanwhile, was safe and sound, having made his escape blindside to the attacking troops.

Larger forces were needed for the murders within Tokyo, to act as rearguards, or to force an entry into the victims' homes. First Lieutenant Naoshi Sakai and three second lieutenants led a force of 150 soldiers from the Third Infantry Regiment in Azabu to attack the private residence of the Lord Keeper of the Privy Seal, Makoto Saito, in Yotsuya. Naïvely, Saito's maids directed Sakai and two of the other officers upstairs to his bedroom. His wife heard the commotion and opened the door, only to slam it again immediately in panic. The assassins burst in, and over her frantic pleas, fired repeatedly at the seventy-eight-year-old Saito. He fell to the floor; as the bullets continued to hit him, his wife threw herself on the corpse.

At about the same time, another squad, led by Captain Teruzo Ando, was in the bedroom of Grand Chamberlain Baron Kantaro Suzuki in Kojimachi. Suzuki's wife too tried to use her own body as a shield against the hail of bullets. When the firing stopped, she implored Ando to allow her to administer the coup de grace to the prostrate body of her dying husband. Saluting, Ando gave permission and left immediately. The grand chamberlain survived to become the prime minister who surrendered his country to the Allies in 1945.

On schedule, also at five A.M., Lieutenant Kurihara, with four other officers and a squad of 300 soldiers, led the attack on Prime Minister Okada, who was asleep in his official residence across the street from the Diet building. This time there was organized resistance, and the assassins had to kill four guards to gain entrance. The delay gave Okada's brother-in-law time to wake him and hide him in a laundry cupboard, before returning to the bedroom to confront the assassins—who mistook him for the prime minister and killed him.

The residence of Finance Minister Takahashi in Akasaka was attacked by a force of about 120 men led by First Lieutenant Motoaki Nakahashi of the Third Regiment of Guards. He had collected his men by conducting an emergency roll call at 4:30 A.M. before setting out, so he informed the guard detail in the barracks, "to visit the Meiji Shrine." Half an hour later, they burst into Takahashi's house, and forced his servants to lead them to the bedroom where their eighty-two-year-old master was asleep. Nakahashi pulled back the covers and shouting "Traitor!" shot his victim at point-blank range while another young officer yelling "Punishment of Heaven!" slashed furiously with his sword.

In terms of creating a political crisis, the least important target was Inspector-General Jotaro Watanabe, whose murder was entrusted to elements of the Saito squad after Saito's own death had been achieved. Even though army officers had been running riot in Tokyo since five A.M., no one had contacted Watanabe, and although they did not reach his house in Ogikubo until six A.M., the conspirators were still able to surprise their victim in his bed. Once again the killers had to get past their victim's wife, screaming, fighting, and begging, before hitting him with a burst of machine-gun fire at close range.

At this point, all was proceeding smoothly. As far as the conspirators knew, they had succeeded in killing all on their original core list, with the exception of Saionji, whose murder had been postponed the previous day because of disagreement on a point of protocol: whether or not enlisted men should participate in the killing. The army minister had even invited them into his official residence and permitted them to read their manifesto and other demands to him. The plan to occupy central Tokyo had also been an unqualified success. By about ten A.M. the rebels controlled the key governmental district in the environs of the palace, including the Diet, Army Ministry and army General Staff offices, government offices, some foreign embassies (including the German), and the official residences of the prime minister, army minister, and other Cabinet ministers. Even the Metropolitan Police Headquarters had succumbed without a struggle.

So successful was the military aspect of the plan, despite all the forewarning that the authorities had been given, that it is hard to resist the suspicion that there was a degree of collusion—that, like their hero Saigo, the rebels were being given enough rope to hang themselves. But as the conspiracy moved into the second stage, it began to go wrong. After leaving Suzuki's house, Ando hurried to the headquarters of the Tokyo garrison to make the crucial appeal for help. Again the shadows of the Satsuma Rebellion seemed to fall over the February 26 Incident. Saigo had approached the garrison at Kumamoto Castle with an equally crucial request for help. He had been refused; and now Ando heard General Kohei Kashii, Tokyo Garrison GOC, congratulate the rebels but give no undertaking to rush into action.

Fatally, the rebels had no leverage, military or political. They could lead the way to the Showa Restoration, but they could not coerce others to follow—unless they could somehow gain control of the authority of the Emperor. This was why the original plan had included the occupation of the Imperial Palace—and this in turn had determined the choice of February 26 as the day of action, when one of the rebel units was detailed for the night relief guard duty there.

Having murdered Finance Minister Takahashi nearby in Akasaka, Lieutenant Nakahashi led his men to the Palace and told the commander of the guard that his squad had been sent to buttress the defenses because of the violence now raging in the city. For a while he was believed, and he and his men were detailed to guard the Sakashita Gate. But they had no time to dig in or to signal to the reinforcements waiting anxiously in the Metropolitan Police building, straining their eyes to see the beckoning torch flashing from the dark palace grounds across the moat. Major Kentaro Homma, in charge of the guard, had quickly realized his mistake. Rushing down to the Sakashita Gate, he ordered Nakahashi out. Tamely, Nakahashi complied and moved his men outside the palace walls.

This reverse, perhaps over all others, fatally damaged the rebels' chances of success. The overriding necessity of capturing the Emperor was one moral they had failed to draw from the story of the Meiji Restoration. Possession of the person of the Emperor was not only a crucial bargaining chip, it was, as the Meiji leaders had discovered in 1868, an infallible means of mobilizing nationalist fervor. And among the officer corps of 1936, such fervor was very widespread indeed.

19

TO THE THRESHOLD
OF POWER

As news of the revolt in Tokyo spread through the army, the authorities faced a highly delicate situation. Even though these young officers had murdered elder statesmen and were occupying the nerve center of government, they were not regarded by many of their fellow officers—company, field grade, or even some generals—as extremists. They had struck a spark that threatened a conflagration throughout the Japanese Empire, wherever men of the Imperial Army were to be found. Contemporary observers testified to "persistent but unconfirmed reports that disaffection showed itself among units stationed in other parts of Japan, notably at Nagoya, Kagoshima and Aomori, and at Hsinking in Manchukuo." Hideki Tojo, then chief of the Kwantung Army Military Police, put his men on alert throughout the crisis in case disaffection spilled over into Manchukuo.

On hearing of the revolt, the Emperor's brother Prince Chichibu had immediately set off on the sixteen-hour train journey from his regimental depot to Tokyo. But he was not allowed to go to the occupied rebel zone; Hirohito had him intercepted and confined to the palace until the rebellion was over. Hirohito himself had first heard at six A.M. of the revolt in progress in his name and he displayed anger on a scale not experienced by his advisers before. In his view, the rebels were mutineers. His military aide-de-camp, General Shigeru Honjo (who had commanded the Kwantung Army at the time of the Manchurian Incident) later tried to argue the Ichigaya line, that the Young Officers' motives were pure: "The spirit in which it was done was one of esteem for Emperor and country and we should not blame them." Hirohito responded passionately: "Why should we forgive them when these brutal officers kill our right-hand advisers? . . . All my most trusted retainers are dead and [the mutineers'] actions are aimed directly at me. . . . We ourselves will lead the Imperial Guards and suppress them."

With Chichibu out of the way, there was little risk that other junior officers might spontaneously lead their units in supportive action. The rebels had struck—but their seniors would pick up the pieces—and in essence, the story of the February uprising after the murders was a rekindling and acting out of the old Kodo-Tosei clique rivalries.

First to move were the Kodo-ha. At eight A.M. on the morning of the twenty-sixth, General Jinzaburo Mazaki, whom a court-martial was later to credit with advance knowledge of the uprising, came to the army minister's residence. He congratulated the rebels and then effectively dismissed them while he went into conference with the army minister, apparently about how best to exploit the situation. Their solution was to arrange an immediate audience with the Emperor for the army minister to put forward the army's recommendation that a new "strong Cabinet" be appointed. Without consulting any other senior officers, they telephoned the palace from the army minister's residence, and an audience was granted for 9:30 A.M. This was a bold move by the Kodo-ha to exploit the situation created by the rebels. Obviously, the "strong Cabinet" would have to be one acceptable to the rebels, and since they were ultimately to recommend Mazaki as the new prime minister, the Kodo-ha would, at a single stroke, see its fortunes restored.

Following up the Kawashima-Mazaki initiative, General Araki made his own contribution to the continuation of the revolt by convening, without Imperial authority, a meeting of the Supreme War Council, a Kodo-ha stronghold. Swiftly the council drafted an "Army Minister's Proclamation" approving the rebels' actions, and sent Tomoyuki Yamashita to read it to them.

Yamashita was a considerable force in the army, but for a man of high intelligence, he lamentably mishandled his involvement in the events of February 26. Long a supporter of the Imperial Way, he had friends and protégés among the younger, more radical officers, including the Captain Ando who had tried (and failed) to kill Baron Suzuki. Weeks ahead of time, they had confided many details of the conspiracy to him, and he had done nothing to interfere. Now he acted as one of the principal go-betweens communicating the rebels' notions to the government. He spent most of the twenty-sixth with the rebels and appears to have become infected by their zeal, to the point of leading a delegation to the palace, apparently at his own suggestion. In the face of the Emperor's anger, Yamashita would back down; but he had already done his career lasting damage.

The Kodo-ha, by acting precipitately, had shown their hand: The prize they sought was political power. They were not alone; the idea of making political capital from the rebellion and securing a favorably inclined Cabinet appears to have occurred to most of the upper echelons of the Imperial Army, but their hopes were short-lived. By now the Emperor, crucially, had intervened to end the maneuvering of the cliques by refusing, on the advice of a senior court official, to accept the resignation of the surviving members of Okada's Cabinet. It was a shrewd tactic: If the rebellion could be suppressed without the Cabinet having to resign, the status quo would be restored as nearly as was possible given the loss of such key figures as Takahashi, and the authorities would have defused much of the tension that the army cliques were trying so hard to exploit.

By now the Kodo-ha were out of power in the army, and Hirohito's stand killed their last chance of a revival. If confirmation was needed of the decline in their fortunes, when Mazaki turned up at the palace on the evening of the twenty-seventh, instead of receiving the Imperial command to head a new Cabinet, he found himself without even the honor of an audience with Hirohito.

As for the Toseiha generals, also hoping to exploit the situation, the Emperor's stand narrowed their options to one: suppressing the rebellion. By the twenty-seventh, a cabal of high-ranking officers in the Tokyo area had formed around Vice-Chief of Staff Gen Sugiyama for the purpose. Ishiwara was appointed to the martial-law headquarters to run the communications and operations sections.

The die was now cast. The Supreme War Council's "Army Minister's Proclamation" was withdrawn and the rebels were isolated. Martial law was declared; on the twenty-seventh, the rebels concentrated their forces around the Diet and barricaded themselves into an area roughly a kilometer square. Defiantly they flew their flags—HONOR THE EMPEROR: DESTROY THE TRAITORS—even as the political maneuvering was making their sacrifice irrelevant. The fundamental realities of the situation, truths about the relationship between army and state, were expressed not in their slogans, however sincere, but in the fact that the financial community was pressing Sugiyama to sort out the mess quickly.

The rebels had erected a barbed-wire cordon around their area. Now the army threw up a ring of its own around the rebel zone; through the day and then the night of February 28 the martial-law commander, General Kashii (originally in sympathy with the rebels), gradually drew it tighter. Civilians were evacuated from the contained area and accommodated in schools; every exit was sealed off.

Tokyo itself, silent under a thick blanket of snow, was also effectively sealed off. The authorities were desperate to avoid regaling the world, or even the Japanese public, with images of Imperial troops killing each other in the streets of the capital. By dawn on the twenty-ninth, Tokyo was silenced, immobilized and isolated. Mainline trains were halted twenty or thirty miles outside the city; suburban railways, tramcars, and buses ceased to run. Long-distance telephone lines were cut, and telegrams were refused. The most powerful impression was of an "unnatural silence brooding over a usually busy scene. . . . No children were heard and the multitudinous familiar figures of the Tokyo streets—bicycle boys, pedlars and newsboys—vanished."

Behind their barricades, the doomed insurgents remained defiant. There was no firing as yet, though the sound of tanks and artillery moving into position could plainly be heard. An intense psychological-warfare campaign was waged with radio broadcasts and leaflets dropped into the occupied zone: "Soldiers, you have obeyed your officers but His Majesty now orders you to return to barracks. If you resist, you will be rebels and have your names stained forever. It is not too late. You must instantly return to the army and you will be pardoned. Your fathers, brothers, and all the people pray for your return."

Tiredness, mental strain, and a growing sense of hopelessness combined to save many lives. Slowly, in batches, the NCOs and men drifted across the barricades and returned to barracks. By lunchtime, still without a shot having been fired, only the Young Officers remained. The only option now seemed to be suicide, and they asked that an Imperial messenger be sent to witness their deaths. At the army minister's residence grisly preparations were made for the ritual. But the Emperor refused to dignify the mutineers even with this much recognition. So instead they decided to surrender themselves to stand trial, at which, like Aizawa, they could at least plead their case and fuel the cause of the Showa Restoration.

By two P.M. on February 29 it was all over and the officers were incarcerated in Tokyo Army Prison. But they were not to be given the limelight they sought. On March 4, a special military tribunal was established by Imperial edict to try them in camera—without counsel for the defense, and with only two hours in which to plead their case. Nine ringleaders, including Kita and Nishida, were executed by firing squad.

The end of the rebellion signaled the start of a larger war against the Kodo-ha and other mutinous elements in the army. By purges and involuntary retirement, the threat to army discipline was eliminated. The Kodo-ha itself was decimated; and the suspicion lingers that this is what the anti–Kodo-ha generals wanted all along, that they permitted the rebellion to take its course in order to draw out the Araki clique.

By the end of 1936, the army was more unified than at any time since Yamagata's heyday; this state of affairs was rooted in Army Order No. 11 of July 24, 1936, which concentrated power in the hands of the army minister. The order itself read simply: "The Chief of the General Staff is charged with the 'supervision' of Officers of the Staff, instead of their 'control.' " But this simple change in wording meant that the army minister was now responsible for the appointment, promotion, transfer, and discharge of all officers throughout the army, including General Staff officers who had previously been "controlled" by their chief.

And the prize of appointment as army minister was put beyond the senior Kodo-ha generals by the simple expedient of limiting the choice of army ministers once more to active-list generals and lieutenant generals—a return to the heyday of the Yamagata era, before the crisis of 1913, when Katsura was ousted from the office of prime minister, had forced the army to concede a small corner of its autonomy.

The revolt not only changed the balance of power within the army, it also profoundly altered the balance between the army and its civilian antagonists. At a stroke, the rebels removed several of Japan's leading proponents of constitutional monarchy, and provided a display of military brute force vicious enough to guarantee the cooperation of others who might otherwise have challenged the army. In the nature of total-war planning, the leaders of the army needed partnership with other technocrats, so the army was never to assume an absolute dictatorship, but direct and overt opposition to its plans ceased after February 1936.

Prince Saionji's power had finally been broken, and in 1937 the initiative for recommending the appointment of the prime minister passed from his hands. Worse, in a way, the rebellion had demonstrated the essential weakness of the Throne against the army. That Hirohito was able to do anything at all stemmed from the fact that the High Command preserved his freedom by defending the gates of the palace. His passionate desire to crush the rebels was fulfilled only because the High Command saw this as essential. He did not "command" the army; the Rescript of February 27, ordering the revolt to be suppressed, was implemented only when it suited the army. But he was not totally without influence. He could and did restrain his brother Prince Chichibu from giving support to the rebels. And by following his counselors' advice and refusing to accept the Cabinet's resignation, he had struck a shrewd blow against individual ambition and factional rivalry in the ranks of senior officers. But ultimately Hirohito was constrained by his dedication to his grandfather's constitution. He sought no personal advantage from the revolt, only to preserve constitutional government as a mechanism—but his influence could not prevent its subversion by powerful forces within the system.

In the wake of the February revolt, the new army minister, Hisaichi Terauchi (son of former prime minister Count Terauchi) announced the "three missions" of the army as the enforcement of discipline, the strengthening of national defense, and the reformation of the administration. In his view, all was "not well with social conditions or with the administration of the country." Lest anyone be unclear as to his meaning, he spelled it out in what amounted to a barely veiled threat: "It would be difficult to restore discipline and obtain a perfectly satisfied and contented army unless steps are taken to reform the administration and also to increase the amount of money available for military expansion." The violence of military extremists was now a weapon with which the army's leaders could hold the country to ransom.

"The military is like an untamed horse left to run wild," confided the new prime minister, Koki Hirota, to a friend. "If you try to stop it head-on you'll get kicked to death. The only hope is to jump on from the side and try to get it under control. . . . Somebody has to do it. That's why I've jumped on." But good intentions, and elegant metaphors, were not enough. After the war Hirota would be hanged by the Allies for the concessions he now had to make to the army.

In the new political landscape, the way seemed open at last to fulfill Nagata's vision of total-war preparation. In his last months, before his death on August 12, 1935, Nagata had worked hard to repair some of the ravages perpetrated on the long-term military program by General Araki during his time as army minister. His first step, as major-general in charge of the Army Ministry's Military Affairs Bureau, was to reassert the primacy of total-war planning. He devoted himself to an endless round of breakfast, lunch, and dinner meetings with industrialists and bureaucrats, persuading them of the need to modernize Japanese industry. His success was apparent when on October 10, 1934, the Army Ministry issued a pamphlet entitled "Fundamental Principles of National Defense and a Plan for Its Strengthening."

The pamphlet was essentially a restatement of Nagata's 1927 thesis. "The ideas of national defence have undergone a remarkable change," it read. "By discarding the idea of relying on actual battles in deciding the outcome of a war, it is considered most urgent to formulate new ideas and plans radically different from those in the past. . . . Prompt measures must be taken to re-examine all the national organs from the point of view of national defence and to readjust fundamentally all policies on finance, economics, diplomacy, education etc and then to control and operate the latent power, spiritual and material, of the Empire to the maximum extent."

In the 1920s, there had been some debate as to whether Japan should seek autarky on British or German lines. The British system rested on the political cohesion of their empire—an approach reflected in Japan's call for a "Co-prosperity Sphere" in Asia—while Germans stressed the military seizure of territory and utilization of the territory's resources. By the mid-1930s, the German system predominated in Japan, largely because of Tatsuhiko Takashima, who was military attaché in Berlin from 1930 to 1934 and who translated into Japanese several German books on total war.

In the resurgence of total-war planning, one of the most significant "fundamental readjustments" to Araki's policies was that toward North China. To Araki, North China had been principally a *cordon sanitaire*, shielding the south against the consequences of war with Russia in the north. With the reinstitution of total-war planning, North China and Inner Mongolia were seen as essential resource areas in the search for autarkic defense.

One of the Okada Cabinet's last acts before the February rebellion had been to approve the Army Ministry's new "Outline Policy to Deal with North China." This explicitly envisioned the ultimate separation from Nanking of the five North China provinces of Shantung, Hopei,

Shansi, Suiyuan, and Chahar. Manchuria had been taken in the teeth of civilian opposition; but this was formal government sanction of an army policy of expansion on the continent.

The government's change of heart toward China and adoption of army policy were voiced unambiguously by Yosuke Matsuoka, the charismatic son of a Choshu samurai, who had led Japan away from the League of Nations in 1933. In August 1935 Matsuoka was appointed to the presidency of the South Manchurian Railway, and summoning his senior staff to his office, he identified the company as the economic spearhead of Japan's expansion into China. "Because of the activities of the Soviet Union and the situation prevailing in China, Japan is going to start operations in North China. Most of the people of Japan do not yet quite understand the great importance of these future operations, and their lack of understanding, I believe, will beyond doubt bring about a really serious crisis in the nation. Regardless of how serious the crisis may become, Japan cannot halt her North China operations. The arrow has already left the bow. The progress of these operations will decide the destiny of the Yamato race."

The early attempts at southward expansion into China failed miserably. The strategy for 1935 had been to make North China an autonomous region under Japanese influence. The Kwantung Army was extremely concerned that the British-backed reform of China's currency would enhance Chiang Kai-shek's hold on North China and "menace the economic foundations of Manchukuo." Though a full-scale Manchukuo-style annexation was not possible—as General Sugiyama explained to the Kwantung Army staff, "Our national policy has not yet developed to the point of carrying out our aims in North China by the use of military force"—the Kwantung Army believed that a coalition of northern warlords could be coerced and bribed into declaring independence from Nanking.

In fact, Chiang Kai-shek promptly preempted the Japanese plan by creating his own "autonomous" government, loyal to Nanking. Maximum publicity was given to Japan's thwarted ambitions, and the resulting nationalist fury reached fever pitch the following November, when the Kwantung Army underwrote a Mongol expeditionary force under Prince Te to establish an Inner Mongolia independent from China. Despite the presence of some Japanese personnel, Te's troops were soundly beaten by Chinese Nationalist forces at Pailingmiao in Suiyuan province. Chinese propagandists painted this as a victory over Japanese dressed in Mongol uniforms and thereby created a false sense of Chinese

military supremacy that was to have serious consequences in the following year.

Expansionism abroad was linked to domestic restructuring. Only
days before his assassination, Nagata had made a number of important
personnel appointments to buttress the total-war lobby within the High
Command. Among them was Kanji Ishiwara, architect of the Manchurian
Incident; on Nagata's death, Ishiwara assumed the leadership of the
campaign. One of his most pressing tasks was to deal with the consequences of promises made by Araki to the Imperial Navy. When Araki
wanted to boost munitions production for the expected war with the
Soviet Union in 1936, he was forced to buy the navy's cooperation with
a promise to support two Imperial Navy demands—one for the abrogation of the naval limitation treaties, the other for finance for a major
shipbuilding program. In December 1934, notice of abrogation of the
treaties was duly given; by January 1, 1937, the navy would become free
to build whatever warships it could afford.

The army was already alarmed at the prospect of a resurgent navy,
and its leaders had been anxious for some time to talk seriously to their
naval counterparts about the overall policy of the armed forces—which
was by now virtually synonymous with the policy of the nation, given the
political strength of the military since the February 26 Incident. On
August 7, 1936, the Five Ministers Conference (the inner cabinet of the
most powerful ministers, including the army minister) approved the
"Fundamental Principles of National Policy." This grandiose statement
represented an idealized summary of both army and navy strategy. The
navy was to become powerful enough to "ensure naval supremacy in the
Western Pacific against the United States," while the army's "military
preparations should be directed to resisting the armed strength Russia
could use in the Far East. We will particularly improve our armed
strength in Manchukuo and Korea in order to launch a major attack at
the outbreak of war." In order to create and supply these expanded
forces, the Fundamental Principles proposed promoting essential trade
and industry, "making the people's thought sound," acquiring "self-
sufficiency in important resources and materials," developing Manchukuo and "by gradual peaceful means" expanding into Southeast Asia.

The navy, with its small officer corps of technical specialists, prudently left the army to ensure that these plans could be achieved; the
responsibility came to rest with Ishiwara. He had certain advantages over
his predecessors in the total-war program. The Imperial Army did at least
have the necessary political muscle now and there was a wide-ranging

consensus among the bureaucracy that Japan required "renovation." Ishiwara could also point to present danger. The U.S. Congress had approved a budget funding what the secretary of the navy called "an unparalleled renaissance" in American naval power. The Soviet Union was continuing its buildup of ground forces; it now had bombers in position in the Maritime Province capable of striking Tokyo and it had begun establishing a Pacific Fleet for the first time since the carnage at Tsushima.

Ishiwara's response was vintage total-war planning. Over a five-year period, Japan's industrial infrastructure would be reconstructed and hugely expanded. Japan would become the central workshop of the Empire, geared to exploiting the available resources, including those in North China and Inner Mongolia. The plan was complete, the relevant ministries had been briefed, and a special meeting of the Diet was scheduled for July 24, 1937, to authorize the program.

Indirectly, the legacy of the February 26 conspirators was to take Japan to the threshold of her own "unparalled renaissance" in military power. But to cross the threshold required every ounce of commitment, the dedicated application of every asset, an incredible degree of sacrifice by the Japanese people. Above all, Japan had to avoid war; she could not afford the cost, nor the risk of offending the Americans, who might refuse to supply the technologies and the machine tools needed to make the renaissance happen.

Nevertheless, just a few days before the Diet was scheduled to meet, war descended on Japan. For eight years, merging into the Second World War, she was to take part in the most savage and bloody conflict waged between two nations in the twentieth century. It was a war that would bleed her dry and ultimately lay her open to the predator she most feared: Stalin's Russia.

PART V

THE CHINA WAR
1937-1941

20

MARCO POLO BRIDGE

A little before midnight on July 7, 1937, a detachment of infantry from the North China Garrison Army was taking a break from their night maneuvers on the banks of the Yunting River near Peking. Suddenly, from the darkness several shots were fired at them. A quick roll call revealed that one soldier, Private Kikujiro Shimura, was missing. His company commander, Captain Setsuro Shimizu, fearing that he was now a prisoner, immediately reported the bare facts of the situation to higher authority, and all on the Japanese side jumped to the conclusion that the incident was the work of Chinese Nationalist troops.

In fact, the question of who fired the shots remains a mystery to this day. After the war a Japanese naval intelligence officer, Tsunezo Wachi, recalled intercepting a signal on July 7 from the U.S. naval attaché in Peking, which read: "According to reliable information, radicals . . . will begin firing at Japanese Army at 19:00." Wachi was talking about extreme Nationalists; but a more likely explanation is that the culprits were Communist agitators anxious to keep the united front active. Japanese signals intelligence picked up a message, emanating from a Communist cell in Peking University, which read simply, "We got it!" And certainly, Japanese military intelligence was convinced that the continuing provocations in the days that followed were the work of Communist agitators.

Whoever they were, the provocateurs had chosen to incite an eruption from the Imperial Army at the epicenter of strategic planning for the annexation of Hopei, the rich province whose capital is Peking. In any conflict in North China, one of the Imperial Army's priorities would be to secure the key bridges across the river near where Captain Shimizu's unit had been resting—the Marco Polo and, more importantly, the railway bridge a little way upstream.

The preoccupation of the Imperial Army with this tactical obstacle made a simple local settlement difficult, despite the fact that Private Shimura reappeared, unhurt, two hours after his disappearance had first been registered. The obvious solution was punishment and apology—but the Japanese tried to profit from the incident by demanding that all Chinese troops withdraw to the far bank of the river, away from the vital bridges.

The Chinese insisted on their sovereign rights, and Japanese officers resented the contempt implied in their resistance. Compromise was ever more remote. During the night, the Japanese demanded to be allowed to search the town of Wan-p'ing at the northern bridgehead, and the next morning, despite Private Shimura's return, they moved toward the town, only to be fired upon once again. This time the transgressors were identifiable Chinese units, and troops under the command of Kiyonao Ichiki went into action.

Briefly, it looked as if the Japanese expeditionary forces and the Chinese leaders in Peking had reached agreement to withdraw across the Yunting River. But new "incidents" ruined any chance of implementing the agreement. As Japanese and Chinese blood flowed, the time for a local settlement passed. From now on the decisions were made in Tokyo and Nanking, bringing into play a range of forces and ambitions at the national level, out of all proportion to the actual incident at the Marco Polo Bridge.

In Nanking on July 8, as the news of the night's events filtered through, Chiang Kai-shek confided to his diary: "The time has come now to make the decision to fight." The hard line he adopted at the outset, which he made public by proclaiming that China had reached her "final critical hour," was in the end the flint that struck the fatal spark from Japanese steel.

It would have been more accurate to say that this was Chiang Kai-shek's own final critical hour. To all outward appearances, this dynamic, charismatic leader was the personification of China, as much as any emperor before him. In the decade from 1926, when he had ridden the Nationalist wave up from the south to take all of North China except Manchuria, his power had become seemingly absolute. Thanks partly to his American-educated "noisy wife," as General Tatekawa liked to call her, he had become a commanding figure on the international stage, beloved by Americans in particular as the bringer of modernism and democracy to China. But his power, though considerable, was not beyond challenge, and by the mid-1930s the ledger of loss and gain had begun to show some disturbing imbalances.

On the positive side, he personally and directly commanded an army of thirty divisions, equipped with modern weapons and efficiently trained by German military advisers. China's economic strength showed signs of improvement, too. Although in the malaise of the 1930s progress was slow, she was acquiring an industrial infrastructure and a rising national income. At last, it seemed, China was coming through the chaos following the collapse of the Ch'ing dynasty and the Japanese-assisted fragmentation of the warlord era.

But to set against these credits was a debit that could not be ignored. Without the resources of Manchuria, China could not become a major military-industrial power. The Imperial Army's monopoly of the abundant coal, iron ore, gold reserves, and other riches of the North, and their obvious determination to hold onto them, presented Chiang with a problem that by 1937 he knew could be resolved only by war.

The proof lay before Chiang. Already in 1933, the world had seen Yosuke Matsuoka lead Japan defiantly from the floor of the League of Nations rather than obey its resolution that Japan should give up this crucial strategic zone. Within Manchukuo, the Imperial Army was building an enduring economic and strategic organization to meet the Empire's needs, with rail lines leading north and a growing industrial machine to process the natural riches of the area. Even politically, the Imperial Army seemed to be succeeding in binding the whole together with an ideology designed to armor-plate the new state against both Nationalist and Communist subversion.

Worse, the Imperial Army had not been content with its gains of the winter of 1931–1932. Under Araki, it had enabled Manchukuo to annex the province of Jehol, and had forced Chiang to create a demilitarized zone south of the Great Wall. Then in 1935, creeping encroachment had continued with the North China "autonomy" movement and the invasion of Suiyuan by Mongol troops covertly sponsored by the Kwantung Army.

After the failure of the autonomy scheme in 1935, careful steps were taken to avoid military confrontation with the Chinese in North China. Though the China Garrison was increased in May 1936 from 2,000 to 5,600 men, to give it equal status with the Kwantung Army, it remained under the direct control of Tokyo, and officers assigned there understood that North China was not intended to become another Manchukuo.

But Japan's new policy of restraint was no comfort to Chiang. He could see himself being rolled back, slowly but surely, to the status of provincial warlord. And while he was losing ground against Japan, he also seemed increasingly out of step with the changing mood within his own country.

Chiang had never wavered from his policy of suppressing the Chinese Communist Party before taking up the Japanese gauntlet. But by 1937 time was running out. Mao's Communists had not only survived Chiang's onslaughts and the Long March, but had also achieved relative security in the northwest in Yenan and were successfully building up their strength on the basis of opposition to Japan. Japan's clumsy bid to sever the five northern provinces stimulated a fresh wave of anti-Japanese feeling among warlords, intellectuals, and the masses alike. And the Kwantung Army's attempt to use Mongolian surrogate troops to conquer Suiyuan—only a few hundred miles north of Yenan, which Chiang was trying to crush—undermined Chiang's policy still further.

It seemed the height of folly for Chinese to fight Chinese while the real enemy inexorably advanced from outside. The fact that the Kwantung Army's surrogates were defeated by local Nationalist troops only added to Chiang's political discomfort. In the upsurge of nationalism following news of the "victory over the Japanese," the Chinese Communist Party seized the political initiative, calling once again (as the Moscow Comintern had instructed) for a united front against Japan.

Circumstance, Comintern propaganda, and the rising tide of revulsion at Japanese encroachment south of the Great Wall slowly propelled Chiang toward grasping the nettle of war. But he was not yet willing to abandon his quest to crush Mao—so when he saw anti-Japanese feeling eroding the commitment of his troops to seek and destroy the Red Army in Yenan, he flew to the headquarters of his "bandit-suppressing" army, at Sian, to remonstrate with his generals.

By a twist of fate, one of these generals was none other than the

Young Marshal, Chang Hsüeh-liang. Ever an opportunist, he saw a chance to evict Japan from Manchuria and regain his domain, if only the Chinese people could present a united front—if, that is to say, the Nationalists could be persuaded to sink their differences with the Communists for long enough at least to defeat Japan. The key to a united front was undoubtedly Chiang Kai-shek, and the Young Marshal did not expect "persuasion" to be easy. So, to the astonishment of China, not to say the world, he and his army declared themselves in revolt against the Nanking regime, occupied Sian, and arrested the generalissimo himself.

For two weeks Chiang Kai-shek, confined to a hotel suite in Sian, was obliged to listen to his generals and invited Communists plead the case for a united front. Heading this delegation was Chou En-lai, and it is said that Chiang went pale as Chou entered the room for the first time. But Chou was in fact Chiang's best ally. He was under orders from Moscow, telegraphed the day before he left for Sian, to keep Chiang alive and to work for a united front, and he had more to offer than words. He was essentially repeating the offer that Stalin had made directly in 1935: Russia would provide the Nationalists with military aid for war against Japan if Chiang would find a place for Mao's Communist Party within the Chinese government structure.

Where Lenin had always regarded the Soviet state as an instrument of world revolution, Stalin saw world revolution as an instrument of the Soviet state. He fostered communism where it was in the Soviet interest to do so. In the China of the mid-1930s, Chiang Kai-shek was of more use than Mao in achieving Stalin's ultimate purpose: war between China and Japan. And if war meant the death of communism in China, then so be it.

But Chiang had his own views on who should be fighting whom— and he saw Japan's natural opponent as Russia, not China. Russia, he was convinced, would be forced to confront Japan in the end, but he had to acknowledge that the moment had not yet come. The paranoia that had gripped Stalin since about mid-1935 was now venting itself in scything, crippling purges of the Soviet Red Army officer corps—purges that pushed back Soviet war readiness all the time. Therefore no distraction was likely in the shape of a new Russo-Japanese war, and China's "critical hour" was, as he knew, upon her.

By early 1937, Chiang also knew that war with Japan would buy him the loyalty and support of the provincial warlords, an end to Communist subversion, and the prospect of military aid from the world's major military-industrial power. He also believed that Japan was unlikely in 1937 to be as resolute in the face of Chinese zeal as she had once been. Even the Soviet ambassador to Tokyo was remarking in private that war was the one thing Japan did not want.

It was not an unreasonable analysis. Internally, the Imperial Army was undergoing a period of reorganization in the wake of the February revolt. "Many experienced and valuable officers" had been retired or purged, inevitably reducing military efficiency, while at the same time significant changes were being made in the administration of the Army Ministry to cope with the "many new problems pressing in on the army": Manchukuo, the newly established air corps, organization of the military police, necessary improvements to counterespionage, industrial mobilization, and control of radical thought.

The reformed Army Ministry, which formally began to operate on August 1, 1936, was not only more efficient, but also exercised influence over a wider area of national life. Army Minister Terauchi proposed the nationalization of electric power and the creation of a Health Ministry: "The number of youths of indifferent physique . . . has steadily grown during the last twenty years. Although the average height has increased . . . there has been no corresponding increase in weight, and cases of tubercular, pulmonary, and eye diseases are ten times as numerous as in 1911." And as the Army Ministry pushed out into the civilian sphere, within the army itself new tactics were introduced. The Imperial Army's main concerns appeared to be nothing more belligerent than building up reserves and the consolidation of Japan's industrial power for a future war with the Soviet Union.

Unfortunately for Chiang, the High Command's analysis of Japan's prospects in a war with China was rather different. The majority of Japanese leaders saw sufficient advantage in such a war to keep them from backing away from the escalating friction following the incident at the Marco Polo Bridge.

Many thought that this might be a quite a good time to fight, with Stalin's purge in progress. After making the journey from England to Manchuria across Russia in the summer of 1937, no less a man than General Masaharu Homma, soon to be director of military intelligence, declared that the Soviet army was "down and out and could do nothing for some time." Russia's forces in the Soviet Far East still possessed a three-to-one superiority over Japanese dispositions in Manchukuo and Korea, but for the first time since the Siberian expedition, the relentless drive of the Soviet Union toward absolute military supremacy seemed to be faltering.

Planners considering war with the Soviet Union had always had to consider how best to safeguard Japanese interests in North China, the southern flank; now suddenly the Marco Polo Bridge incident seemed to be pointing the way. Only a month before, Hideki Tojo (then Chief of Staff of the Kwantung Army) had clearly summarized the two most obvious alternatives. In a telegram on June 9, 1937, to the army vice-minister, Yoshijiro Umezu, and the vice-chief of the General Staff, Kiyoshi Imai, Tojo argued: "Judging the present situation in China from the point of view of military preparation against the Soviet Union, I am convinced that if our military power permits it, we should deliver a blow first of all upon the Nanking regime to get rid of the menace at our back. If our military power will not permit us to take such a step, I think it proper that we keep a strict watch on the Chinese government so that they do not lay a single hand on our present undertakings in China until our national defense system is completed." The Marco Polo Bridge incident seemed positively to invite the blow against the Nanking regime.

More important, the Japanese thought operations would be restricted to an area where the Imperial Army's supply lines were short, secure, and well controlled, and where the terrain was well mapped and well understood. In fact, the army had been preparing for operations in North China at least since 1932, in order to be ready to protect their nationals should anti-Japanese feeling turn violent. After the creation of Manchukuo, the Peking–Mukden Railway was equipped with an exclusively military telegraph, extra sidings, and large marshaling yards at Shanhaikuan. In the summer of 1936, a mechanized brigade was stationed south of the Great Wall, just outside Shanhaikuan, where in the summer artillery units practiced entrainment. In 1936, when the China Garrison was increased to 5,600 men, the Japanese took over barracks formerly occupied by the British at Feng-t'ai, strategically sited near the junction of the Peking–Tientsin Railway, thus controlling Peking's access to the sea; pressure from the local Japanese commanders forced the removal of the Chinese Thirty-seventh Division, entrusted with the protection of this junction. The speed of the Imperial Army's concentration of troops after the Marco Polo Bridge incident showed beyond a doubt that the staff work was already in place.

The last link in the chain of reasoning leading to war was Japan's assessment of the enemy as weak and divided, an uneasy mélange of Nationalists, provincial warlords, and Communists. They had only contempt for the Chinese. Lord Lytton, Britain's delegate to the League of Nations, reported the opinion currently prevailing in Japan: "China is not a civilised state, but a chaotic amorphous mass whose government is powerless to maintain order. Communism is rampant there, and the country is prey to the depredation of the armies of rival war lords, red communist armies and roving bodies of bandits." Not surprisingly, the Japanese thought that the war would be brief; Army Minister Sugiyama advised the Emperor that it would be over in a month.

As the days passed after the first flurries around the Marco Polo Bridge, both sides began moving reinforcements to the area. Now Chiang Kai-shek showed his hand by moving crack Central Army divisions north toward Peking. The increasing belligerency of his public pronouncements had the effect of building a pro-war consensus in Japan. Civilian groups now began hailing the prospect of war as a "golden opportunity" to settle the outstanding differences between the two countries.

These differences had been sharply identified the previous month, when the Chinese ambassador to Tokyo and the Japanese ambassador to Nanking had issued mutually recriminatory statements. The Chinese had insisted that the pro-Japanese regime in the demilitarized zone south of the Great Wall should be dissolved, that all Japanese garrisons in North China should be recalled, and that Japan should cease her unrestricted flights over North China—all these measures to be preconditions of the discussion of Japan's economic complaints against China. The Japanese were equally adamant that economic considerations came first.

Now was the time to cut the Gordian knot. Both the major political parties and most of the leading industrial, commercial, and financial bodies throughout the country threw their weight behind the government's declared intention to prepare for serious resistance should the Chinese continue to show a "lack of sincerity."

As July wore on, war fever gripped Tokyo. Beds were moved into the offices of the Army Ministry and General Staff so that staff could be constantly available. Reinforcements began to pour into North China from farther afield—first from Manchukuo and Korea, then from the home islands. The prime minister, Prince Fumimaro Konoe, called a special meeting of provincial governors on July 15 "to make known to the entire nation the true meaning of the sending of troops." Soon the press began speaking of "the necessity of teaching the Chinese a lesson." Japanese residents in China were evacuated from remoter regions and the navy General Staff instructed Admiral Hasegawa's Third Fleet "to take guard positions to protect Japanese residents at various important cities in China"—precautions taken too late to save the Japanese residents of Tungchow, who were massacred by a mob in July.

On August 11, the newly appointed director of military intelligence,

General Masaharu Homma, said that the massacre at Tungchow had caused within the army "less anger and resentment than the treacherous attack on a company of soldiers [in the early days of the fighting] at one of the gates to Peking." Nevertheless, the army felt itself to blame for Tungchow, and Homma added though there would be no "revenge," the victims had not been "sacrificed" in vain and they would be "avenged." With the Tungchow episode emphasizing the virulent anti-Japanese feeling elsewhere, all Japanese civilians were ordered out of South and Central China—with what proved to be the fatal exception of Shanghai.

Arrogance and utter contempt for the Chinese fighting man blinded most of the High Command to the strategic pitfalls of war with China, and their potentially devastating consequences for Japan's long-term security. The only officers who spoke out in warning were those who still had their eyes on the vision conjured up by Tetzusan Nagata—that Japan might one day be equipped for total war. Ishiwara cried out that war in China would be a quagmire, into which Japan's hopes would sink to oblivion. But he could not hold back the tide, and by mid-September he had been cast out of power into his own oblivion.

From the total-war perspective, by September 1937 Japan was sliding toward disaster, caught up in a war that had already cost over 12,000 dead and injured, and little better prepared for an extended campaign than she had been before the Russo-Japanese War. From now onward, until August 1945, the army would be existing hand to mouth— seeking resources to meet the needs of present conflict, no longer able to prepare for successful war in the future. In this condition, its leaders would make decisions not on the basis of rational calculations by an intellectual like Nagata, but with the desperation of a man drowning.

21

TO THE GATES OF
NANKING

Within eight weeks of the incident at Marco Polo Bridge, there were 200,000 Imperial troops in North China, sixteen divisions grouped as the North China Area Army under General Hisaichi Terauchi. From the beginning, Japanese unit commanders carried with their staff papers a booklet entitled "Criticism of China at War," containing directives for combat. In the attack, never hesitate simply on account of superior Chinese numbers; in the pursuit, rapidity and daring were essential; as for the retreat, this was something "never undertaken as a result of Chinese pressure." The Imperial Army was to be praised for its "accurate understanding of Chinese psychology" by no less a man than General Alexander von Falkenhausen, senior German adviser to Chiang Kai-shek. But this "understanding" was rooted in five decades of contempt for Chinese military power, and Japan would ultimately pay heavily for her blindness to the new face of the Chinese fighting man.

On July 27, the North China Garrison Army, reinforced by units of the Kwantung Army, put into effect their careful plans to drive the

Chinese from the Peking area. The task was not as difficult as it might have been. While the Japanese concentrated their forces, the Chinese had remained divided and unprepared; they had no organized plan of resistance, and troops were widely scattered. "No attempt was made at any concentration, or allotment of defensive areas, and troops of various divisions were hopelessly mixed up." Any troop concentrations the Chinese did achieve were promptly bombed, while a powerful Japanese combined column swept around the north and west of Peking to Wanp'ing, pushing unresisting Chinese forces before it.

On July 28, a brigade of 8,000 men under General Shozo Kawabe moved to attack the Nanuan Barracks some eight miles south of Peking. Kawabe's strategy was eloquent of his disdain for the enemy. He attacked from the south at 4:20 P.M., shelling the barracks with 4.2-inch howitzers—and almost immediately, General Chao Teng-yu, who had only about 1,000 men, decided to evacuate his trucks and artillery to Peking to assist in the defense of the city itself. They set off in an extended, undefended column, and halfway to Peking drove straight into the ambush Kawabe had prepared for them. The column was annihilated, and General Chao and his Chief of Staff were caught by machine guns in their open-topped staff car, trying desperately to overtake the column. With the occupants already dead, the car came finally to rest in the tangled remains of some dead pack ponies.

The Chinese made some semblance of resistance on the twenty-ninth by launching a counterattack against the Japanese barracks, the East (railway) Station, and the airfield at Tientsin. Conceptually, it was a shrewd blow aimed at the hub of Japanese communications in the area; in practice, it was feebly executed with insufficient force. And then it was too late, for the next day saw the arrival from Shanhaikuan of the Suzuki mechanized column: 400 trucks, 3,000 men, 4 field batteries, and 50 tanks. Linking up with Kawabe's unit, this powerful force pushed across the Yunting River and southward for a mile to Changhsiengtien, finally securing all the crucial road and rail bridges into Peking.

Up to this point, Peking itself had not been attacked; but now, encircled and cut off from the sea and the south, without hope of relief, the defenders simply abandoned the city. For a while, the victors hesitated. Suzuki's column did pass through the outskirts of Peking as it redeployed north on August 3–4, but Kawabe and his triumphant troops did not make their formal entry until August 8. An occupation that was to last for eight years, almost to the day, had begun.

The redeployment of the Suzuki Brigade was in many ways more significant than the occupation of Peking. Its aim was to concentrate a large enough force to succeed where Prince Te had failed in November 1936, and carry out the annexation of Inner Mongolia. This was one of the Kwantung Army's most cherished ambitions and the army had always intended to achieve it by force.

The key to Inner Mongolia was domination of the Peking–Suiyuan Railway, and along the railroad the advance proceeded. By August 9, elements of the Suzuki and Kawabe units (together with the Fifth Division under Lieutenant General Seishiro Itagaki, newly arrived from Hiroshima) had reached Nankow, a village some twenty-five miles northwest of Peking, and were confronting their first opposition: troops of the Chinese Central Army augmented by units recently withdrawn from Peking. The Chinese were well dug in, but after twenty-four hours of Japanese shelling they withdrew. The real challenge still awaited the Japanese.

Nankow lies on the plain just outside the mouth of the pass through the mountains flanking Peking. The pass itself is virtually a ravine, never more than four hundred yards wide, with precipitous cliffs on either side. Having advanced some three miles into this killing ground, the Japanese realized that they had far too little force at their disposal, and paused to await reinforcements. As soon as these arrived, they were thrown into costly frontal attacks, which after six days had only pushed the Chinese back about a mile, to a small village on the spur of the Great Wall. Here they stuck, and in resorting to the obvious but time-consuming tactic of an outflanking movement into the mountains, the Japanese were tacitly admitting that this was a stronger foe than they had thought. The flanking movement itself presented few problems; only a single Chinese blockhouse stood in the way, and when it was taken and communications cut, the Chinese in the pass pulled back and the Japanese column continued unchecked.

Coordinated with the attack along the railway was a second thrust by a Kwantung Army detachment south to Kalgan, a city on the Peking–Suiyuan Railway to the west of Nankow. This force, commanded by General Tojo himself, combined Japanese and Mongolian troops, a reminder of the territorial ambition of the Kwantung Army. By August 24 they had taken Kalgan; after consolidating their hold, they pushed on. By September 14, the strategically important town of Tatung, lying on the main route south into Shansi province, was in their hands, together with "a considerable amount of booty."

By November, the Kwantung Army's dream of an autonomous

Inner Mongolia was on the verge of becoming reality. On the twenty-first, the slice of land north of the Great Wall and bordered by Outer Mongolia and Manchukuo was proclaimed the Federation of Mongolia and the Border Territories. On December 8 the state apparatus was inaugurated at Kalgan, with a "Federal Committee" under a Japanese "Supreme Adviser" responsible for developing industry, finance, and communications. Inevitably, Manchukuo took the lead in developing its neighbor's commerce. The Kwantung Army also worked hard to cultivate nationalist fervor among the seven million inhabitants of the new state, to counter Soviet infiltration from Outer Mongolia; the document that proclaimed the Mongolian Federation, though written in Chinese and Japanese as well as Mongolian, was dated "the 732nd Year of Genghis Khan."

This new puppet state was just the first of many signs of Japan's intention to separate North China from Nationalist rule. While the two-pronged attack on Nankow and Kalgan was still in progress, preparations were already being made to strike south from Peking. But before this operation could begin, Chiang Kai-shek snatched the initiative away from Japan by switching the principal arena of combat to Central China. This he did at a stroke, by threatening the only Japanese community remaining in the south—in Shanghai, at the mouth of the Yangtze River.

The Yangtze was Chiang Kai-shek's heartland. His regime was funded by the magnates in Shanghai, and the route west to his capital at Nanking was defended by his German-trained Central Army divisions with their "Hindenburg Line," extending south from Kyiangyin on the Yangtze to Wusieh and from the southern shore of Lake Tai to Hangchow. If he had to fight Japan, then here lay his best chance. Even Shanghai itself suited him better as a battleground than the plains of North China: The 1932 fighting had shown both sides how Japan's advantages in tanks, artillery, and aircraft were partly neutralized there.

After his Sian "conversion" to the idea of the united front against Japan, Chiang set about improving his chances by strengthening the infrastructure of trenches, forts, and pillboxes in the Shanghai area, and even moving into the zone demilitarized by agreement after the 1932 fighting. By June 1937, these preparations had the Japanese consul-general expressing anxiety over the safety of the 30,000 Japanese in the city. After the incident at Marco Polo Bridge, the anxiety level rose as the Chinese hastily began erecting barricades and deployed two crack divisions within easy reach of the city.

Local tension combined with the events in the North to make

confrontation inevitable. Two Japanese were murdered and within four days full-scale fighting was in progress. In the British view as of December 14, 1937, the facts showed "that at all times up to the crucial date of August 12th the Japanese were anxious to avoid getting involved in difficulties at Shanghai and that the outbreak of hostilities was precipitated by the military preparations made by the Chinese prior to that date." But wherever the blame lay for the original flare-up of violence, it was Chiang's determination to use it to threaten the Japanese community in Shanghai, and so lure the Imperial Army out from North China, that made the Yangtze the scene of some of the bitterest fighting of the twentieth century.

The army had failed to anticipate trouble in Shanghai; no soldiers had been sent there, and the brunt of the initial fighting was borne by the Imperial Navy, as it had been in 1932. On the Chinese side were some of the flower of Chiang's army, three German-trained and German-equipped divisions "advised" by Alexander von Falkenhausen; on the Japanese, 8,000 marines of the "Special Landing Force," thoroughly trained in urban warfare. On August 14, two divisions of army troops earmarked for North China—the Third and the Eleventh—were diverted south to relieve the beleaguered marines, who for nine days held out in savage street fighting with their backs to the sea, a testament to their training and to the constant barrage of shells from Japanese warships moored on the Whangpoo and Yangtze. So close in were these ships and so desperately important was their firepower that the Chinese pushed forward men with the heaviest deployable weapons available—knee mortars—to try to check them.

Naval cover notwithstanding, memories of 1932 and awareness of the pillboxes now reinforcing the suburb of Chapei persuaded the commander of the Shanghai Expeditionary Force, General Iwane Matsui, not to feed his men in behind the embattled marines, but to land on the Chinese flank. The sites chosen—at the port of Woosung and at Liuho, along the Yangtze about twenty-five miles northwest of Shanghai—were precisely those used for the landings in 1932, and were held and defended by the Chinese. It was crucial to Chinese success that the invaders be repelled.

At around five A.M. on August 23, the landings began. The moon was bright, and at the central landing points the army took heavy casualties, which would have been heavier had the Chinese had more than machine guns and mines available. At Woosung, the landings were virtually unopposed and the invaluable wharves were captured intact.

The logistical advantage this gave to the Imperial Army was a grave blow to Chiang's hopes of victory on the Shanghai front, and several hundred Chinese soldiers were executed for their cowardice.

Other Chinese units fought harder, and the various Japanese landing forces did not link up until about September 3. But from then on, they drove the Chinese steadily back until the front line was some ten miles inland. At this point the Japanese thrust faltered because the Chinese had moved out of range of the Imperial Navy's guns. Now the army required its own artillery to break through the net of pillboxes and defensive fortifications, but deployment and supply were almost impossible. The terrain given up by the Chinese was a mass of intersecting drainage and irrigation canals, paddy fields and swamps, and devoid of cover—at a time when the Japanese, who had initially only carrier-based planes, had not achieved local air superiority.

By the end of October, Matsui was hopelessly bogged down. A major obstacle facing him was Soochow Creek, a stream between sixty and a hundred meters wide, which ran east–west through Shanghai; it had a moderate current, and flat banks on either side. Lacking sufficient artillery, Matsui could not stop the Chinese from deploying troops in forward positions, with concentrations of reserves in the rear ready to counterattack, and this made crossing the creek extremely hazardous. On November 2, he made the attempt on a frontage of five hundred meters under cover of smoke. Fifty tanks bombarded the Chinese position from a range of between four hundred and a thousand meters, helped by artillery and bombs from forty planes. But this was not overwhelming firepower, and Chinese artillery survived to destroy the troop-laden pontoons on the river, while with bayonet charges their infantry swept the banks clear of survivors. On the following day Matsui dispersed his troops: The crossing was attempted at three points on a twelve-kilometer front with smoke, artillery, and air bombardments, and this time succeeded, though at the cost of 30 percent casualties.

Chiang committed his main strength to containing the Japanese in as confined an area as possible, knowing that if he were to be pushed back he had fixed defenses on which the enemy could exhaust their strength. However, Shanghai is built on the northern edge of a blunt peninsula formed by the Yangtze River in the north and Hangchow Bay in the south; this situation gave the Imperial Army scope for amphibious landings behind Chiang's lines. When, in the second half of October, the High Command shifted priority from North China to the Shanghai front, they made troops available for this obvious tactic.

Ultimately Chiang's forward strategy rested on his ability to maintain a perimeter defense to repel such landings, while keeping the Japanese tied down on the Shanghai front. But as Napoléon had pointed out, a perimeter defense is really good only for smugglers; and the Woosung landing had already pierced the line. Worse was to come.

While Chiang had ensured that the Yangtze was heavily defended, Hangchow Bay had been officially labeled by Chinese defense experts as an "unlikely" place for a landing. The coast there was flat and indeterminate; because of fishing-net stakes and sandbanks, ships could get in no nearer than two miles from the coast; the tide in the area ran at a ferocious five knots; the beaches were flat and exposed, and behind them stretched a treacherous landscape of salt marshes, paddy fields, and creeks.

But here the army decided to land. By dawn on November 5, some forty transports had carried the troops of the Tenth Army under Lieutenant General Heisuke Yanagawa to within two miles of the coast. The assault troops transferred to landing craft, while the bulk of the force was carried ashore in converted fishing boats.

One private remembered: "It was pitch dark on deck. We passed over the ship's side and entered a boat. The swift-running tide astonished us. Filled to capacity with soldiers, the whole fleet of [ninety] boats started together for the beach. We expected to hear bullets flying around us at any moment, and so a light machine gun was fixed in the bows, and all of us crouched down low. We were almost piled on top of one another in that narrow boat, and legs and feet became cramped and sore. We struck the bottom, but it appeared we were still in the middle of the sea. We all went over the side and found that the water came over our knees, and our feet sank down in the mire. . . ."

This private was unlucky: Machine-gun nests raked his platoon until the guns of the support ships knocked them out. But many of the landing parties met no resistance at all. Luck was on the army's side. The old Chinese units had just been replaced, and the newcomers were more concerned with finding food than with defending a torrid, uninviting coast. So the Japanese were able to land and organize three and a half divisions behind the principal Chinese line—and their arrival precipitated, on November 9, a wholesale withdrawal of the defenders west toward Soochow, fifty-odd miles to the west of Shanghai.

The success of the landing had severely demoralized the men of the Chinese Central Army, who already had behind them ten weeks of cruel street fighting in which they had brought total Japanese casualties to over 40,000, with 9,000 killed. By the second week in November, their tight thirty-mile cordon around northwestern Shanghai had become an eighty-mile arc from Hangchow Bay in the south to the Yangtze in the north. Then, at dawn on November 13, General Matsui pulled the Thirteenth Division out of Shanghai and, in a swift operation using the easy loading facilities of the Woosung wharves, landed them twenty miles behind the retreating Chinese near Plover Point, upstream on the Yangtze's southern bank.

At Plover Point the world saw the first tactical use of what had until then been a Japanese secret weapon: the Military Landing Craft Carrier (MLCC). The captain of a British freighter on the Yangtze saw the MLCC "disembarking a large number of the smaller type of [landing] craft. These emerged in quick succession alternately from the fore and aft ends of the main side door on the side of the ship. . . . The craft appeared from inside the ship on two gantries, and were supported by a wire sling to bow and stern. . . . Immediately on being waterborne, they made off for their respective transports to embark a load of troops." The appearance of the MLCC sent a ripple through Western military-intelligence circles because, as the army equivalent of an aircraft carrier, the MLCC gave Japan the capacity for force projection into Southeast Asia on an entirely new scale.

The Plover Point landing, coupled with the deployment of motor torpedo boats on Lake Tai, was particularly effective because it directly threatened the escape routes from Shanghai by road, rail, and river. The Chinese panicked, and Chiang's careful strategy for an unyielding retreat to the prepared defenses of the "Hindenburg Line" was abandoned. With tanks and artillery, with aircraft and with naval gunboats on the Yangtze, the Japanese pursued them west.

The road to Nanking and to the generalissimo himself lay open. For Matsui, now Commander in Chief of Japan's newly created Central China Expeditionary Force, the temptation to push on was irresistible—but the order to advance did not come. On November 3, a peace initiative sponsored by Vice-Chief of Staff Hayao Tada had begun, through the medium of the German ambassadors to Tokyo and Nanking. The terms of peace, including the creation of a demilitarized zone extending south of the Yunting River, and a Nationalist-Japanese partnership against the Communists, were not actually presented to Chiang until November 5. Time was needed to consider and negotiate the terms—but time was running out for Tada and the others who cried restraint, who found themselves locked in a battle as fierce as that on the Yangtze with those who wanted to expand the war.

The debate over whether or not to advance to Nanking laid bare a fundamental flaw which had developed in the character of the army since the nineteenth century. From being simply the executor of policy decided largely by others, the army, through dedicating itself to preparing Japan for total war, had come to take a profound interest in formulating as well as executing policy. But the new interest was not supported by a new system or institutional framework. The army might now be capable intellectually of deciding its own destiny; but organizationally it was still the servant of others.

Such was the personal dynamism of men like Nagata and Araki that organizational frailties were concealed to some extent. The one an effective consensus builder, the other the head of a powerful clique, both were clear in their minds as to what needed to be done, and under their direction the Imperial Army could make policy purposefully and with relative efficiency. In their different ways they acted as clearinghouses for the masses of conflicting opinions rising from every section of the General Staff and Army Ministry and the independent commands on the mainland—assembling, focusing, filtering, integrating, analyzing, interpreting. Had either Nagata or Araki been army minister when the shots were fired at the Marco Polo Bridge, it is quite possible that war would never have developed.

Without this kind of dominant figure, policy-making in the army was haphazard in the extreme, determined on the one hand by temporary coalitions of officers in the Tokyo High Command and on the other by the preemptive action of officers in the field. General Yanagawa, for example, used his field command to try and enforce his view of policy by ordering the Tenth Army to advance on Nanking. This was immediately countermanded by Tada, who repeated his prohibition to Matsui. Neither general disobeyed this direct order, but a cabal of officers in Tokyo who wanted Nanking captured then proceeded to work on Tada to persuade him that his order reflected bad policy.

This was not conspiracy or insubordination; there was no secret about the identity of the expansionist officers. They were sincere in their views—and in the Imperial Army, sincerity was always allowed a voice. As it happened, events on the mainland played into their hands. The landings at Hangchow Bay and Plover Point had been very successful, successful enough to encourage those who wanted to advance—but not enough to convince Chiang that defeat was inevitable. During November the peace initiative gradually withered. On December 1, Tada capitulated and gave the order to move on Nanking; on December 2, Chiang also gave in and agreed to discuss peace—twenty-four hours too late to save his capital.

The Nanking decision illustrated not only the method of policy-making, but its sinister weaknesses. So wide was the spread of the consensus required for action that no one person had a sense of responsibility for what eventually happened, though later an individual might accept personal credit or blame. In effect, Japanese army policy-making was a "system of irresponsibilities," lacking accountability and potentially irrational. And because they were made jointly, decisions tended to reflect the general characteristics of the group. As all the members had been through the same process of indoctrination at Ichigaya, stressing the importance of the attack, the consensual system tended to ensure that army policy was weighted toward action.

The method was also very slow. In the case of Nanking, it had taken nearly a month to make the decision in favor of a campaign that was to last only twelve days—militarily, a disastrous delay. A swift pursuit might have broken the back of Chiang's military strength for good; instead the commanders' vacillation allowed many of Chiang's troops to escape.

Escape, that is, from Nanking. The city itself is a trap, built in the elbow of the Yangtze where the path of the river turns from its westerly course to the south. By November 25, wholesale evacuation of the civilian population was in full swing. By the twenty-eighth, most of the civil and military government officials, including both service ministers, had gone. Not even Chiang Kai-shek stayed. On December 8, his private plane carried him, with his "noisy wife," beyond Matsui's reach to Hankow.

On November 26, the defense of Nanking had been entrusted to General T'ang Sheng-chih, the Chinese director of military training. At his press conference he appeared to be "dazed if not doped," and advised all foreigners to leave the city. The next day he announced his intention to "defend Nanking to the last man." His first task, to rid the city of the disorganized bands of provincial troops, was achieved by about December 5, after which the only soldiers remaining in the city were his own defense force of around 22,500 troops. These were issued with special yellow armbands with the Chinese characters for "Defense Corps" printed on them; for a week up until the actual Japanese assault, no soldiers other than the wounded and those in possession of the yellow armband were allowed into the city.

All the city gates were heavily barricaded with sandbags and large balks of wood; machine-gun redoubts were built along the walls; underground telephone wires were laid. But these preparations did nothing to raise morale. Some 60 percent of Nanking's police force deserted; doctors and nurses abandoned hospitals and patients, and the system for the reception and care of wounded arriving from the front broke down. "The scenes of suffering and misery among these casualties stranded on the railway station and on the wharves along the Yangtze were piteous beyond description."

General Matsui's strategy was to advance with his main strength directly on Nanking from Shanghai along the southern bank of the Yangtze, making occasional forays to the north. At the same time he sent one division to loop south and west and cross the Yangtze upstream of Nanking to cut the retreat by river. In ten days these forces covered 140 miles across the low, rolling hills; here, as in the main advance, the extreme mobility of the Japanese infantry, and its high degree of mechanization (at least by comparison with the Chinese forces), reaped huge rewards.

Matsui's troops were under orders to fire on all shipping on the river. Unfortunately this included American and British vessels, which had been ferrying their nationals upstream to relative safety. The Japanese had been notified of the concentration of foreign vessels, but the authorities failed to inform all the Japanese commanders concerned. Through what Japanese leaders immediately realized was a disastrous excess of zeal, British and American ships were attacked. The U.S.S. *Panay* was sunk and one crewman on the H.M.S. *Ladybird* was killed.

By December 8, when Chiang made his exit, the sound of heavy artillery could clearly be heard within the doomed city. That day Matsui ordered General T'ang to surrender by noon on the tenth. T'ang's response was to order the houses outside the city walls to be burned; gradually Nanking was encircled by a ring of fire.

22

A CARNIVAL OF DEATH

With flames rising around Nanking, Matsui ordered the attack to begin at two P.M. on December 10, 1937. Less than forty-eight hours of aerial and artillery bombardment was enough to convince General T'ang that resistance was useless. By early afternoon on the twelfth, the rout had started and the soldiers who had been fighting outside the walls began streaming in. At dusk T'ang and his senior officers boarded their waiting launch and headed up the Yangtze. As the news broke that their commanders had abandoned them, the defenders of Nanking, orderly until then even in defeat, panicked. To be caught by the Japanese, as they knew only too well, meant certain death.

With the single thought of crossing the Yangtze to safety, they converged on the gates in the north wall. But as their numbers grew, the roads became a ferment of struggling soldiers, pack animals, carts, honking cars, entangled in the debris of an army in full flight. On the evening of the twelfth the Japanese began shelling this mass of humanity. Trapped in the suffocating crush of the narrow gap left in the

Chungshan Gate, the fugitives could not escape the fire that now broke out. Around the gate, houses and vehicles blazed, killing hundreds of men and forcing others in their terror to push on until the gate was filled three feet high with the corpses of their comrades.

In desperation, many climbed onto the high walls and, with the smoke and flames, screams and artillery shells behind them, tried to lower themselves down with puttees and pieces of clothing tied together. Many fell and were killed. Those who made safety joined the rush for the flotilla of junks and sampans moored on the south bank. The crews could not hold the soldiers back, and many of the junks sank or were capsized by the sheer weight of numbers, killing, some said, thousands. Hundreds of others drowned trying to cross on improvised rafts.

On the thirteenth, the Japanese advance troops were in the city, shooting anyone who ran from them. The following day the main force entered with tanks, artillery, and trucks, and then began what has passed into history as the Rape of Nanking. Into the New Year, the occupying troops murdered, raped, looted, and burned the city in a frenzy of evil that still stands as the icon of Imperial Army bestiality.

"It is now Christmas Eve," wrote the American director of the Nanking Refugee Committee.

> In these two short weeks we here in Nanking have been through a siege; the Chinese army has left defeated and the Japanese Army has come in. On that day Nanking was still a beautiful city we were so proud of, with law and order still prevailing; today it is a city laid waste, ravaged, completely looted, much of it burned. Complete anarchy has reigned for ten days—it has been a hell on earth. Not that my life has been in serious danger at any time—though turning lust-mad, sometimes drunken, soldiers out of houses where they were raping the women is not perhaps altogether a safe occupation; nor does one feel too sure of himself when he finds a bayonet at his chest or a revolver at his head and knows it is handled by someone who heartily wishes him out of the way. For the Japanese Army is anything but pleased at our being here. . . . They wanted no observers. But to have to stand by while even the very poor are having their last possession taken away from them—their last coin—their last bit of bedding (and it is freezing winter), the poor rickshaw man his rickshaw; while thousands of disarmed soldiers who had sought sanctuary with you, together with many hundreds of innocent civilians, are taken out before your eyes to be shot or

used for bayonet practice and you have to listen to the sound of the guns that are killing them; and while a thousand women kneel before you crying hysterically, begging you to save them from the beasts who are preying on them; to stand by and do nothing while your flag is taken down and insulted not once but a dozen times, and your own home is being looted; and then to watch the city you have come to love . . . deliberately and systematically burned by fire—this is a hell I had never before envisaged.

The Rape built up to this kind of intensity over a number of days. Despite Japanese casualties now aggregating 52,000—18,000 dead— the expeditionary force of 50,000 Japanese soldiers did not burst on the city as a vengeful mob out of control. There was order of a brutal kind when they first arrived. The official priorities were to secure the city, to find food, fuel, and shelter from the cold, to destroy the industrial and commercial sectors of Nanking, and to kill any Chinese soldiers remaining in the city.

The troops proceeded toward these objectives in an orderly fashion, with platoons under their officers fulfilling instructions—though these were harsh enough. Units with trucks would break into shops, godowns, offices, and houses, loot them, and then set them on fire using special chemical strips. The executions, too, were regulated at first. On the fourteenth, there seems to have been a genuine attempt to isolate Chinese troops who had gone to ground in the city. But on the fifteenth, the Japanese started rounding up men whose hair bore the ring of a tight hat, or whose hands were callused—criteria that took in soldiers, certainly, but also many other manual workers.

Allied and Axis civilians marooned in Nanking at the occupation organized a refugee zone, the sanctity of which they attempted to preserve using the authority of their respective nations. The chairman of this international committee, Herr Rabe, an employee of Siemens, used his swastika insignia to great effect: "He thrusts his Nazi arm band in their faces and points to his Nazi decoration, the highest in the country and asks if they know what that means. It always works." At the height of the Rape, he sent Hitler a telegram asking for his personal intervention to restrain the Japanese.

The moral courage of these civilians was extraordinary. Time and again, unarmed, they confronted Japanese soldiers and stopped attempted rapes and beatings. But sadly, their zone was only partially successful. "That evening came word that soldiers were taking all our

1,300 men in one of our camps near headquarters to shoot them. We knew there were a number of ex-soldiers among them, but Rabe had been promised by an officer that very afternoon that their lives would be spared. It was all too obvious what they were going to do. The men were lined up and roped together in groups of about a hundred by soldiers with fixed bayonets; those who had hats had them roughly torn off and thrown on the ground, and then by the lights of our headlights we watched them marched away to their doom. Not a whimper came from the entire throng. Our hearts were lead."

For the first ten days, this "official" Rape continued unabated, but soon the pall of smoke in the sky from the burned and looted houses, and the episodic machine-gun and rifle fire of the execution squads moved from center stage to become the backdrop to a worse horror as gangs of soldiers drunk and out of control began roaming the streets.

The first rapes were reported on the sixteenth. During the previous night an estimated thousand women had been raped. "One poor woman was raped seven times. Another had her five months infant deliberately smothered by the brute to stop its crying while he abused her. Resistance means the bayonet. The hospital is rapidly filling up with the victims of Japanese cruelty and barbarity. Bob Wilson, our only surgeon, has his hands more than full and has to work into the night. . . . Wilson reported a boy of five years of age brought to the hospital after having been stabbed with a bayonet five times, once through his abdomen; a man with eighteen bayonet wounds; a woman with seventeen cuts on her face and several on her legs."

Sunday, December 19: "A day of complete anarchy . . . The American Flag was torn down. . . . I went to the house of [X] of our Embassy. The Flag was still there, but in the garage his house boy lay dead; another servant, dead, lay under the bed. . . . The Military have no control over the soldiers. . . . We were told that seventeen military police had recently arrived who would help in restoring order. Seventeen for an army of criminals of the most depraved kind . . ."

Monday, December 20: "Vandalism and violence continue absolutely unchecked. Whole sections of the city are being systematically burned. . . . All Taiping Road, the most important shopping street in the city, was in flames. We drove through showers of sparks and over burning embers. Further south we could see the soldiers inside the shops setting fire to them and still further they were loading the loot into army trucks."

Tuesday, December 21: "The problem of feeding is becoming serious. Some refugees, hungry, began rioting at the University. Our coal will soon be finished. . . . The Japanese have sealed all supplies of coal and rice."

Wednesday, December 22: "Firing squad at work very near us at 5am today, counted over 100 shots. . . . Went . . . to see 50 corpses in some ponds a quarter of a mile east of H.Q. All obviously civilians, hands bound behind backs, one with the top half of his head completely cut off. Were they used for sabre practice?"

Thursday, December 23: "At noon, a man was led to HQ with head burned cinder black—eyes and ears gone, nose partly—a ghastly sight. I took him to the hospital in my car where he died a few hours later. His story was that he was one of a gang of some hundred to be tied together, then gasoline thrown over them and set afire."

Friday, December 24: "Military say there are still 20,000 soldiers in the Zone and they must get rid of these 'monsters.' I question if there are a hundred left."

And so it went on. Seven soldiers spent their Christmas in the University Bible Teachers Training School incarcerating and raping the women. On December 31, the terror abated—"for the first time no cases of violence were reported for the night"—because the soldiers were preparing for the New Year: an important festival for the Japanese, but one of dread for the city, "for it means more drunken soldiers." Well into January the atrocities continued, burning out as the front-line troops were redeployed and as the army faced up to the horror it had perpetrated.

The German representatives on the International Committee estimated that twenty thousand women had been raped in the first two weeks; the British thought eight thousand. But the bare statistics, grotesque though they are, convey little of the terror that must have possessed women trapped with nowhere to hide within Nanking's walls. The norm was gang rape. Soldiers would arrive at private houses, university halls of residence, nurses' dormitories, and hospitals, threaten the men present while they raped the women, and then take away women for further molestation at their barracks. The tally of rapes will only ever be an estimate. In March 1938, the Nanking University sociology department carried out a survey of all residents in the city and environs on behalf of the International Committee. Already they found most families unwilling to admit that their women had been abused by Japanese soldiers.

Many women were murdered, the majority of them elderly, staying in their homes to guard their possessions. Many others had been taken away, the survey found, for service as "waitresses, laundry work, or prostitution."

A different kind of inhumanity was shown the refugees, who had everything they possessed stolen from them—pigs and hens, blankets and food, even the clothes they were wearing. Again and again soldiers would come back to rob, and when there was nothing left, would beat them or break up the shelter they had built, leaving them destitute and partially stripped to suffer in the cold of winter.

Figures published later by the Chinese authorities claimed that 250,000 people were murdered in Nanking. The International Committee, however, felt constrained to comment in the preface to the Nanking University report that "statements have been published by China putting upon Japan an exclusive and exaggerated blame for the injuries to the people of the Nanking area." The committee itself also blamed banditry in rural areas, which actually surpassed the violence inflicted by the Japanese.

But it is hardly surprising that the figures should have been inflated. The Rape of Nanking, because it was witnessed by Westerners, gave Chinese propagandists an unparalleled opportunity to consolidate the lead they were building up over Japan in Allied public opinion. As news of the atrocities blazed from the front pages, Japan's reputation was already in decay; feeble attempts to justify the sinking of the *Panay* collapsed as army, navy, and Foreign Ministry sources in America violently contradicted one another. The intensive, widespread bombing of civilian and military targets that started in the latter part of December 1937 further hardened public opinion in the West. To General Matsui's assertion that Japan was "sacrificing so much for the sole purpose of establishing peace in the Far East," or General Homma's remarkable claim that the Imperial Army had not shown conduct "notably inferior" to that of the armies of the First World War, the only responses were outrage and cynical amusement.

In America in particular, revulsion at Japanese behavior produced significant and damaging results by underpinning the "moral embargo" that by the autumn of 1938 had effectively stopped sales of American aircraft to Japan. The British, whose ambassador in China had been strafed and badly wounded by a Japanese fighter, responded to Washington's inquiry in December 1938 as to the action the British were taking over Japan: "In certain cases firms have been discouraged from accepting orders from Japan, although this was not justified by exigencies of British rearmament."

It is simply not possible to establish exactly how many Chinese were killed during the horrors at Nanking. No one knows how many soldiers were actually in the city, because the figures are confused by the wounded of other earlier battles and by soldiers streaming in from outside. No one knows how many tried to escape, or how many were successful. No one knows how many refugees from Shanghai had stayed on in Nanking only to face the Japanese again.

One Englishman writing from Nanking on January 10—"a few hasty jottings amid rape and bayonet stabs and reckless shooting"—put the number killed at ten thousand, adding: "Most of my trusted friends would put the figure much higher." A reading of the eyewitness reports suggests a figure of around fifteen thousand murdered (not including the wounded) for the defense force and the stragglers defending outside the walls. To this must be added the number of civilian residents killed; the Nanking University survey tabulated 3,250 of these, of whom 74 percent died "outside military action," plus the 4,200 men taken away for labor.

Too close a focus on the Rape of Nanking obscures the fact that it was only one tidemark left by a sea of atrocities inflicted by the Imperial Army on the Chinese. This figure of some 22,000 murdered within the city walls or marched from the city to be machine-gunned jumps enormously when murders in the environs of Nanking are included. In an area about the size of Delaware, or of Devon and Somerset combined, 84 percent of the male population up to the age of forty-five were killed, a total of 31,000 men—to whose deaths must be added an unknown number of prisoners and escapees cut off by the Japanese forces looping south and west of Nanking. In addition, the Japanese troops destroyed buildings, animals, farming implements, grain stores, and crops in the fields. Only the winter wheat survived, because "like some of the younger women, it was hidden in the ground during the worst period."

In the months following the incident at the Marco Polo Bridge, the Imperial Army was guilty of both controlled and indiscriminate war crimes all over China. Eyewitness reports are uniform in struggling for words to describe the horror.

Pingting, captured at the end of October: "The first week of occupation by the conquering army will always be an indescribable nightmare." Later the town was turned into a base for supplies "sending soldiers north and south, east and west. . . . Those coming from the front would rest a day or so and rape and loot. . . . Anyone whose clothes had any resemblance to those of a soldier was killed on the spot without questions."

At T'ai-yuan: "Many civilians and gatekeepers shot on sight on suspicion of being plain clothes soldiers. Salvation Army gatekeeper shot dead." On November 8, 1937, many soldiers "shot down on leaving the city to the south and west although leaflets dropped from aeroplanes had advised them to leave and not resist."

Wuhu, taken by the troops looping south and west: "During the first week of occupation, the ruthless treatment and slaughter of civilians and the wanton looting and destruction of the homes of the city far exceeded anything ever seen in my 20 years experience of China. . . . The soldiers seemed especially to seek Chinese women for violation."

K'ai-feng, 1938: "Women dare not go on the streets as they are attacked even in broad daylight in their homes, or dragged off the street to their homes by Japanese soldiers. I never guessed I would ever come into contact with such awful wickedness that is occurring day by day. Multiply anything you have heard about them by twenty and it is only half the truth. Small boys are kidnapped and along with young women are shipped by train to the east. . . ."

At Kihrien: Two thousand civilians were killed at the occupation. "I never thought I should witness such suffering and live."

Christmas 1937 in Hangchow: "Our beautiful Hangchow soon became a filthy, battered, obscene place . . . a city of dread . . . robbery, wounding, murder, rape and burning. . . . Japanese Military Police did their best to help us foreigners but for the city at large there was no help."

Terror in the towns and villages of the Yangtze Basin combined with the destruction of homes, foodstocks, and the means of making a living to create a sea of refugees. Seven hundred fifty thousand of the one million people of Nanking fled before the Imperial Army. Perhaps as many as 20 million Chinese were forced to seek survival elsewhere, and no one knows how many died.

Fifty years on, the horror of these early months of the war with China can be seen as an integral part of a wider pattern of atrocities committed by Japanese troops until 1945, an explanation of which is attempted in chapter 46 of this book. The Rape, while it forms part of this pattern, is particularly revealing in itself, because at Nanking some of the features common to all Japanese atrocities stood out in such stark relief, lurid threads in a dark skein.

The first is the element of strategic calculation amid the havoc. As early as 1935, some analysts were suggesting that Japan wanted to prevent uncontrolled Chinese industrialization and that "she would prefer to create chaos in the Yangtse region rather than allow China to develop industrially and politically." The events of December 1937 bore out this claim. While there was considerable looting in North China, which the Japanese intended ultimately to incorporate into the Empire, they did little damage to potentially valuable industrial resources. But the Yangtze Basin was "devastated." Along the lines of advance, "almost all human and animal life disappeared and a very high proportion of all buildings were destroyed." In Shanghai, machinery in Chinese factories, even good working machinery, was dismantled and shipped to Japan as scrap metal; in Nanking, 80 percent of commercial and industrial buildings was destroyed. Tojo's words echo: "We should deliver a blow first of all upon the Nanking regime to get rid of the menace at our back."

The same kind of strategic reasoning appears to have justified in Japanese minds the "no prisoners" policy. Matsui's army—which was obliged to live off the land—could not have coped with prisoners, and would therefore have had to choose between caging them until they starved to death or releasing them. But if given their freedom, they would either have become guerrillas continuing the fight (as early as November 1937 irregulars were operating near Shanghai), or self-seeking bandits, who would equally have to be suppressed in the end. Immediate execution, on the other hand, reduced Chiang's stock of trained soldiers and had the added advantage of demoralizing his remaining troops—ensuring that when they were threatened, their resolve would break.

But official murder and looting had the inevitable effect of undermining discipline. Not all soldiers were involved in indiscriminate violence (though no one appears to have disobeyed orders to kill prisoners) and even in Nanking some officers tried to restrain their men. But such attempts were meaningless amid the carnival of death. The internal mechanisms of army discipline, which had been so apparent in the prewar army, were retuned by the fact of ordered (and therefore condoned) violence. The consensus now permitted rape, theft from Chinese, and what appears to have been indiscriminate violence based on vengeance for dead comrades.

Where internal discipline failed, only external restraint remained; and here the Imperial Army had a major problem. As an organization, the Imperial Army was not designed to fight in urban areas. A specialist force geared to operations in the relatively depopulated wastes of eastern Siberia, it had no training in the tactics of urban warfare, nor in relations with a large civilian population. In an army of specialized, highly motivated troops unlikely to desert in the face of the enemy and garrisoned in more remote areas, there was less need for the usual control functions performed by military police in Western armies. Accordingly, the number of police remained relatively small, and their purely disciplinary role was diluted by a number of other tasks.

The unlimited opportunities for looting and rape, and the absence of external restraints—there were seventeen military police in Nanking, though later ordinary soldiers were given a policing function—allowed Japanese troops to indulge the tastes of soldiers everywhere. The backgrounds of most of the soldiers, however, probably made these demands more urgent than those of soldiers of Western industrialized countries. Looting by individual soldiers seems to have been motivated at least partly by filial duty, a desire to relieve the extreme poverty of families back home. Rape may also have been condemned less severely at the platoon level because these young men came from a cultural background in which women were considered lesser beings, their thoughts and feelings totally disregarded, their rights not even conceived of.

As the war progressed, the indictment against the Imperial Army stretched far beyond murder, rape, looting, and the wanton destruction of property. The war against insurgents in North China assumed genocidal proportions; medical and biological-warfare experiments were carried out on civilians and prisoners of war; China again suffered widespread propagation of opium and narcotics; the national means of production was expropriated; terrorists and racketeers found themselves Japanese employees in numerous schemes of terror. Cumulatively, the Chinese people were to suffer far worse even than the wretched inhabitants of Nanking in those first weeks of horror.

23

ON TO HANKOW

In August and September 1937, after capturing Peking and starting the drive west through the Nankow Pass to Shansi, the North China Area Army pushed on south along the main rail lines. But this advance, unlike the western thrust, had to be suspended when three divisions were taken for the Shanghai front and one for Manchuria. The halt came, conveniently, at the Yellow River near Tsinan on the border of Shantung province. Here it might well have paused anyway, in view of the strong possibility that Han Fu-chü, the governor of Shantung, might defect to the Japanese cause.

Instead, as the Japanese waited, Governor Han obeyed Chiang Kai-shek's orders to destroy Japanese property. In Tsingtao, the local authorities made a sudden purchase of 10,000 gallons of kerosene and carried out the destruction on December 29 and 30. Given Japan's major investments in Shantung, it was imperative for the province to be taken swiftly, and the North China Area Army resumed its advance. This time Han chose not to fight (for which Chiang had him executed) and the Japanese occupation, including Tsingtao, was unopposed.

Now operations in China came to a halt. The campaigns of 1937 had consumed vast quantities of men and munitions, and the Rape of Nanking had by itself been a breakdown in discipline serious enough to shake the military effectiveness of the mainland armies. Time was needed to consolidate, replenish, and repair the war machine before it could drive on. In addition, the army had to cope with the political repercussions of the Rape. Japan's image had been polluted in the eyes of the world, and the shame and fury of senior figures within the civilian establishment, including the Emperor, precipitated a shake-up in the upper echelons.

During this period of the army's temporary incapacity, a fierce debate broke out among the High Command. General Tada, the vice-chief of the General Staff, who had ordered Matsui to stop the advance on Nanking, again tried to call a halt to the fighting in China. He repeated Ishiwara's warnings that China was a quagmire to suck Japan down, but his stance gained little support. Even the civilians in the government were throwing their weight behind the expansionists in the High Command. On January 16, Prime Minister Prince Konoe publicly declared that as "the Chinese National Government blindly persist in their opposition without regard for the miserable plight of the Chinese people or the tranquillity of East Asia . . . the Japanese Government will cease to deal with that Government."

As the chief secretary to the Cabinet explained, the Chiang regime represented neither the Chinese state, nor the nation, nor the people. Japan, he claimed, was committed to a "holy war . . . for the sake of lasting peace in the Far East," and consequently there had been no declaration of war. The real reason was that formal declaration would trigger American neutrality laws, denying Japan access to the materials she required to prosecute the campaign.

Pressure from those in Tokyo committed to Konoye's "no dealing" declaration, vociferously supported by staff officers in China itself, ensured that not only would the war continue, but that the lull in operations would be short. The Imperial Army had taken control of the northern portion of the Peking–Nanking Railway and most of the Grand Canal, a thousand-mile waterway running from Tientsin to Hangchow Bay; now, with the addition of the port facilities at Tsingtao, it had excellent logistic capacity to embark on the next stage of the war: the capture of Hsuchow.

Hsuchow was a natural target, lying midway between the areas occupied by the armies in Central and North China, and the more tempting because in Chinese history, its fall traditionally signaled the demise of the ruling dynasty. In twentieth-century strategic terms, the city was a crucial rail center, standing at the crossroads of the Peking–Nanking line and the Lunghai Railway (running west from the southern nexus of the Shantung Peninsula six hundred miles to Sian) and its capture would augment Japanese control of the Chinese transportation network, giving them rail and canal links between the two fronts.

By mid-March, the North China Army was moving south, and it looked as though the Japanese desire for a final confrontation was to be fulfilled. Running west along the Lunghai Railway from Hsuchow, Chiang had constructed a defensive line comprising concrete pillboxes, machine-gun emplacements, and rough field defenses, with additional fortifications around Hsuchow itself. Anticipating the Imperial Army's next move after the fall of Nanking, Chiang had pushed large forces into this defensive zone, presenting the Imperial Army with an opportunity to force a decisive battle, which might at last destroy Chiang's main fighting capacity.

But the Japanese mainland armies failed to coordinate their plans, and the Central China Expeditionary Force, instead of circling to the west to cut off the Chinese escape, or even advancing on Hsuchow, halted after the capture of P'eng-p'u. Meanwhile, the North China Army pushed on rapidly and by the beginning of April had broken through the southern Shantung defenses on the Lin-ch'ing–Lin'i line and was approaching the rural town of Taierhchwang, the last major obstacle to be overcome before reaching Hsuchow forty miles to the southwest.

Many military analysts were highly critical of the strategy adopted by the Japanese—fast-moving mobile columns out of touch with each other and having "lines of communication of great length and almost entirely dependent on single track railways." This "rash strategy" was predicated on frontal attacks against Chinese fixed defenses, followed by rapid pursuit when the Chinese withdrew. So far, it had been largely successful. However, by the end of March 1938, Chiang had ordered a general change in his army's strategy. No longer would they meet the Japanese head-on as they had in the north and in Shanghai; instead of positional warfare, the Chinese would now adopt a policy of mobile warfare, giving ground in the center and attacking the flanks of the Japanese as they advanced. In addition, Chiang planned to use guerrillas to cut lines of communication, attack isolated garrisons, and steadily wear away Japanese forces.

Chiang's first opportunity to test his new strategy came at Taierhchwang. For the assault, the North China Area Army had pushed the Tenth

Division—whose supply line now extended over two hundred kilometers—into a narrow salient with orders to attack the town head-on. The Chinese commander, General Li Tsung-jen, reacted by deploying only light forces in Taierhchwang itself while moving the bulk of his troops to the east. As the Japanese battled desperately to dislodge the defenders of Taierhchwang, who held on heroically even when three-quarters of the city was in Japanese hands, the Chinese cut the rail and road links with the north. At dawn on April 6, General Li threw all his forces into an onslaught on the exposed Japanese flank. Luck favored the brave. A single shot ignited the Tenth Division's fuel and ammunition reserves, and by dusk the Japanese were encircled and isolated in the salient their rapid advance had created. During the night of April 6–7 many of them escaped, but for those who remained there was no hope. Itagaki's Fifth Division desperately attempted a rescue but was held off by the forces to the north. The trapped men, some 8,000 of them, were annihilated. The Chinese had won a resounding victory—a Tannenberg, their propagandists trumpeted—but in humiliating their enemy, they made him all the more implacable.

On the day following the Taierhchwang humiliation, the High Command formally sanctioned the escalation that was to drag Japan into the quagmire of war in which she would wallow until her final defeat in 1945. Tokyo ordered the capture of Hsuchow—which fell on May 19—and then an advance into western China along the Lunghai Railway, the first stage in the campaign to take Chiang's new refuge, Hankow.

Hankow lies four hundred miles up the Yangtze from Nanking, forming part of the Wuhan cities, a major industrial conurbation. By mid-1938, Wuhan was the last industrial center remaining to Chiang, and British intelligence echoed Imperial Army thinking when it concluded: "If he hopes to survive he must defend Hankow with everything at his disposal. Chiang will fall with the fall of Hankow."

The east–west axis of the Lunghai Railway offered an ideal approach to Hankow. The key was Chengchow, at the intersection of the Lunghai and Peking–Hankow railways. With Hsuchow secure, the army could now advance west to Chengchow, consolidate, and then turn south to Hankow using their dominance of the port and railway network to transport and supply their mechanized forces. But Chiang and his German advisers had anticipated this obvious stratagem. On the night of June 20, Chiang breached the dikes holding back the Yellow River near Chengchow. Swollen with the melted snows of Mongolia and heavy with loess, the powerful river plunged southeast, returning to its natural course, which it had followed until being rerouted in the nineteenth century. The wall of water that night swept away large sections of the vital Lunghai Railway, and within days huge areas of eastern China as far south as the Yangtze were under water. For the Chinese in the path of the flood, there was no warning, and millions were made homeless while perhaps as many as a million drowned or died from malnutrition or disease as a consequence of the flooding.

With this single action Chiang showed that he, too, understood the meaning of total war. For victory over the Japanese he was prepared for his country to pay any price, endure any suffering—including that inflicted by Chinese upon Chinese. As his armies retreated they destroyed communications networks, crops and buildings, machinery and factories, blighting their own land to deny it to the Japanese. The Japanese press even detailed instances of bacteriological contamination of drinking water by the retreating Chinese.

Dynamiting the dikes at Chengchow took the strategic initiative away from the Imperial Army. As with his decision to switch the fighting to Shanghai, Chiang now forced the Imperial Army to mount the main thrust of their attack where he was strongest, in Hankow—along the Yangtze, where river defenses were in place and the marshy ground harbored cholera and malaria that would kill and debilitate more Japanese than did Chiang's troops in combat.

Already, with the help of General von Falkenhausen, Chiang had spent five months preparing his defenses, and each step of the campaign was bloody and unyielding. By the second week in October 1938, Japanese columns were at last converging on Hankow from the north, east, and south. Until then the enemy they had faced was mainly provincial Chinese troops, as Chiang had held back his German-trained divisions in Hankow. The bloodiest battle of the war seemed in prospect, but now, as the ring tightened, Chinese resistance stiffened—and suddenly broke. On May 13 the evacuation began; Chiang flew upriver to his new capital, Chungking. On the twentieth, Japanese troops entered the undefended city.

The bishop of Hangchow, whose own city had been raped by Japanese troops at Christmas 1937, wrote to a colleague: "We feel sorry for you people and the thought of an occupation of Hankow. Tell everyone you see to go. . . . Women should not stop within a hundred miles of the city." But the lessons of Nanking had been learned. In Hangchow itself, order had been restored by bringing in *kempeitai* and setting up Korean and Japanese brothels. The entry into Hankow was made not by the victorious troops, but by a strong detachment of military police, and the troops themselves were accompanied and supervised by senior officers.

The reason for Chiang's abrupt withdrawal lay only partly in the closing Japanese ring. More compelling was the success of the second strand in Japan's military strategy for 1938—namely, to deny foreign military assistance to Chiang. One crucial source of aid had been Nazi Germany. Hitler saw China as a bulwark against communism, and feared that the outbreak of war would throw China into the Soviet camp. In terms of containing communism, the war was indeed a disaster, and before the fall of Nanking, German diplomats had attempted to mediate a peace.

But Japan, too, had long been seen by Hitler as a buffer against communism and conventional Soviet military might. Besides motivating Chiang's arrest at Sian at Christmas 1936, the Comintern resolution of July 1935 calling for a united front against fascism had also prompted the Anti-Comintern Pact of November 1936 between Germany and Japan. In the published text of the pact, the fiction was maintained that the Comintern was separate from the Soviet state. But annexed to it was a secret protocol, in which Japan and Germany agreed to "immediately consult on measures to safeguard their common interests" in the event of attack by Russia.

By early 1938, indeed, Hitler had come to regard Japan as something more than simply an ally against the Soviet Union. His stated policy of seeking *Lebensraum* would inevitably lead to conflict with Britain; his plan—suggested to him by Ribbentrop—was to overstretch British power by simultaneously threatening her interests at home, in the Mediterranean, and in Asia. In the Mediterranean he would work through Mussolini; in Asia Japan was to be the surrogate, and Ribbentrop himself contacted his personal friend, General Hiroshi Oshima (through whom the Anti-Comintern Pact had been concluded), to suggest alliance.

As far as the China War was concerned, Nazi plans for Japan produced immediate results; in February 1938, Hitler recalled Falkenhausen and curtailed arms sales to China. But these gestures of goodwill were only partial: Falkenhausen remained with Chiang long enough to advise breaching the dikes at Chengchow and to do the staff work for the defense of Hankow. And German arms manufacturers were reluctant to give up a lucrative market; German munitions continued to find their way into Chiang's arsenals, exported from Germany under the Swedish flag and then transshipped at Singapore onto Indian-flag vessels for delivery to Chinese ports.

Chiang needed every weapon he could find. By May 1938, China's pre-war stocks of war matériel were exhausted and she was being sustained only by imports from abroad. At this stage the Soviet Union was her major supplier. In the first two years of the war, Moscow gave Chiang roughly $250 million in credit—represented by a thousand planes, tanks, trucks, and fuel, together with pilots and military advisers. None of this assistance was passed on to Mao's troops, nor did Stalin directly aid the Chinese Communist Party, except by training a few Red Army specialist troops. In the period up to December 1941, America, France, and Britain contributed roughly the same amount, becoming more generous in 1940 and still more so after the passing of the Lend-Lease Act in 1941. Chiang also purchased munitions from international arms dealers abroad, including those in Belgium, Czechoslovakia, and Hungary (where he bought 22.9 million rounds of small-arms ammunition); these munitions were shipped to China along with the Allies' supplies.

The world had no sympathy for Japan's war in China, and the Japanese government could not stem the flow of weapons to Chiang by diplomacy, so the army was left to develop its own stratagems. One method was to erode Chiang's ability to pay the suppliers. Japan now had vast tracts of industrial China under its control and had established "autonomous governments" in both North and Central China under the aegis of the local army commands. In addition to maintaining law and order and essential services, these puppets provided a convenient front behind which the Western powers trading in China might be persuaded to pay over customs duties on imports to the Yokohama Specie Bank and not to the Nationalist government. By the end of 1938, Chiang had been deprived of 70 percent of China's principal hard-currency income.

A second method was to prevent delivery of the munitions. One supply line ran from Siberia; Japanese intelligence agents disbursed "considerable bribes" trying to promote the embryonic Mongol Islamic autonomy movement in the Ningsia and Kansu provinces and thus cut off one access route for Soviet aid. Ultimately, however, the scheme failed, as Japan could not afford to supply the arms the revolutionaries required.

In the south, there were a number of land supply routes into free China: by road from Burma via Lashio to Yunnan, and from Hanoi by rail to Yunnan or by rail and road to Nanning. But none of these could match the handling capacity of Chinese ports; even Soviet supplies came through Hong Kong by British ship from Odessa on the Black Sea coast.

To stem the seaborne trade in arms, the Imperial Navy intercepted shipping in the South China Sea on the basis of information gathered by Japanese intelligence agents posted to Port Said to monitor shipping through the Suez Canal. More effectively, they conducted a series of amphibious attacks on the major Chinese ports—Amoy in May 1938 and Swatow in June 1939—that denied both the arms imports and the Chinese exports that earned the currency to pay for the arms. Swatow, before its capture, was receiving thirty ships a week.

One port Imperial forces could not capture was the British Crown Colony of Hong Kong, through which came the bulk of Chiang's supplies, some 100,000 tons a month. From Hong Kong they were taken by rail to Canton and then north to Hankow. Japanese efforts to close this route began with the bombing of the Hong Kong–Canton Railway on December 27, 1937, and through 1938 the severity of the raids increased.

As in the North, the Imperial Army also hoped to exploit a local autonomy movement in the South, and their agents spent 6 million Chinese dollars in bribes to encourage an uprising in Canton. "Persons dissatisfied either with the central government or present provincial regime and bandits were to rise. . . . Fires were to be started in various places and panic generally caused . . . while plotters were to attempt to seize military HQ and other arms depots." In support, the Japanese intended to bomb Canton and land troops, but the whole exercise came to nothing: Chiang was informed and a hundred of the conspirators summarily executed.

Having failed to bribe the Cantonese into deserting the Nationalists, the army attempted intimidation and began bombing civilian targets in the city. Between May 28 and June 6, 1938, 876 residents of Canton were killed and 2,142 wounded. By September, the intimidation had succeeded to the extent of closing 60 percent of businesses and reducing the normal population by two-thirds.

It could not, however, stop the supplies getting through, and with the costly Hankow campaign still in progress the High Command decided to cut the route by capturing Canton. It was a bold, almost desperate stroke. Militarily it required sending a force into an isolated and apparently well-defended area. Diplomatically, the repercussions would be immense: Japan would be venturing far beyond her previous sphere of interest and challenging the image of white, and particularly British, supremacy in Asia.

Accordingly, the High Command poured resources into this operation to guarantee success. The task force comprised the vaunted Fifth Division together with two reserve divisions, plus strong naval and air support. They chose as their landing site Bias Bay to the east of Hong Kong, where there were good beaches for the landing and easy access to two roads leading to Canton. The build-up and final rehearsal took place in the Pescadores, and the actual landing took place by moonlight on October 12, 1938, the Military Landing Craft Carrier again playing a vital role. The local pirate fraternity operating out of Bias Bay acted as guides and, undetected, the task force quickly grouped and pushed on to Canton. Within ten days they had taken the city, choking off vital supplies to Chiang's beleaguered troops in Hankow. By November 3, the Pearl River defenses had been cleared and the river opened to navigation by Japanese shipping.

What Chiang Kai-shek termed "an unpleasant surprise" startled the Japanese, too, by its ease. But army propagandists turned the reason for Japanese success to good advantage: They produced a leaflet purporting to be a dialogue between two Canton residents who were wondering why they had not been better defended:

A: What has the money we subscribed to the salvation of the country been used for?

B: The whole amount of this money has been put into someone's private purse. It was really my foolishness to have trusted such government leaders.

As for Chiang Kai-shek, the leaflet continued, soon he would be seen "packing up his luggage and fleeing to foreign countries." But this was wishful thinking. After Hankow, Chiang had withdrawn to Chungking on the upper reaches of the Yangtze, a city impregnable to Japanese land attack. With his nucleus of German-trained divisions he remained not only the political leader of China, but also militarily the most powerful warlord. The coalition around him stayed united, and the resistance went on.

24

PLUNDER AND NARCOTICS

By the end of 1938, China was in the grip of the most horrific war in its modern history. The Japanese advance naturally followed the main lines of communication—road, rail, and river; along these lines almost all human and animal life disappeared, and a very high proportion of all buildings were destroyed. The lower Yangtze area alone produced some 20 million refugees, many of whom died of malnutrition or exposure, or in the great flood of June 1938, when the dikes were breached.

Showing extraordinary resilience, by April 1939 some farmers were returning. But without seed or livestock their survival was precarious. Of their families, there was no sign, since "the incessant demand of the Japanese troops is for women, and no female between six and sixty is safe." In Nanking, some streets were designated off limits to troops in an attempt to restore confidence and some semblance of normality to the blighted city.

But for the China of the late 1930s, normality was a memory. In

240

the countryside, Japanese army columns over 20,000 strong, complete with 10,000 pack animals, would pursue their steady progress like a locust swarm living off the land. The troops continued to rape and loot at will, while in those towns and cities where the depredations of the conquering troops were brought under control (partly by the provision of army brothels), the average Chinese found that his energies and wealth were at the mercy of a new breed of exploiters—both military and civilian overlords.

Expropriation was wholesale. Some of it was a rapid response to pressing needs; factories were stripped and machinery pillaged for scrap to produce armaments to continue the war. But on the grandest scale was a carefully planned strategy for the economic development of North and Central China—a plan to take over and develop Chinese industry for Japan's benefit, through huge conglomerates, on the lines of the South Manchurian Railway Company.

The North China Development Company, successor to a South Manchurian Railway subsidiary, was floated on the Tokyo stock exchange in 1938. The prospectus issued by the Japanese government was unashamed in its imperialist language: The combination of North China's resources and the capital and technology of Japan would make it possible to "enrich and stabilize the life of the Chinese people and convert them to pro-Japanese views . . . [and] . . . enrich the supply of our resources for national defense." The capital raised by the stock flotation was not used to purchase assets from the Chinese. The required mines, factories, and businesses dealing in strategically valuable commodities—coal, salt, iron ore—were simply requisitioned by the army and then handed on, the Chinese owners receiving compensation in the form of shares in the new Japanese enterprise.

Aiding and abetting the army were the thousands of Japanese civilians who rushed to share in the easy pickings from China. The expatriate population increased from around 90,000 in mid-1937 to over 500,000 by the spring of 1941. Under the aegis of a paternal military administration, these immigrants took priority in jobs, in access to transport for their goods, in supplies. Many were honest, but floating on the tide was a scum of opportunists, crooks, and extortionists.

In Nanking, a year after the Rape, Chinese shop owners had the choice of operating on a fifty–fifty basis with Japanese or paying protection money. Many shops did not reopen, their burned out interiors instead providing stabling for the Imperial Army's horses. Even the carpetbaggers, the Japanese traders and profiteers whom the army allowed free travel on military transport, were leaving Nanking: "No good—nobody have any money." Instead they went on to Hankow, where in 1939 the Japanese population profited from a military policy of denying shipping rights on the Yangtze to other nationalities, including the United States.

In Shanghai, every day saw the shooting, drowning, beating, and general maltreatment of unarmed Chinese men and women by Japanese soldiers. From soldiers supposedly reined in after Nanking came acts of incredible bestiality. One member of the Shanghai Golf Club described how at lunchtime "yesterday, a young and drunken soldier, with rifle, looked in at the village just behind the Club . . . and called for women and drink. Fortunately, there were no women present, but they did have drink. The soldier consumed all that was put before him. . . . From this village he meandered to the village immediately to the left of our 16th green. As the news of his presence spread, all the younger women departed elsewhere for safety. . . . When he arrived at this village, the soldier enquired of three very old Chinese women, who were sitting together, if there were any young women about. Upon being told there were none, he immediately shot these three women dead from a distance of three feet."

Throughout the Shanghai area, the Imperial Army tightly controlled the population—overtly, by being forbidden to travel without a military pass, and covertly, through the links forged with immensely powerful secret-society bosses. One such link in 1938 was with an organization called the Green League, which had an immense following among the seamen and boatmen of the Yangtze Valley. Another was with the "obese and notorious" racketeer king Chang Yu-ching, who in December 1938 founded the Tranquil and Pure Society dedicated to "the salvation of China, the adoption of a policy of compromise with Japan, and the annihilation of Chiang Kai-shek." At the inaugural ceremony, in front of an altar decorated with the Rising Sun and the five-barred flag of Republican China, enveloped in clouds of incense, the membership took the oath and cheered for the enduring peace of the Orient, for the Imperial Japanese government, the Chinese republic and the reformed government. Chang Yu-ching had rendered assistance to Japan before, in the summer of 1937, when his enforcers had become symbols of terror; now the Shanghai municipal government braced itself for a new wave of violence and fear.

In North China, the story was similar. To Peking, which had a branch of the Tranquil and Pure Society, a war boom brought a veneer of prosperity—small compensation for a community living in constant fear of what they described as "drunken and licentious soldiery." They were treated with overt contempt by the army—"lorries and armoured cars tearing up and down the streets at appalling speed with complete disregard for human life. Every day or two the main thoroughfares are closed for an hour or more so that some Japanese civil, or more often military, potentate may drive from one point to another in becoming state." Native Chinese culture was under assault. The Temple of Heaven became a Japanese barracks; geisha houses and Japanese restaurants and shops cluttered the East City, and the night was "made hideous by glaring neon lights and twanging shamisen."

In Peking too there was expropriation on a massive scale, some of it simple theft. House owners were forcibly dispossessed; Chinese art was looted from private collections and valuable blackwood furniture shipped to Japan for sale. And as a symbol of Japanese dominance, the Nagoya Race Club bought Shanghai's Kiangwan Race Course.

But profits did not derive solely from occupied China. The divisions between "occupied" and "free" China were loose and indistinct, and there were few impediments to smugglers passing between the two. The Nationalists were eager to obtain scarce commodities from whatever source, and the soldiers of the Imperial Army traded actively with the enemy in all manner of goods, to an extent that seriously undermined the High Command's policy of isolating Chungking. The scale of the illicit trade was extraordinary; estimates for 1939–1940 ranged from $21 million to $120 million. And to the strategists planning Chiang's defeat, most depressing of all was the nature of the commodities some Imperial soldiers were prepared to sell—among them medicines, tungsten, and oil, strategic materials critical to the Japanese war effort.

Perhaps the single most glaring act of exploitation throughout occupied China was the deliberate revival of opium addiction and the propagation of narcotics. The principal objective was profit, and much of the money was used to finance clandestine schemes; but the opium trade was also a form of psychochemical warfare to debilitate and degrade Chinese nationalist resistance.

Opium was not a Japanese habit. Yamagata, Ito, and the other nineteenth-century rulers were well aware of the efforts of Western powers, particularly Britain, to promote the opium trade in China, and they took good care to avoid the same happening at home. There could be no vigorous nation-at-arms with a population in thrall to the poppy. This policy, for the home islands, continued into the twentieth century;

in 1938, for instance, there were only 3,600 known addicts, compared with 60,000 in the United States. The acquisition of Formosa, Korea, and the Kwantung Leased Territory, however, plunged the authorities into the thriving opium businesses already in existence there.

Within China, the opium empire had been targeted for extinction by Sun Yat-sen's Republicans, and such was their success that by 1917, the British minister in Peking was able to report that "China was at last on the verge of ridding itself of the opium scourge." But then Japanese traders discovered a ready market for morphine. In 1920 alone, almost a million ounces of morphine and heroin—made in Europe—were imported into China. By then, too, Republican China was fragmenting into warlord fiefdoms, and the warlords were only too aware of the revenue potential of opium. By the early 1920s poppy cultivation and opium addiction in China were once again on the rise.

The Imperial Army had made connections with the drug trade in the 1920s, possibly even earlier; but with the annexation of Manchuria in 1931, drug dealing took center stage. Not only did the new state of Manchukuo inherit the Young Marshal's drug industry, it also acquired the Russian trade in northern Manchuria, previously supplied from Siberia. In Harbin, formerly the center of the Russian trade, an addict could obtain a shot of morphine without ever having to enter one of the many drug emporia; he simply handed over a few coins through a hole in the wall and held out his arm for the needle.

A ready source of income was vitally important to the army. Manchukuo was founded on the anticapitalist sentiments expressed by many of the radical officers in the 1920s; there was no room for the hated *zaibatsu,* which consequently were not prepared to fund Manchukuo's industrialization—and without large-scale finance, it was difficult to create the industrial infrastructure that the total war strategists planned. Opium was seen as a way of filling the coffers; in 1932, the government of Manchukuo floated a 30-million-yen bond issue secured by the profits of the opium monopoly.

Under army guidance, the new state worked hard to boost the trade. Farmers were given cash incentives to grow poppies; supplies were hugely increased when the army took the prime opium-producing province of Jehol in 1933 (and increased again with the creation of the Federation of Mongolia in 1937). Profit did not come simply from the wholesale trade in opium, heroin, and morphine. The *kempeitai* and the clandestine and espionage agents of the army's Special Service Section operated their own opium dens while other enterpreneurs paid license fees for the privilege.

The ancillary vices of gambling and prostitution were also important profit centers in Manchukuo. According to one source, the state held the monopoly of the supply of Korean and Japanese girls. A teahouse owner could visit the offices of the monopoly and place his order; within two or three weeks the girls would arrive, to be paraded around the streets of Harbin or Mukden to drum up custom from among the residents, military and civilian. There were an estimated 70,000 Japanese girls in Manchukuo working in the brothels and teahouses on three- or five-year contracts. They came from peasant families who, hit by the Depression and crop failures and faced with starvation, had little option but to sell their daughters into this kind of servitude.

Manchukuo paid a high price for its cash profits in terms of the corruption and enervation of its bureaucracy; even the Emperor, Pu-yi, was an addict. Part of the problem was that the state could never gain full control of the drug trade in the face of well-entrenched interests dating from the 1920s, powerful gangs that ran their own black-market operations. The cost was human misery on a vast scale. In Mukden, the garbage heaps were littered with the corpses of addicts, gray-faced from the morphine, and usually naked, their clothes having been stripped from them by other addicts.

The Manchukuo army itself appears to have suffered badly from abuse of drugs (probably from the private suppliers). Users could also be found among the ranks of the Kwantung Army, though punishment for a Japanese found with drugs was severe. By and large the officer corps appears to have remained unsullied; their preferred diversion was drinking on a scale rarely seen in the home islands.

South of the Great Wall, between 1931 and the outbreak of war in 1937, the opportunities for profit from drug trading were less than they would have been during the warlord era. In taking up the banner of Sun Yat-sen, Chiang had committed himself to ridding China of the opium menace, and part of his ability to overcome the warlords had lain in taking control of the opium trade routes from western China and choking off the warlord's source of supply.

But opium was profitable to Western traders also—so much so that it served as a useful symbol of Western imperialism and thus as a target for nationalist sentiment. Chiang demanded the abolition of extraterritorial protection from Chinese prosecution of foreign nationals engaged in drug peddling—but the Western powers refused, afraid of even this small erosion of their treaty rights. Consequently, many foreign traders were able to continue the trade, to a more limited extent, from the protection of the international concessions throughout China. After 1931, drugs were smuggled from Manchukuo into North China; and after the 1933 policy decision to separate the five northern provinces from Chiang's regime, the trade was expanded.

The war in China finally ended Chiang's suppression campaign. Opium consumption was heaviest in urban centers, and by the end of 1938 most of these were controlled by the Imperial Army. Soon towns and cities that Chiang had cleared of drugs were once again infested. There were no opium dens in Nanking before the Rape, but within a year there were 50,000 addicts paying a total of $3 million a month for their drugs. In Peking the authorities had established or licensed 600 opium dens by 1940; in Hankow, 460; in Canton, 852. Opium sustained the puppet governments established by the army and was used by the army to pay off laborers, or by soldiers to pay their prostitutes.

Investigators into Japanese war crimes concluded that the trade in China proper was not exclusively an army interest, but was managed by the same official organization, the China Affairs Board, that Prime Minister Konoe had set up to oversee the "legitimate" exploitation of China through the development companies. It was big business; revenue from the drug trade in 1939 was estimated at $300 million—which appears to include income from Japan's participation in international narcotics trafficking. Shanghai, Dairen (in the Kwantung Leased Territory), and the Japanese concession in Tientsin were the largest distribution centers for illicit narcotics in the world. At their peak, Tientsin narcotics producers imported thirty tons of high-grade Iranian opium for processing in one year alone.

America was an easy target; by the early 1920s, the clampdown on the official sale and prescription of narcotics had stimulated a vast clandestine commerce. According to contemporary sources, the United States was "overrun by an army of pedlars who extort exorbitant prices from their helpless victims." Harry J. Anslinger, commissioner of the Federal Bureau of Narcotics, reported that smuggling was "rampant" on Japanese ships calling at American ports in the 1930s. In 1937, a League of Nations investigation into narcotics concluded that 90 percent of all the illicit opium and morphine in the world were of Japanese origin. In 1939, the American and British governments made a joint representation, "out of self-defence," to the Japanese government to bring the trade under control.

The onset of the Pacific War cut supplies from Japanese sources to Europe and America, ensuring a miserable four years for Western addicts. For Japan, the war meant severe oversupply capacity and loss of profits—so the export trade moved with the troops into Southeast Asia.

25

AT WAR WITH MAO

After the fall of Hankow, Chiang Kai-shek retreated with his government and some of his remaining German-trained elite divisions, upriver to Chungking, deep in China's vast, mountainous interior. "No amount of foreign aid can convert the babu-cum-coolie set up in China into a force that can defeat the vigorous Nipponese" was the conclusion reached by the British War Office—but for all its vigor, the Imperial Army did not have the logistical capacity to launch a ground offensive to crush Chiang. Instead, the army resorted to bombing raids of immense ferocity. In May 1939 over four thousand inhabitants of Chungking were killed.

Even from his western fastnesses, Chiang continued to maintain large forces at points along the two-thousand-mile front—over a million men in the Hankow region alone. While this meant sporadic and sometimes large-scale fighting, the Imperial Army had no opportunity to inflict the kind of conclusive defeat that could affect the course of the war. A grinding, bloody stalemate set in, not the stalemate of trench warfare or of opponents too evenly matched, but of a predatory animal unable to chew what it has bitten off.

As 1938 gave way to 1939, Japan needed economic and political strategies to replace military might. But here, too, were intractable problems. China was a developing country; the industrial and agrarian sectors were not integrated. Though industrial China was dependent on rural China, the reverse was not true. Therefore, though the Imperial Army had conquered all the significant industrial centers and the modern communications networks, Chiang retained agrarian China, a power base on such a huge scale that Japan could never hope to dominate it.

Such was the conclusion of the South Manchurian Railway Company's Research Division in their study, commissioned by the Imperial Army, "The Investigation of the Resistance Capacity of the Chinese." The principal author, Tsutomu Nakanishi, traveled to Tokyo to present his findings. "When they were finished there was silence. Finally a young staff officer asked, 'So then, what sites would it be best for us to bomb? I'd like to know the key points.' "

In its political strategies, too, the army lived a waking nightmare. The original intent had been to continue the policy followed since the end of the Ch'ing dynasty—divide and rule. Army strategists were confident that China could be dismembered. The Kwantung Army had established its Federation of Mongolia; in Nanking, amid the agonized aftermath of the Rape, General Matsui called into being a Central "Reformed Government"; and in Peking, the army set up the "Provisional Government of the Chinese Republic." But these creations failed to inspire confidence; they were too obviously collaborators. The North China administration, which consisted of some rather elderly pro-Japanese politicians brought out of retirement, immediately showed its true colors by announcing a policy of cooperation with Japan and Manchukuo, welcoming the Japanese forces who had come "to rescue the people of China from the oppressive yoke of Chiang Kai-shek."

But the army's political ineptitude was only part of the story. They were, in fact, wrong in thinking that it was still possible to divide China. Observed Winston Churchill in May 1938: "Japan has done for the Chinese people what they could perhaps have never done for themselves. It has unified them once more. General Chiang Kai-shek is a national hero among the most numerous race of mankind." This was an overstatement. The intelligentsia may have been united, but many of the peasants in areas under Nationalist control remained oblivious to events outside their villages, however portentous. Nevertheless, when it came to resisting the Japanese, Chiang's regime had sufficient centripetal force to pull together disparate elements in China that the Imperial Army had previously been able to manipulate.

If Japan wanted peace it would have to deal with Chiang or find another national government to take his place. In November 1938, in the aftermath of the fall of Hankow, the Army's Special Service Section organized a "Peoples' Conference" comprising "delegates" from all over China. The conference passed 143 resolutions acknowledging that Japan had "no territorial aims in China. They [the Imperial Army] have helped to form new regimes in North, Central and South China and now, as the government of Chiang Kai-shek is on the verge of ruin, the speedy establishment in its stead of a Central Government is imperative." And the aim of this central government was to "recover the foreign concessions and preserve the sovereignty of China"—among other methods, by abolishing "the unequal treaties imposed on China by the White races."

Empty words, perhaps, and yet behind the scenes just such a central government was being discussed, and with the greatest optimism. As a bolt from the blue, in December 1938 Wang Ching-wei, one of the few figures of genuine stature in the Nationalist Party, announced that he was abandoning the regime in Chungking to assume political leadership in China so as to come to terms with Japan. And while Japan, Wang Ching-wei, and the newly created puppet governments in North and Central China searched for a formula to provide an acceptable alternative government, the army set about further weakening the Nationalist regime.

The emphasis in 1939 was on cutting the flow of arms to Chungking, and on eroding the Nationalists' income. As a base for threatening the sea-lanes, the Imperial Navy occupied Hainan Island and also took the Spratly Islands, far to the south—a clear indicator of their desire to move into Southeast Asia. Within China, three key points were secured: the port of Swatow, and the important rail junctions of Nanchang in Kiangsi and Nanning in the deep south. The Nanning operation, like that against Canton, took the form of an amphibious landing followed by a thrust into the interior. Within ten days of the landing, the army had created a salient a hundred miles deep from the coast to the railway—a risky venture, but one that interrupted the flow of supplies via Haiphong and Hanoi in French Indochina, which after the fall of Canton had become Chungking's principal supply route.

The second part of the strategy was more sophisticated. Despite eighteen months of warfare and the loss of industrialized China, the

Nationalists had still managed to maintain their currency, the *fapi*, trusted and in circulation throughout China, a symbol of Chiang-centered nationalism. To establish genuine economic control, Japan needed to supplant the *fapi* and assume financial direction of China.

With these ends in mind, it created a Federal Reserve Bank, which issued its own currency and declared the *fapi* illegal tender. But public confidence in the Nationalist currency persisted. The British, who had played a major role in the 1936 currency reforms that had created this confidence in the first place, continued to give support, establishing a £10 million stabilization fund. This ensured that the *fapi*—unlike the federal currency, which was inadequately backed by specie—alone remained capable of exchange with foreign currencies; the Western powers, operating from their international settlements, continued to use it for trade, thereby enhancing general confidence.

In North China, where Japan's hopes of economic growth were highest, the intransigence of the Western powers—and their implied support for the Chiang regime—roused the army, and Chief of Staff Tomoyuki Yamashita, to fury. Britain, the largest trader in China, was the principal target of their wrath, and before long the North China Army was confronting the British in Tientsin. A crisis was manufactured by the Japanese demanding that the British release into their custody four terrorists who were suspected of murdering a pro-Japanese Chinese— and, more to the point, that the British refuse to allow Chiang Kai-shek to remove the silver specie he had deposited in banks in the British concession. The incident received wide publicity in Asia, with the help of German propagandists. Ultimately, Japan's attention was diverted by events elsewhere, but not before she had exacted from Britain a humiliatingly equivocal announcement acknowledging Japan's "special requirements" in security matters and undertaking to do nothing "prejudicial" thereto.

In Washington, the mood was one of disgust at Japan's aggression and Britain's conciliation—disgust so pronounced that Roosevelt gave notice of termination of the 1911 commercial treaty between America and Japan; the treaty's end meant harsh duties for Japanese traders in American ports. But this was not the end of the story. Four days after Hitler's invasion of Poland, Japan offered some "friendly advice" to all the European powers now at war: "Withdraw your forces from China." Lacking firm assurances of American support, British gunboats left the Yangtze in October 1939 and her troops marched out of Tientsin and Peking. The Union Jack still flew in Shanghai and the Burma Road—

Chiang's chief supply route—remained open, but for all in Asia to see, the sun was at last beginning to set over the British Empire.

The Japanese army's determination to control China's economy was a symptom of the desperate need for economic success in North China. Only months before, similar need and determination just across the Great Wall had produced a remarkable volte-face in policy. Manchukuo had originally been founded on the principle of state capitalism, and the Kwantung Army had banned the *zaibatsu* from participation. But the *zaibatsu* were Japan's principal source of finance, technology, and managerial skill, without which the new state could not develop. Alarmed by Manchukuo's economic stagnation, the army invited a major industrial conglomerate, Nissan, to fund and manage the country's development. Kwantung Army apologists might argue that Nissan was not one of the old *zaibatsu*, the real enemies of the people. Nevertheless, there had been a considerable climbdown from state capitalism in Manchukuo—underlining once again the army's need for partners in the search for military-industrial strength.

In North China, the army had relied on the *zaibatsu* from the beginning. Under the umbrella of the North China Development Company, *zaibatsu* ran the factories and mines expropriated by the military. In the spring of 1938, it seemed as though the "golden opportunity" presented to Japan by the shooting at the Marco Polo Bridge was to be realized. Chiang's military forces in North China had been dispersed and his political power eradicated. But the destruction of Nationalist power there had left a vacuum, which the overstretched Imperial Army could not fill, and on the scene came an insidious and dangerous enemy—one who knew the crucial importance to Japan of the economic exploitation of China, and was determined to frustrate it.

In 1938, Mao Tse-tung was forty-five years old, a "a gaunt, rather Lincolnesque figure," according to Edgar Snow. He was gaining preeminence in the Chinese Communist movement and his view of the style of communism suited to China had begun to prevail. His hope for revolution rested not with the industrial proletariat, in the Marxist-Leninist synthesis, but with the peasants—an irresistible power with which to encircle the cities and sweep away the forces of reaction. These ideas were developed over a decade of struggle against Chiang Kai-shek and, unfortunately for the Imperial Army, they also provided a perfect platform from which to challenge the Japanese occupation. The Japanese were in the cities, and Mao could kindle the flames of revolution and resistance around them.

Mao provided more than ideological leadership. He was also a strategist of genius, who created a coherent theory of guerrilla warfare. The foundation of his grand strategy was the creation of base areas within what was technically enemy-occupied territory, where his guerrillas could return for rest and replenishment, and where recruits and material support could be assembled.

At first, military units and cadres would infiltrate remote areas— usually in the mountains—link up with local Communist groups, and then begin to expand. They started with the advantage that, after Chiang's departure, the Communists represented Chinese nationalism, and built on this foundation by playing the role of friend and benefactor: eliminating local bandits, paying for food given them by the villagers, leaving women alone. The cadres were well trained, well educated, and highly motivated, "fish swimming in the masses of China"; gradually, as confidence increased, they moved into the next phase—political conversion, with Communist land policies proving irresistible. (The recipients of Communist propaganda were not always as grateful as they might have been. There was a saying current in front-line areas: "Nationalists—too many taxes. Japanese—too many killings. Communists—too many meetings.") From there it was a short step to political organization, and once properly established, these base areas were quite large autonomous units within China, governed by laws devised by the Chinese Communist Party. The oldest-established base area in the north, centered on Yenan, had 1,400,000 inhabitants.

Base areas played an important, if piecemeal, role in mobilizing the masses, but their prime function was to aid the military struggle. The CCP's monopoly of nationalist activism brought them a military windfall: recruits from Chiang's armies who had been dispersed by the Imperial Army and, though still resisting stoutly, were now operating as isolated units. The Red Army in North China grew quickly, from 80,000 in 1937 to 400,000 in 1940.

In the early fighting of the summer of 1937, the Red Army had linked up with Nationalist forces to resist the Japanese invasion. On September 25, 1937, Lin Piao's troops ambushed the supply train of Itagaki's Fifth Division in Pinghsingkuan Pass. The purpose of the attack was to capture weapons; but the Japanese not only fought to the last man, they managed, despite being at the bottom of a narrow defile under murderous fire, to destroy almost the entirety of the Fifth Division's munitions as well. "The enemy soldiers have enormous fighting ability," Lin wrote. "We have never encountered such a strong foe. . . . In combat training we still have a long way to go."

Usually, the Communist forces operated in units no bigger than a platoon. Small groups could move undetected through the tall kaoliang and the ditches of the North China plains, where concentrations might be spotted by reconnaissance aircraft. The units were virtually autonomous, out of contact with their divisional, or even their regimental, commanders for much of the time. Yet they worked to a pattern directed from the top. Thoroughly indoctrinated and motivated, and sharing a common education in guerrilla warfare, they were "an invincible iron army," in Mao's words.

In Yenan, Mao and the senior Communist hierarchy planned strategy and gave instruction in methods. Drawing on the writings of Sun Tzu, the Chinese classics (of which he was a keen student), and his own experience of warfare against Chiang, not least on the Long March to Yenan, Mao gave authoritative, down-to-earth lectures, practical prescriptions for successful guerrilla warfare against a superior enemy.

The Communists' surprise attacks and constant harassment of supply convoys and road and rail links pushed the Imperial Army onto the defensive for much of 1938. Lack of manpower meant that campaigns in Central China denuded garrisons in the North. During the Hsuchow fighting of spring 1938, Japanese garrisons at Peking and Tientsin were "forced to resort to subterfuges such as placing dummy sentries in important places to make the guerrillas believe them still occupied."

This was not, however, the first time the Imperial Army had been challenged by Communist guerrillas. In Manchuria, in the early 1930s, the Kwantung Army had crushed Communist insurgency by moving all bona fide villagers into "protected hamlets," burning their homes, and leaving the guerrillas to face the Manchurian winter without food, shelter, or support. Such a strategy meant uprooting farmers from their land and concentrating them at points far from their fields. Often the "protected hamlets" were unfinished when the farmers and their families were moved in, and many people so transplanted died of starvation.

In North China this policy would not work, thanks to the network of base areas; so as soon as troops became available after the fall of Hankow, the Japanese borrowed a technique that Chiang Kai-shek had used against the Communists, rolling them back with an inexorably advancing line of defended blockhouses. In addition, one technique used in Manchuria did prove effective farther south: employing Chinese bandits to hunt Communists and deter others. In Hopei the army used a "particularly bad organisation," the Huang Hsieh Chun, to create terror off the main lines of communication, burning villages indiscriminately and murdering women and children.

By the fall of 1939, Mao, faced with these ruthless measures, was losing the military struggle. But by then, the CCP had cost Japan dearly in terms of the troops they had been forced to deploy and, more importantly, in terms of political and economic disruption.

The Chinese Communist Party provided a nationalistic alternative to the Japanese puppet government in Peking, and through its guerrilla activities it rendered ungovernable areas outside direct Japanese military occupation. When the Peking government was installed, ten magistrates were dispatched to the local county towns to restore law and order. Six disappeared and four returned in terror, one with his hands chopped off. In August 1938, a year after the events at the Marco Polo Bridge, guerrillas occupied nine of the twenty-two districts of eastern Hopei.

Economically, the Communists were brutally focused. The North China Area Army, in its "Instructions for the Economy" of September 1937, identified its most important task as being "to begin establishing a solid base" to serve Japan's "long-term interests." The CCP objective was to sabotage communications and all Japanese economic plans and industrial expansion; to take or destroy rice and cotton; and to execute anyone trading with the enemy.

As early as October 1938 the guerrillas had prevented trains on the Peking–Hankow Railway from running by night. They intercepted convoys of lorries and any Chinese caught in possession of the Japanese-backed currency was shot out of hand. The Imperial Army had to stand guard over crops being harvested; in September 1941, two whole divisions were dispersed through Hopei and Chahar to prevent the harvests falling into guerrilla hands. The CCP infiltrated the cities, their agents encouraging a policy of passive resistance among the people. The Imperial Army, for example, was obliged to draft Chinese drivers for military transports, but these drivers would ruin new trucks within two weeks. Sometimes they would keep on loading them until the chassis collapsed; the story is told of a sixty-truck convoy that was totally wrecked when the leading vehicle stopped and every single one of the remaining fifty-nine trucks duly crashed into the one in front of it.

All over North China and in Shantung, Communist guerrillas attacked mines, factories, roads, and railways in a strategy of sustained disruption. "The grandiose Japanese plans for economic development cannot be put into effect," concluded British intelligence, "so long as she continues to hold only a small proportion of the country and so long as her lines of communication are perpetually liable to attack."

More importantly, as Joseph Grew, the U.S. ambassador to Tokyo, explained to Foreign Minister Hachiro Arita, there would be no international finance available under conditions of political instability and economic threat. In 1939, the Japanese government applied for a credit of 50 million Swiss francs from a consortium of Swiss banks—and although the application was supported by a guarantee from the German Oerlikon Group, the Swiss government refused permission. Nor would there be Chinese investment, not even from collaborators. "The Celestials," remarked one British intelligence officer, "are not in the least likely to capitalise concerns whose control is entirely out of their hands."

Guaranteeing Mao's success was the fact that Japan herself had little capital available for investment in China. Though the Japanese authorities regularly announced new enterprises capitalized at 10 million or 50 million yen, it was obvious, according to an economic intelligence report from the British Embassy in Peking, that "they have the greatest difficulty in laying hands on any ready cash. . . . One of the original aims of the China Incident was Japan's desire to exploit the iron mines in North Shansi, but up until the present, nothing has been done. Dr. Bidder, councillor to the German Embassy in Peking, has been negotiating for a joint enterprise in which Germany supplies machinery, but the agreement has fallen through because the Japanese Government could not put down US$365,000 in gold."

26

THE PRICE OF WAR

Mao's success ensured that the Japanese people would suffer, in material terms at least, almost as much as Chinese civilians. At the time of the incident at the Marco Polo Bridge, the Imperial Army had been fundamentally unprepared for any kind of war except a short campaign using already existing resources of men and munitions. Since 1931 there had been considerable growth in Japan's industrial base, though development had been patchy. While Japan had the capacity to construct the 64,000-ton leviathans of the *Yamato* class, the largest battleships ever built, she was not capable of producing small, reliable gasoline or diesel engines. Even before the Hankow campaign, armaments factories were working twenty-four hours a day and still needed a full year to complete orders already in hand. Shortages of skilled labor, plants, and machinery had limited Japan's capacity to supply her armies in the field and caused a shortfall that could only be covered by imports from the international arms market.

Increasingly, the army depended on assets—men and materials—

drawn from the civilian side of Japanese life. This need and the initial political and popular will for victory at last made possible the centralization of power required to organize the country for protracted war. In October 1937, civilian and military planners were fused into an all-powerful economic "general staff": the Cabinet Planning Board (CPB) comprised soldiers, bureaucrats, and technical experts divided into sections with specialized concerns—the mobilization of labor, of transport and communications, of materials and production—all under general mobilization and policy sections.

The CPB collated information on Japan's strategic strength and made annual mobilization plans. It was also responsible for devising the legislative framework within which Japan's mobilization for war could be achieved: the National Mobilization Law of April 1938, a wide-ranging totalitarian charter based on the legacy of Tetzusan Nagata. Not only did the law give the government virtually absolute power but, more insidiously, it delegated exercise of that power to the bureaucracy. Any pretense that the Diet could influence Japan's course was gone. Even power within the Cabinet now became concentrated in the hands of five ministers: army, navy, finance, foreign, and the prime minister.

Japan's mobilization effort moved quickly into high gear. In the second half of 1938, the consequences began to make themselves felt. Unaware of the grandiose plans of their masters, the people noticed only the small things: no more metal toys for their children; roads gathering potholes; the neon of the Ginza extinguished; public buildings becoming increasingly shabby; coffee unprocurable. Later the inconveniences became more serious. On one day a month—the "Service Day for the Development of Asia"—families were expected to eat very little. It became illegal to polish rice, because this downgraded its nutritional value and bulk. In 1940, rice was rationed along with salt, sugar, matches, and the other daily necessities. Women were forbidden to perm their hair or wear elaborate clothes, and observers stood on street corners to check that the new regulations were being obeyed.

To stifle opposition, the government turned to the twin instruments of censorship and propaganda. Not until the fall of Saipan did the Japanese hear anything uncensored over the airwaves. The press ceased to express independent opinions, and the official news from the China front was uniformly good. With the truth concealed, the country was subjected to a "National Spiritual Mobilization Campaign." Children no longer walked, they marched to school to hear more about the "Holy War in Asia," while their mothers rolled bandages and carried out other patriotic tasks. "If Japan is to bring about the rebirth of China," the Army Ministry announced, "she must herself be born again."

In the late 1930s, the Japanese were particularly susceptible to such propaganda. The legacy of the Meiji educational system ensured that all children received basic indoctrination at both elementary and middle-school level. The essence of the indoctrination—which occupied some 50 percent of a child's time at school—remained identical: loyalty to the Emperor, the father of the nation. This "most important duty of the Japanese subject" was fulfilled indirectly through obedience to superiors, honesty, frugality, diligence. A child was taught that even his body belonged to the Emperor, and textbooks directed each boy to "make it his duty to cultivate his body and mind from childhood so that he will be able to pass the conscription examinations and join the army and navy to perform the honorable duty of defending his country."

Even fifteen years before, as Shidehara had taken Japan into the Washington Conference system, into the League of Nations, into the era of international cooperation, children in schools were learning that death in the service of their Emperor was rewarded by elevation to the rank of deity: "It is the desire of the Emperor that those loyal heroes who died for the country and Him should be enshrined and be worshiped [at Yasukuni]. . . . We must think of this great benevolence of our Emperor and, like the heroes here enshrined, must serve our country and our Emperor." From 1903 until the Pacific War, the five successive editions of the standard school textbooks issued by the Ministry of Education show an unrelenting progression toward militarism and ultranationalism. The lessons learned in school were compounded at home by moral instruction from parents who had also been raised in the shadow of the Imperial Rescript on Education.

The essence of wartime civilian Japan was contained in two textbooks of public morality produced by the Ministry of Education: *The Cardinal Principles of Japanese Life*, produced in the aftermath of the February 26 revolt in 1936, and *The Way of the Subject*, of 1941. On the face of it, these tracts were simply a strong affirmation of traditional Imperial ideology with its emphasis on loyalty and sacrifice. But taken together they reveal the degree of state interference in the lives of ordinary Japanese. "It is unforgivable to consider private life as the realm of individual freedom where we can do as we like, outside the purview of the State," reads *The Way of the Subject*. "A meal, . . . clothes, none is ours alone, nor are we in a purely personal capacity when at play or asleep. All is related to the concerns of the State. Even in our private lives we should be devoted to the Emperor and never lose our attitude of service to Him."

The seventeenth-century shoguns put a high value on state-sponsored morality. To the eighteenth-century Japanese scholar Sorai, morality was "nothing but the necessary means for controlling the subjects of the Empire and may be regarded as a device for governing the people." The particular morality Sorai and the Tokugawa had in mind was Confucianism, which they propagated in Japan. Confucianism legitimized hierarchy, denied self-interest, and compelled loyalty and obedience to superiors within the hierarchy to which one belonged.

The founders of the Meiji state benefited from the now well-entrenched Confucian nature of Japanese society and used it for nation building, with the Emperor at the apex of the hierarchy. Now, in the twentieth century, political scientists were engaged in pushing the linkage of Confucianism and Emperor ideology to its furthest extreme, to eradicate the tendency toward individualism, insulate against the incursions of foreign ideas, and mold a compliant population, motivated to serve the principal objective of the state: the waging of total war.

To the outsider, it was all mumbo jumbo. To those at the center it was a clinical piece of social engineering utilizing Japan's existing value systems. The scheme even had the approval of modern scholarship. The Emperor ideology had power because, as the anthropologist Bronisław Malinowski explains: "The myth is a statement of primitive reality which still lives in present-day life, and, as a justification by precedent, supplies a retrospective pattern of moral values, sociological order and magic belief."

Cardinal Principles was a thoroughgoing statement of the Imperial Way, and, not surprisingly, a month after the National Mobilization Law was passed, into the Konoe Cabinet came General Sadao Araki, the embodiment of the Imperial Way philosophy. His post was minister of education, and he fulfilled an additional function as national rhetorician: "A Hundred Million Hearts Beating as One!" and "All the World Under Japan's Roof!" were the slogans that spurred the nation now, making the exhortations of the Meiji Restoration's "men of spirit" to "Revere the Emperor and Expel the Barbarian!" seem quite tame.

Cardinal Principles taught that the "mission" of the Imperial Army was to subdue "those who refuse to conform to the august influence of the Emperor's virtues." To fulfill this mission, the army suddenly needed an influx of willing recruits to police the vast territories of occupied China and replenish existing divisions. The 1936 figure of 170,000 conscripts a year was doubled in each of the years up to 1941. So from comprising 24 divisions in 1937, the army grew to 34 divisions in 1938, 41 in 1939, 50 in 1940, 51 in 1941. And the army air force grew from 54 squadrons in March 1937 to 151 in November 1941.

But rapid growth meant a decline in quality. In part this was inevitable, since the army's infrastructure of education and training was stretched too far. But it also seems to have been deliberate policy to draw the requisite manpower from the lower reaches of the reserve pool in order to save the precious reserve of regular troops for defense against the Soviet Union. The army's soldiers now were not professionals who had completed two years with the colors, but increasingly civilians who had had only basic training before finding themselves at the front. A high proportion of the new troops were men in their late thirties. Expatriate Japanese were also pressed to serve their homeland again. The American military attaché took pleasure in telling of the "Japanese" soldier he met in North China—a man who had actually lived in Seattle for twenty years and had a son, aged twelve, in junior high school.

The high proportion of new officers and replacements compounded the decline in efficiency of the Imperial Army in China. The 108th Division in Shansi had a particularly hard time. Over 50 percent of the original officers were killed, and the young replacements introduced in accordance with the policy of using the dregs first were characterized by their seniors as "useless." In order to sustain the anti-Soviet priority, the High Command deliberately held back officers on active service in 1937, preferring instead to send rapidly trained replacements—an ersatz officer corps disparaged by the professionals.

Faced with so ruthless a war, on such a scale, this essentially new Imperial Army began to show fundamental weaknesses. Dr. Robert McClure, field director of the International Red Cross, traveled through Honan and Shansi in the spring of 1938 and found "widespread defeatism among officers and troops all of whom had given up any hope of seeing Japan alive." It was a conclusion reinforced by intercepts of military mail home. On a wall of a bombed-out building someone had written: "Fighting and death everywhere and now I am also wounded. China is limitless and we are like drops of water in an ocean. There is no purpose in this war. I shall never see my home again."

This pervading sense of hopelessness, and the constant fear of death from guerrilla booby traps, ambush, disease, or battle wounds had serious effects on discipline. Many Japanese soldiers explained their persistent predilection for rape as a reaction against certain death. Officers were attacked, even killed, by their own men—a result partly of the common soldier's resentment at seeing his officers profit from opium traffic and smuggling, while he himself, impoverished and needing to send money home, had only limited opportunities for looting and theft.

Poor-quality officers meant poor staff work and poor management generally; even in the early months of fighting there had been failures in supplying the troops, and on one march from the coast to Tientsin, men and pack animals died of thirst. Distrust of the officer corps' abilities aggravated the problems of indiscipline and low morale, and the military effectiveness of the army in China, depending above all on fighting spirit, plumbed depths previously unknown. By 1939, it was becoming obvious that soldiers who had once sought out hand-to-hand conflict now sought equally eagerly to avoid it; where once every man would fight to the last rather than surrender, this was now the exception rather than the rule.

The army's massive superiority in air power, armored vehicles, and artillery (and also chemical-warfare capability) was used to compensate for the decline in fighting spirit. But according to some observers, in rough terrain when armored vehicles could not be employed, experienced Chinese troops were "now proving more than a match for Japan. . . . The myth of the invincibility of Japan is, as far as the Chinese forces is concerned, exploded."

Units used artillery expensively. When searching the surrounding countryside after occupying a town, tanks and guns would blaze away at possible guerrilla concentration points—and then the units sent out to clear the area would not stray beyond artillery range. Communists exploited such hesitancy by "setting off firecrackers in a gasoline tin. . . . They fire into the darkness all night." The excessive reliance on superior weaponry began to show; by May 1938, the Army Ministry had become seriously concerned about "the wholly unexpected expenditure of bombs and field and medium howitzer artillery shells," which was forcing Japan to "mobilize a considerable proportion of her engineering industry."

In the end, it became possible to accuse some units of actual cowardice. The European manager of a coal mine in North China reported one incident near his house. "Hearing sounds of firing he went up a hill at the back of his house when he saw a Japanese column some 500 strong, cavalry and infantry, advancing up the valley when machine guns opened up from hills on either side. . . . Complete panic ensued, some running up and some running down the valley, while others screaming at the tops of their voices ran towards the machine guns with their hands up. No-one succeeded in taking command and no protective measures were taken, nor was any weapon brought into action. The Chinese machine gunners having effected 50% casualties then made off into the hills. The Japanese then collected themselves sufficiently to retrieve their dead and wounded, [and] retraced their steps to the mine where they commandeered a waiting train of empty coal trucks. They were in such a hurry to be off that they pitched dead and wounded indiscriminately into the trucks in heaps, throwing them from the plat-form."

From the High Command's perspective, the decline in military effectiveness was worrying but not catastrophic. China was a contained theater of war and in any event, the enemy was itself in serious decline militarily. The High Command's real anxiety was to be able to match the effectiveness of the country that remained the principal enemy: the Soviet Union.

From the perspective of midsummer 1939, the Soviet Union could be seen to have waged a successful defensive-offensive war against Japan falling only just short of all-out hostilities. Since the Manchurian Inci-dent, diplomatic and propaganda offensives had helped effectively to isolate Japan in the world community, while Russia meanwhile had joined the League of Nations. Militarily, the promise of Soviet support for the united front had influenced Chiang's decision to fight the surro-gate war that Stalin wanted. In Sinkiang province, Russian influence was gaining ground. And around Manchukuo, the Soviets had built a ring of steel.

The success of the Five-Year Plans in the 1930s gave the Red Army the capacity to fight a two-front war, according to the boasts of the Soviet ambassador to Tokyo—which were supported by Japanese intelligence assessments. Manchukuo was surrounded by a giant horseshoe of Soviet-held terrain—from the Mongolian People's Republic in the west, along the Amur in the north, and the Maritime Province in the east. Long stretches of this immense frontier were heavily fortified, and behind stood Soviet forces outnumbering the Kwantung Army by as many as three to one. In addition, long-range bombers based around Vladivostok could strike Japan's cities, and the growing submarine fleet operating out of Vladivostok could wreak havoc on shipping to the home islands.

Unknown to the Japanese, Moscow possessed an additional advan-tage that was the virtual equivalent of the Allied "Magic" decrypting capability: a spy ring in Tokyo, which reached into the inner recesses of the Cabinet. (*Pravda*, in a fit of perestroikan laxity, revealed in 1989 that a second spy ring was also operating at this time.) High-grade intelligence was particularly useful to the Soviets in assessing Japanese intentions because, throughout this period, incidents of violence occurred by the hundreds along the border every year. There would be sniping, kidnaping, intelligence operations—but most usually, simple conflict over where exactly the border line should be drawn. Both the Kwantung Army and the Soviet Union were assertive about their rights and willing to repel by force what they saw as incursions. Among the many clashes in 1937, the First Division (sent to Manchukuo after the February 26 Incident) fired on three Soviet gunboats on the Amur, sinking one.

With the onset of the war in China, the High Command became more reluctant to use force. Therefore, when on July 13, 1938, Soviet troops were spotted atop Changkufeng Hill on the Korean-Russian-Chinese border fifty miles from Vladivostok, the Korean army and Tokyo High Command decided to take no action. The army needed to concentrate all its strength on the Hankow operation. Nevertheless, the commander of the Nineteenth Division was dismayed at the restraint being shown, and when Soviet troops occupied the neighboring Shatsaofeng Hill two weeks later, without seeking prior permission he ordered a night attack.

The operation was successful, and of tactical necessity had taken in the other Soviet position on Changkufeng Hill. But it aroused a storm in Tokyo, as yet another example of insubordination from troops in the field. Only concern for national honor and the potential threat to morale prevented the High Command from ordering immediate withdrawal and persuaded it to hold out for a negotiated solution. In the meantime, the Nineteenth Division was to maintain its position, but there was to be no escalation even in the event of Soviet counterattack, and no use of aircraft except in self-defense.

While Japanese diplomats were seeking peace in Moscow, the Japanese units at Shatsaofeng and Changkufeng were sitting targets. On August 2, the Soviets attacked, and though they were fought off, for the next eight days the Japanese endured an almost continual rain of bombs and artillery shells. "The hill crests seemed one mass of flame which became all the more vivid as darkness fell." Under the avalanche of steel the hilltops turned to mud. The Japanese tunnelled into the mountain to survive, and still they suffered 526 killed and twice that number wounded as they held their positions tenaciously until the cease-fire was arranged.

But their courage had not won them a victory; it merely masked the fact that the Soviets had been highly ineffective. The terrain was partly to blame: The Japanese were well sited on high ground while down below, caught between marshes and a lake, the Soviets found it difficult to mount coherent attacks. In particular, Soviet advantages—air supremacy and armor—were wasted. Bombs missed badly, and strafing runs were too flat to be effective. "The Soviet tactical use of tanks was hopeless. It dated back to 1917," reported an eyewitness. "There was no element of surprise. No attempt at a smoke screen. They came lumbering over the skyline against the sun and no gunner could have wanted a better target."

When they analyzed the Changkufeng incident, the Japanese recognized that in future conflict the Soviets would employ "tactics of attrition . . . to destroy the fighting strength of the adversary by concentrated and large-scale employment of material power." But the lesson had not been driven home hard enough. Consequently, the High Command continued to have faith in the ability of its forces on the continent, and the Kwantung Army in particular, to fulfill their missions. As for the diplomatic isolation that Japan was now experiencing, the High Command hoped to extend the Anti-Comintern Pact into full military alliance with Germany and Italy—a possibility suggested by Ribbentrop to Ambassador Oshima in Berlin at the 1938 New Year. But within twelve months, both these foundation stones of High Command policy were to be smashed by military and diplomatic hammer blows.

On the other side of Manchukuo from Changkufeng lies the Halha River, which the army regarded as the border with the Soviet-controlled Mongolian People's Republic. On May 11, 1939, a small raiding party of M.P.R. troops crossed the Halha and harassed the Japanese garrison at Nomonhan, a remote speck in the endless steppes. It seemed just another border incident; but after M.P.R. troops had annihilated the best part of a Japanese cavalry regiment, and Japanese aircraft had attacked M.P.R. aircraft on the ground deep within the M.P.R., the action escalated. The High Command blamed the Kwantung Army for the escalation: The attack on the M.P.R. airfield had been contrary to Tokyo's will, if not against direct orders.

Nevertheless, it was with the High Command's concurrence that the Kwantung Army now moved a large force—the Twenty-seventh Division, with elements of the Seventh (veterans of the war against the tsar in 1904)—to Nomonhan to "chastise" the invader. Unfortunately, the state of Soviet–M.P.R. relations at that moment was suited to a display of Soviet strength, and the incident turned into full-scale conflict. Under

General Georgy Zhukov, a brilliant and determined commander, the Soviets augmented their strength during August through a massive and unexpected logistical exercise. With almost twice the Japanese force at his disposal, with particular strength in aircraft, tanks, and artillery, Zhukov proceeded to devastate the Japanese.

His generalship was beyond Japanese reckoning. He sent his mechanized forces in wide flanking movements to envelop the Japanese positions, while within the ring, Soviet tanks and infantry, supported by aircraft and artillery, drove wedges deep into the Japanese defenses, isolating and then destroying each redoubt in turn. The Japanese soldiers had no hope. In the early days of the fighting, they had at least been able to destroy tanks with suicide attacks using Molotov cocktails, and mines on the end of bamboo poles. Now Zhukov employed tanks impervious to incendiaries and untroubled by Japanese antitank weapons. A few of the Imperial Army's Twenty-third Division, which was newly formed, turned and fled; some junior officers ordered unauthorized retreats; but the rest stood with the regimental colors until overwhelmed by Soviet technological might. The Twenty-third Division suffered 73 percent casualties. Overall, out of a force of around 56,000 employed at Nomonhan, 8,500 died and a similar number were wounded.

There seemed no reason, apart from logistical problems, why Zhukov could not continue to push deep into Manchukuo and force major concessions from Tokyo. Nevertheless, on August 22, Moscow offered a cease-fire. This was no admission of weakness. Having inflicted a crushing defeat on the Japanese, and knowing full well from the spy ring in Tokyo that the Japanese were desperate to call a halt, Moscow was in full control of events.

While the Kremlin proceeded to resolve the Nomonhan issue with one hand, with the other it dealt Japan a second crushing blow. On August 23, the day after the cease-fire offer, Russia signed a Nonaggression Pact with Nazi Germany, and the Japanese army's high hopes of an Axis alliance to contain communism—all the more urgent after what had happened at Nomonhan—came crashing down. Then Germany and Russia carved up Poland between them; and as the world stood at the threshold of war, Japan could only watch, defeated, betrayed, stunned, and in disarray.

PART VI

THE STRIKE SOUTH
1939-1941

27

SALVATION IN THE
SOUTH

On September 3, 1939, the day the Second World War began in
earnest, the Imperial Japanese Army faced a future more uncertain than at any point in its history. Thousands of the vaunted Kwantung
Army lay on the field at Nomonhan, their bodies uncollected, as their
commanders waited for the cease-fire to be finalized. Unbroken in spirit,
they had been betrayed by equipment unable to counter the twentieth-
century might of the Soviet Union. Although some blame for the defeat
lay with poor generalship, there was no denying Russia's technological
edge. At Nomonhan, Zhukov's artillery had outranged Japanese guns,
and his flame-throwing tanks were a innovation Japan's chemical-warfare
experts could not match until 1942—and then the product never proceeded beyond the prototype stage.

Now that the army's erstwhile ally, Adolf Hitler, had announced his
Nonaggression Pact all hope had gone of extending the Anti-Comintern
Pact into a military alliance capable of deterring the Soviet threat—a
threat that was substantial and growing. By 1941, the Soviet Union had

approximately thirty divisions and 2,800 airplanes in the Soviet Far East.

In China, two years of bitter conflict and half a million casualties had brought not victory, but the prospect of unending war, with the Empire's economy foundering under the strain. Nineteen thirty-nine brought drought to western Japan, floods to Formosa, and to Korea a crop failure amounting to 70 percent in some areas. Equally serious for the army was the partial collapse of the Five-Year Plan for Manchukuo, as the China War drained labor and materials that should have gone into the construction of this industrial powerhouse. Manchukuo authorities tried desperately to attract tourists; Western visitors in 1940 were delighted to find the hotels supplied with cotton dressing gowns decorated with gothic script reading "Prussia," "Nazis," and "Heil Hitler." These tourists bore witness to Manchukuo's sorry plight: "The vast majority of the factories on the outskirts of Mukden are lying idle for want of the essential raw materials. Manchuria's tragedy is that her prosperity depends primarily on the soya-bean. Nobody now wants soya-beans except Germany and the freight costs across Siberia are twice the value of the beans."

With the onset of war in Europe, supplies from the British Empire and Germany virtually dried up, making Japan ever more dependent on America. But as the Chinese and Soviet propaganda offensive saturated the Western consciousness with images of Japanese brutality in China, Americans became increasingly unwilling to succor Japan. Joseph Grew, the American ambassador to Japan, asserted (as late as February 1941) that "Japan in China has a good case and a strong case if she knew how to present it"; but she did not, and she paid the price of a nation's condemnation. In 1938, a "moral embargo" prompted by Japanese terror bombing of civilians stopped sales of aircraft; in June 1939, revocation of the commercial treaty of 1911 laid Japan open to punitive tariffs on imports and exports. Despairing Japanese stratagems just to attract Wall Street money to Manchukuo, let alone North China, were stillborn.

These were desperate times for Japan and the army's continental policy, times that seemed to call for desperate remedies. But none suggested itself in China, and army strategists began thinking of expanding the Empire to the south—Indochina, Thailand, Malaya, and the Indonesian archipelago. Here, as the Cabinet Planning Board pointed out in October 1939, were oil, rubber, tin, nickel, bauxite, and rice, together with a well-established infrastructure for exploiting them. Increasingly, too, thanks to a Japanese campaign of anticolonial propaganda and subversion, Southeast Asia offered populations eager to throw off the yoke of the white oppressors and welcome collaboration with Japan in a Greater East Asian Co-Prosperity Sphere. All this was very different from the situation in North China.

With need came opportunity and incentive. The German blitzkrieg of May and June 1940 crushed Holland and France, leaving Britain, the principal colonial power in Asia, tottering in the eye of the storm. It was an article of faith in the Japanese High Command that Britain would soon fall. In vain the military attachés in Sweden and London argued, quite correctly, that the Germans were not equipped to invade Britain. They had no efficient system of landing troops, so any invasion required the removal of both the Royal Air Force and the Royal Navy from the Channel area. But this was not what the Japanese High Command wanted to hear. In a private letter, the director of military intelligence told his London colleague that reporting such matters to Tokyo was "not good for his future," and General Oshima personally reprimanded the attaché in Sweden.

As France fell and Hitler readied his troops for the invasion of Britain, the riches of Southeast Asia seemed temptingly vulnerable— and, it was felt, they should be grasped before Germany did so. Among the most strident voices advocating the southern advance were inevitably those of Imperial Navy radicals. "Finally the time has come," announced the Navy's War Guidance Office. "This maritime nation, Japan, should today commence its advance to the Bay of Bengal! Moss-covered tundras, vast barren deserts—of what use are they? Today people should begin to follow the grand strategy of the navy."

With similar optimism, the High Command was laying its own plans for Japan's renaissance. Suddenly it seemed possible for the Empire to cut itself free from dependence on the United States and yet still have strength to stand against China and Russia. In a fever of anticipation, the High Command hastened to draft a statement of policy directing Japan's future course. By early July, the task was complete, and the "Outline of the Main Principles for Coping with the Changing World Situation" was formally approved.

It was a pivotal document in the life of the Imperial Army and the history of twentieth-century Japan. In essence, the army was proposing a revolution in both the policies and the political and economic framework of the Empire. This was total-war theory expressed as a political system designed to make Japan a garrison state. In the quest for self-sufficiency, the army argued, Japan should expand into the now vulnerable south, implement the New Order at home to ensure yet more stringent economies, and in addition find a solution to the draining China War. None of these objectives could be easily achieved on its own. Combined, they generated a wind of change in Japan that was ultimately to blow her onto the rocks of catastrophe.

The High Command knew it could not dictate this kind of far-reaching policy to the nation's elites. The army controlled policy in China and it had influence at home, but never the absolute power that the proposed changes required. So it was crucial from the outset to link arms with the navy, particularly as the southward advance was essentially a maritime proposition. The 1936 "Fundamental Principles of National Policy" already enshrined the navy's desire for southward expansion. Nevertheless, the army was still obliged to buy naval support with promises of an enhanced share of strategic resources, particularly steel. In the fevered atmosphere of the times, a deal was struck. Despite the magnitude of what was being proposed, the army was only days away from making its "Main Principles" a joint strategic plan.

One of the navy's concessions concerned Japan's relations with Nazi Germany, a factor crucial to the success of the "Main Principles." Japan was seeking to carve out a zone of special interest from colonies belonging to nations that the Nazis would have to defeat. One fear, particularly with regard to the Dutch East Indies, was that the Germans themselves would take former colonies as spoils of war. To ensure that Germany recognized Japan's paramount interest in the area, the army proposed that—despite the treachery of the Nazi Nonaggression Pact with Russia in the aftermath of Nomonhan—Japan should join the Axis. Previously, the navy had resisted this proposal, fearing it would set Japan against America. Now navy leaders agreed—swayed partly by promises of a larger share of materials for the latter half of 1940, partly by the deterrent effect on America that an alliance with Germany could be expected to have.

In the event, the deterrent effect was an illusion. The announcement of the Tripartite Pact on September 27, 1940, barely registered among policymakers in Washington. Secretary of State Cordell Hull regarded it merely as confirmation of an existing state of affairs. He had good reason. As one move in the propaganda campaign which followed the Rape of Nanking, Washington had been secretly informed by "two very good and independent informants" (probably Comintern agents) of the terms of the secret protocol to Japan's 1935 Anti-Comintern Pact with

Germany. Where the pact preserved the fiction that the Communist International was not a creature of the Kremlin, the protocol specifically named the Soviet Union as the signatories' enemy, and pledged to "immediately consult on measures to safeguard their common interests" in the event of attack. Washington privately informed London of this embryo military alliance, and Russia had successfully widened the growing gap between Japan and the democracies.

With the navy in tow, the army had complete power to dictate the nation's future course. The first step was to ensure that Japan had an administration willing to put the "Main Principles" into effect. The incumbent prime minister, Mitsumasa Yonai, was particularly opposed to the Axis proposal, so his army minister resigned and brought the Cabinet down. Fumimaro Konoe, the army's favorite, returned to form his second administration.

But before Konoe formally accepted the Imperial mandate, he called a conference of the most important of his prospective ministers at his Tokyo home, to establish basic agreement on the "Main Principles." The foreign minister–designate was Yosuke Matsuoka; the navy minister, Zengo Yoshida; and as army minister Konoe proposed appointing the current inspector-general of aviation, Lieutenant General Hideki Tojo. Tojo was then aged fifty-six, a man who, in the words of the *New Yorker*, came "about as close as a Japanese can to looking important." He was also a man in touch with army opinion, an administrator of proven competence, and, unlike other possible nominees, available. He was first and foremost a soldier, not ambitious politically, and he came into the Cabinet almost as a compromise candidate. But the appointment placed him at the nexus of civilian-military relations in Japan at the most crucial moment in her modern history, and was to lead directly to his becoming prime minister some twelve months later.

With his Cabinet in accord, Konoe formally assumed office on July 22, 1940. Part of his popularity with the army stemmed from his desire to create a new political order within which all political parties would be subsumed and which would provide a unitary national structure for directing and controlling the nation's energies. Konoe's private intention—so he said—was in fact to build a political base sufficiently powerful to stand against the military. But as the army saw it, he was a figurehead with sufficient glamour to provide them with a "one party, one nation" mass movement on Nazi lines, which would serve the dual purpose of ensuring full mobilization and all-out sacrifice from the people.

The underlying ideology of the new domestic order was the same as it had always been—nationalism through the medium of the Imperial institution—but greatly intensified. Children were again a key target. Schools became "national schools" and children "national children" studying a curriculum designed to make them "aware of the Imperial system." For the parents, the "spiritual mobilization" inaugurated by General Araki in 1938 reached a climax of artifice in November 1940. Under a bright blue autumn sky, on the plaza before the Imperial Palace gathered Konoe, the Cabinet, senior generals and admirals, and fifty thousand other specially invited guests. Their intent was to commemorate the 2,600th anniversary of Emperor Jimmu's descent from heaven to the divine islands of Japan, and the start of an unbroken line of Emperors.

In the early weeks, Konoe's political initiative appeared promising. The parties in the Diet voluntarily dissolved themselves and, on October 12, 1940, Konoe formally inaugurated his Imperial Rule Assistance Association (IRAA). But beneath the surface, Japan remained as fragmented as ever. The IRAA never became the potent force for which both Konoe and the army had hoped. Political opposition persisted, and national regimentation—one of the supposed strengths of the system— was undercut by the Home Ministry, jealous of its preserves. Preempting any moves the IRAA might have made to ensure popular compliance with wartime regulations, the Home Ministry created a system of "neighborhood associations," groups of ten households collectively responsible for the obedience of each family member.

Almost the first act of Konoe's Cabinet was to approve directives reflecting the new policy. On July 26, the emphasis was on political and economic reform, matters considered by the Cabinet Planning Board. Their document, "The Main Principles of Japan's Basic National Policy," was essentially a totalitarian charter. It had been drafted by Tojo's close colleague, Naoki Hoshino, a graduate of Tokyo University and a former Finance Ministry bureaucrat. From 1932 until his appointment to head the CPB, Hoshino worked in Manchukuo, rising to become the senior civilian in the administration, second only to the army Commander in Chief, and, not surprisingly, the CPB plan reflected the National Socialist sentiments underpinning Manchukuo.

But like Konoe's new political order, the renovation of Japan's economy failed. Those who had predicted that the European war would have disastrous effects on Japan's economy were being amply justified, with prices rising sharply and trade and exports interrupted. The military

services, too, were partly to blame. Despite formal agreement on alloca-
tions, they continued to engage in covert acquisitions and hoarding,
constantly competing to maximize their share of the nation's scarce
resources. Beneath the surface a thriving black market developed among
the Emperor's loyal subjects—which, coupled with the deceit of the
armed services and the unsophisticated fiscal techniques available, made
any calculations by the Cabinet Planning Board merely approximations.

Even more damaging to strategic planning was the high level of
autonomy retained by the industrial conglomerates. Hoshino sought
genuinely centralized control of the economy at a level that denied the
capitalist basis of Japan's development since the mid-nineteenth century.
The *zaibatsu* were bitter in their opposition, and in April 1941 Hoshino
was removed from his post and several of his senior aides imprisoned.
Instead, the principal regulatory mechanism was to be a system of
"control associations," themselves controlled by the *zaibatsu*. This victory ensured that Japan would not start to mobilize fully until almost a
year after the start of the Pacific War.

As the Pacific War loomed, Japan became a totalitarian state only
in its manipulation of the populace. The sacrificial *Way of the Subject* was
for the lower echelons to follow; the elites continued to pursue self-
interest. There was always competition and conflict, with no possibility
of the kind of unity at the top—dictatorship—that true totalitarianism
requires. The July 1940 policy consensus called for the creation of a
"national defense state," but sectional interests stubbornly refused to
make the necessary sacrifices of power.

In the army's eyes, the military problems involved in an advance
south were just as intractable as domestic issues. Despite three years of
war in China, the army had remained essentially a force designed for the
open plains of Manchuria. Now, at short notice, it was trying to plan for
jungle campaigns in areas where it had never seriously contemplated
fighting and about which it knew virtually nothing.

Worse, the Operations Section of the General Staff had very little
to plan with. Commitments in China and the permanent defense of
Manchukuo against the Soviet Union left only eleven divisions and 540
aircraft available for the southward advance. Success depended on careful preparation, attention to detail, and on the troops giving of their best.
Not suprisingly, some of the army's best divisions were earmarked for
southern operations—among them the Imperial Guards and the tough
Fifth Division, which was to lead the attack on Malaya.

The new policy put an immense burden on the Operations Section.

The army was critically deficient in all areas of intelligence about Southeast Asia, from topography to tropical medicine. In haste, staff officers were dispatched to survey the terrain; in early 1941, a captain from the Operations Section spent three months clandestinely traveling down the Malayan peninsula—but the task force ultimately set out for the invasion with British Ordinance Survey maps, which they supplemented with maps of Singapore acquired from an abandoned bookstore in Kuala Lumpur.

The Research Division of the Taiwan Army conducted field exercises on Formosa and Hainan Island to determine the effect of a tropical environment on soldiers and their equipment. On Hainan, troops were sent on a thousand-kilometer march, a simulated advance down the Malayan peninsula, to see how well they could be expected to perform. In October 1940 the Fifth Division was ordered to train for amphibious operations, and on Kyushu the following March, conducted a dress rehearsal for the Malayan landings, followed by an attack on "Singapore," the navy's base at Sasebo.

For a number of reasons, not least the operational range of Japanese military aircraft, the acquisition of bases in southern Indochina was a central strategic imperative of the advance south. Some of the existing French bases were adequate, but there were not enough of them to launch the blitzkrieg campaign being planned, so Japan would be obliged to construct others. Thus the army needed unrestricted access to Indochina for at least twelve weeks before operations could begin. In July and August of 1940, the Operations Section worried away at the problem, which seems to have driven them to commit yet another of the acts of major insubordination that had plagued the army since the assassination of Chang Tso-lin in 1928.

Almost from the beginning of the war in Europe, Japan had been pressuring the authorities in Indochina to close Chiang Kai-shek's supply route via Haiphong and Hanoi. On the day after the fall of France, the colonial governor, Georges Catroux, acted unilaterally to close the border with China, hoping to preempt the inevitable Japanese demands. However, this only encouraged the High Command to seek further concessions that might help in the war against China, and Major General Issaku Nishihara was sent to Hanoi to negotiate.

Nishihara, who had served in Paris and at the League of Nations, asked Catroux to let Japan deploy inspectors to ensure that no supplies reached Chiang, and to help Japan even further by providing military bases in the north and the right of passage for Japanese troops for an attack on Kunming.

Catroux allowed the inspectors in, but refused the use of bases, and there matters rested until Matsuoka resumed the attack from Tokyo. By the end of August, he had extracted from the Vichy government an agreement that formally recognized "the supreme interests of Japan in the economic and political spheres in the Far East" and agreed in principle to the provision of "special military facilities" in northern Indochina.

The details of the "special military facilities" were left to negotiations in Hanoi between Nishihara and Catroux's Vichy successor, Vice-Admiral Jean Decoux. Progress toward a detailed agreement might have been smooth, but the likely outcome did not suit a cabal composed of a number of South China Army headquarters staff and Operations Section chief Kyoji Tominaga. Nishihara was negotiating concessions with a view to aiding the war in China, but Tominaga's group was looking toward the southern advance then being planned by the Operations Section. Already on June 18, the South China Army had deployed the Fifth Division on the Indochina border with orders to prepare for an invasion. Confident in this knowledge, Tominaga flew to Hanoi to join others in the cabal, all intent on finding a pretext to commence military action.

Decoux seemed to provide the pretext by refusing to negotiate, on the ground that he had received no authority from Vichy. Tominaga and the vice-chief of staff of the South China Army, with five other officers, confronted him in his office. Shouting angrily at him, they gripped their swords and promised darkly, "We will meet you on the battlefield!" Decoux's authority to negotiate came through later that evening, and the next day the talks began.

Not wanting a negotiated settlement, Tominaga then began a campaign of disruption, reporting to Tokyo that Decoux was not "sincere." This brought an order from the army vice-chief of staff to begin stationing troops on September 6 or 7, irrespective of French agreement. Late on the fourth, Decoux capitulated, and orders to withdraw were passed down the chain of command to the Fifth Division. One of the commanders decided to postpone compliance with the order, and instead advanced with his battalion into Indochina to reconnoiter French defenses. Two kilometers inside the border he was stopped by the French and politely told to return north. The incursion was reported to Hanoi, and though there had been no bloodshed, Decoux revoked the entire agreement.

While the battalion commander was sent for psychiatric tests, Tojo, Konoe, Matsuoka, and the navy minister pondered their next move. Ultimately, they fell in with Tominaga's suggestion that the government express regret at the incursion and try to resume negotiations. Failing that, they should deploy troops, not later than September 22, both from across the border and by sea via Haiphong. By one P.M. on September 22, agreement had been reached and the orders for peaceful deployment given. At this point, the orders down the line to the Fifth Division appear to have been deliberately delayed at South China Army headquarters so that the division would attack as ordered—presumably in the hope that this would precipitate a more generalized action to take Indochina from the French. At midnight, the division crossed the border and attacked the French defenses.

Even more extraordinary was the behavior of the seaborne troops off Haiphong. In the full knowledge that agreement had been reached with the French, the commander of these troops insisted on an aggressive landing and advance on Haiphong, on the grounds that he had not received direct orders not to attack. As the minutes ticked away toward the dawn launch of the landing craft, the commander and his chief of staff hid themselves—one in a storage cupboard, the other under a lifeboat—to avoid any possibility of receiving the countermanding order. Fortunately, the French were better disciplined, and the landing and subsequent occupation of Haiphong were unopposed.

This time, with Japanese troops within his borders, Decoux did not try to revoke the agreement; nor, after gaining control of the situation, did Tojo order deployments other than those agreed. The cabal had failed to achieve its objective, and Tojo's anger at the adventurism of these officers resulted in a purge not unlike the one following the February 26 revolt in 1936. Some were court-martialed; Tominaga was relegated to a military school in Manchuria. (But he was not abandoned by his clique. Shortly afterward, Tojo was obliged to rehabilitate him, and ultimately he rose to become vice-minister of the army.)

But though the South China Army had failed to manufacture a "Manchurian Incident" style of takeover, serious damage had been done. International suspicion of Japan was deepened, and apart from the closure of the border, little advantage had been gained in the war in China. Once the difficulty of the terrain in North Indochina and Laos was known, the plan to attack Kunming was dropped, and the army was obliged to content itself with a bombing campaign from French airfields.

However, the effect of the border closure on Chungking was severe enough. Through diplomatic pressure, Japan had succeeded also in persuading the British to close the Burma Road. Now the Nationalists were more isolated than ever before, and by the late summer of 1940 an aura of defeatism enveloped Chungking.

It was not, however, a feeling on which Japan could capitalize; for however unsupported he might feel, Chiang could not capitulate as long as his inveterate Communist enemies fought on against the Japanese. Despite the creation of a united front following Chiang's kidnapping at Sian in December 1936, relations had never warmed between the two Chinese factions. Each was jealous of the other's successes, and from time to time fighting even broke out between them. It was in the context of competing with the Nationalists for popular support that the Communists, who until then had been slowly and surely rolled back by an ever-mounting tide of Japanese blockhouses, took the initiative and mounted a "cage-bursting" offensive of extreme ferocity.

On August 20, 1940, around 400,000 Communist troops launched a series of attacks in North China. The offensive caught the Japanese totally by surprise, inflicting major damage on rail installations, roads, industry, and mines, as well as on the hated blockhouses, before the Imperial Army had a chance to regroup and counterattack.

Soon the Japanese had the situation under control, however, and in the end the Communists probably lost more than they gained. But the Imperial Army, obliged now to take Communist military potential seriously, saw the prospect of an end to the war recede even further. Months before, after the military and economic stratagems of 1939 had failed to bring Chiang down, they had already begun to clutch at straws. Even the staff of the China Expeditionary Army wanted the war over by the fall of 1940 and were willing to negotiate directly with Chiang. Ironically, given the huge expenditures on military methods, it was a political ploy that first produced results. The creation of the alternative national government under Wang Ching-wei prompted a positive response from Chungking—but not quite the response for which the Japanese army had hoped.

In December 1939, the Japanese military attaché held secret talks in Hong Kong with a man named T. L. Soong, who purported to be the younger brother of a major figure in the Nationalist camp, on the subject of peace negotiations. The auguries seemed surprisingly favorable, so in mid-February, a staff officer from the China Expeditionary Army was sent to Hong Kong for further talks. In early March, more senior Japanese officers held extended negotiations, detailing peace terms, with Soong and senior Nationalists from Chungking, including one of Chiang's vice-chiefs of staff.

While the negotiations continued, Japan withheld official recognition from Wang Ching-wei's regime. It was clear that once official relations had begun, there was no going back. Konoe's original declaration, in January 1938, that there would be "no further dealings" with Chiang—which was of course being flouted by the talks with Soong— would be carved in stone once Japan recognized Wang's government, and the Japanese hesitated to make the chasm unbridgeable. This was apparently what Chiang Kai-shek and Tai Li, the head of his secret police, were counting on. "T. L. Soong" was an impostor, one of Tai Li's guerrillas; and he managed to keep Japan on the hook until late September 1940, denying legitimacy to the "traitor" Wang and allowing Chiang's propaganda machine to destroy any semblance of popular support for him.

On November 30, 1940, the Japanese government formally recognised the Wang Ching-wei regime as the legitimate government of China. Wang was by then a Japanese puppet, and the gesture did nothing to alter the power configuration in China; but it did bring a change in the conduct of the China War. On January 25, 1941, the General Staff's "Outline Measures for a Protracted War in China" set out a new policy—one of "requisitioning all materials needed for the survival of the army and acquiring from China the full amount of materials needed for Japan's mobilization, especially mineral resources." A new phase in China's agony had begun.

28

FACING REALITY

The failure to bring Chiang to heel profoundly affected the strategy of the southern advance. The "Main Principles for Coping with the Changing World Situation" at their most optimistic directed that if the war in China were settled, then force would be used to achieve Japan's aims in the South at the first favorable opportunity. However, if the war in China continued, then Japan's advance south would proceed on the basis of avoiding hostilities with other nations unless particularly favorable conditions arose. Even in this case, Japan would try to confine hostilities to Britain—though, as the navy insisted that war with America was a possibility, "thorough preparations" were to be made.

This governing principle—that Japan should avoid other hostilities while the China War continued—explains Tojo's anger at the Fifth Division's attack on the French. The Imperial Navy was no less adamant that the troops in theater should adhere to the central policy; so once the commander of the amphibious force had emerged from his storage cupboard and his troops had entered the landing craft, the naval flotilla accompanying them sailed off and left them to it, creating extreme army bitterness at what was regarded as desertion.

But the desire to avoid hostilities did not mean that either army or navy leaders minimized the strategic importance of Indochina or of access to bases in neighboring Thailand. In 1940, Thailand was the one country in Asia that was not under colonial rule; and for years British and Japanese agents had been battling overtly and covertly, through propaganda and subversion, to become the dominant influence over Thai policy. During 1938, five hundred Japanese officers were stationed in Thailand, helping to train the Thai army and air force. Thailand was also the base for subversive operations against Burma: From 1937 onward, arms were smuggled in with a view to creating a rebellion and thus cutting off supplies to Chiang via the Burma Road.

With Japan's adoption of the "Main Principles," this conflict escalated. Thailand was the back door to Malaya and Burma. The head of the Malayan peninsula, the Isthmus of Kra, lay within her borders, and the Operations Section planned that two of its three landings for the Malayan campaign would be on the isthmus. Such was its significance that the British had contingency plans to violate Thai neutrality and occupy the isthmus in the event of war.

The summer of 1940 presented Japan with a golden opportunity to win Thai goodwill. With the fall of France, the Thais decided to demand the return of their portions of Laos and Cambodia, which had been conceded to the French in 1867. While the British were still deciding which side to support, the Imperial Army stepped in and supplied aircraft and munitions to the Thais, who then advanced their forces into the disputed territories.

In mid-January, the French counterattacked, and while the Thais were able to repulse the land assault, the French, with a surprise maneuver, moved warships into position to shell Bangkok. Now the Thais openly appealed to Japan for help, and immediately accepted Tokyo's offer of mediation. The French refused, preferring the British to mediate—which brought a warning from Japan's deputy foreign minister that the army in Indochina would find such a move provocative. The mediation itself took place on a Japanese warship, with the mediator supporting much of the Thai claim. France was deeply unwilling to compromise the territorial integrity of its colony, but faced with the threat of military action from Japan was forced to concede.

So by the early spring of 1941, despite the indiscipline of Tominaga and the South China Army, Japan's expansion had effectively demonstrated that she was now the dominant power on the mainland of southern Asia. But while this was a considerable step in her advance south, it was not enough. To achieve self-sufficiency, the objective of the "Main Principles," Japan needed control of the archipelagoes of Southeast Asia, and in particular of the Dutch East Indies, with its oil and infrastructure of refineries.

In August 1940, the government dispatched negotiators to Batavia to secure supplies of strategic materials in the quantities Japan would need for self-sufficiency. This was ostensibly an economic mission; but the underlying "Principles for Negotiations with the Dutch East Indies" revealed more predatory objectives, not least that the Indies should be made part of the Co-Prosperity Sphere.

But this jewel in the crown was not easy to secure. The Dutch colonial administration remained firmly in the Allied camp, loyal to the government-in-exile. And the Indies were geographically remote: There was no Fifth Division conveniently encamped on the border to bring pressure to bear on the Dutch authorities. If Japan wanted to threaten Batavia, she could only do so overtly, which risked provoking hostilities. With the signature of the Axis Pact in September 1940, the resistance of the Dutch hardened. They knew Japan was acting as Hitler's buying agent and that vital commodities such as lubricating oil were finding their way to Germany on the Trans-Siberian Railway.

As 1940 gave way to 1941 and Japan was no nearer achieving its objectives in the Indies, optimism in the High Command began to fade and voices began to call for a review of policy. One aftereffect of the belligerency of Tominaga and the Operations Division over Indochina had been the setting up of a new General Staff department, the War Guidance Office, to consider the wider implications of the army's strategy; by January 1941, this new think tank was coming to the conclusion that the prospects for expansion were not as favorable as they had appeared the previous July.

The progress of the European war, and a report doubting Japan's ability to wage protracted war, both contributed to this pessimism; but what really influenced the War Guidance Office was the Imperial Navy's contention that in the advance south, war with the United States was unavoidable.

The army had made two dangerous presumptions in drafting the "Main Principles," both of which had led it to believe that America would not intervene. First, it was an article of faith that a German victory was inevitable and therefore that Britain would fall—in which case

British opposition in Asia would remain minimal, and, more important, America would be denied a base from which to mount an offensive against Germany, and so would be obliged to come to terms. And second, in the summer of 1940, the army had had no intention of attacking the Philippines, and so did not recognize that America's vital interests in Southeast Asia would be affected by Japanese actions.

Throughout 1940, the High Command had been reassured by the continuing absence of unequivocal warnings from Washington. They knew of America's isolationist sentiments and the consequent weakness of her armed services, and enjoyed watching her treading a careful path between appeasement and provocation. It was clear that the sanctions America had imposed to punish the Imperial Army's activities in Indochina were carefully gauged not to push Japan too far. For example, on July 26, high-grade scrap metal and aviation gasoline over 86 octane had been embargoed—but Japanese aircraft could fly perfectly well on lower octane levels. As far as the Dutch East Indies were concerned, in May 1940 Roosevelt had stationed the Pacific Fleet at Pearl Harbor, but without ordering mobilization, so the fleet remained under strength and logistically incapable of offensive action. Even the revocation of the 1911 commercial treaty, which followed the Japanese blockade of Tientsin, had not been allowed in practice to affect trade.

But what the army did not see was that American perceptions of Asia, and of its vital interest, were changing as the implications for the world economic system of Axis dominance of Europe and Asia became clear. The linkage of the Axis "New Orders" made Roosevelt conscious of the fact that America's very foundations were under threat. American prosperity, even survival, required global free trade, which the autarkic ambitions of the Axis denied. In April 1940, Roosevelt suggested that "every man, woman and child" in America should think about the question "What is going to happen to the United States if dictatorship wins in Europe and the Far East?"

So while America was behaving cautiously in bilateral relations with Japan, her attitude toward the totalitarian threat in general was hardening. She began rearming. In June and July 1940, Congress voted a huge appropriation for a crash program to augment naval power. On December 27, Roosevelt, victorious in his third presidential election, sat at his fireside chatting with the nation about the sorry state of the world and America's role as the "arsenal of democracy."

From Japan's perspective, America's growing strategic needs were more intrusive than her foreign-policy decisions. The carefully gauged aviation-fuel embargo and limited scrap embargo was followed in late September by a total embargo on scrap iron. The Japanese ambassador to Washington called at the State Department to complain, and was lambasted by Cordell Hull, who accused Tokyo and Berlin of plotting to return the world to the Dark Ages. But despite Hull's rhetoric, this action had not been deliberately punitive, but had been motivated more by the fear that supply would not meet domestic demand. Similarly, it was domestic imperatives that led in December 1940 and January 1941 to an embargo on a wide range of strategic materials—iron ore, copper, nickel, uranium (Japan was never to accumulate enough uranium for even a prototype bomb), and, a little more pointedly, oil drilling and refining equipment.

About the boldest measure directed specifically at Japan was the buttressing of Chiang Kai-shek, continuing the policy of containment that Stalin had been pursuing for years. Roosevelt had no intention of equipping the Nationalists for an all-out assault on the Imperial Army, merely of sustaining the present stalemate. Continued resistance by the Chungking regime would tie down a million Japanese soldiers, easing pressure on Southeast Asia and, as Cordell Hull hoped, ensuring the ultimate failure and humiliation of Japan's "military caste" and its replacement by liberal elements.

By April 1941, the High Command had swung toward the navy's analysis and accepted that American opposition to Japan's southward policy was inevitable. The policy decisions of the previous summer had to be reappraised. On April 17, both army and navy put their seals to a new "Outline of Policy Toward the South." Now Japan would not undertake military operations even if an extremely favorable opportunity arose, but only when "absolutely unavoidable" in self-defense, if the existence of the Empire were threatened.

On the face of it, the navy was pulling the army back from war, but the underlying reality was rather different. The navy was simply ensuring that war would not begin until the sea forces were ready. The earliest the navy could consider hostilities commencing was November 1941, when its mobilization would be complete. But by focusing on preparedness and relative strength, the navy set in motion a new dynamic, which was to play a part in the eventual consensus for war.

Naval strategists gauged relative strength by counting capital warships, taking no interest in the opinion of officers such as Admiral Isoroku Yamamoto, who argued the importance of air power—a point he was to prove with his Pearl Harbor strategy. On this basis, the

Imperial Navy's strength relative to the U.S. Navy would increase through 1942 and into 1943, as the superbattleships—the *Yamato*-class leviathans currently being built—came into commission. But thereafter, the massive U.S. naval augmentation authorized by Congress would steadily erode the Imperial Navy's chances of success.

Consequently, there was a growing feeling among the more radical officers that November 1941 was not simply the earliest date on which operations could commence, but the date on which operations should commence. For eighteen months or so, Japan would have an unrepeatable opportunity to succeed in war against the U.S. Navy. This sense that the Japanese must "use it or lose it" underlay the almost hysterical bellicosity of the navy in the summer of 1941, with Admiral Osami Nagano, chief of the navy General Staff, already calling for war two days before the fateful oil embargo.

However, in the spring of 1941, the emphasis within the government as a whole was more than ever on diplomacy. One key project had nothing to do with the South: the scheme by Foreign Minister Matsuoka to turn the "betrayal" of German-Soviet rapprochement to Japan's advantage. He wanted to build a coalition of "anti–status quo" nations—Germany, Italy, Russia, and Japan—which would not only deter America, but would permit the advance south to proceed without fear of opportunist attack from the North. The first step toward this coalition had been Japan's entry into the Axis in September 1940. Six months later, Matsuoka traveled to Moscow and Berlin to complete his grand alliance.

During the long days and nights in the train across Siberia, he drank vodka and boasted of how Stalin and Hitler would become his puppets. In the Kremlin, paying a preliminary goodwill call on Stalin en route to Berlin, he leaped the ideological chasm separating Russia and Japan with the assertion that while their political and economic systems might differ, at heart the Japanese people were "moral communists" and that on such sentiments could alliance be forged.

In Berlin, Matsuoka tried to persuade the Nazi hierarchy of the advantages of such an alliance. He still had faith in the new world order that would give the "have-not" nations their just deserts—an order in which Germany was to take Western Europe and Central Africa; Italy would push on across North Africa from Ethiopia; Russia would win the "Great Game" and expand into the Gulf and India; and Japan would take Southeast Asia.

But Matsuoka was on a fool's errand. Hitler had long abandoned any thought of alliance with Stalin. In December 1940, he had decided to postpone the invasion of Britain and attack Russia the following summer—a cataclysmic decision, which he ordered concealed from his Axis partners. So when, in early April, Matsuoka returned to Moscow and concluded a Neutrality Pact with Stalin, he was in effect acting as Hitler's dupe; the Axis emissary, fresh from Berlin, seeking diplomatic accord, was a smiling mask over the Führer's savage intentions. Or perhaps he was Stalin's dupe, offering security in the east should Hitler attack from the west.

Either way, Stalin, aware of the Nazi threat even then building on his western border, was naturally delighted by the pact, so much so that he accorded Matsuoka the singular honor of coming to the station to see him off with bear hugs and protestations of goodwill. But only three days after signature of the Neutrality Pact, the High Command, alerted by General Oshima in Berlin, realized the possibility of war between Germany and Russia. Through April and May, Tokyo buzzed with rumor. Then, at the beginning of June, three weeks before the launch of Operation Barbarossa, Oshima found himself invited to Berchtesgaden, where Hitler told him, "A German-Soviet war probably cannot be avoided." Back in Tokyo, the High Command began considering its options.

29

A TIME FOR LEADERSHIP

B y the middle of 1941, some of the options open to Japan since the start of Hitler's war were foreclosed. Despite a death toll of 185,000 Japanese soldiers, peace in China was no nearer and the need for resources from Southeast Asia to sustain the war effort was assuming even greater importance, though the prospect of acquiring them peacefully had all but vanished. On June 6, the Dutch communicated to Japan their final denial of oil and the other strategic materials in anything approaching the quantities the Japanese had demanded, and by June 11 the High Command had agreed with the navy that the advance south must be accelerated, by occupying southern Indochina and preparing military and naval bases.

While Japan teetered on the edge of striking south, Hilter's attack on Russia presented the army with what seemed a genuine opportunity to push the old enemy out of the Maritime Province, off the Amur and back to the far shores of Lake Baikal. The navy was naturally opposed to a land war in which it would play little part, but the army would not forgo the chance completely. On June 24, two days after the start of the Nazi onslaught, the services reached a compromise: Japan was to prepare secretly, while awaiting an "extremely favorable" opportunity to attack Russia.

The fact that the army was prepared to make this kind of compromise seems an acknowledgment of their humiliation at Nomonhan. The High Command recognized the significance of technological superiority and felt confident of success only when Stalin had withdrawn sufficient troops to make possible a Japanese advantage in manpower of two to one. As for the Kwantung Army itself, they wanted not only a three-to-one superiority but also evidence of a decline in the enemy's morale.

Military control over national affairs ensured that the policies were formally adopted at an Imperial Conference on July 2, 1941. Japan was now determined to establish the Greater East Asia Co-Prosperity Sphere and would not be deterred even by the risk of war with the United States.

Twenty days were required to concentrate troops for the occupation of Indochina, and the specter of the Siberian winter made early August the last practicable time to begin operations in Manchuria. On July 21, France agreed to Japan's demands to what amounted to an occupation of Indochina, with special rights to establish bases in the South. Three days later, the first Japanese troops arrived in Saigon. Within three months, control of southern Indochina would give Japan a springboard into Southeast Asia.

As for operations in the North, behind the fiction of major army maneuvers—code-named Kantokuen—troops were building up in Manchukuo. The plan called for sixteen divisions to be readied for the assault, and for a logistical base created for six more. During July 1941, a force of around 850,000 men was assembled in Manchukuo, and there they waited for the "persimmon to ripen," for Stalin to pull enough troops out of the Soviet Far East to give a Japanese attack a hope of success. But Stalin withdrew only a limited number of troops during July, and on August 9 any thought of attack during 1941 was abandoned.

In any event, in the High Command enthusiasm for the attack was on the wane as once again, the kaleidoscope of international dynamics had turned and Japan could not afford to commit to Siberia its last significant forces outside China. Entering the matrix now was Roosevelt's new attitude toward the Soviet Union. The British government rushed to ally itself with "Good old Joe," and Roosevelt followed closely, though his administration and the American people, outraged at Soviet predations in Poland, lagged some way behind him in enthusiasm. Roosevelt saw the value of the Soviet colossus in the ultimate destruction of Nazism and, for his part, immediately ordered the release of Soviet assets frozen in the United States after the invasion of Poland. His personal envoy, Harry Hopkins, traveled to Moscow in late July to meet Stalin. "He will help you to plan for the future victory and for the long-term supply of Russia," Churchill wrote to Stalin, assuring him of America's best intentions, adding "You could talk to him also freely about policy, strategy and Japan."

Japan stood in the forefront of Allied thinking because if Russia were to be helped, particularly if the Red Army were to be pushed east of the Urals, the vital supply route through Vladivostok had to be maintained, as did access to the Allies' supply base in Southeast Asia. Already in July 1941, as the menace of Kantokuen began to make itself felt, a first shipload of Malayan rubber had been off-loaded in Vladivostok's Golden Horn harbor. Japan had to be restrained—from attacking Russia, most important, and from moving south.

From the High Command's perspective, Japan was encircled by an increasingly interlinked ring of enemies, American, British, Chinese, and Dutch. The British and Chinese had been constants since the mid-1930s; in 1941 they began unobtrusively to plan joint action. On Christmas Day 1940, Major General Dennys arrived in Chungking and found the Chinese willing allies—Chiang's Chief of Staff offered 100,000 troops to Britain for use outside China if Britain would equip them—but their situation was "worse than I expected." China "cannot prevent the withdrawal of considerable Japanese forces for action against us elsewhere unless we can somehow stiffen them." The British proposed forming elite guerrilla units to operate in China, and sending some RAF squadrons (for which fuel dumps were being created in early July, under cover of commercial activities), but the key to genuine Chinese resistance lay in American hands.

Roosevelt's attitude to Chungking was a litmus test of his determination to keep Japan from mauling the Soviet Far East. In early July, the U.S. Joint Chiefs of Staff approached the British War Office wanting "full details of British planning so far," and around this time, the first aircraft for Claire Chennault's Flying Tigers arrived in Rangoon. But both the British and American governments had disclaimed any connection with this "International Air Force," and overt aid to China began with the dispatch of U.S. specialists (a de facto military mission) to Chungking to manage the Lend-Lease Program, which had now been extended to China.

Japan had good intelligence sources in Chungking and would have been well aware of American attitudes and the active American presence. Nor were they in any doubt about Roosevelt's other policies. The Philippines had become the base for a novel military enterprise: the creation of a strategic air force designed to deter Japan from striking north or south. With their wood-built cities, the Japanese were believed to be particularly afraid of air attack. The Philippine proposal was part of a wider policy decision, following Japan's advance into southern Indochina, to appoint General Douglas MacArthur as commander of a combined American and Filipino force. There was only a limited supply of B-17s, and not until March 1942 would there have been enough for effective action—but this militarization of the Philippines was clear evidence of American determination.

Roosevelt was walking a tightrope in the weeks following Hitler's invasion of Russia. He wanted to contain Japan, but at the same time could not afford to push her into a situation where she would opt for war. All Roosevelt's advisers warned him of the danger of war on two fronts; America was trying to aid Britain, Russia, and China and to arm herself as rapidly as possible. She could not yet meet every demand on her arsenals, and Roosevelt had to be firm without pushing Japan too far. So the military mission to China was not described as such; Chennault was acting as a private citizen; the State Department press release following the arrival of Japanese troops in Saigon used strong words but was not unequivocal.

Nor was the American freeze on Japanese assets, announced on July 26, intended to be an absolute embargo on sales of strategic commodities to Japan. Roosevelt had conceived the notion of controlling supplies to Japan more subtly by revoking all current export licenses for strategic materials but allowing Japan to apply again, and then controlling the release of frozen funds to pay for the exports. Thus, Japan would receive strategic materials only in the quantities Washington thought fit—namely, sufficient to keep her from risking an advance on the Dutch East Indies. The Japanese government was to be given no guidance on how much might be allowed by either license or release of funds. Roosevelt's was a move similar in its way to the revocation in 1939 of the 1911 commercial treaty, which also had the underlying intention of keeping Japan on the defensive, uncertain of America's intentions.

The idea was worthy of the Japanese in its subtlety, but it was not used in the way Roosevelt intended. On August 1, following the freeze of Japanese assets, all existing licenses to export oil were revoked. The following day, Roosevelt left Washington for a meeting in Newfoundland with Winston Churchill; his under secretary of state, Sumner Welles, left orders that none of Japan's frozen assets were to be released for a week or so.

This was embargo by bureaucratic decision, but when Roosevelt arrived back from Newfoundland, he did not countermand the policy of deliberate vagueness. On September 5, when it was too late to do anything else, the embargo was given formal approval—but still there was no notice given to Japan, and Japanese tankers stayed in American ports until November 1941, waiting hopefully for oil to appear.

By mid-August 1941, the dawning realization that an embargo was in place prompted the Japanese military once again to review security policy. The atmosphere was one of extreme shock. No one had believed that the occupation of Indochina would produce this reaction, because everyone in Japan and in the West recognized that an embargo would provoke Japan into taking drastic action—in all probability invading the Dutch East Indies. On August 16, the navy presented a draft policy document to a meeting with army bureau and section heads. For the next two weeks, war hung in the balance, and finally the scales tipped. At a Liaison Conference of Cabinet ministers and military leaders on September 3, Admiral Nagano, the navy Chief of Staff, explained to those present that while the Allies became stronger, Japan was progressively weakening. While the services were certainly prepared for the present impasse with America to be resolved by diplomacy, if diplomacy failed— and there should be a time limit—then Japan must strike south. "Although I am confident that at the present time we have a chance to win the war," he said, "I fear that this opportunity will disappear with the passage of time."

The policy document adopted by the Liaison Conference—"The Essentials for Carrying Out the Empire's Policies"—went forward to an Imperial conference—Cabinet ministers, military leaders, and the Emperor—on September 6, 1941. Before the conference convened, Hirohito called Nagano and army Chief of Staff Gen Sugiyama to the Palace to express regret that the emphasis seemed to be on war and not diplomacy. He wanted to break with convention and personally debate this issue at the conference, but was restrained by his Lord Keeper of the Privy Seal, Marquis Koichi Kido. Instead, he had to content himself with reading a poem by his grandfather, Meiji, which was understood to indicate his preference for diplomacy: "All the seas in every quarter are as brothers to one another. Why then do the winds and waves of strife rage so turbulently throughout the world?"

The onus fell on Prime Minister Konoe to stage-manage a diplomatic resolution by mid-October at the latest. He proposed a summit meeting with Roosevelt to resolve the differences. But the State Department, which had been negotiating for some months with the Japanese ambassador in Washington, knew the impossibility of achieving a settlement and feared that a meeting would only succeed in demoralizing the Chinese, who would assume that American assistance was about to be withdrawn.

Only the Imperial Army could pay the price America was asking for the restoration of supplies—including withdrawal from China and Indochina, the resumption of free trade, and equal opportunity in China—and the High Command found the conditions unacceptable. The army could see Japanese security only in terms of war-fighting capability. This was in part a consequence of the constant menace of the Soviet Union, but partly also a by-product of twenty-five years of the consensus for total-war preparedness.

The militarists viewed the future Japan as a powerful, self-sufficient empire, while civilian America, without offering any guarantees of Japan's security, was trying to force her to fit into a demilitarized, internationalist framework. The view propounded by Roosevelt and Churchill following their August meeting, a public statement of resolute opposition to fascism known as the Atlantic Charter, was effectively a reiteration of the "weak-kneed" Shidehara approach of the 1920s. The Imperial Army had rejected that policy then, and it continued to do so now.

In Washington, Secretary of State Cordell Hull steadfastly insisted that Japan must conform to American precepts before the summit could take place. In Tokyo, Konoe pressed Tojo to agree to troop withdrawals from China and thereby signal movement in the right direction. Tojo, for his part, insisted that the negotiations had irretrievably broken down and that, as had been agreed in Imperial conference, the final decision for war should be made in mid-October at the latest. The army and navy had been mobilizing for war since September 6, and the time had come for action. It was not a decision Konoe could make. He resigned, and Tojo, the visible tip of the army iceberg on which the negotiations had foundered, was the inevitable choice as his successor.

Still there could be no final decision for war. Tojo's appointment on October 17 was made on the basis that the September 6 decision was no longer binding and that he should reconsider Japan's policy, including the negotiations with the United States, with an open mind. But though the Imperial policy directive might no longer be binding, nothing had changed in the circumstances supporting it—and now there was additional pressure from military planners for a decision before the winter weather forced plans to be abandoned until 1942.

At a marathon seventeen-hour Liaison Conference on November 1, the basis of a "new"—and final—diplomacy was agreed, and two alternative bases for achieving the immediate aim of restoring supplies were drawn up. Plan A took a long-term view and sought a comprehensive agreement on China that did not negate Japan's essential policy; Plan B, an interim agreement, insisted, among other things, on a cessation of American aid to Chiang Kai-shek. The deadline for settlement was November 30; should the talks end in failure, war would ensue.

Japan's position had not changed sufficiently to meet America's minimum requirements, nor were the policymakers in Washington capable of seeing Japan's situation through Japanese eyes. There were a few well-informed individuals who could make the imaginative leap. Joseph Grew, for instance, could see that Japan had a case in China; he argued for a more flexible American policy. Then, almost at the eleventh hour, came a plan—improbably enough, from the lower reaches of the U.S. Treasury Department. Based on a realistic appraisal of Japan's position, it urgently recommended a shift toward meeting Japanese requirements. Ironically, with the first stirrings of the Cold War, America would link arms with Japan to contain communism in Asia. But in 1941 hostility was too deeply entrenched—and for this, the Soviet and Chinese information and propaganda machinery can claim a large part of the credit.

On November 26, the day the Pearl Harbor task force slipped anchor in the Kuriles, Cordell Hull presented a note to the Japanese ambassador in Washington forcefully reiterating his basic position. The die was cast. On December 1, an Imperial conference confirmed the Japanese decision for war. Hirohito remained silent throughout, and the last word fell to Tojo: "At this moment our Empire stands at the threshold of glory or oblivion. We subjects are keenly aware of the great responsibility we must assume from this point on. Once His Majesty reaches a decision to commence hostilities, we will all strive to repay our obligations to him, bring the government and the military ever closer together, resolve that the nation will go on to victory, make an all-out effort to achieve our war aims, and set His Majesty's mind at ease."

Ultimately, the fundamental reasons for making the decision for war were all negative, reducing the options before Japan to one. Within a time frame fixed by the massive American shipbuilding program, the drain of the war in China, and a total embargo on trade with America,

Japan had no option left but to take a shortcut to salvation in the South. But there were some positive inducements. For the navy, as Nagano had said, it was a good time for war—in fact, the last window of opportunity. For the army, too, the strike south could not have been made with a more secure northern border. For a time the Japanese feared that the Soviet Union would negate the Neutrality Pact and allow the Allies to use air bases in the Maritime Provinces; but then Imperial Navy code-breakers deciphered an exchange on the subject between Moscow and the State Department in which, despite $1 billion in Lend-Lease granted in November 1941, the Soviets were unforthcoming.

Other intelligence revelations were a comfort to both army and navy. Cabinet-level papers taken by the Germans from the British ship, the *Automedon*, persuaded the navy that Britain was no longer a significant strategic factor in Asian waters.

The High Command was certain that the initial operations, though extraordinarily complex, would be successful. Japan was choosing both the time and place for the assault, and the enemy was vulnerable. In 1939, the General Staff had deciphered a telegram indicating the blind spots in Singapore's defenses, especially on its northern shore. They had U.S. and British intelligence analysts wrong-footed for most of the autumn: "Japan is now concentrating her forces against the Russians and cannot suddenly change this into a concentration in the south," commented the staff of the Commander in Chief, Far East, on October 1, 1941. Two weeks later, Roosevelt wrote to Churchill, saying: "I think they are headed north."

Both army and navy had luck on their side. On December 6, British reconnaissance planes spotted the Malayan task force of nineteen troop transports and escort battleships, cruisers, and destroyers as it entered the Gulf of Thailand—and then lost it in heavy cloud cover. But the greatest good fortune by far accompanied the navy's opening gambit, the attack on Pearl Harbor.

For the attack to succeed, the Imperial Navy had to secretly assemble, train, and equip a force of six aircraft carriers and accompanying warships and sail it undetected on a twelve-day voyage through the inhospitable waters of the northern Pacific in winter, refueling en route. All this was in the hope of surprising the U.S. Pacific Fleet, which might or might not be in port, and successfully attacking it with newly developed torpedoes and armor-piercing bombs—and then making the long journey home with the capital ships intact.

Those of the Imperial Navy strategists who were privy to the plan from its unveiling in January 1941 were unanimously opposed to it, arguing that at best it had little chance of success and at worst could lose Japan the war on the first day, if the Americans were to trap the task force so far from home. Only the persistence of its progenitor, Commander of the Combined Fleet Admiral Isoroku Yamamoto, ensured that it was put into effect. Yamamoto was short and chubby, an unregenerate womanizer, but also a brilliant and distinguished naval officer, who had taken part in Japan's surprise attack on Port Arthur decades before. He was a gambler, but in his eyes Pearl Harbor was not a gamble, more a last resort, a desperate expedient forced on Japan by her enemies. Traditional naval wisdom on the American threat in Asian waters dictated a Tsushima-style battle of annihilation; this Yamamoto rejected, putting his faith instead in naval air power to destroy America's presence in the Pacific with a preemptive strike.

Some of his arguments were highly persuasive; but there remains a sense that he promoted the scheme in the expectation that it would fail. Like Takamori Saigo leading his men out from Satsuma in 1877, Yamamoto knew his cause was desperate; but, like Saigo, he believed his failure would be noble and worthy of the Imperial Japanese Navy, in the samurai tradition. It was perhaps the Americans' failure to appreciate this self-destructive vein in the Japanese martial character that sustained the belief in the impossibility of an attack (except by saboteurs) on Pearl Harbor, and ultimately explains why they were caught unprepared.

The task of devising a plan of operations was entrusted to Combined Fleet Staff Officer Captain Kameto Kuroshima. Kuroshima was something of a legend in naval circles. When absorbed in a task such as this he was as a man possessed, given to locking himself in his cabin in a perpetual cloud of incense with the portholes shut, and sitting chain-smoking, stark naked, while the muse of naval operations spoke. Somehow he succeeded in producing a plan credible enough to convince the navy General Staff, and the training began. Kagoshima Bay is not unlike Pearl Harbor, and here the attack was tested and refined. Initially only four of the navy's big carriers were to be used, but the trials showed all six were necessary, and Yamamoto unhesitatingly committed them to the operation.

From the moment the task force slipped anchor in the snow-whipped seas of Etorofu on November 26 to the attack at dawn over Oahu, the navy's luck held. The refueling had taken place on seas that were extraordinarily calm for the time of year. The command to attack—

"Climb Mount Niitaka 12.08," a reference to the highest mountain in the Japanese Empire and a fairly obvious metaphor for commencing operations—was intercepted by the British in Hong Kong, who were well on the way to cracking the high-level JN-25b code; but though a junior officer in Hong Kong, Eric Nave, has recorded that he passed the message on to London, there it appears to have stuck. Then, as the first wave of 183 planes under Commander Mitsuo Fuchida approached Oahu, their presence was picked up by a radar operator—a trainee, inevitably at that hour on a Sunday morning—whose excited reports were interpreted as indicating no more than a flight of B-17s en route to the Philippines.

But even with this remarkable run of good luck, the invaders could not steer clear of all the snares and confusions of the battlefield. Commander Fuchida had personal responsibility for assessing whether or not the attack was likely to meet resistance. If Pearl Harbor was not on the alert, he was to order torpedo and high-level bombers to attack first with clear sight of the targets. If the Americans were ready and waiting, he would send in his dive-bombers first to knock out the ground defenses, even though this would mean that the torpedo and high-level bombers would have to locate targets in dense smoke.

Looking down from 10,000 feet on Pearl Harbor sleeping peacefully at dawn, Fuchida opened his canopy and fired the single shot from his Very pistol which was the signal for the torpedo and high-level bombers to attack first. Unfortunately, the commander of the protective screen of Zeros did not see the signal, and Fuchida was obliged to fire again—at which the dive-bombers swooped into the attack. This, in turn, prompted the torpedo commander to initiate his own attack.

Whatever the confusion in their ranks, the mêlée of attacking Japanese took a heavy toll of the U.S. Pacific Fleet and its personnel: 3,695 men killed and wounded. In the two sorties that day, the Japanese lost only twenty-nine aircraft over Pearl Harbor itself—though others crashed into the sea or were written off—at a cost of fifty-five lives. It was a military triumph without parallel in naval warfare—and it could have been even greater. Admiral Chuichi Nagumo, commanding the invasion fleet, could have ordered a second major assault on Pearl Harbor's installations, repair facilities, and huge oil stocks (as large as Japan's entire reserves at the outbreak of war), and pounded the base into irrelevance. Fuchida personally urged him to do so, but instead Nagumo turned his force for home. It was a failure of initiative that would be reproduced by many senior Japanese commanders in the Pacific

War; in Nagumo's case, it seems to have been prompted by the dreadful uncertainty of the preceding voyage and its ravaging effect on his confidence. But such was the importance of preserving the prestige of the leadership that Yamamoto, well aware of the option, refused to override Nagumo and order the subsidiary attacks.

Eyewitnesses of the hours following the attack on Pearl Harbor have recorded that Yamamoto was plunged into depression, sitting silent amid his exuberant and boisterous officers. He was not mourning missed opportunities; he was simply aware that Japan was now doomed to a war she could not win. There were no circumstances in which Japan could defeat America outright; all Japan's military leaders, army and navy, accepted this fact, because Japan could neither project force onto the U.S. mainland nor, given America's vast resources, win a war of attrition. Initial success was all the High Command could hope for. They knew that even were they successfully to seize the oil fields and production facilities of the Dutch East Indies and secure sea-lanes for their tankers, by the end of 1944 the oil would have run out. Yamamoto estimated that the Pearl Harbor operation would buy Japan no more than eighteen months' respite from American counterattack.

The decision to fight was made in the hope of compelling the Americans—an unwarlike and irresolute people, it was believed—to make a compromise peace. The hope of compromise lasted until 1945, when the decision was made not to defend the home islands—and, interestingly, one of the objections voiced within the navy to the Pearl Harbor surprise operation was that it was too provocative, if Japan expected the United States to negotiate. This was a telling point; Yamamoto insisted throughout the planning that the attack should commence no earlier than thirty minutes after a formal declaration of war. It was through no fault of his that the war declaration was delayed and the Japanese found themselves guilty of a sneak attack, which combined with the vitriol of a decade of Russian and Chinese propaganda to generate a deep-rooted moralistic animosity against Japan that was to last throughout the war and beyond.

The whole question of how to bring the coming war with America to an end without a victory was one that concerned the army greatly, and had there been full consultation over the Pearl Harbor proposal, Yamamoto might well have been defeated in his ambitions. On Tojo's instructions, the Army Ministry drew up a strategy for peace. The paper—"Outline of War Guidance Against the United States, Great Britain and the Netherlands"—was accepted at a Liaison Conference almost two weeks before the Pearl Harbor task force sailed. In the context of the times, with the Wehrmacht plunging deep into Soviet territory and England and America still not formally allied, it gave some hope that a negotiated peace might be possible.

Japan, the paper stated, would create a "strategically superior position" by a speedy armed offensive to capture American, British, and Dutch strongholds in East Asia and the Southwest Pacific. She would consolidate these gains by further fortifying the former German islands she held in the Pacific and endeavoring to "draw out the main strength of the United States navy at an appropriate time and destroy it in a decisive battle"—a policy that reflected the Army Ministry's general ignorance of the Pearl Harbor planning.

From this position of strength, efforts could be made to end the war after the capture of the South—or alternatively after the fall of Chiang Kai-shek, or the defeat of Britain. A British collapse was crucial to the favorable scenario painted by the planners. Japan would cooperate with Germany and Italy to force the British to surrender—and then, rather than concluding a separate peace, would use Britain to force the United States to sue for peace, "thus ending the war." If Britain had fallen, America would have been without a viable base of operations and the fate of Europe would have rested entirely with the Soviet Union. With the fall of Russia, America, though undefeated, would have had no option but to cease fighting.

For the Imperial Army, these military and political rationales were relatively new. They concerned enemies against whom the army had only recently considered war, enemies about whom they knew little and against whom they had made virtually no preparations. But though the targets might be different, the purpose of initiating conflict was that which had preoccupied the leadership of the Imperial Army since 1916. "By firmly securing the southern vital resources areas and the main lines of communication," ran the "Outline of War Guidance," "Japan will establish a structure that will make her self-sufficient for an extended period of time." The quest for total-war preparedness legitimized the strike south; twenty-five years from its inception, it had led Japan to the gates of Armageddon.

PART VII

THE PACIFIC WAR: THE ATTACK

30

"FIRECRACKER ATTACK": THE HUNDRED DAYS

At Pearl Harbor, the Imperial Navy had achieved a spectacular success. But in Southeast Asia, the Imperial Army was to conduct a campaign that would rival and even surpass the navy's achievement, following a strategy that for a hundred days enabled it to relive some of the triumphs of the Russo-Japanese War.

The oil fields of the Dutch East Indies were the primary target. But in advancing south, the Japanese had to protect their flanks and secure supply lines running through waters that, if carefully managed, might become virtually an Imperial lake, permitting Japan's precious fleet of tankers to ply back and forth unmolested to fuel the military and the war machine. From the bases previously established in Thailand and French Indochina, the Japanese must dislodge the Americans and British from their footholds in the Far East: the Philippines, Hong Kong, and, crucially, Singapore, which they feared the British might turn over to the Americans. Then they could advance in comfort toward the Indonesian islands on three fronts—by way of the South China Sea, the Molucca

303

Passage, and the Makassar Strait. Once their resources were secure, they envisaged themselves advancing to a line running from the India-Burma border through the Indian Ocean, skirting the East Indies, to New Guinea and the Solomons, up to the Gilbert Islands and on, by way of the Marshalls and Wake Island, to the Aleutians.

Japan's fate rested with four generals and the pick of the Imperial troops. The first landings were to be made in Malaya, where General Tomoyuki Yamashita—bull-necked, resentful, and unorthodox—would command the crack Twenty-fifth Army. To the Philippines would go the Fourteenth Army under General Masaharu Homma, Japan's military attaché in London at the time of the Manchurian Incident, Anglophile, humane, sensitive, and doomed. The vital Dutch East Indies were entrusted to General Hitoshi Imamura, reputedly the most intelligent strategist in the army, a figure of great popularity and prestige. And to Burma was posted the Fifteenth Army under General Shojiro Iida, unusual in his sympathy for the people of the territory he was to conquer. The Burmese leader Ba Maw would describe Iida as a man of "almost mystical devotion" to his Emperor; but it was an emotion that enabled him to understand the devotion of others to their own gods, and in this he was a most unmilitarist military man.

In each theater, the fundamental strategic principles were the same: Attack first and surprise the enemy; attack fast and aim for a short campaign and a decisive victory. Give the enemy time to gather strength, and Japan would surely lose.

Japanese troops were supposed to land at Kota Bharu on the northeast coast of Malaya just as the attack was going in at Pearl Harbor. Through a single officer's error, however, the invasion and the accompanying push from prepared positions in southern Thailand began over two hours early. The targets for Yamashita's force were Penang, Kuala Lumpur, Johore, and Singapore, in accordance with plans made over the previous six months by Masanobu Tsuji and the Taiwan Army Research Section.

Malaya is shaped like an elongated lozenge, attached to Thailand in the north by the narrow Isthmus of Kra, with the tiny island of Singapore lying off its southern tip. The Malayan peninsula down which the Japanese would advance en route to Singapore was then three-quarters covered with tropical rain forest sprawling over a spine of mountains and running into swampy coastal plains. Most of the significant development—the larger cities, roads, railways, and industries—spread down the west coast; the east was fringed with sandy beaches interspersed with tangled mangrove thickets.

The British had nearly twice as many men in Malaya, some 120,000, and twice as much artillery and armor. But the Japanese had the advantage of surprise, and in Malaya at least they had air superiority. The forces at Yamashita's disposal were, too, the pick of the Imperial Army, well trained and keyed up. The Fifth Division, fresh from Shanghai, had a distinguished record of combat in China, and brought to the Malayan campaign a specialty in disembarkation techniques. The Eighteenth Division contained a high proportion of coal miners from Kyushu, whose quarrelsome, violent energies had been carefully channeled by strict discipline. At the other end of the spectrum was the Imperial Guards Division. This was still a prestige formation, physically superior and groomed in elegant ceremonial. But it had last seen active service in 1905 and its staff officers had too good an opinion of themselves to respond well to orders.

But the Japanese army's greatest advantages in Malaya were, perhaps, mental readiness and adaptability. The British, who had ruled Malaya for years, saw only an expanse of impenetrable jungle, unfit for anything except the profitable business of growing rubber. Tsuji, on a lightning reconnaissance flight, saw an asphalt road stretching down the peninsula, a natural battlefront. Too narrow for the British to deploy their superior strength, too cramped for anything except the hand-to-hand fighting at which the Japanese excelled, the road put the Imperial Army potentially on an equal footing with its powerful adversaries.

Parity soon turned to dominance. "Moving over corpses," wrote Tsuji of the Eighteenth Division's landing at Kota Bharu, "the wire-cutters kept at their work. Behind them followed a few men, piling up the sand ahead of them with their steel helmets and creeping forward like moles. . . . Suddenly one of our men covered a loophole with his body and a group of the moles sprang to their feet in a spurt of sand and rushed into the enemy's fortified position." After that, the advance down the peninsula barely paused for breath.

Having failed to move into Thailand to preempt the invasion, despite the definite sighting of the invasion fleet on the previous day, the British now failed even to fall back in time on their planned defenses at Jitra. News of the landings took, inexplicably, almost three hours to reach Singapore; General Arthur Percival took another three hours to issue his orders, and it was another two hours still before the troops actually began to fall back—by which time Jitra was practically indefensible. In the torrential rain of the northeast monsoon, trenches and gunpits were flooded and field telephones ruined. Miserably, men of the Eleventh Indian Division huddled under the trees by the side of the road,

305

seeking shelter from the downpour; their guns, which constituted the rear guard's antitank screen, were unmanned. Less than seventy-two hours after the first landings, a small infantry force and ten light tanks of the Japanese Fifth Division broke through the gap and drove deep into the only fully prepared position in the north of the peninsula.

The loss of Jitra was crucial in determining the adversaries' initial impressions of each other, powerfully influencing the events of the months to come. The Jitra line had taken six months to fortify, and was expected to hold the Japanese for three months; it lasted less than three days. Thousands of British and Indian troops surrendered, abandoning fifty field guns, fifty heavy machine guns, three hundred trucks and armored cars (almost half the first-line transport), and enough gasoline, food, and ammunition for a division for a month—"the Churchill ration," Yamashita's men called it. Later, when they took the vital Alor Star airfield, it became "Churchill Airfield," from which they flew many sorties, "tanking up with British fuel to drop British bombs on British positions."

Colonel Tsuji was an unashamed racist; but he was not alone in forming an unflattering picture of Indian soldiers after the hasty retreats at Jitra and Alor Star. In his memoirs, he managed to make their feeble performance a reproach both to them and to the imperialists who had put them in the field. "The first prisoners-of-war taken were all Indian soldiers, short of stature like the Japanese," he wrote, displaying the familiar national sensitivity to physical appearances. "It appeared that these prisoners typified the mentality of the Indian soldiers who would be fighting against us, and that they were the British Army's 'goods for consumption.' "

The Japanese, on the other hand, were beginning to take on the aspect of some kind of jungle supermen in the eyes of the Allies. Penang fell, then Kuala Lumpur, before the entire army had even finished landing. Now there was a race for Johore, one side hastening forward, the other falling back at full speed; during this contest the Japanese showed a total and, to the British, terrifying disregard for natural obstacles.

If British troops were outflanked and their supply lines broken, their commanders seemed to see no alternative to surrender. When the inexorable advance of the Japanese was blocked on the road, they simply struck out into the uncharted jungle, wading chest-high in swamp, hacking through the tangles of vines and cane, braving snakes, leeches, and mosquitoes. Where roads were impassable to cars, they mounted bicycles; when they came to rivers where the bridges were blown, they shouldered the bicycles and waded, while with extraordinary speed their engineers repaired the bridges for the tanks and artillery to follow. "On an average," boasted Tsuji, "our troops had fought two battles, repaired four or five bridges, and advanced twenty kilometers every day." Smashing through the inadequate defenses of Johore province, Yamashita's army found itself, only eight weeks after the first landings, on the shores of the Strait of Singapore.

Singapore was "Britain's pivotal point in the domination of Asia," in Tsuji's phrase. "It was the eastern gate for the defense of India and the northern gate for the defense of Australia. It was the axis of the steamship route from Europe to the Orient, north to Hong Kong and through to Shanghai, and to the treasures of the Dutch East Indies to the south and east. Through these two arteries alone, during a period of many years, Britain controlled the Pacific Ocean with Singapore as the very heart of the area." For the sake of her supply lines, not to mention her proclaimed crusade to liberate Eastern countries from the grip of the West, Japan could not afford to leave Singapore unsecured.

The island was the shape of a flattened diamond, some twenty-seven miles west to east at its widest point and thirteen miles north to south, joined to the mainland by a causeway just west of its northern apex. Singapore City itself was on the opposite side of the island, a seething mass of contrasts—extreme grinding poverty among the native work force, Malay, Chinese and Tamil, set against the huge wealth of a minority, both expatriate and local, and the gracious gentility of the colonial superstructure of tennis, cricket, the Raffles Hotel, Palm Court teas, and British-only clubs.

In 1941 the colony's beach defenses were concentrated largely on that southern seaward side. Fuel, supply, and ammunition dumps were distributed through the north and center of the island, as were three of the four airfields, all highly vulnerable to attack from the land. But the northern beaches were virtually defenseless, some without so much as a trench or a barrier of barbed wire.

As the British troops retreated from the mainland over the causeway, making an ineffectual attempt to dynamite it behind them, Yamashita chose as his battle headquarters the palace of the Sultan of Johore, a stately red-brick and green-tiled edifice with a five-story observation tower at the eastern end. At the top of this tower, a spiral ladder led to a four-and-a-half-mat room glassed in on all sides like a submarine conning tower. Here, for a week before the battle, Yamashita and his staff confined themselves, eating dry bread and food out of tins, and laying their plans.

The tower was so ludicrously exposed to air attack, artillery barrage, and even machine-gun fire that it occurred to no one that Yamashita would use it. But it was ideal for communications and gave a view of the whole battle line; with field glasses it was possible to see single figures moving. "The spiritual effect alone," commented Tsuji, "of being able to see every detail of the battle was of sufficient importance to override all opposition." And this spiritual stimulation was relayed to other ranks by Yamashita's first telegram from headquarters: "I, this whole day, pushing forward the command post to the heights of the Johore Imperial Palace, will observe directly the strenuous efforts of every divisional commander."

The British had 85,000 men at Singapore, against Japan's 30,000. But they had also lost 25,000 men in the course of the Malayan campaign, as against Japan's 4,500; and once again Yamashita's men could do almost nothing wrong, while the unhappy British commanders could do very little right. General Percival was greatly handicapped by having more than just his troops to consider. He had originally resisted the upgrading of Singapore's defenses on the grounds that it would demoralize the civilian population, but for weeks refugees had been pouring onto the island from the rest of the peninsula. So now he had a large, frightened civilian community putting a severe strain on rations and resources, a very vulnerable water supply, and entirely inadequate defenses. It would have taken a far more ruthless character to respond to Churchill's demand that he hold Singapore to the last man.

After weeks of uncertainty, he decided to defend on the northern beaches—a hazardous maneuver, with jungle blocking his lines of fire and communications poor between strongpoints, even had he not been totally deceived as to the direction of the main attack. Meanwhile Yamashita's men advanced with ferocious speed, hauling collapsible assault boats through the jungle, fighting off crocodiles at the water's edge, and launching devastating bombing raids across the Strait. Then on the night of February 8, the engineers who had repaired bridges the length of the peninsula now braved the barrage to ferry the troops across the Strait, and the Japanese hurled themselves against Singapore Island.

The end was not long in coming. Percival's field commanders had put all their troops on forward defense. Stunned by the murderous onslaught, they ordered the fallback prematurely, with no troops in reserve and no strong rear positions in front of the city. Once the causeway and the water pipeline to the mainland were both demolished, Singapore had water for only a few days. It had become a nightmare city, the streets littered with burnt-out cars, broken glass, tangled telegraph wires, and the mangled victims of air raids. At the main hospital a huge pit had to be dug in the manicured lawn to take the bodies of the dead; and on all sides officials shredded papers and smashed and burned anything that might help or cheer the Japanese. Everywhere deserters looted, got drunk, or simply hid from the advance of the unknown. Percival felt he had no realistic alternative.

Yamashita's staff were taken by surprise at the abruptness of the surrender, when Percival appeared to have large numbers of troops remaining. Nor was Tsuji impressed by the demeanor of the survivors. "Groups of them were squatting on the road smoking, talking and shouting in rather loud voices. Strangely enough, however, there was no sign whatever of hostility in their faces. Rather was there an expression of resignation such as is shown by the losers in fierce sporting contests. . . . The British soldiers looked like men who had finished their work by contract at a suitable salary, and were now taking a rest free from the anxiety of the battlefield. They even bowed courteously to us Japanese, whom they hated." His contempt is chilling.

Percival's defeated troops had no inkling of what might be in store for them in captivity. Paradoxically, had they been more hostile, had they compensated (in Japanese eyes) for their weakness in battle with defiance in defeat, their treatment might have been better. As it was, the Japanese were encouraged to view them as having no further significance at all in the context of the war, no claim to be treated as individual human beings.

Some were simply massacred, most notoriously those already sick and wounded in the Alexandra Hospital, along with all the medical staff. Thousands spent the remainder of the war in Changi jail. Some were taken to Korea to be exploited for psychological purposes—in the words of General Itagaki, to "stamp out the respect and admiration of the Korean people for Britain and America and establish a strong faith in Japanese victory." Others were dispersed to camps all over Japanese-occupied territory for use as slave labor on military projects, in defiance of the Geneva Convention. Airfields in Borneo, coal mines in Japan, roads, bridges, ammunition dumps in Sumatra, Thailand, Java, Formosa, New Guinea were all built and operated by Allied prisoners. The largest project was the Burma–Siam Railway, planned in a race against time to supply Japanese troops in Burma, and pushed with agonizing effort through the densest jungle in the world apart from the Amazon Basin. The railway was later estimated to have cost the life of one prisoner or native coolie for every seventeen and a half feet of track. The literature— British, Australian, Dutch, and Indian—of journeys to the camps and of life there for those taken prisoner in Singapore and the rest of Malaya is vast and appalling, telling of starvation, filth, disease, humiliation, torture, murder, death marches, and coffin ships.

To some extent the Singapore pattern would be repeated in Burma, in a campaign that confirmed the Japanese High Command in its arrogant disdain for the enemy. Here, too, an ill-equipped, ill-prepared army incorporating a large number of Indian troops was crushingly defeated, forced into the longest retreat in British military history.

Japanese strategists could see several pressing reasons for invading Burma. Most obviously, it was necessary in order to safeguard Japan's gains in Malaya by blocking a British counteroffensive from India. Burma is shaped like a hand with a long forefinger pointing south; most of the hand is an extension of the mountain mass of Central Asia known as "the roof of the world." "As your hand divides itself into fingers," wrote an official historian, "so does Burma split up into ranges stretching southwards. Between them are the valleys with their three chief rivers, Chindwin, Irrawaddy and Salween; together they make up four-fifths of Burma." These ranges made Burma a barrier rather than a corridor between its neighbors, and a perfect strategic shield for Japanese conquests against Allied attack from the west.

But the Japanese were also anxious both to improve their own supply position, by exploiting Burma's rice resources, and to damage that of Chiang Kai-shek in China. The Soviet-Japanese nonaggression pact had stopped Russian aid to Chiang, and the occupation of Indochina had closed the road and rail routes from Hanoi. This had left the Burma Road, hand-hewn between 1937 and 1938 by 100,000 Chinese coolies, as China's only lifeline. America was sending the desperately needed supplies by sea to Rangoon, then by rail north through the Irrawaddy valley to Mandalay, and on over the mountains to Lashio in east-central Burma. From there the goods traveled by truck on the Burma Road over the border to Kunming, provincial capital of Yunnan and the communications hub of southwest China. It was one of the oldest trade routes in history, and Chiang's survival—and with it the contribution he might make to the Allied war effort—seemed to depend on its being kept open.

Blocking the Burma Road should have been made harder for the Japanese than it was. Unlike the Americans, who wanted to use China as a base for attacks on Japan, the British were less concerned to support

Chiang than they were to avoid provoking Japan, and they gave Burma the lowest of priorities. Responsibility for its defense was tossed from one authority to another. Intelligence gathering was negligible, crippled by respect for the neutrality of neighboring Thailand. "Our ignorance of Japanese movements," wrote General William Slim, who commanded the First Burma Corps from 1942 to 1945, "was profound"; with only one officer in the whole of Burma Corps who could speak and read Japanese well, it would be unsullied for some time. With attention focused on Singapore, troops in Burma were under strength, poorly armed, and ill prepared. The front line consisted of the Seventeenth Indian Division, trained and equipped to fight in the deserts of the Middle East, and the First Burma Division, barely trained at all; neither had battle experience.

The main obstacle confronting the Japanese on their march from the Thai border toward Rangoon, Burma's capital and the actual and symbolic core of British strength, was the Sittang River, some sixty miles northeast of the city. There a large part of the Seventeenth Indian Division was lost on February 23 when the divisional commander decided to blow the Sittang Bridge in a despairing attempt to halt the Japanese advance, leaving two out of three brigades on the enemy side. Now there was little hope of holding Rangoon. It fell on March 8; and but for a rare stroke of good luck for the Allies, the campaign might have ended there and then.

One of the Japanese divisional commanders, swooping down on Rangoon from the east, had received orders to bypass the city and swing round to attack it from the west. To cover his flank as he crossed above Rangoon, he set up a strong roadblock on the main road north—and inadvertently bottled up the British garrison, which at this point included the Burma front commander, General Harold Alexander, and his headquarters, as it tried to get away from the city. "All the Japanese commander had to do then," observed Slim later, "was to keep his road-block in position and with the rest of his troops attack the forty-mile column strung out along the road. Nothing could have saved the British, tied as they were by their mechanical transport to the ribbon of road." Luckily for them, the Japanese commander stuck rigidly to the letter of his orders, and pressed on to complete his flanking maneuver, withdrawing the roadblock once his main body had crossed. "The Japanese division thus entered Rangoon from the west, according to plan; the British, finding the cork removed, flowed on, bag and baggage, to the north, also according to plan."

The British ground troops could look for little help elsewhere. The paper plans for Burma's defense had placed great reliance on air power; yet in December 1941 Burma had been allocated a single RAF squadron and a flight of the Indian Air Force, equipped with Buffalo fighters and other obsolete machines quite incapable of equaling the Zero and other Japanese planes.

Resistance was stiffened by the P-40s and Hurricanes of the American Volunteer Group under Colonel Claire Chennault, a former pilot who had left the U.S. Air Force in 1937 to act as Chiang's air adviser and assembled a group of daring and experienced pilots round him. These "Flying Tigers" happened to be fitting out in Rangoon at the time of the Japanese advance, and with the RAF did their utmost to harass the invaders as they progressed north from Rangoon.

But they were hopelessly outnumbered. With massive raids on the virtually defenseless Allied airfields, the Japanese had secured control of the air by the end of March. Reconnaissance planes in the air and disaffected Burmese informers on the ground made it relatively simple to locate the British ground forces as they positioned themselves to defend the line from Toungoo to Prome, stretching between the Irrawaddy and the Sittang about 150 miles north of Rangoon, and crucial if the Allies were going to save the vital oil fields at Yenangyaung.

The British were reinforced at this point by Chinese troops under the orders of General "Vinegar Joe" Stilwell, sent by Roosevelt and accepted by Chiang as the nominal commander of Chinese forces in Burma. The Chinese performed better than Stilwell's reports would suggest, but it was not enough. Prome fell, then Toungoo; the British themselves fired the oil fields before retreating. The Chinese force was overwhelmed south of Mandalay, and the Japanese attack drove a wedge between them and their Western allies. Once the Japanese had captured Lashio, the southern terminus of the Burma Road, resistance was over. The Japanese established a screen of troops along the Indian border and eastward, between China to the north and Burma, Thailand, and Indochina to the south, pushing all before them.

The Chinese withdrew to the northeast up the Salween River and back over the border into Yunnan; the British pulled back to the northwest across the Chindwin River into India, with Lieutenant General Shozo Sakurai, commander of the Thirty-third Division, in hot pursuit. Marching as much as thirty miles a day, Sakurai fought 34 battles in 127 days and inflicted heavy casualties. In the end he could not stop the British forces reaching India; but the cost of safety was appalling.

After Mandalay, the British were falling back away from their supplies, struggling in the wet and filth of an early monsoon, on roads clogged with hundreds of thousands of Indian civilians trying to get home. The first of the army survivors to reach India were, in Slim's phrase, "an undisciplined mob of fugitives intent only on escape." Behind them came the organized formations, in the most pitiful condition. Most had ghastly sores, or were so crippled by dysentery that they left a trail of blood behind them; some were on the verge of insanity. During the 900-mile trek, over 13,000 British, Indian, Gurkha, and Burmese troops died of wounds, disease, and starvation. As for the civilian refugees, it was impossible to keep count, but the death toll may have been as high as 50,000.

In neither Malaya nor Burma did the Japanese have the chance to measure their skills against strong resistance. Hong Kong, in contrast, had provided a brief opportunity. The mainland enclave of Kowloon fell far more easily than anticipated, when a lieutenant on a scouting mission noticed that the British forces along the "Gin-Drinkers' Line," the forward line of defense, were stretched very thin; he took a platoon through the barbed wire at night and launched a brilliantly successful surprise attack, deep in enemy territory, which left the colony's defenses off balance and tottering.

But on Hong Kong Island the defenders, spurred by desperation, were harder to dislodge. Their defiant resistance was a catalyst for some of the most savage Japanese atrocities of the Pacific War—nuns raped and murdered in the streets, hospital patients bayoneted and mutilated in their beds, nurses raped on the bodies of the dead. But however brave, the garrison was little more than a police force, hopelessly isolated from command headquarters in Malaya. With Kowloon taken, Hong Kong was essentially indefensible, and on Christmas Day, 1941, it fell.

In the Philippines the Japanese would come far nearer to defeat. By the time the island fortress of Corregidor finally surrendered on May 6, 1942, the besiegers, outnumbered three to one, were almost as short of ammunition as the besieged. The campaign had also put some of the weaknesses of the High Command on show—most conspicuously the clashes of personality, differing priorities, and individual ambitions.

Fortunately for the Japanese, Allied strategy too was riven by disagreement. America's policy toward its colony had veered between a determination to use the islands as a spearhead in any conflict with Japan, and the desire to abandon them and fall back on Hawaii. But even if the Americans had been unequivocally determined to hold the Philippines, on December 8, 1941, when the Japanese attacked, they were not ready to do so.

The "old" U.S. Army in the islands, in the words of one American commentator was "an army of polo ponies and long golf games, of cheap domestic help, and shopping trips to Shanghai and Hong Kong. At the Army and Navy Club, officers gathered each year on the lawn to listen to the Army-Navy football game during the early hours of the morning. When Army made a touchdown, a mule would be ceremoniously paraded around the lawn. When Navy scored, a goat was similarly honored."

As for the auxiliary Filipino forces, most were lamentably ill-trained. In 1939 Manuel Quezon had visited Japan; convinced by the crushing strength of the Imperial war machine that it was futile for the Philippines to resist, he cut the arms budget, halved reserve training, and postponed mobilization. As a result many Filipino troops would go into action without ever previously having fired their rifles—obsolete Enfields and Springfields—and with such basic equipment as helmets and shoes missing. Seventy different dialects made this makeshift force next to impossible to command.

In the circumstances, the rapid progress of the Japanese advance under General Masaharu Homma was hardly surprising. Bad luck and thick fog had grounded the U.S. air forces at Clark Field when Japanese planes raced over. Many of the American planes had taken off for action, but had returned; they were sitting targets for an attack that destroyed nearly a hundred of them on the ground and temporarily paralyzed American air forces in the Philippines. The subsequent landings were virtually unopposed, and with a relentless Japanese pincer movement closing on Manila, the Americans declared it an open city and retreated fast toward the Bataan peninsula before their forces could be trapped and divided.

At this point, some of Homma's advisers pointed out that enemy possession of Bataan would present a permanent threat to Manila Harbor and urged him to intercept the retreat. But Homma had strict instructions from Tojo—whom he disliked but needed to impress—to win a spectacular victory, readily convertible into political points; only the capture of the capital would meet requirements. Underestimating the tenacity of the defenders, Homma put off the mopping-up operation until he had taken Manila, by which time the Americans had had time to conduct an almost leisurely evacuation; they were firmly dug in, and the High Command had begun to withdraw troops for the invasion of Java.

What conspired to defeat the retreat to Bataan was the "Europe First" policy. Homma was saved from the full consequences of his neglect of Bataan by the Allies' failure to honor any of their constant promises of reinforcements and food. Gradually the morale of the "Battling Bastards" of Bataan was destroyed, by uninterrupted bombing, the broadcasts of Tokyo Rose, malaria, and night blindness, but above all by the suspicion, turning to certainty, of having been abandoned. On February 22, Roosevelt ordered MacArthur to leave the Philippines for Australia; his last words as he handed over his command to General Jonathan Wainwright were received by his men with some skepticism: "I shall return."

By the time the surviving Americans had finally been forced into the cellars and tunnels of Corregidor, Homma's career was in jeopardy. The southward surge had lost some of its impetus and the Americans had been allowed to sustain a last-ditch stand that would be used as an inspiration and rallying cry for the rest of the war. Four thousand men had crammed on to the Rock, with most of the wounded huddled underground in the Malinta Tunnel. General Wainwright was able to visualize what would happen if the Japanese took the tunnel, and he could not face the prospect, either on humanitarian or on political grounds; the American generals, unlike the Japanese, had to consider the feelings of the electorate, which had no taste for suicidal gallantry. He surrendered, at a moment when the Japanese themselves had reached the verge of exhaustion, having sustained three times the number of the American casualties.

Many of the men Wainwright had saved were to die tragically in the days that followed. The Japanese were anxious to clear the strategically significant tip of the Bataan peninsula, and had made plans for the evacuation of 25,000 prisoners north to Camp O'Donnell, near San Fernando on the western coast of Luzon. They had not anticipated that the actual number of American and Filipino prisoners would be almost three times that number, or that their physical condition would already be very poor, and the arrangements for transport, food, and medical attention were totally inadequate. The nineteen-mile march the Japanese military officials had planned—and which they would have considered well within the powers of a Japanese force—turned into an excruciating sixty-five-mile ordeal.

Most of the casualties died of heatstroke, starvation, exhaustion and disease. The remainder were tortured and murdered by guards who grew increasingly brutal as the horrible fiasco of the plan became more obvious. Prisoners were killed for their scanty possessions, or bayoneted when they could not keep up. One elderly captain begged a guard to put him out of his misery with a single shot; a young American soldier was taken from the line and forced at riflepoint to beat the captain and bury

315

him alive. The young soldier later committed suicide. At several points along the way there were bloody, motiveless massacres. Almost 11,000 American and Filipino prisoners died on the road between Mariveles and San Fernando; thousands more died after reaching Camp O'Donnell, where the captives were forced to exist in indescribable squalor.

Beyond the Philippines, the original objectives of the Hundred Days campaign had been achieved long ago. After the stunning success at Singapore, the invasion of the East Indies had been brought forward by a month and carried through triumphantly with a giant pincer movement on Java. In the end the Allies, shaken and full of mutual recriminations after the naval calamity in the Battle of the Java Sea, offered little credible defense of the precious oil fields. Flushed with triumph, the Army Ministry and General Staff now recommended leaving the southward advance to rest on its laurels, and moving troops back north again to confront the old enemies in China and Manchuria. A mere twenty-one battalions, the Army Ministry suggested, would be enough to secure the gains in the south. The war in the Pacific, they seemed to imply, was as good as over.

31

"BENEATH THE SKIN": THE JAPANESE FIGHTING MAN

"To attempt an estimate of the Japanese Army is something like attempting to describe the other side of the moon. . . ." In the wake of the Hundred Days, America and Britain did not know what had hit them. How had they been routed by forces that had fought themselves to a standstill in China, of whose declining discipline and morale there had been so many rumors? Whom exactly were they fighting? The heroes of the Russo-Japanese War? The apparent insurgents of the Manchurian Incident and the other attempted coups of the 1930s? The barbarians of Nanking?

In truth, in those early weeks the Allies had been their own worst enemies, defeated by their own weaknesses as much as by Japanese strength. Japan's principal assets were surprise, brilliantly exploited, and a far greater degree of readiness.

The Imperial Army, after all, was already at battle stations. On the other hand, the U.S. Army at the time of Pearl Harbor was, in the view of one American critic, "a tight-knit, hard-drinking, hard-bitten long-service army: an army of inspections and close-order drill, and of long evenings over drinks at the officers' club"—a force in which most NCOs had over twenty years' service and it could take that long for a first lieutenant to make captain. A new ethos was, perforce, on the way. Figures like General George C. Marshall had laid the theoretical foundations for a new and innovative approach to war, with major projected changes in organization and battlefield tactics. But these plans were far from full implementation. The years of isolationism had held the services' budget to 2 percent of GNP; and in 1941 only three divisions were anywhere near full strength.

The Japanese at this point had been mobilizing officially and in earnest for four years. After the war the High Command would insist that they had prepared only for battle on the Asian mainland, against China and to counter the Russian threat, not for large-scale war against the Allies. The fact remained that in 1941 there were two and a quarter million men—however variable their quality—on active service: one and a quarter million in Manchuria and North China, the rest divided between Korea, Formosa, and the home islands. In Japan itself, four and a half million reserves stood by. Once Aritomo Yamagata had intended the army to be a school for the nation; now it seemed that the nation had become a school for the military—a "nation-in-reserve," with military values being implanted in its citizens at every turn.

Within the ranks of the Imperial Army stood the forces of its colonies and "protégés." Korea, notoriously, would supply many of the guards in Japanese prison camps, and thousands of its people were forcibly transported to Japan as laborers. Formosan aborigines—hardy, skilled in mountain lore, and well used to living off the land—made excellent commandos. The pick of the Manchukuo army were sent to Japan for further education, and the other puppet regimes in China had "Peace Preservation Armies" as potential allies in fighting on the mainland. Some 41,000 more Chinese served Japan as coolies, carried to the front or to the homeland like cattle, in freight cars in whose sleeping area it was barely possible to sit up, let alone stand.

The prospect of shaking off European rule was dangled before the nationalist armies of Burma, India, and Indonesia, and the bait was taken—though sometimes the freedom fighters may have wondered what they were being offered instead. "Before the war, the East people was thought for animal by our enemy English and USA," explained a Japanese spokesman attempting through the medium of the English language to recruit Naga tribesmen. "Now we treat for a dear friend by Nippon, and build a happy countries by their own hands. . . . India has many guns, balls, swords, tanks and motor cars which is presenting by Nippon. You can strike English by your own hands. . . . To capture a happy India please you will give me much rices, grains, cows, pigs, hens, eggs and so on. Rice is equal to a hard hammer knocks down our enemies."

The Japanese had quantity—and in the troops which had stormed down the Malayan peninsula they had had the highest quality, well trained and well equipped for their task. But they did not have this kind of strength in depth. The remainder even of the five corps specially assembled for the strike south were inferior; one outstanding corps, drawn mainly from Kyushu, had led the charge on Singapore, and the rest simply followed along behind, in the view of Lieutenant General Yoshio Tanaka, then serving in the mobilization section of the Imperial General Staff.

In order to raise even five corps, the army had had to scrape the bottom of the manpower barrel still further. The demands of the China War had already forced the army to look beyond its reserves to civilian conscripts. Now every mobilization plan had to be extended to its outer limit. Categories of men who had previously been scorned—like the hard-case inner-city draftees, more resistant to the attentions of the Imperial Military Reservists Association—suddenly had important roles to play. Soon the age limits would be widened in both directions, and student deferments abolished.

Nor did many of these new recruits have anything resembling the kind of training given to the crack Fifth and Eighteenth Divisions for Malaya. "It should be borne deeply in mind that a drop of sweat before the battle is well worth a drop of blood after the fighting has started." The influx of raw conscripts put intolerable pressure on training facilities, and thousands of Japanese warriors would go overseas with the most rudimentary skills and a mere three months' training behind them. The pool of qualified instructors had already been drained once to meet the needs of troops in China and Manchuria. Now the shortage of teachers was making it necessary to curtail courses and exercises. Admiral Yamamoto presumably had some casualty statistic in mind when he announced suddenly that he considered death in training to be a hero's death. Certainly both regimen and ethos were becoming much harsher.

The longer the new war lasted, the worse the manpower situation would get, as the caliber of the material available to the Imperial Army in the Pacific deteriorated. The vast bulk of the forces stationed on the Asian mainland were of variable quality. The elite forces of the Kwantung Army were, generally speaking, being held in reserve against the Soviet Union; the thirty divisions mobilized in Manchuria for the Kantokuen "maneuvers" were to stay there on the alert. The troops in China were worn, battered, and coarsened by four years of brutal war.

Their military effectiveness had been significantly impaired, their morale eroded—and a lack of faith in victory was readily translated into indiscipline. Even the Army Ministry was prepared to admit that standards of conduct were on the decline. In September 1940 Naoichi Kawara, adjutant of the ministry, went so far as to issue a small printed pamphlet entitled "Plan for Improving Discipline," which listed "special characteristics of crimes and misbehavior in the China Incident."

Official priorities were quite clear. Crimes against superiors within the army—insolence, threatening behavior, violence, even the occasional murder—were considered a far more serious menace to good order than crimes against the native population. But both were admitted to be increasing. "From the outbreak of the China incident to 1939, 588 men were punished by courts-martial for threatening a superior with violence or being insolent; 78 for insubordination. . . . Compare this with the 120 crimes against superiors which developed during the whole of the Russo-Japanese War. Even though there has been an increase in the overall number of soldiers, the ratio of crime can be seen to have increased. From the outbreak of the China Incident to 1939, 420 men were punished by courts-martial for plundering or for plundering accompanied by rape resulting in death; 312 for rape or for rape resulting in death; and 494 men for gambling. Beside these we find other cases of violence, incendiarism and murder inflicted on Chinese."

The bloodless, matter-of-fact phraseology is chilling when one even begins to visualize the horrible scenes which "plundering accompanied by rape resulting in death" actually represents. And the court-martial statistics are derisory when set against the vast totals of suffering that the Imperial Army left behind it in China. But the pamphlet is at least an indication that the military acknowledged some fraction of the truth; and its diagnosis of the causes of war crimes is illuminating.

> In order to suppress crime and misbehaviour . . . the following important facts should be borne in mind.
> 1. The majority of the offenders were drunk at the time.
> 2. Those responsible for the crimes are principally called-up reservists, especially those from the first and second reserve services.
> 3. Comparatively few of the crimes are committed by men facing

the enemy. They are mostly by men on guard duty and rear-area duty.

4. These acts increase directly after combat and during halt. When the men are on the move, especially during combat, they are few.

5. Many of these crimes are motivated by a feeling of superiority toward the people of the territories involved in the Incident.

6. Many result from lax interior administration.

7. With the lengthening of the Incident:
   a. There is a tendency for crimes and misconduct to become more perverse and skillful.
   b. There is a tendency for incidents involving regular servicemen to increase.
   c. There is a tendency for crimes motivated by a desire for material gain to increase in accordance with length of halt.
   d. A great deal of talk and action requiring attention springs from combat fatigue, desire for a triumphal return home, and dislike of army life.

8. There are incidents springing from mental derangement in places with unseasonable weather.

Every officer in the Imperial Army should have committed this document to memory if there was to be any chance of forestalling the horrors of Japanese misconduct in the Pacific War. And the pamphlet shows clearly that not only was this army not the force that had won the Russo-Japanese War in 1905, it was not even the same army that had entered the Sino-Japanese War in 1937.

32

"FAITH IS STRENGTH":
FIGHTING SPIRIT

D isciplinary problems were the more worrying in the Imperial Army
because they ate away at the foundations of its principal bastion,
the one feature in which its leaders claimed clear superiority over any
force in the world: its fighting spirit. The Japanese soldier was heir, the
High Command insisted, to a martial tradition that made him an invincible opponent.

Spirit was indeed a military advantage, and one which was relied
upon to compensate for deficiencies in training, equipment, and the basic
caliber of recruits as the conscription net was thrown ever wider. For the
army leaders, all the qualities listed in the Emperor Meiji's Rescript to
Soldiers and Sailors and given practical application in the Field Service
Code were bankable. The individual soldier's willingness to endure
hunger and cold was essential to the economies that the Japanese Army
was always going to be obliged to make. His obedience underwrote every
commander's tactics. His feeling of invulnerability gave him resilience
and forward momentum. "Faith is Strength" was the credo, in contrast

to the English-speaking soldier's ethos of self-deprecation, understatement, and wary realism. "It was very galling to us," complained the commander of the First U.S. Marines, "to sit on Guadalcanal and listen to the radio at night; we would sit there and listen to these people make a statement, well, they *hoped* we could hold Guadalcanal. One Army Air Force general even said it was foolish to try."

The Japanese soldier was required to display qualities that every army covertly hopes for, even expects, but shrinks from demanding directly. From the commander's point of view, the most useful practical property of the Japanese soldier was his willingness to die, which removed all limits on what his leaders could attempt. A legacy of the authentic samurai ethic, as the war progressed acceptance of death became ever more heavily stressed—just as it was ever more necessary.

It was an attribute that all armies would have preferred their troops to possess—one that the wholly efficient fighting man *must* possess. In the words of one chronicler of the U.S. Army, the soldier must aim for "a final, full acceptance that his name is already written down in the rolls of the already dead. . . . Only then can he function as he ought to function under fire." But in other armies these ideas are implicit, kept decently hidden for the sake of morale. In the Imperial Japanese Army they were flourished for the sake of morale.

The Japanese Thirty-third Division was told when about to attack Imphal that the division would be annihilated but they would win a victory; troops in the Arakan were informed that they would die and their bodies would lie rotting in the sand dunes, but they would turn to grass, which would sway in the breezes blowing from Japan. Promises like these would not have put fire in the bellies of many Allied troops; and in the mouths of Allied leaders, exhortations to fight to the last man failed to persuade.

"Battle must be fought to the bitter end. Commanders and senior officers should die with their troops. The honour of the British Empire is at stake. With the Russians fighting as they are and the Americans so stubbornly at Luzon, the whole reputation of our country is at stake." Churchill's message to General Percival at Singapore sounds like what it was: a political gesture aimed at persuading the Australians that Britain was trying its hardest to forestall a Japanese invasion of Australia. No British soldier would have been happy to die simply to keep Britain's end up in what Churchill presented as a kind of "bravest nation" contest. Percival's military record put his personal courage beyond question, but he refused the command to sacrifice his men.

At the beginning of the war, even after decades of moral instruction and the transformation of the concept of Japan's national essence into an official printed creed, the Japanese notion of spirit was less crude, simplistic, and inflexible than it is sometimes depicted as being. In some respects, it was a heightening of normal standards and values rather than otherworldly dogma, and there was room within it for the shrewd and practical. Between the lofty exhortations of the Field Service Code gleams a sometimes surprising understanding of human weakness. "Remember that 'Do not allow yourself to become bored' is the saying of an ancient general. . . . Do not despise your enemy or the natives. Do not be negligent after a small success. . . . Control your anger and suppress your grudges. . . . Do not allow yourself to worry about the fate of those at home in the event of your death."

But as Japan's material strength was eroding, the pressure on her spiritual resources became ever more intense, and it was these human qualities that were crushed out of the Japanese fighting spirit. Only the everlasting readiness for death remained, by which all other qualities were measured and to which they were often reduced. "Responsibility" was often cited as an important element of the Japanese spirit; but rarely did the term convey any sense of initiative or self-respect, simply overtones of duty to a higher power. Most often it simply meant "obedience."

"The Japanese Army's absolute obedience to orders," wrote one Japanese veteran, "is grounded . . . upon a psychology of submission to those who have power. As soldiers, we were unable to hold the conviction . . . that you must not surrender to power when it fails to live up to your own idea of what is right."

Mindless or not, "spirit" produced behavior of extraordinary heroism in the Pacific War. Citations were very rarely given to individuals in the Japanese army, more usually to units, as one might expect in a group-oriented society. Nevertheless, General Slim was convinced from his observations, which were thorough enough, that Japanese courage was "distinctly an individual rather than a collective characteristic." Certainly the Japanese had elaborated some highly effective methods for fighting in teams, like the assault technique that enabled a team of seven to knock out a pillbox. But when isolated, the Japanese soldier fought on alone. His courage was often so spectacular as to have an element of the theatrical in Western eyes; when his comrades were dead, Slim suggested, his ancestors were his audience.

During the invasion of Singapore, men of the Fifteenth Independent Engineer Regiment were helping to transport troops across the

Johore Straits in open barges lashed together for stability. Lance Corporal Kiyoichi Yamamoto was steering a group of three when suddenly the two outer ones were destroyed by shellfire. "Lance Corporal Yamamoto's chest was torn open, exposing his right lung through his ribs," wrote Colonel Tsuji later, describing his personal citation. "He continued, however, to direct the boat forward and single-handed maneuvered it to the disembarkation point, and without a hitch landed the troops aboard. Then, saying, 'Long live his Majesty the Emperor,' and praying for the certain victory of the Imperial Army, he closed his eyes with composure and died."

The soldiers did not have to be bullied to behave like this; to a large extent, compulsion had been successfully internalized. There seems to have been no deliberate psychological preparation for individual banzai charges. "It was gathered that there may have been impromptu exhortations from unit commanders," concluded American researchers later, "and there was reported definitely a 'mutual exhortation' which started between unit members and increased to the point of mob hysteria. [But] this was a spontaneous affair and not maneuvered by the commanding officers, who merely explained the tactical situation and placed the challenge before the men."

Unlike the Allies, who tried to "manage" fear, admitting it, analyzing it, and learning to live with it, the Japanese simply rejected it. "There is a philosophy of both ancient and modern times that a large and imposing building may be destroyed by an ant hole. For this reason, there must not be even one soldier without spirit."

The Japanese tended to regard "spirit" as their main strength, with almost mystical potency—an amulet, whose loss would be fatal. Beyond doubt it carried them to some startling victories; but at the same time, it carried within it Japan's undoing. The more convinced the Allies became that they were dealing with no ordinary enemy, the less willing they were to take chances or to offer the Japanese the benefit of any doubt; their responses were conditioned by fear and incomprehension. In a sense, the Japanese conception of spirit governed the behavior of armies on both sides, pushing back the borders of what was considered taboo and opening the way to excess.

33

"GANGSTERS,
CAT-BURGLARS
AND POACHERS":
THE PHILOSOPHY OF
THE ATTACK

"It has begun to dawn on the Japanese," wrote a Western observer in 1930, "that they must evolve a school of tactics suitable to their own peculiar needs." Japan's "peculiar need" was to make the most of her principal resource—to find a means of transplanting the spirit of her soldiers into effective action. As a result, the strategy and tactics of the Imperial Army were dominated by the attack.

The attack does not simply give an army the initiative and freedom of action, it carries with it a certain moral superiority. In island caves and jungle pillboxes, the Japanese would later find a way of making the defense a very special kind of tribute to the Emperor. But at the start of the Pacific War, as in the China War—and the Russo-Japanese War thirty years before—Japanese soldiers of all ranks were "thoroughly imbued with the spirit of offence, in which they tend to see the solution of all problems. The almost instinctive reaction of any Japanese commander in a new, unexpected or difficult situation is to look for some way to assume the offensive."

This was no longer the massed frontal assault against fixed defenses learned, with the help of Major Meckel, from Prussia. Weapons had developed far beyond the capacity of the largest number of troops to overcome them, as World War I had demonstrated twenty years before, and the Germans themselves had long abandoned the massed infantry charge against prepared positions. Under the direst pressure, the Japanese might on occasion revert to something resembling it, but in general they had chosen to break away from the kind of large-scale slogging match, ruinously expensive of men and weapons, which in the long run they could only expect to lose.

Instead they devised methods of warfare that played to their own strengths—not weight of arms, but speed, mobility, and surprise. Fundamental to the new approach was the decision to switch to the triangular divisional structure (a move also adopted by the U.S. Army once General Marshall became Chief of Staff in 1939). Previously, each Japanese division had contained four regiments, falling into two symmetrical combat teams that were deployed in columns to penetrate and destroy the enemy head-on—a structure that put the emphasis on firepower. The new triangular structure provided three units: one for attack, one for envelopment, and one in reserve to support either the attacking or the enveloping force. This was a far more flexible arrangement, which made for greatly increased mobility.

In mobility and surprise, the Japanese were employing the weapons of the underdog. They knew the Allies' artillery and armor to be greatly superior to their own; hence the need to move the emphasis away from firepower. If they stayed on the base line, as it were, and exchanged ground strokes, they could only lose; to score, they had to come in hard and fast behind an unpredictable serve and take on their opponents at the net.

They had to lure the enemy in close for what they hoped would be a decisive encounter. All their unique strengths were short-range: hand-to-hand fighting, which was the most direct expression of spirit; skill with the sword and bayonet, which had the power to frighten Western enemies out of all proportion to the damage the weapons actually caused. "They seemed to exult in struggle body to body," complained one Western observer later. "They produced gestures of defiance and glee and also of fear which, by most other soldiers, were regarded as childish. A skirmish was accompanied by grunts, gasps and bloodcurdling yells. Later, when Japanese films became popular in the West, it was seen that the Japanese soldier had fought very much as Japanese actors tradition-

327

ally represented him as doing. It made him a surprising and alarming adversary."

The Allies felt the force of the new tactics at once, as the successive waves of invaders broke on the shores of Southeast Asia. Hitting the beaches and overwhelming hastily assembled defenses, they moved inland as fast as they could, breaking into wide envelopment formation. Lead elements fanned out, shouting and shooting to draw enemy fire; in the center, frontal assault was delayed while small parties carried out flanking attacks on their own initiative—overall, a most skillful and alarming infiltration of enemy positions. "The speed with which the advance is conducted cannot be over-emphasized," an Allied training manual of 1942 warned gloomily. After that, the battle would develop very quickly, as a leapfrogging system brought fresh troops into action constantly.

The approach was the same once the early battles were over and the advance established. Frontal attacks on a small scale were, obviously, still part of the tactical repertoire—to capture a specific feature, say, or engineer a breakthrough toward an enemy command center. But where possible, the Japanese preferred flank and rear attacks, pushing through jungle that their opponents had dismissed as "impenetrable," or, on the Malayan peninsula, hopping down the coast in small boats to come up behind the Allied troops and force, or accelerate, their retreat. "The Japanese use of small launches captured at Penang to tow barges filled with infantry," remembered one veteran of the Malayan campaign, "meant they could land, remain hidden, and attack at will, wherever required. It was this uncertainty, never knowing whether they would appear at your rear, which was one of the most demoralizing factors to the British and Indian soldiers in that withdrawal down Malaysia."

Fears and apprehensions were exaggerated by darkness; and from the beginning the Japanese made the night attack their specialty. "The night is one million reinforcements," ran a training slogan—and the night attack one means of neutralizing superior enemy strength, in particular artillery strength. With some ingenuity, the General Staff traced the Japanese fondness for the night attack to their emotional attachment to the sword. To be effective against an enemy armed with bazooka and machine gun, close combat with the sword needed an element of surprise, and this was most easily achieved at night; thus, a central tactical maneuver was wrapped in the aura of "spirit" from the outset.

Most people function worst between three and six in the morning, when the metabolic rate is at its lowest. The soldier woken from sleep by an attack (like the men at Pearl Harbor, in Malaya, the Philippines, Kowloon, Singapore, Guam, and Wake Island) is dazed, disoriented, breathless, and virtually blind for the crucial first moments. The attacker has been awake long enough for his system to make some of the necessary adjustments, and for his eyes to reach peak nighttime vision, a process that can take up to an hour. Even a small group of Japanese night raiders, if well organized, could spread confusion and fear intense enough to start a large-scale panic, with the Allied troops firing wildly and turning on each other.

"During the nights," remembered a marine who had been at Munda, on New Georgia, "men rested in foxholes three or four feet deep. Usually there were four men in a foxhole, sometimes less. Japs sneaked in pairs towards the foxholes. One would often jump into the middle of our men and try to stab them. The other stood by to see the outcome. Sometimes, the Japs would jump in the foxhole and then jump out quickly, hoping our troops would become excited and stab each other. 'They must have springs on their feet,' one soldier said."

General Slim attributed much of the Japanese success at night to the high proportion of troops from a rural background. "The more civilized we become, the more we draw our soldiers from well-lighted towns, the more clumsy and frightened shall we be in the dark, and the greater the odds in favour of a more primitive foe." He was overlooking, or choosing to ignore, the intensive training that night attacks required and that all Japanese soldiers, rural or urban, were obliged to undergo.

The first essentials were the ability to move in silence and identify sounds and objects in the dark. British officers in Burma, trying to turn raw reinforcements into jungle fighters, deeply envied the Japanese capacity for stealth. They found their own men far too noisy, especially the Gurkha officers, who were possibly coarsened by an excess of blitz and assault courses in training. "Although we *do* want 'gangsters,' " one complained, "we also want cat-burglars and poachers, and every man must combine the qualities of all three."

The Japanese were believed to possess these qualities by nature. In fact, the Japanese soldier spent a significant proportion of his training acquiring them. He spent long hours mastering techniques of crawling— moving forward with his weight on his left palm and on his left leg below the knee (this was the fastest, but also the noisiest way); lifting himself on his left elbow and right toe, with his left hip or, alternatively, his stomach, touching the ground; and inching forward using both elbows and both toes, with the whole body flat on the ground and his rifle cradled in the crook of both arms.

He was trained to wrap the metal blade of his bayonet and the hobnails on his boots in cloth to avoid telltale glints; to fill his canteen to the top and stuff his ammunition pouch with paper, to quiet slopping water and rattling bullets; to keep calm and quiet whatever happened. "A dog bays the moon and a thousand curs follow suit," he was told. He learned how to adapt his fighting techniques. In the dark, nine out of ten soldiers would make their bayonet thrusts too short. One training routine showed him how to "thrust several dummies successively"—a horrible reminder of the havoc a determined night attacker could wreak in a sleeping camp.

First with dark glasses, then in bright moonlight on the barrack square, then finally in pitch blackness across difficult country, he accustomed himself to the new conditions, taking his bearings from compass, moon and stars, and natural features, with occasional help from star shells, whistles, and trails laid with flour or chalk by others in his patrol. Assault leaders would stretch strips of white material across their backs, even sometimes drench themselves in a distinctive scent, to keep their men in line behind them.

The trainee learned to disguise his own silhouette, and to recognize the shapes of others and the effects that the phase and angle of the moon might have on what he saw. "Groves of small pine trees are often mistaken for enemy patrols and a low bank is sometimes taken for an enemy column." He was encouraged to fall flat at regular intervals and scan the horizon for suspect outlines. Army medical researchers had a theory that off-center was sharper than forward vision, because it used the part of the retina which contained most of the rods, the red cells enabling the eye to see objects in the dark. Trainees practiced looking at an angle toward objects they were trying to identify. They discovered that in the dark they were likely to overestimate the distance to an obstacle but underestimate their distance from a flash.

Noises, too, gradually began to form identifiable patterns—the sounds of weapons being primed, vehicles moving at different distances, communications equipment being operated, positions being constructed. The soldier learned that it was easy to overestimate the number of men in a patrol from the sound of their footsteps, and that "barking dogs may indicate troops passing through a village and the sudden stopping of insects' singing may indicate an approaching enemy."

"Though cunning, he is stupid and unoriginal, and so subject to ruses," wrote British military intelligence of the Japanese soldier, with the open-minded humility that had endeared the British to millions of imperial subjects. "He is evidently intensely inquisitive in a small 'Native' way." As their supply situation got worse, Japanese troops found it very difficult to resist bait in the form of caches of food and ammunition, and their antipathy to the retreat laid them open to ambush. But whatever they endured in the way of Allied ruses and ploys, they were more than able to repay.

The Japanese scout was unequaled in the art of drawing fire, because he was willing to take any risk. "Sometimes an enemy soldier in plain sight would walk slowly towards the American lines," wrote an American marine in horrified admiration. "Fire from all directions easily knocked him down, but this gave our positions away." A less expensive method was to work a rifle bolt backward and forward, or crack two pieces of bamboo together to simulate rifle fire.

Drawing fire could be a joint maneuver. "On several occasions," reported U.S. Marine Corps intelligence officers in New Guinea, "on first contact the Japs in large numbers attacked. On being met by strong fire from our troops, they immediately turned around and fled. When our troops followed up to take advantage of the apparent demoralisation, the retreating Japs threw themselves on the ground, and our men ran into machine-gun fire from the Japanese rear."

Another specialty was the "jitter attack"—an all-out effort to cause the kind of panic that would induce the enemy to destroy themselves. Voices would call out in English, Hindi, or Gurkhali to distract and mislead: "OK Johnny, cease fire," "OK Bill, stand down." Sometimes the aim was simply to terrify. Troops recently arrived at the battlefront found it hard to express the horror of hearing all around them in the night, among the other unfamiliar screeches, whistles, and rustles of the jungle, spectral wails and yells—"Marine, you die!" "U.S. Marines be dead tomorrow."

The jungles of Southeast Asia were ideal terrain for ruses and ploys, ambushes and misinformation. To many Allied troops, uneasy and acutely uncomfortable in alien surroundings, the jungle seemed to offer an unfair advantage to the Japanese, whom they assumed to be at home there—an insular and ill-informed view, since Japan has no jungle. The Japanese enjoyed fighting in the jungle no more than anyone else. A common saying among Japanese generals, from 1942 onwards, was "I've upset Tojo, I'll probably end up in Burma." But they had taken the precaution of preparing thoroughly and intelligently for it.

Officers and men destined for jungle warfare were briefed on the conditions they could expect and the adjustments they would have to make. Thicker undergrowth would limit fields of fire, enabling enemy patrols to approach positions much more closely; very often one would hear or smell them before one could see them. The lowering canopy of foliage could be unbearably claustrophobic and yet at the same time offer inadequate cover against air attack, since any disturbance or clearing of the vegetation was easily visible from above. Likewise, rice paddies and tea and cultivated palm groves, being laid out in formal patterns, offered almost no cover at all.

Troops were required to be remarkably fit, and prepared mentally for constant suspense and frequent isolation. The holding of a continuous line was out of the question in the jungle. The effect was more of a number of strongpoints held in an enormous no-man's-land through which ranged the patrols and raiders of both sides. "Though the total battle front may be very large and cover thousands of miles," wrote an Allied observer, "the actual battle will usually be small scale, at Platoon or Company level; there can be few general's battles."

In many places the conflict was virtually reduced to guerrilla war. The Japanese army had a tendency to form special units for specific tasks, rather than maintaining permanent "specialist" formations. Japanese commando troops were not a force apart, but were selected from ordinary units for particular missions and returned to them afterward— those who survived. Increasingly, as the initiative slipped from the Japanese and surprise became harder to achieve, it seemed prudent not to launch night attacks blind but to neutralize the enemy's defenses beforehand. This was the unenviable task allotted to the commandos, making every raid a suicide mission.

The troops had their own ideas on guerrilla tactics, which grew wilder as their actual position became more difficult. Japanese officers instructed to canvass suggestions were rewarded with a rich and unpleasant crop of fantasies: "blinding squads" carrying a device to paralyze the enemy's optic nerves, or hydrocyanic acid dischargers, which would work like flamethrowers; explosives carried by kites, or fitted to caterpillar tracks and operated by means of spring and time fuse; bullet-shaped "human tanks" made of wood and towed behind a submarine, for transporting troops underwater; turtle-shaped midget tanks for penetrating enemy positions. "The tanks will each be mounted by one man," wrote the proud inventor. "They will scatter and swarm like baby spiders over enemy positions and attack independently."

Some favored using the native population to pass on tobacco tainted with opium, or attempting economic disruption through counterfeit currency. Others toyed with the idea of "uprooting barbed wire entanglements by using a harpoon"; of installing in aircraft "an optical instrument . . . to locate submerged enemy submarines"; of flying cheap "disposable" planes by automatic pilot at low altitude to lure enemy aircraft to their destruction by crack fighters lurking above the cloud cover.

Psychological warfare was recommended with a frequency that said much about the state of the inventors' own nerves. "We should lower morale in the enemy front lines by broadcasting sentimental music, thus appealing to the enemy's appetite for pleasure," wrote one. Alternatively, the amplified sounds of aircraft, advancing tanks, and artillery barrage might be used to fool the microphones that American forces sometimes planted along their perimeters instead of sentries.

One writer drafted propaganda leaflets with more venom than care for credibility. "From Your Lonely Wife," they began: "Since you left for the front, the days have been lonely, prices are going up every day. . . . Now we must get along with a ration of meat once every ten days. . . . Every evening your old friend Roosevelt the Cripple comes around for a chat and gives me a line. It's disgusting. How I hate war. . . . Please stay alive, even if you have to surrender to the Japanese."

A more direct approach was "promotion of war weariness among the enemy by butchering his troops. It would also be good to distribute photographs of atrocities and photographs of the self-indulgent and deplorable conditions in their country. . . . Badly battered, evil-smelling bodies will be scattered in the path of the enemy's advance, pictures of ghosts, vengeful spirits, betrayers of Christ, etc. will be used to terrify the enemy." What is truly frightening is that several of these ideas, which were presented with the gusto of a children's comic, had already been tried by the High Command, and had close parallels among Allied propaganda ploys.

The Japanese attack did have weaknesses, hard though these might have been to perceive at the time. It was often less than well coordinated, with infantry, artillery, tanks, and air strength failing to interlock and fuse. "The Jap is an absolutely first-class infantryman," wrote one observer, "but he lacks the equipment, communications and perhaps knowledge and desire to use all his arms as a coordinated whole. He will as soon attack a target by patrol as he will by artillery or aircraft. He fights all his weapons as infantry weapons including his artillery and, latterly, his low level attacking aircraft."

The infantryman himself might have found this argument lopsided.

All the onus is on the infantry, and none on the other arms; whereas he might have claimed that he was consistently let down by artillery that was too thin on the ground, underweight, short-ranged, and liable to run out of ammunition. As for the air force, communications between air and ground were often faulty, and pilots were too attached to one-to-one combat to accept team tactics readily.

Often attacks were not followed through as they should have been. Sometimes the resources—transport, supplies and reinforcements—were lacking; but often the problem was a want of flexibility, an inability to see beyond the prescribed objective or to exploit a changing situation. Mistakes were repeated as if by rote. The death of a commander could throw a company into lasting confusion.

Nonetheless, the Japanese attack unit, powered by martial spirit that looked back to one of the world's great military traditions, was one of the world's most formidable fighting forces. The Imperial Army's tragedy was that its other resources—leadership, weaponry, air power, logistics, intelligence—were not equal to the task it had set itself.

34

"DO YOUR BEST AND LEAVE THE REST TO PROVIDENCE": THE SENIOR COMMANDERS

Just as enigmatic as the ordinary—or extraordinary—Japanese soldier were the men who commanded him on and off the field. Yamashita, Homma, Hitoshi Imamura, Terauchi, Renya Mutaguchi, Tsuji: These men were bywords in the Imperial Army and yet, except in military circles, none was known at all outside Japan. Only the name of General Hideki Tojo, who was, after all, prime minister, had some resonance in the West; and even then the perceived image of the brutal, bullet-headed, bespectacled bully bore only partial resemblance to the reality of a shrewd, conscientious administrator, emotional in his dedication to the Emperor, constantly on guard against his enemies, vulnerable in his two noncombatant sons and his overbearing wife.

Japan's senior commanders in the field have frequently been dismissed with hindsight as mediocre, and various accusations have been leveled against them. "Japanese commanders were little better than what Liddell Hart called 'bow and arrow generals.' . . . Operational thinking remained essentially primitive, unscientific, complacent, narrow and sim-

335

plistic." The Japanese placed far too much stress, it was said, on the traditional fighting spirit of their men, at the expense of monstrous casualty rates, and neglected the study of modern theory—the significance of air power, for instance, or the new roles for artillery. Operational orders were often vague and repetitive, leaving the means of implementing them to junior officers. Commanders ignored the possible reaction of the enemy, and concentrated instead on irrelevancies, such as injunctions to lace the boots tightly before marching.

Senior officers are charged with having been simultaneously rash and inflexible. There was certainly an element of unreason in many of their actions, of explicit trusting to luck or destiny, which would not have been tolerated in a Western military leader. In 1943 Lieutenant General Ryotaro Nagai wrote in his essay "On Generals": "It is a fact that victory or defeat in warfare is ascribable to something transcending logic, namely, fate or the *grace of Heaven*. . . . I presume there is hardly a commander who, being responsible for many lives, does not fall into the idea of doing his best first, then praying for the *grace of Heaven.*"

Japan's entry into war was a reckless advance into the unknown—a leap, in Tojo's phrase, from the verandah of the Kiyomizu Temple. He himself admitted to having no idea in 1941 of what the future might bring; the army, he thought, would "manage somehow" in 1942 and even 1943, but beyond that anything might happen. The word he used to describe the leadership once the decision for war had been made was "carefree"; but "unthinking" might have been more fitting. "From fatalism to passivity to the giving up of thought—the path is distinctly cut."

This was a Buddhist attitude reflecting the religious leanings of most of the officer corps, including Tojo. It was honored in the Japanese martial tradition and found at its most perfect in the Zen Buddhism practiced by the samurai. It may help to explain the extraordinarily casual attitude of some generals to the practicalities of their campaigns. General Slim noted with Western-style incredulity that they attacked with a very narrow margin of administrative safety, generally with not more than nine days' supplies in terrain where operations could reasonably be expected to last for weeks. If it was heaven's will that they should win, then something would turn up—perhaps the supply dumps of their enemies; the same cast of mind may have lain beneath the army's dogged refusal to negotiate long after defeat was inevitable. Reason and logic dictated that Japan should surrender; but many commanders seem to have turned away from the thought processes that would have led them to that conclusion, filling their minds instead with the belief that the army's way, the Emperor's way, was the Way of Heaven, and that somehow they would be saved—or die; either way there was little to be done.

"Risk, as a correlate of strategic objectives, stakes and consequences, is not a word that one finds in the ordinary vocabulary of the Japanese military." Neither before nor after operations did leaders care to calculate the human or material costs. Emotion and impulse did much to govern policy; and yet, having rushed into action, commanders often displayed a disastrous rigidity. "The Japanese were ruthless and bold as ants while their designs went well," wrote Slim, "but if those plans were disturbed or thrown out—ant-like again—they fell into confusion, were slow to adjust themselves, and invariably clung to their original schemes. . . . The fundamental fault of their generalship was a lack of moral, as distinct from physical, courage. They were not prepared to admit that they had made a mistake, that their plans had misfired and needed recasting. . . . Rather than confess that, they passed on to their subordinates, unchanged, the orders they had themselves received, well knowing that with the resources available the tasks demanded were impossible."

Each of these charges—strategic crudity, rashness, inflexibility—has some truth, and adds a patch of color to the overall picture of the Japanese military leadership. But the organization was far too complex and varied to be covered by a handful of blanket epithets. Far from displaying the relentless uniformity suggested by the "anthill" simile so dear to Westerners, Japanese leaders were a remarkably disparate group, more so, perhaps, than their Allied counterparts. Though all Japanese commanders were molded by similar backgrounds and training, and welded into informal alliances and power blocs, still there was scope for considerable individual eccentricity and waywardness.

General Renya Mutaguchi conformed in many ways to the Western stereotype of the Japanese officer. Square-faced, with beetling black brows, a heavy moustache, and a sullen jaw, he was brave, aggressive, fanatically stubborn, evil-tempered, and totally indifferent to the human cost of his plans. He displayed more obvious personal ambition than most; he liked to see himself as a prime mover in the outbreak of war in China, and five years later his vanity would be one of the principal motive forces behind the ill-fated march into India.

But at the other end of the scale was Kiyotake Kawaguchi, whose career was effectively blighted by his refusal to throw away the lives of his men. Kawaguchi first attracted the disapproving stare of Imperial

General Headquarters in May 1942 as commander of Japanese forces on Cebu, for his objections to revenge killings of senior Philippine officials. He had worked in a prisoner-of-war camp during World War I and been proud of Japan's humanitarian treatment of the German inmates. To shoot defeated opponents in cold blood was, he argued, a violation of the true Bushido.

Kawaguchi confirmed his suspect reputation when he was appointed commander of one of the detachments sent to retake Guadalcanal. He made a brave and conscientious attempt to carry out his mission, with two desperate attacks on the hill called, with good reason, Bloody Ridge. But the task had, in truth, been hopeless for some time; only the ruthless determination of senior officers ignorant of the appalling conditions on the island kept the offensive alive. Kawaguchi was openly critical of headquarters; a realist, he remarked, "No matter what the Staff College says, it's extremely difficult to take an enemy position by night assault. ... There were a few cases in the Russo-Japanese war but they were only small-scale actions. If we succeed here on Guadalcanal, it will be a wonder in the military history of the world."

Kawaguchi had genuine sympathy for the sufferings of his men; sending a scout out on a particularly hazardous mission, he pressed into his hands a tin of sardines, the only food he had brought personally from Japan, and a gift of incredible value at a moment when hundreds of men were starving every day on the island. Now he was ordered to launch an extraordinarily foolhardy frontal attack, and found that he was not prepared to sacrifice any more lives. Risking the charge of cowardice, he proposed a more circuitous approach—a plan that was never given serious consideration; and then, in circumstances of some confusion, he was accused of having failed to advance. He was abruptly relieved of his command; the frontal assault went ahead and was effectively obliterated.

Far more acceptable to the High Command were death-and-glory eccentrics like Tokutaro Sakurai and Takeichi Nishi. Sakurai was a veteran of the China War, a major in intelligence on the staff of the China Expeditionary Force. Here he had rapidly made his name as a fearless specialist in night attacks; fame turned to notoriety when he experimented with "Dirty Dozen" raids that recruited the talents of thugs and criminals and were too often unacceptably violent. The same Sakurai, however, liked to wear a long and beautiful string of pearls, and was in some demand for his party trick—a Chinese dance performed naked, with lighted cigarettes protruding from his nostrils and the corners of his mouth.

Nishi's glamour was less grotesque. He was a baron, from an exceedingly wealthy family connected to the Imperial household, and before the war his life-style had resembled that of many European aristocrats. His passions were racing boats, fast cars, and show jumping; he toured the European horse shows for years, and eventually won a gold medal at the Los Angeles Olympics. Now a celebrity, he loved other celebrities, and was very proud of the photographs taken of him in Hollywood with Mary Pickford, Douglas Fairbanks, and Spencer Tracy.

As a lieutenant colonel commanding an armored detachment on Iwo Jima, Nishi was a dedicated exponent of Bushido. When his tanks were disabled, he ordered them to be partially buried so that their turrets could be used as artillery weapons. He himself fought to the death on Iwo Jima, as an infantryman. For years he had been a popular figure in Japan, and various legends grew up around his end. In one, though virtually blinded by artillery blast, he had taken part in a night attack, with a devoted orderly guiding his steps; desperately wounded by machine-gun fire, he asked an aide to point him in the direction of the Imperial Palace, and shot himself. In another, still more romantic, he waded into the surf off the northernmost tip of Iwo Jima, the point nearest Japan; with a lock from the mane of his favorite horse, Uranus, in his breast pocket, and the riding crop with which he had won the Olympics in one hand, he shot himself in the head with the other.

Not all Japanese officers were heroes in this mold. General Masafumi Yamauchi was a gentle, frail, pessimistic man. During his years of service as a military attaché in Washington he had become greatly attached to Western food and hygiene. In northern Burma, dying of tuberculosis, he traveled with a Western-style latrine and continued to insist, under impossible conditions, on a diet of milk, oatmeal, and fresh-baked bread. His attitude was anything but gung ho. "The hills of Arakan I have crossed," he wrote in verse, "my journey to the next world." But he showed courage of his own in resisting, silently but stubbornly, Mutaguchi's bullying toward an objective he considered criminally stupid.

Masaharu Homma might more accurately be termed an antihero. His capacities were civilian and, for an officer of the Imperial Army, unconventional: a taste for good paintings and furniture, a modest talent for verse, a flair for Western languages. As for his emotional life, he was regarded as something of a curiosity: the man who had married, disastrously, for love. His first wife, Toshiko, whom he married over the protests of all his friends, was the daughter of a Meiji general; she was

339

notorious for her amours. During his posting to England in 1919, she became an actress, first on the stage and then in the cinema—at that time, considered an extremely dubious occupation; devastated, Homma was only saved with difficulty from throwing himself out of the window of the Langham Hotel in London's Portland Place. When eventually he was persuaded to divorce Toshiko, he promptly made another unorthodox marriage, to the Westernized, independent-minded Fujiko, with whom he was extremely happy until his death.

Homma was forgiven much because of his intellectual brilliance; he graduated from Staff College with the second-highest mark of his year, lower only than Hitoshi Imamura, widely considered one of the most outstanding officers the Imperial Army ever had. But he used his intelligence to examine orders in the light of common sense and humanity, which did not always make him popular. He was considered indulgent to the point of negligence toward the people of the Philippines after the Japanese invasion. (Ironically, it was ultimately for being too easygoing that he would be hanged by MacArthur. Almost certainly he knew nothing about the Bataan Death March, but it took place while he was the commander in charge, and he should perhaps have been more carefully monitoring the conduct of his troops, who were angry and frustrated after the long siege. In that context, a liberal and detached attitude and a distaste for routine administrative chores were defects.)

Tomoyuki Yamashita, known to Western armies as the Tiger of Malaya, was another curiously isolated figure within the ranks of the Japanese leaders. He was one of the most effective commanders in the Imperial Army, and inspired unusually strong loyalty and affection in his men, who knew he would ask of them nothing he was not prepared to do himself. For the first landings in Malaya, he insisted on putting army headquarters in one of the lead ships in the convoy so he would share the fate of the frontline troops. And during the last stand in the Philippines, he refused to set himself apart from his men in any way, enduring rain, fever, leeches, hunger, and filth at their side.

But Yamashita's career might also be taken as an object lesson on the perils of political involvement. Suspicions that he might be "unsound" were first raised when he was closely associated with implementing cuts in the armed forces after the First World War. In the late twenties and early thirties his sympathies with the Imperial Way philosophy brought him into conflict with Tojo, and for the rest of his life Yamashita felt his movements watched.

He was lucky to emerge from his deeply compromising involvement in the February 26 Incident in 1936 without standing trial. His two young protégés, Ando and Nonaka, whom he seems to have encouraged right up to the moment of the coup, were the only two rebels to commit seppuku, again at his urging; he himself effectively recanted in the face of the Emperor's anger. His part in the affair was surprisingly discreditable, and he made more powerful enemies. His punishment was comparatively light—an unwelcome posting to Korea and later China. But this was enough to keep him away from the hub of policy-making while Tojo was consolidating his influence. In future, Yamashita's most conspicuous characteristic would be suspicion of his peers, from whom he doubtless turned with relief to the company of his men.

Even had the mixture of characters been less rich, the pattern of Japanese military leadership would still have been highly complex, subtly blurred and distorted by two threads running, indistinct but persistent, against the warp. Two features of the decision-making process make it peculiarly difficult to identify precisely those who truly deserve to be called army leaders.

First, obeying emotion and instinct rather than logic, commanders relied too often on nonverbal communication, to avoid the necessity of putting unpleasant or compromising realities into words. Rules might be flouted by tacit consent, and unpalatable decisions made without anyone having to voice them and thus accept responsibility. In the last stages of the disastrous Imphal operation, General Mutaguchi confronted his commander in Burma. "The sentence 'The time has come to give up the operation as soon as possible' got as far as my throat," he wrote later, "but I could not force it out in words. But I wanted him to get it from my expression." Combined with the conspiratorial secretiveness bred of factionalism, this kind of obliquity was a real obstacle to lucid policy-making and decisive action.

In a quandary, a Japanese officer would often take refuge in the technique of *mokusatsu:* silence, as lofty as he could manage. He might not agree with an order, or simply not understand it, but if he could avoid saying so, awkwardness would be avoided—for the immediate present. Major problems, of course, would simply not go away, and the throwing up of a smokescreen of ambiguity and evasiveness could have dire consequences. On July 30, 1945, when Prime Minister Kantaro Suzuki, announcing Japan's response to the Potsdam Proclamation used the term *"mokusatsu,"* he intended to imply that for the moment, the Japanese government had no comment on the Allied conditions for peace. He was construed as having said that Japan proposed to ignore them; days later, the bomb was dropped on Hiroshima.

Another phenomenon subverting conventional army methods of

making decisions was the notorious *gekokujo,* the peculiar brand of insubordination that had come to permeate the middle ranks of the Imperial Army in the 1930s. To impatient, immoderate, ambitious young officers, it often seemed that their seniors in the High Command were intellectually lazy, outmoded in their military thinking, and, more important, seriously compromised politically by their close relations with the despised civilian government. What they needed was firm, decisive direction from below.

Gekokujo had been viewed by some as a positive trait, a habit of helping one's superior to interpret and implement his orders from above by taking the initiative oneself. Staff officers and subordinate commanders routinely offered their own views, openly expressing doubts about their seniors' thinking. Generally speaking, staff officers were responsible for drafting orders; because of inertia, overwork, and even a curious desire to curry favor, it became increasingly common for commanders to approve these orders against their own instincts and experience.

This dependence on their juniors was damaging, because the young officers, for all their zeal, lacked experience and a broad grounding in politics, economics, or diplomacy. The quality of leadership inevitably suffered. The habit of acquiescence was dangerous, because it could be interpreted too widely; in the majority of the attempted coups of the militarist era, right up until the last desperate fling of August 14, 1945, the middle-ranking extremist leaders acted under the impression that they had the support of some of the highest officials in the army—Ugaki, Araki, Yamashita, Korechika Anami.

The career of Colonel Masanobu Tsuji offers an outstanding example of *gekokujo* and the harm it could do. Tsuji was an exceptionally intelligent staff officer with a flair for operational planning—talent vitiated by megalomaniac ambition, violent prejudices, and ruthless disregard for human life. In his own eyes he was an idealistic prophet of Asian unity and an anticommunist crusader. He strides through the pages of his own numerous books as the architect of every successful stratagem, the hero of death-defying encounters—flying over enemy lines in tiny spotter planes, storming enemy dugouts in tanks—prescient, dynamic, and misunderstood.

During the retreat from Burma, he helped General Masaki Honda, commander of the Thirty-third Army, to make a remarkable escape from encirclement, and left a cheeky note for the thwarted British commander: "Sorry to cause you so much trouble. This spot is where Lt. Gen. Honda was. Try harder next time. Sayonara." He himself felt practically immune to harm at enemy hands. "My body," he once boasted, "carried the bullets of five countries—Russian from Nomonhan, American from Guadalcanal, Chinese from Shanghai, British from Burma, and Australian from the Philippines."

He was understandably more reticent about the outcome of his exploits in these five countries, for his career was punctuated with hasty transfers ordered by outraged or exasperated superiors. As a young staff officer in China, he was transferred from headquarters after chastising his seniors for spending secret funds on women and drink. At Nomonhan he was blamed for the crushing failure of an overambitious advance. He left the Eleventh Army at Hankow after persistently attempting to take control of headquarters. A firm believer in "the iron hand in the iron glove," he was directly responsible in Singapore and the Philippines for brutal treatment of the native populations. On Guadalcanal he would overrule all objections to what proved to be one of the most wasteful operations of the entire campaign.

Tsuji was the nail that sticks up and is hammered down—but no amount of hammering could flatten him for long. He seems sometimes like a Japanese Rasputin, bobbing up in every theater of war with his taste for violence and his capacity for escalating it unimpaired. In many Japanese accounts of the war he is a convenient scapegoat, a kind of Moriarty, responsible for an impossible number of the Japanese army's misdeeds and miscalculations. But even allowing for exaggeration, for an officer of his rank he played a remarkably significant part in accelerating Japan's progress toward war, and his seniors' failure to nip his particular brand of *gekokujo* in the bud was especially disastrous.

"It was the Ishiwara-Tsuji clique—the personification of *gekokujo*—that brought the Japanese Army to this deplorable situation," complained General Sosaku Suzuki toward the end of the war. "In Malaya, Tsuji's speech and conduct were often insolent; and there was this problem of inhumane treatment of Chinese merchants, so I advised General Yamashita to punish Tsuji severely and then dismiss him. But he feigned ignorance. I tell you, so long as they exert influence on the Army, it can only lead to ruin. Extermination of these poisonous insects should take precedence over all other problems."

As the war went on and sweeping changes affected the lower echelons of the officer corps, it became more rather than less difficult to control junior officers. China and then Nomonhan had killed many good leaders. Then the rapid expansion of the army led to an influx of ersatz officers, an unprecedented number of them promoted from the ranks, imperfectly trained, and forced to assume managerial duties above their station—junior officers performing the duties of seniors, NCOs the duties of subalterns. Commissions in the army were now even less of an upper-class preserve than they had been in the Meiji era; by the late 1920s almost one-third of the officer corps was drawn from the lower middle class, and the proportion was growing.

This did not mean, however, that there were no divisions between officers and men. In barracks, during training, the "family" bonds within a company were still stressed, and there was nothing like the pronounced social gulf between officers and men that existed in the British army. But under the extraordinary stresses of battle the ranks drew apart. The Japanese infantryman was as likely as any Western soldier to complain about the folly of the High Command and their indifference to the plight of the combat soldier—and he had some justification, in the view of General Ichiji Sugita, who was then a colonel on the General Staff.

The Chief of Staff never went near the front, and senior officers visited it rarely if at all. (Sugita himself was in action throughout the Malayan campaign, and he endured all the rigors of defeat and with-drawal from Guadalcanal.) The troops received no direct encouragement, and they deduced that their leaders were forming plans with no real understanding of local conditions. Some high-ranking officers were known to be living in conspicuous comfort amid their exhausted, hungry men. General Iwao Matsuda's quarters at Egaroppu on New Britain incorporated a four-poster bed, a luxury bathroom, a prayer room, and a personal air-raid shelter; cans of Coca-Cola and Philippine beer were scattered around, with evidence of expensive imported food everywhere.

At a lower level, though the proportion of officer casualties in battle was comparable to the ratios in other armies, once the battles were lost, officers sometimes showed a distinct unwillingness to perish with their men. At Buna and Sananda, officers reserved the bulk of the scanty remaining rations for themselves, and got out wherever they could, abandoning their men. When the island of Mereyon was bypassed by the American advance, the Japanese garrison was abandoned by headquarters; it can be no coincidence that the officers suffered only a 38 percent fatality rate from starvation and disease against a horrifying 74 percent for their men.

The relationship between officers and men in the Imperial Army might have deteriorated since the Meiji era, but that did not radically affect the conduct of the war. Far more significant was the shifting pattern of power balances between different subdivisions of the military establishment; on the outcome of this constant jockeying for influence depended crucial policy decisions.

The relations between frontline officers and General Headquarters continued to be volatile. As ever, those in the field felt themselves entitled to act on their own initiative to take advantage of local developments, as they had done since the nineteenth century—in Korea in 1894; at Amoy in 1900; in Siberia after the First World War; at Mukden in 1928, with the murder of Chang Tso-lin; Mukden again in 1931, precipitating the invasion of Manchuria; after the incident at the Marco Polo Bridge in 1937; at Nomonhan in 1939. Field officers considered themselves much the best qualified to judge the chances of a plan's success; Headquarters staff had no business meddling in operational details. But in this war, in the later years at least, the instinct of those at the front line was no longer always to push on while those at Headquarters, their eyes fixed on diplomatic, economic, or other outside imperatives, counseled caution. This time it was often Headquarters doing the pushing, working to a paper plan, while the leaders on the ground argued for realism in the face of overwhelming odds.

There was still tension, too, in the parallel existence of General Staff and Army Ministry. *Tosui-ken,* the independence of the Supreme Command from civilian control, was still the single most important attribute of the army; but the fortunes of the General Staff fluctuated with the progress of the war, and as battles began to go against Japan in the field, the balance of power began to tip towards the Army Ministry at home.

Within the General Staff, the most powerful group in wartime was inevitably the First Bureau (Operations), which hedged its discussions and decisions around with a barrier of secrecy and acted as a law unto itself. Its only concerns were the armies in the field; military operations might have direst implications for international relations, the Japanese economy, or the steadily worsening condition of millions of Japanese civilians, but to the Operations Bureau these were irrelevancies.

After Tojo took over the position of Chief of Staff in 1944, while still serving as army minister, the balance tipped gently toward the ministry, helped by the increasing focus on logistics and home defense as the situation in the field remorselessly deteriorated. Within the ministry, the Military Affairs Bureau wielded most power, with its control of budgets and its position at the shoulder of the minister, drafting his directives and regulating his dealings with the General Staff.

In one sense, the division between ministry and General Staff was illusory; both were manned by staff officers, with the same officers moving between the highest planning posts in both hierarchies, or holding positions in both concurrently. Often the bonds of personal affection and obligation cemented during the years at the Military Academy were far stronger than any organizational loyalties; some cabals were powerful enough to resist virtually all control. The nexus of connections between classmates twined in and out of the structure of policy-making, pulling it this way and that and even altering its overall shape. Staff officers who had not been through military preparatory school and then on to the Academy together, but had entered the army by the less prestigious path of middle school and in-service training, frequently found themselves excluded from the centers of power, and their paths to promotion blocked.

Far more clear-cut was the rift between all army officers, wherever they served, and the officers of the Imperial Japanese Navy. By the 1930s the traditional rivalry had hardened into implacable hostility and mistrust. Seizo Arisue, later to become head of military intelligence and one of the most powerful figures in the High Command, went to Italy in 1936 as a military attaché and spent much of his time in negotiations—not with the Italians but with the Japanese naval attaché. Arisue would issue his invitations and make his appointments—and within hours the naval attaché would have duplicated them, lest the army somehow steal a march.

At this time, the services were jostling primarily for political power, as the route to adequate funding and a loud voice in foreign policy. The creation of Manchukuo gave the army a power base and a significant political edge; the navy urgently sought to send its own political representatives to the area and to build up naval strength on the Sungari River—the "Sungari Fleet." By the time of the February 26 Incident in 1936, the navy in all seriousness feared that it, too, would be attacked by the army on the rampage. And it had made its own plans to "rescue" the Emperor.

To Arisue and other army stalwarts, the navy was the enemy, far more obvious a menace than any outside power, even in 1941. One of the leading candidates for the Navy Ministry in that year summed up his attitude to the army succinctly: "Horseshit." Hardly surprisingly, the bitter mutual dislike and competition would have disastrous effects on the conduct of the Pacific War. There was no genuinely unified leadership at Imperial Headquarters, no Joint Chief of Staff. There was no coordinated air force, no shared research in such crucial areas as radar technology, where a pooling of knowledge might have revolutionized

Japan's advance-warning capability. In the Mitsubishi factory at Nagoya a curtain running the length of the shop floor screened work carried out under navy contract from work carried out for the army. Even when raw materials and mineral resources were relatively plentiful, they were not shared according to need; and as shortages became more acute, neither service would hand over a fraction of its stocks, though the future of a campaign might depend on it.

In the early days of success, army and navy occasionally cooperated effectively—brilliantly, in the case of the Malayan campaign. But there was far too little genuine trust or sympathy for this to last. At heart, army officers felt they had been inveigled by the navy into an alien and unnecessary war, and been promised support which the navy then totally failed to provide. The navy misrepresented its own strength as compared with the American fleet, encouraging the army to advance farther than was prudent. "We were confident of the Navy's ability to hold back the American fleet," complained army planner Colonel Kumao Imoto. "Why didn't they tell us they weren't so confident! We trusted them; they didn't come out and warn us of their limitations. . . . We Japanese have a tendency not to push matters too far. . . . This was never discussed openly . . . they were not open enough!"

The navy also failed to inform the army of its short-term plans. Minutes before the first naval air attack on Clark Field in the Philippines in December 1941, nine army bombers on a routine training mission flew into the path of the incoming assault, having had no warning of anything out of the ordinary. Then after battles, the navy grossly misled the army as to the results, concealing losses and exaggerating gains, allowing the army to build its future strategy on foundations of sand. It was 1945 before some of the most senior army officers discovered how catastrophic the Battle of Midway had been for Japanese air power. Even at the very end, with Japan's cities pounded every night by firebombing, with the air forces reduced to a single large suicide squad, and the greater part of the fleet destroyed or disabled, the services could find no way of settling their differences and working together in the final despairing defense of the home islands.

35

"MY SWORD IS MY SOUL":
WEAPONS

For every American soldier in the field during the Pacific War, there were four tons of equipment available; for every Japanese soldier, there were two pounds. This was essentially a war of resources—started in pursuit of them, and lost, as the total-war planners had always feared, for lack of them.

As far as weapons were concerned, Amane Nishi, philosopher of the Meiji army, had perceived the importance of technology as early as the 1880s. Modern armies, he argued, were all based on the concept of "mechanism"—mechanized equipment and the use of men like instruments. Nevertheless, the Japanese may have failed to see precisely how the new technological developments might apply to the Imperial Army. The war that army planners kept constantly in mind throughout the 1930s was a war against the Soviet Union, most probably on the plains of Manchuria. In this type of battle, the infantryman would have had a crucial role to play, traveling fast and light, with room to maneuver and a minimum of heavy equipment. The war the Japanese army actually fought in the 1930s was not a Russian but a Chinese war, but it was still one that gave some scope to Japan's strengths and helped to conceal her weaknesses.

The Chinese had little air power, few tanks, and a miscellany of outdated firearms. As an enemy, they were hardly an accurate yardstick of technological prowess. The arms Japan possessed in the late 1930s may have been adequate for their conception of warfare at the time; but in absolute terms they were dangerously weak.

Two arms in particular were vulnerable: artillery and armor. Western observers liked to attribute these weaknesses, which were quite obvious, to a sentimental attachment to the classical military tradition, with its stress on the individual, finely crafted blade. This had led, it was claimed, to a temperamental disdain for the crude, remote strength of the tank or shell. All the new tanks used in the Jehol campaign in 1933 were out of action within thirty-six hours, through "a lack of sympathy on the part of the ordinary Japanese soldier with machinery," and a tendency to drive their tanks into the ground without proper maintenance.

Japan—mountainous, intersected by rivers, and carpeted with rice paddies—was geographically quite unsuited to the use of tanks. And it was true that Japanese tank technology was well behind that of the Allies, which Japan copied assiduously well into the 1930s, most commonly producing versions of Renault and Vickers models. The most advanced tank designed and built in Japan between the wars was the Type 97 of 1937; already this betrayed the Japanese tendency to think of the tank as a glorified armored personnel carrier, or as an infantry support weapon with no combat role of its own.

As for artillery, many of the howitzers used in coastal defense in 1922 were made of bronze and dated from well before the Russo-Japanese War. Fifteen years later the Japanese had still not developed their artillery to the level one might expect of a first-class power—and in particular, the power that had been the first to use super-heavy artillery, during the siege of Port Arthur. In the China War, the weakness did not matter; heavy prearranged fire at long range was rarely needed, and Chinese artillery was even more limited. In the Pacific, it would be disastrous.

Nor could the Japanese forces feel sanguine about their rifles or machine guns. The failure to develop a serviceable machine gun between the wars was particularly surprising, given the heavy reliance in Japanese tactics on the machine-gun unit as suicidally determined support for the infantry.

It is worth remembering that most of the armies entering the Pacific

War used a significant proportion of weapons that were obsolescent if not actually obsolete. The Americans did not start large-scale production of automatic rifles until well after they were at war; and many British troops were using bolt-action weapons until the end of the war. The difference was, perhaps, that the Japanese made less effort to remedy the shortcomings of their weapons. The overall quality, in fact, deteriorated; differences in finish, and even in shape, size, and materials are quite obvious in some Japanese weapons manufactured at the end of the war when the shortage of raw materials had reached crisis levels. The Americans, on the other hand, had weapons in prototype at the start of the war which would soon give them a clear lead.

It is symptomatic of the Japanese attitude to arms on the modern battlefield—at first slightly contemptuous and then fatalistic—that they laid such disproportionate emphasis on cold steel. Japanese infantrymen were taught that their primary weapon was the bayonet, a rough but strong 15½-inch blade, weighing about a quarter of a pound, which most kept fixed to their rifles all the time. "The fixing of bayonets is more than a fixing of steel to the rifle since it puts iron into the soul of the soldier doing the fixing." To Allied soldiers the bayonet was a symbol of the ferocity and determination of the enemy, and it achieved results out of all proportion to its practical effectiveness.

The sword, too, had great symbolic value, but to the wearer rather than the victim. "Lay to heart the saying of an ancient warrior: 'My sword is my soul,' " directed the Japanese Field Service Code. As nationalist feeling grew in the 1930s, the Western-style swords issued routinely to officers were replaced by traditional samurai-style weapons, and the sword-making profession was rescued from oblivion. Individuals could have their standard-pattern weapons mounted with ancestral blades, some of which were of exceptional value and beauty. When officers were required to surrender their swords at the end of the war, many had plaques attached to the weapons detailing their history and significance. But swords were far from simply decorative: "Both the cavalry sabres and the classic single-edged blades of Japan's feudal era were capable of slicing a handkerchief in mid-air or of parting a man's body from collar-bone to waist in a single clean slash."

The sword was a principal focus for Japanese hylozoism, the belief that some material objects possess spirit and should be revered: books; the desk at which a man's work is done; and, in wartime, weapons wielded in the Emperor's name. A soldier's rifle was both a symbol of his military spirit and the property of the Emperor, so rough handling became desecration and irreverence, and rust became corruption of the soul. To damage one's rifle was an offense whose gravity depended on the part of the "body" affected. In his novel *A Sense of Collapse,* Hiroshi Noma describes the penance of one culprit: " 'Mr. 38-M Rifle, I, Second Class Private Ryuichi Oikawa, am a donkey, a dunce, and a fool. I have injured your precious head by mistake. I will never make such a mistake as this again, so please forgive me!' This Ryuichi Oikawa was beaten with a wooden chair, dragged down to the cold dirt floor, and forced to sit on it because he broke the spring of Rifle No. 10296 while repairing it."

The Arisaka M-38 rifle was now some thirty-five years old. It was a clumsy weapon, especially in the jungle, and a good example of a Western weapon adapted for Eastern use despite being fundamentally unsuitable—quite simply, too big for the average Japanese soldier, who had difficulty holding the weapon to his shoulder while operating the bolt. On the M-38 6.5 caliber sniper's rifle, the telescopic sight had to be mounted well back to cater to short Japanese necks; and the 20mm antitank rifle had to be fitted with carrying handles in order to be readily transportable. The M-44 carbine was well liked because it was short and had a permanent folding bayonet; this did away with the need for a scabbard hanging down from the belt, tangling and tripping the wearer. But an attempt to create a folding rifle for the use of parachute troops failed because the hinged stock weakened the weapon too seriously.

There was no shortage of ammunition for rifles after the government withdrew the copper one-sen coin in 1940 and used the metal; but packing and storage were sloppy. Cartons were not hermetically sealed, nor was waxed or waterproof paper much used—both essentials in the salty, sandy, humid conditions of the Pacific. Ants, damp, and corrosion contributed to a rate of misfires far higher than with American, British, or German weapons. Many of the handguns issued to officers were notoriously prone to jamming; at best, they did not pretend to be much more than single-shot weapons for self-defense—or self-destruction.

Far more serviceable was the grenade, which had been the mainstay of the infantryman since 1931. It was particularly useful during night raids, as it did not need such careful aiming, nor did it flash like a rifle and give away one's own position. A close-range weapon, it was well suited to jungle warfare, and the Japanese used a wide variety: fragmentation grenades, stick grenades, and antitank grenades used with a launcher, "a flexible and economical means of bringing high explosive directly into the front line."

But it was in high explosives that the Imperial Army was generally most deficient. Unlike the Chinese, the Allies made crushing use of long-range artillery bombardments, and the Japanese had nothing with which to reply. Their artillery was, generally speaking, underweight. This suited it to the way in which it was used: well forward, in close support of infantry, with the stress on speed and surprise. But all too often the infantry were setting off into the teeth of an enemy barrage that the artillery had failed to neutralize. The Japanese made little use of counterbattery fire—possibly because they had such limited experience and awareness of its value, possibly because they simply did not have the industrial capacity to produce heavy weapons and ammunition in any quantity—and the Allies did not regard Japanese artillery as much of a threat.

But they reserved their most pungent criticisms for Japanese tanks. "The free traverse of the gun is, to me, rather disturbing," reported a British officer about a light tank he had been asked to test-drive. "If it happens to swing right (breech left), only a dehydrated Jap could survive. I tried three of the smallest Gurkhas I could find inside it, and my impression was that the little yellow perils would be able to work the tank quite efficiently, but limited by the inherent design inefficiency."

The main "inefficiency" he listed was the commander's position within the tank, which was quite hopeless for fighting. Until the end of the war, Japanese tanks remained infantry-support vehicles, thin-skinned and undergunned. By the time the Japanese realized the need for a heavier machine capable of slugging it out with enemy tanks in defense, they had run out of the raw materials necessary to make it.

Japan had not been alone in undervaluing tanks between the wars. Few countries had appreciated their potential for operating independently as attacking weapons, the heavier the better. But Western powers accumulated experience and their attitudes evolved, whereas Japan, more isolated, persisted in her disregard. The Spanish Civil War had shown Europeans the pointlessness of tankettes; but against the Chinese, who had virtually no antitank weapons, any tank, however fragile and lightly armed, had seemed to work. So the Japanese persevered with armor that could be penetrated by Allied small arms. It took the crushing defeat at Nomonhan to alert them to the dangers of massed heavy armor, and they began to contemplate separate tank divisions which might eventually form an armored army with an independent command.

The first two tank divisions were not activated until the summer of 1942—and by the following year the Japanese had been forced by production and shipping problems to abandon the idea of the armored army. From then on, consciousness of relative weakness would blight Japanese tank tactics; commanders were often hesitant and unenterprising, using their tanks in twos and threes to support small infantry actions (with limited success), as mobile pillboxes, or simply dug in as defensive artillery. The massed drive would be virtually unknown until near the end of the war in China, in 1944.

It was also too late, by the time the Japanese realized they had completely underestimated the scale on which the Allies would use tanks, to evolve adequate antitank equipment. In the Philippines, Burma, and the Pacific atolls the Japanese faced larger, heavier, more maneuverable tanks in far greater numbers than they had expected and in places that they in their turn had believed to be quite unsuitable for tanks.

"The heavily wounded had jumped into the muck intent only on fleeing from the terror of the tanks. I could hear them moaning, 'Ugh, it's all over,' their mouths full of mud. Such a miserable plight made one wonder if these men really were the brave warriors of the most highly respected unit in the Imperial Japanese Army." Tanks had much the same effect on the Japanese infantryman as the bayonet and jitter attack did on the Allied soldier, and Allied tank commanders learned to exploit this fear. One described toying with his prey during a tank action in the Arakan. "Half-way through an assault and by pre-arrangement the infantry would halt and the tanks would cease fire. This was almost always more than the inquisitive little NIP could stand, especially if the tanks 'revved up' their engines and gave the appearance of moving off. He almost inevitably came up from underground to have a look and then, by radio-telephony to all tanks, 'WALLOP.' "

The Japanese found tank attacks so desperately frightening because they had nothing that was certain to stop them. In the absence of any heavy antitank guns, they had to improvise. They hollowed out coconuts, stuffed them with black powder, and then fitted grenades inside with just the percussion caps protruding, held in with chicken wire. They attempted to blind oncoming tanks by hurling paper bags of mud or lime at the observation ports. They planted terra-cotta mines in rubbish heaps, cane fields and cabbage patches, camouflaged with broken tiles, stalks of bamboo, and heads of cabbage. They hurled glass globes containing hydrocyanic acid gas at the ventilating slits and the driver's ports. Above all, they used themselves as mines and missiles.

"In the open ground across the tanks' approach routes, they dug a series of holes and installed a man in each of them. Between his knees he held a fused 250kg aerial bomb, nose uppermost, and clutched a brick in his hand, the idea being to wait until a tank was on top of him, then smack the brick down on the bomb cap and blow himself and the tank to kingdom come." These human mines, awaiting one of the biggest Allied tank attacks of the war, at Meiktila in Burma, were destroyed by a British colonel who spotted the suspiciously regular marks where the holes had been dug, went forward under cover of the tanks' guns, and shot each bomber in the head. "None of the Japanese detonated their bombs because they had been told to do it only for tanks."

In the attempt to compensate for their inferiority in mainstream weapons, the Japanese experimented with a variety of more esoteric devices. A novel kind of swamp-crossing vehicle; an armored-car trolley that ran on rails, to protect railway battalions from bandits; an infrared homing bomb whose sensors could detect the heat from a man's face at one hundred meters; a television-controlled boat and a radio-controlled bomb, intended as long-term substitutes for the kamikaze pilot; a cathode-ray personnel-detection device; echo-ranging underwater equipment—American teams studying Japanese wartime research would draw up a long and remarkably diverse list of projects, most of them thwarted by shortage of materials.

There were other impediments to research, some of them self-imposed. The most senseless was the lack of coordination that had crippled Japan's scientific research and development program for years. The army had its own considerable research organization with a separate branch of technical officers of all grades up to lieutenant general, and twenty-one different laboratories—ten for the ground forces, eight for the air forces, plus specialist facilities for studying radar, fuels, and ordnance.

Then there were the laboratories owned and operated by the *zaibatsu*, and three active civilian establishments. In addition, there were the science faculties of all the universities in Japan—an intellectual resource that could have transformed the military's research and one that they signally failed to tap. Very few official research programs were formally instituted in universities; suspicious, perhaps, of their intellectual and political independence, the military mobilized less than a tenth as many civilian scientists as the Allies.

Lastly, of course, there was the navy, which had a research organization of comparable size and scope to the army's. Its technical personnel were undoubtedly superior and its research was in many respects more sophisticated. But the results were guarded as closely from the army as from the enemy.

One of the most notable casualties of this failure to work together was Japan's atomic research program, if it can be given the name. At the Institute for Physical and Chemical Research in Tokyo, Dr. Nishina, a pupil of Niels Bohr, was studying the theory of atomic power, and there were other professors in Kyoto and Osaka working in the same field. Nishina had one cyclotron, and there were three or four others in Japan; some effort had also been made to obtain uranium-235. But Nishina was primarily concerned with atomic power as an alternative source of energy, and those army and navy scientists who were interested in its military application greatly reduced their chances of success by declining to pool their research. The ultimate weapon was still well beyond Japan's reach when the end came.

In the crucial field of radar, too, army and navy proceeded independently. Japanese physicists fully comprehended the basic principles; a limited exchange of technical information was one of the few concrete advantages that Japan derived, briefly, from the alliance with Germany before the Allies broke Axis codes and were able to check the blockade-running operations that brought the information through. Japanese scientists also avidly studied the Allied equipment that fell into their hands during the Hundred Days; they even sent divers down to the *Prince of Wales* (sunk in the Gulf of Siam in late 1941) in the hope of locating its radar. But very few of their own designs ever reached production.

This was not due simply to the lack of materials; there was also a severe shortage of skilled workers, as conscription bit ever deeper. In particular, though Japan's physicists might have mastered the theoretical basis of radar, her production engineers did not have the mathematical skills to make a working model. Japan achieved some land-based early-warning equipment, and some ships were eventually fitted with radar, but airborne radar never reached production. The Americans described Japan's efforts as "a halting, makeshift application of recognized microwave techniques" and concluded that for all their labors, by 1945 the Japanese had barely reached the point from which Allied scientists had departed in 1941.

The Japanese trailed, too, in rocket technology, though the Allies would find some of their discoveries interesting. The *Baka* or "crazy" bomb was rocket propelled—a piloted glider, packing 1,135 pounds of high explosives, which was carried under the fuselage of an airplane. At a height of 27,000 feet and a range of fifty-five miles, the glider was launched and the pilot directed it toward its target, either airplane or ship, choosing the right moment to activate the rockets that would hurtle him to extinction at over five hundred miles an hour.

The Japanese made serious efforts to develop a "death ray" to be used against enemy air crews. The basis was a high-frequency electromagnetic wave tube or magnetron, which emitted a four-meter wavelength with fifty kilowatts continuous power. It could stop a gasoline engine at close range, kill a rabbit at three meters in less than a minute and a monkey in three, by producing lung and brain hemorrhages. Mercifully, the death-ray project never amounted to more than a series of cruel experiments.

On the other hand, there was one weapon that the Japanese had ready but rarely used. "I had heard that from early childhood they are warned against fire and forbidden to use it under any circumstances likely to endanger the flimsy houses in which they lived. Evidently the lesson was well learned," concluded one American chemical officer serving on Biak. The Japanese had developed a flamethrower that could be operated by one man. Fueled with petrol that had been thickened with latex, it shot out flames thirty meters long, six bursts to a container. But the Japanese fear of fire was so strong, almost pathological, that they gave the Order of the Golden Kite to flamethrower operators who returned alive, and often held back from using the apparatus that would eventually claim so many of them as victims.

Fear—this time, fear of retaliation—also inhibited them from using poison gas and bacteriological weapons in the Pacific War; but these had long been ready.

With only limited battle experience in World War I, the Japanese were later into the field of chemical warfare than the European nations. It was not until 1925 that they invited one Dr. Mezzner from Germany to organize a research program. The drive to acquire a chemical-warfare capacity, including production of the principal poison gases, began in earnest—and in private—in 1926, as part of the Ugaki reforms.

By 1930 it had come out into the open. "Chemical warfare is prohibited by international treaties," the army vice-minister observed in October 1931, "but in actual fact military authorities in all countries consider chemical warfare in future wars as inevitable. Even in the recently drafted disarmament treaty, while germ warfare is absolutely prohibited, chemical warfare as a means of reprisal in wartime is not actually prohibited. This being the case . . . it has been decided to establish a School of Chemical Warfare for the study of gas and the perfection of drill in gas defense." The school was built at Okubo in Tokyo, with a second one two years later at Narashino in Chiba prefecture, and from then on all infantry divisions had selected men trained as "gas personnel" and organized in both defensive and offensive units. By 1933 Japan possessed the technology and production capacity for the gases and was turning more toward perfecting delivery systems.

Once Mussolini had used chemical warfare in Abyssinia, from then on, despite international prohibitions, it was once more the specter hanging over each new battlefield. Most armies had chemical weapons— this was no longer in doubt; in producing blister gases like lewisite, lung irritants like phosgene, tear gases, and toxic smoke, Japan was going no farther than any of the major Western powers—until she started actually to use the weapons against the Chinese.

There was a standing authorization for commanders in the China theater to use gas in a critical situation. One such situation was the fighting at I-ch'ang in October 1941. "Ten minutes after the explosion a darkish fluid issued which gave rise to a grayish white yellow and orange smoke. The vapour released affected the skin and mucous membranes like red pepper. It was fragrant like flowers and in certain cases smelled like putrid fruit. . . . Soldiers and civilians affected became unconscious instantly. Some died within a few minutes to half an hour while others suffered from blisters and died a few hours later. Still others suffered from watering eyes, sneezing and bleeding from the nose. The skin of corpses turned black and blue."

This was lewisite, or a mixture of lewisite and mustard gas. More routinely, tear and sneezing gas, as well as smoke flares, were used— highly effectively, as Chinese chemical-warfare defenses were pitiably poor. A Japanese handbook entitled *Lessons of the China Incident* described how some Chinese soldiers "carried their gas masks without canisters fitted to them; some did not uncover the lid of the canister and were asphyxiated by the mask; some died by asphyxiation sticking their noses and mouths into the ground."

The scale of use in China varied widely. The Twentieth Division in an attack on Kyukyo used eighteen thousand toxic smoke candles to screen an advance on a nine-kilometer front. At Shangyo, where the advance was halted by strongly entrenched Chinese forces, Major Mamiya, the detachment commander, "sought all possible means to continue the advance and finally decided to resort to the use of special smokes. . . . By our special smokes the enemy was thrown into utter confusion. . . . Mopping up was done of those enemies who lay prostrated in houses and shelters suffering from the smoke."

Gas seems to have been the standard means of knocking out blockhouses; the ventilators were blocked with mud, toxic smoke candles were thrown in, and as soon as the enemy stopped firing, NCOs and enlisted men wearing their masks charged in. Poison gas was also used to kill Communist guerrillas hiding in their maze of tunnels under the plains of Hopei.

But the prospect of engaging in chemical warfare with the United States, with its clear margin of technical superiority, was another matter entirely. From Pearl Harbor onward there was a strict embargo on its use in the Imperial Army—and discovery of a U.S. poison-gas shell in Singapore only increased the High Command's alarm. One recurring nightmare was the possibility that Germany would use chemical warfare in the European theater, bringing swift retaliation against their Axis ally in the East.

Nevertheless, in extremis the Japanese army did still resort to chemical weapons. They may have assumed that there was some margin of safety before the Americans were likely to retaliate—in which case they were right. "It is the common policy of the US and British Governments," reads a top-secret Allied report of 1944, "only to use chemical warfare after its use has been begun by the enemy. . . . The unplanned, unauthorised use of chemical weapons locally and on a very small scale would not necessarily constitute an adequate reason for starting gas warfare, though this point can obviously not be expressed in open international declarations."

"Unplanned and unauthorised use" would seem to cover the various occasions on which the Japanese army employed chemical weapons in the Pacific War. On the heights of Modbung in Burma, faced with a tank advance to which they had no conventional answer, Japanese units used the *chibi-dan,* or tich bomb—one of the few contributions made by German scientists to Japanese strength. The bomb was a thick glass sphere the size of a baseball, containing prussic acid in liquid form; this turned to gas when the glass shattered against a tank's armor, and streams of white smoke were drawn in through the aperture, asphyxiating the crew.

Elsewhere in Burma, casualties displayed the curious symptoms of chemical warfare. A British officer collecting wounded from the field found one man with his clothes and equipment smoldering—only to burst into flames when water was poured on, as they might have done if they had been impregnated with phosphorus. "Heavy fire drawn," reported the officer grimly, "and man had to be abandoned." While another casualty was being cleaned with ether, "in application to skin which appeared burnt, skin began to smoulder, filling operating tent with sulphurous fumes."

In frantic house-to-house skirmishes during the bloody retreat from Manila in March 1945, "special smoke" was used—but this was, in a British observer's view, an "aberrational act, which one might expect from fanatical rear-guard suicides." In general, the Japanese were more anxious than most to avoid provoking large-scale chemical retaliation, acutely conscious of the inferiority of their chemical industry to those of the Allies. "There must not be the least disclosure to the enemy of our readiness for gas warfare," one staff officer warned units in Batu, lest they be contemplating the use of tear gas or prussic-acid grenades. In August 1945 large quantities of poison gas were dumped into the sea around the home islands to destroy the evidence of Japan's preparations to use it against the Allied invasion—but this was perhaps the only use of gas to be planned rather than impromptu.

In studying techniques of bacteriological warfare, again Japan was not alone, nor did she keep secret the fact that she was engaged in such research. Most countries had research establishments preparing counter-measures against such terrors as anthrax, bubonic plague, rabies, and salmonella. A staff paper entitled "Defence against bacteriological warfare," captured in the Philippines in March 1945, reveals just how much thought the Japanese had given to the subject; but the writer also constantly betrays Japan's concern with offensive germ-warfare capacity.

Tetanus and gas gangrene, the report maintains, are best spread by bullets, as infection develops through an open wound. Yellow fever and glanders are especially suitable for military use, because they are difficult to immunize against and their toxicity does not deteriorate when they are cultured. Diphtheria and anthrax, which cause infection through the respiratory system, might be sprayed in solution from the air—though low-level or diving attacks would be needed if the bacterial clouds were not to be blown off target. "It is conceivable," mused the writer, "that ground tissues, containing diseases which are impossible to cultivate, such as rabies and hoof and mouth disease, ground internal organs of animals dying from plague, anthrax or glanders, and excreta from patients with cholera, typhoid or dysentery may be converted to liquids and used as sprays." More ambitious was the notion of dropping whole creatures: fleas, lice, and mosquitoes in containers, rabid dogs by parachute.

There is little evidence, however, to show that the Japanese actually used germ warfare on any significant scale. Almost certainly they dropped grains of rice contaminated with plague in China. Mao's forces alleged that in occupied areas the Japanese had forced the Chinese inhabitants to provide as part of their land tax two rats per acre; these were then infected with plague and let loose. There is some suggestion that the troops which devastated the Chekiang region of China in 1942 consolidated their efforts with cholera, dysentery, anthrax, bubonic plague, and paratyphoid—only to be affected themselves, in uncertain wind and weather conditions, by the same germs. Of parachuting dogs, diphtherial mists, and ground tubercular animal organs there was no trace.

What distinguished Japan's bacteriological warfare program was not the tactics proposed, but the grotesque cruelty of the experiments on which the program was founded. The story of Unit 731, the Manchurian center of the Japanese army's researches into the potential of biological weapons, is a story of hideous suffering inflicted on thousands of victims, most of them Chinese, labeled and treated by their captors as *maruta*, "blocks of wood." Skulls drilled into and entrails removed from live bodies; limbs frozen until they gave off a sound like a plank of wood when struck; eyeballs forced out by the application of massive pressure to the head; bodies reduced to a fifth of their weight by dehydration; knives inserted into the various organs of living subjects to see which produced the quickest death; malnutrition and frostbite carefully simulated, with all their agonies; Chinese civilians, Russian "spies," Manchurian "bandits," American and British prisoners of war, infected with germs of every kind, sprayed invisibly, shot into them with bullets and shrapnel, injected with needles, concealed in cake, carried by fleas and rats let loose in thousands.

In the contest with larger and more prosperous opponents, Japan felt she needed every advantage she could contrive for herself. At Pearl Harbor, Kota Bharu, and Clark Field she had exploited the element of surprise. Now the Kwantung Army's scientists took advantage of the moral scruples which made similar experiments by the Allies unlikely. Tojo is said to have shared these scruples to the extent that he declined after a while to watch the films that the scientists made of their experiments. But at every level of the High Command, and some departments of the civilian government as well, the work of the "Epidemic Prevention and Water Supply Unit" was an open secret. Tetzusan Nagata and Sadao Araki, to name only two, are known to have supported or condoned the program in outline, though it is unlikely that they knew the detail of individual experiments.

"You couldn't say I want to do this or that in war, however good or bad," recalled the printer of Unit 731's scientific treatises, Uezono

Naoji, of what he saw in the human experimental unit. "The Japanese way is to obey a superior. It was the same as if the order came from the Emperor. Sometimes there were no anaesthetics. They screamed and screamed. But we didn't regard the maruta as human beings. They were lumps of meat on a chopping block."

36

THE MISSING LINK: AIR POWER

From the moment in 1914 when Japanese pilots were involved in the first aerial combat over Tsingtao, they set about acquiring practical and technical know-how in the air. With raids on Vladivostok (1920), Tsinan (1928), Manchuria (1931), Shanghai (1932), and Jehol (1933), and four years of sustained combat in China behind them, in 1941 Japanese pilots of both army and navy air forces had far more recent battle experience than most of their rivals; the flyers who bombed Pearl Harbor had an aggregate of eight hundred flying hours.

But Japanese air strength was one of the best-kept secrets of the 1930s. British and Americans alike clung to the comforting fiction that the Japanese airman was a dwarf with poor eyesight and no mechanical aptitude, flying planes that were cheap copies of Western technical achievements. In reality, Japan's aircraft at the start of the Pacific War equaled and in several respects excelled the air strength of the Allies. The Zero was the fastest and most maneuverable fighter in existence, the first carrier-based plane to equal land-based machines for range and power; and the smoking wrecks at Oahu, the *Repulse* and the *Prince of Wales* sunk from Indochinese airfields, could testify to the effectiveness of Japanese torpedo-bombers and dive-bombers. All this came, however, only after years of expensive trial and error; and it is possible that the seeds of the decay that was to overtake Japan's air forces were present from the start.

Twenty-five years after the Imperial Army had shifted its allegiance to Prussia in the mid-1880s, the founders of the air forces found themselves looking back to the French for military assistance. In 1910 Japan was making no combustion engines of her own, and her first flying machine was an imported French Farman biplane. For several years Japanese aviation proceeded in fits and starts. In 1911 the army established the Tokorozawa airfield twenty miles northwest of Tokyo, and in 1912 enlisted five trainee pilots. The same year the Naval Air Service was founded with a handful of pilots—competent and tough, in the opinion of the French military observer Bertin (who was slightly *parti pris,* since two of them had trained in France). But they were handicapped by a severe shortage of good mechanics, and ended up performing amateur repairs and maintenance themselves, with predictable results. Bertin saw an additional drawback in the scarcity of good roads and modern motor vehicles. "Il est donc impossible, au Japon, à un chauffeur d'automobile de s'entrainer aux grandes vitesses en vue de dresser ses nerfs pour l'aviation."*

The army air force that fought at Tsingtao consisted of eight pilots and five planes, as against the navy's seven pilots and four planes; none of them succeeded in bringing down the lone German flier. But after this brief baptism, both services tried hard to build up their air power. In 1915 the Army Flying Corps was founded, as the role of military aircraft broadened beyond reconnaissance to artillery spotting, photography, bombing, strafing, and the prototype dogfight. In 1916 a small seaplane was the first machine to be both designed and built in Japan; the next five years saw the start of the Japanese aircraft industry, as major industrial concerns like Kawasaki and Mitsubishi set up aircraft divisions.

By 1918 the army had two air battalions taking part regularly in maneuvers, but policy and tactics were still relatively unsophisticated. In 1919 a Japanese mission was sent to Italy to benefit from the lessons

*"It is therefore impossible, in Japan, for an automobile driver to accustom himself to great speeds with a view to steeling his nerves for aviation."

learned in Europe during the war, while at the same time a variety of foreign advisers came to Japan. Under the guidance of a Lieutenant Deckert of France, a large number of Japanese planes took part in an air raid on Seoul in 1919, where an uprising was being bloodily repressed by Terauchi. They acquitted themselves well, but Deckert complained that the effects of his training seemed to be wearing off distressingly quickly, and the pilots reverting to their old slaphappy ways under the influence of a homegrown instructor, one Lieutenant Wada. "I saw his flights in 1919," observed Deckert. "His descents were vertical, stalling the engine every time. I saw him again in 1920, descending like a parachute, risking life and limb."

But the French Faure mission of 1919 felt able to claim some success, albeit modest. "Three sets of less than talented pupils completed their course with only one accident, and that to a pilot since discovered to be mentally afflicted," read the report. Progress accelerated in the 1920s. The Army Ministry set up a separate Aviation Bureau, and by 1924 there were six air battalions. But the Japanese airplane was not yet a very sophisticated machine; according to the Air Service manual of 1924, the engine fitter's kit consisted of six spanners and two pairs of pliers.

By the start of the 1930s, however, with the pressure for rearmament growing, the army had developed its own aerial design facilities, working closely with civilian manufacturers. Doctrine evolved more slowly. Most senior army officers were still impervious to the real value of air power, and persisted in seeing it as a supplement to ground forces in short-range operations. Reconnaissance was considered to be its principal function; few army men had any conception of the positive use of aircraft for attack.

Not until mid-decade did attitudes change significantly. The conquest of Manchuria gave Japan a prime base from which to reach out into the Asian landmass; in the event of a war on the continent, the role of the army air force was now seen as gaining air superiority, not merely supporting troops on the ground. Faster, more wide-ranging planes were at last encouraged. Japanese machines were still far from revolutionary; their new fighters, "Claude" (the Mitsubishi A5M) and "Nate" (the Nakajima Ki 27) had old-style radial engines and fixed landing gear, and "Claude" had an open cockpit. But they were evolving all the time to meet Japan's particular needs.

In general, these needs were perceived to be range and speed rather than weight. Far from both Russian and American cities and industrial plants, the Japanese planners could see no need for heavy bombers, and concentrated on fast, maneuverable attacking planes with a long range (though, in the event, not long enough). Too many of these machines were under-protected. The "Betty" Type 1 G4M bomber was a notorious "flamer," with little protection for either crew or fuel tanks; similarly, the Zero (Mitsubishi A6M *Reisen*) fighter achieved much of its speed, climb, firepower and maneuverability at the expense of armor. Crucially, it did not have self-sealing fuel tanks, a defect mercilessly exploited once Allied pilots had grown familiar with the plane.

But in the end the real weakness of Japan's air forces was not their state of readiness in 1941, but their failure to support the strength they had managed to build up. The Army Air Force in particular lagged behind in reliability and maintenance of its machines, and in the upkeep of its ground installations, where conditions were often poor enough to depress morale seriously and threaten efficiency. Pilots, as one Japanese veteran pointed out, need perfect vision; in too many units, this was impaired by malnutrition.

"By American standards," remarked the U.S. Strategic Bombing Survey pityingly after the war, "the Japanese never fully appreciated the importance of adequate maintenance, logistic support, communications and control, and air fields and bases sufficiently prepared to handle large numbers of planes. As a result, they were unable to concentrate any large percentage of their air strength at any one time or place." For this, the perennially poor coordination between army and navy was also to blame.

Nor, as the war progressed, could Japan maintain the relative advantages she had enjoyed at the start. After initial success, the Japanese air forces seemed unable to develop sufficiently—and here a familiar scenario begins to unfold. Hard though Japan had tried, and remarkable though her achievements had been, in some fields she was never going to catch up with the West, and was in fact falling farther behind. Here at the cutting edge of industrial-technological strength, the failure to prepare adequately for total war became all too apparent.

Until 1941, much of Japan's technical progress depended (as it had since the Meiji Restoration) on "tailgating." At every level and in every aspect of an industry as complex as airplane manufacture, Japan had been dependent on Western skills, plugged into the latest Western research into airframe construction, metallurgy, the science of resins. Even the designers had mostly been trained in the United States, and many of the designs had been bought there. The war cut off the lifeblood of Japanese aircraft development, which then simply stagnated, for there was not the industrial technological momentum within the Empire's borders to compensate.

The High Command had always hoped to gain the same kind of technological assistance from Germany that the Soviet Union had enjoyed until the rise of Hitler. But when Hitler handed over the blueprint for his Messerschmidt jet aircraft, the Japanese lacked the technical know-how even to make a prototype.

"In spite of the fact that nationwide efforts were made to increase the production of aircraft in Japan," gloomily reflected Major General Morimoto (Chief of Staff at the headquarters of the Southern Area Army), "because of the general low standard of Japanese machine industry, the forced use of substitutes owing to the shortage of the necessary raw materials and the increased employment of temporary unskilled labor, the execution of plans was extremely difficult and the records achieved were unsatisfactory."

He might also have mentioned the unreasonableness of some of the demands made on designers and engineers. The High Commands of both army and navy, anxious to acquire the world's leading fighters and bombers, issued performance specifications far beyond the capacity of the industry, and called for an impractical number of new models. Engineers were constantly being forced to slow production of existing types in order to construct new prototypes. These experimental aircraft often went into production without proper tests, sometimes without maintenance manuals; this led inevitably to malfunctions, breakages, and time constantly wasted in expensive modifications.

Just as fatal as the shortage of planes was the wastage of experienced airmen. By 1941, both army and navy air forces had already produced large numbers of skilled and adventurous pilots, blooded over Nanking, Hankow, and Nomonhan. Although the ethos of both services discouraged the exaltation of the individual, and there was no official tradition of recording pilots' tallies separately, the Japanese had their aces just as Western air forces did, decorating their planes and competing for "kills"—Nobuo Ogiya, trained as a swordsman, with thirty-two cherry blossoms painted on the fuselage of his plane; Kaneyoshi Muto, who was known to have shot down four enemy aircraft in one engagement with single bursts; Hiroyoshi Nishizawa, Japan's top air ace with 102 victories, who believed he had a charmed life and died aboard an air transport piloted by someone else.

Around navy pilot Junichi Sasai, "the Richthofen of Rabaul," gathered a small circus of air aces, close friends and passionate rivals. Among them was Saburo Sakai—60 victories—who became a folk hero after being critically wounded in a burst of enemy machine-gun fire over Guadalcanal. With several bullet fragments in his brain, with shrapnel in his back and chest, having lost the sight of his right eye, intermittently blind in his left, paralyzed down his left-hand side, he brought his crippled plane home to Rabaul in an epic eight-hour flight. By 1944, he was back in combat.

Many of these pilots died in acts of near-suicidal bravery—hopelessly outnumbered by enemy fighters, or using their planes as battering rams. As the war went on, other less glamorous though no less courageous fliers died simply from lack of skill, as pilot training contracted. Aircraft were becoming scarcer for training or any other purposes, fuel was in short supply, and experienced pilots were too precious to be spared as instructors. The U.S. Navy rotated experienced pilots between combat and training duties, to maintain a permanent nucleus of veteran instructors. The Japanese kept their best pilots flying combat until they were annihilated. So poor were the skills of some pilots in the later years of the war that they adopted defensive maneuvers dating from the First World War; the habit, for instance, of flying line astern in a circle made them sitting ducks against fighters with Second World War speed, maneuverability, and armaments.

Then, with the commanders despairing of conventional air victories, the planes in which Japan had once taken much pride—the Zero, "Kate," "Frank," "Peggy," "Val," and "George"—were turned over for use as kamikaze weapons by pilots with scarcely the training to take off. The navy was the first to introduce the "Divine Wind" Special Attack Corps; the army was slower to establish permanent suicide units, but in October 1944 founded the Banda unit, or "Ten Thousand Petals," seeing in the kamikaze dive, perhaps, another manifestation of the banzai charge that had been for so long the pinnacle of infantry tactics. In all, 1,388 army airmen would die in "special attacks"—though to some of the air aces, the suicide tactic seemed a pointless and repulsive waste of skill; several, including Sakai, refused the order to self-destruct. "It is essential," warned the training manual, "not to miss the target because of shutting one's eyes for a moment"—a reminder that not all of these pilots were volunteers, and many were eighteen and nineteen years old.

For Japan's ground forces, the loss of air superiority had disastrous consequences. Amphibious landings were more exposed to enemy air attack, and it became more difficult to maintain positions, with enemy planes sinking the convoys that brought reinforcements, and disrupting troop concentrations and overextended supply lines. Air reconnaissance and supply drops, vital aids to survival in the jungle, were restricted if not ruled out. And the men on the ground were increasingly easily demoralized, knowing that if the enemy chose to attack from the air, there was nothing to stop him. The air force is generally the most visible of the three services. Its actions are frequently watched by the other two at a distance, and its failures cannot be concealed. The end of the Japanese air forces would mark the beginning of the end for the Imperial Army as a whole.

KYODO

The charismatic Takamori Saigo, first commander of the Imperial forces, negotiates the surrender of the Shogun's castle in January 1868.

KYODO

The Emperor Meiji—here in his middle years—was a boy of sixteen in 1868, a pawn in the hands of Japan's new masters.

KYODO

The architect of the Imperial Army, Aritomo Yamagata.

The new Imperial Army in action in 1877, advancing against the rebel samurai warriors of the Satsuma clan.

Taro Katsura, one of Yamagata's protégés, had a key role in the 1880s molding the modern military machine along Prussian lines.

In the Russo-Japanese War of 1904–5, General Maresuke Nogi's rigid adherence to the Prussian philosophy of massed frontal attacks left the corpses of Japanese infantrymen— including his own son—piled high before the defenses of Port Arthur.

Japan's staggering victory against Russia confronted the West with startling images such as this—Asian soldiers standing guard over European prisoners.

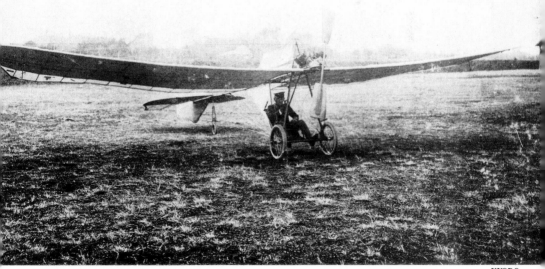

Pioneer Japanese aviators like Captain Kumazo Hino, pictured here in a monoplane brought back from Germany in 1910, claimed the first recorded air-to-air combat during the siege of Tsingtao in 1914.

The Siberian Expedition—an illusion of international cooperation amidst the chaos following the Bolshevik Revolution of 1917.

In the 1920s, the Imperial Army developed as a highly mobile force geared to warfare in the vast tundras of eastern Siberia: artillerymen (*left bottom*) could manhandle their weapons over the most difficult terrain; Norwegian instructors trained the peasant conscripts to ski (*above*); and daily Kendo practice (*below*) honed the spirit of the attack.

Menaced by Bolshevism, strategists like Tetsuzan Nagata looked to Manchuria and China for the raw materials with which to sustain the battles of attrition demanded by the twentieth-century philosophy of total war.

Manchuria was the first territory to be annexed. Here Pu Yi, puppet Emperor of the new "Manchukuo," rides with Emperor Hirohito during a state visit to Tokyo.

The search for autarky led to a savage war against China in 1937. Infantrymen struggled to hold the railway lines, the arteries of Japanese power in China, against Nationalist and Communist guerrilla attacks (*left bottom*), and to take the fight to Chiang Kai-shek by any means possible (*above*); but ultimately all efforts stalled in the logistical quagmire (*below*).

72

The China War drained Japan's manpower reserves: In China, young girls were trained to defend the crucial railway lines (*above left*) and child "soldiers" drilled in Tokyo (*above right*). As the army ballooned from twenty-four divisions in 1937 to fifty-one in 1941, crash training programs like this one in communications for headquarters staff were launched (*below*).

The domestic propaganda machine ground incessantly: Here the sounds of triumphal marching feet are relayed to radio listeners.

The reality was more often death, the only consolation being the elaborate ritual with which the soldier's remains were returned to his family.

By December 1941, after four years of war in China, the army had units fully equipped for a blitzkrieg in Southeast Asia. Under generals like Tomoyuki Yamashita (*left top*), they routed the ill-prepared British and took Singapore. U.S. forces on Bataan proved more tenacious, even against Japanese flamethrowers (*right top*). But Japan's objective—the oilfields of Indonesia (*below*)—was quickly obtained, and the surrender of Corregidor (*right*) provided a triumphant finale to the Imperial Army's hundred days of glory.

Japan's weakness—her vulnerability to strategic bombing—was first revealed by the risky Doolittle Raid of April 18, 1942; only some of the fliers (*left*) were lucky enough to come down behind Chinese Nationalist lines. Japan's civil defense preparations were wholly inadequate. Tokyo postmen (*below*) were protected against gas attack, but not against the incendiary bombing that was to destroy more than half their city.

After the fall of Saipan in July 1944, the B-29 bombing campaign was still threatened by the radar and fighters based on Iwo Jima. This key target was fortified with virtually impregnable tunnels and cave hideouts. Here a Japanese prisoner is being used as a "missionary," appealing to his comrades to surrender.

The myth of the "jungle superman" was destroyed as the Allies took prisoners. These captives—taken in Burma (*right*) and New Guinea (*below*)—were victims as much of the failings of their own high command as the strengths of their adversaries.

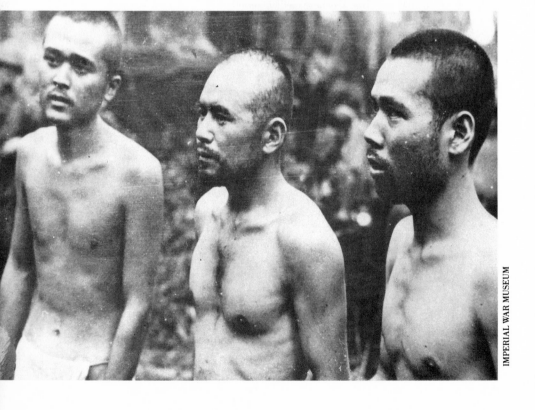

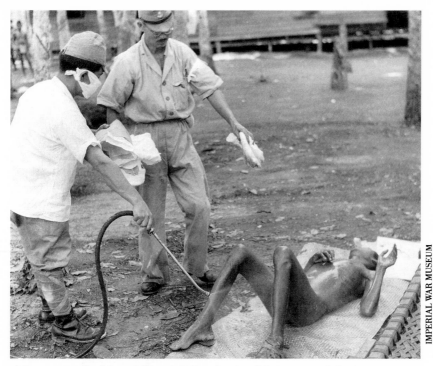

A Javanese coolie dying of disease and neglect in a labor camp at Seletah is sprayed with disinfectant by a Japanese medical orderly in an attempt to conceal the evidence of atrocity from the approaching Allies—who caught him in the act.

Japanese officers surrender their swords—some of them priceless heirlooms—at Kuala Lumpur in October 1945.

September 1945: Soldiers wait in a Tokyo street for their demobilization papers.

For more than 1.5 million, there was no return. Many took their own lives, falling on hand grenades or curling a toe around the trigger of a rifle.

37

STAYING ALIVE:
LOGISTICS

I n September 1942, a senior Japanese staff officer on colonial service in Kuala Lumpur wrote in his diary with some concern: "A certain native said, 'I have never seen such a strong army as the Japanese army; I have never seen such a poor administrator as the Japanese.' "

During the Pacific War, operational effectiveness was too often limited by curbs that had nothing to do with strategy or tactics, or with the quality of the soldiers or their weapons. Problems of logistics, transport, communications, medical support, and other services behind the line forced the Imperial Army to pay a price in suffering and inefficiency that would greatly have distressed Meckel, Kawakami, and the others who had reformed army organization in the 1880s.

Many felt it was entirely to the Japanese army's credit that its ratio of service to combat troops was so low. Where the Americans needed approximately eighteen soldiers in supply services to keep one rifleman firing, and the average ratio for other Western armies was about eight to one, Japan was alleged to have no more men behind the lines than she kept in the field.

But there were dangers in the relatively low priority given by the Japanese to administration. The cream of the General Staff went straight to the Operations Bureau, whose power and prestige increased rapidly in the early years of the war at the expense of all the other sections, with logistics trailing badly in the competition for good men. Less-influential officers were unable to command a generous share of resources, and it was hard sometimes for Japanese administrators and soldiers alike not to envy the wealth that was obvious in every bulge of the well-fleshed administrative organizations of the Allies, especially the Americans. "Even though they are the work of the enemy," one Japanese officer confided to his diary in Guadalcanal, "newly established automobile roads, the strengthening of positions . . . the setting up of a network of communications etc. are beautiful things."

Even before the China War had reached a stalemate, the army was having to come to terms with serious shortages both of essential goods and the means of transporting them—ammunition, motor vehicles, gasoline, shipping. Nothing to do with supply or transport was easy; and as the war went on and the shortages—food, drinking water, medicines—became even more painful, Japanese soldiers were increasingly tempted to compare their own hardships with the life led by the G.I., whose supply of everything seemed so effortless and so extraordinarily abundant.

Taking prisoners or seizing abandoned supplies, the Japanese were often stunned by what Allied quartermasters considered necessities. They themselves still subsisted primarily on rice, cooked on the battlefield despite the inconvenience and frequent danger. America's revised K ration (though much reviled by G.I.s) included—besides a variety of food—lavatory paper and an ingenious type of general-purpose soap, which could be used in salt water to shave, wash clothes, even brush teeth (though the shaving equipment itself was not included, an omission that the British considered bad for morale). For situations in which it might not be possible to take full advantage of the K ration, the "Candy Assault Ration" had been developed. Experience on Tarawa and Makin would show that in the early stages of an amphibious assault there was not enough time to eat the full ration; the Marine Corps' Seventh Division in the Marshalls would be issued instead with twenty-eight pieces of hard candy, a chocolate-peanut bar, cigarettes, and gum.

Lieutenant Hiroo Onoda was particularly impressed by the degree of ease which chewing gum implied. Onoda was one of the very last Japanese soldiers to surrender, emerging from the Philippine jungle twenty-nine years after the official capitulation. During this long guerrilla existence he had eaten leaves, roots, and even bark to survive, and he later wrote incredulously, "In one place a wad of chewing gum was sticking to the leaf of a weed. Here we were holding on for dear life, and these characters were chewing gum while they fought! I was more sad than angry. The chewing gum tinfoil told me just how miserably we had been beaten."

Huddled in a cave on Angaur in the Palau islands, filthy, starving and desperately wounded, Sergeant Hiroshi Funasaka looked down on an American encampment. "I could imagine the Americans sleeping soundly inside those tents. They might even be soothing their tiredness by reading a novel. And in the morning, they'd rise leisurely, shave, eat a hearty breakfast, then come after us again as usual. That sea of shining electric lights was a powerful, silent commentary on their 'battle of abundance.' . . . I had an image of the island divided in half with heaven and hell lying next to each other, separated by only a few hundred metres."

The price of luxury, of course, was a heavier pack. The U.S. infantryman was often grossly overloaded, carrying up to 132 pounds and suffering a serious risk of drowning if he overbalanced coming off the landing craft. It was more common for the Japanese soldier, except on special missions, to carry between sixty-five and seventy pounds, including rifle and bayonet, ammunition, rations, water bottle and mess tin, water purifier and mosquito net, gas mask, camouflage nets, pick and shovel, tent sheet, greatcoat in season, bandages, and a compass. (Occasionally there were unforeseen burdens. Curiously, the Japanese seemed not to have devised an effective sleeping bag, and relied on blankets with an impractically high percentage of cotton. After the landings on the frozen soil of Attu in the Aleutians, each soldier was issued with no less than seven.)

Japanese equipment was not without its occasional flourish. Inventors had devised a helmet of compressed silk or sorghum that was one-third the usual weight, yet was proof against shrapnel and offered no magnetic interference. Senior officers were sometimes issued with bulletproof vests fitted with canvas pockets that held eight-inch-thick metal plates. For the piercing cold of North China, a lucky few were to be offered electrically heated *tabi* (the Japanese split-toed socks), and aviators were equipped with heated goggles and flying-suit liners. For the horses there were camouflage suits for snow. British experts also admired the Japanese gas-decontamination suit—"of excellent quality, pure rubber, and comprised a hat, a pair of shoulder-length rubber gloves, trousers, and shoes—all made up into a packet about $12 \times 5 \times 3''$."

But the Japanese infantryman was still a functional rather than a parade-ground soldier, and continued to distress the Allied stickler (like the British commanding officer at Imphal, who singled out the work of Mobile Bath Units as keeping divisions at fighting pitch). The Japanese soldier walked rather than marching, picking up firewood en route and swigging from his water bottle whenever he felt like it. His buttons were often undone, his cap sat at an irregular angle, and he was unshaven. But he was extremely fit; his unorthodox "marching" covered remarkable distances, and Allied troops found themselves shelled from unexpected directions as his regimental guns were manhandled deep into the jungle.

Keeping him supplied was often more complicated than it need have been. Until November 1943, when the Ministry of Munitions was established, there was no coordination between army, navy, and civilian supply systems. Some generals, too, paid no attention at all to the practicalities of transport and supplies when formulating their plans (though there were honorable exceptions like Yamashita, who turned down the offer of five divisions for the invasion of Malaya on the grounds that it would only be practical to supply three—unheard-of restraint amid the battle for resources).

Logistical systems devised to suit operations against the Soviet Union in the freezing wastes of Manchuria took some adapting to battles on Pacific islands and in the jungles of Burma. As the pressure on Japan increased and it became necessary to transfer troops from the northern to the southern theater, whole divisions would arrive at the front with the wrong equipment. The Fifteenth Division outside Kohima, for instance, had nothing but motor transport in terrain where only pack transport was viable.

In general, however, the army suffered from a shortage of motor transport—though this was far less damaging in a war fought in jungle and on islands than it would have been in Europe. Bicycles were far better suited to the conditions, and in Japanese hands they became an effective weapon. The average division was allocated roughly five hundred motor vehicles for its whole strength, and six thousand bicycles. In official bicycle companies, troops lashed their rifles to the handlebars, and mortars were transported on iron-wheeled vehicles towed behind tandems; in Manchuria a number of Harley-Davidson motorcycles operated with machine-gunners in the sidecar. Some paratroops carried folding bicycles.

Perhaps out of concern for the imperial image, few British troops in Malaya had bicycles. They also had no alternative to walking on some of the tracks over which they were forced to fight, whereas the Japanese made brilliant use of the machines that before the war had been one of their principal exports to Malaya. "Thanks to Britain's dear money spent on the excellent paved roads," gloated Tsuji, "and to the cheap Japanese bicycles, the assault on Malaya was easy." Bicycles made it possible to carry out hot pursuit, giving the enemy no time to rest or reorganize. The main problem was the heat, which caused tires to puncture spontaneously. A repair squad of two mechanics was attached to every bicycle company, but if necessary the cyclists rode on their rims—in itself an asset, as the noise was colossal, more than once convincing a nervous enemy that they were facing a tank advance.

In emergencies, when bridges could not be quickly repaired, Japanese forces were often to be seen wading streams with bicycles on their shoulders. In general, though, they were extremely well served by their engineers. All Japanese support troops were armed and trained to fight as infantrymen if necessary, but more was expected of the engineers than most. "In addition to their strictly engineer duties—fieldwork, demolitions, mine-clearing, river crossing and so on—they were often called upon to provide assault detachments for tasks which would clearly be costly and even suicidal." It was usually engineers who had the unpopular job of manning the flamethrowers.

Jungle conditions also greatly complicated the work of the communications corps on both sides. The Americans had by now developed a global radio/radio-telephone network, but it helped them very little amid the dense vegetation and heavy humidity of the Pacific islands and Burma. The sacrifice of power for portability had made light radio inadequate in these conditions; and in any event, every transmission longer than thirty seconds attracted a deluge of artillery fire.

On the Japanese side, signaling had always been made more difficult by the complexities of the language. In Japanese, many words with similar pronunciation have totally different meanings, offering endless possibilities for confusion in both telephone and telegraph messages. Back in Tokyo scientists might be hard at work on the development of a "photophone for voice transmission by infra-red or invisible light with an effective range of 4–5 kilometers," but there was still great scope for the carrier pigeon, the messenger, and the runner in the Pacific War.

In their casualty-evacuation procedure, too, Japanese methods were sometimes strangely antiquated, though this was often unavoidable given the shortage of air and motor transport in many areas. By 1941 the medical services that had once been the envy of American military surgeons would seem to have deteriorated significantly.

Professional knowledge of tropical diseases was "not of a very high grade," according to a British expert. "As an example, scrub typhus was not recognized by them for a long time, although it is certain that they must have had an appreciable incidence of it. It was termed Wewak fever and Hansa fever, and was undoubtedly confused with malaria." As for malaria itself, neither preventive nor curative treatment was standardized, instead depending a good deal on the whim of the individual medical officer. "It is certain that a large number of deaths was due to insufficient early treatment and the failure to use intravenous quinine for cerebral malaria." Every possible combination of quinine, atabrine, and plasmoquin was employed—but not the invaluable mepacrine, which the Japanese did not possess, although they knew of it. (They also knew how valuable it was to the Allies in keeping troops in action, so they put out a rumor that it caused impotence. But this had little obvious effect in spreading despondency.)

The Japanese medical system offered no prophylactic injections against tetanus; thus troops were left highly vulnerable to wounds received in the agricultural land that saw much fighting in Burma and the Philippines. At the start of the war Japanese medical officers had apparently not heard of penicillin, and it never became universally available, though scientists claimed later to have developed a strain superior to Fleming's. Nor was sulfaguanidine prescribed for the treatment of dysentery.

These shortcomings were partly due to the interruption of supply lines by bombing and shipping losses, leading to acute shortages of drugs and food. In New Guinea and the Solomons, all health problems were aggravated by malnutrition. Vast quantities of vitamin tablets and injections were used, but it seems they proved of very little use; beriberi, night blindness, and other signs of deficiency were common.

Even in hospitals there was not enough food, and the patients' lives were less than secure. Medical officers were armed with sword and pistol, orderlies with bayonets, and stretcher bearers with grenades. When the Allies closed in on Japanese positions later in the war, it was not unusual for the staff to put their patients out of their misery, or at the very least offer them the means of committing suicide, solving the problems of transport and supplies and leaving no one to tell of the Japanese army's desperate predicament.

38

HIDDEN ASSET:
JAPANESE MILITARY
INTELLIGENCE

There was one other resource in which the Japanese were seriously deficient. The inadequacy of their military intelligence, as compared with that of the Americans, was almost as crippling as their inferiority in oil supplies. Japan had no source of information on the Allies comparable with the Allies' access to Japanese codes; even when the Japanese obtained hard information, their instincts and common sense often betrayed them. "Their estimates of strategic objectives are sometimes wide of the mark," commented an American intelligence report in surprise, "although the general pattern of Allied strategy has been announced frequently by Allied spokesmen."

Military intelligence, as far as the army was concerned, was primarily the responsibility of the Second Bureau of the Army General Staff. Under this came the intelligence departments of each field command, and the bureau also sent representatives abroad as military attachés. Around the Second Bureau were ranged a variety of other agencies—such as the Central Special Intelligence Department, dealing with code-breaking; the Special Service Agency, in charge of espionage; and the *kempeitai* intelligence personnel, who focused mainly on counterintelligence. In parallel ran the intelligence functions of the navy General Staff, the Foreign Ministry, and the Greater East Asia Ministry.

"Intelligence" incorporated not just the gathering of information but also its dissemination—though the outgoing material was not so much misinformation as propaganda. Agents were trained as much in the techniques of propaganda as in infiltration, code-breaking and disguise; and the Japanese seemed often to be better at speaking than listening. "The Japanese does not play chess with his army," observed one Allied intelligence expert. "He makes a plan and goes ahead without respect to our moves or possible moves. . . . He is supremely conceited, and is thoroughly contemptuous of us."

Ideological disdain for the enemy may indeed have discouraged Japanese leaders from learning what he was really like and what he was doing. Certainly, the High Command frequently failed to take advantage of the data their intelligence services did obtain. Right at the start of the war, through a cashiered American major who pumped his old friends in the Army and Navy Club in Farragut Square in Washington, they were notified in some detail of the Allies' "Europe First" decision at the "Arcadia" conference of December 22, 1941–January 14, 1942. The implication was that Japan need not expect an immediate all-out attack, but should take measures against a long-term blockade that would use submarine packs and aerial bombardment. Elated by their early victories, the High Command ignored the warning.

This inertia may have been partly a matter of temperament; it is a characteristic of the authoritarian personality to reject unwelcome information, and many of the Japanese leaders certainly fell into this category. The failure to appreciate intelligence adequately was also due to mechanical difficulties, to a lack of system in the way information was processed and used. No policy-making body used intelligence reports on a regular basis. Intelligence work as a profession was not highly regarded in the Imperial Army. It seemed in many ways the antithesis of action, requiring caution, stealth, patience, forethought—none of these being prized martial virtues. "High fliers" generally chose to go into operations, not intelligence or administration. In 1941 only one member of the army General Staff—Ichiji Sugita—had specialized training in intelligence.

But attitude was not the only problem. Code-breaking was severely hampered by a lack of resources, human and material. In general, Japan was not producing mathematicians of the same sophistication as the

West's. Almost more important, there was no individual genius to make the crucial, almost intuitive breakthroughs. Nor did the government allocate sufficient resources to finance research and development, or even to supply the code-breaking equipment that was already available.

The Japanese army had not been particularly late in entering the field of military intelligence. At the turn of the century, their agents had been as ingenious and flamboyant as any—men like Makiyo Ishimitsu, who had posed as a Japanese businessman in Korea, lived rough with Chinese bandits while reconnoitering the Russian-built Chinese Eastern Railway, and run a laundry in Harbin, Manchuria, that enjoyed considerable success with talkative Russian administrators in the years before the Russo-Japanese War. But the Japanese entered the Pacific War lagging seriously behind in knowledge of their enemies simply because they had been concentrating for years on the wrong enemy.

The army did not share the Imperial Navy's keen interest in the threat of American power, and in the 1930s army intelligence agencies did not study the United States very closely. Nor did the navy choose to pool its intelligence. To a large extent, army agencies were preoccupied with the role that intelligence might play in the war with Russia which they felt must come. Plans were made for a program of subversion to accompany hostilities, using Koreans, defectors, and White Russian émigrés in Manchuria, just as during the Russo-Japanese War Motojiro Akashi had sought to distract the authorities' attention from the front line in the east by sending aid to the Bolsheviks and ethnic minorities.

Russian, not English, was the foreign language learned by the fast-lane candidates in the Military Academy. English was not taught in military preparatory schools, so only those entering the academy from ordinary middle schools, at some disadvantage, could speak it fluently. Of twenty officers from captain to colonel in the Operations Bureau of the General Staff in 1941, only one had ever been to America, and only for a few days. The American section of the General Staff's Second Bureau was not set up until 1942, and even then it had only three permanent officers; of the fifteen other members of staff, only five had been through the Staff College, and only two of these had ever visited America or Britain. The remainder of the section were businessmen mobilized for their foreign connections and experience.

Relatively few agents worked in America (their central clearinghouse was the Japanese Imperial Railway Company in New York), but the Japanese military intelligence organizations still put great faith in espionage in general. The principal training establishment was the

Nakano School in Tokyo, founded in 1938 by young officers of field rank who felt the need for systematic training of agents to work against Russia; the army formally acknowledged it two years later. In its early days Nakano breathed some of the mystery and glamour that the spy's profession had traditionally possessed in Japan, and tried to fire its trainees with the spirit of the ninja, who possessed virtually supernatural powers of stealth, speed, and invisibility.

Later Nagano became more severely practical. The students learned the techniques of disguise, codes and code-breaking, infiltration, propaganda, the use of explosives, and guerrilla warfare. Some were trained with a view to resisting an invader; others were destined to go ashore with the first wave of an invasion force, infiltrate the local population in disguise, and then cause trouble behind enemy lines. Nakano graduates led most of the organizations that encouraged independence movements in Asia—training native armies, keeping up links with puppet governments, offering "political guidance." They trained the officers who became the nucleus of the Burmese National Army; they attempted to destabilize the French in Indochina with propaganda and fifth-column tactics; they coached Papuans in New Guinea in secret-police methods; they set up and "ran" Subhas Chandra Bose in India.

But many Japanese spies also tended to the credulous. They were far more often deceived by Allied ploys than successful in laying false trails themselves. At one point the High Command was persuaded to set British and Indian strength in Burma at forty-eight divisions, whereas in fact there were never more than eighteen there, and they identified nonexistent American divisions in Australia, Alaska, and the Pacific islands. The intelligence agencies bought a good deal of misleading information from dubious free-lances; a significant number of their contacts were double agents.

Instead of focusing on espionage, they should perhaps have concentrated harder on codes and code-breaking. It was the area from which they were themselves to hemorrhage information to the Americans, but throughout the war they managed to break no high-grade Allied codes.

Japanese cryptologists were not without their coups. In 1939 the Second Bureau had deciphered a British telegram that indicated in some detail the weaknesses in Singapore's land defenses; and the navy would have some success with British interdepartmental codes. Most of the Chinese codes were cracked, and these provided some incidental information on the Allies; the Chinese quite often, for instance, relayed British situation reports from Burma. Some low-grade American codes gave the Japanese information on aircraft movements—including, for a time, the probability of B-29 bombing raids. A navy signal-intercept station picked up U.S. Air Force messages from Ch'eng-tu directing all stations to turn on their homing beacons for a specified period the following day, and it did not take long to realize that these messages were generally transmitted shortly before a B-29 raid into Manchuria or the home islands—not that a great deal could be done with the information.

Japanese intelligence also cracked codes that gave them American unit dispositions in the Pacific, though at the start of the war they could glean almost as much from the American press, given the original U.S. military policy of identifying all divisions participating in a campaign. At the very least, open sources like radio and newspapers confirmed Japanese suspicions, and at worst they volunteered fresh information, until the rules were tightened. Much of the crucial intelligence about Pearl Harbor, which enabled the Japanese navy to draw up a "bomb plot" precisely locating all the American vessels and the harbor's de-- fenses, was gathered by a single officer visiting public places as "a very observing tourist."

Traffic analysis reaped considerable rewards. Signals-intelligence analysts monitored unusual message routings, radio silences, heavy volumes of traffic, reconnaissance flights, concentrations of submarines, the activities of merchant transport, the appearance of new units or new aircraft call signs, and drew what conclusions they could from them. (In mid-1942, for instance, navy intelligence officer Haruki Ito deduced from the existence of two new Allied call signs in the southwest Pacific—which tended to suggest the headquarters of a new task force— that there might soon be a counteroffensive in the Solomons or New Guinea. This was shortly before the American landings on Guadalcanal; Ito was ignored.)

Useful though this kind of detail was to the Japanese, it dwindled into insignificance beside the information on their own movements that had been cascading through Allied intelligence channels virtually from the beginning. The system for breaking the principal Japanese diplo- matic "Purple" codes gave the Americans the body of information known, aptly enough, as Magic; among other feats, Magic alerted the Allies to the crucial battles of the Coral Sea and Midway. (It also gave the Allies vital clues to the intentions of the Germans, as relayed to Tokyo by the Japanese ambassador in Berlin.) In addition, both British and American cryptographers had cracked the key naval code, JN-25b, used by the admirals for strategic matters, by the spring of 1942, a matter of days before it was replaced as the Japanese carrier strike force set out for Midway.

And then, in 1943, at least some of the Imperial Army's codes succumbed. Compared with the diplomatic signals, the codes used by the military were highly complex, and the messages were usually deliberately incomplete. Nevertheless, the breakthrough was made—after which, in February 1944, a copy of the principal army code was captured with some of the cryptographic equipment, giving the Americans knowledge in several areas of the disposition of Japanese forces, the shipping organization that supplied them, the replenishment of oil stocks, air strengths (or weaknesses), casualty figures, troop movements, and states of readiness. Knowing Japanese intentions, the Allies could set up elaborate deception programs. They were aware of how much, or how little, the Japanese knew of Allied plans. The Japanese did not even know that their codes had been broken.

Had their code-breakers been more successful, the Japanese army would not have had to rely so heavily on other sources of intelligence—sources that dried up as the fortunes of war changed. The value of aerial reconnaissance, for instance, was always limited by the jungle terrain in which so many of the Pacific battles were fought, but even this fitful illumination was snuffed out as the Japanese air forces progressively lost control of the skies.

The mass seizures of matériel, documents, and, most important, prisoners in the aftermath of the Hundred Days would never be repeated, and very little fell into Japanese hands once the Imperial forces had gone into retreat. There was the radar system from the American submarine *Darter,* which ran aground off Palawan in October 1944; and the radar and bomb-sight adjusters on a B-29 that crashed in Japan after the first raid on Yawata in June 1944. The Germans had been able to supply useful information on the far greater quantities of matériel they had seized in Europe, but soon this conduit, too, would dry up.

As for personnel, the Japanese had developed fairly sophisticated techniques of interrogation and persuasion, to be used on prisoners "where time allows." There were comprehensive instructions on interrogation methods. Prisoners were always to be kept apart, so they had no time to compare their stories; the first interrogation was crucial, while the prisoner was unprepared and in "a state of spiritual unrest." "In examining a young person or woman," wrote the instructor, "advantage should be taken of his or her vanity. . . . In regard to women, advantage should be taken of their shyness, and they should be made to confess with intimidation. . . . If the prisoner looks repeatedly and inquisitively at the interrogator's face and steals a glance at the interrogator's eyes, this is a sign that the prisoner is concealing vital knowledge. . . . During questioning, if the prisoner complains repeatedly that he is thirsty and asks for water, this is a sign that he is in agony such as one experiences just before confessing matters of a vital nature."

But the Japanese had fewer and fewer opportunities to put these precepts into practice. Most of the prisoners they took in the latter years were airmen, who occasionally divulged interesting details—about the alleged presence of chemical weapons on Guadalcanal, for instance, or reinforcements flown into Imphal—but were rarely senior enough to know a great deal about strategy.

In contrast, the outflow of material from the Japanese ranks was torrential. The excellence of American counterintelligence impressed and frustrated the Japanese intelligence staff—but they failed to convince their own troops of the importance of tight security. Quite senior officers had to be warned against disseminating intelligence material without proper security; several directives were issued against transmitting in plaintext information that had been derived from code-breaking, a habit that betrayed to the enemy the fact that his codes were no longer secure.

"If victory is divinely decreed and if retreats do not take place, security training is a luxury which can easily be dispensed with," gibed a document entitled "The Exploitation of Japanese Documents," issued to the staff of the Allied Translator and Interpreter Section (ATIS). Against instructions, Japanese troops persisted in carrying into battle their operational orders, maps, and diaries, which the Allies gratefully removed from their corpses and from overrun command posts. Seven tons of documents were seized on Saipan, of which about 60 percent had some value and a few were immediately useful in the conduct of the American operations.

Documents, claimed the ATIS report, were "the normal means of access to the Japanese understanding"; the Japanese relied heavily on written records, because homonyms made their spoken communication so ambiguous. Fortunately for the Allies, the Japanese were careless with these records through overconfidence in the impenetrability of their own language—which did amount, the writer admitted, "almost to a cryptographic system." The authorities who produced documents did not envisage them being read by enemies, so there was relatively little risk of deliberate misinformation—other than that designed for Japanese consumption. Allied readers were warned that in Japanese documents Japanese forces never retreated, they merely "changed the direction of their advance," and the Allies were always "stricken and annihilated," even in battles they had won.

Japanese prisoners were likely to be franker, within the limits of their knowledge. The Allies were startled by the freedom, even avidity, with which their prisoners volunteered information. But the Japanese had not been trained, as Allied servicemen had, in how to behave in captivity, since capture was not a possibility that could be contemplated. The military code dictated that the soldier who surrendered was as good as dead to his family, his village, and his comrades—and so, suddenly, he was liberated from the ethical ties that had bound him all his life. This was the Japanese fighting spirit rebounding on itself.

PART VIII

THE PACIFIC WAR: THE RETREAT

39

"ADVANCING TO THE REAR": THE DEFENSIVE

Historians are fond of identifying turning points, pivots, hinges of fate, watersheds. To pick the moment when triumph turned to disaster for Japan is not easy. Disaster for which service precisely? Though obviously linked, the fortunes of war moved at different speeds for army and navy. And in the army's case, one might even ask, Disaster in which war? It was fighting two at once, and their crises, their peaks and troughs, never coincided.

Within the Pacific War, the fulcrum is constantly being relocated. Some trace the slide to defeat back to Pearl Harbor and the failure to eliminate American air power completely. Others blame the failure, by early 1942, to have built a large enough merchant fleet; before long there were too few ships to meet the needs of both trade and troop transport. Still others would say that the real reverse came only with the acceptance of defeat—and for the army's hard core, this was not until the very end, after the dropping of the "cruel and unnatural" bomb.

Midway, Port Moresby, Guadalcanal, Saipan, Okinawa—each has

been labeled the turning point of the Pacific War. But it is tempting, where the army alone is concerned, to place the crux immediately after the Hundred Days. The Japanese had established a position of strength that had astonished even the most sanguine of them. Now they allowed themselves to be persuaded to take a further step; they moved, faltered— and the nature of the war changed, to become precisely the kind of battle they were least equipped to win: a war of defense, and a war of attrition.

"You keep repeating that the Imperial Army is invulnerable," Tojo reported the Emperor as saying quite late in the war, "yet whenever the enemy lands you lose the battle. You've never been able to repulse an enemy landing." The Japanese were not comfortable with defense; it was not part of the ethos of the officer corps. They had never had to fight a battle against a foreign enemy on their own territory, and in three major wars they had held the initiative virtually all the time. Even the word "defense" was avoided. In its "Intention" paragraph, the operation order for what in other armies would have been called a defensive maneuver stated firmly, "The unit will secure its present positions for an advance. While continuing generally to disrupt the enemy's activities it will prepare for future attack."

In planning war with America and Britain, the army had placed all its emphasis on the attack. Defensive principles were neglected to the point where Japanese commanders sometimes found it hard to anticipate or even comprehend the defense tactics of the enemy. As intelligent a general as Masaharu Homma totally misjudged the tactical significance of the American withdrawal to the Bataan peninsula, construing it simply as a sign of weakness. When the defenders proceeded to hold out for no less than four months, his schedule of operations was ruined, and with it much of his credibility at Imperial Headquarters.

Traditionally, the compromise solution had been an "offensive" concept of defense—active rather than passive, mobile rather than static, with the counterattack a favorite defensive weapon. The primary principle of Japanese defense was to have one extremely strong defensive zone—a continuous infantry line based on natural obstacles, with a good field of fire, strengthened with the main artillery positions. Behind this lay the rear defensive zone, as sheltered and as well fortified as possible, where reserve troops waited. But in front of the main zone was a crucial band of observation posts and outposts, always well forward and, where possible, dug in close to the enemy. Here the army commander would carry out vigorous patrolling night and day, so that enemy attacks might be anticipated and broken up in front of the main defensive line.

Even if enemy pressure became too strong to be resisted and the outer "protective" zone was invaded, snipers could be posted in the rear of the advancing forces. It is obvious from the way Allied troops talked about the Japanese sniper that they considered him an aggressor, and a dangerous and frightening one.

The Japanese put their snipers everywhere—covering the enemy's advanced outposts and paths behind the front line, covering the lines of approach to their own main positions, covering tempting gaps in barricades, and breaks in telephone cables that would need repairing. They were under bushes and hedges, even nestling in tree roots, in and under buildings, in holes and dips in the ground. "Forward enemy troops lay 'doggo,' " reported one Allied observer in Burma, "concealed in the jungle till attackers had passed through, then shot them from the rear. Many riflemen were found in holes dug under trees, to which covered communication trenches ran from positions twenty or thirty yards away."

With spikes and belts, snipers climbed forty-foot palm trees, sometimes with machine guns, and tied themselves in position so that they would not fall even if wounded. Some were sent out for weeks on end, carrying with them concentrated food, coffee, vitamin pills, water-purifying tablets, a respirator and antidote against mustard gas, quinine for malaria and pills against dysentery, a green eyescreen, green mosquito hood, and green camouflage net.

Camouflage was another Japanese forte. Everything could be concealed—uniforms, weapons, gun emplacements, the mouths of caves to protect them against air attack; elephants could be painted green if need be. The individual soldier was issued with head and body nets of greenish straw to which a garnish of vegetation could be added; nets also covered horses, machine guns and anti-aircraft positions. Otherwise the main material was half-inch-thick rope, whose strands were opened (as in splicing); tufts of grass fifteen to eighteen inches long were slipped in and fluffed out; then the rope was retwisted and coiled over the object to be disguised. For extra protection the sniper had a cape woven from the brown fiber at the base of fronds on coconut palms, which sat like a thatch on his shoulders; and hands and face could be dyed green.

The invisible enemy also set lethal obstacles and traps in the path of the advancing Allies. In the jungle, panjis were particularly loathed and feared. These were sharpened bamboo spikes about three feet long, set upright at the bottom of pits, or in rows at an angle of 60 degrees, or, nastiest of all, at the sides of paths, at a height of about four feet "in such a position that if a patrol were met by fire, personnel dashing for cover into the side would be impaled on the stakes." Booby traps were everywhere—radios whose battery cavities had been filled with explosives, and gramophones whose pickup arms acted as electric contacts triggering a charge; camera cases, ammunition cartridges, even bars of soap concealed explosives or incendiary devices; grenades were jammed in the forks of trees, and green coconuts were injected with picric acid. A favorite device, because of its underpinning of natural justice, was the watch on the wrist of the corpse, primed to explode if disturbed in any way.

Each of these elements in the Japanese defense had to be taken seriously. But until the end of 1942 the overall quality of Japan's defensive system had been little tested. Then, as the infantry began to outrun its transport capacity, gradually the advances ground to a halt for lack of support, and the enemy took the offensive. Now, suddenly, defense was the order of the day—and a rather different kind of defense.

The old tactics had essentially been adapted from techniques evolved in the open spaces of Manchuria, where mobility, dash, and flexibility were at a premium. Defense centered on the tiny coral islands of the Pacific would be more static, with less insistence on the primacy of spirit and more reliance on firepower. Resistance on the beaches along a wide front would give way to a defensive line drawn farther inland from the start; and at the heart of the new concept would be the deep dugout.

The forward defense was pushed off the beaches essentially by the rapid development of naval armaments, which soon had the strength to overpower land fortifications. The old methods were not, of course, obliterated immediately or completely. Machine-gun units would still try to sink landing craft with coastal fire, and suicide ships continued their ramming attacks on troop transports offshore.

For Tokyo Bay there would be plans until the end of the war for a very special kind of offshore coastal defense. Japanese scientists had been working on self-contained diving equipment and had succeeded in developing a suit that enabled a diver to operate underwater for eight hours at a stretch—longer than American divers could then manage. The proposed special units—"Special Harbor Defense and Underwater Attack Units"—would enter the water before dawn and remain there until darkness fell again at night, drawn up in rows under about fifteen feet of water.

Farther out to sea would be a barrier of anchored mines, which the divers could release with a trip rope. Then they themselves would be armed with mines and torpedoes, which they were expected to launch against an invader at close range—hence the minimum prescribed distance of forty meters between divers. "It was explained that from a morale standpoint, while a man was willing to die when he himself made the charge, he was not willing to die as a 'by-product' of another man's charge."

While the divers waited in their serried underwater ranks, they were expected to communicate with each other by either hitting pieces of metal together or using their breathing equipment as megaphones. There would also be a good deal of time to think about the purpose of their mission. "It is interesting to note," remarked the American technical researchers gathering data after the war, "that each diver was given an ensign to wear, placing him in the same category as a combatant ship. The idea was to bolster morale on the theory that each man was taking the place of a ship which had been put out of the fight."

But away from the home islands, for the Pacific theater in general, after beach positions had been repeatedly torn apart by naval bombardments the army General Staff issued instructions on "Essentials of Island Defense," which made it clear that main positions were to be constructed well back from the shoreline.

In constructing these main positions chiefly from bunkers and foxholes, the Japanese may have been drawing on information gleaned during the First World War, when they had observed the French, Germans, and Turks all making successful use of deep underground chambers roofed with reinforced concrete. They took the information, modified it, and improved on it to devise the ultimate dugout defense system. "By Christ, them little bastards can dig," observed a British sergeant at Imphal. "They're underground before our blokes have stopped spitting on their bloody 'ands."

Dugouts took many forms. The one-man weapon pit was about two feet across and four feet deep, with a trip wire strung around the top and sometimes a necklace of empty tins to act as an early warning system. Tank turrets sunk securely in the ground made instant defenses, and once, in Kohima, a Japanese raiding party took cover in bread ovens, pulling the heavy iron lids down on top of them. Pillboxes and bunkers ranged from small hollowed-out mounds to elaborate constructions on more than one floor; when the bunker was bombed, the occupants simply dropped through trapdoors to the story below.

Generally speaking, the capacity to attack had developed faster since World War I than the capacity to defend. But the Allies would spend an inordinate amount of time, money and energy trying to penetrate these Japanese static defenses. A report prepared by the British Directorate of Tactical Investigation in August 1944, entitled "Trials of Weapons Against Bunkers" and classified "Most Secret," summarized the results of tests carried out with various weapons against "typical Japanese bunker-type defensive positions" and vividly illuminated the problems involved.

The aim was to explode a round of ammunition either inside the bunker; or in the embrasure, sending fragments through the loophole; or in front of the bunker, to close the loophole with debris. Then the researchers measured the degree of damage, both to the structures and to the personnel inside them, represented on this occasion by animals—two white rabbits, one already "somewhat dull in behaviour and suffering from mange," two cockerels, and two half-grown billy goats, one "salivating freely." The animals were protected from a direct hit—perhaps too well, for when a two-inch mortar bomb was exploded inside, the animals were found to be "coated in dust; they appeared mildly surprised but in other respects were apparently normal. The goat was coughing slightly." In response to a PIAT missile, the goat's blood pressure and pulse rate actually went down. Driven to extreme lengths, the researchers exploded three bombs at once. "Both the goat and the observer started, while the cockerel and rabbit remained apparently unaffected."

The M9A1 grenade was the only weapon to emerge with any credit at all from these tests—but the problem was getting it inside the bunker, where it could inflict serious damage. The embrasure was often too well concealed for the attacker simply to shove the grenade through, and to penetrate the walls or roof he needed high-velocity weapons. Air attack had the force but probably not the necessary accuracy, especially in the jungle, where bombers might prove more of a danger to their own leading troops. Recoilless rifles were accurate enough for the firer to pierce the loophole, but they were only just beginning to be introduced when the war ended.

As the fighting wore on and the bunkers remained stubbornly in place, the Allies were driven to ever more desperate and ruthless measures. Where tanks were available, they could be driven to and fro over the top of deep dugouts till the roof collapsed. Otherwise flames seemed to be the most effective weapon against an enemy whose fear of fire was known to be inordinate. Where the entrances to bunkers sloped away underground, gasoline could be poured down and set alight. On the larger scale, "it is believed that in one RAF raid on Hamburg many thousands were suffocated by lack of oxygen in the centre of a ring of large fire," explained one British expert dispassionately. "On this analogy it is thought that after a preliminary bombardment by 2000-pound HE [high explosive] and AP [armor-piercing] bombs, the most effective final reduction might well be by fire. The target could be plastered with very large bomb containers of petrol, dieselite or other inflammable liquid and the whole subsequently fired to suffocate any remaining occupants." Fortunately for the Japanese, no such very large bombs were then available; but in the meantime, flamethrowers were quite intimidating enough.

"Flame has a good material effect if it can be projected into the bunker. The morale effect should also be high," commented a technical report, with ugly understatement. The medium flamethrowing tank could inject fire into a bunker from sixty yards; manpacks used by individual operators were effective only from about twenty yards. The jets of flame were defeated by winding tunnels, but they could follow the gentle curve of a cave; used with smoke shells, and with small-arms fire covering all possible exits, they were deadly. One soldier on Peleliu, seeing the flamethrower raised by a marine, blew himself up with a grenade; the flame fell short. On another occasion, the flamethrower fired into one opening of a cave; two hundred Japanese ran headlong out of the other entrance, straight into machine-gun fire, which killed a hundred and fifty of them.

In the end, the very stubbornness of the Japanese defense in depth would become a danger rather than a strength, because of the ferocity of the response it provoked from the Allies—including, eventually, the thought of escalating the attack beyond conventional weapons. "It appears that there is no existing weapon which is entirely suitable for taking on Japanese defences under difficult jungle conditions," concluded Allied experts in 1944. "Their reduction has therefore to be a carefully prepared deliberate operation which may last for a matter of days or even weeks. The fact that these positions exist in considerable depth necessitates an endless repetition of the lengthy process, and thus introduces a considerable measure of attrition into the war in the Pacific. In considering the possible use of chemical warfare in the Pacific, therefore, its application to the bunker problem should be an important factor."

Japanese defensive tactics alarmed the Allies because they were extreme. There was virtually no place within them for skilled withdrawal, and only one outcome could realistically be anticipated. Where the Allies referred to "foxholes," the Japanese preferred the term "octopus pots"—the difference being that the fox, having taken temporary shelter in his earth, can get out to hunt another day, but the octopus is in the pot for good. Some Japanese gunners, having set up their weapons in the pillbox, would cement the door closed for a stronger defense and, in what was now effectively a ten-foot coffin, wait for death. The only question left was how many of the enemy they could take with them.

This was the attitude their leaders would have expected. They themselves counted no cost in holding defensive positions. "This tendency to place troops and leave them isolated without apparent intention of relief or supply at points behind our lines, the retention of which they consider vital to their plan, has been repeatedly noticed," observed Allied staff officers with distaste. "It does not appear to matter to them as to what finally happens to these troops once their purpose has been fulfilled." Their Japanese counterparts had no hesitation in spelling out what they expected to happen to these troops. "Every man," they ordered, "must regard his position as his grave."

40

"THE PACIFIC IS ALSO BIG":
JAPAN'S LONG DECLINE

W hen Seizo Arisue was ordered home from North China in 1943
to become the Imperial Army's director of military intelligence,
he was invited to report to Chief of Staff Sugiyama at a geisha restaurant
in the Shimbashi district of Tokyo. Relaxing, kimono-clad, the two men
were joined by Sugiyama's deputy, stiff and nervous in his uniform, who
reported that he had just been to the Meiji Shrine to pray for the success
of the Japanese counterattack at Guadalcanal. "Where's Guadalcanal?"
enquired the new director of military intelligence.

The story may be apocryphal, but the point it makes is valid. The
Japanese army's main preoccupations were not in the Pacific, but on the
mainland, and some of its most influential commanders knew little about
fighting an island war. After a hundred days of triumph, its soldiers
would struggle, out of their element, for more than two years.

For many in the Imperial Army, once the resources of the Dutch
East Indies were secure the war in the Pacific might just as well have
been over. Their attention swiveled back automatically to the "real war,"

393

the war against China; before the summer of 1942 troops were moving back there as well. But some ending had to be contrived for the Pacific campaign. Several leading figures pointed out that these adversaries were too strong, and their bases too distant, to be knocked out for good; better to negotiate with them now while they had been fought temporarily to a standstill, and achieve a compromise peace.

The majority, however, would not consider making any concessions to the enemy. What they wanted was time to consolidate the advantages they had already obtained—to fortify the territory they had captured and build a political and military structure capable of withstanding a long war.

There was, of course, a third option, which the army had not seriously considered until they found it urged upon them by the navy— and this was to advance. That way Japanese forces would retain the initiative and capitalize on their obvious superiority, before the United States had time to mobilize its industrial capacity to the full and while it was pursuing a "Europe First" policy.

In hindsight, the army's instinct to sit tight and consolidate was far sounder. Expansion in the Pacific would contribute little to the quest in China, and had serious risks attached. Japan's short-term military superiority was more apparent than real. The modest standing forces she had shattered in Malaya and the Philippines were not typical, and gave little indication of the strength that the Allies would possess if they mobilized their emergency forces. It was also highly dangerous to overestimate the shock effect that the defeats of the Hundred Days had had on the Allies. Not wedded to the concept of the "decisive battle," they were able to accept and absorb their losses as a temporary setback, and never showed any sign of being frightened into negotiating an unfavorable peace.

Against this, the long-term weaknesses in the Japanese military machine were glaring. They were essentially weaknesses of scale. The smaller and shorter the operation, the better the Imperial Army's chances of success—a moral the High Command might have drawn already from observing the progress of the China War. Initial operations had been fast and flexible; as the war escalated and the army was drawn farther and farther into the interior, it outran its operational capacity, and efficiency declined drastically.

The lesson was not lost on the Emperor, at least. At the start of the Pacific War, Army Chief of Staff General Sugiyama had to report to him again with an estimate of how long this new fighting would continue. "Last time," Hirohito complained, "you said it would only be three months." "China is bigger than we thought," Sugiyama explained. "The Pacific is also big," said the Emperor.

The war contemplated in the Pacific was, even at the beginning, on a larger scale than the Japanese economy could support, and it required resources that Japan simply did not have. In 1941 her 4,000 oil wells (which left her the twenty-second-largest oil producer in the world) yielded 1,941,000 barrels. America's 400,000 wells produced 1,403,784,000 barrels—700 times as much. American superiority in munitions, steel, and coal was comparable. In that sense the war was lost for Japan before it even started; she might, perhaps, have been better advised to take the fruits of the battle and abandon the war—to hang on to a proportion of the oil somehow, and retire.

Defeat was not a possibility that Japanese leaders were prepared consciously to contemplate; but some experienced qualms the moment the army relinquished the idea of consolidation and moved beyond the Dutch East Indies. Certainly the consequences of the new strategy were almost immediately apparent. The war in Greater East Asia had now emerged from the first stage, which was full of surprise attacks and blitzkriegs, reported Tojo in the House of Peers in December 1942, and had become a long-drawn-out affair.

Understandably enough, Tojo omitted to mention that blitzkrieg could in fact no longer be sustained. The enemy was stronger; conditions for battle were worse; logistical problems were more severe; and the Imperial Army had no alternative but to settle for a war of attrition. The real conflict, Tojo warned, was just beginning. But this time Japan was entering the fray without the secret weapon of surprise, and at a serious disadvantage in many respects. "By stretching and overextending her line of advance," the Americans concluded later, "Japan was committed to an expensive and exacting supply problem, she delayed the fortification of the perimeter originally decided upon, jeopardized her economic program for exploiting the resources of the area already captured, and laid herself open to early counterattack in far advanced and as yet weak positions."

How, in those crucial months in 1942 following the Hundred Days of triumph, had the army been persuaded to embark on this disastrous advance? The answer seems to lie in a combination of ignorance and insecurity. Few commanders had any real conception of what an island war, hopping from atoll to atoll, would involve. War in the Pacific was secondary in their minds, and the army's role in it would be secondary too. Having given it little thought, they did not realize how impossible the atoll strategy actually was—and always would have been, even with adequate air power. Misled by the navy's economy with the truth about the failures of mid-1942, they came to expect far more naval support than could realistically be supplied, and they seriously underestimated American strength in the region.

Oblivious of the long-term hazards of war in the Pacific islands, the Japanese army had in addition been pushed to the brink of supporting action there by a sudden threat much closer to home. On April 18, 1942, onetime world airspeed record holder Colonel James Doolittle led a squadron of medium bombers on one of the most significant raids of the war. Taking off from a carrier in mid-ocean, with no intention of trying to return, he flew his planes over Tokyo, Yokohama, Kobe and Nagoya, dropped a small number of bombs, and flew on to mainland China. All but eleven of the eighty pilots reached the safety of Nationalist lines. Of those eleven, three were killed in crash landings. The remaining eight were captured, paraded through the streets of Shanghai and Nanking, tortured for information, and eventually executed after a token trial.

They had killed fifty civilians and destroyed ninety buildings— minimal casualties, from the grim perspective of strategic bombing in Europe and Asia. But the impact of the Doolittle raid on the Japanese nation was out of all proportion. To a profoundly insular people, the unthinkable had happened; invaders had flown over the Imperial Palace and brought the threat of direct attack to the homeland.

So great was the shock, the Japanese could not at first believe it. (Nor, indeed, could Western observers; American ambassador Joseph Grew bet the Swiss ambassador $100 that it was not true.) Schoolteacher Takaaki Aikawa later described his reaction: "It was warm and clear and we were in our classrooms as usual, carrying on the regular study of our lessons. Suddenly the siren blew warning of an air raid. . . . We climbed to the roof garden and hundreds of students and teachers, leaning on the rails, looked at the strange-looking airplanes flying very low over the city of Yokohama. Even then we still believed it was a drill, and standing close-packed like sardines in a can, we waved our hands at the planes. Some of us did feel a little strange when we noticed that one of the planes dropped something which caused some smoke when it reached the ground. Doolittle's flying groups thus flew over us, just a few hundred meters away, without being recognized as enemy planes by most of us."

The prestige of the military was sharply dented. In their efforts to counter the blow, they made serious strategic errors. The navy sent out almost every warship it possessed to search for the planes and their carrier. This generated a great deal of signal traffic, which the Americans, well aware of what had prompted it, were able to analyze closely. Unwittingly, Doolittle had made an important contribution to the American breaking of JN-25b, the Japanese naval code. For their part, the army leaders were jostled into giving their support to what could now be presented as a retaliatory strike against a presumptuous enemy.

In March and April 1942, the navy had been pushing various proposals for the advance. They were eager to seize the island of Midway, far out in the Central Pacific, as a forward base from which they might even menace Hawaii, but from which they could certainly hope to lure the U.S. fleet into the chimerical "decisive battle." At the very least, possession of Midway would threaten the Allies' lifeline to Australia, the prime base for a counterattack. Given a choice, the navy would have preferred to attack Australia directly; but the size of the ground force that would have been needed, and the prodigious problems involved in supplying that force, were more than the army could accept.

Instead, in early April the two services reached a compromise on a new outer perimeter, which would push Japanese control as far as New Caledonia, Fiji, and Samoa in the South Pacific, Midway in the center, and the Aleutians in the north. The army had got the worst of both worlds. They were committed to a southward attack in the Pacific, but without conviction—the absolute negation of the Japanese military ethos. With much of its attention and enthusiasm elsewhere, the Southern Army scrapped its separate intelligence section for the Pacific—and forfeited the chance to forecast either the timing or the strength of Allied counterattacks. The Japanese army had lost the initiative in the Pacific War, never to recover it.

Crucial to the defense of the southern line against Allied operations in the Coral Sea and the possibility of a counteroffensive from Australia were eastern New Guinea and the southern Solomon Islands. Gradually three operations evolved, separate but bound together closely and, as it turned out, fatally. The two that concerned the army were invasions of New Guinea—with Port Moresby as the ultimate objective—and of Tulagi and Guadalcanal, in the Solomons. In the third, land troops would never go into action. But the naval battle of Midway, and its precursor in the Coral Sea, were nonetheless crucial for the army and its operations in New Guinea and the Solomons, for both of those island campaigns took place while Japan was losing control of the sea.

Midway, for the pleasing coincidence of its name and the fact that here the Japanese navy suffered the crippling loss of its aircraft carriers, is often taken as the most decisive battle of the Pacific War. But from the perspective of the army, the Battle of the Coral Sea, in May 1942, had more momentous consequences. In the first naval battle in history in which opposing ships did not exchange a shot (all the offensive action being carried on by carrier-based planes), numerically the Japanese navy was the winner in terms of enemy ships sunk, thanks to its superior air strength. American casualties included the carriers *Lexington,* sunk, and *Yorktown,* badly damaged. But the Japanese sea attack on Port Moresby was turned back nonetheless, the first check to the southward advance. The New Guinea campaign had suffered a serious reverse at the outset— and the careful timing of the three-pronged Japanese advance had been knocked disastrously awry.

Looking back, Ichiji Sugita recognized clearly that the High Command should have reevaluated the entire strategy. But at the time, the full extent of the damage was not known and the advance blundered on. A small naval contingent was landed to build an airfield on Guadalcanal, and invasion forces hit the northeast coast of New Guinea. With awesome overconfidence, the two tasks, as well as being contemporaneous, had been allocated to the same force, the Seventeenth Army.

Japanese bombers operating from Guadalcanal would have posed a serious threat to the Allies; and America lost little time in sending a large force of marines to stop the building of the air base. They met little resistance at the base itself, which was promptly rechristened Henderson Field and converted to American use. But the marine landings were interrupted and the offensive weakened by a successful night attack from the Japanese navy off Savo Island. Landing reinforcements had now become very difficult; and those marines already on the island were left short of food, heavy weapons, and other necessities, without naval or air support.

Nevertheless, the troops had landed. Admiral Gunichi Mikawa, in charge of the Savo attack, had failed to press his advantage; he had destroyed most of the protecting warships, but left most of the American transports intact. Almost casually, the Imperial Navy asked the Imperial Army to clear the island. Unfortunately, they grossly misled the army as to the scale of the task. The navy's estimate of the size of the American force was 2,000; the true figure was nearer 11,000. Partly from overconfidence, partly out of concern for the parallel operation in New Guinea, the army sent only 6,000 reinforcements to Guadalcanal, and these in dribs and drabs. Two weak forces confronted each other on the island; at sea the battle was on to supply and strengthen them.

Every night the Japanese tried to run reinforcements from Rabaul down The Slot (the channel separating the outer islands of Choiseul and Santa Isabel from New Georgia), in a supply system the Japanese called "grocery runs" and the Americans the "Tokyo Express." Supplies were loaded in metal drums roped together and hung from the gunwales of destroyers. Each ship would sail at high speed toward a targeted point on the beach; as it approached shoal water the drums were cut loose, and the vessel turned sharply and ran for base, while a shore party hauled the chain of provisions ashore.

But by day the Americans dominated the sea with the air power established at Henderson Field. The Japanese destroyers stayed at their moorings at Bougainville island—and even there they were not safe from American bombs. "When the air-raid alarm sounded," wrote Japanese military commentator Masanori Ito, "all ships would get under way and maneuver violently, swinging their bows hard left or right to dodge the falling bombs. These attacks came so frequently and regularly that the destroyer skippers began to look forward to them as a chance for practicing evasive tactics. Admiral Tomiji Koyanagi, commander of the destroyer squadrons, nicknamed these evasive maneuvers the 'Bon Dance' because of their left and right swinging movements, so reminiscent of the dancing in the annual Bon Festival of Lanterns. The dance of the destroyers was laughable, if one could ignore the deadly consequences of a misstep."

Inexorably the American garrison swelled. The campaign on Guadalcanal now took the form of a series of Japanese offensives hurled at the airfield in a frantic attempt to push the Americans out and off the island. Japanese historians would come to call Guadalcanal "the Port Arthur of the Pacific."

The Guadalcanal battle was a foretaste of the rest of the army's war in the Pacific—the first of many they would fight without control of the air, by itself a crippling disadvantage, and the first in which hunger and disease would kill almost as many men as combat. Conditions were horrible beyond words. Arriving in their transports, the marines had smelled Guadalcanal almost before they saw it—a miasma of rotting vegetation hanging on the water. The extinct volcanoes at the core of the island were impossibly steep and ringed with tangled, sweaty jungle, hiding crocodiles, leeches, spiders, and scorpions; the coconut palms fringing the coast harbored white ants and were surrounded by razor-edged grass. The climate was brutal, alternately stifling and bone-chilling, with rain heavy and persistent enough to leave fingers permanently puckered, like a washerwoman's hands.

Troops on both sides lived in intense discomfort and fear, magnified for the Japanese by the decay of their logistics. Food was running out and disease rampant. It was an effort to move anywhere with the jungle thick on every side. The Japanese had no maps, no reliable communications, no worthwhile intelligence on the enemy, and no protection overhead. They were also undermined by the demoralizing conviction that the navy, having made its unreasonable demands on them, was letting them down, even betraying them—quietly losing the war while the Imperial Army struggled against the tide. In a few agonizing weeks, Guadalcanal became known to the Japanese as the "island of Death."

The first attack on Henderson Field had been led by Colonel Kiyonao Ichiki, the officer who had commanded the battalion involved in the start of the incident at the Marco Polo Bridge. Ichiki, a former instructor at the Infantry School with a fondness for the night attack and a low opinion of the American marine, was a hasty man, with an exaggerated faith in his own powers. On August 18, 1942, he landed about half his 2,000-man detachment on Guadalcanal with almost no resistance at the beachhead. Elated, he saw an opportunity for immortal fame, and decided not to wait for the remaining troops. Leaving 125 men to guard the beach, he set off up the coast toward the airfield. Each of his men carried only 250 rounds of ammunition and seven days' rations; Ichiki did not anticipate much trouble from the Americans, and had already asked if he might go on to occupy Tulagi.

It was not long before his advance was detected, deflected, and trapped with ease in a coconut grove at the Ilu River where, at one-thirty in the morning his men launched a desperate banzai assault with fixed bayonets, firing from the hip and lobbing grenades. In the crushing American riposte, almost all the Japanese were killed.

Then the American tanks went in, leaving their tracks on piles of Japanese bodies on the sandbar as they headed for the coconut grove. Blasting canister shot as they went, they jolted snipers from the surrounding palm trees and ran down fugitives until their treads looked "like meat grinders." As night fell, only a handful of the 800-strong Ichiki detachment were alive. Ichiki himself lay critically wounded amid the debris of mutilated bodies, but found the strength to order the color-bearer to burn the regimental flag as a tank bore down on them. Before Ichiki could be crushed with the others, he committed hara-kiri. After dying Japanese soldiers had fired on marine souvenir hunters and corpsmen bringing help, anything that moved in the grove was riddled with rifle and pistol shots.

The defeat of the Ichiki detachment was not just the obliteration of a significant proportion of the Japanese troops originally allocated to Guadalcanal; it was the first American victory over the "jungle supermen"—proof that "spirit," even spirit as remarkable as Ichiki's, was not enough.

Ichiki had shown a reckless, fatalistic disdain for reconnaissance, which had revealed facts to him that he did not want to accept. He had gambled and lost at least 777 lives on his faith in his own and his army's moral superiority. The second offensive was led by a man of very different temperament. Major General Kiyotake Kawaguchi had deep and well-founded reservations about the feasibility of what he was being asked to do. Planning ahead, he had put far too much faith in what had become known in Malaya as the Churchill ration—supplies captured from a retreating enemy. On Guadalcanal there were none, and the Japanese army was having increasing difficulty in bringing in its own. The Americans sank two-thirds of the ships coming down The Slot, and most of the rations and ammunition were lost.

The Kawaguchi detachment went ahead with their advance on Henderson Field regardless, "hacking a way through the jungle with hatchets and swords, scaling cliffs, and crossing gorges in order to attack the United States air base from the rear. Along the way they encountered the living remnants of the Ichiki Detachment. They were so much skin and bone, with a heavy growth of beard, clothes torn and boots falling to pieces; some had no footwear at all. They bowed repeatedly and asked for food." On the nights of September 12–14, Kawaguchi fought the Battle of Bloody Ridge, a natural barrier standing between his troops and the airfield. Time after time he sent banzai charges howling up the slopes towards the marine positions; every charge was cut down by concentrated machine-gun fire.

By now Imperial Headquarters was desperate to repair the prestige of the army. Having at first taken the Allied threat in the Solomons too lightly, the High Command had now decided that the battle for Guadalcanal would be the decisive one, and on September 18 it was given priority over all other operations. The commanding officer on the island, Lt. Gen. Harukichi Hyakutake, came under overwhelming pressure once more to attack the airfield, from the General Staff and in particular the ubiquitous Colonel Tsuji.

Tsuji had an elaborate plan for a third assault, involving a massive naval bombardment and complicated troop movements converging on the field from different directions. Hyakutake allowed himself to be persuaded, his confidence artificially boosted in the teeth of all the evidence; he set about planning the details of the ceremony in which he would receive the American surrender. But Tsuji too had greatly underestimated American strength on the island, which had now reached some 20,000; and the condition of the Japanese forces was desperate. As Hyakutake's Second Division landed for the new offensive, they were confronted with the last survivors of Bloody Ridge stumbling out of the jungle. "Their ribs protruded. Their black hair had turned a dirty brown and could be pulled out in patches. Their eyebrows and eyelashes were dropping off and their teeth were loose. For almost three weeks no one had had a bowel movement and their bodies were so starved of salt that the sea water tasted sweet."

Tsuji's plan began to fall apart. Supply and transport arrangements were too unpredictable for him to achieve the degree of coordination on which success depended. The operation fell behind schedule—but no one told the commander of a diversionary attack, which went in on the day originally appointed and was eliminated. An officer gazing fixedly at the southern perimeter of Henderson, his field glasses flashing in the sun, gave away the direction and timing of the main attack; forewarned, the defenders were able to force apart the two arms of the Japanese pincer movement and defeat them separately. Tactics were the same as at Bloody Ridge—and so was the result. But this time Kawaguchi put his scruples into practice and refused to launch a suicidal frontal assault. He was relieved of his command; the assault went ahead, with sickening casualties.

By November American losses were also huge. The Japanese navy bombarded the island relentlessly, and for the first time Japanese bombers caused serious damage at Henderson Field. But American control of the airspace was tightening all the time, and the Japanese were reduced to smuggling in supplies by submarine. Hyakutake was losing two hundred men a day from starvation. A grisly timetable of mortality was drawn up:

He who can rise to his feet	—	30 days to live.
He who can sit up	—	20 days to live.
He who must urinate while lying down	—	3 days to live.
He who cannot speak	—	2 days to live.
He who cannot blink his eyes	—	dead at dawn.

Tojo and the Army Ministry now felt that Guadalcanal was costing more than it was worth, and that the troops could be more usefully employed elsewhere on the defensive perimeter. Kenryo Sato, chief of the powerful Military Affairs Bureau, found the courage to recommend withdrawing, and had the support of the navy, which was reeling from a string of damaging defeats. But in the time-honored manner, the General Staff disagreed. The Emperor, they recalled, had personally ordered the retaking of Guadalcanal with tears in his eyes, and they should never give up. The answer, according to Shinichi Tanaka, chief of the Operations Bureau, was 370,000 tons of shipping, carrying more supplies.

Rather than explicitly ordering a withdrawal, the ministry simply withheld the shipping, without which the garrison could no longer be supplied. Tanaka, beside himself with frustration and rage, publicly punched Sato, and burst into Tojo's deputy's house in the middle of the night, screaming abuse at Tojo. He was promptly transferred; and on January 4, 1943, the decision was taken to evacuate Guadalcanal. For the 13,000 surviving troops, Colonel Sugita devised a mass retreat to Bougainville—though the men were told only that they were being redeployed for a new assault; the word "retreat" was never uttered. The phrase favored by Imperial General Headquarters was "advance by turning."

Rumors spread that the troops withdrawn from Guadalcanal were being imprisoned outside Japan, to conceal the full extent of the catastrophe for as long as possible. In seven months the Imperial Army had lost 25,000 of the 40,000-odd men it had deployed, almost 10,000 of them from starvation and disease. The southward advance was stalled, and Japan was unambiguously on the defensive. There was no longer any uncertainty in Seizo Arisue's mind as to where Guadalcanal might be; it was not in his makeup to contemplate a Japanese defeat, but at a subterranean level he had misgivings.

The operation had not only been disastrous in itself, it had seriously jeopardized the campaign in New Guinea. Here, the original naval expedition had been abandoned after defeat in the Coral Sea in May 1942; but the substitute plan to take Port Moresby over land had got off to a flying start in July when the crack South Sea Detachment under Major General Tomitaro Horii was landed near Buna and rushed without reconnaissance over the Kokoda Trail across the Owen Stanley Range toward the south coast, remorselessly forcing back the ill-prepared Australian defenders.

The Kokoda Trail was so grueling as to make even Guadalcanal look inviting—endless steps traversing a series of jungle-covered ridges, in which for every thousand feet gained, six hundred were lost in the drop to the foot of the next ascent. Advancing through dripping moss forest, over log bridges phosphorescent with decay, the troops had to clear every inch of the way with machetes for the coiling vines, and spades for the mud.

Men would disappear between points no more than sixty yards apart, seized noiselessly by enemies lying hidden only inches off the track. Rain fell relentlessly, an inch in as little as five minutes; boots rotted in less than a week. Men staggered along with their arms permanently lifted in the "New Guinea salute," brushing away flies fat from feeding on corpses. For supplies they were dependent on native bearers and on airdrops, which in this terrain were practically impossible to target reliably; hundreds of precious consignments fell into enemy hands or simply into the swamp and jungle. Some days, progress was to be measured in yards rather than miles.

While this force was struggling over the spine of Papua, another was detailed to land on its eastern tip and advance round the coast to join the Kokoda detachment. But at Milne Bay in August 1942 the Australians were ready for the Japanese, and inflicted on them their first full-scale defeat on land. This reverse was then compounded by the tilting of the balance on the Kokoda Trail.

The Japanese had scored a convincing victory at Ioribaiwa, some thirty miles away from Port Moresby, greatly alarming the Australian commanders. But as they approached The Gap, the steepest part of the trail, the advance gradually slowed and finally stalled altogether, only thirty miles short of the objective. Once again the problem was not military losses but inadequate supplies. Many shipments failed to reach the island; much of the food that did arrive was stolen by the carriers. Again the Japanese had counted on living off enemy rations—but here the strategy backfired, due to the Australians' habit of abandoning tainted food, which multiplied the existing risks of gastric chaos.

The strength displayed at Ioribaiwa had been bred of despair, and it was transient. "The Japanese literally swarmed onto Ioribaiwa Ridge, impatient to see the Australians go. Victory meant food—or so they thought. Whatever quantity of food remained, they coveted it. . . . The sight of so much food disappearing southward on carriers' backs out of his grasp, and the destruction of the unsalvaged remnants, distressed every hungry Japanese who witnessed it. In the scramble for punctured tins and mud-stained rice, the warrior spirit evaporated. The Australian rearguard went unmolested."

Horii, the detachment's commander, had had no doubts that they would be reinforced, properly supplied, and ordered ahead to Port Moresby. His September 20 "Address of Instruction" referred to a final advance. But two days earlier Guadalcanal had been given top priority; and back at Buna on the north coast an American attack was imminently expected. The designated reinforcements were sidetracked; and by September 25 Horii had been ordered to turn back.

The retreat over the same dreadful terrain, with the problem of supplies becoming ever more acute, defies description. It is beyond doubt that many Japanese soldiers were forced to cannibalism. Enemy corpses were found curiously mutilated; and so, in the end, were those of their own comrades. It was even rumored that men were killed for food. One terrified Japanese infantryman surrendered at Aitape: "He was ordered to report to the cookhouse without his dixie (cooking pail)," commented the Australian officer who took his surrender, "so he shot through [ran away]."

The South Sea Detachment reached the north coast in a pathetic condition, barefoot and hobbling, wearing rice sacks because their uniforms had rotted. "The soldiers had eaten anything to appease hunger," reported one Japanese journalist, "young shoots of trees, roots of grass, even cakes of earth. These things had injured their stomachs so badly that when they were brought into the field hospital they could no longer digest any food. Many of them vomited blood and died."

After the war, top-ranking Japanese officers, including General Arisue, concluded that the New Guinea campaign contributed a good deal to Japan losing the war. "Within the period 1942–4, the Japanese General Staff poured tremendous amounts of troops, weapons, equipment, shipping and planes into the Southwest Pacific area. It can be said, without exaggeration, that on this front the Japanese war machine received not only its first definite setback at Milne Bay and on the Kokoda Trail, but bled itself white continuously thereafter. Of the masses of troops and material committed to that area—the critical area upon which Japan pinned its hopes of an integrated Asiatic Empire—none were ever successfully evacuated or withdrawn to fight elsewhere than in the defeated or bypassed sectors of their initial historical advance."

41

"THE WORLD'S WORST COUNTRY": IMPHAL

Of the tens of thousands who try to climb Mount Fuji, many stop about four-fifths of the way up for what is commonly known as the milk break, a pause for rest and refreshment. After Guadalcanal and New Guinea, both sides in the Pacific War took a milk break for much of 1943. But the Japanese at least might have reflected that in the case of Fujisan, the last fifth of the climb is the steepest and the most difficult. As they paused to recruit their strength, the Japanese military "climbers" faltered and started to slide back down.

The Americans spent much of their time debating the relative merits of Nimitz's proposal for a central advance through the Marshalls, and MacArthur's for a southern push to the Philippines. In the event, both were approved; but the first operation to proceed was "Cartwheel"—an advance zigzagging between New Guinea and the Solomons and beyond to throw a ring round the key Japanese base at Rabaul.

The Japanese, on the other hand, could only consider how best to protect themselves; they formulated the policy of the "Absolute National

Defense Sphere." The territories to be defended at all costs lay behind a line running Burma–Malaya–East Indies–western New Guinea–Carolines–Marianas–Kuriles. Everything beyond this inner defensive line—and this included the Solomons and the rest of New Guinea—was to be held for a maximum of six months and then abandoned. The aim was to make time, by reducing commitments, to treble aircraft production and rebuild the fleet.

The political leaders were perhaps more ardent advocates of the new concept than the army. "They had the whole nation and the whole Army chanting 'Absolute National Defense Zone!' " It had more meaning as a slogan of national solidarity, a rallying cry, than as a military strategy; the Japanese position was too vulnerable, with the loss of air control, for any military thinker seriously to admit the possibility of "absolute" defense. The slogan had, besides, heavy overtones of the war of attrition—and this was the one kind of war that Japan could never hope to win.

One could ask for no clearer proof of this than the catastrophe of Kohima and Imphal—an expedition in which an entire Japanese army was worn down by grinding combat, hunger and disease, almost to nothing.

The Imphal campaign of March–July 1944 has sometimes been presented as a "March on India," undertaken in collaboration with Subhas Chandra Bose and the Indian National Army (INA), the military arm of the Free India movement among Indians living in Southeast Asia. The suggestion is that Japan had some intention of setting up a puppet government in India to undermine the British Raj.

In his official appreciation of the situation in Burma in June 1943, Masakazu Kawabe, the Commander in Chief of the Burma Area Army there, referred to "the future intention . . . to invade India." But he also mentioned that, Burma and India having the lowest priority of the three theaters of war (the Pacific, China, and Burma/India), he would not be permitted to risk a reverse of any seriousness—and a Japanese-led invasion was most unlikely to have the all-important support of Indian political leaders like Gandhi and Nehru.

The Japanese high command certainly proposed to cross the border from Burma into Assam; and Bose may have cherished dreams of exploiting Japanese success against the British in Assam to lead his troops into India and raise the standard of revolt against the Raj. But even he questioned the wisdom of Japanese forces pressing farther into India. "Bose was most emphatic that INA troops should be the first to cross the frontier," wrote Kawabe. "He maintained that the success of his plans depended on this, and that an advance by the Japanese would only cause an unfavorable reaction amongst the Indian populace."

Kawabe's analysis and projections for the future in Burma were prudent and cautious, couched in terms of defense and reaction, not attack and action. The most he was prepared to consider was an "offensive defense" against the Allied counterattack that had long been threatened by the British in Assam, the Americans under General "Vinegar Joe" Stilwell in north Burma, and the Chinese Nationalist forces trained and supplied by America.

The "Report on Operations in Burma 1943–5" by Commander in Chief Hisaichi Terauchi makes it even clearer that Japan's overall intentions in 1944 were far less grandiose than an invasion of India. The British seemed likely soon to strike back into the territory they had lost when the Japanese invaded Burma; and the Americans were determined, with the aid of the Chinese, to reopen the Burma Road, the main conduit of supplies to the Nationalist army. The most economical defense against this dual threat, rather than an attempt to defend the long line of the Chindwin River, seemed to be for the Imperial Army to command key points in the mountains of Assam.

Specifically, the Fifteenth Army should occupy the garrison towns of Imphal and Kohima and hold the mountain passes west of them. The loss of Imphal, with its supply dumps, all-weather airfield, technical installations, and transport base would be a blow serious enough to cripple any proposed British attack on Burma, and the occupation of the Imphal plain would also cut Stilwell's supply lines. At the same time, Kawabe's "offensive defense" would be launched in the coastal state of Arakan, both as a diversion from the Imphal expedition and to check the slow British advance toward Akyab.

The Imphal project was invested with greater glamour and turned into something of a crusade by the commander of the Fifteenth Army, Renya Mutaguchi, who saw in himself a potential historic figure and cherished grandiose ideas that chimed with Bose's. Mutaguchi had commanded the regiment that had been at the eye of the storm at the Marco Polo Bridge, and he had played a significant role in the surrender of Singapore. Now he had visions of helping to liberate India—which might in its turn encourage Britain to pull out of the war, isolating the United States and forcing it to negotiate. He was already suspect within the army as a glory-seeker—a reputation that can only have been confirmed when, as the Fifteenth Army set out, he reissued the signal made famous by

Admiral Togo at Tsushima: "On this one battle rests the fate of our nation." But with public morale sagging after Midway, Guadalcanal and New Guinea, Tojo was eager for a success to bolster his political fortunes; and no one acted effectively to curb Mutaguchi's vaulting ambitions.

He had in fact chosen a most unpromising star to which to hitch his wagon. Quite apart from the dubious value of Bose as an ally, Imphal was a dreadful battlefield on which to open a campaign. Assam was, in the words of General Slim, "some of the world's worst country, breeding the world's worst diseases, and having for half the year at least the world's worst climate." And in this unattractive landscape, Imphal was one of the most forbidding spots—built on a high, remote plateau infested with snakes, leeches, mosquitoes, malaria, scrub typhus, and amoebic dysentery.

Most important, the supply lines feeding the approach to Imphal were precarious in the extreme. For declaring that not even one division could be supplied with any security, Mutaguchi's original chief of staff was sacked, and replaced by a man with more positive ideas—though not as positive as those of Mutaguchi himself. Cows, goats, and elephants were all potential pack animals in his eyes; he had fifteen thousand cows trained for the purpose.

Mutaguchi was confident enough to order the Fifteenth Army's prostitutes and geishas to be ready to fly into Imphal ten days after the launching of the attack. He also had no qualms in starting the operation in March 1944, with the May monsoon only weeks away; he was convinced that victory could be secured in time for the Emperor's birthday on April 29.

But by the start of the Imphal expedition, the diversion in Arakan—Operation Ha-Go—which had begun on February 3, was nearing a sorry end. "As [the British] have previously suffered defeat," declared General Sakurai, the Twenty-eighth Army's commander, "should a portion of them waver, the whole of them will at once get confused and victory is certain." Unhappily for the Twenty-eighth Army, in the principal engagement of the Ha-Go campaign there was no wavering. The battle took place at the "Admin Box," a cluster of administrative headquarters of the British army in the Sinzweya basin. Here, in a tiny area cluttered with huts, vehicles and ammunition dumps, the Japanese divisional commander, Hanatani Tanahashi, had pinned the British Seventh Indian Division.

But these were not the British forces of the Hundred Days. With air superiority, they could now mount a multidimensional defense against an attack which was consistently one-dimensional. Repeated attacks on the Box failed, the besiegers' supplies started to run out, and Tanahashi began to lose faith. A force which had numbered 2,190 men on February 11 had been reduced by the twenty-first to 400; and on the twenty-second Tanahashi cut radio contact so that he could not be ordered to advance again. On February 24 he began to withdraw without orders.

Many of the troops the Japanese were encountering now were those whom they had pushed out of Burma so ignominiously in 1942. But the positions were strikingly reversed. Where the British and Indian troops at the Admin Box had shown daring and inventiveness, the Japanese had been unimaginative and inflexible. At one point on the southern perimeter there was a possible entry to the besieged area by way of a small gully coming down from the hills, where a bend in it was overlooked by a British defense post. On the fourth night of the siege two Japanese trying to infiltrate were killed there. The next night a larger group came exactly the same way and was wiped out. From maps captured later, it became clear that this was a prearranged rendezvous point and that, defying common sense, the second group had been diligently following instructions. By the end of the siege, 110 bodies had been counted at the same spot. The Battle of the Admin Box was a significant defeat for the Japanese, comparable with the slaughter of the Ichiki detachment on Guadalcanal and the battle of Milne Bay. Now the British, like the Americans and the Australians, had fought off a strong Japanese attack in the jungle.

Meanwhile, however, Mutaguchi's advance on the Imphal plain had made a promising start. "Stretched over a 150-mile front, his army went on advancing in nine giant columns, contemptuously brushing aside opposition, and thrusting over mountains and through jungles and rivers as if they barely existed." He had three commanders under him— Kotoku Sato in charge of the Thirty-first Division, Genzo Yanagida in charge of the Thirty-third, and Masafumi Yamauchi at the head of the Fifteenth. Yanagida pushed across into Assam below Tiddim (incidentally cutting off the Seventeenth Indian Division's retreat to base), and turned northward to Imphal. Yamauchi advanced on Ukhrul and succeeded, at least temporarily, in blocking the vital road leading from Imphal back across the mountains into India, while pushing north towards Kohima, a hill station sixty miles up that road.

Sato moved straight toward Kohima. He had an outstanding record, including a night attack at Changkufeng that was a model of its kind, and now he was moving so fast that in two days at the beginning of April

1944 he succeeded in cutting off the enemy garrison from the relieving brigade being sent from Dimapur, thirty miles up the road. Kohima was besieged. Mutaguchi wanted to push on to Dimapur; the town was a prime source of ammunition and supplies for the Allies and its capture would have dislocated their communications and ruined the prospects for a new offensive into Burma. But an advance to Dimapur would have turned the Imphal operation from a defensive to an offensive one. Kawabe, constantly on the alert for any attempt by Mutaguchi to exceed his authority, refused him air cover and, to the intense relief of the Allied commanders, Dimapur was spared.

So Sato's energies were focused on Kohima, which during two weeks in April 1944 witnessed one of the bloodiest battles of the Pacific War. The town was built on steep terraces amid thick woods, and the fighting raged over the incongruous terrain of the district commissioner's bungalow, his tennis court, the club square, and the badminton court. Most of the horror of it sprang from the impossibly confined space within which the two sides were fighting. All the actions took place at close quarters, "hand-to-hand combat, fierce and ruthless, by filthy, bedraggled, worn-out men, whose lungs were rarely free of the noxious smell of decaying corpses inside and outside the perimeter." At one point, a Japanese soldier deepening his dugout was throwing his spoil into British trenches only inches away. Nearby, British troops were mesmerized by the performance of a Japanese sentry who dug in in full view of their positions, sang at night, and chalked up rising suns on his dugout.

Inside the garrison, conditions were appalling. Space was so limited that it was impossible to stick a spade in the ground without uncovering graves or latrines, jumbled among the dugouts and kitchens. The wounded could not be evacuated, and were often wounded again as they lay waiting for treatment. But the situation was little more comfortable for the besiegers, and in one critical respect worse, for the Japanese had no aerial supply route and all other systems had broken down, with the fifteen thousand cows, long ago.

Supplies were desperately short and the transportation to forward units of what was left was complicated by the fact that all the mules had been eaten some time before. For over a month at the beginning of the campaign, Mutaguchi was directing operations from Maymyo, hundreds of miles away in Burma, at a safe distance from problems he refused to acknowledge. Sato, on the spot, had criticized the logistical arrangements from the start and had been struggling almost as desperately with his superiors as with the enemy.

Held back by hunger and by Sato's refusal to proceed without

411

adequate supplies—he also had personal reasons for disliking Mutaguchi, rooted in the faction fights of the 1930s—the offensive began to fade. On April 18, British relieving forces broke through to Kohima. Within three days the Japanese had been ordered onto the defensive, and it was the British who were trying to drive them off the heights.

The defenders who remained had little real hope, and spent much of their scanty leisure writing memorial notes, making packages of hair and fingernails for their next of kin to bury, and burning letters and photos. One company, scheduled to lead an assault, threw away their bayonet scabbards, not expecting to sheath their weapons again. Sato became increasingly determined to save at least a fraction of his men from what appeared to be certain death.

Mutaguchi had ordered him to take Kohima by the Emperor's birthday on April 29, and then—a flight of fantasy—transfer three infantry battalions to Imphal in trucks, which he was expected to capture from the British. Sato refused, and took the drastic step of signaling direct to Commander in Chief Kawabe that Mutaguchi was killing his men through incompetence and neglect. On May 25 Sato announced that his men were going to withdraw to a position where they could receive supplies. "It seems Army cannot grasp the real situation," he added on May 31, "no supplies and men wounded and sick. I wish to inform you that, according to the situation, the divisional commander will act on his own initiative." To his men of the Fifteenth Army he signaled, "We have fought for two months with the utmost courage and have reached the limits of human fortitude. Our strength is exhausted [lit. our swords are broken and our arrows gone]. Shedding bitter tears, I now leave Kohima. The very thought is enough to break a general's heart."

Mutaguchi threatened him with court-martial, but Sato simply replied, "Do as you please. I will bring you down with me. . . . The tactical ability of the 15th Army staff lies below that of cadets." When he finally took the step of pulling back without authority, his men were unrecognizable as soldiers—staggering, half-naked, eating grass and slugs. The collapse that followed was precipitous. "Two great days on the Kohima front," reported a young British captain involved in the pursuit. "Jap going back along the Imphal road so fast that we lost contact. . . . Bold driving marches over enormous hills and valleys. Japs nervous about communications and show signs about being ordered suddenly to withdraw—so suddenly that they have left arms, ammunition, beautifully built dugouts and roadblocks and only three bridges blown for more than six miles. A dozen could have been blown. And even left men who are being hunted from dugout to dugout. . . . An hour ago I saw one spring out of the ground. He held a grenade to his chest and blew up 20 yards away."

The long resistance of the enemy at Kohima had detained troops desperately needed by the Japanese commanders attacking Imphal—an operation already compromised by the failure of Ha-Go to stop reinforcements reaching the British garrison from the Arakan.

The Japanese had succeeded in closing a ring of attackers around Imphal; but the assault soon ground to a bloody stalemate. The road between Tiddim and Imphal became known as "Yasukuni Avenue," the quickest route to posthumous glory. When Sato began to fade at Kohima, Mutaguchi had already been having trouble persuading another divisional commander to go forward. Yanagida, committing an elementary blunder, had allowed the Seventeenth Indian Division to escape from encirclement; when Mutaguchi ordered hot pursuit, Yanagida sent an extraordinary signal that was a symptom of how far standards of discipline had declined. "Regret 33rd Division unable to comply with orders of 15th Army. Suggest you give alternative orders so that some failure does not occur elsewhere." He then remained inactive for a week.

Mutaguchi was driven to issue an order of the day that became famous—or notorious—as a rubric of Japanese spirit. "The struggle has developed into a fight between the material strength of the enemy and our spiritual strength," he proclaimed. "Continue in the task till all your ammunition is expended. If your hands are broken fight with your feet. If your hands and feet are broken use your teeth. If there is no breath left in your body, fight with your spirit. Lack of weapons is no excuse for defeat."

Despite his fighting words throughout the campaign, Mutaguchi came seriously to doubt that he could achieve his aims and advance in Assam. Once the monsoon arrived in May, he might just as well have called a halt to the offensive. Instead it was allowed to drag on, at terrible cost, until July, because neither he nor Kawabe could think of a reputable way out. There were some 60,000 Japanese casualties at Kohima/Imphal, as compared with 17,000 British and Indian losses. The army's strength in Burma was effectively shattered; for once, the Japanese had found a genuinely "decisive" battle.

Mutaguchi, Kawabe, and most of the senior staff officers involved in the operation were relieved of their posts. Both Sato and Yanagida were placed on the transfer list, Sato with the comment that he was "mentally disturbed under the stress of the acute war situation." If he was, he behaved no more oddly than Mutaguchi. Mutaguchi's language was increasingly wild—his orders to Sato had included the phrases "Get off your fat ass" and "Pull your finger out"—and his behavior erratic. He had a little clearing made near his tactical headquarters and put up a stand of bamboo pointing in the four directions of the compass. He then decorated it, and early every morning would approach it and call on the eight hundred myriad gods of Japan. He would also get up, according to his batman, in the middle of the night and shout out, "There's something strange under the floor of my hut, get troops here at once and chase it away!" The troops never found anything.

Some said that Mutaguchi was racked with guilt at the suffering and death he had inflicted on the Fifteenth Army. Certainly he had done much to reduce Japanese troops to a pitiful state as they retreated into Burma.

> The tatterdemalion divisions staggered along the mountain roads. Weapons gone, clutching a stick in one hand and a rice tin in the other, the Japanese stumbled painfully through the torrential rain. The lucky casualties were taken to the Chindwin on horse-drawn sledges, others bounced to and fro on sodden stretchers. The more seriously wounded lay by the side of the tracks. The pain from untended wounds, the frantic hunger, and the inward racking of malaria and dysentery pushed them inexorably to the moment when they would beg passers-by for hand-grenades with which to finish themselves off. Some were too weak even to ask for that and lay with the maggots of putrefaction squirming and wriggling in eyes, noses, mouths. Even the walking wounded were too exhausted to brush off the white worms that gathered in their long, matted hair, so that they gave the odd appearance of hoary sages tottering down the jungle tracks, pursued by agonized cries of "Soldier . . . give me a grenade . . . A grenade, soldier!"

And then even when they reached the Chindwin River and safety, many drowned because they were too weak to keep their heads above the rising flood.

42

"POWERFUL ENEMIES": WEAKNESSES IN THE JAPANESE ARMY

"After the Americans had penetrated through the canal, they began to lob incendiary bombs and grenades into the caves, and constantly used flame throwers, as they set out to cook us to death, just like we were *tanuki ibushi* [raccoon dogs to be smoked out]. We were trapped inside the caves, jolted by terror and wrath. The air became more and more bloody. The injured men's wounds festered, and filled the air with a sickening stench that assaulted our noses. Their features and forms, covered in the dust of battle, were transfigured in the gloom in an especially eerie way. Then, in starvation and despair, everyone began to reveal their various instincts. Outside, the enemy attacked us heartlessly with flames, but inside, we were attacked by those powerful enemies— hunger, thirst and pain." Thus wrote Sergeant Hiroshi Funasaka of the struggle in the Palau islands in 1944.

On Guadalcanal, at Milne Bay, the Admin Box, Kohima and Imphal, the Allies saw a different Japanese soldier from the conqueror of Singapore, Hong Kong, and Corregidor—one who could be wounded, starved, frightened, defeated, slaughtered. The fanatic "banzai" warrior had not vanished completely; the effects of indoctrination persisted until the end of the war, and dazzling courage and self-sacrifice were not extinguished. But other characteristics were superimposed on him—or perhaps it would be more accurate to say that these traits had been present from the start, but now came to the foreground of the picture. To those who chose to look, a complex three-dimensional figure was visible, in place of the crude, flat caricatures that the Allies had previously devised for themselves.

Their initial image of the Japanese fighting man had been the one cherished by the cartoonists: the scrawny runt with buck teeth, and thick spectacles masking eyes that were the wrong shape for night vision—an object of complete contempt. The British persevered in their preoccupation with physical stature. "I suppose you'll shove the little men off," remarked the governor of Singapore breezily to the British military commanders as the Japanese advanced inexorably down the Malay peninsula. (In defense of the British, it is worth mentioning that the Indonesians referred to the Japanese as *Si Pendet* ["Short One"] and the Burmese called him *Loo Poo* ["Shortass"]. One British battalion commander boasted to another of the caliber of his men: "Don't you think they are worthy of some better enemy than the Japanese?"

This gross underestimation of the enemy was one of the Allies' principal weaknesses. There were others almost as crippling: disagreements between the partners, for instance—on the relative priority of European and Pacific theaters, on the reliability of China as an ally, on the future of colonialism in the Far East, on the right to Supreme Command—and disagreements between the different services every bit as virulent as the rivalry between the Imperial Army and Navy.

The way was paved to the Japanese victories of the Hundred Days by the Allies' chronic lack of preparation. In the late 1930s the United States had shown a conspicuous reluctance to mobilize and arm. Research and development had been neglected; weapons were obsolescent and in short supply; and the military intelligence system was far from watertight. However much advance warning of the attack on Pearl Harbor might have been possible, the fact remains that there were no fighters on alert there, the radar was only operating part-time, and the antiaircraft gunners had not been issued with live ammunition. As for British unreadiness in Malaya, it was almost willful. As early as 1924, strategists had been "very interested in Japanese heavy artillery" and the bearing it might have on the landward defense of Singapore. But no action was taken, and seventeen years later there was still no landward defense; with Japanese troops approaching Johore, the British authorities yet hesitated to prepare wire and trenches on the beaches of Singapore, for fear of dismaying the civilian inhabitants.

Today these failings seem glaring; but in time of war people are reluctant to consider their own weaknesses, and in 1942 it was more appealing to explain Japanese victories in terms not of Allied defects but of Japanese strength. "Defeated soldiers in their own defence have to protest that their adversary was something out of the ordinary," observed General Slim, "that he had all the advantages of preparation, equipment and terrain, and that they themselves suffered from every corresponding handicap. The harder they have run away, the more they must exaggerate the unfair superiority of the enemy."

Thus was born the specter of the Japanese superman. Ignorance made it as easy now to magnify the Japanese soldier as it had once been to despise him. Within days of arriving in the jungle, raw recruits could be reduced almost to hysteria by their fear of the unknown and invisible enemy.

Both Americans and British authorities found it necessary explicitly to debunk the myth. "The Japanese," argued a British pamphlet entitled "The Japanese in Battle," "are an island race who have mastered the art of war not through any mysterious or indefinable quality inherited from their Emperor, their islands, or their ancestors—during your grandfather's time they were still in the bow and arrow stage—but through serious study of ancient and modern methods and by intensive training." The parallel American document, entitled "Exploding the Japanese 'Superman' Myth," set out a wide variety of curious notions about the enemy and his powers and went to often unconvincing lengths to rebut them.

"The Japanese are more resistant to hunger, cold and disease." No, argued the authorities, but they do observe hygiene precautions conscientiously. "They have a special affinity with jungle conditions." Actually they chatter loudly and their local security is poor. (Yamashita could have confirmed this; during the Malayan campaign he often fumed at noisy progress through the undergrowth, lamentable map-reading, and clumsy patrolling.) "Their snipers are infallible." In fact they were reputed to be mediocre shots.

"Exploding the Japanese 'Superman' Myth" perhaps revealed more about the vulnerability of the average G.I. than about flaws in the makeup of the Japanese. The tone veered uncertainly toward the awe-struck in places, and the weaknesses the pamphlet did identify were more bad habits than serious limitations. But limitations did exist, and sooner or later they would become obvious to all.

Leaving aside the material weakness that essentially lost the Japanese the war—that is to say, the shortage of raw materials and the limited production capacity that left them fatally and decisively undersupplied— their most serious defect was a reciprocal ignorance of the enemy. Issei and nisei (first- and second-generation Japanese-Americans) returning to Japan in the months before the war disparaged the American soldier to an exaggerated degree, and were believed.

They overestimated the decadence of the Americans, confident that they would lack the moral fiber to retaliate quickly after Pearl Harbor. They exaggerated American disunity, in particular the rifts between black and white. Other critics denigrated American character, discipline, and technical skills. "It is judged that vigorous operations and daring manoeuvres will not be carried out for the present by large forces," wrote one Japanese observer. "One reason for this probably is that their officers of middle rank and below possess little tactical ability. Furthermore, if . . . any one opposes [the enemy] he becomes radically less aggressive at once. This is seen to be the usual attitude of foreigners."

The British too were felt to be figures of fun. As clever a man as Masanobu Tsuji had a ludicrously low opinion of their intelligence. As part of the invasion of Malaya, he had evolved an elaborate plan to masquerade in Thai uniform and win over Thai troops, with whom the Japanese would trick British defenders and seize one of the bridges crucial to the advance. "On disembarkation flags of the three nations— Thailand, Japan and Great Britain—would be issued to the disguised troops, who would advance waving in one hand the Thai and in the other the Union Jack, calling out in English 'Japanese soldier is frightful' and 'Hurrah for the English,' and would thus break right through the frontier line."

But the more complacent the Japanese soldier, the more devastating the discovery of the real caliber of the enemy; and from the beginning the Allies were on the lookout for signs of the crumbling of what had seemed almost miraculous moral strength.

According to an Australian Station intelligence report in 1938, "Recent reports . . . from merchant service sources serve to suggest that the traditional blind patriotism of the Japanese is ceasing to be as universal as it has been in the past." The writer cited the case of the man asking to be excused from service in China on the grounds that not only was he the sole support of his parents, but he had also built up a thriving business. "Before long he was paraded before the whole regiment. The commanding officer announced, 'Here is a man who wished to make money in his shop rather than fight for the Emperor. This is what we do to men like this'—and the prisoner was shot."

There was a strong element of wishful thinking in this story. But unquestionably morale did decline in China as the war dragged on; and there were signs of the rot spreading to the Pacific War in its later stages. All soldiers are liable to complain about their superior officers to some degree, but a few of the criticisms rising from the Japanese ranks went well beyond the time-honored grouse. "If that drunken sot Yonekawa hadn't been so damn drunk most of the time," declared a prisoner taken on Attu, "we might have had an airfield there and done some good."

Beleaguered in New Guinea, Staff Officer Nakamoto set out to analyze in his diary the causes of death of senior officers, and reached gloomy conclusions.

> Great numbers of high-ranking officers have been killed in the southern area not only because this is the day of mechanized warfare but also because the ability of the Army has decreased. Officers who have been killed—
>> Admiral Yamamoto (in the air)—poor protection by Navy fighter planes
>> MajGen Oda (suicide)—orders issued by Yamagata Force CG were suicidal
>> MajGen Horii (at sea)—due to long continued duty
>> LtGen Abe (apoplexy)
>> LtGen Aoki (Malaya)—fatigue
>> Chief of Staff Hongo (sniper)—poor security leaks
>> Staff Officer Toyoshige Tanaka (at sea)—due to long continued duties
>> Staff Officer Aoyanagi (sniper)—poor security.

Nothing was sacred. Nakamoto examined the Japanese military tradition and found it wanting. "In Buna and in the recent operation those who applied the tactics of historical heroes failed in their operations." Others even questioned the divine authority of the Emperor and the sense of commitment to his cause. A copy of the Imperial Rescript to Soldiers and Sailors was given to each combatant unit. In later battles turning to retreats, the Rescript—the unit's "one and sole 'sacred treasure' "—was quite often to be found among the detritus left behind. The official line was that every Japanese serviceman died with the Emperor's name on his lips. In fact, like the G.I., he was more likely to cry "Mother!" A waitress in Manila told of a meal held in the restaurant for kamikaze pilots the night before an attack. "I believe a good many of them were under twenty, judging from the high-pitched 'Sayonara' and 'Momotaro' sung in falsetto. . . . One of the airmen, when they were about to get on a truck, suddenly spoke to the proprietress and asked her, 'Would you mind very much if I called you "Mum" just once?' "

Sometimes the lack of respect for authority was taken to its logical conclusion in actual disobedience of orders—and this at a level where it could have serious consequences for the conduct of the war. Often enough there was tension between men and their officers; this became clear after the war, in the prison camps. The 1940s equivalent of fragging—the "accidental" killing of unpopular officers by their own men—was a recognized phenomenon, mostly in China. But more startling perhaps was the readiness of some officers to disobey their superiors.

In the thirties, disobedience might be said to have been institutionalized in *gekokujo,* but very often this was more a political conflict—the resistance of young officers to their superiors' convictions—than a military one. Disobedience in the Pacific War sometimes meant disregard of specific military orders as well. And where the Kwantung Army had become famous—at Mukden, Changkufeng, and elsewhere—for disobeying orders to hold back, these officers were disobeying orders to press on.

Mutaguchi's divisional commanders provided the most obvious examples. But elsewhere in Burma, where the front was very long, with poor communications between battlefields and more initiative required of commanders, the phenomenon repeated itself. Major Ito, leading part of the Yamamoto Detachment in the attempt to fight free after the catastrophe at Imphal, and ordered to press an advance under impossible conditions, called the whole disciplinary edifice into question by saying: "The Emperor couldn't possibly give orders as stupid as these." At the very highest level, Heitaro Kimura, commander of the Burma Area Army, would refuse the order from Field-Marshal Hisaichi Terauchi, Commander in Chief of the whole Southern Area Army, to try to hold Rangoon. "I admired the sentiment expressed in the message, but I was at the same time astounded by the complete ignorance of the actual situation shown by the staff of Southern Army."

In a society with so profound a respect for hierarchy, so intense a dislike of internal controversy, where for over a thousand years obedience had been the most highly rated virtue, insubordination of this sort, however sporadic, must have been significant. At the very least, it suggests that discipline within the army was less than watertight.

The widespread abuse of personal punishment supports this idea. "Personal" punishment was that handed out by an officer at his own discretion, without reference to official procedure; as often as not it consisted of a beating with his clenched fist. The practice had always been extralegal; but for years it had been considered a useful tool for reinforcing discipline, "morally excellent, though harsh." Now, however, officers were abusing it to the point where it was wholly destructive.

At all levels, systematic brutality was taking over. Teachers at the Military Academy struck student officers, and they reacted by relaying the harsh treatment to NCOs and to men returning to their units. The principal victims were those at the bottom of the pecking order, the new recruits.

Two damning reports prepared by an anxious Imperial General Staff listed the forms persecution might take. The veteran might be annoyed by the recruit's lack of respect and failure to listen to sage advice; by his different educational level; by his sloppy performance of administrative chores, or neglect of his weapons and clothing; by his bad memory for all the myriad new details he was expected to absorb. The methods of punishment included not just slapping, punching, kicking, assault "with fists, overshoes, belts, cleaning rods, tent poles, tent pegs, dispensary broomsticks, bamboo swords, wooden rifles," but, more subtly, forcing recruits to assault each other, putting them on constant fatigues, forcing them to double-time or sit at attention for hours, keeping them from the stove, stopping them from bathing, making them pay for drinks, exposing their secrets. In the washrooms and latrines, the canteen, the stables, during roll call, in the field maneuver areas—abuse took place everywhere.

Brutality was hardly a novelty in the Imperial Army, but its consequences were new. "Even those who are at fault will become offended if slapped," concluded the official report. "Without fail, deep within, they will harbor a lesser or greater feeling of antipathy and discontent. They act like those who have received an education embodying ideals of liberty and popular rights"—and worse than that the military man could not say.

The High Command was forced to recognize that the abuse of personal punishment had dire effects. Recruitment was inhibited; the victims were often seriously hurt. But in addition—and this was the novel phenomenon—they were beginning to take independent action and retaliate. Some damaged army property, misappropriated army funds, inflicted violence on sentries. Others simply deserted, like Private Shintaro Hiratsuka, who had been posted to border duty in Manchuria. On the transport going there, he mislaid his overcoat, for which he was struck several times in the face by a sergeant. Permanently unsettled and hostile, Hiratsuka led a dissolute life in his new post, and eventually stole government goods. Beaten again, he ran away and was caught, court-martialed, and sentenced to death.

One enlisted man was drunk and obstreperous in the mess at the New Year. He was slapped by the leader of a different squad—whereupon he threw his bayonet at the senior man, and followed it with the sake bottle. Another soldier overslept roll call, and when reprimanded was insolent to the lieutenant in charge on the drill ground. The lieutenant hit him twice and then, when challenged, twice more. "At this turn of events, screaming 'What the hell do you think you're doing,' the accused struck the Lieutenant behind the left ear with his right fist and inflicted a bruise which required three days to heal." A private, blind drunk, abused his company commander, who slapped his face thirty times. "This enraged the accused. A short time later he exploded a Type 89 Hand Grenade on the road outside the entrance to the room in which the company commander was sleeping."

These threats and insults to superiors were to the authorities the most reprehensible offenses of all, because they tended "to contravene the first principles of building up the Army and the national structure." In the sorry catalog of petty crimes and misdemeanors provoked by personal punishment, it is possible to see the death throes of the Imperial Japanese Army, or at least the army as Yamagata had known it. "Even when [brutality] does not result in crimes, it causes men to lose confidence in their superiors and become recalcitrant. . . . What can a unit in such a condition do on the terrible bullet-swept battlefield? . . . Personal enmity will prevent a man under a hail of bullets and in sight of flashing bayonets from immediately and gladly carrying out an order involving death. If the cause of this is extra-legal punishment, then it can indeed be said that extra-legal punishment is the greatest concealed evil hampering the fighting power of the company."

Skepticism, suspicion, fear, resentment, defiance—all were eroding the foundations of the Imperial Army's strength: its spirit or *seishin*. And *seishin* was a doctrine of absolutes; the soldier could not be *partially* committed to "death before surrender." The fabric of discipline and dedication had been very tightly stretched; once the slightest rent was made in it, it was liable to tear itself to shreds.

By mid-1944 the British were maintaining that it was quite common for Japanese troops to withdraw in defiance of orders to fight to the last man. The Japanese High Command might not have accepted this sweeping claim, but they had their own misgivings. "Withdrawing into caves during artillery and air attacks, and then emerging to fight when the enemy approaches is extremely hazardous," urged instructions issued by the General Staff. "To seek the safer course, to shirk one's duty and take refuge in a cave, is the natural impulse of every soldier, but before one notices it, security is neglected and the envelopment of our positions by a small enemy force has been made possible. There have been numerous such instances where large numbers of our troops have been put out of action and annihilated. . . . Your fire will immediately draw fierce enemy artillery and air attacks. Restraint must be exercised. After firing one or two rounds, do not change position or take cover." It is impossible to imagine Yamagata issuing any such orders.

Nor would he have tolerated the steep rise in numbers of deserters during the war. In 1939, 669 desertions and defections were recorded; in the first half of 1944 alone this had risen to 40 defections and 1,085 desertions.

It would seem that rational calculation—incompatible with indoctrination and fanaticism—was creeping into the Japanese soldier's thought patterns. "It is necessary that training be given in the doctrine of committing suicide without hesitation," warned one intelligence report in 1943, "in circumstances such as when, after the ship has been sunk and one is adrift, he is unfortunately sighted and about to be taken prisoner by an enemy craft." Where suicide was concerned, hesitation could indeed be ruinous. Two Japanese scouts were roused from sleep by the American landing at Massacre Bay on Attu in the Aleutians. Later, as prisoners, they told how when they were first awakened in their tent by rifle fire they had fled. "Kawamura ran part of the way with his pants dragging around his knees. Kawamura had gotten a slight flesh wound in his buttock, so the two men stopped and decided to commit suicide. Then Kawamura's companion had to move his bowels and so told him to hold up until he finished. 'Now, how can you commit suicide after a silly thing like that?' "

The frankness of these prisoners was not unusual in the later stages of the war—nor, indeed, was the very existence of prisoners, which at the start of the war was the great unthinkable. Chinese sources had reported an interesting progression in the attitude of Japanese soldiers to surrender. The first prisoners taken during the China War were described as being in a state of almost hysterical shame and anger; many of them were suicidal. By the time of the Hankow campaign they were often willing to talk; and by the stalemate of the early 1940s, some were positively anxious to work for the Chinese government.

One must allow for a heavy dose of Chinese propaganda. There remained a large majority of Japanese troops who never contemplated giving in, and many who after capture still attempted suicide in painful and improbable ways, such as trying to choke on the blood from a bitten tongue. "Declining morale" was a meaningless concept to the doomed defenders of Peleliu, to whom the Emperor sent an unprecedented total of eleven telegrams of thanks before, abandoned by the High Command, they died to a man, their last signal reading "Sakura! Sakura!"— "Cherry blossoms" . . .

But there were others whose resolve was less stern, and who were becoming less afraid to show their true feelings. In Burma villagers reported seeing soldiers arguing fiercely with their officers, throwing their arms into a railway wagon, and then setting fire to it. Surrenders were more frequent. There were enough prisoners now to provide fodder for the statisticians. A survey run by the Morale Analysis Section of the Office of Wartime Intelligence in Washington came up with some interesting if inconclusive ideas. The majority of captives had come from the towns, from industrial and commercial occupations rather than from agriculture, and had a better-than-average standard of education. More than half of the sample were officers or NCOs. Slightly less than half considered Japan's military leaders competent or honest.

Natives were used to bring in stragglers (or to kill them) in New Guinea and Bougainville. Even more effective were the "missionaries"— early prisoners sent back behind their own lines to persuade comrades that they would be reasonably treated if they gave themselves up. By the time Okinawa was invaded, as military chains of command broke down and knowledge of Japan's defeats spread, the number of surrenders would rise steeply; and the manner of submission was sometimes abject. One soldier carried a dictionary and declared: "Me vanquished, miserable, dishonourable, depraved."

Those surrendering were still in a tiny minority. But the fact of their existence was a wedge driven into the uniform, impregnable façade originally presented by the Imperial Army. It shattered the myth, dispelled the shadows—and this was a crucial part of the final victory. The Allies needed to defeat the image as well as the reality of the Japanese fighting man.

The Allies fell eagerly on each and every sign of declining morale, and analyzed it as avidly as once they had analyzed the Japanese spirit in full flower. The British War Cabinet set up a separate subcommittee on Japanese battle morale, which concluded that the decisive element in the decline was the loss of the strategic initiative. "In general, it appears that Japanese morale is a structure which, being founded in the national way of life, is of very considerable strength. If it has weaknesses they are not likely to be in details . . . but in the limitations of the whole Japanese social structure and philosophy. The concept of formal situations calling for appropriate responses conditioned by long training has great strength, but it is a somewhat rigid strength. Over-training is always liable to make a man muscle-bound. He is strong but he cannot use his full strength flexibly and quickly when a sudden demand is made upon him from an unexpected angle. It is our general conclusion that, to a greater extent than with western races, Japanese morale is dependent upon the ability of the Japanese to dictate the nature of the battle, or, by correctly forecasting its nature, mentally to prepare for it."

Perhaps it was not necessary to look for abstract reasons for any weakening of the Japanese fighting man. He was suffering just like the soldiers of any other country fighting a losing war under the most atrocious physical conditions.

Disease was as vicious a killer as battle, by the end; but even minor illnesses and wounds became fatal for lack of medical treatment. In the Palaus, Sergeant Funasaka was wounded repeatedly, and watched his own condition progressively deteriorate. "Screwing up my face and twisting my body in agony, I tried to appeal to the medic. 'Can't you at least do something to prevent gangrene?' The medic, who had not spoken a word, slowly and deliberately brought something out and placed it by my shoulder so it wouldn't drop. This was neither medicine nor a bandage. Giving off a dim black luster in the deepening gloom, with a heavy feeling like lead, it was a hand grenade."

The effects of all injuries and illnesses were intensified by the generally feeble physical condition of the victims. In every theater, hunger became the main enemy as supplies dwindled and ran out. "My insteps were emaciated, and my feet looked shriveled like a chicken's," wrote Shohei Ooka on Leyte. "It hurt as I immersed them in the water. I looked at my hands. Here too the skin was stretched tightly over the bones; the flesh had receded and my fingers looked almost twice their normal length." The quest for food became a second campaign. "It's a matter of life and death to be in charge of rations," wrote one private on Bougainville, after an attempt had been made to murder the corporal in charge of the rice allocation. "It's much more frightening than meeting the enemy's assaults. There is a vicious war going on within our ranks."

The very thought of food became an obsession. Allied intelligence recovered a diary from the pocket of one young infantryman. Scrawled across the last three pages were his dying thoughts: "When I reach home . . . the faces . . . raw fish, vegetables, five bowls of red-bean soup with rice cake—first day. Second day—pork cutlets, vegetable salad. Third day—sukiyaki, fish. Fourth day—tempura [writing gets fainter] . . . Sixth day—fish. Seventh day—fried oysters, slaw. Eighth day [fainter still]—rice ball wrapped with dried seasoned. . . . . . . Ninth day—cutlets, curry and rice. Tenth day—ten plates of fried noodles a la Wan Tun. . . . . [fades out]."

Military surgeon Tadashi Moriya, part of a detachment abandoned in the Philippines, noted two solutions to the problem of hunger. One was to eat the bats infesting the caves where they were sheltering. "We tore off the wings, roasted them until they were done brown, flayed and munched from the heads, holding them with the legs. The brain was relishable. The tiny eyes cracked lightly in the mouth. The teeth were small but sharp, so we crunched and swallowed them down. We ate everything, bones and intestines, except the legs. The abdomen felt rough to the tongue, as they seemed to eat small insects like mosquitoes. We never minded that, and devoured them ravenously. . . . Hunger is the best sauce, indeed, for I ate fifteen bats a day."

The other solution was more sinister. "Takahara reported he saw a group of soldiers cooking meat. When he approached, they tried to conceal the contents of a mess-tin, but he had a peep of them. A good deal of fat swam on the surface of the stew they were cooking, and he saw at once it couldn't be the karabaw meat. Then I had the news that an officer of another unit was eaten up by his orderly as soon as he breathed his last. I believe the officer was so attached to his orderly that he bequeathed his body to his servant, and the devoted orderly faithfully executed the last will and testament of his lord and master, and buried him in his belly instead of the earth."

To destroy the stereotyped image of the Japanese as invulnerable robot soldier, fanatical automaton, one has only to read the diary of a medical orderly awaiting death on Attu. This is a human being caught in a nightmare, with responses that are both alien and entirely familiar.

MAY 16. If Shitagata-Dai is occupied by the enemy, the fate of East Army is decided. So, burnt documents and prepared to destroy the patients.

MAY 21. Was strafed when amputating a patient's arm. . . . Nervousness of our CO is severe and he has said his last word to his officers and NCOs—that he will die tomorrow; gave all his articles away. . . . Everyone who heard this became desperate, and things became disorderly. . . .

MAY 23. Everybody looked around for food and stole everything they could find.

MAY 26. [Amidst huge naval bombardment] Consciousness becomes vague. . . . Strafing planes hit the next room, two hits from a 500 caliber shell, one stopped on the ceiling and the other penetrated. My room looks like an awful mess from the sand and pebbles that came down from the roof. . . . No hope for reinforcement, will die for the cause of Imperial Edict.

MAY 28. Heard that they gave four shots of morphine to severely wounded and killed them. Ate half fried thistle. It is the first time I have eaten something fresh in six months. It is a delicacy.

MAY 29. Today we assembled in front of headquarters. . . . The last assault is to be carried out. All the patients in the hospital were made to commit suicide. Only 33 years of living—and I am to die here. I have no regrets. . . . Banzai to Emperor. . . . I am grateful that I have kept the peace in my soul. . . . At 18 [o'clock] took care of all the patients with grenades. Goodbye, Taeko, my beloved wife who loved me to the last. Until we meet again, greet you God-speed. Misako, who just became four years old, will grow up unhindered. I feel sorry for you, Tokiko, born February of this year and gone without seeing your father. Well, be good. Matsue (brother), Dochan, Sukechan, Masachan, Mittichan, goodbye."

43

"DESPERATE AND CRAZY TO DIE": LAST STANDS

To suggest that the "Japanese superman" was a figment, that the Japanese soldier had much in common with the fighting man of any other nation, including his weaknesses, is not to deny that in the last eighteen months of the war he often displayed quite preternatural courage. But this courage was itself, paradoxically, one facet of weakness. The utter disregard for danger was rooted not in hope but in resignation to the inevitability of defeat. "Dash forward bravely and with joy when meeting difficult situations," urged one of the most famous Bushido texts. "Common sense will not accomplish great things. Simply become desperate and crazy to die." Both in the vulnerabilities and in the heroics of its men, the desperate Imperial Japanese Army was tending toward its end.

By the end of 1943, Operation Cartwheel, gradually edging up New Guinea and the Solomons, had been superseded. The Americans had the Japanese homeland in view; they had simply to agree their route. MacArthur, hell-bent on fulfilling his promise to return, wanted to continue the advance in the Southwest Pacific up through the Philippines and on to Tokyo. Nimitz wanted to take the shorter route through the atolls of the Central Pacific—the Gilberts, Marshalls, Carolines, and Marianas—projecting American power to points that cut Japanese supply lines to the south and were within striking distance of the home islands, now that the strategic bombing offensive from China was acknowledged to have failed. In the end, the Americans went ahead with both advances, and the Japanese faced attack over an enormous area. However profound the army's indifference might once have been toward war in the Pacific, from now on they would be required to take at least an equal share in the fighting there, as successive strings of tiny islands, which the navy wanted as "unsinkable aircraft carriers," at the same time became bases for land battles, however unsuitable and hazardous the terrain. All too often land battles were simple suicide missions, designed only to stall the American advance temporarily. Once battle was joined, the island garrisons could expect neither supplies nor reinforcements; they themselves were not expected to win, but to defend, delay, and die. The defense of Peleliu was a prime example—a venture that Tojo himself saw as little more than a kamikaze mission on the grand scale. But it was not the only instance.

To meet the two-pronged American thrust, the Japanese army evolved new methods of defense. On Guadalcanal, Attu, and other beleaguered islands, the defenders had operated flexibly on a wide front along the beach. Now beach defenses would become far more massive and static. The Americans had encountered heavy Japanese fortifications before, but now they seemed to be confronted with the dugout as an entire philosophy of war.

The first demonstration came in November 1943 on Tarawa, an atoll in the Gilbert Islands, which the High Command had designated the principal bastion in the outer line of defense, beyond the Absolute National Defense Sphere. The Japanese were fighting on Tarawa to hold up the American advance while other fortifications were built farther in, on Timor, New Guinea, the Carolines, the Marianas, the Bonins, and the home islands themselves.

The defenders were under instructions to "withstand assault by a million men for a hundred years"; the method selected was an all-round decisive defense on the beach. The obstacles started offshore, with layers of teak posts set up at ten-foot intervals, antiboat mines, and large concrete tetrahedrons strategically sited half-submerged on the reefs to divert incoming boats into areas that could be raked by fire. At the water's edge were more mines (including some British bombs captured in 1942, made over as mines); beaches that the commanders considered less likely targets were "protected" by pairs of wooden sticks simulating the horns on underwater mines, bamboo "guns," and "barbed wire" made of vines. Five to ten feet inland came a five-foot-high breastwork and retaining wall of palm logs and sandbags, with a coral bank behind it, and then the machine-gun and rifle emplacements. Anyone who passed these had the pillboxes and blockhouses of poured concrete to contend with. The eight-inch naval guns at the three corners of the island were all Vickers-built, taken from Singapore.

These precautions, though they were not quite complete when the American assault began, were nearly enough. The preliminary naval bombardment—the heaviest yet delivered on an invasion beach—did damage, but it did not destroy the deeper defenses. Worse, it threw up dense clouds of smoke and dust, which disrupted the precise timing of the operation. Many of the amphibious transports were still between ten and thirty minutes away from the beach when the firing stopped, and it was then that they discovered that they could go no farther. Admiral Richmond Turner, under severe pressure to push the invasion through as quickly as possible, had not carried out thorough reconnaissance of the beach defenses, and he was using nineteenth-century maps, taking a chance on the tides.

As ill luck would have it, neap tides—known locally as "dodging tides"—were exposing acres of coral flats in the lagoon. Half a mile out from the shore, the marines were having to disembark and wade chest-deep, unprotected against machine guns and mortars and offering larger and larger targets as the beach began to shelve upward. For those who reached the beach there was still little shelter, and the shallow water made it impossible for landing craft to bring in supplies or reinforcements, or the tanks and artillery needed to take out the lethal fixed defenses.

By the late afternoon, the tide still had not risen. A handful of American troops were clinging to a few yards of beach below the breastwork; behind them the lagoon was choked with corpses and wreckage. Only about one-third of the first wave of marines had survived the landing, less of the second wave, and virtually none of the third. The agony lasted almost another twenty-four hours—and then at noon the next day the tide rose, the tanks and artillery landed, and the picture altered. By the following morning Rear Admiral Keiji Shibasaki, the Japanese commander, was sending his final message: "Our weapons have been destroyed and from now on everyone is attempting final charge. May Japan exist for 10,000 years." With three hundred of his men, he was incinerated in the command bunker when marines sealed the entrances with sand, pumped petrol down the ventilation shaft and lit it with a grenade.

Makin, the Truk Islands, and the Marshalls all fell in the next three months, and the outer defensive perimeter lay in ruins. "The Marshalls really cracked the Japanese shell," remembered U.S. Admiral Richard Conolly. "It broke the crust of their defenses on a scale that could be exploited at once. It gave them no time adequately to fortify their inner defensive line that ran through the Marianas." In fact, with the decision to reopen land campaigns in Burma and China in the spring of 1944, the Imperial Army was fighting a two-front war and there were not enough troops to garrison the inner line.

Many within the army had no real confidence in this defense line of atolls, and would have greatly preferred to withdraw to Formosa or the Philippines, where they could fight a genuine land war. But it had become essential, however difficult, to hold islands like Saipan, Tinian, and Guam. Should the Americans seize them, they would have breached the much-trumpeted and psychologically sensitive Absolute National Defense Sphere; they would be able to disrupt Japanese forward communications and would be within bombing range of Japan itself.

The island of Saipan had excellent natural defenses in the form of a spine of mountains in the north, pitted with thousands of caves; work was also in progress on heavy artificial fortifications. But time was running out. Saipan urgently needed concrete, steel, and lumber to complete its defenses, but the Allied blockade in the Pacific was denying these supplies, and well over 100,000 American troops were converging on the island. However, the battle for Saipan was really lost in the air, almost before it had begun on the ground, in what became famous as the Great Marianas Turkey Shoot, which more or less completed the destruction of the Japanese carrier air forces. Had the Japanese ground forces won on Saipan, they would only have succeeded in postponing the inevitable.

It was still army orthodoxy to defend islands on the beaches, and initially on Saipan the line held. Once again, the massive American bombardment had left many emplacements intact, and the defenders had a chance to stall the advance until reinforcements could arrive. On June 15, 1944, 8,000 Marines landed in twenty minutes, carried by 719 amphtracs (amphibious tractors) that were supposed to carry them to high ground. But many bogged down in deep sand, to become sitting targets for artillery fire.

The Japanese resistance could not last, however, because there was no help coming from outside. The Japanese navy, unable to decide where the next American blow would fall, had concentrated its strength too far south in a vain attempt to retake Biak. Now the American thrust had lured Admiral Jisaburo Ozawa's carrier fleet north in pursuit of the chimerical "decisive battle," but the Japanese were hopelessly outweighed. American radar gave ample warning of each enemy strike, and a seemingly inexhaustible supply of U.S. fighters was available with which to shoot them down. Admiral Ozawa lost three out of six carriers and almost four hundred carrier planes, 280 of them in a single day. There were no Japanese reinforcements, while Americans continued to pour ashore on Saipan, and the Japanese leaders had no coherent policy other than to exact a high price for enemy victory. Their own success seems never to have been seriously considered.

By the first week in July, the surviving Japanese troops had all been herded into the rugged northern quarter of the island, but as a disorderly crowd, not in organized defensive formations. The three commanders had set up their headquarters in a cave, and sent a staff officer to inspect the front lines. Aghast, he reported that these no longer existed, as the men had retreated against instructions. The message was received in incredulous silence. The same evening, the commanders received orders from Tojo to hold out as long as possible, to gain time for forces elsewhere. Now it was their turn to disobey. They prepared orders for a final sacrificial attack, and the next morning all three committed suicide; there was no time to execute hara-kiri, so they required their aides to shoot them in the base of the skull—a hasty and inglorious death.

Surrender was now the only alternative to death, and on Saipan almost nobody took it. The remnants of the troops carried out the largest banzai raid of the war so far, stumbling down the slopes towards Tanapag Harbor, emboldened or perhaps just numbed by sake. Officers armed only with swords led desperate charges straight into the path of machine guns; and in the rear came all the wounded who could move, hobbling into the attack on crutches.

All over the island, civilians followed the army to their deaths— partly from fear of inhuman treatment by the enemy, partly because the army impelled them to do so, thinking perhaps of the samurai tradition that when the warrior lord died, his vassals and their families accompanied him. Some fell on grenades, others waded out to sea; most threw themselves off the cliffs, mothers clutching their babies, fathers pushing their children over the edge before rushing to meet their own deaths. Horrified marines coming ashore in small craft could not steer a clear course through waters choked with corpses.

Two out of three civilians on Saipan died, some 22,000 of them. There were virtually no survivors from the 30,000-strong garrison. Bull-dozers had to be brought in to shovel the dead into mass graves—2,000 corpses from the last banzai charge alone. It was also the costliest battle of the war so far for the Americans: Over 14,000 were killed or wounded.

Now the inner defensive ring, too, had been cracked. All the army propagandists could do was claim that the Japanese people had been transformed by the loss into "one great adamantine rock with a ball of infernal fire within." The sphere of absolute national defense was shrink-ing fast. All the "outer" territories, which Japan had hoped to hold for six months—the Aleutians in the north, the Solomons and New Guinea in the south, the Marshalls, Gilberts, and Carolines in the middle—had been seized in less than that, and the gate to the final buffer zone lay open. Troops began to be moved from Manchuria in earnest now—another turning point for the Imperial Army as a whole, reflecting a reluctant but inevitable shift in priorities to the defense of the home islands.

There were four possible centers for the defense effort, the "Sho Go," or "Victory Operation," as it was defiantly called: Formosa, the Philippines, the Kurile islands, and the home island of Honshu itself. The Americans aimed to provoke the Japanese forces into advancing on Formosa, thus weakening their resistance in the Philippines. Ships and planes were drawn to the Formosa Sea—and here, in October 1944, the Japanese military authorities proclaimed a resounding naval victory, with all the American carriers wiped out. The Emperor at once declared a public holiday, the first for two years.

The gesture may have been politically motivated. Saipan had been the straw that broke the back of the Tojo government. Tojo's attempt to establish himself as the unquestioned war leader, assuming the posts of army Chief of Staff and munitions minister as well as army minister and prime minister, had made him many enemies. (Sugiyama, the man he replaced as Chief of Staff, sent a memorandum to the Emperor warning him that Tojo threatened to become a modern shogun.) The catastrophe of Imphal, the first B-29 bombing raids on the home islands, the Great Turkey Shoot, and then the appalling casualty figures on Saipan co-alesced the opposition and forced him to resign in July 1944. The

Formosan "victory" may have been cooked up to boost the status of his successor, General Kuniaki Koiso, and to stimulate the production of munitions. Whatever the reasons, the consequences of the lie were disastrous.

The truth could not have been more different. There had indeed been a huge air battle as the Americans made a show of raiding Formosa, but the results actually demanded not a holiday for the Japanese but a day of mourning. "The Imperial Navy's 6th Air Fleet was ordered aloft into the battle. Most of Admiral [Shigeru] Fukudome's flyers were green trainees whose combat experience was limited to film simulators (employed to save fuel). Over 500 were shot down like 'so many eggs thrown against the stone wall of indomitable enemy formations,' as Fukudome sorrowfully reported." Many planes intended for the defense of the Philippines were siphoned off to Formosa, straight down the drain; now the in-depth air defense of the Philippines was impossible.

And the Philippines—a crucial link in the supply chain from the home islands to the southeast theater—were the next target. The Japanese navy had decided in September that they offered one final opportunity for the "decisive battle." Into this struggle would be thrown the last remnants of the air forces. If the Japanese fleet was to have any chance of success at Leyte, the Philippine island selected as the core of the defense effort, the American carriers must somehow be sunk or disabled; and the only means left was the kamikaze attack. Examples of Japanese suicide tactics had already been seen on land, at sea, and in the air; but they were exalted by the kamikaze into a system.

The navy seemed to be expecting a similar commitment from the army in the Philippines. And once again, just as in the decision to advance beyond the conquests of the Hundred Days, the army was induced to conform to navy plans against its better judgment. In the case of the Midway project, army leaders had been spurred to action by the Doolittle raid. This time it was the mythical victory in Formosa that convinced General Headquarters that the enemy had been seriously weakened by the loss of his carriers, and that the army should aim for a decisive ground battle.

The army's leaders had originally intended to limit its involvement in the operation, because its presence in the Philippines was relatively weak. The previous army commander in Luzon, Shigenori Kuroda, had made few preparations for battle, considering the islands "obviously indefensible." Succeeding him, Tomoyuki Yamashita was inclined to agree. Certainly he felt he had too few troops and insufficient equipment for a decisive encounter—and he himself was badly prepared. After their successful feint in Formosa in the second week of October, the Americans moved very fast on the Philippines, and many of the Japanese commanders were barely in place. The landings at Leyte went ahead on October 20, 1944, and Yamashita had only been in Luzon since the sixth. (His Chief of Staff arrived on the actual day of the invasion.) He had had little time to familiarize himself with the command. Supplies and transport arrangements were inadequate, local labor unreliable, training incomplete. Naval ground troops were operating within his command area but outside his authority. His relations with his immediate superior, Field Marshal Hisaichi Terauchi of the Southern Area Army, and with Imperial General Headquarters were strained.

Yamashita's misgivings were entirely justified. The navy's vague aspirations eventually crystallized on October 25, in the series of battles at Leyte Gulf, a hopelessly optimistic attempt to smash the American Third Fleet, which was providing distant cover for 430 transport ships carrying 174,000 men of the U.S. Sixth Army to Leyte.

The defeat of the Imperial Navy at Leyte Gulf was not entirely due to numerical inferiority; bad luck and confusion played an important part in a battle during which commanders on both sides made remarkable errors of judgment. The Japanese could only field twenty-nine destroyers against the Americans' one hundred, but seven battleships remained undamaged, and two of the unique *Yamato*-type super-battleships had joined the fleet. The surviving carriers were virtually useless after the ravages of the Turkey Shoot, with few planes or pilots, but with them the Japanese succeeded in luring Admiral William Halsey and the U.S. Third Fleet to the north, away from the Leyte beaches, leaving one of the approaches to the gulf unguarded. Admiral Takeo Kurita, commanding one of the two Japanese task forces converging on Leyte, came very near to reaching his objective, despite heavy air attack. Then, for reasons that have been endlessly discussed but never convincingly explained, he decided to turn away from Leyte Gulf. The slim chance of halting the American advance was lost, and the Japanese navy ended the engagement in ruins, with thirty-four ships, including all four carriers, lost. Now the battle for survival was left to the army, in a trial of strength it had desperately wanted to avoid.

The land battle of Leyte was complicated by the fact that, for once, the Japanese had air superiority, as all their surviving planes were concentrated in Luzon; they contrived to stall the American advance for a month. Few had hopes of winning anything more than a breathing space for those desperately preparing the last-ditch defenses in the homeland; but this was enough to make the fighting especially bitter.

Of one encounter an American observer wrote, "The cemetery was filled with weeds seven to ten feet high, and with old-fashioned Spanish-type crypts built off the ground. . . . The 1st platoon, Company L, in company support, followed the lead elements of the company, beating the brush with no results. Just as this platoon crossed the cemetery path, a headstone tilted back revealing four Japs in the grave with rifles and an American BAR (Browning automatic rifle). Small arms fire was immediately opened on the enemy, but they could not be dislodged until a flamethrower was brought forward to burn them out." Company L then organized itself into small "killing details" and pushed through the cemetery, destroying the enemy as they were located. "Company K . . . too reached the center path without incident, but upon pushing through the weeds, received heavy fire from the stone crypts; the enemy had removed the bodies, punched small holes through the stone and were using the crypts as individual pillboxes."

But Japanese resistance on Leyte was doomed, as Yamashita had always feared, by the lack of reinforcements and the progressive severing of supply lines. Yamashita turned his attention north to Manila. The metropolis itself, he felt, could not be defended, and, declaring it an open city, he withdrew to make his stand to the north. The naval ground troops garrisoning Manila, however, were not under his direct command; Admiral Sanji Iwabuchi had no intention of abandoning the city, and ordered some 21,000 soldiers to fight to the death to hold it.

MacArthur had forbidden bombing, because of the civilian population, so these troops had to be blasted out with heavy artillery, building by building. The Americans were taking their revenge for the spring of 1942, when positions had been reversed. The Japanese threatened to hold out in the Malinta Tunnel as long as the Americans had done; but then a huge charge of TNT (with which they had hoped to blow their way out) ignited prematurely and much of the tunnel caved in. Forced into the open, the survivors of the explosion were totally obliterated. After nearly two months of fighting, during which time Iwabuchi's troops plundered, raped, and murdered, his stronghold in the Intramuros district was overrun on February 24, 1945. The battle for Manila cost the deaths of almost 100,000 Filipino civilians, as well as thousands of American soldiers; even MacArthur could not bring himself to organize a victory parade.

To the north, Yamashita had abandoned all idea of a pitched battle, and turned to "self-sufficient combat," a type of large-scale guerrilla warfare. He had some 275,000 troops, but they were drastically under-supplied, forced to live off the land. The Americans had the initiative, as they had done from the beginning of the Philippine campaign, and Yamashita found it increasingly difficult to stage effective counterattacks. Then one of his key subordinates deserted. Five years before, Kyoji Tominaga had been the aggressive radical staff officer who had led the cabal scheming for the invasion of Indochina. He had become the com-mander of the Fourth Air Army and was one of the architects of the kamikaze campaign. Now he fled to Formosa with most of his pilots and, it was alleged, an attractive nurse, to minister to a mild case of malaria.

Yamashita's forces, left without air cover, were pushed back inexo-rably, retreating ever farther into the mountains. He willingly shared every hardship with his troops and had their entire respect and affection, but he could see that there was no escape. Briefly, he toyed with the idea that they should stage a mass breakout and then scatter to conduct guerrilla raids. Not for him the futile glory of the mass suicide attack and his own hara-kiri—that, he felt, would have been an abdication of responsibility on his part. In the end he simply surrendered, to halt the deaths of his men from starvation and disease. "My men have been gathered from the mountains/Like wildflowers," he wrote. "Now it is my turn to go/and I go gladly."

The Philippine campaign had become a tragically expensive hold-ing operation. The Japanese lost 9,000 planes, the best part of their navy, almost all the troops already in the islands, plus three and a half divisions brought in from China and Manchuria—about 320,000 casual-ties in all. There were also, significantly, 7,000 surrenders.

On every front, war aims were dwindling and simplifying, reducing themselves to the short-range defense of the home islands. Yamashita's stand in the mountains had served no real strategic purpose; once Leyte had fallen, the most pressing task for the Southern Area Army was to keep the Allies out of French Indochina. In the same way, the complex strands of the war in Burma had thinned out, or been roughly broken, leaving only a determination to hold the south of the country as an advance base for the defense of Indochina, Sumatra, Thailand, and Malaya.

Even before Imphal, the Japanese position in North Burma was becoming precarious, under acute pressure from Stilwell in the north and Chiang at Yunnan in the northeast. The British victory at Imphal opened up the additional prospect of an immediate overland attack to retake the south. The three Japanese armies in Burma—the Fifteenth, Twenty-eighth, and Thirty-third—had a variety of objectives in the beginning: to keep the Burma Road blocked; to keep Stilwell and Chiang apart; to keep the Allies from Rangoon, which might be used as a stepping-stone to Malaya; to protect the crucial oil and rice resources of the south.

But the disaster at Imphal, which had absorbed large numbers of troops originally intended for other fronts, left Japanese strength in Burma reeling, with the Philippine campaign in view and little prospect of reinforcement. First the Thirty-third Army failed to keep Stilwell out of Myitkyina, his gateway across North Burma in the quest to reopen the Nationalists' supply routes. Then the Thirty-third and the remnants of the Fifteenth Army were crushed at Meiktila by an overwhelming British tank attack, and the Japanese had lost their last real chance of holding Central Burma. After the fall of Rangoon, which was surrendered with minimal resistance, the oil fields were surrounded, and there was little left for the Twenty-eighth Army to do except retreat into the Pegu Yoma mountains to plan a breakout. The Burma campaign was rapidly turning into a nightmare for Japan, proportionally one of the most expensive of the whole war.

Meanwhile, the slaughter was also reaching a climax in the Central Pacific, on "Sulphur Island"—Iwo Jima. Possession of the Bonin Islands, of which Iwo Jima formed a part, had gradually become crucial to the Americans. Japanese fighters on the islands, and the early-warning radar system there, were interfering with the strategic bombing campaign against Japan. The B-29s were having to fly a dogleg around the islands, consuming extra fuel and reducing the bomb load accordingly. If Iwo were to become an American possession, on the other hand, the bombing run would be shortened, and the United States would have, besides an emergency landing field for the bombers, an invaluable advance base for the invasion of Japan.

Strategic value was Iwo Jima's only attraction. It was a tiny island five miles long and two and a half miles wide, one-third the size of Manhattan—"nothing but sands and clay, hump-backed hills, stunted trees, knife-edge Kunai grass in which mites who carry scrub typhus live, and a steady, dry, dusty wind." It was the shape of a pork chop, and at the "bone" end stood the inactive volcano of Mount Suribachi like a natural fortress, overlooking the only possible landing beach on the southern shore. The beaches were of sharp, slippery volcanic ash and tufa, offering no foothold to the invaders—"like trying to fight in a bin of loose wheat," said one observer—and across the island ran barren wastes of rock, torn and pitted with fissures and caves. Everywhere was the stink of sulphur.

The marines attacked Iwo Jima on February 19, 1945. For six weeks American planes had been pounding the island; air superiority was complete, and a huge fleet prowled offshore. The landings were on an enormous scale; within a seven-mile semicircle of ships, an "alphabet soup" of landing craft, amphibious craft, destroyers, and other vessels disgorged troops toward the beaches. And yet on the first day the assault came near to failing, defeated by the terrain.

Landing craft struggling desperately to find a grip in the sand stalled and were obliterated by shellfire from Mount Suribachi. Infantrymen found themselves pinned down under a series of fifteen-foot ridges of sand. Fire from the heights above the beach was too heavy for the artillery to land. "Never have I seen such badly mangled bodies," wrote one war correspondent. "Many were cut squarely in half. Legs and arms lay fifty feet away from any body." Soon there was no room at the edge of the sea for reserves to land, as the beach piled up with wreckage and the dead. There was an atrocious smell of burning flesh.

Most of the damage, however, was done at a distance. Japanese defensive strategy had been modified again, to become even more static and fatalistic. Beach defenses had been seen to achieve very little at Tarawa and Guam, Tinian and Saipan, and here they had been abandoned. "There were no organized attempts made to counterattack our beachhead, no large scale night counterattacks, no 'all-out' banzai charge. Instead, the enemy committed a minimum number of troops to the southern beach area and defended it by delivering heavy volumes of fire from both Suribachi and the north so that even when the southern area was finally taken, the bulk of the enemy's forces remained intact and were well entrenched in the most heavily fortified part of the island. . . . It was this simple tactic, coupled with the incredible rocky terrain and the maximum use the enemy had made of this terrain in constructing fortified positions, which made the capture of Iwo Jima so difficult."

"Entrenched" and "fortified" were understatements for the mode of defense the Japanese had adopted in these last stages of the war. The digging had started on Iwo very soon after the fall of Saipan. Fortification engineers and cave specialists had come and drawn up specifications for cave hideouts—the backbone of the defensive system. A belt of fortifications stretched across the island, hundreds of armed positions joined by tunnels. "Most of the positions showed excellent engineering and terrain appreciation," wrote an American engineer after the battle. "Communications were maintained by trenched wire, radios, and a labyrinth of underground tunnels connecting all areas. One of these tunnels was explored for 800 yards, and fourteen entrances were found; it housed two battalion command posts and was equipped with lights and telephones." Then the northern plateau was riddled with caves, both natural and man-made, in a fantastic lunar landscape of dust, ravines, and rocky cliffs. "One bluff, forming something similar to an amphitheater, contained two terraces and three tiers of concrete pillboxes and caves."

It took the Allied invaders four days to take Mount Suribachi; four more weeks to push up through the lines of fortifications and across the plateau. After the battle, one American corporal described the death of a dozen Japanese troops, revealed by the light of a parachute flare while taking cover in a ravine. "They looked like little devils running through the gates of Hell. All they needed were pitchforks." "The gates of Hell" was a good description for Iwo Jima. The Americans lost over 6,000 dead, making this the greatest single loss, by ratio of men participating, in the history of the Marine Corps, worse even than Peleliu. Of the original Japanese garrison of 21,000, almost 18,000 had died, with a mere 216 prisoners. An unknown number remained in hiding in their dugouts. As for Iwo Jima, it never became a forward offensive base after all.

Before the fighting had finished on Iwo Jima, Imperial General Headquarters had reached a critical decision. No further supplies were to be sent to ground forces outside the home islands. This was emblematic of the overwhelming priority now being given to the defense of Japan itself; at last the long-sought "decisive battle" had found its natural home.

The implications were immense for the remaining garrisons lying across the Allies' path to Tokyo, which were effectively to be left to fend for themselves. Chief among them was the force guarding the island of Okinawa, one of the Ryukyu Islands, 350 miles southwest of Kyushu; the Ryukus had been made a prefecture of Japan in 1879. The garrison was large, more than 100,000 men, and it had commandeered the support, much of it enthusiastic, of Japanese civilian settlers and thousands of Okinawans. But it had little help from anywhere else.

Imperial General Headquarters had had to decide whether after Iwo Jima the Allies would strike at Formosa or Okinawa; they had guessed Formosa, and moved the crack Ninth Division there from Okinawa. Even after they realized that they were wrong, they refused to replace the Ninth with reinforcements from the homeland, where every single soldier would be needed if the Americans invaded. Once again, the role of the defenders in the outposts was to fight to the death, winning time for others to survive.

Nor, after Leyte Gulf, was there a fleet to protect Okinawa against amphibious assault. In one of the most gallant and pointless gestures of the Pacific War, Japan's largest super-battleship, the *Yamato,* set off for the island with, so the legend goes, no fuel for a return journey—her mission being to draw the fire of the American carriers and then ground herself on the coast so that her guns might be used to pound enemy positions. She was less than halfway to her destination when she was effortlessly ripped apart from above and below by enemy bombs and torpedoes. There were 269 survivors from her crew of 3,332. Her captain, Kosaku Aruga, was not among them; after three hours of steady attack, he turned to his executive officer and said, "I am one with the *Yamato*, but, once in the water, I might swim and survive. Take this rope and tie me to the binnacle. This is my last request, and it is an order!"

The only weapon offered to the Okinawa garrison and its commander Lieutenant General Mitsuru Ushijima was the kamikazes. The "Floating Chrysanthemums" campaign, begun at Leyte, reached a climax at Okinawa, as thousands of planes, sometimes 350 at a time, hurled themselves at American vessels; between April and June 1945, there were over three thousand raids. The onslaught was relentless; after one especially grueling battle, the sailors on a destroyer assigned to radar picket duty put up on deck a huge arrow pointing rearward and a sign reading "CARRIERS THIS WAY."

Nothing larger than a destroyer was sunk by a single plane; but some thirty-six smaller American vessels went down, and the kamikazes succeeded in keeping about 375 ships out of the war. Almost more important, they helped to disrupt the bombing of the home islands, by forcing American commanders to divert over two thousand B-29 sorties away from the cities and toward kamikaze airfields in Kyushu. At a cost of around 1,500 of their own lives, the kamikazes killed 4,907 American sailors, the U.S. Navy's heaviest casualties of the war. Had their attacks been more concentrated and less random, they might conceivably have forced a naval withdrawal, seriously affecting the progress of the land battle. As it was, towards the end of May, when it became clear that air attacks alone could not tip the balance, the High Command transferred its air strength, too, to Japan.

Japanese leaders may have been reluctant to pay a high price in ground troops for Okinawa; but the Americans had no such inhibitions. They saw Okinawa as a base for attacks not only on Japan but also on China, Manchuria, and Korea, and they planned an assault on the same scale as the D-Day operation. Eventually 170,000 men were committed, with a high proportion of battle-hardened veterans, and the biggest naval force ever seen—1,500 ships, assembled from California, Hawaii, Leyte, and Guadalcanal. The naval barrage of April 19 was the largest of the Pacific War, hurling 19,000 shells onto the island in a single hour.

But the Imperial Army put up an unexpectedly stiff resistance. Ushijima had based his defense in the southernmost third of the island, which was rough, hilly terrain, narrowing to an isthmus dominated by Shuri Castle. Here he had his headquarters, dug down a hundred feet below the battlements; on a series of defiles round the castle, he deployed an impressive array of artillery—far more heavy weapons than most Japanese commanders had had at their disposal elsewhere.

Once again the Japanese let the invaders land almost unopposed. Ushijima wanted them to press forward to the point where any fighting would be out of range of their naval bombardment and air barrage. Then he hoped to tie the enemy forces down, forcing the fleet and its planes to linger at the mercy of the kamikazes. The tactic was sound; he achieved a stalemate, and after two weeks a combination of their own casualties and the anxiety of the navy under air attack was really troubling the American army commanders.

Every yard of the advance on Shuri was bought with blood. For a time American tactics resembled the traditional Japanese infantry charge, with wave after wave of men thrown forward to break against apparently impregnable defenses. But even as its front line was battered and torn, the enormous American force was being steadily increased from the rear. Men, guns, ammunition, food, vehicles poured onto the island, and pressure built up on the watching Japanese. It was this pressure which induced Ushijima to make his fatal mistake. His more volatile subordinates (and in particular his Chief of Staff, General Isamu Cho) could no longer endure the tension of the waiting game, and between them they bullied him into coming off the defensive. On May 3 he tried to break out of Shuri Castle; but his counterattack collapsed for lack of support, and by the end of the month the castle had been taken, with 60,000 Japanese casualties.

Backing down the island towards the sea, Ushijima would hold out for three more weeks. Toward the end of June 1945, squeezed into the southernmost tip of Okinawa, his forces made their last stand. A thousand died per day, until on June 23 Ushijima committed seppuku. He, like Yamashita, ordered the survivors to resist the temptation of the banzai charge, and continue the battle as guerrillas.

In fact, the morale of the ground troops on Okinawa was not above question. An article written during the long retreat by a signal officer, First Lieutenant Tadashi Tachihara, suggested various reasons for a decline. The most serious was simply the fact of withdrawal. "To the Japanese Army, retreat is the greatest cause of the loss of morale. . . . Men of the units which have retreated have already lost their fighting power and are only taking shelter in the caves." In addition, the defeats in Saipan, Iwo Jima, and Leyte could not be concealed within the army. The loss of Leyte in particular was a blow, since General Headquarters had declared, most unwisely, that everything hinged on a victory there. The rapid changes of government after Tojo's fall had deepened the unsettling effect.

Like any ground force, the Japanese infantry were deeply demoralized by the complete absence of any visible air cover; the bombing of Naha, Okinawa's capital, had lasted ten hours, yet during that time not a single Japanese plane had risen to combat it. Overall, America's superior material strength was glaring in the confines of an island; the troops were especially shaken by the abundance of that most feared weapon, the tank.

Confidence in the officer corps was eroding; under stress, many officers had resorted to drink and women, regardless of the dangers their negligence might pose to their men. Serious disagreements between reserves and regular officers were emerging; Tachihara considered this a major factor in the weakening of fighting power. The zeal of the regulars was quite often inflamed by adversity, but the reaction of the reservists was quite different—and the clash between the two was almost more damaging than any defeatism itself. Enemy propaganda was intensifying the effect of all these other disruptive influences. Tachihara was a graduate of the elite Tokyo University, far more likely than most conscripts to articulate his feelings in what amounted to a damaging critique of the army's position. But he was undoubtedly a shrewd and intelligent observer, sensitive to genuine undercurrents of feeling within the doomed force.

Of the 107,539 Japanese who died on Okinawa, 27,769 were cremated with flamethrowers or blown up with grenades in caves which, as on Iwo Jima, could not be taken in any other way, so stubborn was the defense. There were 75,000 Okinawan civilian casualties, and 7,000 U.S. G.I.'s and marines were killed. It was by far the bloodiest battle of the war, and every American saw in it a mere shadow of the horrors to come.

44

DEATH MARCH:
THE ROAD TO SURRENDER

B y the time American troops started landing on Okinawa at the
beginning of April 1945, defeat and death were staring at the
Imperial Japanese Army from all sides. Yamashita's men were still
fighting in Luzon, but without hope. The collapse in Burma was gathering momentum, and the only thought in the minds of the men massing
in the Pegu Yoma mountains was the best moment to make a break for
survival. Only in China was there forward movement—and soon that,
too, would be halted. On April 5 the Soviet Union warned Japan that the
Neutrality Pact would not be renewed. That day the Koiso cabinet
resigned en bloc. Then, on May 8, Germany surrendered uncondition-
ally, releasing the full strength of the Allies against Japan.

Yet the Imperial Army went on fighting, with a determination that
some contemporary Japanese see as an atrocity against the Japanese
people, criminal manslaughter. "Bataan Death March!" wrote Takaaki
Aikawa, teaching during the war at a Baptist mission school. "We heard
about it even in those days. But our military leaders did not make only

American captives participate in such (a) march. They made our whole civilian population take part in it! We marched day after day, not knowing our destination nor the time of the end."

Life in wartime Japan was a combination of misery, absurdity, and horror. Food shortages, forced labor, brutal paramilitary training, civildefense exercises of utter, obvious futility—there was no relief. As fish and meat became harder to find, the authorities urged the *Hinomarubento,* or ":Sun-Flag Lunch," on schoolchildren and students doing labor service. The lunch consisted of a red plum–pickle in a bed of boiled white rice, and was deficient both in calories and nutrients; but by that time even rice was a luxury.

Those least able to withstand such hardships—the old and the very young—were beginning to die now, adding their numbers to the victims of the bombing. "I myself cremated a few friends on our school ground," wrote Aikawa, "because the crematory was not available to common people. I watched those bodies burn and curve in the flame and smelled the nasty smell. We picked up the remaining bones, and the relatives took them with them to their dwellings. I remember, just now as I write, how hard it was at that time to get a match. When smoke was seen, the neighbors rushed to the fire to get some for their cooking."

All this was taking place amid an unrelenting hail of high explosives, napalm, and incendiaries. Japan was within range of American warships now as well as the B-29 bombers. Between March and August 1945, 40 percent of Osaka was destroyed, 50 percent of Tokyo, Kobe and Yokohama, 90 percent of Aomori; 241,000 people were killed, 313,000 more wounded.

The devastation was the product of a change in tactics ordered by General Curtis LeMay, architect of the strategic bombing of Hamburg, now in command of the fire campaign against Japan. High-level precision bombing in daylight with explosives had produced disappointing results, hampered by weather conditions, mechanical failure in the B-29's fuel system, and air crews' indifferent handling of the radar equipment used for bomb aiming. LeMay was convinced that low-altitude incendiary raids would be less difficult, less dangerous, and infinitely more destructive.

Replicas of typical Japanese houses were erected at the Dugway Proving Ground in Utah; tests showed that the average model would burn to the ground in twelve minutes. And the area selected for the first low-altitude firebombing had a "fire susceptibility . . . probably greater than that of any other similar area in the world." "There was probably no other residential area in the world," remarked the U.S. Strategic Bombing Survey, "of a comparable size which equaled the built-upness of Zone 1." The houses packed together in the *shitamachi* (downtown) district of southern Tokyo were mostly (95 percent) wood-frame buildings with tile-and-wood roofs, and wood floors covered with straw matting. About a million people lived in them; between 83,000 and 120,000 died on the night of March 9–10, 1945, when 334 B-29 Superfortresses dropped a mixture of oil, phosphorus and napalm, and a high wind spread the conflagration even beyond the target area.

Accurate casualty figures were quite impossible to obtain, not least because tens of thousands of people drowned and boiled in the Sumida River in their desperate efforts to escape fire that came "bouncing along like volleyballs." The surface of the river was black and solid, with corpses indistinguishable from charred logs and other debris; large numbers of these corpses were washed out to sea. But it is known that more people were killed in a six-hour period with a smaller expenditure of bombs than in any other recorded attack; and almost twice as many died in LeMay's incendiary raids as at Hiroshima and Nagasaki.

The city was effectively defenseless. There were only two units of effective night fighters left, and many interceptors were being held in reserve for Okinawa and the defense of the home islands against invasion. Tokyo had few anti-aircraft guns heavy enough to deal with low-level attack. Such civil-defense preparations as there were—and the government had played down the risk of bombing in order to protect its own prestige—were geared to high-explosive attacks. Citizens had been issued with clothing padded against blast, and now found that this material was flammable. Mothers carrying their babies strapped to their backs in traditional Japanese style discovered too late that the padding swaddling the children had caught fire. Other babies were simply snatched from the slings by the winds of the firestorm.

Whatever the nature of the bombs, the preparations were pathetically inadequate—bucket chains and sandbags to deal with a blaze so fierce that entire block fronts burst into flames before the actual fire even reached them, and all combustible materials were consumed completely, leaving no charred remains. The M-50 incendiary bomb, in the words of the Strategic Bombing Survey, "achieved unusual, if unexpected, success by breaking buried water mains in unpaved streets, thereby reducing the supply of water available for fire fighting." In other cities, the raiders would drop twenty-pound fragmentation bombs and five-hundred-pound bombs with airburst fuses "for antipersonnel effect and to discourage fire fighting."

The government's original advice to its citizens had been to hide in the clothes cupboard. Later they recommended digging individual shelters; there were few public shelters in Tokyo, and several of the city's modern ferro-concrete structures proved the worst deathtraps of all, as hundreds of fugitives packed them to the point where escape was completely impossible if the fire got in. Hundreds died in the Meiji Theater after they lowered the steel curtain to protect themselves against the smoke, and discovered only after the heat had welded the curtain shut that burning air had already seeped in. All the doors were jammed with bodies when the roof caved in.

Many of the hospitals, like the fire stations, had been destroyed, and those that remained were completely overwhelmed. Doctors were reduced to using already soiled dressings; vaccines against epidemic diseases were in chronically short supply, being largely reserved for troops. The streets were filled with black twisted bodies "like enormous ginseng roots"; in some places the remains were not cleared for twenty days.

To Japan's military leaders, civilian suffering was a secondary consideration, relevant only in its implications for the national defense effort. Would the population have the will and the strength to wield the bamboo spears that were their principal weapons against the enemy? ("If we could have three million bamboo spears," General Araki is reputed to have said, "we would be able to conquer Russia easily." "One bold critic," Aikawa remembered, "said privately that if the same speech had been made in the French or English Diet, the speaker would have been found in a lunatic asylum the next day.")

However apprehensive the Allies may have felt about the fanaticism with which the battle for the homeland was likely to be fought, there were in fact serious weaknesses in the Japanese preparations.

The whole edifice was, of course, built on sand, in that Japan's material resources had long since been inadequate. Oil was a critical commodity, as it had always been; the problem, however, was no longer supply but transport. One could say that the oil fields of the East Indies were what the Pacific War was about; and yet the Japanese ended by destroying them because they lacked the merchant shipping with which to carry the precious cargo to the home islands. The navy's early obsession with surface engagements between grand fleets in the quest for the "decisive battle" had distracted attention from the construction of an adequate merchant fleet; and even if the ships had existed, by this time they would have been virtually immobilized by the efficient Allied blockade, which isolated Japan both from the Asian mainland and from the South Pacific.

For the same reasons, Japan lacked iron ore, aluminum, magnesium, crude rubber, copper, zinc, lead, tin, and coal. Her heavy industry had been badly damaged by bombing, and almost as seriously affected by chronic labor shortages as skilled workmen were conscripted. The air forces suffered perhaps most heavily from the shortfalls in materials and labor. (High school children were helping to build planes by the end of 1944; the standards were low enough to make every practice flight an anxiety and emergency landings an everyday event.) There was a dramatic drop in the number of planes produced, from 28,180 in 1944 to 11,066 in 1945—and by that year there was virtually no fuel to fly them. Despairing efforts had been made to manufacture substitute fuels from potatoes and pine resin to sustain the kamikaze attacks, but still it was estimated that by mid-year motor fuel of all types would have been completely exhausted.

It was also becoming impossible to meet demands for ammunition, ordnance, arms, and equipment. Light tanks, for instance, had almost ceased production; whereas in 1940, 708 had been manufactured, in 1945 there were only five. So the defenders would face the material might of the Americans—what Funasaka had called their "awesome, gaudy power"—at an even worse disadvantage than before. On the most fundamental level, they would not even be properly fed. Soldiers got priority in the rice ration; but there had been food shortages in the home islands since 1939, and the rice crop for 1945 was expected to fall well below that of 1944, with no hope of importing foreign rice and with the ever-present fear that the B-29s would bomb the paddies before the harvest. In America before the war, the average intake of calories per day was 3,400; in Japan by 1945 the average was around 1,600.

The problems of organizing a credible defense were endless, and the Imperial General Staff may at last have begun to regret the heavy stress it had placed throughout the war years on strategy at the expense of administration.

A very large proportion of the Imperial Army still survived—5.4 million men—but more than half were overseas, in China, Korea, Manchuria, or farther afield, in Burma or the Pacific; and with so many ships destroyed, the difficulty of getting the scattered garrisons home was considerable. Mobilization of fresh troops continued, but too many Japanese observers took heart from the size of the force available without critically assessing its quality.

The army was dredging deeper and deeper into the manpower supply, competing with industry for even the least desirable recruits. In

1941, of the men passed fit for service, only 51 percent were actually called up; by 1945 this figure had rocketed to 90 percent. "Active-duty troops"—that is, regulars and first reserves—formed only 15 percent of the army now, as compared with 60 percent before the war and 40 percent at the end of 1944. Physical, intellectual, and, it was rumored, moral standards were deteriorating fast, and there was no time to remedy the defects with thorough training. "Untrained comrades are more to be feared than the enemy" ran an oft-repeated motto of the night-training instructors, and the new intake would have every opportunity to prove its wisdom. There was also a severe shortage of officers; large numbers of posts were filled from the rank or ranks below by men without the necessary experience or training. Less than 12 percent of all officers had been to the Military Academy now, as compared with 36 percent before the war.

Food, billets, labor, even rifles and bayonets were all in short supply. To foster a sense of national unity and purpose, men who could be neither fed, nor clothed, nor armed were being called up and formed into units. Thus, hunger aggravated instead the tension between soldiers and civilians in garrison towns; discipline slackened; drunkenness, bullying and disorder increased among troops; and resentment of the military became less theoretical and more personal.

There was disharmony at a higher level, too, between the military and civilian leadership. General Kuniaki Koiso, though a military man, had proved a wholly unsatisfactory figurehead for the army; and from his perspective as prime minister, he had also found himself quite unable to control the military. In the early thirties, he had been close to the core of the policy-making structure, as chief of the Army Ministry's Military Affairs Bureau, deeply implicated in the Manchurian Incident; and his influence had continued, as Chief of Staff in the Kwantung Army and the head of its special section. But since then he had spent some ten years in Korea, as the Commander in Chief of its army and then as governor-general. Now, cushioned by a clique of Korea cronies, he was "a snobbish, senile general on the reserve list, without any influence whatever in the Army."

In preparation for home defense, Koiso proposed amalgamating Cabinet and General Headquarters into a single entity that would both control the population and command the troops; he himself, like Tojo before him, would hold the posts of both prime minister and army minister. But the army leaders had no intention of compromising their prerogative of supreme command by merging with the Cabinet, and they refused to reinstate Koiso on the active list so that he could become army minister. He resigned on April 5, 1945, after only eight and a half months in office.

His successor, Baron Kantaro Suzuki, had cleaner military credentials—he was a hero of the Russo-Japanese War, and one of the survivors of the Young Officers uprising on February 26, 1936. But he had two grave flaws in the army's sight. He was a navy man, and he was suspected (with reason) of wanting an end to the war. Tojo, still convinced of the possibility of a military victory, despised Suzuki, seventy-eight years old and rather deaf, and described his government as the Japanese equivalent of the Badoglio Cabinet, the Italian Cabinet that had signed an armistice with the Allies in September 1943.

Perhaps most serious of all the flaws in Japan's defenses was the complete failure to unify army and navy. To have any success at all in the air, it was crucial that they combine their combat strength. But even at the last ditch, they could not put aside their differences. The army, presumably confident of its ability to dominate the drastically weakened navy, put forward a proposal for a unified service with a single minister and a combined but not fully merged bureaucracy. Army Minister Korechika Anami even expressed his willingness to serve as vice-minister to the navy minister, Mitsumasa Yonai, but Yonai was concerned, on the brink of extinction, to preserve the navy's individual identity and traditions, and refused to countenance the idea.

In the circumstances, it is hardly surprising that no coherent or realistic strategy for the defense effort had been devised. "The Japanese Army should establish a strategic setup to doom the American forces," ran a General Headquarters directive in April 1945, without elaborating greatly; and Army Minister Anami's "Precepts Concerning the Decisive Battle" contained no practical or technical advice at all, only moral exhortation. Plans had advanced little beyond the traditional massed charges on the beaches. Members of the High Command managed to convince themselves that it would not be beyond the bounds of possibility to repel a first attack in this way, and so improve Japan's position at the negotiating table. What would happen if the Allies preferred instead to launch a second or third onslaught, they chose not to contemplate. There was a suspiciously heavy stress on the correct mental attitude, suggesting to the cynic that the defenders would be armed with little else. Chief of Staff Yoshijiro Umezu went so far as to urge cultivation of "a metaphysical spirit" to rise above mere material difficulties such as the lack of tanks, planes, and heavy artillery.

With all these areas of vulnerability as a background to the defeats in the field, the destruction of the navy, the obliteration of the qualified pilots, why did the army persist in fighting on? On all sides there were those who counseled surrender. The Foreign Ministry's position was spelled out in its paper, "The Present State of National Power," of June 6, 1945, which left little room for optimism. Elsewhere in the civilian government, defeat had been privately forecast months, even years ago. Marquis Koichi Kido, Lord Keeper of the Privy Seal, rated Japan's prospects of victory as less than fifty-fifty. Prince Konoe had never given even half a chance. Prince Mikasa, Hirohito's brother and a major with the army in China, had urged the military leaders in April 1944 to consider making Kyoto an open city, to protect its treasures when the Allies invaded. Prince Higashikuni, the Emperor's uncle, had told Hirohito after Guadalcanal that the army was going to learn a lesson as harsh as that of Nomonhan.

Even within the forces, many acknowledged that defeat seemed inevitable. As early as 1943 the Army Ordnance Department, confronted daily with failure—failure to supply iron and steel, failure to produce tanks and planes—had despaired of the situation ever improving. At the end of February 1944 a study group led by Rear Admiral Sokichi Takagi of the navy General Staff had registered serious misgivings as to the outcome of the war. Just before the fall of Iwo Jima in March 1945, the deputy chief of staff himself had warned that Tokyo would "become a battleground in a month."

But anticipating defeat and recommending surrender were two different things. Suspecting, even knowing, that he was not going to win was not enough to stop the Japanese soldier from feeling that he must fight. Intellectual perception of defeat was quite different from emotional acceptance of it—and in the last days of the army emotions ruled. In the Japanese military tradition, honor had never been inextricably associated with winning; and now honor was all that was left. One staff officer at headquarters spoke for many: "We merely prepared for the final operations with the philosophy that we must fight in order to glorify our national and military traditions, that it was an engagement which transcended victory or defeat." A battle on home soil was the only fitting end for the Imperial Army.

At the middle levels of the officer corps, isolated individuals could not resist the dictates of logic, and were prepared to risk their careers for it. In the spring of 1944 Colonel Sei Matsutani drafted a thesis entitled "Measures for the Termination of the Greater East Asia War," to be implemented in the event of a German defeat, and was transferred to China for his pains; at the same time Colonel Ichiji Sugita was circulating a discussion paper on the same theme among military intelligence staff, only to be summarily ordered to withdraw and destroy all copies. But below this level, among junior officers in the field, optimism rooted in ignorance prevailed, and there was passionate resistance to a negotiated peace.

Farther up the hierarchy the stakes were too high. Quite simply, none of the military leaders had the courage openly to suggest surrender, although no one knew better than they did how many lives resistance was costing. Several of them would have been quite happy for Japan to have surrendered—provided they themselves had had nothing to do with the process.

There were various strands in the desperate, blinkered desire to hold out. Especially among field officers, duty to the glorious dead was deeply felt—and by the middle of 1945, there were well over a million of them in the army alone: around 1,140,000 dead, 240,000 missing, and 295,000 wounded. Unconditional surrender, which was what the Allies demanded, would mean losing China, where so many of these lives had been lost, and Manchuria, at the heart of Japanese military thinking for almost seven decades. In both territories the specter of communism beckoned, anathema to the Japanese military mind. The end of the war, too, would almost certainly mean the end of the Imperial Army, and an occupation which had been more a way of life than simply a career.

Above all, they could not allow themselves to be party to the possible destruction of the Throne. The army was the Emperor's army, and its sense of the importance of the direct link with the Throne had not diminished since the independence of the Supreme Command had first been established seventy years before. There were those within the General Staff who had seriously proposed replacing Hirohito and his peace plans with the most bellicose of his brothers—but they had no notion of attacking the Imperial institution itself.

To overcome this resistance, a potent combination of forces was needed. One important factor in the equation that had kept the army fighting was canceled out when it became apparent that the war in China was lost. In April 1944 Japan had broken the long stalemate with an ambitious offensive designed to open the way to a negotiated settlement with the Nationalists. Its aims were to secure communications between Japanese forces in Manchuria and northern China and those in occupied Southeast Asia, and to neutralize the American air bases from which the B-29s were then planning to bomb the homeland.

The Ichi Go, or "Number One offensive," which was carried out in terrain and under conditions far more congenial to the Japanese ground forces than the island fighting in the Pacific, was for months a smashing success. The Japanese forces drove down the seaboard of central China, and pressed inland toward the Nationalist headquarters of Chungking. And then gradually forces outside China and beyond the China Expeditionary Force's control began to undermine the operation. As the Americans pushed the Japanese defense line back across the Pacific, it seemed more important to the Japanese to fortify the coast of China against Allied invasion than to attack its heart themselves. In May 1945 the Chungking offensive was suspended; after seven years of fighting, the momentum of the Japanese campaign in China had been reversed.

One strong prop to the army's resolve had therefore been kicked away as it faced up to a dual menace. The Americans were rumored to have all but completed a new weapon of horrifying destructive power; and the Russians, having agreed in principle to enter the war against Japan once Germany was beaten, were clearly making preparations to do so by seizing Manchuria and southern Sakhalin. These two chilling threats were linked more closely than the General Staff perhaps appreciated, and in such a way as to bring both nearer. Looking to the future, the Americans wanted to bring about a Japanese surrender by any means at their disposal before the Russians had time to invade, while the Russians brought forward their invasion in an attempt to forestall a surrender induced by the A-bomb, which would leave Japan largely in American hands.

The Americans got in first. The atomic bombs dropped on Hiroshima and Nagasaki on August 6 and 8, 1945, killed more people than the entire Russo-Japanese War, and were a final crippling blow against the civilian population of Japan. But by themselves they were not the conclusive military strike that the Americans intended them to be. The full horror of their effects would not become clear for months, even years; and it was possible for some military leaders to convince themselves, and even others, that the damage had not been overwhelming. People who had been wearing white, it was claimed, had been only slightly burned; and the fire that had consumed thousands of people in an instant had reached this intensity because the bomb had struck at breakfast time, when most people had their stoves alight. Even those who acknowledged that this was a monstrous new weapon could argue that the Americans were unlikely to have more than the two they had used. Hours after the destruction of Nagasaki, Army Minister Korechika Anami assured the Cabinet that the High Command did not believe the war was lost.

It was the blow that had fallen in between the two atomic explosions which finally halted the Japanese army—a blow from the direction long expected, from the power that had been the primary enemy of Japan since the Meiji Restoration. On August 8, 1945, Soviet forces launched a four-pronged offensive into Manchuria in great strength; more than one and a half million men in 80 divisions, with 26,000 artillery pieces, 3,700 tanks, and some 500 combat planes swept down on a Japanese force that had been being progressively depleted for over two years.

"The inevitable has come at last," remarked Anami; Aritomo Yamagata's nightmare had come true, and Russia had finally taken revenge for the first Russo-Japanese War. The Soviets wanted back everything they had lost at the Treaty of Portsmouth in 1905: a secure presence in Manchuria and access to its industrial wealth; possession of the railways; international acceptance of the satellite status of Mongolia; occupation of the Kuriles and southern Sakhalin. American intervention had lost them these prizes in 1905, and now, in a series of summit meetings with America and her allies between October 1943 and February 1945, the Soviets had made these gains the condition of their entry into the war against Japan.

The Japanese army leaders had been perfectly aware of the threat in theory. The revised, defensive policy in China early in 1945 incorporated preparations "to cope with any sudden changes in Soviet-Japanese relations"; and the leaders knew that the Russians had been transferring troops from Europe to the Far East from February onward, weeks before they renounced the Neutrality Pact. In May and June intelligence agents reported troop movements across Siberia, and they noted the unusual recall of Soviet diplomats and their dependents from Japan. But they believed that Russia would adopt a policy of "waiting for the ripe persimmon to fall," rather than shaking the tree, and were expecting nothing before the end of August.

As late as the beginning of the Potsdam Conference in mid-July, this had in fact been the Soviets' target; but the dropping of the Bomb on Hiroshima prompted them to bring forward the attack. Their buildup was not complete, but their forces were more than strong enough to destroy an army that had by this time been reduced by as much as 50 percent, as troops were taken for New Guinea, Guadalcanal, the Philippines, China, the home islands. Latterly, from mid-June onward as the Soviet threat became less hypothetical, the process had begun to go into reverse, but still some of the Kwantung Army's divisions were no more than empty shells. All hope of a forward strategy had been abandoned for tactics of endurance and defense, but even these restricted objectives were unrealistic.

Many of the Japanese troops being fed back into Manchuria were untrained; up to a quarter of those present when the Russians attacked had been mobilized within the previous ten days. Much first-line equipment had been moved as well, and what remained was obsolete and underweight. The most glaring deficiencies were in tanks and antitank weapons, tactical planes, and heavy artillery; Japan's effective strength in Manchuria in August 1945 has been estimated at no more than eight divisions out of the twenty-four positioned there.

In the end, the fighting in Manchuria was over before more than a fraction of the Kwantung Army had been committed to battle. The Russian forces simply crushed everything in their path, including large numbers of Japanese civilian settlers and youth volunteer corps; over 80,000 died, though many of these were killed by local Chinese, seeing a chance to vent the anti-Japanese resentments of years. The Soviets claimed to have killed 83,737 Japanese soldiers and taken 594,000 prisoners; under cover of the fighting, they also committed large-scale atrocities against White Russians and Eastern European refugees in Manchuria.

Otozo Yamada, commander in chief of the Kwantung Army, heard the Emperor's broadcast on August 15. Hopelessly ill-informed by their intelligence services about the scale of the Soviet attack, most of his field officers wanted to continue the struggle. But after holding out for two days for written verification, Yamada faced reality. On August 18, the order to surrender was read to all Chiefs of Staff; on the following day headquarters ceased to function, and by September 17 the Kwantung Army, pride of the Japanese military, had been formally dissolved.

Revealing their prime motive for entering the fray, the Russians first proposed that 80 percent of all heavy industry in Manchuria should be operated jointly by themselves and the Chinese. Later they tried to argue that all industry that had contributed to the Japanese war effort was booty subject to unilateral Soviet removal, and they refused to budge from Manchuria until the matter was settled. In the meantime, leaving nothing to chance, they were systematically stripping factories, plants, refineries, and mines of materials and equipment with a replacement value of $2 billion. Among their plunder were the stockpiles accumulated by the Japanese in 1941 when they were planning "Kantokuen," their Grand Maneuver against the Soviet Union; with a nice sense of irony, Stalin handed most of the matériel to Mao Tse-tung.

45

AFTERMATH

Critical as the crushing defeat in Manchuria had been in persuading the Japanese military leaders that the war was lost, it was the Emperor's intervention that ultimately made surrender possible. By forcefully and unequivocally expressing his desire for peace, Hirohito provided his military commanders with an escape, a screen behind which they could preserve their personal honor in defeat.

Not all wished to take advantage of it. Astonishingly, even after the atomic bombs and the Russian onslaught, Army Minister Anami and the two Chiefs of Staff argued for fighting on, to improve Japan's position at the negotiating table to the point where she could insist on certain key conditions: her survival as a national entity; the preservation of the Throne; the right to disarm herself and try her own war criminals. The civilian leaders feared further catastrophe—a third bomb, perhaps—if they prevaricated any longer, and the Cabinet was deadlocked; so Prime Minister Suzuki appealed directly to the Emperor. In the early hours of August 10, Hirohito made his true feelings known. The army and navy's plans to fight for the divine homeland were, he said, "erroneous and untimely. . . . To subject the people to further suffering, to witness the destruction of civilisation, and to invite the misfortune of mankind are entirely contrary to my wishes."

Still the zealots held out, apparently more concerned than the Emperor himself with the inviolability of the Imperial institution. In the Potsdam Declaration of July 26, the thirteen-point ultimatum in which the Allies had set out their conditions for ending the war, they had insisted on unconditional surrender; the only alternative, they warned, was "prompt and utter destruction." The Japanese narrowed their own conditions down to one: respect for the Emperor's status. But the Allies would not be drawn. Though they had in fact resolved for their own purposes to maintain the Emperor in place, they would say only that his authority would be subject to that of the Supreme Commander of the Allied Powers, and that Japan's form of government would be decided by the freely expressed will of the people.

Without doubt, the people's will would have been that the Emperor's rule be preserved, but the three military leaders still found it impossible to contemplate the end of the old order and with it the end of the army. Each advised resisting the demand for unconditional surrender. Anami visited Prince Mikasa, the youngest of the Emperor's three brothers, urging him to make the army's feelings known to Hirohito. But the prince turned on him angrily—"The Army has been acting contrary to the will of the Emperor, ever since the time of the Manchurian incident"—and Anami faltered. He had, in fact, no intention of challenging authority with a coup, but there were others who had. He was surrounded by young diehards, most of them from the Military Affairs Bureau of his own Ministry, warning that unless he resisted the Potsdam Declaration, order in the army could not be guaranteed—and this was a threat, not a prediction. Fatally, he neither disassociated himself completely nor discouraged them convincingly.

On August 14, the Emperor once again declared his willingness to accept unconditional surrender, and this time he insisted on obedience. The government, the army, the people of Japan must "endure the unendurable." In a high-pitched, uncertain voice, he recorded his acceptance of the Potsdam Declaration, and the two sets of discs were locked away for safety—not at the radio station, where the broadcast would take place the following day, but in a small and unobtrusive safe in the Imperial Household Ministry.

Now that the decision had been made, Anami and Umezu gave

instructions that the end of the Imperial Army should come about with honor. Instead, for twenty-four hours chaos prevailed. All over the Army Ministry and General Headquarters, heaps of papers were burned indiscriminately. Large numbers of the guards and gendarmerie guarding the two establishments deserted. Everywhere young and middle-ranking officers, passionately opposed to surrender, argued about their next move.

One group, led by Major Kenji Hatanaka, decided that for the Emperor's own sake and that of the army, he must be stopped from delivering his speech of surrender, and those who had brought him to such a predicament must die. The first step was to isolate the Imperial Palace and declare martial law, then to confiscate the surrender recording, persuade the Emperor of the virtue of resisting the Potsdam Declaration, and arrest those who had advised him to accept it.

To seize the palace, they needed the cooperation of the commander of the troops garrisoning the grounds—General Takeshi Mori of the First Division of the Imperial Guard. Feverishly, they tried to win him over. When he refused, they shot him, deployed his troops to isolate the palace, and used his seal to forge orders activating reinforcements. But the confusion was too great, their own desperation too obvious; no one moved to their support. Panicking, the conspirators failed to find the Emperor's recording—and to all intents and purposes, the revolt was over; the troops melted away, and the ringleaders shot themselves. But the debacle precipitated the death of Anami, who could not bear the prospect of hearing the Emperor reading the surrender declaration. His son had been killed in action on almost exactly the same date; now Anami sat cross-legged in the corridor outside his living room, facing the Imperial Palace, and committed seppuku.

At noon on August 15, traffic halted all over Japan as people gathered round their radios to hear how the Emperor had decided to respond to the Potsdam Declaration. His voice, which the populace had never heard before, was halting, his diction archaic and obscure, and his thought elliptical; the word "surrender" was never used, and it took time for his meaning to sink in. People knew few details of the terrible military losses of the last months, and had been indoctrinated for years to exclude the possibility of defeat from their minds. They were not merely grieved and humiliated by the realization that the war was lost, they were profoundly shocked.

The reaction of the armed forces was a mixture of incredulity, shame, horror—and, among the mass of conscript soldiers at least, relief. But many of the younger field officers found the decision impossible to reconcile with all they had been taught and all they had fought for; commanders in both the Japanese and Allied armies anticipated widespread disobedience, and peace envoys were sent to every theater to convince all units that the order to surrender was genuine, and persuade them of their duty to obey the Emperor.

Both the Southern Army and the China Expeditionary Force had long planned to hold out, subsisting on their own resources, even if the civilian government surrendered. The Commander in Chief in China, General Yasuji Okamura, sent a personal telegram to the Emperor begging permission to continue fighting; and on Terauchi's staff in the Southern Army, suicide was openly discussed. Members of the Imperial family were dispatched to use their special authority in urging surrender—Prince Haruhito Kanin to the south and Prince Asaka to China, while the Emperor's cousin Prince Takeda went to Manchuria.

In some areas the Allies faced a dual problem. They had to guard their own troops against the possibility of being killed by enemies who did not believe the war was really over; and they had to guard enemies who did surrender against being killed by "clandestines"—guerrillas operating on the Allied side. In Burma, a startling number of Japanese were reported as being preyed upon by dacoits after the surrender, and a hasty telegram was sent to Twelfth Army commanders instructing them to check that these "dacoits" were not in fact their own clandestines taking a little private revenge. Occasionally, this revenge was connived at. In British Northern Borneo, a large number of Japanese soldiers surrendering to an Australian infantry unit were marched into the jungle; here they were massacred by Borneo tribesmen while the Australians looked on.

For those soldiers taken prisoner by the Allies, conditions varied. Japanese commanders had two principal requests: that they be allowed to maintain their own command structures in order to disarm their troops and maintain discipline within the prison camps; and that their men be known not as prisoners but as "surrendered personnel." Both were granted, but there were still complaints of the way in which the "surrendered personnel" were treated.

In Burma, General Slim was adamant that all senior officers were to surrender their swords in front of their troops, regardless of warnings that they might be so shamed that they would commit suicide. "No Japanese soldier," he wrote, "who had seen his general march up and hand over his sword, would ever doubt that the Invincible Army was invincible no longer. We did not want a repetition of the German First

War legend of an unconquered army.... If the officers committed suicide
I had already prepared for this by broadcasting that any Japanese officer
wishing to commit suicide would be given every facility."

Slim's professed, rather uncharacteristic, disregard for the Japanese
code of honor suggests the kind of contemptuous attitude that some
Japanese prisoners claimed to find more lacerating than physical brutality. Most Allied observers would feel that they were lucky in having so
little opportunity to compare the two. In letters home, some prisoners
told of slappings, abuse, and stolen valuables. Allied commanders themselves admitted to supply problems, which led to short rations in some
camps; nor were the camps immune to health problems. Reporting in
1946 on the "condition of Japanese personnel in Southern Regions,"
General Numata (who had been Terauchi's Chief of Staff with the Southern Army) noted 20 percent of the 59,900 prisoners on Rempang down
with malaria, dysentery, and beri-beri, with fifty-six deaths in recent
months. But it was never suggested that the Allies were guilty of anything resembling the extreme and systematic ill-treatment of prisoners
in Japanese-run camps.

Numata also noted more than six hundred Japanese casualties, 384
of them troops, of "actions since surrender" in Java. Both sides in the
battles that raged after the war between local independence movements
and colonial powers attempting to regain their former influence were
afraid that Japanese prisoners might be somehow sucked in. British
intelligence experts in Indonesia warned against allowing Japanese
weapons to fall into native hands. On the other hand, there were repeated
allegations that the British were thinking of rearming Japanese prisoners
and using them to fight a colonial war against the Indonesians.

There is little evidence, or indeed likelihood, that this was true.
What is incontrovertible is the use of Japanese prisoners in the reconstruction of countries that they themselves had occupied and helped to
lay waste. Many Japanese prisoners protested bitterly at being used as
a labor force, and found some sympathy from outside; in particular, the
retention of thousands of prisoners by the British in Singapore and
elsewhere was a serious source of friction with the Americans, who
mistrusted what they saw as attempts to rebuild the Empire.

But the British were unrepentant. Mountbatten, as Supreme Allied
Commander in the South East, had visited one camp in India in April
1945, and was disgusted by the indulgence with which he felt prisoners
were treated. The Japanese, he complained, absolutely refused either to
salute enemy officers or to work for them, though both duties were laid

down in the Geneva Convention. This refusal, he conceded, might have been due to ignorance, but it was nonetheless highly undesirable.

> One knows . . . that the Japanese authorities make no allowance for their fighting services being taken prisoner. They are not told about the white flag, or how to surrender; and they do not know of the existence of the Geneva Convention, let alone that their own government was a signatory to it. . . . In these circumstances, it is understandable that they think our attempt to make them work and salute is . . . an attempt on the part of the individual officers in the camp to degrade and humiliate them. Whatever their reasons may be, however, I am sure you will agree that it is intolerable that they should get away with it. . . . I do not wish to bring up the question of the way in which we know our own people who have fallen into Japanese hands have been treated. Two wrongs do not make a right, and I am not for a moment suggesting that we should behave in any retaliatory way to these men. But I think, in view of the feeling among British people on this subject, it will be gravely detrimental to the morale of our own troops if it becomes known that Japanese prisoners are allowed to get away with insubordination and mutinous conduct which would never be tolerated among our own troops.

There was one group of Japanese soldiers to whom the conditions in prison camps, and even the surrender itself, were an irrelevance. The change in American policy in 1944 from island-hopping to leapfrogging had left Japanese garrisons scattered throughout the Pacific, ignored by the Allies and written off by their own strategists, to wither on the vine. There were those troops who had dug in so successfully to defend the Pacific atolls that they were never rooted out and remained in hiding long after the attackers had moved on. In Burma and the Philippines, too, there were areas that had been taken but not cleared by the victorious Allies; Japanese soldiers were still coming out of these jungles twenty-five years later, unaware—in their conscious minds at least—that the war was over.

In all these places troops were dying of disease and starvation—so many of them that a signal went out from the chief of staff of the Japanese Fourth Fleet ordering that "all personnel who have died of illness as a result of [the] food situation since July 1 [1944] are to be considered as killed in action." On the eve of surrender, Japanese troops still held 40 percent of the Central Pacific islands, including the Marshalls and Carolines, though these no longer had any real strategic significance. Their staple diet included lizards, beetles, and weeds; dozens died every day—of disease, of starvation, in quarrels over food, in despair by their own hands. On Iwo Jima, the entire garrison had been listed as dead; but hundreds in fact survived, unwilling to choose either death or surrender. Some held out for six years, hiding until 1951 "beneath the crust of the little island, like dead souls on a distant planet."

Troops cut off on the mainland at least had a third option denied to island stragglers—the headlong break for freedom. In July 1945 the 30,000 troops of the Twenty-eighth Army sheltering in the Pegu Yoma range of Central Burma were finally driven by hunger from their hiding places in a futile, despairing bid to reach and cross the Sittang River and rejoin the rest of the retreating Japanese army.

"As an example of military stupidity," wrote one British clandestine who witnessed the Burma breakout, "it must rival the Charge of the Light Brigade and in the same way it has an epic quality." Whichever way the fugitives turned, the British seemed to be waiting for them. They had first to reach the river, without weapons, carrying only short lengths of bamboo to help in the crossing. "They started to cross the tarmac Toungoo–Pegu road in a steady stream and make straight for the river bank as fast as they could. The slaughter was terrific. British, Indian and Gurkha troops were strongly entrenched along the road and railway line and patrols of tanks and armored cars moved in between the various posts. Heavy concentrations of artillery were firing almost continually day and night. On the river bank fighter aircraft kept up an almost continuous daylight patrol." Among the Indian troops carrying out the slaughter was the Seventeenth Division, so badly mangled during the Japanese advance in 1942.

And then there was the river itself, in spate during the monsoon. At one point it had burst its banks, and the fugitives were confronted with "a vast lake, not marked on any map, but which stretched for miles. . . . It was no lake, just the result of the Sittang overflowing and obliterating the banks between patches of land. It wasn't deep, therefore, and they put together banana stalks . . . for buoyancy and pushed these little 'rafts' ahead of them as they swam through the water. They had finished off the last of their food before they began. For five days they swam, resting every fifty yards, and snatching what sleep they could at night in the branches of submerged trees. They did not dare to leave their mouths open for fear of water leeches, and to save themselves falling in the water as they slept, they strapped themselves to a branch with their gaiters." Elsewhere the river raged past chest-high, whirling along corpses and frantic figures shouting "54 Division here! Help, for God's sake, don't let us go!"

No one knows exactly how many men died on the killing grounds and in the river during the breakout in Burma—anywhere between 10,000 and 17,000, with about 1,400 prisoners taken. British deaths totaled 97. The vast majority of the Japanese dead were killed after the armistice.

For the officers and men who survived to return to the wreckage of the homeland, the future was uncertain. One of the first problems confronting the officials of the Allied occupation force—nominally an international body but dominated, for all practical purposes, by Americans, under Supreme Commander MacArthur—was what to do with the Imperial Army.

Those suspected of committing war crimes were a case apart. The Allies distinguished between "major" criminals—military and political leaders implicated in what their enemies saw as a pernicious conspiracy to wage aggressive war—and "minor" criminals—soldiers accused of specific acts of murder, rape, torture, and looting. For the "minor" crimes, tribunals were staged in Japan, and by each Ally within its own territory or command area, on the basis of evidence accumulated during the war years by a branch of the United Nations War Crimes Commission centered in Chungking.

The lists of potential defendants were appallingly long; but only 5,700 Japanese were ever brought to trial. Many escaped because those responsible for tracking them down were themselves implicated in war crimes and feared exposure. Others were given immunity by the Allies in return for information on other criminals or Japan's military secrets. (It was by giving immunity to some of the men who had experimented with the lives of Allied nationals that the United States acquired much of Unit 731's research into bacteriological warfare.) In 1949, for reasons of political expediency, an arbitrary halt was called to proceedings, with thousands of cases unheard. "Revenge," declared Winston Churchill, "is, of all satisfactions, the most costly and long drawn out; retributive persecution is, of all policies, the most pernicious. Our policy . . . should henceforth be to draw the sponge across the crimes and horrors of the past—hard as that may be—and look, for the sake of all our salvation, towards the future." Nine hundred and eighty-four war criminals had been sentenced to death and around 3,500 to imprisonment, as compared with the hundreds of thousands of noncombatants who had suffered and died at Japanese hands in contravention of the rules of war.

The standards of justice applied by the Allied tribunals varied measurably from country to country. The trials held in the Philippines, scene of so many hideous Japanese atrocities, were particularly fiercely criticized after the event. At some of them, undoubtedly little better than kangaroo courts, no one but the defendant knew Japanese, and witnesses consistently confused names and faces. But the basis of existing military law on which they were held was perfectly sound, and the procedures were sound in principle, even if they were sometimes badly implemented.

The same could not be said of the trials of Japan's leaders. The intention was that men like Tojo, Homma, and Yamashita should be held up before the Japanese people as exemplars of the cruel, irresponsible militarism that had destroyed Japan; instead they were converted into near-martyrs, invested with an aura of heroism they had hardly possessed in life.

Yamashita and Homma were held responsible respectively for the sack of Manila and the Bataan Death March, though both could argue that they were unable to control the actual perpetrators of the atrocities. (Yamashita was cut off in the mountains of north Luzon from contact with Admiral Iwabuchi and his Naval Defense Force. Homma had delegated responsibility for the prisoners from Bataan, who were not expected in such great numbers, in so poor a condition, or so early; arrangements for food, medicine and transport broke down completely, and discipline collapsed, without his knowledge.) Each was accorded by the Americans the dubious privilege of a separate trial. These trials were set up on MacArthur's instructions and to his specifications, and reflect extraordinary discredit on him.

In each case judgment was delivered by a panel of five generals, none with legal training; the rules of evidence were relaxed to admit anything at all that could have "probative value in the mind of a reasonable man." Yamashita's chief prosecutor was a Major Kerr, who boasted that he had come to the Far East to fight "Japs" but would gladly hang them instead. The results were much the same as if MacArthur had simply passed judgment himself on the basis of personal opinion. As it was, he loomed over both trials, exerting stultifying pressure for quick results and personally rejecting appeals for review of the inevitable death penalties. (It can hardly have been coincidence that Yamashita's fate was announced on the fourth anniversary of Pearl Harbor.) MacArthur also

influenced the decision that both should be denied the death by beheading that the Japanese considered befitting a warrior. Homma was to be
shot, in civilian clothes, and Yamashita hanged—an intentionally degrading form of execution. "The world I knew is now a shameful place,"
wrote Yamashita before his death. "There will never come a better
time / For me to die."

The deficiencies in the International Military Tribunal for the Far
East, by which the so-called major criminals were tried, were generally
less glaring; but they were none the less deadly in their effect. Most
significantly, the IMTFE had no solid foundation in established law. Like
the Nuremberg Tribunal, on which it was modeled, it had lofty and
impractical aims. Instead of simply seeking punishment for the overt and
innumerable war crimes of the Imperial armed forces—murder, torture,
rape, looting, drug trafficking, abuse of prisoners—they sought to try
"crimes against peace," to establish the defendants' criminal conspiracy
over a period of seventeen years to wage an aggressive war.

In fact, though there was no conspiracy in the Anglo-American
jurisprudential sense, there was the distinct smell of it in the dedicated
quest for autarky that since 1916 had been the common purpose of the
total-war officers. To that extent the indictment was justified. But in other
ways it was gravely flawed. Before Pearl Harbor it was not regarded as
possible to attribute responsibility for acts of war to specific individuals,
nor was aggressive war seen as a crime under international law. In effect,
Tojo, Doihara, Itagaki, Araki, Koiso, Kido, and the other twenty-two
defendants indicted, whatever their other crimes may have been, were
being tried for acts which were not illegal at the time when they were
committed, and had only been made illegal ex post facto by the victorious
Allies.

The choice of defendants was in some ways curious. Tojo, who had
attempted to make himself the sole war leader, was an obvious candidate;
so too were Iwane Matsui, in overall command at Nanking; Akira Muto,
commanding troops at Nanking in 1938 and Manila in 1944, and responsible for the maltreatment of prisoners and native laborers in Sumatra;
Heitaro Kimura, who had explicitly approved the brutalization of prisoners of war, and had had detailed knowledge of conditions on the Burma–
Siam railway. But there were those even among the judges who
questioned the justice of including Koki Hirota, Shigenori Togo, and
Marquis Kido, whom some saw as nothing but a proxy for a most
conspicuous absentee from the list: the Emperor himself.

The choice of judges was almost equally controversial. The president of the Tribunal, the Australian Sir William Webb, came fresh from a protracted enquiry into Japanese atrocities in New Guinea, and had the (undeserved) reputation of being a hanging judge. There was no neutral or Japanese representation, and the only Asian representatives were India and Nationalist China. Burma was allowed to attach a prosecutor to the British team, but none of the other Asian countries that had suffered under Japanese occupation was given a voice. In many ways, the trial was the last bastion of colonialism.

As for procedure, once again the court was instructed not to be "burdened" by technical rules of evidence, and to allow anything that appeared superficially to be genuine—hearsay, opinion, unsubstantiated documents like the diaries of the dead. War criminals had no rights; all purported confessions or statements made by them were admissible. Tojo was interrogated on over 50 occasions, for 124 hours in all, before being charged, and defense counsel was present at none of these interviews.

More dubious still was the heavy reliance on the evidence of General Ryukichi Tanaka, whose blend of vindictiveness and mental instability would have disqualified him as a witness in any other trial on earth. His motive for testifying, he said, was that Tojo had put him in a mental asylum for expressing opposition to the war. In fact, he had suffered a severe breakdown, and his medical record (even in the opaque official translation) would have made the average lawyer hesitate to accept his uncorroborated testimony, with its references to amnesia, melancholia, and manic-depression. "Since six months, observed physical exhaustion and isomunia [insomnia]. These symtons [sic] grew worst [sic], feeling of anxiety and unrest, palpitation and feeling of strong pressure in the breast. Since two weeks sense of fear due to the old syphilis for paralysis specially noticed. Syphilis past treatment . . . Family History: mental disease disposition positive. Father and grandfather committed suicide."

Translation difficulties were not confined to the prosecution. In this respect, as in every other, the defense was far worse off. Disastrously underfunded in comparison with the well-oiled prosecution machine, the defense lawyers were forced to make a radio appeal to the Japanese people for money, revealing their lack not only of facilities like translators and communications, but even food and lodgings. To have even a chance of survival in an Anglo-American trial, the defendants needed Anglo-American lawyers trained in Western legal procedure; instead, for the most part they were provided with Japanese lawyers whose idea of the duty of a criminal defense attorney "was, figuratively speaking, to put flowers gracefully on his client's grave."

Seven of the defendants did indeed go to their graves—Tojo,

Doihara, Itagaki, Kimura, Muto, Matsui, and Hirota. Sixteen others (including Araki, Koiso, Umezu, Kido and Kenryo Sato) were sentenced to life imprisonment, though most were paroled shortly after the end of the Allied occupation.

Punishing war crimes can never be anything but a distasteful, untidy, incomplete, profoundly depressing task, and it is all too easy to criticize with hindsight those who struggled to exact some retribution for barbarism. But the fact remains that the imperfections of the IMTFE and the trials of Homma and Yamashita colored the way in which Japanese people regard their past; they provided an excuse for those who were, and are, unwilling to confront the realities of Japanese actions in the 1930s and 1940s.

The destinies of the rank and file were both less dramatic and less certain. The first task was to bring home the millions of soldiers scattered through Manchuria, Korea, China, Formosa, Thailand, Malaya, Burma, the Philippines, and the islands of the South Pacific. This operation was complicated by the acute lack of shipping, and the simultaneous repatriation of a million non-Japanese from the homeland—Koreans, Formosans, and others who had been imported and used as forced labor. There were other problems, too, that had nothing to do with logistics. During the brief, shattering Soviet invasion of Manchuria in the very last days of the war, morale in the Kwantung Army collapsed, and there were mass surrenders on a far larger scale than anything the Allies had seen on Okinawa. Thousands were simply overpowered, and the Russians held some 1.3 million prisoners whom, despite constant pressure from MacArthur, they insisted on keeping as slave labor under extremely harsh conditions. During the Cold War years repatriation was gradual and grudging; as late as the 1970s, 300,000 Japanese soldiers remained unaccounted for in Russia.

The vast horde that did disembark in Japan had next to be demobilized and disarmed—in the words of the Japanese government, "a most delicate task." Showing a sudden interest in the niceties of the Hague Convention, the Japanese pointed out that Article 35 demanded respect for defeated soldiers' honor, and asked that they be allowed to demobilize themselves. MacArthur was well aware that the Americans could not disarm an army of this size without its cooperation, and that it made sense for the Army and Navy Ministries to disperse the forces they had assembled—but at the same time the Japanese people had to be impressed with the fact of the complete defeat of their armed forces. The result was a compromise.

In reality, demobilization was effectively in Japanese hands—but it was not to be perceived that way. The central war-making apparatus was dismantled. The General Staff, creation of Meckel, Katsura, Kodama, and Kawakami in the 1880s, was abolished; and the Army and Navy Ministries, initially renamed the First and Second Demobilization Ministries, had shrunk by June 1946 to mere "bureaus." Nor was there to be a heroes' welcome for the troops; MacArthur forbade them to return to their homes in military formations "with bands playing or with any display of flags, banners, or emblems of distinction." It was all to be very different from the manner in which they had originally left their villages to go to war.

As for the Imperial Army's weapons, their removal was a lengthy but profitable business. Planes, tanks, field guns, and anti-aircraft installations were cut up with oxyacetylene torches, or sprayed with liquid gas and set on fire. Ammunition dumps were exploded. Ships were distributed among the Allies, scuttled, or scrapped. The *Nagato,* Japan's only surviving battleship, was used as a target in the American atomic tests at Bikini Atoll in July 1946. Small arms were collected from the soldiers or the caches in the home islands where they had been stored in readiness for the last battle. A hundred thousand tons of materials for chemical warfare, which had also been waiting for the invading Allies, were taken into custody.

MacArthur had then to neutralize Japan's capacity to replace her lost arms. A total ban was imposed on weapons research; the atomic program was suspended, the scientists were taken into custody, and all five Japanese cyclotrons were destroyed, despite MacArthur having sanctioned their use for medicine, metallurgy, and agriculture. For the time being, no Japanese was to learn to fly, as trained pilots would be a military asset, and airfields were to be turned over, where practicable, to agriculture. Weapons were neither to be imported nor produced, and war-related industries were limited to supplying "peacetime domestic needs," which were defined as being approximately equal to Japan's requirements in 1930, before expansion had begun in earnest. In consequence, heavy industry was cut to one-tenth the capacity of the mid-1930s, and the surplus was to be distributed as reparations to the Allies.

Few of the Allies failed to benefit from the disarmament program. America made valiant efforts to monopolize any scientific knowledge that might be useful; the Russians complained that the Americans were also taking more than their fair share of the hardware. Some of MacArthur's excuses were a trifle lame; a large number of "tanks, assorted" in American possession were, he maintained, "containers, not combat vehicles." More often he did not bother to justify his actions, and weapons were described baldly as being "in U.S. Army custody for possible future use." The British, too, found items they could use; a "Self-Contained Mobile Command Post for Four AA Gun Positions" was sent to India where, with Partition approaching, it was obviously felt to be needed.

But the Allies did not get everything. There had been a crucial interval of two weeks between capitulation and occupation, during which huge quantities of the Japanese army's supplies, like its paperwork, mysteriously disappeared. The phenomenon is partly explained by Army Ministry Order No. 363 of August 18, 1945, instructing local command-ers to distribute to the public stores of fuel, oil, vehicles, gunpowder, and other commodities, for purposes of "reconstruction."

The Army Ministry's motives may have been humanitarian; but supplies worth 10 billion yen were hoarded at this time and later found their way on to the black market. There was also some "distribution" of weapons. In September 1945 a correspondent for *The New York Times* reported seeing armed but unmarked trucks entering and leaving tunnels into a mountainside in the Tokyo/Yokohama area by night. In remote rural areas, Allied troops found pillboxes, housing tons of field artillery and ammunition, disguised as traditional Japanese houses complete with sliding screens.

Next the disarmed, demobilized men had to be reintegrated into the shattered Japanese infrastructure. The authorities had two separate prob-lems. They had to find employment for millions of workers, some of whom had been away from home for as much as eight years. But agricul-ture and industry were both in ruins, and in the months following the surrender, crime rates doubled—fraud, gambling, black-marketeering, armed robbery. The Occupationaires saw a particular challenge in those soldiers who had been taken prisoner by the Allies. Successful rehabilita-tion of these renegades would be a shrewd blow at the militarists' code of death or dishonor; and some, though not all, did welcome the unex-pected opportunity for a fresh start.

One group of returning prisoners were intractable, through no real fault of their own. These were a fraction of the captives held by the Soviets, who besides cold and hunger also subjected them to intensive indoctrination. The prisoners in the lumber camps of Siberia ate their meager meals to the accompaniment of diatribes against the *zaibatsu,* and were taught to see their ordeal as preparation for "the struggle upon returning home." The most promising were sent to four indoctrination schools in or around Moscow for special training as intelligence agents;

in 1949 Russia seemingly unbent to MacArthur's pleas and poured no less than 95,000 Communist "converts" back into Japan. "What a terrifying lot our returned countrymen are!" wrote one wife to her war-criminal husband, imprisoned in Singapore. "Grim and unsmiling, their hearts are as frozen as the country they left, and [they are] bellowing to everyone that the only true freedom is to be found in the teachings of Marx and Lenin."

While trying to fit these millions of fighting men back into the lower echelons of Japanese society, the authorities also had to prise out of influential positions anyone who had helped the war effort at a loftier and more abstract level. "There must be eliminated for all time," trumpeted the Potsdam Declaration, "the authority and influence of those who have deceived and misled the people of Japan into embarking on world conquest." This description covered, beside the war criminals, all members of the General Staff, everyone who had served in General Headquarters, all the *kempeitai,* all career officers of both army and navy, and all civil servants at policy-making level in the service ministries. None was to be allowed to take part in national politics; they were to be excluded or removed from the Cabinet, the Diet, and senior ranks of the central ministries. The purge was later extended to include members of local government, the press, business—and even the statues that ornamented Tokyo. At the Yasukuni Shrine, the figure of Masujiro Omura, the first proponent of conscription in 1869, was solemnly removed.

Not content with dispersing the troops, destroying the administrative structure, and confiscating the weapons of the Japanese army, the Allies aimed also to obliterate what had been its greatest strength: its spirit.

Seishin was the product of years—decades—of indoctrination, and no one expected that it would evaporate overnight. Public feeling may have been running strongly against the military by the time of the surrender, and there may have been many who were eager to embrace American-style "democratization." But for the soldiers, defeat did not automatically erase the beliefs for which they had been fighting. Correspondence between "minor" war criminals and their families in the immediate postwar years revealed regret but not guilt, and continuing loyalty to the old values. Veterans kept in touch with each other—and in some cases did rather more than that. Much of the Imperial Army's land had been redistributed to the Ministry of Agriculture, and its property to the Ministry of Finance, immediately after the surrender; and when ex-soldiers applied to Local Assistance Bureaus for work on the land, the Japanese authorities made available to them the land and buildings of former arsenals and installations, rent-free, with large quantities of military supplies. Scandalized foreign press correspondents reported the existence of communities run entirely on prewar lines: positions within society determined by army rank, paramilitary drill and discipline, and tanks used as tractors.

The British and Americans had characteristically differing solutions to the Japanese attitude problem. For the Americans, the immediate priority was to instill a sense of guilt and encourage repentance. The British Foreign Office followed a less moral and more severely practical line. "Japanese believe success to be right and failure to be wrong. They have failed; we have succeeded and we are therefore to be adjudged as right. We should make fullest use of this situation to undermine any prestige remaining to the Japanese War Machine and militarists. . . . However much we should like the Japanese to wish to follow our ways for reasons other than opportunism, it would be wise for some time to come to ESCHEW subtle argument and to concentrate particularly for the consumption of Japanese military personnel on impressing the same simple lesson that we have won and they have been defeated."

But neither conscience nor pragmatism was enough to guarantee the permanent extinction of the Japanese martial spirit. Some kind of ultimate safeguard was still needed, a legal buttress against human changeability. The war itself had done more than the Occupation ever could to dampen the Japanese people's appetite for fighting, which was in any case an artificial creation of the long campaign for total war. But lest they forget, the means of waging war was to be denied them. Under Article 9 of the new Constitution, drafted and promulgated under American auspices in 1946, Japan forfeited the sovereign right to wage war and renounced the possession of arms.

Almost at once, as the shadows of the Cold War lengthened and Japan became a valuable potential ally in the fight against communism, many American and Japanese leaders began to regret this gesture, and no one cared to take responsibility for it. Most had agreed that Japan should repudiate war as an instrument of diplomacy; but to renounce arms completely was an altogether more drastic move. The opposite of militarism, after all, was not full-blown pacifism, but civilianism, the control of the military by civilians. What was most probably intended was a compromise, with Japan losing the immediate capacity to attack America, without being deprived of the future right to bear arms.

But there were those on the left wing of the Occupation, liberal idealists within the Government Section of MacArthur's headquarters, who were rapt by the vision of a pacifist Japan. For a short time in 1946 the time was ripe for a grand gesture—and MacArthur was the man for it. It seems likely that once the idea had been implanted, he was unwilling to relinquish it, and he had the power to translate wishful thinking into concrete action.

The full implications of Article 9 may have been more extreme than most people intended, and it continues to be debated and attacked to this day. But the emotional impulse behind Japan's involuntary renunciation of war in 1946 was clear enough. The Imperial Japanese Army, with all its strengths and weaknesses, had been destroyed, and nothing like it must ever be allowed to exist again.

PART IX

THE SHROUDED PAST

46

"LONGSTANDING REGRETTABLE PRACTICES": ATROCITIES AND THEIR ORIGINS

"The prisoners were made to kneel down by the grave and were killed one by one. . . . The mother and child were killed towards the last. The mother was holding the child, who was crying, in her arms when she was shot with a pistol. The child was then shot with a pistol. . . . The other prisoners were all stabbed with bayonets." Another soldier describing the same incident, in which seven Australians were murdered near Buna Government Station in New Guinea, told of the death of the sixteen-year-old girl in the group, whom the soldiers failed to kill cleanly. They held her down screaming and crying while they cut off her head. "The soldier who told me this said the sight was more than he could stand. I am told they threw the heads and bodies into the sea. It is said that many ghost fires fly about in the vicinity. Some soldiers are said to have suffered burns."

The atrocities committed by the Imperial Japanese Army are impossible to catalog. The number and the hideous variety of the crimes defy even the most twisted imagination: murder on a scale amounting to genocide; rapes beyond counting; vivisection; cannibalism; torture; American prisoners of war allowed to drown in excrement in the "hell ships" taking them back to Japan for use as forced labor; civilian prisoners used as human sandbags during air raids; Burmese coolies, dead and dying, stuffed under the sleeping platforms of other laborers on the Burma–Siam Railway.

More than a quarter of all prisoners taken by the Japanese died under interrogation, from starvation and untreated disease, or simply through random brutality. "Against a calm person who thinks it is natural to become a prisoner of war, threats must be made," ordered a guide to interrogation procedure. At a dire disadvantage where operational intelligence was concerned, Japanese commanders regarded prisoners as a crucial source of information, and third-degree methods were simply a matter of common sense, though it was best, the instructions continued, to leave no scar. The *kempeitai* routinely used electric and water tortures, filling a man's stomach and then jumping on him until the water was expelled through every orifice.

"At every turn we see men displaying an attitude of indifference in directing prisoners, as though the latter were on an equal footing with themselves," complained the commander of a Japanese engineer regiment. "It is necessary that subordinates be trained so that in the future they will be capable of dominating white men and putting them to work. ... You must have sufficient self-respect to place yourselves on a higher level and use them as Canton coolies. In giving orders, use bugles, whistles or Japanese words of command and make them move smartly. ... There are some forces which, out of a feeling of compassion for the prisoners, give them too much rest. ... Why should we waste compassion on a crafty enemy who has killed and wounded thousands of our comrades? ... These men should be made to realise the feelings of their dead comrades." All too often, bugles, whistles, and words of command were replaced by the fist, the club, and the bayonet. At the Tanbyuzayat base camp of the Burma–Siam Railway, prisoners were welcomed with the words, "You are the remnants of a decadent white race and fragments of a rabble army. This railway will go through even if your bodies are to be used as sleepers."

The doctrine of collective responsibility devised in Manchuria and China (and operating in the Japanese homeland) was applied ruthlessly in prisoner-of-war camps. Prisoners would be formed into "shooting squads" of between ten and twenty men, all of whom would be shot if one tried to escape. In the Philippines, three civilians were caught escaping from an internment camp and sentenced to death. "The firing party used automatic pistols, but the three men were not killed outright. . . . Even in their grave the men were still moaning and groaning, but the Japanese officer in charge ordered the Filipino grave-diggers, on pain of death, to fill it in." On Guadalcanal, reported a Japanese private dispassionately in his diary, "two prisoners were dissected while still alive by M.O. Yamaji and their livers were taken out. For the first time I saw the internal organs of a human being. It was very informative."

Prisoner-of-war casualties would have been hugely multiplied had the invasion of Japan taken place. The diary of a camp commandant in Taiwan detailed plans to entomb prisoners in the mine where they were forced to work. "Whether they are destroyed individually or in groups, or however it is done, with mass bombing, poisonous smoke, poisons, drowning, decapitation or whatever, dispose of them as the situation decrees."

There is no arguing with the facts of atrocity, displayed in captured Japanese documents as well as in the thousands of files maintained by the United Nations War Crimes Commission, and in other testimony by victims who survived. There is no way of reducing their horror. They are incidents locked in the past and it is not for people who were not there, were not born then, to try and excuse or justify what happened. But events of such magnitude do need to be understood. Perhaps if the behavior of the Imperial Army had been analyzed in the years after the war, the American deployment of a conscript army in a counterinsurgent war might have been more sensitively managed. For this reason, it is perhaps permissible for those who were not there to attempt an objective explanation of Japanese behavior.

No war atrocity has a single cause. The nature of the individual perpetrator, the ethics of the society and the ethos of the military organization from which he comes, the aims of the campaign in which he is involved, the state of the war and of the soldier himself at the moment of committing the crime—all play their part.

It is a crass but common racist assumption that the Japanese are somehow cruel by nature. One Japanese commentator, himself a prisoner of the British, dignified this argument with a sociological rationale. Historically, he maintained, the Japanese have not kept animals for food, and have therefore had little experience of slaughtering them. Accordingly, "they tend to flap and get into a frenzy when they see blood. Thus, though many nations might have committed acts of cruelty towards enemy prisoners or enemy civilians, Japanese cruelty was peculiar in that those who inflicted it were usually in an uncontrollable frenzy, and often behaved wildly, wounding people without any purpose, continuing to strike and injure people after they were dead, as if possessed. This naturally gave the impression to the Europeans that the Japanese were a cruel race." Similarly, the inefficiencies of the Bataan Death March—the failure to provide food, water, or shelter to the marchers—were explained as being partly due to Japanese inexperience as herdsmen.

Setting these hypotheses aside, it is doubtless true that the Japanese army, like any other, had its share of sadists and psychopaths. It is likely, too, that a high proportion of these may have found their way to guarding prisoners of war, since this duty was considered almost as dishonorable as being a captive, and many misfits were assigned to it—drunks, troublemakers, even the insane. (Mental illness was the more dangerous in the Imperial Army because it was recognized so late and consequently left untreated for so long. Only toward the end of the war did the military authorities acknowledge the existence of battle fatigue and permit the use of psychiatrists to handle it.)

But there were far too many atrocities all to be the product of madness. More influential was a lack of moral sense, in Western eyes. Japanese war criminals rarely expressed guilt or even regret; sometimes it seemed that they saw nothing wrong in what they and their comrades had done. The Japanese soldier admitted no higher authority than the Emperor, represented in practical terms by his superior officers. His only criteria for action were the decree of the Emperor and the collective will of those groups to which the soldier belonged—his family, village, unit. (Ironically, Hirohito had expressed his abhorrence of atrocities; but the feeling grew up that the more violent one's participation in the war, the greater one's commitment to his service.)

In part this was military conditioning, but it was paralleled in civilian society by a similar lack of a transcendent moral authority, comparable to God in the Judeo-Christian system—to guide the individual's actions, to which he could appeal, by which he could be judged. There were no absolute moral values. The Japanese did of course distinguish between "right" and "wrong" along the same lines as Western cultures; but the distinction could more easily be overridden according to the demands of a particular situation. "Right" tended to be what was deemed right by the group in a particular situation. In this context, individual conscience was a meaningless concept.

The lack of an overriding moral authority meant that there was little resistance to orders to commit atrocities. It was not unknown; there were, for example, a number of suicides among officers on the Yangtze who found themselves incapable of executing the scorched-earth instructions given them. But generally speaking, if an order was issued as being from the Emperor and accepted by the rest of the unit, the soldier had no other source of reference by which to evaluate it; he simply obeyed, as he had been so carefully trained to do. Thus, there was no recorded resistance to the practice of using prisoners for bayonet drill, and the order to take no prisoners at Nanking was obeyed to the letter, though many must have seen the absurdity of the dictum that any man with calluses on his hands was a soldier and should be murdered accordingly. Shame might hold the army back—after Nanking, Prince Kanin, the Japanese Chief of Staff, issued a printed order (classified "very secret") calling for discipline on the grounds that atrocities were ruinous to Japan's reputation—but guilt did not.

In an early war-crimes trial, the Japanese defense counsel tried to argue that the defense of "acting on superior orders" should be absolute in all cases for the Japanese soldier. In terms of the ethical system in which the Japanese soldier operated, counsel was correct; but this was not acceptable in Anglo-American jurisprudence, where some weight is given to the soldier's duty to obey transcendent moral imperatives. The cultural divide was wide enough to prevent the court from recognizing that the Japanese soldier had no moral imperatives outside the orders of his superiors and the ethic of the group. The soldier could not even cite the Geneva Conventions. Though Japan was a signatory, they were not incorporated in the training of either officers or the rank and file.

A closed moral system of this kind makes peer pressure the more overwhelming. Once brutality of various descriptions was accepted as a norm, even as a proof of manhood, it was hard for the individual soldier to resist. Rape in particular, for which the Japanese army was notorious, had much to do with boasts, challenges, and competitive virility in a male subculture. It also grew out of Japanese society's generally demeaning attitude to women. "While a Japanese woman or child is practically helpless before the power of the male," wrote a liberal Japanese professor in 1934, in despair at reports of the army's conduct overseas, "it can be imagined that in the case of millions who are not of the race, the result is even more terrible. The young Korean girls and those of Formosa are absolutely beyond help."

Another crucial feature of the Japanese ethical system was its insistence on hierarchy, both within Japanese society and within the world as a whole. Japanese consciousness of superiority was fed from two

479

sources: Confucianism, which revolved round the notion of hierarchy and proper place, and Shinto, which insisted on the unique and divine origins of the Japanese race. Japanese racism was the more dangerous for being firmly rooted in religion.

This made it omnidirectional; whereas British and American racism was directed at specific targets, the Japanese regarded *all* other races as inferior. Thus even the peoples of Asia whom they claimed to liberate were put at a distance and, in time of war, dehumanized to a greater or lesser extent, which made their enslavement easier.

But particularly savage contempt was reserved for the Chinese (who had been guilty of much the same racial arrogance throughout the centuries when China had called itself the Middle Kingdom, the center of the universe). Ever since vague feelings of cultural affinity had given way in the middle of the nineteenth century to territorial rivalry, hostility between Japan and China had been hardening into racial hatred—from the First Sino-Japanese War, through the Boxer Rebellion, the Twenty-one Demands, the seizure of Tsingtao, and the Tsinan Massacre, to the Manchurian Incident and the bombing of Shanghai. China in the 1930s began to pay the full price of the heavy indoctrination of the Imperial Army's officer corps.

Cold-bloodedly, the Imperial Army set out in the 1930s to exploit the narcotics trade in China for the sake of both profit and power. "The use of narcotics is unworthy of a superior race like the Japanese," proclaimed the Army Handbook. "Only inferior races that are decadent, like the Chinese, Europeans and East Indians, are addicted to the use of narcotics. This is why they are destined to become our servants and eventually to disappear."

There are records in Japanese war memoirs of peculiarly brutal rapes and murders committed by Chinese soldiers against Japanese civilians in the 1920s and 1930s. But it is equally certain that during the China War, every type of atrocity was committed by the Japanese against the Chinese on the mainland—crimes that grew out of conventional battles; crimes associated with guerrilla warfare; rape, murder, looting, drug-pushing. War crimes had become a part of the Imperial Army's life and mentality, as the High Command acknowledged in a chilling Supplement to Sixteenth Army Operation Orders, issued in Saigon on January 15, 1942. The soldiers, stated the directive, must not treat the new Western enemies *"as if they were Chinese* [emphasis added]. . . . We hear of not few units which have not yet got over the long-standing, regrettable practices of the operations against China." The "regrettable practices" would indeed be employed until the end of the Pacific War against expatriate Chinese wherever they could be found in Southeast Asia.

The International Military Tribunal for the Far East was severe in its condemnation of Bushido as a major factor in atrocities, and these strictures have helped to warp and harden Western perceptions of the samurai ethic. In fact, the original Bushido left room for honorable surrender and laid great stress on compassion towards the vulnerable. But the twentieth-century version, though it did its best to derive legitimacy from its samurai origins, was a perversion, and did indeed contribute to the committing of war crimes. It generated a range of mental attitudes that bordered on psychopathy: a view of death as sublime and beautiful, the fall of a cherry blossom; surrender as the ultimate dishonor, a belief whose corollary was total contempt for the captive; reverence for the sword, inherited directly from the samurai, which gave beheading as a punishment a special mystical significance.

The Japanese code of ethics had its impact on the army's philosophy of total war. There were no constraints on the methods the army might use to secure its ends. Any weapons that it could secure were legitimate, including the chemical armory and bacteriological weapons personally sanctioned and funded by Nagata. Any ploy was acceptable on the battlefield in a war to the death: wearing enemy uniforms, boobytrapping enemy corpses for the benefit of stretcher parties, luring enemy troops into ambushes with the white flag of surrender. (One battalion's "Hand Flag Regulations" included the information that the signal "Wave a white flag above the head" was to be interpreted as "sudden attack.")

The total-war policy resulted in death and destruction to Japan's enemies on an unlimited scale. The need for the army, including its thousands of pack animals, to live off the land was a permanent menace to civilian supplies—and it also meant that resources were usually lacking to care for prisoners. The constant demand for money to finance the vast effort prompted the drug traffic. And the urgent need to develop Chinese resources after 1941 led to unrivaled horrors. Suddenly, from being a nuisance gradually coming under control, the Chinese Red Army was perceived as a major military threat, and the response was swift and savage. Recognizing that Communist strength rested on secure base areas, the army (borrowing Nazi counterinsurgency tactics) began what the Chinese came to call the Three Alls Campaign: "Loot all, burn all, kill all." The full story of the pogrom will never be known. Good intelligence probably saved many from death, but their homes were burned, their livestock destroyed; virtually all the villages in the province of Hopei were burned, wholly or partially. And when the Imperial Army did surprise civilians, it showed no mercy.

There were elements in the training of the Japanese soldier that made for extreme and senseless violence on and off the battlefield—elements to which other soldiers also succumbed; for the effect of military basic training is brutalizing in all armies alike. Basic training has been called a "socialization for death." Its essential purpose is to implant a lethal combination of willingness to be led and readiness to kill, by breaking down the recruit's consciousness of self and sense of independent responsibility, and at the same time putting a gun in his hand and teaching him how to fire it against an enemy who is presented as less than human. The recruit is no longer expected to make judgments for himself; he has become part of a machine operating to a prearranged program. "The group . . . has a sensation of power, springing from its numbers. . . . Feelings can be communicated within the group by an almost hypnotic 'contagion,' and the group has a wide suggestibility of which this contagion is only a small element. . . . Groups go to extremes: suspicions become certainties and antipathies become hatred."

The recruit is trained to accept the possibility of violent death—his own or that of others—as being in certain circumstances right. He is abused verbally and often physically; his hair and clothes are made uniform; he is routinely humiliated to cut away his civilian self-esteem. Each of these steps is potentially dangerous, a degradation of human feeling opening the way to inhuman behavior.

Physical brutalization was especially conspicuous in the Imperial Army, where the most common disciplinary measure, sanctified by tradition, was face-slapping. As early as August 1919 the captain of an American warship was writing from Vladivostok to his Commander in Chief: "An interesting sidelight on the discipline of the Japanese troops was shown when the Japanese captain struck one of the soldiers several times in the face . . . for failure to transmit a message." Soldiers in China were often lined up in double file and made to slap each other until the blood ran. After the fall of Singapore, Colonel Tsuji was incensed to catch a junior officer and ten men bullying a watchmaker into selling them his wares cheap. "For me . . . questions and answers were unnecessary. 'Fools!' I cried, as I instantly smacked the faces of the officer and men concerned." As the war went on, the rapid expansion of the army led to pressure on training facilities and the introduction of short-cut methods, with greater emphasis on brute force.

The inflation of the army also led to a decline in the caliber of its officers. Too often individuals were given managerial tasks beyond their competence, which contributed to supply problems and the consequent ill-treatment of prisoners. More serious, large numbers of NCOs were pushed into junior officer positions to fill the gaps—and NCOs were the key to brutalization of the rank and file, through "personal punishment." It has been suggested that the NCOs who abused draftees were simply passing on both oppression from above and social pressures applied to them before they even joined the army. "Former peasants who became NCOs and regular army men were able to vent all their pent-up anger and frustration, the rage accumulated from the social and economic deprivation they had suffered in the countryside." A large proportion of the ordinary soldiers themselves came from extremely harsh backgrounds, and now they found themselves at the mercy of their surroundings again. Conscious efforts were made to convert simmering resentment into fighting strength; but the energies generated could not always be contained within the army. In the ladder of oppression, beneath the Japanese rank and file came prisoners of war and the natives of occupied countries, and by the time transferred fury and brutality touched them, it had been magnified to a terrible intensity.

Indiscipline became more and more noticeable, partly as a by-product of a war developing "not necessarily to Japan's advantage," partly because the policing system was inadequate. In conception, the Imperial Army was a specialist force designed to operate in the depopulated zones of northern Manchuria, where military–civilian relations were not expected to be sensitive and discipline was less of an issue. It had a low quota of military police, and these were also responsible for intelligence work. So controlling the troops' behavior was a problem even when senior officers did feel the need. Drunkenness was endemic in the army, and contributed to the vast majority of excesses, as well as to the fervor of many banzai charges. During the last days, even weeks, of the Japanese occupation of Manila, when Admiral Iwabuchi's men were running amok, most of them were drunk all the time.

The Rape of Manila was not an authorized orgy of plunder, rape, and murder by the licentious soldiery, as the Rape of Nanking had been. It was an expression of bewilderment, outrage, and despair at the predicament in which the entire Imperial Army found itself. Many atrocities were generated as much from without as from within, in response to situations that were themselves hideous.

The Japanese were fighting an insurgent war in many places, surrounded by hostile natives, and this can be a particularly dirty kind of battle. The enemy is organized in cells totally independent of each other and very difficult to suppress singly. The occupying force has either to obliterate whole areas on the principle that some insurgents are bound to be included, or try to crack the will of prisoners in the hope that they will give access to others. Either method leads inexorably to atrocities. Lack of contact with the enemy keeps troops in a state of permanent tension—and the Japanese were fighting these guerrilla wars most often in the jungle, which, contrary to Western belief, imposed exactly the same stresses on them as on Allied soldiers.

They were also, for a long time, fighting a losing war (though it cannot be ignored that some of the worst excesses were committed during or just after the Hundred Days, when none of these mitigating circumstances applied). The vengeance they took on the Doolittle flyers was directly provoked by the shock to the national psyche of the prospect of aerial bombing—the first attack on the Japanese homeland since Genghis Khan's, in the thirteenth century.

As the Allied stranglehold tightened, supplies dwindled; prisoners of war were the first to suffer. But conditions for the Japanese troops were also desperate, and in some places all normal restraints on behavior were gone. One Japanese prisoner told his captors of the situation in his unit on one of the bypassed islands: "Japanese troops had been under such conditions that they were not normal human beings at the time when the cannibalism took place." These conditions were described by the prisoner as "continuous standing in swamp water up to the arm pits, suffering from malaria with 40°C of fever, and such lack of food, particularly vitamin B, as to cause night blindness. . . . They were also deaf and reduced to such a state of delirium that their only reaction was to discharge their rifles in the general direction of any sound they might hear." In committing dreadful acts of cruelty and violence against others, many of the soldiers of the Imperial Army were taking revenge in advance for their own imminent deaths.

47

FACING THE PAST

All over Asia there are reminders of the career of the Imperial Japanese Army. From the River Kwai in Burma, across Asia to the remote northern boundary of Manchuria, on the Amur west of Khabarovsk, stand countless memorials to the victims of military occupation and exploitation. The monuments to independence from colonial rule are a different type of reminder. But within Japan itself, little physical evidence of the army's later years survives.

Ueno Park in Tokyo boasts a statue of the great Saigo, and on a small hill in the park is a shrine for the Shogun's samurai, who in 1868 made a last futile stand against the embryo Imperial Army. General Nogi, conqueror of the Russians, has his shrine in Tokyo, like Admiral Togo, hero of the battle of Tsushima. In the old Choshu capital town, Shoin Yoshida, inspiration to Yamagata and the other Choshu men of spirit, has a museum; and in Kyoto, the huge statue of the Goddess of Mercy serves as a memorial to the unknown dead of all nations in the Pacific War.

But there is no national army museum. Even Sugamo Prison, where Generals Tojo, Itagaki, Matsui, Muto, Doihara, and Kimura, and the civilian Hirota were hanged, is buried under a glossy hotel and shopping complex called Sunshine City. The ashes of these war leaders are interred at the Yasukuni Shrine, where the spirits of all those who have died for their Emperor since the Meiji Restoration are worshiped. For some in Japan this is the national memorial, and there is a small museum housing memorabilia, notably of the kamikaze; but the status of Yasukuni is uncertain. It is not Arlington Cemetery or the Cenotaph, because it stands as a perpetual reminder of the abuse of Shinto to support the militarists' creed. For almost forty years after the war, official state visits to the shrine were outlawed, in obedience to the Occupation decree that state and religion must be strictly separate. Then in 1985 Yasuhiro Nakasone attempted to reinstate the practice—but the vision of a Japanese prime minister bowing in reverence in the presence of Tojo's ashes aroused furious protest in Asia.

The archives of the Imperial Army—those that survived the incendiarism of both the B-29s and, in the aftermath of surrender, the General Staff—are discreetly stored. Some are held in the offices of the Kaikosha (the Officers' Association), near Ichigaya, where ex-officers meet daily to conduct seminars on the battles in which they took part. Most are kept at the National Institute for Defense Studies, where they are open for public inspection but are consulted most often by ex-officers come to pore over the past.

The possession of the ex-army's archives by the present army administration gives a misleading impression of continuity between the two. In fact, the Self-Defense Forces inherited little from the Imperial Army, though the hiatus between the death of the latter and the birth of the prototype for the former was very short.

From the moment of the surrender, there were those on both the Japanese and American sides who regretted the grand gesture of Article 9 and worked to rebuild a Japanese fighting force, with an eye to the intensifying conflict with Russia. General Charles Willoughby, MacArthur's intelligence chief, worked in close collaboration with his opposite number, General Seizo Arisue. Together they contrived to keep together some of the best brains in the Japanese General Staff, in the guise of a "historical research" team and a covert Japanese intelligence organization operating within Willoughby's G-2 Section of Occupation Headquarters. Willoughby also managed to keep track of Japanese army veterans through the records of the Demobilization Bureau.

These surreptitious maneuvers were foundations to be built upon when Washington began considering Japan's potential as an ally in the Cold War of the late 1940s. Some American strategists feared that without an army, Japan would become a power vacuum destabilizing East Asia; on the other hand, with a minimum of expense the Japanese might be equipped to hold a key segment of the defensive line against the Russians in the Pacific. "Dollar for dollar there is no cheaper fighting man in the world than the Japanese," remarked General Robert Eichelberger. "He is already a veteran. His food is simple."

In 1948 the proposals first took shape. "Even though created originally for the maintenance of domestic law and order," explained an American War Department report, "an augmented Civilian Police Force would be a vehicle for possible organization of Japanese armed forces at a later date"—a possibility that Willoughby had discussed with Arisue almost three years earlier. The explosion of the first Russian atom bomb brought a sense of urgency to the discussions, and the thin end of the wedge was tapped in. In 1950 Japan instituted a National Police Reserve of 75,000 men, equipped and trained by the United States but drawing heavily on the experience of Japanese veterans; as the purge of "militarists" was progressively abandoned during 1951, the Japanese government wrote individually to ex-officers of the Imperial Army "drawing their attention" to the opportunity that awaited them in the new force.

By 1952 the Police Reserve had been converted into a National Security Force of 110,000 men, with tanks and heavy artillery. In 1953, Richard Nixon, on a vice-presidential visit to Tokyo, declared that Article 9 had been "an honest mistake." The following year saw the creation, by government ordinance, of the Self-Defense Forces—ground, air, and maritime—authorized to defend Japan against external attack. Today Japan has the third most expensive army in the world, ahead of Britain, Germany, Israel, and South Africa.

At the beginning, the Self-Defense Forces contained large numbers of veterans, both officers and men; but this in itself does not seem to have made for any significant continuity. The same kind of familial tie still bound officers and their men, but the fanatical essence of the old army had gone, along with the agrarian social structure that nourished it.

In 1951, in an indignant "representation" to MacArthur, a young Yasuhiro Nakasone warned against the "salaried-man-like position of the member of the Force which has nothing to do with one's soul or the moral values," and over forty years he has seen his forebodings realized. Many recruits do indeed join up less to satisfy their souls than to acquire marketable skills. They are encouraged neither to keep themselves apart from civilians—they do not even have a separate judicial system—nor to express pride in the military ethos. Naturally, as the cadets of any army study their country's military past, the SDF recruits study the Pacific War and the operations of the Imperial Army. But these are studied as history and for the lessons in tactics and strategy they may teach, not for moral inspiration. The official military history of the war runs to over one hundred volumes; but these vary in reliability, and put a far heavier emphasis upon narrative than analysis, let alone evaluation or comment.

In an army composed entirely of volunteers, obedience is no longer emphasized to the near-exclusion of other virtues. The modern SDF is among the most highly technological armies in the world. For technology to function, independent decision-making in tactical encounters must be delegated to low levels; blind obedience and a spirit of self-sacrifice could only impair military effectiveness. As the automated battlefield increasingly becomes a reality, the need will grow for soldier-technicians, not indoctrinated fighting men.

Politically, the position of the military in Japan has changed out of all recognition. There is, deliberately, the most tenuous of connections between the forces and the Emperor. Even the firing of a ceremonial salute at the enthronement of Emperor Akihito in November 1990 caused much public agonizing. The Self-Defense Forces are nowhere near the center of the nation's policy-making; they have, in fact, remarkably little influence considering the size of their budget. On the contrary, the defense establishment is under strict civilian control. The director-general of the Defense Agency (the modern equivalent of the Army and Navy Ministries) must be a civilian; the prime minister is the forces' Commander in Chief, and frontline commanders need his authorization to act even in the event of a surprise attack.

Paradoxically, the Imperial Army, in its fall as well as in its heyday, has had a more obvious impact on other elements in Japanese society than on the Self-Defense Forces. Where business and industry are concerned, the total-war planners provided at least part of the impetus toward a planned economy conceived on strategic lines. And the defeat at the hands of high technology of an army powered primarily by spirit pointed a moral that the Japanese did not ignore.

Japan's foreign relations, too, bear the imprint of the Imperial Army—though not in the ways that Yoshida, Yamagata, Nagata, Itagaki, Tojo, and the others would have wished. The army encouraged Japan to think of herself as playing a part on the world stage, and today she is very much a world power; but she is a particular kind of international operator, unpopular in Asia and dependent on the United States—the very antithesis of what her military leaders had in mind when they initiated the Greater East Asian War under the banner of Pan-Asianism. The SDF was never intended to be an independent force; its profile is that of an adjunct to the U.S. Army. By demonstrating that Japan, with her lack of strategic depth and material resources, could not survive alone, the Imperial Army contributed greatly to a situation in which the American alliance is an integral feature of Japanese national identity.

The only lasting effect that the Imperial Army has had on the Japanese people in general has been to make a large proportion of them turn away—away from the wartime military, and away from the whole idea of war. For years, since the first bout of heart-searching in the immediate postwar era, there has been relatively little discussion of the war, in comparison with the torrents of military history and war novels in most Western countries. Many individual Japanese soldiers have written memoirs of the war; but senior officers tended to keep complete or partial silence while Hirohito was alive. And more generally, while so many ex-servicemen survive, Japanese people will always be inclined not to raise the painful subject for fear of embarrassing conflict.

At the official level, too, frank discussion has been made difficult by the political implications—the link between war memories and declining sales in Asia; residual racial hatred in America pervading and aggravating the trade war; the continuing propaganda war with China. Military history has near-pariah status in some academic quarters, and there are cases of official military historians, whatever their individual ideals and aspirations, being excluded by other academics from peace-studies groups.

"The people who were so eager to defend their country before the war," wrote Nakasone in 1951, "are now astonishingly negative toward war." Forty years later, much of that negative feeling persists. The fearful suffering of the home population as well as the slaughter of millions of soldiers, the shame of defeat, and the existence of Article 9 institutionalizing pacifism have ingrained in the Japanese people an authentic resistance to war that is more widespread than in most Western countries, with the possible exception of Germany.

The peace movement in Japan has many strands: the support of religious organizations like the Nichiren Buddhist Soka Gakkai; the women's vote, taken increasingly seriously; less predictably, some sympathy within industry, the major power lobby in Japan, unwilling to deflect the nation's energies from peaceful commerce; the advocacy of the political opposition. Beneath these identifiable groups, there is a groundswell of popular emotion, inexplicit but heartfelt, that rejects all things military.

Conventional pacifism is underwritten and greatly intensified by the Japanese people's unique abhorrence of nuclear weapons. Over 300,000 people in Japan are still entitled to special medical care for the aftereffects of atomic bombing, and the emotional and ideological fallout is just as severe. Perhaps more than anything else, the legacy of Hiroshima and Nagasaki has shaped the way the Japanese people look at—or refuse to look at—the war.

The passionate desire, born of the atomic horror, to have nothing to do with war (and this includes the history of war) is entirely natural, genuine, and shared by people of all nations, including the alliance that dropped the bombs. What is less valid is the tendency to discount or ignore the history of the Imperial Japanese Army on the grounds (not always expressed) that what happened at Hiroshima and Nagasaki somehow blotted out Japanese war crimes—that the dazzling light of the explosions cast all else into shadow.

Hiroshima and Nagasaki have been distanced from their appalling human realities and manipulated as a phenomenon. The memory of the atomic holocaust, whose right function is as the focus of antinuclear sentiment in Japan, has been made to serve less worthy ends, as a means of evading responsibility for other crimes.

The events of the 1930s, the progress toward the fatal plunge into war, can all be blamed on "the militarists," rather as the Nazis can be blamed for the Third Reich. But in reality there was no coherent group like the Nazis in Japan; the day-to-day murders, rapes, and tortures of eight years of war were committed by ordinary Japanese people, "civilians in uniform." They were the work of members of a huge conscript army, not a brutal specialist force somehow apart from the people. As Lieutenant William Calley, emerging from the court where he had been convicted of command responsibility for the murder of Vietnamese civilians, told reporters, "The guilt . . . we all as American citizens share it. . . . I say if there's guilt, we must all suffer it." My Lai and other horrors of the war in Vietnam plunged America into a welter of national self-analysis, which, although perhaps pushed to the borders of masochism, yielded a great deal of information and understanding, within America and beyond. The Japanese have never been seen by the West as trying to confront their national responsibility in this way.

As a result, Japan remains an outsider among the Western-style democracies. The self-image of the Japanese stubbornly fails to match the image that other nations have of them, and this rules out the possibility of mutually intelligible and productive debate about Japan's position in the world. Japan's past and her attitude to her past will continue to be a barrier between nations as long as they remain unexamined. Singapore's Lee Kuan Yew, for instance, has stated publicly that the Asian nations can never trust a Japan that cannot acknowledge its own misdeeds. Anti-Japanism is not diminishing of its own accord; it is likely, in fact, to flourish unless the Japanese take steps to counter it—partly because for many Southeast Asian countries it serves as a buttress to nationalism, just as it once did in China.

While turning resolutely away from the militarism of the past, the Japanese are also averting their eyes from the fact that Japan is rearming at considerable speed. Where home defense, as opposed to the dispatch of troops overseas, is concerned, Article 9 has become more of a talisman than a restraint. Though the Gulf Crisis of 1990–91 has helped to bring security issues into sharper focus, the debate has traditionally been vague, uninformed, and abstract. Whether Japanese rearmament really presents a threat to the security of the Asian region is questionable. But it is perhaps dangerous for a nation to be spending this heavily on arms when its democratic processes make no specific provision for handling a strong military.

Japan is psychologically better equipped than many other nations to entertain the concept of international harmony, the peaceful coexistence of nations, as a precondition of life in the postindustrial state. At the same time, she shows a greater insensitivity than many other nations to international standards of conduct. The Japanese have, for instance, displayed an almost total lack of concern for the effects of their industrialization on the resources of the outside world; their despoliation of the rain forests and their ruthless plundering of marine resources are cases in point.

It is entirely true, as they suggest, that other nations are guilty of the same crimes; but not on the same scale, and not with the same apparent disregard for foreign protests. The Japanese would be wise to look at this clash with world opinion from the perspective of their wartime reputation—because without doubt, other nations do. Japan exterminates whales, clubs dolphins to death, trawls with nets thirty miles long—and we hear again the argument that the Japanese are naturally cruel and rapacious. They open factories in Wales and refuse to relax trade barriers against British merchandise—they have always

been tricky and untrustworthy. They buy shares in Rockefeller Center—
and it is part of a hundred-year plan for world domination.

By refusing to look clearly at the Imperial Army and its history, the
Japanese are losing in other respects. They are missing much that was
remarkable, heroic, impressive, and tragic, as well as hideous and
shameful. Japan's discussion of national security can never be more than
partial as long as her people decline to discuss the issues that underlie
the anomalous status and role of their present military forces. And it is
becoming increasingly urgent for Japan to resolve the uncertainties, even
absurdities of her national defense posture. It is possible to consider
what a nation's army has done and suffered for her sake without becoming a jingoist or a ghoul. It is not possible to avoid wars or control armies
without understanding them.

A NOTE ON SOURCES

The Imperial Army was not just an instrument of conquest, but a child of necessity, of Japan's urgent need to preserve her independence from the nineteenth-century imperialist powers. Its story, as we have tried to tell it here, is inextricably woven into the fabric of Japanese and Asian development and Japan's relations with the West, and the sources we have used are correspondingly diverse: Japanese, French, Nationalist Chinese, American, and British.

In Paris, at the Archives of the French Army at Vincennes, and at the Ministry of Foreign Affairs, we found the reports of the early French instructors to the fathers of modern Japan in their efforts to create a modern military force.

Archival sources in London and Sheffield were of immense value for the period from the 1870s all the way through to 1941. The British Empire had enormous interests and ambitions in China, and from 1901 to 1922 Britain was formally allied to Japan; a constant stream of military attachés, diplomats, and officers on secondment visited Japan, and there is an unparalleled wealth of day-to-day reporting, analysis, and intelligence on all aspects of the evolution of the Imperial Army from the Russo-Japanese War of 1904–1905 through the First World War all through the 1920s and 1930s, even as Japan's relations with the West deteriorated. The British Public Record Office at Kew also gave us access to the reports of the Allied Translators and Interpreters Service, 1941–1945; the reports are mostly translations of captured Japanese documents, with some commentary and analysis—an invaluable source for all researchers on the Pacific War that has only recently been indexed and microfilmed by UPA Academic Editions.

Japan has its own military archive of both Imperial Army and Imperial Navy documents, at the National Institute for Defense Studies (NIDS), where we have deposited photocopies of our research papers from Paris. This archive is the basis of the Japan Defense Agency's 104-volume war history series. We are very grateful to Professor Kanji Akagi (formerly of NIDS, now of Keio University) both for arranging a discount on the volumes of the series we purchased, and for his advice and enthusiasm during a day's book hunt in Kanda, Tokyo's secondhand-book district. There is little Japanese archival material on military intelligence, as far as we are aware, and we owe a particular debt to Professor Akagi and to Professor Hisao Iwashima for sharing their findings—and, of course, to General Ichiji Sugita, who headed the General Staff's American intelligence section.

The other archives we visited in Japan were those of the Kaikosha, or Officers Association (we are particularly grateful to Professor Toshio Morimatsu for permitting us to photocopy certain of Tetzusan Nagata's *Kaikosha Kiji* articles); the Ministry of International Trade and Industry's Institute for the Study of Developing Economies at Ichigaya (which contains papers of the South Manchurian Railway); and the National Defense Academy (NDA) at Yokosuka, with its extensive and underused library holdings. We owe an enormous debt to Professor Ryoichi Tobe of the NDA for his detailed bibliographical advice and for supplying us with many journal articles that we would not have found for ourselves.

Our two research trips to Tokyo, in the summer of 1989 and fall of 1990, were valuable above all for the opportunity to meet Imperial Army General Staff officers. We were invited to their homes, entertained, and given their valuable time—not as a propaganda exercise, but because with the passing of Emperor Hirohito, the time had come to talk. For Westerners too young to have known the war or even its immediate aftermath, this was an extraordinary experience and one that has left us with an impression of the General Staff not as trumpeting militarists, but as highly intelligent men devoted to duty as they saw it. Had the Imperial Army not committed the atrocities it did, or were there a Nazi party or SS-type organization to take the blame, the reputation of these men would be considerably different.

This question of blame hung over the research and writing from the beginning. One of the major problems we encountered was the uncertainty over many of the army's actions and motivations, an uncertainty caused by their wholesale destruction of their own documents. This was compounded by the deliberate and perhaps inevitable distortion of the truth by the International Military Tribunal of the Far East, the Tokyo equivalent of the Nuremberg trials, and by postwar propagandists who relied on the evidence accumulated by the prosecution. From the start, therefore, we decided to tell the story of the Imperial Army using materials of the period as far as possible, tempered only by genuine postwar scholarship and avoiding the retrospective propaganda of both sides. In this way, we hoped to find some objectivity between the "victors' justice" of the Tokyo trial and the apologetics of the Japanese revisionists.

We have used the following abbreviations:

AAV	Archives of the Service Historique de l'Armée, Vincennes, Paris
FO	Papers of the British Foreign Office in the Public Record Office, Kew, London
NAW	National Archives, Washington, D.C.
WO	Papers of the British War Office in the Public Record Office, Kew, London

NOTES

CHAPTER 1: SAMURAI AND SQUINT-EYED BARBARIANS

4   "To attempt an estimate": P. Thompson, *How the Japanese Army Fights* (London: Penguin, 1942), p. 7.

6   international telephone calls: Interview with Prof. Ikeda, who speaks Satsuma dialect, May 1989.

6   The Choshu details are taken from A. M. Craig, *Choshu in the Meiji Restoration* (Cambridge, Mass.: Harvard University Press, 1961).

7   *Hagakure*: Yukio Mishima, *On Hagakure: the Samurai Ethic and Modern Japan,* trans. Kathryn Sparling (London: Penguin, 1979).

7   "Morality is nothing": quoted in K. C. Moloney, *Understanding the Japanese Mind* (Westport, Connecticut: Greenwood, 1968), p. 148.

8   "Be frugal": N. Umetani, *The Role of Foreign Employees in the*

Meiji Era in Japan, (Tokyo: Institute of Developing Economies Occasional Papers, Series no. 9, 1971), p. 8.

8   students of "foreign learning" now concentrated: ibid., p. 9.

9   The Stevenson account is from R. L. Stevenson, *Familiar Studies of Men and Books* (New York: Scribner, 1923), p. 158.
Quoted in H. Timperley, "Yoshida Shoin, Martyred Prophet
of Japanese Expansionism," *Far Eastern Quarterly,* vol. 1, no.
4 (August 1942), p. 338.

9   "The general prosperity": Moloney, op. cit., p. 103.

10   Perry's strategy: See Michio Kitahara, "Knock, Knock! The
Story of the Perry Mission and the Reopening of Japan,"
Japan Digest, vol. 1, no. 4 (April 1991).

10   "Sixty or seventy": ibid. p. 57.

10   When a samurai force assembled: H. Sonoda, "The Decline of
the Japanese Warrior Class, 1840–80," *Japan Review*, no. 1
(1990), p. 84.

11   The account of the rifle borrowed by the Satsuma lord is from
W. Beasley, *The Meiji Restoration* (Stanford, California: Stanford University Press, 1973), p. 123.

11   "What a disgrace": FO 46/24, Dec. 3, 1862, Neale/Russell.

11   "barbarian-subjugating": J. Crowley, "From Closed Door to
Empire: The Formation of the Meiji Military Establishment,"
in B. Silberman and H. Harootunian, eds., *Modern Japanese
Leadership: Transition and Change* (Tucson: Arizona University Press, 1966), p. 264.

11   "The commonest sound": FO 46/6, Jan. 7, 1860, Alcock/FO.

12   The description of Yamada's interest in the Western military is
from A. Craig, *Choshu in the Meiji Restoration 1853–68*
(Cambridge, Mass.: Harvard University Press, 1961), p. 135.

12   The account of the *shotai* is taken from R. Hackett, *Yamagata
Aritomo in the Rise of Modern Japan 1838–1922* (Cambridge,
Mass.: Harvard University Press, 1971), p. 27.

13   "The ugly English barbarians": ibid. p. 19.

13   feminine grammatical forms: ibid. p. 34.

14   100,000 new rifles: Seiho Arima, "Military Science," in *Accept-
ance of Western Cultures in Japan from the Sixteenth to the
Nineteenth Centuries* (Tokyo: Center for East Asian Cultural
Studies, 1964), p. 141.

14   the British Foreign Office pointed: FO 46/34, April 29, 1863,
Neale/Russell.

14   Jardine, Matheson: C. Totman, *The Collapse of the Tokugawa Bakufu 1862–8* (Berkeley and Los Angeles: University of California Press, 1980), pp. 212, 396.

14   the Tokugawa turned to the French: See, e.g., J. P. Lehmann, "The French Military Mission to Japan, 1866–8, and Bakumatsu Politics," in *Proceedings of the British Association for Japanese Studies,* vol. 1 (1976, Part 1).

15   "They still wore": M. Medzini, *French Policy in Japan During the Closing Years of the Tokugawa Regime* (Cambridge, Mass.: Harvard University Press, 1971), Chapter XII, no. 29, p. 218.

15   gave him a six-shooter: Hackett, op. cit., p. 45.

15   The account of the battle at Toba-Fushimi is from Totman, op. cit., pp. 434–35.

16   an artillery captain named Brunet: Lehmann, op. cit., pp. 7–16.

CHAPTER 2: EMPEROR AND ARMY

19   Competing religions were attacked: H. Kishimoto, ed. *Japanese Religion in the Meiji Era,* trans. J. Howes (Tokyo: Obunsha, 1956), p. 7.

19   a massive campaign . . . "Three Great Principles": See generally H. Hardacre, "Creating State Shinto—the Great Promulgation Campaign and the New Religions," *Journal of Japanese Studies* vol. 12, no. 1 (Winter, 1968), p. 29.

20   For factional rivalries among the Meiji leaders, see, e.g., M. Umegaki, *After the Restoration: The Beginning of Japan's Modern State* (New York: New York University Press, 1988), pp. 5–8.

20   For the account of Nishi, see generally Thomas R. Havens, *Nishi Amane and Modern Japanese Thought* (Princeton, N.J.: Princeton University Press, 1970).

22   The daimyo of Tosa . . . 9,000 troops: S. Yamamura, *Politics and Education in Early Meiji Japan: The Modern Military System* (Ph.D. thesis 1979), (Ann Arbor, Michigan: University Microfilms International, 80-00577).

22   "Rather than face collapse": H. Sonoda, "The Decline of the Japanese Warrior Class, 1840–80," *Japan Review,* vol. 1 (1990), p. 74.

23 But the burden was initially light: G. Ogata and Y. Takata, *Conscription System in Japan* (Oxford: Oxford University Press, 1921).

23 In ancient times: E. H. Norman, *Soldier and Peasant in Japan: The Origins of Conscription* (New York: Institute of Pacific Research, 1943).

24 The second French military mission: E. Presseissen, *Before Aggression: Europeans Prepare the Japanese Army* (Tucson: Arizona University Press, 1965), pp. 34–67.

24 Tokuho: Hackett, op. cit., p. 83.

24 "A military man": N. Bamba and J. Howes, eds., *Pacifism in Japan: The Christian and Socialist Tradition* (Kyoto: Minerva, 1978), p. 8.

24 "To be incited": Tokihiko Tanaka and Shigeru Ikuta, eds., *Meiji Japan Through Contemporary Sources* (Tokyo: Center for East Asian Studies, 1972), p. 235.

25 [Nishi's] emphasis had been: Havens, op. cit., p. 214.

CHAPTER 3: THE END OF THE SAMURAI

26 "I think there are some methods": Sonoda, op. cit., p. 106.

26 Korea's aggressive and insulting refusal: See B. Oh, "Sino-Japanese Rivalry in Korea," in A. Iriye, ed., *The Chinese and the Japanese: Essays in Political and Cultural Interactions* (Princeton, N.J.: Princeton University Press, 1980).

27 The samurai of Kanagawa: Umegaki, op. cit., p. 197.

28 "another India": N. Ike, "Triumph of the Peace Party in Japan in 1873," *Far Eastern Quarterly*, vol. II, no. 3 (May 1943), p. 294.

28 "If we open fire": Quoted in H. Conroy, *The Japanese Seizure of Korea* (Philadelphia: University of Pennsylvania Press, 1960), p. 48.

28 the intervention was largely instigated: H. Conroy, "Meiji Imperialism: Mostly Ad Hoc," in H. Conroy and H. Wray, eds., *Japan Examined,* (Honolulu: University of Hawaii Press, 1983), pp. 138–39.

29 Saigo became a lodestar: See J. Buck, "The Satsuma Rebellion of 1877: From Kagashima Through the Siege of Kumamoto Castle," in *Monumenta Nipponica*, vol. 28, no. 4 (1973); and

NOTES

A. Mounsey, *The Satsuma Rebellion: An Episode of Modern Japanese History* (London: Murray, 1879).

29   "a sort of independent country": Takayoshi Kido, *Diary*, Vol. III (1874–77), trans. Sidney Devere Brown and Akiko Hirota, (Tokyo: Tokyo University Press 1986), p. xxxiv.

29   "Although observing outwardly": FO 46/216, Feb. 19, 1877, Parkes/Derby.

30   The "spy's" confession is from FO 46/216, Feb. 18, 1877, Satow/Parkes.

30   "to encounter in arms": FO 46/217, March 12, 1877, Parkes/Derby.

30   "Political thought": T. Ideishi, *The True Story of the Siege of Kumamoto Castle*, trans. J. Buck (New York: Vantage Press, 1976), p. 8.

31   These samurai paramilitaries: FO 46/217, March 29, 1877, Parkes/Derby; and FO 46/217, April 12, 1877, Parkes/Derby.

31   "were in need of men": FO 46/217, April 12, 1877, Parkes/Derby.

31   "women of rank": FO 46/217, March 29, 1877, Parkes/Derby.

31   "rifle pits": FO 46/218, May 23, 1877, Parkes/Derby.

31   The account of Saigo's head is from Hackett, op. cit., p. 81.

32   "noble failure": Ivan Morris, *The Nobility of Failure: Tragic Heroes in the History of Japan* (London: Secker, 1975), Chapter 9.

32   a precedent for military overspending: U. Kobayashi, *War and Armament Loans of Japan* (Oxford: Oxford University Press, 1922), Chapters 1 and 2.

32   the clerical staff's tea: AAV 1690, Dossier 6, Rapport No. 6, Nov. 27, 1880, Bougouin.

33   "the want of familiarity": FO 46/217, March 19, 1877, Parkes/Derby.

33   "le commencement": AAV 1708, Feb. 24, 1879, Munier.

33   "La fantasia": AAV 1690, Dossier 7, Rapport No. 6, Sept. 10, 1881, Bougouin.

34   Then, with effective control of all the military forces: S. Lone, "Factional Discord in the Meiji Army: Katsura Taro and the Getsuyokai 1881–89," in *Papers on Far Eastern History* (Australian National University), no. 37 (March 1988), p. 83.

CHAPTER 4: THE NATION IN ARMS

35   whist, velocipedes: B. Chamberlain Hall, *Things Japanese*, (London: Kegan Paul, 1890), p. 157.

36   Nishi's theory of two societies: Havens, op. cit., pp. 202–3.

37   "deploring the times": The Admonition to Soldiers and Sailors is to be found in Tanaka and Ikura, op. cit., p. 220.

37   command function of the General Staff: See generally R. Minear, "A Taisho Democrat's Challenge to the Military: Yoshino Sakuzo on Dual Government," A. Craig and J. Fairbank, eds., in *Papers on Japan*, vol. 2, (Cambridge, Mass.: Harvard University Press, 1963).

37   "a senior officer": E. Norman, "Feudal Background of Japanese Politics," reprinted in J. Dower, ed., *Origins of the Modern Japanese State* (New York: Pantheon, 1975), p. 439.

38   Albert Mosse: Hackett, op. cit., pp. 108–11.

38   "very gentle to the people": I. Bird, *Unbeaten Tracks in Japan* (London: Virago, 1984; originally published 1880), pp. 164–65.

39   "remarkable trinity": Michael Howard, *Clausewitz*, (Oxford: Oxford University Press, 1983), p. 20.

39   "nation-in-arms": At an interview Professor Toshio Morimatsu made the point that this concept was introduced into Japan in the 1870s, May 1989.

39   "Every great nation": W. Gorlitz, *The German General Staff: Its History and Structure* (New York: Hollis and Carter, 1953), p. 63.

39   "a free people militarily organised": Conroy, *Japanese Seizure of Korea*, p. 97.

39   "In the olden days": Hackett, op. cit., p. 65.

40   "Know ye, Our Subjects": ibid., pp. 132–33.

41   From now on, moral education: See, e.g., W. Fridell, "Government Ethics Textbooks in Late Meiji Japan," in E. Beauchamp, ed., *Learning to Be Japanese: Selected Readings on Japanese Society and Education* (Hamden, Connecticut: Linnet, 1978); and H. Passin, *Society and Education in Japan* (New York: Columbia University Press, 1965), pp. 154–57.

41   "with the company": J. Weland, *The Japanese Army in Manchuria: Covert Operations and the Roots of Kwantung Army Insubordination* (Ph.D. thesis, University of Arizona, 1977).

And cf. WO 106/5659, "Letter from O/C 1st Regiment of Heavy Artillery to the Relatives of the Recruits who entered in December 1913." This letter was written in *Sosho,* a style neither the recruits nor their families could read; the letter would likely be placed with the family treasures, unread.

41   French observers commented: AAV 1706, July 1, 1909, Duval, p. 16.

CHAPTER 5: A MODERN ARMY EMERGES

46   "To annex a territory": FO 46/13, Aug. 2, 1861, Alcock/ Russell.

46   "Allow me to assure you": FO 46/24, Nov. 3, 1862, Enslie/ Neale.

47   "radiating military power": Lone, op. cit., p. 84.

48   Across the whole spectrum: C. Black, M. Jansen, et al., *The Modernization of Japan and Russia: A Comparative Study* (New York: Free Press, 1975), p. 131.

48   the three pushed . . . a program of reform: Lone, op. cit., p. 88.

49   "It is rather difficult": Rudyard Kipling, *From Sea to Sea and Other Sketches: Letters of Travel* (London: Macmillan, 1900), p. 428.

49   Meckel did not, so far as is known: I. Nish, "Japanese Intelligence and the Approach of the Russo-Japanese War," in C. Andrew and D. Dilks, eds., *The Missing Dimension: Governments and Intelligence Communities in the Twentieth Century* (New York: Macmillan, 1984), p. 17.

49   The Japanese had originally believed: AAV 1691, June 12, 1885, Berthaut.

50   maneuvers held to test the network: WO 106/5548, "Notes on the Japanese Army," 1891.

50   In the realm of battlefield tactics: Presseissen, op. cit., pp. 139–48.

CHAPTER 6: LINE OF ADVANTAGE: THE FIRST SINO-JAPANESE WAR

54   "In order to defend": Hackett, op. cit., p. 157.

54   army leaders had had provisional plans: A. Iriye, entry on

"Sino-Japanese War of 1894–5," in *Kodansha Encyclopaedia of Japan* (Tokyo: Kodaha, 1983).

55 For a detailed description of Kawakami's involvement see generally E. Young, "A Study of Groups and Personalities in Japan Influencing the Events Leading to the Sino-Japanese War," in *Papers on Japan*, vol. II (Cambridge, Mass.: East Asian Research Center, Harvard University Press, 1963).

55 "How could this old fellow": Young, op.cit., p. 258.

55 For the description of Mutsu's views, see generally G. Berger, ed. and trans., *Kenkenroku: A Diplomatic Record of the Sino-Japanese War 1894–5* (Tokyo: Japan Foundation, 1982).

55 Mutsu . . . contrived to conceal: C. Lee, *The Politics of Korean Nationalism* (Berkeley and Los Angeles: University of California Press, 1963), p. 38; and Berger, op. cit., p. 259.

55 Kawakami's plan: Lee, op. cit., pp. 36–37. (But *contra*, Berger, op. cit., p. 263, n. 4.)

56 For the genro, see R. Hackett, "Political Modernization and the Meiji Genro," in R. Ward, ed., *Political Development in Modern Japan* (Princeton, N.J.: Princeton University Press, 1973); and cf. I. Nish, *Japanese Foreign Policy 1869–1942* (London: Routledge, 1977), pp. 62–63.

56 The first Imperial General Headquarters: Berger, op. cit., p. 264 n. 10; and Young, op. cit., pp. 249–50.

57 . . . moved on Seoul: Young, op. cit., p. 275.

57 "an encounter": "Vladimir," *The China-Japan War* (London: Sampson Low, Marston, 1896), p. 7.

57 A precision instrument factory: U. Kobayashi, *Military Industries of Japan* (Oxford: Oxford University Press, 1922), p. 34.

57 "baggy trousers": R. Powell, *The Rise of Chinese Military Power* (Princeton, N.J.: Princeton University Press, 1955), p. 31.

58 D'Anethan detailed their arms: d'Anethan to Merode, Nov. 6, 1894, G. Lensen, ed., *The D'Anethan Despatches from Japan, 1894–1910,* (Tokyo: Sophia/Diplomatic Press, 1967), p. 34.

58 "to fire off all their . . . ammunition": WO 106/48, May 27, 1903, Churchill/Director-General of Mobilisation and Military Intelligence.

58 "a sense of self-assurance": S. Chu, "China's Attitudes Toward Japan at the Time of the Sino-Japanese War," in A. Iriye, ed., *The Chinese and the Japanese: Essays in Political and Cultural Interactions* (Princeton, N.J.: Princeton University Press, 1980), p. 93.

58   "dwarf pirates": ibid., p. 76.

58   "We operate": ibid., p. 92.

59   Plans for birthday celebrations of the Empress Dowager: ibid.,
      p. 77.

59   "So many old samurai": M. Jansen, "Modernization and For-
      eign Policy in Meiji Japan," in R. Ward, op. cit., p. 186.

61   "The spectacle of this Eastern nation": *Illustrated London News,*
      October 20, 1894. Quoted in D. Keene, "The Sino-Japanese
      War of 1894–5 and its Cultural Effects in Japan," in D.
      Shively, ed., *Tradition and Modernization in Japanese Culture*
      (Princeton, N.J.: Princeton University Press, 1971), p. 132

61   "If we are not excessive": Bismarck, July 9, 1866. Quoted in
      G. Craig, *Germany 1866–1945* (Oxford: Oxford University
      Press, 1978), p. 4.

CHAPTER 7: THE RUSSIAN MENACE

64   "We are under an illusion": Nitobe, July 11, 1930. In I. Nitobe,
      The Works (Tokyo: Tokyo University Press, 1972), p. 53.

64   "At present Japan must": *Jiji Shimpo [Current Events]*, June
      1895; quoted in R. Storry, *Japan and the Decline of the West
      in Asia 1894–1943* (New York: Macmillan, 1979), p. 30.

65   the industrial revolution was taking hold: G. Ono, *War and
      Armament Expenditures of Japan* (Oxford: Oxford University
      Press, 1922), p. 252.

66   "as if by sudden epidemic": U. Iwasaki, *The Working Forces in
      Japanese Politics* (New York: Columbia University Press,
      1921), p. 74.

66   cutting of the topknot: Lee, op. cit., pp. 47–48.

66   "bully-like samurai": Lee, op. cit., pp. 43–45.

68   "The Japanese": d'Anethan to Favereau, August 27, 1896.
      Quoted in Lensen, op. cit., p. 65.

69   "Educational Fund": Ono, op. cit., p. 53.

69   "The foreigners are like fish": Empress Dowager to Prince
      Tuan, February 21, 1900. Quoted in Peter Fleming, *The
      Siege at Peking* (London: Readers' Union/Hart-Davis, 1960),
      p. 97.

69   The *Daily Mail* report is taken from Fleming, op. cit., p. 116.

69   Russian accounts: J. N. Westwood, *Russia Against Japan*

1904–5: A New Look at the Russo-Japanese War (London: Macmillan, 1986), p. 11.

69   They had many of the virtues: A. Henry Savage Landor, *China and the Allies* (London: Heinemann, 1901), p. 341.

70   "Luckily for us": Lancelot Giles, *The Siege of the Peking Legation: A Diary* (University of Western Australia, 1970), p. 145.

70   "The Japs are perfectly splendid": Richard A. Steel, *Through Peking's Sewer Gate: Relief of the Boxer Siege, 1900–1,* (New York: Vantage Press, 1985), p. 21.

70   "The Japanese," wrote . . . Landor: Landor, op. cit., pp. 196–98.

71   "The real reason": WO 106/48: Col. Churchill's report on the Japanese Army, 1903.

71   an expedition to . . . Amoy: I. Nish, "Japan's Indecision During the Boxer Disturbances," *Journal of Asian Studies,* vol. 20, no. 4 (August 1961), pp. 451–56.

72   Woodblock prints: Keene, op. cit., pp. 135–39.

72   notorious picture of a Buddha: R. Valliant, "The Selling of Japan: Japanese Manipulation of Western Opinion 1900–5," in *Monumenta Nipponica,* vol. XXIX, no. 4 (1974), pp. 416–17.

73   "As long as Japan indulged": Kakuzo Okakura in *The Book of Tea;* quoted by Keene, op. cit. p. 174.

CHAPTER 8: WAR WITH RUSSIA

75   He was anxious to protect the . . . Trans-Siberian Railway: Nish, *Japanese Foreign Policy,* p. 240.

75   "It is inevitable": Dec. 30, 1903.

75   For the Kogetsukai, see S. Okamoto, *The Japanese Oligarchy and the Russo-Japanese War* (New York: Columbia University Press, 1970), pp. 72–75, 250–51.

76   Kodama was "gifted . . .": AAV 1692, Corvisart, August 1906.

76   On paper the move involved demotion: Okamoto, op. cit., pp. 35, 97.

76   "We must defeat Russia": Iwasaki, op. cit., p. 67.

76   200 yen or less: Lensen, op. cit., p. 184.

77   D'Anethan's remark about "warlike sentiments," and his de-

scription of the remarkable banquet, are taken from Lensen,
op. cit. pp. 176–77.

77   Tsukahara Bokuden: Stephen Turnbull, *The Lone Samurai and
the Martial Arts* (London: Arms and Armour Press, 1990),
pp. 62–63.

78   267 trains: R. Connaughton, *The War of the Rising Sun and
Tumbling Bear: A Military History of the Russo-Japanese War
1904–5* (London: Routledge, 1988), p. 16.

78   Siberian frontier guardsmen: A. Fujiwara, "The Role of the
Japanese Army," in D. Borg and S. Okamoto, eds., *Pearl
Harbor as History: Japanese-American Relations 1931–41*
(New York: Columbia University Press, 1973), p. 192.

78   "Lions led by assess": Col. J. Grierson, quoted in Connaughton,
op. cit., p. 18.

79   "Seize the submarine": Quoted in ibid., p. 44.

79   Kuropatkin would later claim: General A. N. Kuropatkin, *The
Russian Army and the Japanese War* (Westport, Connecticut:
Hyperion, 1977), pp. 206–207.

80   "The saddest thing": Kipling, op. cit., p. 434.

80   Nitroglycerin . . . had recently been tested: U. Kobayashi,
Military Industries, p. 68.

80   "one of the men": Report of Captain Peyton March in *Reports
of Military Observers Attached to the Armies in Manchuria
during the Russo-Japanese War: Part 1* (Washington: Government Printing Office, 1906), p. 7.

80   "The Foreign Office": Quoted in Capt. M. D. Kennedy, *The
Military Side of Japanese Life* (Westport, Connecticut: Greenwood Press, 1973; originally published 1924), p. 321.

80   The account of Yasumasa Fukushima is from I. Nish, "Japanese
Intelligence," pp. 19–21.

80   The account of Tanaka in St. Petersburg is from ibid., pp.
21–24.

81   The account of Akashi is from Motojiro Akashi, *Rakka ryusui:
Col. Akashi's Report on His Secret Cooperation with the Russian
Revolutionary Parties During the Russo-Japanese War*, C.
Inaba, trans.; O. Falt and A. Kiyala, eds., *Studia Historica 31*
(Helsinki: Finnish Historical Society, 1988); and cf. Nish,
"Japanese Intelligence," pp. 25–26.

81   "At great self-sacrifice": Kuropatkin, op. cit., p. 212.

81   shaved and coiffed: Connaughton, op. cit., p. 109.

83   Seaman's remarks are from Louis Seaman, *The Real Triumph of Japan: The Conquest of the Silent Foe* (London, 1906)

83   The description of Kuroki's alternative crossing is from Connaughton, op.cit., pp. 50–58.

84   telegram . . . to Meckel: Presseissen, op. cit., p. 148.

84   "a certain vague apprehension": Lt. Gen. Sir Ian Hamilton, *A Staff Officer's Scrapbook During the Russo-Japanese War*, (London: Edward Arnold, 1905), Vol.I, p. 133.

84   "the cooperation of the nation": Kuropatkin, op. cit., p. 216.

85   The description of the battle for the Nanshan Heights is from Connaughton, op. cit., pp. 75–76.

86   "The story of the Siege": Ellis Ashmead Bartlett, *Port Arthur: The Siege and Capitulation* (London: Blackwood, 1906).

87   a . . . face like a bath sponge: Hamilton, op. cit., p. 23.

88   "the Japanese Moltke": AAV 1692, Aug. 1, 1906, Corvisart.

88   "Here the corpses": Quoted in Connaughton, op. cit., p. 201.

91   five of his vice-admirals: ibid., p. 259.

91   the Togo turn: Stephen Howarth, *Morning Glory: A History of the Imperial Japanese Navy* (London: Hamish Hamilton, 1983), p. 91.

92   Japan had also gained control . . . bridgehead: Y. Inoue, "Russo-Japanese Relations and Railway Construction in Korea, 1894–1904," *Proceedings of the British Association for Japanese Studies*, vol. 4, 1979, Part 1, p. 96.

CHAPTER 9: THE ARMY UNDER ATTACK

94   "What o'clock": Nitobe, op. cit., p. 271.

95   "the gallant little Gurkhas": Hamilton, op. cit., p. 8.

95   "little anatomies": Kipling, op. cit., p. 435.

95   "I have still not been able": AAV 1706, March 1, 1909, "Rapport du Capitaine d'Infanterie Breveté Duval, stagiaire au 6ème Regt. d'Infanterie Japonaise sur la période novembre 1908–février 1909, Nagoya."

96   Officers considered it effeminate: Kennedy, op. cit., p. 8.

96   "pinned on the breast": Hamilton, op. cit., p. 264.

96   Schroeder's verse is quoted in Keene, op. cit., p. 149.

97   Roosevelt was said to have bought . . . sixty copies: *Asahi Shimbun* staff, *The Pacific Rivals: A Japanese View of*

NOTES

Japanese-American Relations, (New York and Tokyo: Wea-
therhill/Asahi, 1972), p. 62.

97 "I wish I were certain": A. Iriye, *Pacific Estrangement: Japanese
and American Expansion 1897–1911* (Cambridge, Mass.:
Harvard University Press, 1972), p. 112.

97 "the real yellow man": Charles Neu, *The Troubled Encounter:
The United States and Japan* (New York: John Wiley, 1975),
p. 45.

97 full-blown nationalism: William L. Neumann, *America Encounters Japan: From Perry to MacArthur* (New York: Harper Colo-
phon, 1963), p. 107.

97 Japanese had been spotted . . . "the Negroes": Iriye, *Pacific
Estrangement,* p. 159.

98 an overt economic incentive: P. Duus, "The Takeoff Point of
Japanese Imperialism," in Conroy and Wray, op. cit., p. 155.

99 "a poor, effeminate people": Nitobe, op. cit., p. 255.

99 Righteous Armies: Lee, op. cit., pp. 79–84.

100 The remarks by Bland are in a letter from Bland to G. E.
Morrison (May 27, 1905). Quoted in H. Lo, ed., *The Corre-
spondence of G. E. Morrison, Vol. 1 1895–1912* (Cambridge:
Cambridge University Press, 1976).

101 Koseki's Army Branch Information: AAV 1698.

101 But a far more powerful weapon: See, e.g., M. Peattie, *Ishiwara
Kanji and Japan's Confrontation with the West* (Princeton,
N.J.: Princeton University Press, 1975), pp. 5–6.

101 "their respect—which": AAV 1706, March 1, 1909, Duval.

102 "The cold-steel principle": *Jiji [Current events]*, Jan. 4, 1910.

102 Between 1908 and 1911 statistics of crime: AAV 1695, May 29,
1913, LeRond.

102 casualties in training: *Asahi,* July 18, 1909.

102 "A handsome old warrior": Hamilton, op. cit., p. 22.

103 a second generation of leaders: See, e.g., Okamoto, op. cit., pp.
24–33.

103 "a rotund, contented . . . man": Hamilton, op. cit. p. 24.

103 "Japan . . . private individual": WO 106/5549, March 25,
1902. Report by DAQMG Peach on "The Value of Japan as
an Ally."

104 the Finance Department's accounts: Ono, op. cit.

104 the navy had to wait: I. Gow, "The Evolution of a General Staff

509

System in the Imperial Japanese Navy," *Proceedings of the British Association for Japanese Studies,* vol. 4, 1979, Part 1.

104   prided themselves on being more liberal: Ikeda interview, May 1989.

105   "choice territory": T. Suganuma, quoted by T. Yano, "Southern Expansion Doctrine," in *Kodansha Encyclopaedia.*

105   "I had been doing my best": Foster R. Dulles, *Forty Years of American-Japanese Relations* (New York: Appleton-Century, 1937), p. 79.

107   The account of the Siemens scandal is from WO 106/5553. Report by Captain Brand RN, Nov. 28, 1913.

CHAPTER 10: FALLING BACK: THE GREAT WAR

109   an approach made by a Canadian insurance company: WO 106/5553, Oct. 29, 1914, Greene.

110   "Engagement with Miss Butterfly": WO 106/5552, Aug. 12, 1914, Jordan/Grey.

110   For the battle in Tsingtao, see generally C. Burdick, *The Japanese Siege of Tsingtao* (Hamden, Connecticut: Archon, 1976).

110   The Japanese minister . . . warned strongly: WO 106/5552, Sept. 29, 1914, Jordan/Grey.

110   "wishing their German friends": J. Jones, *The Fall of Tsingtau, with a Study of Japan's Ambitions in China* (Boston: Houghton Mifflin, 1915), p. 118.

110   The first German prisoners: C. Burdick and U. Moessner, *The German Prisoner-of-War in Japan 1914–20* (Lanham, Maryland: University Press of America, 1984).

111   As at Peking, the Japanese . . . complained: WO 106/5552.

111   The various inventions, including Uchida's, are described in Koseki, op. cit., 1909.

112   both Churchill and Lloyd George: V. Rothwell, "The British Government and Japanese Military Assistance, 1914–18," in *History,* vol. 56, no. 186, (February 1971).

112   Repington would present proposals: Rothwell, op. cit., p. 40; and WO 106/5553.

112   "Byrons and Lafayettes": WO 106/5553, Feb. 16, 1915, Calthrop.

112   The Japanese soldier . . . was conscripted: WO 106/5553, Sept. 3, 1914, Greene.

112   Public opinion, too, was against it: WO 106/5553, Sept. 9, 1914, Greene.

113   Japan's approach . . . was . . . self-serving: J. Banno, "The Japanese Army's China Policy from 1911: Split or Division of Labour?", in *Papers on Far Eastern History* 19 (Australian National University), (March 1979); and cf. WO 106/869, July 14, 1917, military intelligence memo on "Japanese Policy and Aspirations in Asia and the Pacific."

113   These the army supported clandestinely: See, e.g., J. Fairbank and A. Feuerwerker, eds., *Cambridge History of China*, Vol. 13: *Republican China 1912–49, Part II* (Cambridge: Cambridge University Press, 1986), p. 94.

113   helped . . . Sun's defeated rebels: See generally M. Jansen, *The Japanese and Sun Yat-sen* (Cambridge, Mass.: Harvard University Press, 1954).

113   Akashi . . . had recommended sorting out "pending questions": Akashi/Terauchi, Aug. 20, 1914. I. Nish, "Japan 1914–18," in A. Millett and W. Murray, eds., *Military Effectiveness*, vol. 1, (London: Allen and Unwin, 1988), p. 236.

CHAPTER 11: RETHINKING WAR

119   an obsolescent relic: I. Nish, *Japanese Foreign Policy 1869–1942: Kasumigaseki to Miyakezaka* (London: Routledge, 1977), p. 5.

119   the unconditional surrender of the enemy: J.-H. Kim, *The Garrison State in Pre-War Japan and Post-War Korea: A Comparative Analysis of Military Politics* (Tucson: Arizona University Press, 1978), p. 5.

119   "nation at war": B. H. Liddell Hart, *History of the First World War* (London: Cassell/BCA, 1973), p. 52.

120   "doctrinal stodginess": letter from Leonard Humphreys to Mark Peattie, in Peattie, op. cit., p. 11.

120   "the fact is": WO 106/5554, April 21, 1922, Prinsep/Milit. Att. Tokyo.

120   Japanese officers observed . . . America: F. Kurosawa, "Japanese Military Perceptions of the United States in the 1920s," in *Kokusaiseiji* [*International Affairs*] (special issue 1989).

120   "For the achievement": WO 106/5479, July 2, 1918.

120 "The outcome of wars": W. Morton, *Tanaka Giichi and Japan's China Policy* (Folkestone, Kent: Dawson, 1980), p. 20.

121 to wage total war successfully: See generally M. Barnhart, *Japan Prepares for Total War: The Search for Economic Security, 1919–41,* (Ithaca, N.Y.: Cornell University Press, 1987); W. Beasley, *Japanese Imperialism, 1894–1945* (Oxford: Oxford University Press, 1987); J. Crowley, *Japan's Quest for Autonomy: National Security and Foreign Policy 1930–38,* (Princeton, N.J.: Princeton University Press, 1966); A. Milward, *War, Economy and Society 1939–45* (London: Pelican, 1987); I. Nish, *Japanese Foreign Policy.*

121 From the home islands: WO 106/5479, "Certain Minerals Essential for War Munitions."

121 Akashi . . . sent a survey team: Morton, op. cit., p. 223 n.50.

121 "The Exploitation of China's Resources": ibid., p. 28.

121 "a limitless treasure trove": M. Ikei, "Ugaki Mazushige's View of China and his China Policy 1915–30," R. Toby, trans., in A. Iriye, ed., *The Chinese and the Japanese,* p. 201.

121 "China's abundant natural resources": J. Welfield, *An Empire in Eclipse: Japan in the Postwar American Alliance System,* (London: Athlone, 1988), p. 16.

122 Japan set up a military administration: Tsing Yuan, "The Japanese Intervention in Shantung during World War I," in A. Coox and H. Conroy, eds., *China and Japan: The Search for Balance Since World War I* (Santa Barbara, California: ABC-Clio, 1978).

122 loans made to Tuan Ch'i-jui: Hsi-ping Shao, "From the 21 Demands to the Sino-Japanese Military Agreements 1915–18: Ambivalent Relations," in Coox and Conroy, op. cit., p. 47ff.

122 "It is by the grace of Heaven": Morton, op. cit., p. 343.

122 Siberia Planning Committee: For the Siberian Expedition, see generally M. Kettle, *Russia and the Allies, 1917–20* (projected 5 vol., various publishers, 1981–   ); and J. Morley, *The Japanese Thrust into Siberia, 1918* (New York: Columbia University Press, 1957).

122 Czechoslovak troops: A. B. Ulam, *Expansion and Co-Existence: The History of Soviet Foreign Policy 1917–67* (London: Secker, 1968), p. 90ff.

123 the army had in its grip: WO 106/5555, July 13, 1922, and Sept. 28, 1922.

123   "to integrate the economy": Morley, *Japanese Thrust,* p. 309.

123   "The Japanese have been": WO 106/5554, April 21, 1922,
        Prinsep/Milit. Att. Tokyo.

124   For Semenov's gold, see WO 106/5555, June 27, 1922.

124   "Black Jumbo": ibid.

124   by August 15th: WO 106/5555 and *Japan Times,* Sept. 20,
        1922.

125   significant quantities had been deployed: G. McCormack, *Chang
        Tso-lin in North East China 1911–28: China, Japan and the
        Manchurian Idea* (Folkestone, Kent: Dawson, 1977), p. 58.

125   He was a tiny man: McCormack, op. cit. p. 1.

125   in particular with the Imperial Army: WO 106/5555, Oct. 11,
        1922.

CHAPTER 12: THE GREAT DIVIDE

126   "Nothing of any importance": WO 106/5479, July 2, 1918.

127   "voluntariness": Kurosawa, op. cit.

127   Marumiya Shoten: WO 106/5479, July 31, 1918.

127   Tanaka accused of . . . misappropriation: Morton, op. cit, p. 45.

127   the "Mad Baron": P. Hopkirk, *Setting the East Ablaze,* (Oxford:
        Oxford University Press, 1986), pp. 123–25.

127   bandits attacked . . . Hunchun: WO 106/5548.

127   cycle of rural conscription: Ikeda interview, May 1989.

128   carefully defined boundaries: See generally R. Mitchell, *Censor-
        ship in Imperial Japan* (Princeton, N.J.: Princeton University
        Press, 1984).

129   "Japan's prosperity": Buyei Nakano, in *Japan to Her Allies: A
        Message of Practical Sympathy from the Japanese Association
        for Aiding the Sick and Wounded Soldiers and Others Suffering
        from the War in the Allied Countries* (Tokyo: 1916).

129   "So far as Japan": WO 106/5553, Oct. 2, 1916.

130   plans for an invasion of the Philippines: AAV 1695, April 30,
        1914, "Conditions d'une invasion japonaise aux Philippines
        en cas de guerre avec les Etats-Unis," LeRond/Ministre de
        la Guerre.

130   "The Japanese cannot understand": WO 106/869, July 1916.

130   "Apart from the selling of guns": Dec. 30, 1916; quoted by
        Stephen Howarth, *Morning Glory* (London: Arrow, 1985), p.
        128.

130   For British suspicion of Japan, see, e.g., WO 106/869, May 9, 1916, "The growing dissatisfaction in Japan with the Anglo-Japanese Alliance," Cardew/Director Criminal Intelligence; Sept. 26, 1916, Cunningham-Greene/Viscount Grey; May 30, 1916, General Staff memorandum; July 14, 1917, memo on "Japanese policy and aspirations in Asia and the Pacific."

131   "Prior to the war": WO 106/869, Sept. 26, 1916, Greene/Grey.

133   "The age of Machiavellian": Ikei, op. cit., p. 203.

134   Yamanashi achieved: "Japanese Army Reorganisation and Reduction," Oct. 17, 1924. Papers of Captain M. Kennedy, Sheffield University, Group 10.1.

CHAPTER 13: COUNTERATTACK

135   Munitions Bureau and Council . . . abolished: WO 106/5479, Feb. 25, 1925.

135   "We must substitute": A. Iriye, "The Failure of Economic Expansionism 1918–31," in B. Silberman and H. Haratoonian, eds., *Japan in Crisis: Essays on Taisho Democracy* (Princeton, N.J.: Princeton University Press, 1974), p. 245.

135   Baron Oi: WO 106/5479, June 29, 1925.

136   For Germany in 1923, see G. A. Craig, op. cit., pp. 450, 461.

136   The *Kaikosha-Kiji* articles were discussed in our interview with Toshio Morimatsu, May 1989.

137   the Resources Bureau: WO 106/5479, Jan. 13, 1928: "Shigen Kyoku." And cf. correspondence, June 24, 1930.

137   "control and direction": WO 106/5479, Jan. 13, 1928.

137   "Regulations for the Investigation of Resources": WO 106/5479, April 1930 report.

138   For the Osaka experiment, see WO 106/5479, March 5, 1929; *Daily Telegraph*, June 25, 1929; July 1929 report.

138   "grave crisis": WO 106/5478, March 3, 1924.

139   For Soviet military power, see generally R. W. Davies, *The Soviet Economy in Turmoil 1920–30* (New York: Macmillan, 1989) and E. F. Ziemke, "The Soviet Armed Forces in the Interwar Period," in A. Millett and W. Murray, eds., *Military Effectiveness* (London: Allen and Unwin, 1988), vol. II, pp. 1–38.

139   the mainspring of the army's elite: Y. Nakamura and R. Tobe, "The Imperial Japanese Army and Politics," *Armed Forces and Society*, vol. 14, no. 4 (Summer 1988), p. 521.

139   Soviet heavy bomber: Davies, op. cit., p. 452.

140   The Comintern was active: Clive Rose, *The Soviet Propaganda Network* (London: Pinter, 1988), pp. 27ff.

140   For the Kumamoto high school, see WO 106/5656, 1934 Report, p. 18.

140   For Comintern aid to China, see Ulam, op. cit., p. 174.

140   Ho Chi Minh: F. Ansprenger, *The Dissolution of the Colonial Empires* (London: Routledge, 1989), p. 83.

140   "A genius": Han Su-yin, *Destination Chungking* (London: Penguin, 1959), p. 21.

141   "northern expedition": See generally D. Jordan, *The Northern Expedition: China's National Revolution of 1926–28* (Honolulu: Hawaii University Press, 1976).

141   "The peculiar element": WO 106/5478, Annual Report, Japan 1928.

141   "In the light of the Washington Conference": Jordan, op. cit., p. 166.

142   Tsinan in 1928: Morton, op. cit., p. 118.

143   the weakest of the powers: R. Garthoff, ed., *Sino-Soviet Military Relations* (New York: Praeger, 1966), p. 20.

143   For the fighting at Manchouli, see Garthoff, op. cit., pp. 20–25.

CHAPTER 14: THE HARD CHIEF AND THE VISIONARY

145   an excuse to intervene in Manchuria: See generally T. Yoshihashi, *Conspiracy at Mukden* (New Haven, Conn.: Yale University Press, 1963); Peattie, op. cit.; S. Ogata, *Defiance in Manchuria: The Making of Japanese Foreign Policy, 1931–2* (Berkeley, Calif.: University of California Press, 1954); J. Morley, ed., *Japan Erupts: The London Naval Conference and the Manchurian Incident 1928–32* (New York: Columbia University Press, 1984); Crowley, op. cit.; A. Iriye, *After Imperialism: The Search for a New Order in the Far East 1921–31* (Cambridge, Mass.: Harvard University Press, 1965).

145   the lessons of his failure: Peattie, op. cit., p. 102.

145   Japanese infantry virtues: ibid., p. 106.

146   For Itagaki's character, see WO 208/4597, May 27, 1938.

146   For Ishiwara's character, see generally Peattie, op. cit.

146   they must not lose sight: Nakamura and Tobe, op. cit., p. 520.

147   they ordered . . . Hashimoto to plan a coup: H. Seki, "The Manchurian Incident 1931," M. B. Jansen, trans., in Morley, *Japan Erupts*, p. 163.

147   the army by itself could not supply: C. Clapham and G. Philip, eds., *The Political Dilemmas of Military Regimes* (London: Croom Helm, 1985), p. 1; and cf. S. Finer, *The Man on Horseback: The Role of the Military in Politics* (London: Peregrine, 1976), p. 14.

147   "tightening the links": WO 106/5479 Report April 1930 and correspondence, Feb. 16, 1931.

148   Japan's bureaucrats: R. Spaulding, "The Bureaucracy as a Political Force 1920–45," in J. Morley, ed., *Dilemmas of Growth in Prewar Japan* (Princeton, N.J.: Princeton University Press, 1971), p. 33ff.

148   "renovation": See, e.g., I. Nish, "The Renovationist Faction in the Japanese Foreign Ministry: A Case Study," in *Proceedings of the British Association for Japanese Studies,* vol. 1, 1976, Part 1, p. 95ff; and cf. Spaulding, op. cit., p. 61ff.

148   The Issekikai: Seki, op. cit., in Morley, *Japan Erupts,* p. 132.

149   an opportunity to call the army to heel: L. Connors, *The Emperor's Adviser: Saionji Kinmochi and Pre-war Japanese Politics* (London: Croom Helm, 1987), p. 114.

150   "This is different": Morton, op. cit.

150   trump card: Connors, op. cit., p. 117.

151   "the overwhelming burden": FO 800/287, June 22, 1932.

151   "It is extremely bad": ibid., p. 128.

151   The account of the Mukden Incident follows WO 106/5561, Report, Oct. 22, 1931.

153   repeated the order not to resist: WO 106/5559, Oct. 1, 1931.

153   "back and forwards among the wounded": WO 106/5560, Oct. 19, 1931.

154   For the tableau of corpses, see WO 106/5558, Sept. 25, 1931, Kinney memo.

CHAPTER 15: TURNING SOUR IN SHANGHAI

156   "To have any point at all": WO 106/5559, Oct. 1, 1931.

156   widespread sympathy: Ogata, op. cit., p. 142.

157   "the financial condition": WO 106/5561, Dec. 4, 1931.

157   "can possibly meet this demand": WO 106/5559, Nov. 2, 1931.

157   "Nanking had made up its mind": WO 106/5561, Dec. 4, 1931.

157   "a very precarious position": WO 106/5560, Dec. 17, 1931.

157   "unusually reliable source": WO 106/5560, Dec. 31, 1931.

158   For the Karakhan warnings, see WO 106/5558, Oct. 30, 1931, Intelligence Summary 118.

158   "unavoidable destiny": Jonathan Haslam, *Soviet Foreign Policy 1930–33*, (London: Macmillan, 1983).

159   "there will be no question": WO 106/5558, Oct. 3, 1931.

159   "Today the state is dragged": Ogata, op. cit., p. 103, Katakura diary.

159   paper swords: WO 106/5558, Oct. 14, 1931.

160   deny Chiang Kai-shek . . . financial backing: WO 106/5562, Jan. 29, 1932.

160   "The Chinese did not understand": WO 106/5562, Jan. 31, 1932.

160   "They have quite unnecessarily": WO 106/5562, Jan. 31, 1932.

160   "incessantly and indiscriminately": WO 106/5562, Jan. 31, 1932.

161   Stimson's . . . feelings were clear: A. Rappaport, *Henry L. Stimson and Japan 1931–33* (Chicago: Chicago University Press, 1963).

161   "China has conducted": M. Wilkins, "The Role of U.S. Business," in Borg and Okamoto, op. cit., p. 353.

162   a ten-year propaganda war: Crowley, op. cit., p. 192; and for the state of planning on the eve of the Sino-Japanese War, see B. Lasker and A. Roman, *Propaganda from China and Japan* (New York: Institute of Pacific Affairs, 1938); also E. R. May, "U.S. Press Coverage of Japan 1931–41," in Borg and Okamoto, op. cit., pp. 511–32.

162   Khruschev warned: Morton, op. cit., p. 209.

162   For the Tanaka Memorial, see ibid., p. 205.

NOTES

162   *Blood on the Sun:* M. Mayo, ed., *The Emergence of Imperial Japan: Self-Defence or Calculated Aggression?* (New York: Heath, 1970).

162   For the Karakhan map, see WO 106/5492, Sept. 22, 1931.

CHAPTER 16: THE OFFICER CORPS DIVIDES

167   "so much so that any Minister": WO 106/5558, Oct. 13, 1931.

168   "talk to the Emperor": Connors, op. cit., p. 131.

168   *tenko*: A. Tiedemann, "Big Business and Politics in Prewar Japan," in Morley, *Dilemmas,* p. 285ff.

168   "Modern industries": C. Johnson, *MITI and the Japanese Miracle: The Growth of Industrial Policy 1925–75* (Stanford, Calif.: Stanford University Press, 1982), p. 108.

168   "regardless of the consequences": Crowley, *Quest,* p. 191.

168   For the social composition of the officer corps, see the detailed discussion in T. Cook, *The Japanese Officer Corps: The Making of a Military Elite* (Ph.D. thesis) (Ann Arbor, Michigan: University Microfilms International 87-12515), Chaps. 4–6; statistics pp. 243, 247.

168   half were from urban areas: B. Shillony, *Revolt in Japan: The Young Officers and the February 26th, 1936, Incident* (Princeton, N.J.: Princeton University Press, 1973), p. 22.

169   highly committed infantry tactics: WO 106/5656. Reports by officers on attachment 1929, 1934, 1936, 1937, 1938, 1939.

169   premium on fitness: WO 106/5656, 1937 Report, Appendix III.

169   a regiment would be expected to march: WO 106/5656, 1934 Report.

170   The account of the regional military preparatory schools is drawn from WO 106/5515, "General Report on the Japanese System of Military Education and Training, 1906."

171   The account of Military Academy life is drawn from the Reports of 1922, 1928, 1932, 1933, and 1937 by British Army language officers on three months' attachment at Ichigaya. See also Cook, op. cit., chap. 3.

172   1,372 hours: WO 106/5485, February 1928 Report, p. 136.

172   poem in common currency: ibid., p. 141.

174   Infantry School at Chiba: WO 106/5494, Aug. 25, 1931, Report.

518

174   Even at Staff College: WO 208/1429, January 1937 Report.
174   "after 3 years": WO 106/5485, February 1928 Report, p. 84.

CHAPTER 17: THE SPUR TO ACTION

177   *A Plan for the Reorganisation of Japan:* M. Masaki, "Kita Ikki's Political Ideas and the February Meeting of 1936," in J. Hunter, ed., *Aspects of Pan-Asianism* (Suntory-Toyota International Centre for Economics and Related Disciplines, London School of Economics, 1987/II).
177   Mitsugi Nishida: Shillony, op. cit., p. 15.
178   "the realisation of a system": FO 371/20283, March 27, 1936.
178   "a pulpit": WO 106/5581, Sept. 20, 1934.
178   80 percent of their men: WO 106/5498, June 6, 1934, Report, and WO 106/5582 Report: "The Influence of the Army on the Government and People of Japan."
178   For the October Incident, see R. Storry, *The Double Patriots: A Study of Japanese Nationalism* (Boston: Houghton Mifflin, 1957), pp. 86–93.
179   "There is a shining sun": FO 371/20283, quoting Araki speech of March 1933.
179   "unusually attractive": Kennedy papers, 7/2 "Far Eastern History in the Making," p. 448.
179   Araki firmly believed: M. Barnhart, *Japan Prepares for Total War: The Search for Economic Security, 1919–41* (Ithaca, N.Y.: Cornell University Press, 1987), p. 34.
180   "a Shinto inquisition": *Manchester Guardian*, Aug. 27, 1934.
180   imports of war resources: WO 106/5496 and 5525.
181   The account of Aizawa's visit to Nagata is drawn from Shillony, op. cit., p. 52.
181   pinning him briefly: J. Toland, *The Rising Sun: The Decline and Fall of the Japanese Empire 1936–45* (New York: Random House, 1970), p. 11.
182   "Our object is": FO 371/20282, Feb. 5, 1936.

CHAPTER 18: THE FEBRUARY 26 REVOLT

183   *Nihon Hyoron*: Shillony, *Revolt*, p. 120.
183   "no sincerity": WO 106/5585(2); *Japan Advertiser*, Jan. 12, 1936.

184 "clarification of national polity": *Japan Advertiser*, Jan. 12, 1936.

184 "Manifesto": Shillony, *Revolt*, pp. 146–48.

184 The narrative of the February 26 Revolt is drawn from FO 371/20283, *Japan Advertiser*, July 8, 1936; and see Shillony, *Revolt*, pp. 135–42; Toland, op. cit., pp. 12–29; Butow, *Tojo*, p. 65ff.

184 "When you rise up": M. Hane, *Emperor Hirohito and His Chief Aide de Camp: The Honjo Diary 1933–6* (Tokyo: Tokyo University Press, 1982), p. 50.

185 "I went poking around": WO 106/5585(1), March 3, 1936.

188 choice of February 26: Shillony, *Revolt*, p. 129.

188 For events at the Palace, see ibid., pp. 142–43.

CHAPTER 19: TO THE THRESHOLD OF POWER

189 "persistent but unconfirmed": FO 371/20283, March 12, 1936.

190 anger on a scale: Shillony, *Revolt*, p. 173.

190 "The spirit in which": Connors, op. cit., p. 168; and cf. Hane, op. cit., p. 213.

190 "strong Cabinet": Shillony, *Revolt*, p. 149.

191 refusing . . . to accept the resignation: ibid., pp. 173–74.

191 without even the honor: Letter from Professor Ryoichi Tobe, February 1991.

192 the financial community was pressing Sugiyama: ibid.

192 "unnatural silence": WO 106/5585(2) London *Times*, March 2, 1936.

192 "Soldiers, you have": London *Times*, March 2, 1936.

192 grisly preparations: FO 371/20283, March 12, 1936.

193 suspicion lingers: Shillony, *Revolt*, pp. 119–22; and cf. Hane, op.cit., p. 248 n. 81.

193 Army Order No. 11: FO 371/20283, Report No. 15; and cf. WO 106/5582, Aug. 26, 1936.

194 essential weakness of the Throne: See Stephen Large's discussion of Hirohito in *Proceedings of the Japan Society*, no. 115 (March 1990), pp. 65–78.

194 "not well with social conditions": WO 106/5585(1), May 6, 1936.

194 "The military is like an untamed horse": S. Shiroyama, *War Criminal: The Life and Death of Hirota Koki*, J. Bester, trans. (Tokyo: Kodansha, 1974).

195 endless round: interview with Professor Inoki, May 1989.

195 "The ideas of national defence": WO 106/5582, Oct. 25, 1934.

195 autarky on British or German lines: interview with Prof. Morimatsu, May 1989.

196 "Because of the activities of the Soviet Union": WO 106/5581, Aug. 5, 1935.

197 promise to support two navy demands: Barnhart, op. cit., pp. 36, 44.

197 "Fundamental Principles": Quoted in J. Lebra, ed., *Japan's Greater East Asia Co-Prosperity Sphere in World War II: Selected Readings and Documents* (Oxford: Oxford University Press, 1975), p. 63.

197 prudently left the army: interview with Prof. Ikeda, May 1989.

198 a special meeting of the Diet: Barnhart, op.cit., p. 49.

CHAPTER 20: MARCO POLO BRIDGE

201 mystery to this day: For the Marco Polo Bridge Incident, see generally David Lu's introduction to and translation of Ikuhiko Hata's "The Marco Polo Bridge Incident 1937," in J. W. Morley, ed., *The China Quagmire: Japan's Expansion on the Asian Continent 1933–41,* (New York: Columbia University Press, 1983), pp. 233–88; D. Lu, *From the Marco Polo Bridge to Pearl Harbor: Japan's Entry into World War II* (Washington: Public Affairs, 1961).

201 Wachi: T. Wachi, *Two Remorse Episodes in Sugamo Prison* (unpublished ms., 1977).

202 "We got it!": interview with Professor Kanji Akagi, Nov. 21, 1990.

202 one of the Imperial Army's priorities: WO 106/5576, Secret Memo G/1647/1.4.

202 "The time has now come": I. Hata, "Continental Expansion 1905–41," A. Coox, trans., in P. Duus, ed., *The Cambridge History of Japan,* vol. 6: *The Twentieth Century* (Cambridge: Cambridge University Press, 1988), p. 305 n. 65.

204 officers assigned there understood: Crowley, op. cit., p. 293.

NOTES

205 Chou was . . . under orders: J. Haslam, "The Sian Incident: Moscow, the KMT and the CCP 1936," in I. Nish, ed., *The Soviet Union in East Asia* (Suntory-Toyota International Centre for Economics and Related Disciplines IS/90/213, 1990), p. 14.

205 By early 1937, Chiang also knew: See the discussion of Chiang's position in WO 106/5576, Sept. 8, 1937.

206 "Many experienced": WO 106/5585(1), May 6, 1936.

206 For the Army Ministry changes, see FO 371/20283, Aug. 26, 1936.

206 The Imperial Army's main concerns: WO 106/5656, 1936 Report.

206 "down and out": WO 106/5576, Dec. 18, 1937.

207 "Judging the present situation": P. Calvocoressi, G. Wint, and J. Pritchard, *Total War: The Causes and Courses of the Second World War* (New York: Viking, 1989), p. 797.

207 protect their nationals: Tobe correspondence, February 1991.

207 After the creation of Manchukuo: WO 106/5576, Secret Memo G/1647/1.

208 mutually recriminatory statements: WO 106/5576, Aug. 16, 1937.

208 threw their weight: WO 106/5576, Aug. 16, 1937.

208 "to make known": WO 106/5576, Aug. 20, 1937.

208 Hasegawa's Third Fleet: WO 106/5576, Aug. 16, 1937.

209 "less anger and resentment": WO 106/5572, Aug. 11, 1937.

CHAPTER 21: TO THE GATES OF NANKING

210 From the beginning: See generally J. Boyle, *China and Japan at War, 1937–45: The Politics of Collaboration* (Stanford, Calif.: Stanford University Press, 1972); C. B. Burdick and D. Detwiler, *War in Asia and the Pacific 1937–49* (New York: Garland, 1980), vols. 8, 9, 13, 14; F. Dorn, *The Sino-Japanese War, 1937–41: From the Marco Polo Bridge to Pearl Harbor* (New York: Macmillan, 1974); C. Johnson, *Peasant Nationalism and Communist Power: The Emergence of Revolutionary China 1937–45*, (Stanford, Calif.: Stanford University Press, 1963); Lincoln Li, *The Imperial Japanese Army in North China, July 1937–December 1941: Problems of Political and*

Economic Control, (Oxford: Oxford University Press, 1975); D. Lu, *From the Marco Polo Bridge to Pearl Harbor: Japan's Entry into World War II* (Washington: Public Affairs, 1961).

210   "Criticism of China at War": WO 106/5376.

210   "accurate understanding": WO 106/5376, Jan. 16–28, 1938, Hankow interviews with German Military Mission.

211   "No attempt": WO 106/5576, Secret Memo G/1647/1.

211   Nanuan Barracks: WO 106/5576, Aug. 2, 1937.

212   For the Nankow Pass fighting, see WO 106/5576, Sept. 9, 1937.

212   "a considerable amount of booty": WO 106/5576, Sit. Rep., Sept. 1–20, 1937.

213   Federation of Mongolia: WO 106/5574, Jan. 26, 1938; and cf. K. Usui, "The Politics of War," D. Lu, trans., in Morley, *Quagmire*, p. 318ff.

213   "the 732nd year": WO 106/5574, Jan. 26, 1938.

213   30,000 Japanese: FO 371/20960, Dec. 14, 1937.

214   "that at all times up to the crucial date": FO 371/20960, Dec. 14, 1937.

214   thoroughly trained in urban warfare: letter from Professor Kanji Akagi, March 1991.

214   For the Woosung landing, see WO 106/5352, November 1937 Report of Belgian Military Attaché. And cf. WO 208/229, compilation of reports on Japanese landings.

215   the Japanese thrust faltered: *Army and Navy Journal*, Sept. 18, 1937; extracted in WO 106/5572.

215   Soochow Creek: WO 106/5376, article "The Capture of River Crossings by Japanese Forces"; and cf. FO 371/20961, Nov. 15, 1937.

216   Hangchow Bay had been labeled: WO 208/229, compilation of reports on landings.

216   "It was pitch dark": ibid.

217   "disembarking a large": ibid.

217   Tada and the others: Boyle, op. cit.

219   "defend Nanking": WO 106/5353, Nov. 28, 1937.

220   "The scenes of suffering": WO 106/5574, Jan. 2, 1938.

220   140 miles: WO 106/5322, map of campaign.

220   the authorities failed to inform: WO 106/5574, Jan. 2, 1938.

CHAPTER 22: A CARNIVAL OF DEATH

221   converged on the gates: FO 371/22147, June 18, 1938.

222   "It is now Christmas Eve": in FO 371/22147.

223   did not burst on the city: H. J. Timperley, ed., *The Japanese Terror in China* (New York: New York Books for Libraries, 1938), p. 27.

223   chemical strips: FO 371/22146, Jan. 10, 1938.

223   For Herr Rabe, see WO 106/5576.

223   "That evening came word": FO 371/22147, American Director's Report.

224   "One poor woman": FO 371/22147, American Director's Report.

225   For the rape statistics, see FO 371/22146, Jan. 10, 1938.

225   Nanking University survey: L.S.C. Smythe, *War Damage in the Nanking Area, December 1937–March 1938* (Nanking: June 1938).

227   "a few hasty jottings": FO 371/22147, Jan. 10, 1938.

227   84 percent of the male population: Smythe report, op. cit., p. 22.

227   "like some of the younger women": ibid., p. 17.

227   Pingting: Timperley, op. cit., p. 64.

227   T'ai-yüan: FO 371/22043, Jan. 7, 1938.

228   Wuhu: Timperley, op. cit., pp. 78–81.

228   K'ai-feng and Kihrien: WO 106/5573, July 26, 1938.

228   Hangchow: FO 371/22043, Feb. 27, 1938.

229   "We should deliver a blow": Calvocoressi, op. cit., p. 797.

230   seventeen military police: FO 371/22146, Jan. 10, 1938.

CHAPTER 23: ON TO HANKOW

231   Han Fu-chü . . . might defect: FO 371/20960, Weekly Intelligence No. 15, Nov. 25, 1937.

232   Tada . . . again tried: Boyle, op. cit.

232   "the Chinese National Government": WO 106/5574, Jan. 16, 1938, Summary.

234   two hundred kilometers: WO 106/5376, April 14, 1939.

234   a single shot ignited: ibid.

234   "If he hopes to survive": WO 208/234, May 25, 1938.

234   Chiang breached the dikes: WO 106/5351, June 20, 1938.

235   bacteriological contamination: *Japan Advertiser*, Sept. 22, 1938.

235   The entry into Hankow: WO 106/5352, Nov. 24, 1938.

236   Swedish flag: WO 106/5575, Sept. 21, 1938.

237   China's pre-war stocks . . . exhausted: WO 106/5575, May 7, 1938.

237   Moscow gave Chiang: Garthoff, op. cit., pp. 54–55.

237   By the end of 1938: Morley, *Quagmire*, pp. 343–44.

237   Mongol Islamic autonomy: WO 106/5352, April 24, 1938.

238   agents posted to Port Said: WO 106/5575, Nov. 16, 1937.

238   6 million Chinese dollars: WO 106/5351, Feb. 9, 1938.

238   Between May 28 and June 6: WO 106/5351, June 8, 1938.

239   The text of the army propaganda leaflet is in FO 371/22044, Nov. 22, 1938.

CHAPTER 24: PLUNDER AND NARCOTICS

240   "The incessant demand": WO 106/5575, April 14, 1938.

240   streets off limits: WO 106/5574, Oct. 21, 1938.

241   living off the land: WO 106/5576, Oct. 11, 1938.

241   "enrich and stabilize": WO 106/5575, July 23, 1938.

241   expatriate population: Usui, op.cit., in Morley, *Quagmire*, p. 429.

242   "No good": WO 106/5574, Oct. 21, 1938.

242   "yesterday, a . . . drunken soldier": FO 371/22146, p. 45.

242   For Chang Yu-ching, see WO 106/5575, Dec. 23, 1938.

242   For the situation in Peking, see WO 106/5574, March 23, 1938, and Dec. 1, 1938, Reports.

243   For trade between the Nationalists and the Imperial Army, see L. Eastman, "Facets of an Ambivalent Relationship: Smuggling, Puppets and Atrocities during the War 1937–45," in A. Iriye, ed., *The Chinese and the Japanese*, pp. 275–303, especially p. 278.

244   3,600 addicts: L. Craig Parker, *The Japanese Police System Today—An American Perspective* (Tokyo: Kodansha, 1984), p. 169.

244   "China was . . . on the verge": F. T. Merrill, *Japan and the Opium Menace* (New York: Institute of Pacific Relations, 1942), p. 19.

244 By the early 1920s: *The Opium Trade 1910–41*, vol. 6, 1927–41 (Wilmington, Delaware: Scholarly Resources, 1974), pp. 14–15.

244 a hole in the wall: Amleto Vespa, *Secret Agent of Japan* (London: Gollancz, 1938), p. 97.

244 30-million-yen bond issue: T. D. Reins, *China and the International Politics of Opium 1900–37* (Ph.D. thesis) (Ann Arbor, Michigan: University Microfilms International 81-19948), p. 258.

244 *kempeitai* and Special Service Sections: J. J. Stephan, *The Russian Fascists: Tragedy and Farce in Exile 1925–45* (London: Hamish Hamilton, 1978), p. 65.

244 For prostitution, see Vespa, op.cit., pp. 86–96.

245 drinking on a scale rarely seen: unpublished reminiscences of Joseph Ballantine, 1961, Oral History Research Office, Columbia University, New York.

245 from the protection of the international concessions: Reins, op. cit., p. 244.

246 For the Nanking addicts, see A. Brackman, *The Other Nuremberg* (New York: Morrow, 1987), p. 191.

246 $300 million: R. Butow, *Tojo and the Coming of the War* (Stanford, Calif.: Stanford University Press, 1961), p. 109 n.3.

246 thirty tons of . . . Iranian opium: Merrill, op.cit., p. 89.

CHAPTER 25: AT WAR WITH MAO

247 "No amount of foreign aid": WO 208/234, November 1938 Report.

248 "When they were finished": J. Fogel, ed. and trans., *Life Along the South Manchurian Railway: The Memoirs of Ito Takeo* (New York: M. E. Sharpe, 1988), p. xxi.

248 "Japan has done": W. Churchill, *Daily Telegraph*, May 26, 1938.

249 "People's Conference": WO 106/5575, Dec. 1, 1938.

249 For Wang Ching-wei, see generally Boyle, op. cit.

250 Federal Reserve Bank: WO 106/5575, Nov. 5, 1938.

250 A crisis was manufactured: See generally F. C. Jones, *Japan's New Order in East Asia: Its Rise and Fall 1937–45* (Oxford: Oxford University Press, 1954), p. 147ff; Usui, op. cit., in Morley, *Quagmire*, pp. 356ff; Calvocoressi, op.cit.; D. C.

Watt, *How War Came* (London: Heinemann, 1989); K. Akagi, *Anglo-Japanese Relations and Japan's Strategy Against Britain 1936–41* (unpublished manuscript), pp. 9–15.

250   "friendly advice": Jones, op. cit., p. 153.

251   "Lincolnesque": E. Snow, *Red Star over China* (New York: Grove, 1973), p. 90.

252   "Nationalists—too many taxes": M. Lindsay, *The Unknown War: North China, 1937–45* (London: Bergstrom and Boyle, 1975).

252   base areas: W. Laqueur, *Guerrilla* (London: Weidenfeld, 1977), p. 257.

252   Red Army . . . grew quickly: L. van Slyke, "The Chinese Communist Movement During the Sino-Japanese War, 1937–41," in J. Fairbank and A. Feuerwerker, eds., *Cambridge History of China* (Cambridge: Cambridge University Press, 1986), vol. 13, part 2, p. 621.

252   "The enemy soldiers": van Slyke, op. cit., pp. 639–40.

253   "an invincible iron army": Mao Tse-tung, *Basic Tactics*, S. R. Schram, trans. (London: Pall Mall, 1967), p. 32.

253   practical prescriptions: ibid.

253   "forced to resort": WO 106/5576, Oct. 11, 1938.

253   "protected hamlets": Research pamphlet published by Rand Corporation, RAND RM-5012-ARPA.

253   "particularly bad": WO 208/254, July 26, 1939.

254   hands chopped off: WO 106/5574, Dec. 30, 1937.

254   nine of the twenty-two: FO 371/22044, Aug. 4, 1938.

254   "Instructions for the Economy": See T. Nakamura, "Japan's Economic Thrust into North China 1933–38," R. Angel, trans., in A. Iriye, ed., *The Chinese and the Japanese*, p. 243.

254   The CCP objective: WO 106/5576, Oct. 11, 1938.

254   "The grandiose Japanese plans": FO 371/22044, Aug. 19, 1938.

255   Oerlikon: FO 371/ 23573/ F7284.

255   "The Celestials": WO 106/5576, Oct. 11, 1938.

255   "They have the greatest difficulty": ibid.

CHAPTER 26: THE PRICE OF WAR

256   development had been patchy: interview with Prof. Akagi, May 1989.

NOTES

256   twenty-four hours a day: WO 106/5575, July 19, 1938.
257   economic "general staff": C. Johnson, *MITI* op. cit., p. 137.
257   legacy of . . . Nagata: interview with Prof. Ikeda, May 1989.
257   no more metal toys: T. Marks, "Life in Wartime Japan," in I. Nish, ed., *Japan and the Second World War* (London: Suntory-Toyota International Center for Economics and Related Disciplines, London School of Economics, IS/89/197).
257   The press ceased: O. K. Falt, "Fascism, Militarism or Japanism?" (*Studia Historica Septentrionalia*, 8, 1985).
257   uniformly good: WO 106/5576, G. T. Ward's report.
257   "National Spiritual Mobilisation Campaign": Y. Oka, *Konoe Fumimaro: A Political Biography*, S. Okamoto and P. Murray, trans. (Tokyo: Tokyo University Press, 1983), pp. 72–73.
258   "born again": WO 106/5585(1), Nov. 1938, *Kakushiri.*
258   From 1903 until the Pacific War: Un Sun Song, "A Sociological Analysis of the Value System of Pre-War Japan as revealed in the Japanese Government Elementary School Textbooks 1933–41," (Ph.D. thesis, University of Maryland, 1958), pp. 43–47.
258   "It is unforgiveable": V. Koschmann, ed., *Authority and the Individual in Japan: Citizen Protest in Historical Perspective* (Tokyo: Tokyo University Press, 1978), p. 48.
259   "nothing but the necessary means": J. C. Moloney, *Understanding the Japanese Mind* (Westport, Connecticut: Greenwood, 1968), p. 148.
259   Tokugawa . . . Confucianism: R. Scalapino, *Democracy and the Party Movement in Prewar Japan: The Failure of the First Attempt* (Berkeley and Los Angeles: University of California Press, 1953), pp. 5–7.
259   linkage of Confucianism and Emperor: Song, op.cit., p. 46.
259   "The myth is": Quoted in Moloney, op. cit., p. 148; and see D. Titus, "Watsuji Tetsuro and the Intellectual Basis of Emperorism," *Proceedings of the British Association for Japanese Studies*, vol. 4, 1979, part 1, p. 122ff.
259   "those who refuse": Moloney, op. cit., p. 141.
259   For the growth of the Imperial Japanese Army, see C. Boyd, "Japanese Military Effectiveness: The Interwar Period," in *Military Effectiveness*, vol. II, p. 138.
260   lower reaches of the reserve pool: FO 371/20961, Dec. 21, 1937.

260   Seattle: WO 106/5376, Jan. 28, 1938.

260   ersatz officer corps: interview with Professor Inoki, May 1989.

260   McClure: FO 371/22044, June 21, 1938.

260   "Fighting and death": Agnes Smedley, *China Correspondent* (London: Pandora, 1984), p. 209.

261   died of thirst: WO 106/5576, Dec. 18, 1937.

261   "now proving more than a match": WO 106/5376, April 1939.

261   "setting off firecrackers": Smedley, op.cit., p. 177.

261   "wholly unexpected": WO 106/5575, May 7, 1938.

262   boasts of the Soviet ambassador: WO 106/5585(1), Sept. 11, 1936.

262   three to one: Tobe correspondence, February 1991.

262   a spy ring in Tokyo: See C. Johnson, *An Instance of Treason* (London: Heinemann, 1965).

262   second spy ring: *Pravda*, May 9, 1989.

263   For Changkufeng, see generally A. Coox, *The Anatomy of a Small War: The Soviet-Japanese Struggle for Changkufeng/ Khasan 1938* (Westport, Connecticut: Greenwood, 1977); I. Hata, "The Japanese-Soviet Confrontation, 1935–39," A. Coox, trans., in J. Morley, ed., *Deterrent Diplomacy: Japan, Germany and the USSR, 1935–40* (New York: Columbia University Press, 1976); and Ziemke, op. cit., pp. 22–23.

263   "The hill crests": FO 371/22146, Aug. 20, 1938.

264   "The Soviet tactical use": ibid.

264   "tactics of attrition": Imperial War Museum, London, British Intelligence documents BIOSJAP "Chemical Warfare."

264   Nomonhan is comprehensively described by A. Coox, *Nomonhan: Japan Against Russia 1939* (Stanford, Calif.: Stanford University Press, 1985), 2 vols. See also Morley, *Deterrent Diplomacy*, pp. 115–78; Ziemke, op. cit., pp. 23–25.

CHAPTER 27: SALVATION IN THE SOUTH

269   Salvation in the South: See generally *Kokusaiseiji*, "From the Sino-Japanese War to the Anglo-American War."

269   their bodies uncollected: Coox, *Nomonhan*, p. 923.

269   Nonaggression Pact: For the IJA attitude to the Soviet Union, see Ryoichi Tobe, "The Imperial Japanese Army and a Next World War," in *Kokusaiseiji*, op. cit.

269   For Soviet strength, see C. Hosoya, "The Japanese-Soviet Neutrality Pact," in J. Morley, ed., *The Fateful Choice: Japan's Advance into Southeast Asia, 1939–41* (New York: Columbia University Press, 1980), p. 102.

270   crop failure amounting to 70 percent: FO 371/23572, Annual Report for Korea, 1939.

270   dressing gowns . . . "The vast majority": FO 371/24699, 1940 Morrison Report.

270   "Japan in China has": Quoted in J. G. Utley, *Going to War with Japan 1937–41* (Knoxville: Tennessee University Press, 1985), p. 80.

270   Wall Street money: Y. Cho, "An Inquiry into the Problem of Importing American Capital into Manchuria: A Note on Japanese-American Relations, 1931–41," E. Harrell, trans., in Borg and Okamoto, op.cit., p. 377.

270   Cabinet Planning Board: W. Beasley, *The Rise of Modern Japan,* (London: Weidenfeld, 1990), p. 201.

271   "Finally the time has come": J. Tsunoda, "The Navy's Role in the Southern Strategy," R. Scalapino, trans., in Morley, *Fateful Choice,* p. 242.

271   "Outline of the Main Principles": text in Burdick and Detwiler, op. cit., vol. 2, monograph 146, "Political Strategy Prior to Outbreak of War," part II, appendix 2. And see generally Tsunoda, op. cit., and Morley, *Fateful Choice.*

271   "garrison state": J.-H. Kim, *The Garrison State in Pre-War Japan and Post-War Korea: A Comparative Analysis of Military Politics* (Tucson: Arizona University Press, 1977), p. 5.

272   "two very good . . . informants": FO 371/20960, Nov. 1937.

273   "immediately consult": Morley, *Deterrent Diplomacy,* pp. 261–64.

273   "about as close": Quoted in Butow, *Tojo,* p. 435.

274   2,600th anniversary: Oka, op. cit., pp. 110–11. And see R. Storry, *A History of Modern Japan* (London: Penguin, 1985), p. 23.

274   IRAA: Oka, op.cit., p. 106ff.

274   For Hoshino, see NAW International Military Tribunal of the Far East, Prosecution Document, Dec. 29, 1945.

274   underpinning Manchukuo: Ogata, op.cit., p. 124.

275   made any calculations . . . approximations: Johnson, *MITI,* op. cit., p. 141.

275   would not start to mobilize: ibid., p. 160.

275   trying to plan for jungle campaigns: Akagi, op. cit., p. 28.

275   only eleven divisions: Tsunoda, op. cit., p. 287.

276   three months clandestinely traveling: Akagi, op. cit., p. 23.

276   maps of Singapore: interview with General Sugita, May 1989.

276   Japan pressuring . . . Indo-China: I. Hata, "The Army's Move
         into Northern Indo-China," R. Scalapino, trans., in Morley,
         Fateful Choice, pp. 155–208.

277   "the supreme interests of Japan": ibid.

277   "We will meet you on the battlefield!": ibid., p. 177.

279   400,000 Communist troops: Johnson, *Peasant Nationalism*, pp.
         57–58.

279   T. L. Soong: K. Usui, "The Politics of War," D. Lu, trans., in
         Morley, *Fateful Choice*, p. 406ff.

280   "Outline Measures": ibid., p. 430.

CHAPTER 28: FACING REALITY

281   "thorough preparations": Burdick and Detwiler, op. cit., vol. 2,
         Monograph 146, p. 45.

282   British and Japanese agents . . . battling: FO 371/23572/
         F10495.

282   For the Thai demands, see S. Nagaoka, "The Drive into South-
         ern Indo-China and Thailand," R. Scalapino, trans., in Mor-
         ley, *Fateful Choice*, pp. 209–34.

282   shell Bangkok: Lu, op.cit., p. 145.

282   For Japan's mediation, see Burdick and Detwiler, op. cit., vol.2,
         Monograph 147, p. 15ff. And cf. Lu, op. cit., p. 144ff.

283   more predatory objectives: S. Nagaoka, "Economic Demands on
         the Dutch East Indies," in Morley, *Fateful Choice*, pp. 143–
         44.

283   Hitler's buying agent: ibid., p. 145.

284   without ordering mobilization: Utley, op. cit., p. 84.

284   "every man, woman": Quoted in ibid., p. 86.

284   America's growing strategic needs: ibid., p. 106.

285   humiliation of Japan's "military caste": ibid., p. 146.

285   "Outline of Policy Toward the South": text in Morley, *Fateful
         Choice*, Appendix 3.

285   For Imperial Navy's strength vs. the U.S. Navy's, see S. Pelz,

Race to Pearl Harbor (Cambridge, Mass.: Harvard University Press, 1974), p. 224. And cf. S. Asada, "The Japanese Navy and the United States," in Borg and Okamoto, op. cit., p. 236.

286 Nagano . . . calling for war: Pelz, op. cit., p. 223.

286 "moral communists": Hosoya, "The Japanese-Soviet Neutrality pact," p. 72.

287 "A German-Soviet war": ibid., p. 91.

CHAPTER 29: A TIME FOR LEADERSHIP

289 the services reached a compromise: Hosoya, op. cit., p. 96.

289 advantage . . . of two to one: Morley, *Fateful Choice*, p. 102.

289 For the Kantokuen details, see Hosoya, op. cit., p. 104. And cf. Coox, *Nomonhan*, p. 1035ff.

290 "He will help you": July 28, 1941. *Correspondence between the Chairman of Ministers of the U.S.S.R. and the Presidents of the U.S.A. and the Prime Ministers of Great Britain During the Great Patriotic War of 1941–45* (Moscow: Progress Publishers, 1957), vol. 1, p. 19.

290 joint action: British assistance to China up until Sept. 9, 1941, summarized in WO 208/304 A.

290 100,000 troops: WO 208/304 A, Feb. 7, 1941.

290 under cover of commercial activities: WO 208/304 A, July 2, 1941.

291 Philippines . . . strategic air force: W. Heinrichs, *Threshold of War: Franklin D. Roosevelt and America's Entry into World War II* (Oxford: Oxford University Press, 1988), pp. 144, 175ff, 194ff.

291 For the oil embargo, see ibid., pp. 135, 141.

292 "Although I am confident": N. Ike, *Japan's Decision for War* (Stanford, Calif.: Stanford University Press, 1967), p. 131.

292 All the seas: Butow, *Tojo*, p. 258.

293 not a decision Konoe could make: Oka, op. cit., pp. 150–51.

294 For Plans A and B, see the bases of plans in Burdick and Detwiler, op. cit., vol. 2, Monograph 147, pp. 66–67.

294 U.S. Treasury Department: Utley, op. cit., p. 170.

294 "At this moment": Ike, op. cit., p. 283.

295 Imperial Navy code-breakers: J. Chapman, ed. and trans., *The*

NOTES

War Diary of the German Naval Attaché in Japan 1939–43 (Lewes, Sussex: Saltire, 1990), vol. IV.

295   *Automedon:* Akagi, op. cit., pp. 26–27. And of Chapman, op. cit., p. xxxix.

295   blind spots in Singapore's defenses: interview with Prof. Akagi, May 1989.

295   "Japan is now concentrating": WO 208/304 A, Oct. 1, 1941.

295   "I think they are headed north": Quoted in G. Prange, *Pearl Harbor: The Verdict of History* (New York: McGraw-Hill, 1986), p. 126.

295   British reconnaissance: Heinrichs, op. cit., p. 218.

296   Kuroshima was something: Hiroyuki Agawa, *The Reluctant Admiral: Yamamoto and the Imperial Navy,* (Tokyo: Kodansha, 1979), p. 222.

297   JN-25b code: Described in A. Stripp, *Codebreaker in the Far East* (London: Frank Cass, 1989), p. 68ff.

298   Yamamoto plunged into depression: Agawa, op. cit., p. 259.

298   "Outline of War Guidance": Burdick and Detwiler, op. cit., vol. 2, Monograph 147, p. 40.

CHAPTER 30: "FIRECRACKER ATTACK": THE HUNDRED DAYS

304   Ba Maw is quoted in Louis Allen, *Burma: The Longest War* (London: Dent, 1984), pp. 561–62.

304   The description of Malaya comes from R. Holmes and A. Kemp, *The Bitter End,* (London: Antony Bird, 1982), p. 12.

305   a lightning reconnaissance flight: Masanobu Tsuji, *Singapore: The Japanese Version* (London: Constable, 1962), p. 49.

305   "Moving over corpses": ibid., p. 95.

306   "tanking up": John Costello, *The Pacific War* (London: Collins, 1981), p. 165.

306   "The first prisoners-of-war": Tsuji, op. cit., p. 111.

307   "On an average": ibid., p. 213.

307   "Britain's pivotal point": ibid., p. 216.

307   The description of Singapore comes from Holmes and Kemp, op. cit., pp. 102–3

308   "The spiritual effect alone": ibid., p. 228.

309   nightmare city: Holmes and Kemp, op. cit., p. 111.

309   "Groups of them": ibid., p. 272.

309   "stamp out the respect": Quoted in Lord Russell of Liverpool, *The Knights of Bushido* (London: Cassell, 1958), p. 60.

310   "As your hand divides itself": Lt. Col. F. Owen, *The Campaign in Burma* (London: HMSO/Central Office of Information, 1946), p. 10.

311   "Our ignorance": W. Slim, *Defeat into Victory* (London: Cassell, 1956), p. 13.

311   "All the Japanese commander": ibid., p. 15.

313   "an undisciplined mob": ibid., p. 196; and cf. Allen, *Burma*, p. 73.

313   civilian refugees: Allen, *Burma*, pp. 80–90.

313   most savage Japanese atrocities: Russell, op. cit., p. 98.

314   "an army of polo ponies": R. Spector, *Eagle Against the Sun: The American War Against Japan* (New York: Viking, 1985), p. 106.

314   The auxiliary Filipino forces: ibid., p. 73. And see also R. Hunt and B. Norling, *Behind Japanese Lines: An American Guerrilla in the Philippines* (Lexington, Ky.: Kentucky University Press, 1986).

315   one elderly captain: Teodoro A. Agoncillo, *The Fateful Years: Japan's Adventure in the Pacific 1941–5* (Quezon City, Philippines: R. P. Garcia, 1965).

CHAPTER 31: "BENEATH THE SKIN": THE JAPANESE FIGHTING MAN

317   "To attempt": P. Thompson, *How the Japanese Army Fights* (London: Penguin, 1942), p. 7.

317   "a tight-knit": Spector, op. cit., p. 10.

318   Once . . . Yamagata had intended: T. Cook, "The Japanese Reserve Experience: From Nation-in-Arms to Baseline Defense," in L. Zurcher and G. Harries-Jenkins, eds., *Supplementary Military Forces: Reserves, Militias, Auxiliaries*, vol. 8 (Los Angeles: Sage, 1978), pp. 269–70.

318   Formosan aborigines: WO 208/949, Oct. 6, 1944, Interrogation Report 499, "Intelligence Methods Gleaned from PoW Interrogation."

318   The pick of the Manchukuo Army: WO 208/313, Feb. 29, 1940, Military Attaché, Tokyo, Memo 33.

318   "Before the war": WO 203/4637, Appendix B to HQ 33 Ind. Corps Intelligence Summary No. 12.

319 the rest simply followed: interview with Yoshio Tanaka, Nov. 13, 1990.

319 "It should be borne": WO 208/2595, "Lessons from the Saipan Operation."

CHAPTER 32: "FAITH IS STRENGTH": FIGHTING SPIRIT

323 "It was very galling": Clifton B. Cates, First Marines. Quoted in Spector, op. cit., p. 195.

323 "a final, full acceptance": J. Jones, *World War II*, p. 41. Quoted in J. Ellis, *The Sharp End of War: The Fighting Man in World War II* (Newton Abbot, Devon: David and Charles, 1980), p. 240.

323 Thirty-third Division: Allen, op. cit., p. 610.

324 The Field Service Code is reproduced in Tsuji, op. cit.

324 "The Japanese Army's absolute obedience" H. Minami, *Psychology of the Japanese People*, Translation Series 36 (Honolulu: East-West Center, 1970), pp. 8, 12–13.

324 "distinctly an individual": Imperial War Museum, London, Record Group AL 5403, Sept. 8, 1948, Notes of Meeting at Chatham House.

325 Kiyoichi Yamamoto: Tsuji, op. cit., p. 294.

325 "impromptu exhortations": Imperial War Museum, London, British Intelligence documents, BIOSJAP 564.

325 "there is a philosophy": WO 208/2372, ATIS, October 1942, "Morale and Welfare" lectures given by Medical Officers.

CHAPTER 33: "GANGSTERS, CAT-BURGLARS AND POACHERS": THE PHILOSOPHY OF THE ATTACK

326 "It has begun to dawn": WO 106/5683, Oct. 15, 1930, Military Attaché, Tokyo, Report 28.

326 "thoroughly imbued" WO 208/3854 "Japanese in Battle" II, 1944.

327 For changes in divisional structure, see the general principles discussed in J. B. Wilson, "Mobility vs. Firepower: The Post–World War I Infantry Division," in *Parameters*, vol. 13, no. 3 (1983), p. 47.

327 "They seemed to exult": Calvocoressi, *Total War*, p. 992.

328   "The speed": WO 208/3854

328   "The Japanese use": J. Edwards, *Banzai, You Bastards!* (Hong Kong: Corporate Communications, 1988), p. 19.

329   metabolic rate: R. Holmes, *Firing Line* (London: Cape, 1985), p. 124.

329   "During the nights": Ellis, op. cit., p. 95.

329   "The more civilized": Slim, op. cit., p. 538.

329   " 'gangsters' ": WO 203/2607 "Lessons from Operations."

330   For Japanese night training, see generally C. Burdick and D. Detwiler, eds., *War in Asia and the Pacific 1937–49*, vol. 3: *Command, Administration and Special Operations: "Night Fighting"* (New York: Garland, 1980).

330   "Though cunning": WO 208/1393, July 30, 1944, MS/17.

331   "Sometimes an enemy soldier": Holmes, op. cit., p. 95.

331   Marine Corps intelligence: July 26, 1943, Marine Corps M-2 Information Bulletin 70, "Tactics in New Guinea."

331   "A common saying": A. Swinson, *Four Samurai—A Quartet of Japanese Army Commanders in the Second World War* (London: Hutchinson, 1968), p. 154.

332   "Though the total battle front": WO 208/1393, July 30, 1944, MS/17.

333   crop of fantasies: WO 203/1263, "Guerrilla Tactics."

333   "The Jap is": WO 208/1393.

CHAPTER 34: "DO YOUR BEST AND LEAVE THE REST TO PROVIDENCE":
THE SENIOR COMMANDERS

335   "Japanese commanders": A. Coox, "The Pacific War," in *The Cambridge History of Japan*, vol. VI: *The Twentieth Century* (Cambridge: Cambridge University Press, 1988), p. 322.

335   lace the boots: WO 208/147, "Burma Intelligence Notes."

335   "It is a fact": Minami, op. cit.

335   "manage somehow": Coox, "The Pacific War," p. 334.

336   "From fatalism": Minami, op. cit.

337   "Risk, as a correlate": A. Coox, "The Effectiveness of the Japanese Military Establishment in the Second World War," in *Military Effectiveness*, vol. III.

337   "The Japanese were ruthless": Slim, quoted in Swinson, op. cit., p. 252.

337   "No matter what": Toland, op. cit., p. 377.

338   For Sakurai, see Allen, op. cit., p. 171.

339   Nishi's glamour: B. Ross, *Iwo Jima: Legacy of Valor* (New York: Vanguard, 1985), pp. 346–47.

339   For Yamauchi, see Allen, op. cit., pp. 247, 296–97.

339   For Homma, see Swinson, op. cit., pp. 39–41.

341   "The sentence": Allen, op. cit., p. 266.

341   *mokusatsu:* ibid., p. 287.

342   *Gekokujo* had been viewed: interview with General Yoshio Tanaka, Nov. 13, 1990.

342   increasingly common: Ryoichi Tobe, letter to authors, Aug. 1990.

342   a cheeky note: Allen, op. cit., p. 471.

343   "My body": Swinson, op. cit., p. 162.

343   "It was the Ishiwara-Tsuji clique": Toland, op. cit., p. 533.

344   in the view of . . . Sugita: interview with General Ichiji Sugita, Nov. 8, 1990.

344   Matsuda's quarters: U.S. Marine Corps, *The Campaign on New Britain,* p. 42.

344   For Buna and Mereyon, see S. Ienaga, *Japan's Last War: World War II and the Japanese 1931–45* (Oxford: Blackwell, 1979), chapter 5, n. 44, p. 268.

346   The nexus of connections: interview with General Sugita, Nov. 8, 1990.

346   For Arisue and the Japanese naval attaché: interview with General Seizo Arisue, Nov. 14, 1990.

346   "Sungari Fleet": ibid.

346   "Horseshit": H. Agawa, *The Reluctant Admiral: Yamamoto and the Imperial Navy* (Tokyo: Kodansha, 1979), p. 129.

347   In the Mitsubishi factory: interview with General Tanaka, Nov. 13, 1990.

347   "We were confident": Spector, op. cit., p. 76.

CHAPTER 35: "MY SWORD IS MY SOUL": WEAPONS

348   "mechanism": Havens, *Nishi Amane,* op. cit., p. 198.

349   "a lack of sympathy": WO 106/5487, Oct. 31, 1933, Mil. Att. Tokyo.

349   Japanese tank technology: See generally D. McLean, ed., *Japa-*

nese Tanks, Tactics, and Anti-Tank Weapons (Normount Technical Publications, 1970).

349　many of the howitzers: WO 106/5660, Nov. 28, 1922, Capt. Russell/Mil. Att. Tokyo.

350　large-scale production of automatic rifles: interview with Paul Cornish of the Imperial War Museum, Oct. 31, 1990.

350　weapons in prototype: A. Millett, "The U.S. Armed Forces in the Second World War," in *Military Effectiveness*, vol. III, p. 72.

350　"The fixing of bayonets": R. G. Lee, quoted in Ellis, op. cit., p. 378.

350　the sword-making profession: R. Fuller and R. Gregory, *Military Swords of Japan 1868–1945* (London: Arms and Armour Press, 1986), p. 79.

350　"Both the cavalry sabres": A. Barker, ed., *Japanese Army Handbook 1939–45* (London: Ian Allen, 1979), p. 49.

350　hylozoism: Hiroshi Noma, *A Sense of Collapse,* quoted in Minami, op. cit., p. 149.

351　telescopic sight: Barker, op. cit., p. 35.

351　carrying handles . . . folding rifle . . . single shot: interview with Paul Cornish, Oct. 31, 1990.

351　"a flexible and economical": WO 232/78.

352　"The free traverse": WO 208/2223, Aug. 16, 1944.

353　"The heavily wounded": Hiroshi Funasaka, *Falling Blossoms* (New York: Times Books, 1986), p. 13.

353　"Half-way through an assault": WO 208/1401.

353　chicken wire: McLean, op. cit., p. 192.

353　"In the open ground": Allen, op. cit., p. 439.

354　swamp-crossing vehicle: Imperial War Museum, London, British Intelligence documents, BIOSJAP 1705.

354　armored-car trolley: Barker, op. cit., p. 72.

354　infrared homing bomb: BIOSJAP 1301.

354　television-controlled boat: BIOSJAP 742, Scientific Intelligence Survey.

354　cathode-ray personnel-detection device: BIOSJAP 743.

354　army . . . research organization: BIOSJAP 742.

355　atomic power: BIOSJAP 743, Appendices 3-A-4, 5-A-2, 6-A-2.

355　radar: BIOSJAP 742.

355　"a halting, makeshift application": ibid.

356　"death ray": BIOSJAP 742 and 743.

356   "I had heard": H. Riegelman, *Caves of Biak* (New York: Dial, 1955).

356   Japanese . . . flamethrower: WO 208/2206, ATIS SWPA 628.

356   For the chemical-warfare school, see WO 208/1437, Oct. 30, 1931, Mil. Att. Report 22.

357   chemical warfare in Abyssinia: *Army,* vol. 35, no. 1 (January 1985), p. 44.

357   "Ten minutes": WO 208/3044, Jan. 28, 1942, CX 32431/III/61022.

357   For "Lessons of the China Incident," Major Mamiya, and the blockhouses, see BIOSJAP 742.

358   "It is the common policy": WO 203/3679, Dec. 9, 1944, "Reports on the Use of Gas by the Japanese."

358   *chibi-dan:* Allen, op. cit., p. 301.

358   For the Burmese incidents of chemical warfare, see WO 208/3044, C in C India/GHQ Melbourne.

359   "aberrational act": WO 208/2199.

359   "There must not be": WO 203/3679, CoS on Batu.

359   "Defence against bacteriological warfare": WO 208/2648, ATIS 381.

359   Mao's forces alleged: WO 208/3044, April 10, 1942, 18th Army Group, China Army, "Reports from China."

360   Unit 731: See generally P. Williams and D. Wallace, *Unit 731: The Japanese Army's Secret of Secrets* (London: Hodder, 1989); and cf. Ienaga, op. cit.

360   "You couldn't say": Williams and Wallace, op. cit., p. 44.

CHAPTER 36: THE MISSING LINK: AIR POWER

362   For Japanese aviation, see generally Eiichiro Sekigawa, *Pictorial History of Japanese Aviation* (London: Ian Allen, 1974).

363   Bertin saw an additional drawback: AAV 1694, March 15, 1911, Bertin.

363   start of the Japanese aircraft industry: B. Collier, *Japanese Aircraft of World War II* (London: Sidgwick, 1979), pp. 14–15.

364   Deckert: AAV 1707, March 31, 1920, Report of Deckert Mission.

364   "Three sets": AAV 1707, April 8, 1920, Report of Faure Mission.

364   Air Service manual: WO 106/5484

364   army officers . . . still impervious: M. Okumiya, J. Horikoshi, and M. Caidin, *Zero!* (London: Transworld/Corgi, 1958), p. 28; and cf. Sekigawa, op. cit., p. 26.

365   "By American standards": Summary report, July 1, 1946, in *U.S. Strategic Bombing Survey,* vol. 7 (Washington: U.S. Government Printing Office, 1946), pp. 9–10.

366   When Hitler handed over the blueprint: A. Milward, *War, Economy and Society 1939–45* (London: Pelican, 1987), p. 176.

366   "In spite of the fact": WO 106/5895, Interrogations at Singapore. "On the Causes of the Defeat of the Japanese Air Force."

366   demands made on designers: Okumiya, Horikoshi, and Caidin, op. cit., pp. 339–40.

366   air aces: See generally I. Hata and Y. Izawa, *Japanese Naval Aces and Fighter Units in World War II* (Annapolis, Maryland: Naval Institute Press, 1989).

367   Saburo Sakai: S. Sakai, with M. Caidin and F. Saito, *Samurai* (London: Kimber, 1959).

367   U.S. Navy rotated: Spector, op. cit., pp. 148–49.

367   Banda Unit: D. Warner and P. Warner, *The Sacred Warriors: Japan's Suicide Legions* (New York: Van Nostrand Reinhold, 1982), p. 123.

367   "It is essential": ibid., p. 238.

CHAPTER 37: STAYING ALIVE: LOGISTICS

369   "A certain native said": WO 325/2, Sept. 6, 1942, Great East Asia War Diary.

369   Americans needed eighteen: Ellis, op. cit., p. 157.

370   "Even though": WO 208/2350, "US Combat Methods on Guadalcanal."

370   revised K ration: WO 232/78.

371   "In one place": Hiroo Onoda, *No Surrender: My Thirty-Year War* (London: Deutsch, 1975), p. 72.

371   "I could imagine": Funasaka, op. cit., p. 151.

371   seventy pounds: WO 208/1255, Japanese Military Handbook, "Infantry."

371   sleeping bag: Oct. 1, 1944, U.S. War Department Handbook on

Japanese Military Forces (Washington: Department of the Army).

371   compressed silk: WO 208/2223.

371   bulletproof vests: WO 208/1658, JICPOA, Supp. 1., "Tarawa Defenses."

372   mortars were transported: WO 208/1255.

372   Harley-Davidson: WO 208/1255, March 20, 1943, Handbook "Infantry" (updated).

373   "Thanks to Britain's": Tsuji, op. cit., p. 185.

373   rode on their rims: Costello, op. cit., p. 182.

373   "In addition to their . . . engineer duties": Barker, op. cit., p. 24.

373   Jungle . . . communications: WO 232/78.

373   "photophone": Imperial War Museum, London, British Intelligence documents, BIOSJAP 742.

374   "not of a very high grade": WO 208/1000.

374   For mepacrine and impotence, see J. Baty, *Surgeon in the Jungle War* (London: Kimber, 1979).

374   Medical officers were armed: WO 208/1000.

CHAPTER 38: HIDDEN ASSET: JAPANESE MILITARY INTELLIGENCE

375   "Their estimates": J. Bennett, W. Hobart, and J. Spitzer, *Intelligence and Cryptanalytic Activities of the Japanese During World War II: SRH 254, the Japanese Intelligence System, MIS/WDGS 4.9.45* (Los Angeles: Aegean Park Press, 1986), p. 56.

376   "The Japanese does not play chess": WO 208/1393, July 30, 1944, MS/17.

376   cashiered American major: Toland, op. cit., p. 257.

376   not highly regarded: Coox, *Military Effectiveness,* vol. III.

376   only one member: interview with General Sugita, Nov. 8, 1990.

376   mathematicians . . . genius: interview with Professor Kanji Akagi, Nov. 21, 1990.

377   Ishimitsu: I. Nish, "A Spy in Manchuria: Ishimitsu Makiyo," in *Proceedings of the British Association for Japanese Studies,* vol. 10 (1985).

377   Nakano school: L. Allen, "The Nakano School," in *Proceedings*

of the British Association for Japanese Studies, vol. 10 (1985), pp. 9–18.

378   forty-eight divisions: Bennett, Hobart, and Spitzer, op. cit., p. 46.

378   British telegram: interview with Akagi, Nov. 21, 1990.

378   Chinese codes: Bennett, Hobart, and Spitzer, op. cit., pp. 12–14.

379   B-29 bombing raids: ibid., p. 15. And cf. R. Spector, *Listening to the Enemy: Key Documents in the Role of Communications Intelligence in the War with Japan* (Wilmington, Delaware: Scholarly Resources, 1988), pp. 225–34.

379   "bomb plot": Prange, *Pearl Harbor*, pp. 485–87.

380   the Imperial Army's codes succumbed: R. Lewin, *The Other Ultra: Codes, Ciphers, and the Defeat of Japan* (London: Hutchinson, 1982), pp. 196–99.

380   instructions on interrogation: Bennett, Hobart, and Spitzer, op. cit., pp. 35–37.

381   "The Exploitation of Japanese Documents": Library of the School of Oriental and African Studies, London University: ATIS, Dec. 14, 1944.

CHAPTER 39: "ADVANCING TO THE REAR": THE DEFENSIVE

385   trade and troop transport: WO 106/5547 JIC (42) 515, "Strategical Implications of the Shortage of Japanese Shipping."

386   "You keep repeating": Toland, op. cit., p. 446.

386   "The unit will secure": WO 208/3853, "Japanese in Battle," I, p. 15.

387   "Forward enemy troops": WO 208/1401, Sept. 10, 1943, MI2 (c), "Operations in New Guinea."

387   For Japanese snipers, see WO 208/12167 and 208/1401.

387   elephants could be painted: WO 208/1393, Sept. 10, 1942, "Technical and Tactical Trends No. 7."

387   half-inch-thick rope: WO 208/1393.

387   panjis: WO 208/2223.

388   Booby traps were everywhere: WO 208/2223 and 208/1658.

388   Fukuryu: Imperial War Museum, London, British Intelligence Documents, BIOSJAP 776.

389   "It was explained": ibid.

389   "It is interesting to note": ibid.

389   "By Christ": Holmes, op. cit., p. 84.

389   capacity to attack: B. Buzan, *An Introduction to Strategic Studies: Military Technology and International Relations* (New York: Macmillan, 1987), p. 21.

390   "Trials of Weapons Against Bunkers": WO 232/35.

390   recoilless rifles: S. Hayashi and A. Coox, *Kogun: The Japanese Army in the Pacific War* (Quantico, Va.: Marine Corps Association, 1959), p. 214, n. 16.

390   "it is believed": WO 208/966.

391   "Flame has a good . . . effect": WO 232/35, "The attack on Japanese bunkers," DTI report, 86/Res/33.

391   "It appears": WO 232/35.

392   "This tendency": WO 208/3854.

CHAPTER 40: "THE PACIFIC IS ALSO BIG": JAPAN'S LONG DECLINE

393   When Seizo Arisue: interview with General Arisue, Nov. 14, 1990.

395   1,941,000 barrels: Coox, *Military Effectiveness,* vol. III.

395   reported Tojo: WO 208/4598, *Domei,* Dec. 27, 1942.

395   "By stretching and overextending": U.S. Strategic Bombing Survey, Office of the Chairman, No. 1 (Washington: U.S. Government Printing Office, 1947).

396   "It was warm": Takaaki Aikawa, *Unwilling Patriot* (Jordan Press, 1960), p. 23.

397   JN-25b: Costello, op. cit., p. 235.

398   Sugita recognized clearly: interview with General Sugita, May 19, 1989.

399   "grocery runs": Masanori Ito, *The End of the Imperial Japanese Navy* (New York: Norton, 1984), p. 80.

399   "When the air-raid alarm sounded": ibid., p. 81.

400   For Ichiki, see Richard B. Frank, *Guadalcanal* (New York: Random House, 1990), pp. 145–46, 151–55.

400   souvenir hunters: ibid., p. 156.

401   777 lives: ibid., p. 156.

401   "hacking a way": H. Murakami, *Japan: The Years of Trial 1919–52* (Tokyo: Kodansha International, 1983), p. 124.

402   "Their ribs": Toland, op. cit., p. 392.

402   timetable of mortality: ibid., p. 421.

403   Rumors spread: WO 208/1446.

404   "The Japanese . . . swarmed onto Ioribaiwa": R. Paull, *Retreat from Kokoda*, p. 227.

405   "He was ordered": ibid., p. 273.

405   "The soldiers had eaten": Costello, op. cit., p. 376.

405   "Within the period 1942–4": WO 208/3917, "Japanese Reaction to Allied Conduct of the War in the Pacific."

CHAPTER 41: "THE WORLD'S WORST COUNTRY": IMPHAL

406   milk break: interview with General Tanaka, Nov. 13, 1990.

407   "They had the whole nation": Funasaka, op. cit., p. 18.

407   "absolute" defense: interview with Professor Hisashi Takahashi, Nov. 16, 1990.

407   In his official appreciation: WO 203/1171, July 7, 1943.

407   "Bose was most emphatic": WO 208/3924, May 26, 1948, Memo by Lt. Col. J. Figgess, UK Liaison Mission, Tokyo: "Enquiry for Historical Section of Cabinet Office."

408   For the Terauchi report, see WO 208/149, Report on Operations in Burma 1943–5.

409   "Some of the world's worst country": Slim, op. cit., p. 169.

409   "As [the British] have previously": WO 208/3750, Japanese Campaign in Arakan, Dec. 1943–Feb. 1944.

409   multidimensional defense: Allen, *Burma*, p. 187.

410   110 bodies: ibid., p. 184.

410   "Stretched over": Swinson, op. cit., p. 133.

411   "hand-to-hand": Allen, *Burma*, p. 236.

411   British troops were mesmerized: WO 203/2607.

412   "It seems Army cannot grasp": Allen, op. cit., p. 289.

412   "Do as you please": Swinson, op. cit., p. 143.

412   "Two great days": WO 203/4367, April 18, 1944, Capt. Kitchen.

413   "Regret 33rd Division": Swinson, op. cit., p. 134.

413   "The struggle has developed": ibid., p. 141.

414   "Get off your fat ass": ibid., p. 142.

414   a little clearing: Allen, *Burma*, p. 311.

414   "The tatterdemalion divisions": ibid., p. 313.

CHAPTER 42: "POWERFUL ENEMIES":
WEAKNESSES IN THE IMPERIAL ARMY

415   "After the Americans": Funasaka, op. cit., p. 59.

416   Si Pendet: WO 203/5184, "Psychological Warfare."

416   As early as 1924: WO 106/5660, April 1924, Register No.M.I.1.2/2481/2-11.

417   "Defeated soldiers": Slim, op. cit. p. 187.

417   "in close . . . country": WO 232/35, Notes on interview with Brigadier Stewart.

417   "The Japanese in Battle": WO 208/3853, "Japanese in Battle," I.

417   "Exploding the Japanese 'Superman' Myth": WO 208/1446.

418   Issei and nisei: interview with General Sugita, Nov. 8, 1990.

418   "It is judged": WO 208/2350.

418   "On disembarkation": Tsuji, op. cit., pp. 65–66.

418   Australian Station intelligence report: WO 208/1202a, Report 2/38, Feb. 1938, quoted by Dir. Nav. Intell. Adm./Dir. Mil. Ops. and Intell. WO, April 12, 1938.

419   "If that drunken sot": WO 208/1446.

419   The Nakamoto diary is in WO 208/2568, ATIS Enemy Publication 300.

420   "I believe a good many": T. Moriya, *No Requiem* (Tokyo: Hokuseido, 1968), p. 77.

420   "The Emperor couldn't": Quoted in Allen, *Burma,* p. 225.

420   "I admired the sentiment": ibid., p. 482.

421   "personal" punishment: See generally WO 208/2505, Dec. 3, 1944, ATIS Enemy Publication 237: "Personal punishment and military discipline"; and WO 208/2603, March 25, 1945, ATIS Enemy Publication 336: "Extra-legal Punishment."

423   "Withdrawing into caves": WO 208/1401, April 9, 1945, ATIS Information and Combat Instructions File of Tagawa Unit, 24th Infantry Division.

423   rise in . . . deserters: Ienaga, op. cit., p. 214.

423   "It is necessary": WO 208/1446, March 4, 1943, HQ USA FISPA G-2 Report 19, "Value of the Army for War."

423   "Kawamura ran": WO 208/1446.

424   Chinese sources: ibid.

424   Burma villagers: WO 203/5184.

424   A survey: WO 203/5418, Interrogation Bulletins Nos. 4 and 5, Nov.–Dec. 1944.

424   Natives were used: WO 203/959, July 12, 1944, SACSEA/34 Corps; and cf. WO 208/1010, "Enemy Morale at Okinawa."

424   "Me vanquished": Toland, op. cit., p. 723.

425   subcommittee on Japanese battle morale: WO 203/692.

425   "Screwing up": Funasaka, op. cit., p. 42.

425   "My insteps": Shohei Ooka, *Fires on the Plain*, I. Morris, trans. (New York: Knopf, 1957), p. 57.

426   "It's a matter": WO 208/1503, Sept. 14, 1944, War Diaries.

426   "When I reach home": WO 203/5184.

426   "We tore off": Moriya, op. cit., pp. 289, 297.

426   medical orderly . . . Attu: WO 208/1446, May 1943.

CHAPTER 43: "DESPERATE AND CRAZY TO DIE": LAST STANDS

428   "Dash forward": Tsunetomo Yamamoto, *Hagakure: The Book of the Samurai* W. Wilson trans. (Tokyo: Kodansha, 1979), pp. 45, 171.

429   For the Tarawa defenses, see WO 208/966 and 208/1658.

431   "The Marshalls really cracked": Costello, op. cit., p. 452.

432   Admiral Ozawa lost: Masanori Ito, op. cit., pp. 98–99, 108–113.

432   The three commanders had set up: Toland, op. cit., pp. 511–12.

433   "one great adamantine": L. Meo, *Japan's Radio War on Australia 1941–5* (Melbourne: Melbourne University Press, 1960), p. 85.

434   cooked up to boost the status: WO 203/5184.

434   "The . . . 6th Air Fleet": Costello, op. cit., p. 499.

436   "The cemetery was filled": WO 208/1010, "The Battle for Dagami," Oct. 29, 1944. RCT 17, HQ 7th Infantry Div.

437   an attractive nurse: Tetsuro Ogawa, *Terraced Hell: A Japanese Memoir of Defeat and Death in Luzon, Philippines* (Tokyo: Tuttle, 1972).

437   "My men have been gathered": Swinson, op. cit., p. 220.

438   "nothing but sands": J. Lardner, *The New Yorker*, quoted in Costello, op. cit., p. 543.

438   "loose wheat": R. Heinl, *Soldiers of the Sea: The US Marine Corps,* quoted in Costello, op. cit., p. 543.

439   "Never have I seen": R. Sherrod, quoted in Spector, op. cit., p. 501.
439   "There were no organized attempts": WO 208/1021.
439   "Most of the positions": WO 208/1021.
440   "They looked like little devils": Ross, *Iwo Jima*, p. 306.
441   "I am one with Yamato": Ito, op. cit., p. 204.
441   "CARRIERS THIS WAY": Spector, op. cit., p. 537.
443   "To the Japanese Army": WO 208/1010, Aug. 4–11, 1945, G-2 Periodic Report No. 6, "The Decline of Morale in the Japanese 62nd Division."

CHAPTER 44: DEATH MARCH: THE ROAD TO SURRENDER

444   criminal manslaughter: Ienaga, op. cit., p. 182.
444   "Bataan Death March!": Aikawa, op. cit., p. 75.
445   "I myself cremated": ibid.
445   Replicas of . . . houses: United States Strategic Bombing Survey, vol. X (New York: Garland, 1976), p. 81.
445   "fire susceptibility": ibid., p. 87.
446   "bouncing along like volleyballs": Hato Edoin, *The Night Tokyo Burned* (New York: St. Martin's, 1987), p. 84.
446   effectively defenseless: Gordon Daniels, "The Great Tokyo Air Raid," in William Beasley, ed., *Modern Japan* (London: Allen and Unwin, 1975).
446   Mothers . . . discovered too late: Robert Guillain, *I Saw Tokyo Burning* (London: Murray, 1981), p. 185.
447   "enormous ginseng roots": Edoin, op. cit., p. 85.
447   "one bold critic": Aikawa, op. cit., p. 46.
447   For the destruction of oil fields, see interview with Professor Takahashi, Nov. 16, 1990.
448   substitute fuels: WO 208/3917, "Japanese Reaction to Allied Conduct of the War in the Pacific." Daily Report 72-1320.
449   Thus, hunger aggravated: Hayashi and Coox, op. cit., p. 151.
449   "a snobbish, senile general": Calvocoressi, op. cit., p. 1179.
451   "We merely prepared": Coox, "The Pacific War," p. 372.
451   For Matsutani, see R. Butow, *Japan's Decision to Surrender* (Stanford, Calif.: Stanford University Press, 1954), p. 27.
452   a discussion paper: interview with Sugita, May 19, 1989.
453   the Russians brought forward their invasion: R. Garthoff, "The

Soviet Intervention in Manchuria 1945–6," in R. Garthoff, ed., *Sino-Soviet Military Relations* (New York: Praeger, 1966), p. 63.

CHAPTER 45: AFTERMATH

457   "erroneous and untimely": Coox, "The Pacific War," p. 375.

457   The prince turned on him: Hayashi and Coox, op. cit., p. 181.

459   For Okamura's telegram see L. Allen, *The End of the War in Asia* (London: Hart-Davis, 1976), pp. 233–34.

459   clandestines . . . dacoits: WO 203/4989.

459   "No Japanese soldier": Slim, op. cit., p. 533.

460   letters home: FO 371/84036, POW Correspondence.

460   For the Numata report, see WO 203/4587.

460   rearming Japanese prisoners: WO 203/6045 and 203/4587.

460   For Mountbatten's complaint, see WO 203/4348, Supreme Allied Commander's Memo of his Visit to Japanese Prisoners [sic] of War Camp, Bikaner, on April 14, 1945.

461   "all personnel who have died": R. Lewin, *The Other Ultra* (London, 1982), p. 261; and cf. WO 208/3908, "Bypassed Enemy Garrisons."

462   "beneath the crust": Toland, op. cit., p. 736.

462   "As an example": J. Bowen, *Undercover in the Jungle* (London: Kimber, 1978), pp. 191–92.

462   "a vast lake": Allen, *Burma*, p. 530.

463   "Revenge": FO 371/92699 FJ 1664/1.

464   Information on the Philippine trials is from the interview with Professor Takahashi, Nov. 16, 1990.

465   "The world I knew": Swinson, op. cit., p. 232.

465   For deficiencies in IMTFE, see generally M. and S. Harries, *Sheathing the Sword: the Demilitarisation of Japan 1945–52* (London: Hamish Hamilton, 1987), chapters 11–19.

466   "Since six months": NAW RG 331, IPS-11, Case 234.

466   "to put flowers": *The New York Times*, Dec. 19, 1948.

467   Russians held some 1.3 million prisoners: Harries and Harries, op. cit., pp. 35–36.

467   demobilized and disarmed: See generally ibid., chapter 4.

468   "tanks, assorted": NAW Record Group 319 (Army Staff) P & O Div. 1946–8, 091 Japan CinCFE/DoA WDGPO Radio, Oct. 9, 1947

469 armed but unmarked trucks: *The New York Times*, Sept. 9, 1945.

470 "What a terrifying lot": FO 371/84036, FJ 1662/2, Oct.–Dec. 1949.

471 "Japanese believe success": WO 203/2190.

471 Article 9: see Harries and Harries, op. cit., chapters 20–22.

CHAPTER 46: "LONGSTANDING REGRETTABLE PRACTICES":
ATROCITIES AND THEIR ORIGINS

475 "The prisoners": WO 208/4605, ATIS, "Japanese Violations of the Laws of War," PW JA 100037 p. 21.

476 human sandbags: H. Rodriguez, *Helen of Burma: The Autobiography of a Wartime Nurse* (London: Corgi, 1988), p. 131.

476 "Against a calm person": Bennett, Hobart, and Spitzer, op. cit., p. 36.

476 At a dire disadvantage: WO 208/4605, ATIS, May 1943, 51 Div. Intelligence Plan.

476 "At every turn": WO 208/4605.

476 "You are the remnants": A. Apthorp, *The British Sumatra Battalion* (London: Book Guild, 1988).

477 "The firing party": WO 208/3047, Foreign Secretary's statement to the House of Commons, January 1944.

477 "two prisoners . . . dissected": WO 208/4605 PW JA 100037, p. 37.

477 "Whether they are destroyed": *South China Morning Post*, June 17, 1988, quoting Taiwan POW camp journal, Aug. 1, 1944.

477 One Japanese commentator: Yuji Aida, *Prisoner of the British—A Japanese Soldier's Experiences in Burma*, H. Ishiguro and L. Allen, trans. (London: Cresset Press, 1966), p. 45.

478 Mental illness: Imperial War Museum, London, British Intelligence documents, BIOSJAP 564, "Neuropsychiatry in the Japanese Armed Forces."

478 rarely expressed guilt: FO 371/76250 and LC02/2982 "Report on the Mentality of Families of War Criminals in Jail in Singapore and the Federation as Deduced from Incoming Correspondence During the Years 1948–9."

478 lack of a transcendent moral authority: M. Maruyama, "Theory and Psychology of Ultra-Nationalism," in *Thought and Be-*

haviour in Modern Japanese Politics (Oxford: Oxford University Press, 1963), pp. 4–5.

479 For Prince Kanin's order, see WO 106/5571, Jan. 7, 1938, "Sino-Japanese Hostilities."

479 "acting on superior orders": The case was *In re Masuda*, 1945. L. Green, *Superior Orders in National and International Law* (Leyden, Holland: A. W. Sijthoff, 1976), p. 304.

479 "While a Japanese woman or child": Vespa, op. cit., p. 90.

480 savage contempt: Ienaga, op. cit., p. 12.

480 "The use of narcotics": A. S. Candlin, *Psychochemical Warfare: The Chinese Communist Drug Offensive Against the West*, p. 43.

480 "*as if they were Chinese*": WO 208/4605.

481 "Hand Flag Regulations": WO 208/4605, Document 2696.

481 Three Alls: letter from Professor Ryoichi Tobe, March 17, 1991. Cf. Johnson, *Peasant Nationalism*, pp. 58–59.

482 "socialisation for death": Kazuko Tsurumi, *Social Change and the Individual: Japan Before and After Defeat in World War II* (Princeton, N.J.: Princeton University Press, 1970), pp. 99–138.

482 "The group": Holmes, op. cit., p. 242.

482 "An interesting sidelight": NAW Roland S. Morris Information Data 1917–34, Aug. 5, 1919, C/O USS *New Orleans*/CinC US Asiatic Fleet.

482 Tsuji was incensed: Tsuji, op. cit., p. 279.

483 "Former peasants": Ienaga, op. cit., p. 125.

483 insurgent war: See, e.g., Major W. Hayes Parks, "Crimes in Hostilities," in *Marine Corps Gazette*, vol. LX, no. 8 (August 1976); Capt. A. Bevilacqua, "Intelligence and Insurgency," in *Marine Corps Gazette*, vol. LX, no. 1 (January 1976).

484 exactly the same stresses: Swinson, op. cit., p. 154.

484 "Japanese troops had been under such conditions": WO 208/4605, PW JA 145121, p. 44.

CHAPTER 47: FACING THE PAST

486 rebuild a Japanese fighting force: See Harries and Harries, op. cit., chapters 20–24.

487 "Dollar for dollar": Osaka *Mainichi*, Feb. 12, 1949.

487   "Even though created": NAW RG 319, P & O Div. Decimal File
        1946–8, 091 Japan TS Section Ia., Part 1, April 19, 1948.

487   "salaried-man-like": Justin Williams Papers, Group 166.01, in
        the East Asia Collection, McKeldin Library, University of
        Maryland.

489   "The people who were so eager": ibid.

490   Calley is quoted by P. French, "Morally Blaming Whole Popu-
        lations," in V. Held, ed., *Toward Conceptual Order*, p. 266.

490   The Japanese have never been seen: Junji Kinoshita, "What the
        Tokyo Trial Made Me Think About," in C. Hosoya, N. Ando,
        Y. Onuma, and R. Minear, eds., *The Tokyo War Crimes Trial:
        An International Symposium* (Tokyo: Kodansha, 1986), p.
        147: "Why Did I Fail to Pursue War Responsibility?"

INDEX

INDEX

INDEX

Kumamoto Castle, 30–1, 76, 187
Kunming, 276, 278, 310
Kuomintang, 113, and see Chiang Kai-shek;
  Nationalist China
Kurihara, Yasuhide, 183, 186
Kurile Islands, 407, 433, 454
Kurita, Takeo, 435
Kuroda, Shigenori, 434
Kuroki, Tamemoto, 82–4
Kuropatkin, A. N., 79, 81–4, 87–90, 92
Kwai, 485
Kwantung Army, 100, 142, 145–6,
  149–50, 157, 196, 207, 210–13, 251,
  263, 269, 289, 319, 360, 420, 433,
  449, 454–5, 467, and see Chang
  Hsueh-liang; Changkufeng; Chang
  Tso-lin; China: North Chinese
  autonomy; drugs; Imperial Army:
  officer corps; Kwantung Leased
  Territories; Manchouli; Manchukuo;
  Manchurian Incident; Nomonhan;
  Second Sino-Japanese War; South
  Manchurian Railway; surrender, 1945
Kwantung Leased Territories, 100, 129,
  145, 246
Kwantung Peninsula, 85
Kyoto, 355, 451, 485

Lashio, 310, 312
League of Nations, 133, 157, 159, 163,
  167, 181, 196, 203, 207, 246, 258
LeMay, Curtis, 445–6
Lend-Lease program, 290
Leyte, 434–7, 441–3
Li Hung-chang, 62
Li Tsung-jen, 234
Liaotung Peninsula, 47, 59, 61–2, 67,
  76–7, 82, 84–5, 92, 98, 100, 128
Liaoyang, 82, 84, 87–9
Lienchun Force (Chinese Army), 57
Lin Piao, 252
Lloyd George, David, 112
Lobanov-Rostovsky, Prince, 46
London Naval Treaty (1930), 142–3, 151
Lunghai Railway, 233–5
Lytton Commission, 163
Lytton, Lord, 159, 207

Ma Chan-shan, 158
MacArthur, Douglas, vii, 291, 315, 340,
  428, 436, 463–4, 467–8, 470, 472,
  486–7
"Magic," 379
Mahan, Alfred, 78, 105
Makino, Count Nobuaki, 147, 184–6
Malaya, 181, 275–6, 282, 304–10, 313,
  319, 328–9, 340, 343–4, 347, 372–3,
  394, 401, 407, 416–19, 437, 438,
  467
Malinta Tunnel, 315, 436
Manchouli, 143–4, 158
Manchukuo, 159, 168, 180
  resources and development, 197, 203,
    251, 270, 274
  and drugs, 244–6
  prostitution, 244–5
  Russians surround, 197–8, 206, 269–70
  communist suppression, 253
  army, 318, 346
  and see Mongolia, Federation of
Manchuria:
  resources, 47, 121, 203
  Japan and, 47, 59–62, 81, 83, 92, 98,
    100, 106, 110, 113–14, 122, 141–2,
    145–59, 348, 483, and see Chang
    Hsueh-liang; Chang Tso-lin;
    Manchurian Incident
  Russia and, 47, 67, 71–2, 74–5, 92,
    100, 106, 114, 143, and see
    Russo-Japanese War
  invasion by Soviet Union, 1945, 316,
    454–6, 467
  Pacific War, 318–20, 348, 372, 388,
    394, 422, 433, 437, 441, 448, 452,
    467, 470
Manchurian Incident (1931), 145–59, 304,
  317, 345, 362, 364, 449, 457, 480
Mandalay, 310, 312
Manila, 314, 359, 420, 436, 464–5, 483
Mao Tse-tung, 140, 204–5, 237, 251–5,
  359, 455, and see China: Chinese
  Communist Party
Marco Polo Bridge Incident, 201–2, 213,
  345, 400, 408, and see Second China
  War: causes

563

INDEX

ABOUT THE AUTHORS

MEIRION HARRIES was born in 1951, studied law at Cambridge University, and worked as an attorney in Japan and Hong Kong before taking up his appointment as deputy director-general of the Society of Authors. He is also a member of the International Institute for Strategic Studies and of the Executive Committee of English PEN.

SUSIE HARRIES was also born in 1951, studied classics at Cambridge and Oxford universities, and worked for several years in the Independent Commission Against Corruption in Hong Kong.

Mr. and Mrs. Harries began their writing partnership in 1979 and have since co-authored six books on diverse subjects, as well as writing on Japanese security and environmental policy for English and Japanese newspapers. Two of their books have been nominated for national prizes in England. *Soldiers of the Sun* is their second book on Japanese military history.